American Environmental Leaders

Volume I

American Environmental Leaders
From Colonial Times to the Present

Volume I
A–L

Anne Becher
Joseph Richey

Grey House Publishing

PUBLISHER:	Leslie Mackenzie
EDITORIAL DIRECTOR:	Laura Mars-Proietti
EDITORIAL ASSISTANT:	Jael Bridgemahon
MARKETING DIRECTOR:	Jessica Moody
AUTHORS:	Anne Becher
	Joseph Richey
COPYEDITOR:	Elaine Alibrandi
COMPOSITION & DESIGN:	ATLIS Systems

Grey House Publishing, Inc.
185 Millerton Road
Millerton, NY 12546
518.789.8700
FAX 518.789.0545
www.greyhouse.com
e-mail: books @greyhouse.com

While every effort has been made to ensure the reliability of the information presented in this publication, Grey House Publishing neither guarantees the accuracy of the data contained herein nor assumes any responsibility for errors, omissions or discrepancies. Grey House accepts no payment for listing; inclusion in the publication of any organization, agency, institution, publication, service or individual does not imply endorsement of the editors or publisher.

Errors brought to the attention of the publisher and verified to the satisfaction of the publisher will be corrected in future editions.

Except by express prior written permission of the Copyright Proprietor no part of this work may be copied by any means of publication or communication now known or developed hereafter including, but not limited to, use in any directory or compilation or other print publication, in any information storage and retrieval system, in any other electronic device, or in any visual or audio-visual device or product.

This publication is an original and creative work, copyrighted by Grey House Publishing, Inc. and is fully protected by all applicable copyright laws, as well as by laws covering misappropriation, trade secrets and unfair competition.

Grey House has added value to the underlying factual material through one or more of the following efforts: unique and original selection; expression; arrangement; coordination; and classification.

Grey House Publishing, Inc. will defend its rights in this publication.

Copyright © 2008 by Grey House Publishing, Inc.
All rights reserved. No part of this publication may be reproduced, stored in a retrieval system, or transmitted, in any form or by any means, electronic, mechanical, photocopying, recording, or otherwise, except for the inclusion of brief quotations in a review, without prior permission in writing from the publishers.

Publisher's Cataloging-In-Publication Data
(Prepared by The Donohue Group, Inc.)

Becher, Anne. American environmental leaders : colonial times to the present / Anne
   Becher, Joseph Richey. — 2nd ed.
     2 v. : ill. ; 28 cm.
   Includes bibliographical references and index.
   Content: v. 1. A-L — v. 2. M-Z.
   ISBN: 978-1-59237-119-8

1. Environmentalists—United States—Biography. I. Richey, Joseph. II. Title.
GE55 .B43 2008
363.7/0092/273

DUST STORM DISASTER
   Words and Music by Woody Guthrie
   TRO-© Copyright 1960 (Renewed) 1963 (Renewed) Ludlow Music, Inc., New York, NY.
   Used by permission.

ROLL ON, COLUMBIA
   Words by Woody Guthrie
   Music based on GOODNIGHT, IRENE by Huddie Ledbetter and John A. Lomax
   TRO-© Copyright 1936 (Renewed) 1957 (Renewed) and 1963 (Renewed)
   Ludlow Music, Inc., New York, NY. Used by permission.

THIS LAND IS YOUR LAND
   Words and Music by Woody Guthrie
   TRO-© Copyright 1956 (Renewed) 1958 (Renewed) 1970 (Renewed) 1972
   (Renewed) Ludlow Music, Inc., New York, NY. Used by permission.

SAILING DOWN MY GOLDEN RIVER
   Words and Music by Pete Seeger
   TRO-© Copyright 1971 (Renewed) Melody Trails, Inc., New York, NY. Used by permission.

DIRTY STREAM
   Written by Pete Seeger
   Published by SANGA MUSIC, INC. Administered by The Royalty Network. Used by permission.

Table of Contents

Volume I

List of American Environmental Leaders, vii

Preface, xiii

Acknowledgments, xv

Introduction, xix

Biographical Profiles A–L, 1

Volume II

List of American Environmental Leaders, vii

Biographical Profiles M–Z, 499

Key Documents, 897

Timeline, 1003

List of Leaders by Occupation/Focus, 1015

Index, 1025

About the Authors, 1051

List of American Environmental Leaders

Volume I

Abbey, Edward, 3
Ackerman, Diane, 4
Adams, Ansel, 6
Adams, Henry, 8
Adams, John Hamilton, 10
Adams, John Quincy, 12
Addams, Jane, 13
Albright, Horace, 15
Alston, Dana, 17
Amidon, Elias, and Elizabeth Roberts, 19
Anderson, Adrienne, 21
Anderson, Ray, 25
Andrus, Cecil, 27
Anthony, Carl, 29
Audubon, John James, 31
Austin, Mary, 33
Ausubel, Kenny, 36
Ayres, Richard, 38
Babbitt, Bruce, 43
Bahouth, Peter, 44
Bailey, Florence Augusta Merriam, 46
Ball, Betty, and Gary Ball, 48
Balog, James D., 51
Bari, Judi, 52
Bartlett, Albert, 55
Bartram, John, and William Bartram, 58
Bates, Marston, 60
Bauer, Catherine, 61
Bavaria, Joan, 63
Bean, Michael, 65
Beattie, Mollie, 67
Beebe, C. William, 69
Begley, Ed, Jr., 71
Bennett, Hugh Hammond, 73
Benyus, Janine, 76
Berg, Peter, 74
Berle, Peter, 78
Berry, Friar Thomas, 80
Berry, Wendell, 82
Bertell, Rosalie, 84
Bien, Amos, 86
Bierstadt, Albert, 89
Bingham, Eula, 91
Bixby, Kevin, 93
Blackgoat, Roberta, 94
Blaeloch, Janine, 96
Bloomberg, Michael, 98
Bookchin, Murray, 100
Boulding, Kenneth, 102
Bramble, Barbara, 104
Brand, Stewart, 107
Brandborg, Stewart, 109
Bresette, Walt, 113
Brower, David, 115
Brown, Janet, 118
Brown, Lester, 119
Brown, Michael, 122
Browner, Carol, 124
Bullard, Robert D., 126
Burroughs, John, 129
Butcher, Devereux, 131
Cade, Thomas, 135
Caldwell, Lynton, 137
Callicott, J. Baird, 139
Carhart, Arthur, 141
Carlton, Jasper, 143
Carr, Archie, 145
Carr, Marjorie Harris, 148
Carson, Rachel, 150
Carter, Jimmy, 152
Carter, Majora, 155
Carver, George Washington, 157
Castillo, Aurora, 159
Catlin, George, 160
Caudill, Harry, 162
Chafee, John, 164
Chapman, Frank, 166
Chappell, Kate, and Tom Chappell, 167
Chase, Robin, 170
Chávez, César, 172
Chavis, Benjamin, 174
Chief Sealth (Seattle), 734
Christy, Elizabeth, 176
Cizik, Richard, 178
Clawson, Marion, 179
Cobb, John B., Jr., 181
Colborn, Theo, 183
Colby, William, 186
Cole, Thomas, 188

LIST OF AMERICAN ENVIRONMENTAL LEADERS

Collom, Jack, 190
Commoner, Barry, 192
Connett, Ellen, and Paul Connett, 194
Conway, Stuart, 197
Cook, Richard A., 198
Cooper, James Fenimore, 201
Costle, Douglas, 202
Cowles, Henry, 204
Cox, Paul, 206
Craighead, Frank, and John Craighead, 208
Cronon, William, 211
Daly, Herman, 215
Darley, Julian and Celine Fanny Rich, 217
Darling, Jay Norwood "Ding", 220
David, Laurie Ellen, 224
Dawson, Richard, 226
DeBonis, Jeff, 228
Desser, Christina Louise, 231
Devall, Bill, 233
Devoto, Bernard, 234
DiCaprio, Leonardo, 236
Dilg, Will, 238
Dingell, John, Jr., 239
Dittmar, Hank, 241
Dombeck, Michael, 244
Donovan, Richard, 246
Douglas, Marjory Stoneman, 249
Douglas, William Orville, 251
Dowie, Mark, 253
Downing, Andrew Jackson, 255
Drayton, William, 257
Drury, Newton, 259
Dubos, René, 262
Dunlap, Louise, 264
Durning, Alan, 265
Dutcher, William, 267
Dyer, Polly, 270
Earle, Sylvia, 275
Edge, Rosalie, 277
Ehrenfeld, David, 279
Ehrlich, Anne, and Paul Ehrlich, 281
Eisner, Thomas, 284
Ellis, Juliet, 286
Elton, Charles S., 288
Emerson, Ralph Waldo, 290
Figueroa, Rogelio, 295
Fontenot, Willie, 296
Foreman, Dave, 299

Fossey, Dian, 302
Franklin, Jerry, 304
Frome, Michael, 306
Fuller, Buckminster, 309
Fuller, Kathryn, 312
Futrell, J. William, 314
Gagliano, Sherwood M., 319
Geisel, Theodor (Dr. Seuss), 320
Gelbspan, Ross, 323
Gibbs, Lois, 325
Gleason, Henry Allan, 327
Gold, Lou, 329
Golten, Robert, 331
Goodman, Paul, 333
Gore, Albert, Jr., 335
Gottlieb, Robert, 338
Gould, Stephen Jay, 341
Gray, Asa, 343
Grinnell, George Bird, 345
Grogan, Pete, 347
Grossman, Richard L., 349
Gussow, Joan Dye, 352
Guthrie, Woody, 354
Gutiérrez, Juana Beatriz, 357
Hair, Jay, 363
Hamilton, Alice, 365
Hansen, James E., 367
Hardin, Garrett, 370
Harrelson, Woody, 372
Harry, Debra, 374
Harvey, Dorothy Webster, 376
Hawken, Paul, 379
Hayes, Denis, 382
Hayes, Randy, 383
Hays, Samuel P., 385
Henderson, Hazel, 387
Hermach, Tim, 390
Hill, Julia Butterfly, 392
Hoagland, Edward, 395
Hornaday, William Temple, 397
House, Donna, 399
Huerta, Dolores, 402
Ickes, Harold, 409
Ingram, Helen, 411
Jackson, Henry, 415
Jackson, Wes, 417
Jacobson, Michael, 419
Janzen, Daniel H., 421

Jensen, Derrick, 424
Johnson, Glenn S., 425
Johnson, Hazel, 428
Johnson, Lady Bird (Claudia Alta), 431
Johnson, Robert Underwood, 433
Jones, Van, 435
Jontz, Jim, 437
Jordan, Chris, 439
Jukofsky, Diane, 441
Kamp, Dick, 445
Kane, Hal, 446
Katz, Daniel, 449
Kaufman, Hugh, 451
Kellert, Stephen, 453
Kendall, Henry, 456
Kennedy, Robert F., Jr., 457
Kingsolver, Barbara, 460
Kratt, Chris, and Martin Kratt, 461
Krupp, Fred, 463
LaBudde, Samuel, 469
LaDuke, Winona, 471
Lammers, Owen, 473
Lappé, Frances Moore, 475
Leopold, Aldo, 478
Lindbergh, Anne Morrow, and Charles Augustus Lindbergh, 480
Littletree, Alicia, 482
Lopez, Barry, 484
Louv, Richard, 486
Lovejoy, Thomas, 488
Lovins, Amory, and Hunter Lovins, 490
Luce, Benjamin, 492
Lyons, Oren, 494

Volume II
MacKaye, Benton, 499
Mader, Ron, 500
Mander, Jerry, 503
Mann, Michael E., 505
Manning, Richard, 507
Marsh, George Perkins, 510
Marshall, Robert, 512
Marston, Betsy, and Ed Marston, 514
Martínez, Dennis, 516
Mather, Stephen, 519
Matthiessen, Peter, 521
McCloskey, Michael, 523
McDonough, William, 525

McDowell, Mary, 528
McHarg, Ian, 530
McKibben, Bill, 532
McPhee, John, 534
Meadows, Donella H., 536
Meany, Edmond, 538
Merchant, Carolyn, 540
Merculieff, Ilarion (Larry), 542
Miller, Laura, 545
Mills, Enos, 546
Mills, Stephanie, 548
Mitchell, George J., 550
Mittermeier, Russell, 553
Montague, Peter, 554
Moses, Marion, 556
Moss, Cynthia, 558
Moss, Doug, 560
Muir, John, 562
Mumford, Lewis, 565
Murie, Mardy, and Olaus Murie, 568
Muskie, Edmund, 570
Nabhan, Gary, 575
Nader, Ralph, 577
Nagel, Carlos, 579
Nash, Roderick, 581
Nearing, Helen, and Scott Nearing, 584
Needleman, Herbert, 586
Nelson, Gaylord, 588
Nelson, Willie, 590
Newman, Nell, 591
Nickels, Greg, 594
Norton, Bryan, 596
Noss, Reed, 598
Odum, Eugene, 603
Oliver, Mary, 605
Olmsted, Frederick Law, Jr., 609
Olmsted, Frederick Law, Sr., 607
Olson, Molly Harriss, 610
Olson, Sigurd, 612
Orr, David, 615
Osborn, Fairfield, 616
Owings, Margaret, 618
Packard, Steve, 623
Palmer, Paula, 625
Parkman, Francis, 627
Peacock, Doug, 629
Perkins, Jane, 631
Peterson, Roger Tory, 633

LIST OF AMERICAN ENVIRONMENTAL LEADERS

Peterson, Russell, 635
Pinchot, Gifford, 637
Plotkin, Mark, 639
Pollan, Michael, 642
Popper, Deborah, and Frank Popper, 643
Postel, Sandra, 647
Pough, Richard, 649
Powell, John Wesley, 652
Pritchard, Paul C., 654
Pryor, Cynthia, 657
Pulido, Laura, 658
Raven, Peter, 663
Red Cloud, Henry, 665
Reilly, William K., 667
Reisner, Marc, 669
Reynolds, Michael, 670
Richards, Ellen Swallow, 673
Rifkin, Jeremy, 675
Ringo, Jerome C., 677
Ritter, Bill, Jr., 679
Robbins, John, 682
Robin, Vicki, 684
Rockefeller, John D., Jr., 686
Rockefeller, Laurance, 689
Rodale, Robert, 691
Rolfes, Anne, 693
Rolston, Holmes, III, 695
Roosevelt, Franklin D., 697
Roosevelt, Theodore, 699
Rosenfeld, Arthur H., 702
Roszak, Theodore, 703
Ruether, Rosemary Radford, 705
Safina, Carl, 709
Sagan, Carl, 712
Sale, Kirkpatrick, 714
Sandoval, Arturo, 716
Sanjour, William, 718
Sargent, Charles Sprague, 719
Sawhill, John, 721
Schlickeisen, Rodger, 724
Schneider, Stephen, 725
Schultes, Richard Evans, 728
Schurz, Carl, 730
Schwarzenegger, Arnold, 732
Seeger, Pete, 736
Selikoff, Irving, 738
Seo, Danny, 740
Sessions, George, 742
Seton, Ernest Thompson, 743
Shabecoff, Philip, 746
Shapiro, Andrew L., 748
Shuey, Chris, 750
Silkwood, Karen, 753
Sive, David, 754
Smith, Rocky, 757
Sneed, Cathrine, 758
Snyder, Gary, 760
Soleri, Paolo, 762
Solomon, Susan, 765
Soulé, Michael, 766
Speth, James Gustave, 769
Standing Bear, Chief Luther, 771
Steel, William, 773
Stegner, Wallace, 775
Steingraber, Sandra, 776
Stone, Christopher, 779
Stone-Manning, Tracy, 780
Subra, Wilma, 783
Suckling, Kierán, 785
Susanka, Sarah, 787
Swearingen, Terri, 789
Tall, JoAnn, 795
Tamminen, Terry, 797
Tchozewski, D. Chet, 799
Tewa, Debby, 802
Thompson, Chief Tommy Kuni, 804
Thoreau, Henry David, 806
Thorne, Oakleigh, II, 809
Thorpe, Grace, 812
Tidwell, Michael, 814
Tokar, Brian, 817
Tompkins, Douglas, 819
Toor, Will, 821
Turner, Frederick Jackson, 823
Turner, Ted, 824
Udall, Morris, 829
Udall, Stewart, 831
Vogt, William, 837
Walter, Martin, 841
Warburton, Barbara, 843
Waring, George, 844
Warshall, Peter, 846
Watson, Paul, 848
Waxman, Henry, 850
Werbach, Adam, 852
Whealy, Diane, and Kent Whealy, 854

White, Gilbert F., 857
White, Lynn, Jr., 859
Whitman, Walt, 861
Willcox, Louisa, 864
Wille, Chris, 866
Williams, Terry Tempest, 868
Wilson, Diane, 871
Wilson, Edward O., 872

Winter, Paul, 874
Wolf, Hazel, 877
Wolke, Howie, 879
Woodwell, George, 881
Worster, Donald, 883
Yard, Robert Sterling, 889
Zahniser, Howard, 893
Zwick, David, 895

Preface

American Environmental Leaders: From Colonial Times to the Present, covers the confluence of the multifaceted environmental movement and its protagonists' many heroic acts on behalf of the natural world, over a two-hundred year period of history. This biographical dictionary refers readers to individuals who have forged lasting positive environmental impacts on their immediate surroundings, the nation, or the planet at large.

Along with historical environmental champions, we include living forward thinkers and doers, those who conceive and implement new best practices and positive visions for the future. Fortunately, there are many more environmental leaders than we could profile in this tome. For this second edition, we have especially tried to capture recent developments in the fast changing fields of earth science, policy making, environmental activism and the arts.

The book honors about 400 American environmental leaders—well-known founders and leaders of the diversified strands of the environmental movement, as well as some unsung local, regional, or behind-the-scenes actors, without whose work, vital advances may have remained mere concepts or proposals. A special effort was made to include not only the most well-known movers and shakers, but also those who collaborate on important levels that are often less visible.

The struggles to preserve spectacular tracks of wilderness present a panorama of heroes and heroines. Among the best known are John Muir, the voice of Yosemite and founding president of the Sierra Club, and Stephen Mather, the dynamic first director of the National Park Service, who with staff members Robert Sterling Yard and Horace Albright, convinced Congress and the American people of the value of national parks.

Others have dedicated themselves to preserving endangered species and habitats. Species loss emerged as a concern during the late 19th century when the once-commonplace passenger pigeons were exterminated by hunters. American Bison almost disappeared as well, but were saved by the efforts of big-game hunters like Theodore Roosevelt and George Bird Grinnell, and the first Audubon Society president, William Dutcher, who fought for the earliest state and federal bird protection laws. Efforts to preserve endangered species and their habitats have continued through the work of innumerable activists–people and organizations like Kierán Suckling who co-founded the Center for Biological Diversity, and Louisa Willcox who works in the Northern Rockies to protect the habitat of grizzlies and wolves. Given the real and present danger that global climate change presents to large mammals, leaders like Cynthia Moss seek to preserve the elephant population; mariner Paul Watson of Sea Shepherd defends whales, dolphins, and sea lions; Henry Red Cloud of the Lakota is helping to bring back herds of buffalo.

Protecting natural resources such as forests, water, minerals and soil, and promoting more efficient and sustainable use of them has steadily gained importance since colonial times. Nineteenth-century scholar George Perkins Marsh first wrote about how human activity could damage the environment in his *Man and Nature, or Physical Geography as Modified by Human Action* (1864). Since then there have been full-scale efforts to reduce the negative impact of agriculture and the extractive industries on the health of the environment. Agricultural scientist George Washington Carver taught impoverished Southern farmers to grow such soil-enriching crops as peanuts, sweet potatoes, and black-eyed peas, showed them how to prepare these foods, and convinced the U.S. Congress in the 1920s to provide economic incentives for their production. This work contains profiles of several subsequent promoters of sustainable agriculture, including Soil Conservation Service director Hugh Hammond Bennett, organic gardening guru Robert Rodale, and philosopher-farmer Wes Jackson. We have highlighted the recent work of novelist Barbara

Kingsolver and journalist Michael Pollan as it helps expand the locally-grown food movement.

Seeing the potential of industry to help solve global energy and environmental problems, contemporary visionaries such as entrepreneur Paul Hawken and Rocky Mountain Institute-founders Amory and Hunter Lovins have helped private businesses—including some of the largest in the United States—to become more efficient and sustainable in their practices. One of their clients, Ray Anderson of Interface, Inc., the largest commercial carpet, tile, and interior fabrics company in the world, has converted his company into a model of sustainability and environmental responsibility.

Unfortunately, most industry leaders are not as environmentally-conscientious as Anderson, and many of the environmental fAUTHORleaders featured in this book are activists who have felt called to fight the industrial pollution that ruins their homes. One of these activists was Grace Thorpe who founded the national Environmental Council of Native Americans in 1993 to support Indian nations that refused the persistent requests by nuclear industry and the federal government to store nuclear waste on their land.

Improving urban landscapes is another piece of the complete picture of environmental work taking place in our country. We have profiled inner-city environmental justice organizers like Marjora Carter in the South Bronx, and Van Jones and Juliet Ellis in the San Francisco Bay Area enhancing urban ecology and reducing metropolitan areas' carbon footprint.

As with the first edition, this second edition focuses on those individuals whose work leads new trends in early 21st century American environmentalism. One such trend has been the growth in climate science. Climatologists, meteorologists and geomorphologists now make headline news. More evidence of severe climate change appears on a weekly basis: reductions in diversity of flora and fauna, rising ocean temperatures, more frequent storms and severe weather, receding coastlines as ice caps melt north and south. As a result, innovations have been conceived, proposed, and actualized in the areas of urban design, sustainable building practices, landscape architecture, mass transit, renewable energy, and localized food production. This second edition includes several prominent individuals who specialize in these areas.

Driving some of the conversion toward renewable and sustainable systems are business executives, investment bankers and philanthropists. We included Joan Bavaria, an investment banker who founded the Coalition for Environmentally Responsible Economies, and New York City Mayor Michael Bloomberg who, with the power of capital and political position, helps move private sector drivers to run cleaner industries.

The subjects chosen for these volumes are diverse, and their diversity strengthens and enhances the environmental movement. Poets, lawyers, economists, farmers, grassroots activists, scientists, theologians, sanitary engineers, and musicians—their stories are lessons in conscience, creativity, and commitment. Many are guided by strong convictions and an inner knowledge of how to make the world a healthier place.

A lofty goal of *American Environmental Leaders* is to inspire effective environmental work from its readers. A less lofty, yet still vital goal, is encouraging readers to follow up with additional research using the excellent, up-to-date bibliographic resources available about the leaders we've profiled and their work—provided at the conclusion of each entry.

This second edition significantly improves the first edition, which was published in 2000. In addition to expanding the list of subjects to nearly 400, we include a colorful Timeline of the environmental movement and a collection of Key Documents. We are delighted to offer this contribution to the great and ever-expanding bibliography of works about our environment and those working to protect and conserve it.

Anne Becher
Joseph Richey

Acknowledgments

We are grateful to Grey House Publishing for the opportunity to compile and edit this second edition of *American Environmental Leaders*. Thanks to our kind, cheerful and ever-helpful editorial assistant at Grey House, Jael Powell and to Laura Mars-Proietti who communicated her vision for this expanded and improved edition. They gave us the chance to improve the first edition, and gently mid-wived the book to its completion.

Friends and colleagues who helped us compile the subject list include:

Cain Allen, David Augeri, Richard Ayres, Matt Baker, David Barsamian, Ingrid Becher, Amos Bien, Stewart Brandborg, Charlotte Caldwell, Duncan Campbell, Bill Chaloupka, Eric Doub, Paul Dresman, Elizabeth Dubrulle, Michael Egan, Willie Fontenot, Robert Gass, Tom Goldtooth, Bob Golten, Robert Gottlieb, Marie Gould, Diane Hadley, Benjamin Hale, Jennifer Heath, Theron Horton, Linda Irvine, Frank Joyce, Diane Jukofsky, Gwyn Kirk, Kamala Kempadoo, Marda Kirn, Meg Knox, Ron Mader, Bob McFarland, John Opie, Paula Palmer, Jane Perkins, Lori Lea Pourier, Annette Ramos, Gretchen Reinhardt, Randy Roark, Brian Russell, Rachel White Scheuering, Mark Schleifstein, Chet Tchozewski, Will Toor, Jeff Wagenheim, Marty Walter, Howard Wapner, Paul Wapner, Peter Warshall, and Chris Wille.

Special thanks to Mariella Colvin who helped with on-line bibliographic research. Ingrid and Ted Becher fortified the timeline with copious library research and synopsized the passage of key bills of legislation. Angie Layton gave tips on recent environmental legislation. Patricia Romero Lankao pointed us to useful documents on climate change policy. Christy Jespersen saw how our summer was going and invited our kids out for a splendid full day of climbing at a key point in our attempt to meet a deadline.

*

The following subjects provided information for and/or reviewed their own entries, or an assistant did this; if this was done only for the version in the first edition of the book, that is indicated parenthetically:

John Hamilton Adams (with Ann Roach)
Dana Alston (1st edition, Larry Kressley and Adisa Douglas)
Elias Amidon and Elizabeth Roberts
Adrienne Anderson
Ray Anderson (Lisa Cape Lilienthal)
Carl Anthony (Martha Olson)
Kenny Ausubel (Aaron Leventman)
Richard Ayres (1st edition)
Betty and Gary Ball
James Balog (Sport)
Judi Bari (1st edition, Alicia Littletree)
Albert Bartlett
Michael Bean
Ed Begley, Jr. (1st edition)
Peter Berg
Peter Berle (1st edition)
Amos Bien
Eula Bingham
Kevin Bixby
Janine Blaeloch
Murray Bookchin (1st edition, with Janet Biehl)
Barbara Bramble (1st edition)
Stewart Brandborg (with Anna Vee Brandborg)
Walt Bresette (1st edition, Rick Whaley and Tom Goldtooth)
Robert Bullard (Glenn S. Johnson)
Tom Cade
Lynton Caldwell (1st edition)
J. Baird Callicott
Jasper Carlton (1st edition)
Majora Carter (James Chase)
Robin Chase
John B. Cobb, Jr. (with Trisha Famisaran)
Theo Colborn (with Rose Baeur)
Jack Collom
Ellen and Paul Connett

ACKNOWLEDGMENTS

Stuart Conway
Richard A. Cook (Alice Hartley)
Paul Cox (1st edition)
Frank and John Craighead, (1st edition, with John Willis Craighead, Charlie Craighead)
Herman Daly
Richard Dawson
Jeff DeBonis
Chris Desser
Bill Devall (1st edition)
Hank Dittmar
Michael Dombeck
Richard Donovan
Mark Dowie (1st edition)
Louise Dunlap (Joe Browder)
Alan Durning
Polly Dyer
Anne and Paul Ehrlich
Thomas Eisner (with Janis Strope)
Juliet Ellis
Rogelio Figueroa
William Fontenot
Jerry Franklin (1st edition)
Michael Frome (1st edition)
Kathryn Fuller (1st edition, with Lisa Clark)
J. William Futrell
Ross Gelbspan (1st edition)
Lois Marie Gibbs (1st edition)
Lou Gold (1st edition)
Bob Golten
Robert Gottlieb
Pete Grogan
Richard Grossman
Joan Gussow
James E. Hansen
Debra Harry (1st edition)
Dorothy Harvey (with Mark Harvey)
Paul Hawken (1st edition)
Randy Hayes (1st edition)
Samuel P. Hays
Tim Herrnach
Donna House
Daniel Janzen
Glenn S. Johnson
Hazel Johnson (1st edition)
Van Jones (Marni Tomljanovic)
Chris Jordan (Mike Lengel)
Diane Jukowski (with Gretchen Ruethling)

Richard Kamp
Hal Kane
Daniel Katz
Hugh Kaufman (1st edition)
Stephen Kellert
Robert F. Kennedy, Jr. (1st edition)
Chris and Martin Kratt (Susan McLennan)
Samuel LaBudde (1st edition)
Alicia Littletree (1st edition)
Richard Louv
Amory and Hunter Lovins (1st edition)
Ron Mader
Michael Mann
Richard Manning (1st edition)
Ed and Betsy Marston
Dennis Martinez (1st edition)
Carolyn Merchant (1st edition)
Ilarion Merculieff
Stephanie Mills
Peter Montague (1st edition, Maria Pellerano)
Doug Moss
Carlos Nagel (1st edition)
Nell Newman (Sally Shepard)
Greg Nickels (Sue Nakamura)
Reed Noss
Eugene Odurn (1st edition)
Molly Olson (1st edition)
David Orr (1st edition)
Steve Packard (1st edition)
Paula Palmer
Jane Perkins (1st edition)
Michael Pollan
Frank and Deborah Popper
Sandra Postel
Paul Pritchard
Cynthia Pryor
Laura Pulido (1st edition)
Peter Raven
Jerome Ringo (Daphne Butler, Keith Schneider)
Bill Ritter Jr. (Evan Dreyer)
John Robbins (1st edition, with Deo Robbins)
Vicki Robin (1st edition)
Holmes Rolston, III
Rosemary Radford Ruether
Carl Safina (with Megan Smith)
Arturo Sandoval
Bill Sanjour (1st edition)

Arnold Schwarzenegger (Kira Heinrichs)
Rodger Schlickeisen (1st edition, with Aimee Delach)
Stephen Schneider (1st edition, with Sue Evans)
Danny Seo (1st edition)
Philip Shabecoff (1st edition)
Andrew L. Shapiro (Leslie Benson)
Chris Shuey
David Sive (1st edition)
Rocky Smith
Gary Snyder (1st edition)
Susan Solomon (Jim Roberts)
Michael Soulé
Tracy Stone-Manning
Wilma Subra
Susanka, Sarah (Katie Kiefer)
Chet Tchozewski
Oakleigh Thorne (with Stephanie Muirhead)
Brian Tokar
Will Toor
Martin Walter
Barbara Warburton (1st edition, María Alma Solís and Larry Lof)
Adam Werbach (1st edition, Kelly Braucht)
Kent and Diane Whealy (1st edition)
Gilbert White (1st edition)
Louisa Willcox
Chris Wille (with Gretchen Ruethling)
Howie Wolke
Donald Worster
Howard Zahniser (1st edition, with Ed Zahniser)
David Zwick (Jon Scott)

CONTRIBUTORS

Many of the entries in this book were written by contributors. Following are the names of the contributors with the entries they wrote. Entries that are unlisted were written by Anne Becher or Joe Richey. Entries included in the First Edition were updated by Anne Becher for the Second Edition.

First Edition Contributors

Cain Allen: Chief Sealth (Seattle), William Steel, Chief Tommy Thompson

Eleanor Crandall: Paul Pritchard

Kris Daehler: Jerry Mander

Kevin Dahl: Gary Nabhan

Michael Egan: John James Audubon, Marston Bates, Peter Berg, J. Baird Callicott, William Colby, William Cronon, Bill Devall, William O. Douglas, Newton Drury, Alan Durning, Albert Gore, Jr., Stephen Jay Gould, Asa Gray, Alice Hamilton, Samuel P. Hays, Chris and Martin Kratt, Edmund Meany, Olaus and Margaret Murie, John D. Rockefeller, Jr., Holmes Rolston, III, Richard Evans Schultes, George Sessions, Michael Soulé, Morris Udall, Stewart Udall, Walt Whitman, Donald Worster

Joan Erben: Samuel LaBudde, Donella Meadows

Erica Ferg: Karen Silkwood, Carol Browner

T. L. Freeman-Toole: Fred Krupp, Wes Jackson, Owen Lammers, William McDonough, Roderick Nash, Sigurd Olson

Harah Frost: Hazel Johnson

Jennifer Heath: Dolores Huerta, Bill McKibben, Lewis Mumford

Sarah W. Heim-Jonson: John Hamilton Adams, Richard Ayres, Michael Bean, Barbara Bramble, William Dutcher

Cassandra Kircher: Frederick Jackson Turner

Meghan McCarthy: Rodger Schlickeisen, Luther Standing Bear, Peter Warshall

Kyle McClure: Ansel Adams, Henry Adams, Cecil Andrus, Mary Austin, Bruce Babbit, Peter Berle, Albert Bierstadt, Lester Brown, John Burroughs, Lynton Caldwell, Jimmy Carter, John Chafee, Marion Clawson, Thomas Cole, Douglas Costle, Herman Daly, Jeff DeBonis, Christina Desser, Bernard Devoto, John Dingell, Richard Grossman, Juana Gutierrez, Jay Hair, Paul Hawken, Hazel Henderson, Edward Hoagland, Michael McCloskey, Ian McHarg, John McPhee, Stephanie Mills, Edmund Muskie, Helen and Scott Nearing, Marc Reisner, Theodore Roszak, John Sawhill, Stephen Schneider,

Acknowledgments

JoAnn Tall, Wallace Stegner, Ted Turner, Howie Wolke

Bob Macfarland: Ernest Seton Thompson, Oakleigh Thorne, Gilbert White

Susan Muldowney: Debra Harry, Laura Pulido

Katherine Noble-Goodman: Eugene Odum, David Sive

Brian Russell: Dorothy Harvey

Rachel White Scheuering: John Quincy Adams, Jane Addams, Peter Bahouth, William Beebe, Stewart Brand, Michael Brown, Tom Cade, Archie Carr, Marjorie Carr, Harry Caudill, James Fenimore Cooper, Mark Dowie, Silvia Earle, David Ehrenfeld, Buckminster Fuller, Theodore Geisel, Ross Gelbspan, Joan Gussow, Julia Butterfly Hill, Helen Ingram, Stephen Kellert, Francis Moore Lappé, Anne Morrow and Charles Lindbergh, Richard Manning, Carolyn Merchant, Carlos Nagel, Margaret Owings, Steve Packard, Roger Tory Peterson, Russell Peterson, Deborah and Frank Popper, Peter Raven, Jeremy Rifkin, John Robbins, Robert Rodale, Carl Safina, Cathrine Sneed, Sandra Steingraber, Terry Tempest Williams, Diane and Kent Whealy, Louisa Willcox, Paul Winter, Hazel Wolf, George Woodwell

Noelle Sullivan: George Mitchell, Laurance Rockefeller, Kirkpatrick Sale, Philip Shabecoff, Enos Mills, Sandra Postel

Horace Voice: Henry David Thoreau

Deena Wade: Ed Begley, Jr., Woody Harrelson, Carl Sagan

Jeff Wagenheim: Vicky Robin

Ray Watt: Christopher Shuey, Henry Waxman

Julia Willis: Catherine Baeur, Mollie Beattie, Eula Bingham, Janet Brown, Aurora Castillo, Kate and Tom Chappell, John B. Cobb, Jr., Henry Cowles, Dian Fossey, Henry Jackson, Lady Bird Johnson, Jim Jontz, Hugh Kaufman, Henry Kendall, Oren Lyons, Mary McDowell, Marion Moses, Herbert Needleman, Bryan Norton, Francis Parkman, William K. Reilly, Rosemary Radford Reuther, Bill Sanjour, Carl Schurz, Irving Selikoff, Paolo Soleri, Christopher Stone, Brian Tokar, Will Toor, William Vogt, Lynn White, Jr.

Hilary Wood: Diane Ackerman, Archie Carr

Josh Zaffos: Reed Noss

*

Second Edition Contributors

Kate Sloan Fiffer: Janine Benyus, Janine Blaeloch, Louise B. Dunlap

Rosemary Gabriel: Rosalie Bertell

Rodrigo Gonzalez: Derrick Jensen, Art Rosenfeld

Vince Leibowitz: Michael Bloomberg, Laura Miller

Emily Marturana: Robin Chase, Elizabeth Christy, Stuart Conway, Michael F. Jacobson, Cynthia Moss, Nell Newman

Jim McVey: Gary Peacock, Paul Watson

Jesse Morse: Julian Darley and Celine Rich, Willie Nelson, Greg Nickels

Laura Paskus: Ben Luce, Diane Wilson

Annette Ramos: Florence Bailey, Richard Cook, Leonardo DiCaprio, Juliet Ellis, Charles Elton, Rogelio Figueroa, James Hansen, Michael Mann, Jerome Ringo, Andrew Shapiro, Arnold Schwarzenegger, Terry Tamminen, Mike Tidwell, Doug Tompkins

Sue Salinger: Kenny Ausubel, Joan Bavaria, Laurie David, Van Jones

Paul Wapner (with Diedre Zoll): Michael Pollan

John Weiss: Richard Cizik

Shawna Williams: Thomas Berry, Kevin Bixby, Marjora Carter, Andrew Jackson Downing, Woody Gagliano, Henry Gleason, Mary Oliver, Cynthia Pryor, Anne Rolfes, Michael Reynolds, Arturo Sandoval, Tracy Stone-Manning

Diedre Zoll: Henry Red Cloud

Introduction

This second edition of *American Environmental Leaders: From Colonial Times to the Present* is the first published by Grey House Publishing. The previous edition was published by ABC-CLIO in 2000. This 2-volume second edition is significantly revised and expanded with new material and added features:

- **NEW Key Documents**—a 100-page section includes 23 articles, book excerpts and speeches by the foremost authorities in the field. It comprises an incredibly expansive perspective—nine centuries—including excerpts from the 13th century *Constitution of the Iroquois Nation* to the 2008 title *Global Warming: Twenty Years Later* by James Hansen. The detailed introduction to these Key Documents on page 901 offers insight into the criteria for inclusion and the actions these documents have prompted.
- **NEW and Updated Entries**—64 brand new essays, primarily focusing on recent environmental developments, from science to policy making to the arts. This second edition, like the first, includes biographies of well-known shakers and movers, as well as less visible heroes. In addition, all articles from the first edition have been revised as needed. This new edition offers a total of 390 biographies, many with new images, that address the most pressing topics of environmental concern.
- **NEW Contributors**—this edition adds 14 names to the list of contributors to the first edition, creating a group of 41 of the strongest, most experienced authorities on the environment in the country today.
- **NEW Timeline** –detailing important firsts in areas vital to the environment—and its protection—such as accomplishments of various social movements, significant legislation, and technological advances.
- **Updated Leaders by Occupation or Work Focus**—lists all covered individuals under one—or more—category, from *Activists* to *Whistleblowers*. There are 27 occupations in all, comprising a varied, sometime unlikely, list including *Advertising Executive*, *Cartoonist* and *Theologian*.
- **Updated Index**

American Environmental Leaders

Volume I

American Environmental Leaders

From Colonial Times to the Present

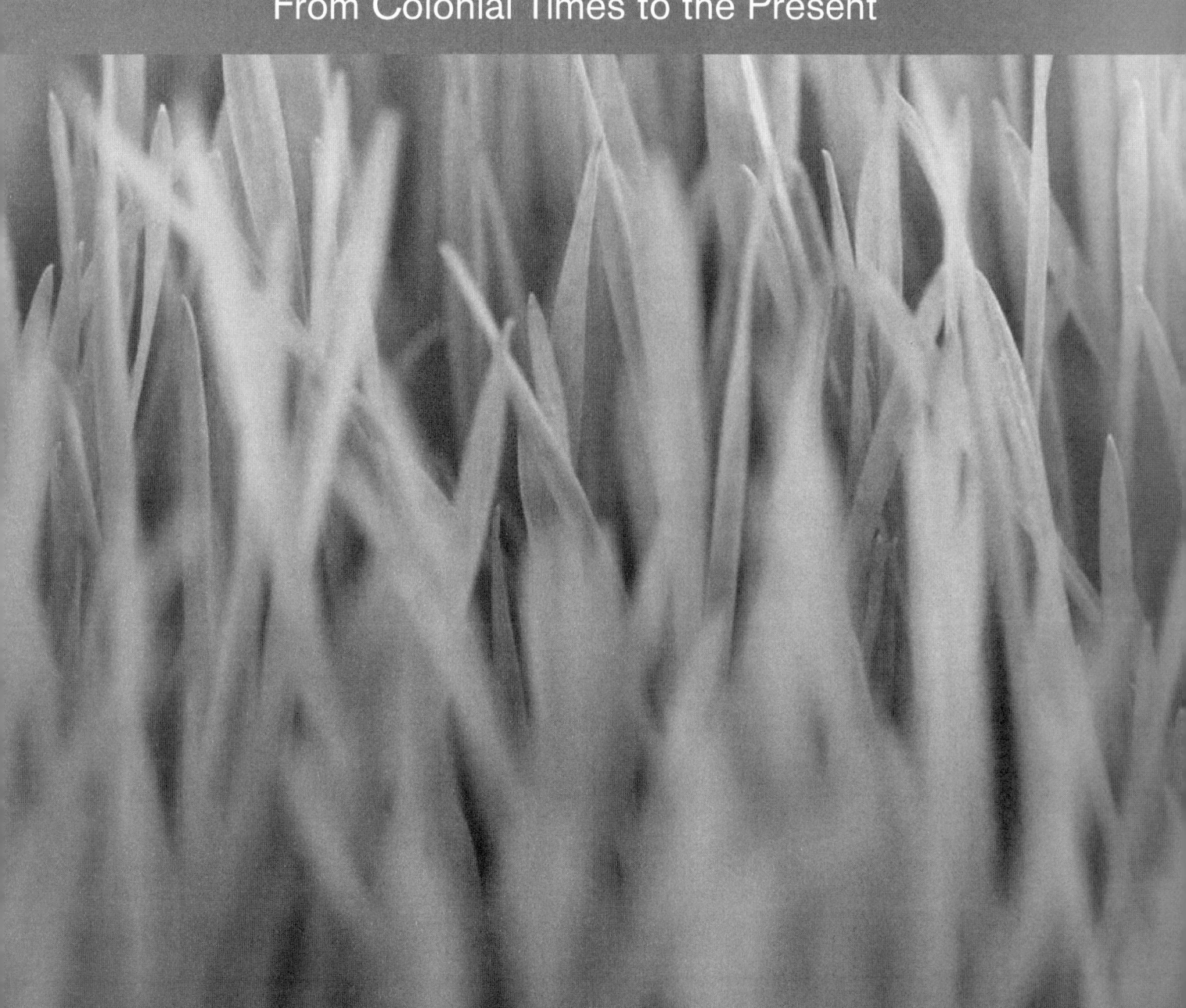

Abbey, Edward

(January 29, 1927–March 14, 1989)
Writer

Edward Abbey, wild man of the American West and the author of 22 books, defies literary definitions. He is known for his exquisite descriptions of his beloved Southwestern desert, for his bitter diatribes against those who defile such pristine areas (ranchers, loggers, even dumb tourists), and for the unruly characters—some autobiographical—who people his novels.

Edward Paul Abbey was born on January 29, 1927, in Home, Pennsylvania, a rural Allegheny community. His mother, Mildred, was an activist for the Woman's Christian Temperance Union, and his father, Paul Revere Abbey, was a Socialist union organizer who earned his livelihood cutting hickory fence posts. As a child Abbey wrote comic books, and he became a journalist while in high school (though he flunked his journalism class). During the summer of his seventeenth year, Abbey hitchhiked and rode buses and trains on an exploratory tour of the West. He fell in love with the deserts and canyons. And at the age of 19, after one year in the Army and another at Indiana State Teachers College, Abbey moved west, where he was to stay except for a few brief periods of his life. Abbey studied philosophy and English at the University of New Mexico, earning his B.A. in 1951 and his M.A. in 1956. His master's degree thesis, entitled "Anarchism and the Morality of Violence," examined political situations in which violence could be justified. His conclusion was that it was most justifiable when used in self-defense.

While working at varied jobs after completing his M.A., including inspecting roads for the U.S. Forest Service and being a ranger for the National Park Service, Abbey wrote several novels. His first widely acclaimed work was *Desert Solitaire* (1968), a compilation of his journals from the time he was working as a seasonal ranger in Arches National Monument in Utah. Many critics call this book his best. It is a medley of crystalline nature writing and enraged rants against the incursion of civilization into the pristine Southwest deserts. The author's note in *Desert Solitaire* warns the reader:

> Do not jump into your automobile next June and rush out to the canyon country hoping to see some of that which I have attempted to evoke in these pages. In the first place you can't see *anything* from a car; you've got to get out of the goddamned contraption and walk, better yet crawl, on hands and knees, over the sandstone and through the thornbush and cactus. When traces of blood begin to mark your trail you'll see something, maybe. Probably not.

The direct action arm of the environmental movement remembers Abbey best for *The Monkey Wrench Gang* (1975), an account of the exploits of a group of iconoclasts who specialized in what was later termed *monkeywrenching*, the deliberate damaging of equipment used to destroy nature. The Monkey Wrench Gang practiced by pouring sugar and dirt into the gas tanks of bulldozers and tractors at desert construction projects, but their ultimate goal was to blow up the Glen Canyon Dam. True to Abbey's master's thesis conclusions, the Monkey Wrench Gang's violence was undertaken in self-defense, for the gang identified so closely with the desert that the development was an attack on their very beings. This book inspired DAVE FOREMAN, HOWIE WOLKE, and three other friends to found Earth First! in 1979. Their first public action was at a Glen Canyon Dam protest during which Abbey spoke. From that time on, Abbey served as an elder adviser and shaman to the group.

During his lifetime, Abbey wrote 22 books. The literary establishment pegged him as a Western environmentalist writer. Abbey himself said in an interview published in *Resist*

Much, Obey Little (1996) that he was content to remain in that pigeonhole because it assured him easy access to publishers and earned him a comfortable living. However environmentalists who wanted to see him as a spokesman for their causes were often disturbed by some of his assertions. He spouted brash, disturbing opinions in some of his books. He insulted literary critics who did not like his work; called on the U.S. Border Patrol to turn back all Mexican immigrants, hand them guns, and tell them to finish their revolution; and criticized mainstream environmentalist organizations for their compromises.

Abbey's friends and fans admired his dedication to the truth—about the world and his own life—even if his words were sometimes difficult to digest or undiplomatic. Abbey was continually outraged, wrote WENDELL BERRY in his contribution to *Resist Much, Obey Little*, but Abbey's humor made his outrage tolerable to his readers. During his life Abbey married five times and fathered six children.

Abbey died of internal bleeding on March 19, 1989, shortly after being informed that he had a terminal circulatory disorder. His death and burial have achieved the same mythological status that was given his life while he was alive. Two days before he died, he asked his friends to take him out of the hospital, into the desert where he enjoyed one last campfire circle. He died in a sleeping bag on the floor of his writing cabin, and his friends followed the instructions he had left them to drive his body as far as possible into the desert and bury him under a pile of rocks.

BIBLIOGRAPHY
Abbey, Edward and David Petersen, *Postcards from Ed: dispatches and salvos from an American iconoclast*, 2006; Bishop, James Jr., *Epitaph for a Desert Anarchist*, 1994; Cahahan, James M., *Edward Abbey: a life*, 2001; Hepworth, James R., and Gregory McNamee, *Resist Much, Obey Little: Remembering Ed Abbey*, 1996; Hoagland, Edward, "Edward Abbey: Standing Tough in the Desert," *New York Times Book Review*, 1989; Loeffler, Jack, *Adventures with Ed: a portrait of Abbey*, 2002; Petersen, David, "Where Phantoms Brood and Mourn," *Backpacker*, 1993.

Ackerman, Diane
(October 7, 1948-)
Poet, Nature Writer

Writer Diane Ackerman is best known for her ability to combine the seemingly disparate disciplines of art and science. Her writing, which includes poetry, nonfiction, stories for children, and plays, is unique in its ambition to use creative expression as she explores and describes the natural world. In 1990, Ackerman's book, *A Natural History of the Senses*, became a national bestseller and inspired a miniseries that aired as part of public television's *Nova* in 1995.

Diane Ackerman was born in Waukegan, Illinois, on October 7, 1948. Eight years later, her family moved to the more rural location of Allentown, Pennsylvania. The change suited the young writer, who remembers herself as an outgoing tomboy who spent most of her time outside. When she was indoors, Ackerman spent her time reading and writing, the latter becoming a major passion that resulted in limericks, stories, and articles for the local newspaper. After spending her freshman year at Boston University, Ackerman transferred to Pennsylvania State University in 1968. It was there that she met British novelist Paul West, a professor who later became her life companion.

Ackerman graduated in 1970 with a B.A. degree in English. During the same year she began studying for her M.F.A. at Cornell University in Ithaca, New York. Eight years later, Ackerman had not only completed her intended degree but had also earned an M.A. and a Ph.D. in English literature. During this period she won two prestigious awards, the Academy of American Poets Prize and the Corson Bishop Prize for Poetry and published her first book of poetry, *The Planets: A Cosmic Pastoral*, in 1976. Even at this early point in her career, Ackerman showed signs of her future ambition to bring science and poetic writing into the same medium. *The Planets*, written entirely about astronomy, introduced readers to the author's unusual articulation of the natural world, a perception that did not distinguish hard data from passionate observation. This unique blend of disciplines was to be Ackerman's trademark, a result of what she terms her "nomadic curiosity."

Ackerman's fascination with the universe is reflected in the diversity of subjects she investigates in her writing. In 1980, *Twilight of the Tenderfoot*, a book detailing her experiences as a ranch hand in New Mexico, was published to wide acclaim. After earning her pilot's license, she wrote *On Extended Wings* (1985), a book exploring the implications of learning to fly, which was later adapted to the stage. During this time, Ackerman continued to write poetry. *Lady Faustus*, a collection of poems published in 1983, covered such diverse subjects as soccer, flying, and meditations on amphibians. Despite the wide spectrum of subject matter, Ackerman's work remains infused with a central theme. Whether branding cattle or staring at the stars, there is always a fascination and a deep enthusiasm for the natural world. Though this point of view received criticism from those who believed that poetry must be free of science, Ackerman's approach shows that the two can be combined gracefully.

In 1988, Ackerman published *Reverse Thunder: A Dramatic Poem*, detailing the life and times of Sor Juana de la Cruz, a nun who lived in seventeenth-century Spain. A play written in verse, *Reverse Thunder* is a tribute to a woman Ackerman deeply admires. Despite the restrictions of the times, Sor Juana was both a poet and a scientist, a woman who shared Ackerman's awe at the complexities of creation. Her meditations reveal a creative mind unafraid to combine religion with science or poetry with data, an unpopular concept in her day.

Ackerman's most popular book, *A Natural History of the Senses*, became a bestseller shortly after its publication in 1990. A celebration of the five senses, the book uses essays, vignettes, and observations to investigate the ways in which humans perceive the natural world. The sweeping success of *Senses* was a surprise, as very few scientifically based works become bestsellers. No doubt the success of the book can be attributed to Ackerman's skill as a writer and her ability to mix potentially dry material with humor, myth, and poetic description. In February 1995, the television series *Nova* invited Ackerman to host a five-part miniseries entitled "Mystery of the Senses," which received some of the highest ratings of the season. *Senses* is Ackerman's crowning achievement to date, a work that introduced countless readers to her unique genius.

In 1991, Ackerman returned to poetry with *Jaguar of Sweet Laughter: New and Selected Poems*, which was nominated for the National Book Critics Circle Award. Another publication, *The Moon by Whale Light: And Other Adventures among Bats, Penguins, Crocodilians, and Whales*, expanded upon a series of articles that had been previously published in the *New Yorker*. In 1994, Ackerman's *A Natural History of Love*, which was modeled upon her earlier book, received mixed reviews from critics who believed that the subject of love, unlike that of our senses, was broader than could be covered in a single volume. Despite these hesitations, *Love* was widely enjoyed by the public, many of whom savored the beauty of Ackerman's prose in its investigation of the many different concepts of love.

Ackerman's 1995 *The Rarest of the Rare: Vanishing Animals, Timeless Worlds* resulted from a series of pilgrimages to the world's rarest ecosystems, during which she paid homage to rare and unusual species. The book contains chapters on the monk seal, the short-tailed albatross, the golden lion tamarin, and other endangered species. Ackerman mixes descriptions of habitats and animals with biographical data about her human companions, biologists who study and strive to protect their chosen species.

Ackerman's latest non-fiction books include *Deep Play* (1999), which examines the state of mind one enters when focused passionately and entirely on something one loves; *Cultivating Delight* (2001). 52 essays that range from the sensory pleasures of a garden to detailed botanic and zoological description; and *The Zookeeper's Wife (2007)*, which tells the story of Antonina Zabinski, the wife of the keeper of the Warsaw Zoo, who after her husband's zoo was pillaged during the Nazi occupation of Poland, rescued and harbored more than 300 Jews. Another focus of *The Zookeeper's Wife* is a forest in Poland called Bialowieza, home to free-ranging "living fossils," descendents of ancient bison and horses.

Diane Ackerman resides in upstate New York..She has received many awards for her writing, including the Black Warrior Review Poetry Prize in 1981, the Pushcart Prize VIII in 1984, the Lowell Thomas Award from the Society of American Travel Writers in 1990, in 1992 the Wordsmith Award, and the New and Noteworthy Book of the Year for *The Moon by Whale Light* from the *New York Times Book Review*, in 1998 a John Burroughs Nature Award, and most recently, in 2003, a Guggenheim Fellowship.

BIBLIOGRAPHY
Brainard, Dulay, "Diane Ackerman," *Publisher's Weekly*, 1991; "Diane Ackerman," www.dianeackerman.com; Dowd, Maureen, "Diane Ackerman," Vogue, 1991; Elder, John, ed., *American Nature Writers Volume 1*, 1996; Shelton, Pamela, ed., *Contemporary Woman Poets*, 1998.

Adams, Ansel
(February 20, 1902–April 22, 1984)
Photographer, Preservation Activist

Ansel Adams was a photographer and a preservationist. His pictures played an important role in defining how Americans think about wilderness, and they have been vital in supporting its preservation. Adams served on the board of directors of the Sierra Club for nearly 40 years.

Ansel Easton Adams was born on February 20, 1902, in San Francisco, California, the only child of Charles Hitchcock Adams and Olive Bray Adams. His father was a businessman whose enterprises included an insurance agency and a chemical plant. Adams grew up among the sand dunes on the westernmost edge of the San Francisco Peninsula, where from his early childhood he was surrounded by natural beauty. His education was erratic and largely self-acquired. He attended both public and private schools, and he also received some instruction at home from his father.

A significant event in Adams's early life was a vacation his family took to Yosemite National Park in 1916, when he was 14 years old. He brought along a Kodak Box Brownie camera that he used to take his first photographs. As a result of this experience, Adams persuaded Frank Ditmman, the owner of a San Francisco photo finishing plant, to take him on as an apprentice in developing and other techniques in the darkroom. While Adams's enthusiasm for photography was growing, music, at this time, was his main concern. He was receiving four hours of instruction every day from Fredrich Zech, who had studied under Hans von Bulow, one of the great German pianists and conductors of the nineteenth century. By the time he was 18, Adams was convinced that he would be a professional pianist. It was not until 1930 that he decided to abandon his music studies and devote all of his time to photography. The study of technique and the attention to detail he acquired in his musical training, however, never left him. In a 1977 interview he stated that there is a very definite relationship between music and photography, all art being "essentially the same thing," and that he really benefited from two factors, a sense of discipline and a sense of aesthetics.

It was in 1930, two years after he had married Virginia Best, that Adams met Paul Strand, a photographer whom Adams credited with opening his eyes to the artistic possibilities of the stark, crisp photographic image. Most photographers of the time were practicing hand-tinted, soft-focus photography, creating images more like paintings than photographs. Adams helped to found a group called f/64 (the name f/64 being a reference to the small lens opening of the camera) in opposition to the general photographic practices of the time. The members of this group sought, through "straight photography," to create images with sharp focus, and great depth of field, to "create photographs which actually looked like photographs."

Adams is best known for his black and white photographs of nature and the American landscape. He pioneered the Zone System, a technique designed to enable the photographer to anticipate and control the tonal range of the print. He believed that a photograph is made, not taken. And in his photographs he sought to capture the spiritual excitement he felt about the subject.

Adams once said that "everybody needs something to believe in. Conservation is my point of focus." His involvement with conservation dates back to his first photographs. He joined the Sierra Club in 1919, and he worked for four summers as caretaker of the club's headquarters in Yosemite Valley. He later sat on the board of directors of the club for nearly 40 years, strongly influencing the club's philosophy and activities and encouraging activism and a national focus, in what until then had been primarily a California-based organization. In 1936, when the Sierra Club was lobbying for the creation of a national park in the King's Canyon area of California, Adams sent copies of his book, *Sierra Nevada: The John Muir Trail*, which contains many pictures of this area, to Pres. FRANKLIN D. ROOSEVELT and to other important political figures. He also made a trip to Washington to personally advocate the designation of this national park.

Adams was also active in protesting the widening of Yosemite's Tioga road as a part of the National Park Service's Mission 66 in 1952. He even went so far as to resign from the board of directors because of the Sierra Club's unwillingness to take a stance on the issue. As a private citizen, he denounced the plan as a violation of the National Park Service Act, bordering on criminal negligence. The Sierra Club board was not willing to accept his resignation, and its members persuaded him to return, stating that his "purist voice was needed to keep the club true to its ideals." Throughout his time on the board of directors, Adams wielded a powerful voice for cooperation and compromise. This would eventually estrange him somewhat, as younger members of the Sierra Club moved toward more aggressive and antagonistic means of promoting wilderness preservation.

The California Wilderness Act established the Ansel Adams Wilderness in 1984, south of Yosemite, doubling the area of the already-existing Minarets Wilderness and changing its name to honor Ansel Adams. It is an area of almost 230,000 acres, characterized by steep gorges and rocky peaks and spires, and shelters the headwaters of the San Joaquin River. Adams received two other major honors from the U.S. government: the Conservation Service Award from the U.S Department of the Interior, in 1968, and the Presidential Medal of Freedom, in 1980.

Adams's interest in the national parks and wilderness was an abiding one. And, while he never specifically made pictures for environmental purposes, his pictures have been invaluable to environmental work. Indeed, his images of national parks, Yosemite especially, have virtually defined the way people see and experience these places. For many, Yosemite *is* what Adams captured with his camera.

Adams left a legacy in two parts, one being the result of his conservation work, his advocacy of wilderness, and national parks. The other was his photographs that record the beauty and majesty of these places for the enjoyment and education of future generations. He died on April 22, 1984, of heart failure in San Francisco. He left his wife, his son, Michael, and daughter, Anne Helms.

BIBLIOGRAPHY

"Ansel Adams," *Current Biography Yearbook*, 1977; "Ansel Adams Main—Sierra Club" www.sierraclub.org/ansel_adams/; Callahan, Harry M., ed., *Ansel Adams in Color*, 1993; Maack, Richard, "The 'Lost' Photographs of Ansel Adams," *Arizona Highways*, 2005; Spaulding, Jonathan, *Ansel Adams and the American Landscape*, 1995.

Adams, Henry
(February 16, 1838–March 27, 1918)
Writer, Historian

Henry Adams was a historian, social critic, and travel writer. He was an incessant traveler, and he used his experiences as a tourist and outsider not only to understand the changing human society of the 1800s but also to understand the human soul. In his writings he examined the meaning and importance of wilderness as an idea and as a geographical location. He believed that the rapid technological advances and social changes occurring at the turn of the nineteenth century could only lead to economic and social collapse.

Henry Brooks Adams was born February 16, 1838, into the famous and successful Adams family that included presidents John Adams and JOHN QUINCY ADAMS, respectively his great-grandfather and grandfather. As a member of such a prominent family, Adams grew up believing that he too would enter into public service and would eventually take his own turn as president of the United States. Despite all of his other, major accomplishments, Adams carried with him a certain sense of failure at not having lived up to the example set by his forebears.

Adams grew up in Boston, Massachusetts, attending the Dixwell School and graduating from Harvard University in 1858. Following college, he spent two years visiting Belgium, Holland, Italy, Sicily, France, Germany, and England as a newspaper correspondent to the

Boston Courier. He returned to the United States in 1860 and took a position as private secretary to his father, who was a congressman at that time. Later that year, when Abraham Lincoln appointed Adams's father minister to Great Britain, Adams accompanied him in his capacity as private secretary and remained in England until 1868. During this time, he came into contact with many distinguished artists and intellectuals, including Robert Browning, Charles Dickens, and one of Britain's foremost geologists, Sir Charles Lyell.

Upon returning to Washington, D.C., in 1868, Adams began working as a freelance journalist, contributing articles to various U.S. and British periodicals. In 1870, Adams was offered a position as an assistant professor of medieval history at Harvard. He spent seven years there, during which time he edited the *North American Review* and developed a very popular seminar style of classroom instruction. He gave up his teaching post in 1877 to concentrate on researching and writing history, moving to Washington, D.C., where he could make use of the government archives for his historical research. During the period between 1877 and 1885, he wrote and took many trips to Europe with his wife, Marian Hooper, whom he had married in 1872. He published two biographies, one of Secretary of the Treasury, diplomat and ethnographer Albert Gallatin (1879) and one of Senator and Congressman John Randolph (1882), and two novels, *Democracy* (1880) and *Esther* (1884), while also working on his nine-volume work, *The History of the United States during the Administrations of Thomas Jefferson and James Madison* (1889–1891). Adams published *Esther* under the pseudonymn Frances Snow Compton, and many believe that its main character, who grapples with the disharmonies inherent in science and religion, was modeled after his wife. The character, Esther, nearly commits suicide in the book. Adams's own wife, Marian, actually did kill herself in 1885 after a period of deep depression, a loss from which Adams would never fully recover.

Democracy was published anonymously. In this book, Adams writes about "wilderness" but in a way that completely reverses the original usage of the term. On the first page of the novel, referring to New York City, he writes, "What was it all worth, this wilderness of men and women as monotonous as the brown stone houses they lived in?" This "urban wilderness" became a theme of Adams's as he reflected through his writings on the rapidly changing Western world. He saw civilization, as it was developing during his life, as being just as bewildering and intimidating as any wilderness of trees and animals. He believed that society was too organized and that this organization stripped individuals of their autonomy, eventually leading to social and economic collapse. Which, from one perspective, it eventually did, in the form of two global wars and the Great Depression of the 1930s in the United States. These ideas, which were shared by others such as Oswald Spengler and Arnold Toynbee, led to an intellectual movement that believed that the shrinking natural wilderness should be preserved as an escape for humans from the growing oppressive urban social wilderness.

For the remainder of his life, Adams was an avid traveler and a prolific writer. He published a total of 18 books. He visited Japan and Russia and began spending half of every year in France until the onset of World War I. In his most famous book, *The Education of Henry Adams* (1918), for which he received a posthumous Pulitzer Prize for autobiography, he tracks his lifelong education. It was travel, not formal education, that truly provided Adams with an education, an education that was usually "accidental" and adventurous. This book also provides an in-depth look at the changes occurring in the society of the 1800s. Adams attributed these changes to the increasing attempts by humans to control the forces of nature, compounded by the rapid technological advances of the time—which together made life more complicated. He found himself in a state of amazement at the emerging "modern world." In a letter quoted by Viola Winner for an *American Heritage* magazine article, he writes, "Out of a medieval, primitive, crawling infant of 1838, to find oneself a howling, steaming, exploding, Marconing, radiummating, automobiling maniac of 1904 exceeds belief."

Winner also points out that Adams was concerned with environmental issues. He wrote, "Cities are now growing uninhabitable everywhere. The noise and wear are impossible. Paris is as bad as any. New York is already abandoned by everyone who can escape." "Nature," he believed simply, "has got to turn on us."

Adams suffered a cerebral thrombosis on April 24, 1912. He never entirely recovered but continued to travel and write. His health declined gradually over the next few years, and he died at his home in Washington on March 27, 1918.

BIBLIOGRAPHY

Adams, Henry, *Democracy*, 1880; Adams, Henry, *The Education of Henry Adams*, 1907; Blackmur, R. P., *Henry Adams*, 1980; Chalfant, Edward, *Both Sides of the Ocean*, 1982; Nash, Roderick, *Wilderness and the American Mind*, 1967; Wills, Garry, *Henry Adams and the Making of America*, 2005; Winner, Viola Hopkins, "The Virgin and the Carburetor," *American Heritage*, 1995.

Adams, John Hamilton
(February 15, 1936–)
Co-founder of Natural Resources Defense Council (NRDC)

John Hamilton Adams cofounded the Natural Resources Defense Council (NRDC) in 1970, an organization of public interest lawyers focused on the formation and enforcement of emerging environmental laws. As its executive director from 1970 to 1998, Adams created an influential nonprofit organization of lawyers and scientists with a membership that has grown to 1.2 million members and online activists nationwide. As president of NRDC from October 1998 to December 2006 and still today in his current role as founding director, Adams advises politicians and members of industry on the need to create environmental policy that will help protect the nation's natural resources for future generations.

Adams was born on February 15, 1936, in New York City and grew up on a farm in the Catskills of New York State. He graduated from Michigan State University in 1959 with a B.A. in history. After college he attended law school at Duke University, graduating in 1962 with his LL.B. He returned to New York and worked as an associate at Cadwalader, Wickersham, and Taft on Wall Street from 1962 to 1965. From 1965 to 1970, Adams worked as the assistant U.S. attorney for the Southern District of New York.

At the U.S. attorney's office in Manhattan, Adams met a number of other young attorneys who were attracted to environmentally oriented public interest law. They cofounded the NRDC in 1970, and Adams became its first paid staff member. NRDC's first case was to represent a coalition of environmental groups that had been working throughout the 1960s against the construction of the Storm King Mountain pump storage plant on the Hudson River. In addition to marring one of the most spectacular sites on the river—Storm Mountain was a popular subject for THOMAS COLE and other painters of the Hudson River School—the plant would have resulted in devastating fish kills. NRDC's lawyers eventually won the Storm King case, which is still significant because it provided a historical precedent for environmental lawsuits brought on by citizen plaintiffs.

NRDC has won a reputation as one of the nation's most influential environmental organizations, and today includes 1.2 million members and online activists. NRDC seeks to safeguard the health of humans and the natural world, attempting to persuade governments, business, and other institutions to adopt more environmentally friendly policies. NRDC is credited with having major impacts on national and international policies in many areas, including air and water pollution, toxic chemicals, energy, transportation and urban development, protection of old-growth forests and other terrestrial and marine habitat, limitation of nuclear proliferation, and global warming, an area in which the NRDC has served a particularly important role in recent years. Adams served as President of the NRDC until he stepped down in 2006.

In 1972, Adams joined the adjunct faculty of New York University's School of Law, where he taught Clinical Environmental Law for 26 years. Although Adams no longer teaches in this program, NYU law students still have the option of participating in the environmental clinic, through which they attend lectures and discussions on a range of environmental subjects and work on projects at NRDC. In 1973, Adams joined the board of the Open Space Institute, a conservancy devoted to the protection of open space lands in the Northeast. Since 1973, Adams has served as the chairman of the board. The Institute has purchased thousands of acres of land in the Hudson Valley, the Adirondacks, and the Catskills. One of its most successful projects was ensuring the protection of Sterling Forest, an area of 20,000 acres between New York and New Jersey. He is also on the boards of the Catskill Center for Conservation, the League of Conservation Voters, and the Woods Hole Research Center. He served on the President's Council on Sustainable Development and participated in the Environmental Protection Agency's Common Sense Initiative.

Over the years, Adams has received several notable honors and environmental awards, including the Wilderness Society's Robert Marshall Award, the Judge Lumbard Cup for public service from the U.S. Attorney's Southern District of New York, the National Conservation Achievement Award from the National Wildlife Federation, the Francis K. Hutchinson Conservation Award from the Garden Club of America, Duke University's Distinguished Alumni Award, Duke University Law School's Charles J. Murphy Award, as well as an Honorary Doctor of Laws from Duke University. Adams was named one of the National Audubon Society's 100 Champions of Conservation.

Adams lives in upstate New York with his wife. They and their three grown children and grandchildren enjoy time spent at their home in the Catskills on the Beaverkill River.

BIBLIOGRAPHY

Adams, John, "Are Higher Fuel-Efficiency Standards a Good Idea?" *Insight*, 1996; Adams, John, "The Future of Environmental Management," *Environmental Management*, 2000; Adams, John, "Leadership on the Right Track," *Conservation Voice*, 1997; Adams, John, "On Environmental Cost-Benefit Scale, Prevention Scores High," *New York Times*, 1993, "The Litigator: John Adams," *Rolling Stone, 2005.*

Adams, John Quincy
(July 11, 1767–February 23, 1848)
President of the United States

John Quincy Adams was far ahead of his time in recognizing the need for conservation. While most of America's attention in the early nineteenth century was focused on expansion, he understood the problem of overusing the land. He was the first president to show any interest in setting land aside to be protected from the unchecked degradation that came with building a civilization. He was interested in natural history and did much to promote scientific study and discovery, at a time when these ideas were politically unpopular.

Born on July 11, 1767, in Braintree (now Quincy) Massachusetts, John Quincy Adams grew up as a child of the American Revolution, which began when he was seven years old. His father, John Adams, would later become the second president, and his mother, Abigail Smith Adams, was an accomplished and outspoken woman. He was educated in the village school and was urged along in his studies through letters from his absent father, who was serving in the Continental Congress in Philadelphia. He occasionally accompanied his father on diplomatic missions to Europe, and there was no question that his parents were grooming him for the presidency later in his life. After graduating from Harvard College in 1787, he became a lawyer and established a practice in Boston. On July 26, 1797, he married Louisa Catherine Johnson, with whom he would have a long and passionate marriage and four children.

His career as a politician began in 1802, when he was elected as a state senator from Suffolk County, Massachusetts. He then served in the United States Senate from Massachusetts, from 1803 to 1808. For the next few years he taught at Harvard, practiced law, and served as foreign minister to Russia. From 1817 to 1825, he served as President Monroe's secretary of state. And in 1825 he became president himself.

During his only term as president, he showed himself to be remarkably conscious of the need to protect the nation's forests. He was up against the frenzy to expand the nation, and very few people considered the cost to the environment. There seemed to exist an endless supply of timber, and there was an insatiable demand for it—which created an opportunity for great profit. Thus there was heavy pressure on politicians to provide policies favorable to the continued plundering of the forests.

Instead, Adams acted in the opposite direction. Understanding the need to preserve for the future, he set aside live oak lands along the Gulf Coast to be used as naval timber reserves. Santa Rosa Island off Pensacola was one of the reserves he established. Unfortunately his term in office was only four years, and his successor, Andrew Jackson, was opposed to all of Adams's conservation efforts. During Adams's terms in the House of Representatives following his presidency, an act decreed that it was unlawful to cut timber on public lands, but President Jackson saw to it that it was never implemented.

Adams also had a high regard for science and learning. He believed that the quest for knowledge was the greatest thing a person could aspire to, and once said "it prolongs life itself and enlarges the sphere of existence." He was a great supporter in Congress of scientific expeditions and led the movement for establishing the Smithsonian Institution in Washington, D.C., one of the nation's foremost centers of learning. In an age when most of his country cared more about productivity and progress, he had the foresight to advocate greater scientific knowledge of the land. In the early nineteenth century, his cry for knowledge was a precursor to today's concern for the environment. Indeed, as science progressed in that century, it produced sobering data about the consequences of human exploitation of the environment.

After his presidential term, Adams returned to politics in 1831, serving in the U.S. House of Representatives for the rest of his life. He died on February 23, 1848, in Washington, D.C., and was buried at First Parish Church in Quincy, Massachusetts.

BIBLIOGRAPHY
Bartlett, Richard A., *The New Country*, 1974; Goetzmann, William H., *New Lands, New Men: America and the Second Great Age of Discovery*, 1986; Lipsky, George A., *John Quincy Adams: His Theory and Ideas*, 1950; Nagel, Paul C., *John Quincy Adams: A Public Life, A Private Life*, 1997; Remini, Robert Vincent, *John Quincy Adams*, 2002; Shabecoff, Philip, *A Fierce Green Fire: The American Environmental Movement*, 1993.

Addams, Jane
(September 6, 1860–May 21, 1935)
Social Reformer, Peace Activist

A relentless reformer and a humanitarian activist, Jane Addams confronted the urban and industrial environmental realities of the Progressive era in the late nineteenth and early twentieth centuries. She founded Hull House in Chicago, an advocacy and education center run largely by women that provided cultural, social, and medical services to those who needed them. She centered her efforts on the quality of life of industrial workers and sought to abolish the urban miseries she saw daily, such as polluted and unsanitary neighborhoods, overcrowded tenements, inadequate schools, and unsafe working conditions. Hull House became a meeting ground for reformers and activists of all kinds, and Addams's work paved the way for better conditions in urban work environments.

Laura Jane Addams was born on September 6, 1860, in Cedarville, Illinois, to John Huy Addams and Sarah (Weber) Addams. She was the eighth of nine children, though only she and three others lived past childhood. When she was two years old her mother died, and as she grew up she became very close to her father. She was a bright and ambitious child but

Jane Addams (Library of Congress, Prints & Photographs Division, LC-DIG-ggbain-39054)

was plagued by constant back pain, caused by tuberculosis of the spine. Also, she sometimes felt she was an ugly duckling and was ashamed of the overwhelming adoration she felt for her father. He was a successful banker, miller, and later an admired state senator. He was strongly antislavery and was a friend and correspondent of Abraham Lincoln. His abolitionist views and his benevolent outlook were strong forces in Jane's life and influenced her own perception of the world. Though she admired and loved her father, she also felt occasionally restricted by him. After graduating from high school, she hoped to attend Smith College in Massachusetts, one of the few schools that offered women the same caliber of education as men. But her father objected, saying Smith was too far from home and that she did not need such a rigorous education. Though frustrated, she relented and ended up going to Rockford Female Seminary in Illinois, a religious school that did not even offer degrees. With her determination and vision, though, she quickly became an outstanding student and leader and worked hard in the hopes that her school would eventually decide to confer college degrees. In 1881 she graduated at the head of her class, and a year later Rockford Seminary became a degree-granting institution and she was granted a B.A.

In the same year that she completed her studies, her father died. She was devastated by this and had difficulty getting a career in order. In the fall of 1881 she enrolled in the Women's Medical College in Pennsylvania but dropped out a few months later, realizing she did not want to be a doctor. Her own health was deteriorating, and she soon had to have surgery on her spine, which confined her to bed for six months. Increasingly, she felt aimless and hindered by the fact that there were few options at this time for aspiring women. In the end, her circumstances combined forces against her, and she fell into a depression that lasted for years.

During this period, she occasionally traveled with her stepmother overseas. On one visit to London, Addams was shocked by the poverty and filth in the slums there. It had a profound impact on her and provoked her to action, and she finally began to feel as if she had a purpose. She and her close friend Ellen Gates Starr began making plans to buy a house in a poor neighborhood in Chicago where they and other interested women could attempt to reverse some of the abuses of industrialization. In 1889, they moved into Hull House in the nineteenth ward, a poor district in west Chicago inhabited by thousands of immigrants. Their goal was to establish a "settlement," or a center for ideas and reform.

Cities in the nineteenth and early twentieth centuries were experiencing industrial expansion, economic growth, and urban restructuring—all of which contributed to new forms of environmental degradation. Some of the most widespread problems included solid and hazardous waste disposal, inadequate sewerage and sanitation systems, loss of water quality, and other public health issues. For Addams, the boom in industry offered an opportunity to expand the nation's sense of civic responsibility. When the Hull House settlement was established, it became a major force for social reform in industrial cities. Addams worked aggressively to provide programs that addressed the immediate needs of the community. Hull House included a library, a nursery, an art studio, a cooperative boardinghouse for working women, a community kitchen, and a music school. With the help of her growing numbers of settlement activists, including MARY MCDOWELL and physician ALICE HAMILTON, Addams also fought for other social and environmental reforms, such as abolishing sweatshops, child labor, unsafe factories, and overcrowded tenements; and for the establishment of effective urban infrastructure that would provide such services as adequate garbage collection. The garbage problem was a major symptom of the environmental downfall of the times and created a serious health threat in the urban neighborhoods—and Addams undertook a large-scale investigation of the city's garbage collection system. Conditions improved little as a result of her complaints, so in sheer desperation she submitted her own bid to collect the garbage in the nineteenth ward. Her application was thrown out on a technicality, but nevertheless, she started rising early every morning to follow the garbage trucks on their rounds and in general made enough of a ruckus that the city decided to restructure the garbage collection system.

In an era when very few women had significant public status, Addams became an international celebrity through her work. She wrote several books that became best sellers and traveled around the world attending conferences of the Women's International League for Peace and Freedom. Her pacifist stance brought her much criticism during World War I, but she never wavered. In 1931 she became the first woman in the United States to receive the Nobel Peace Prize. She died of cancer on May 21, 1935, in Chicago and is buried in Cedarville, Illinois.

BIBLIOGRAPHY

Addams, Jane, *Twenty Years at Hull House*, 1910; Farrell, John C., *Beloved Lady: A History of Jane Addams' Ideas on Reform and Peace*, 1967; Gottlieb, Robert, *Forcing the Spring: The Transformation of the American Environmental Movement*, 1993; Knight, Louise W., *Citizen: Jane Addams and the struggle for democracy*, 2005.

Albright, Horace

(January 6, 1890–March 28, 1987)
National Park Service Director

Responsible for drafting the National Park Service Act, lobbying Congress to pass it, serving as assistant director of the National Park Service under its first director, STEPHEN MATHER, and eventually becoming director himself, Horace Albright played the roles of midwife and nanny to the U.S. National Parks movement.

Horace Marden Albright was born on January 6, 1890, in Bishop, California, just north of Sequoia National Park, east of Kings Canyon, and south of Yosemite. He graduated from the University of California at Berkeley in 1912 and received his law degree from Georgetown University in 1914. At the age of 24, when he thought he was finishing up a temporary job assisting Interior Secretary Franklin Lane and preparing to return to California to marry and begin practicing law, Albright met the man who was to influence the course of the rest of his life. Secretary Lane was courting wealthy industrialist Stephen Mather for a near-volunteer job directing the national parks, and Lane asked Albright to tell Mather about the job's duties. By the end of the evening, Albright had convinced Mather to take the job, and Mather, in turn, had persuaded Albright to become his assistant.

Several national parks already existed in 1915 when the Mather-Albright team began its work: Crater Lake in Oregon; Glacier in Montana; Rocky Mountain in Colorado; Yellowstone straddling Wyoming, Montana, and Idaho; Yosemite in California—13 in total. But they lacked infrastructure for visitors, their administration was underfunded and uncoordinated, and most alarming, they were threatened by logging or mining at their borders and by unscrupulous profiteers catering to the few visitors that made their way there.

Mather and Albright made a list of priorities when they began work. Foremost was to draft and pass a National Park Service Act that would give them the authority they needed to reorganize park management and implement protection laws. They drafted the Na-

Horace M. Albright (Library of Congress, Prints & Photographs Division, LC-USZ62-37302)

tional Park Service Act, and thanks to publicity assistant ROBERT STERLING YARD's prolific and effusive articles about the national parks and to Mather's personal charisma and generosity in inviting the most influential congressmen and their wives on spectacular park tours, a majority of Congress voted for it. Albright's Capitol Hill connections got the bill to Pres. Woodrow Wilson ahead of schedule, and the bill became law August 25, 1916.

From 1916 to 1919, Assistant Director Albright continued to work at the National Park Service (NPS) in Washington, D.C., and to accompany Mather and groups of elite politicians or private donors on tours designed to convert them into committed conservationists. In 1919 he felt ready to move on to the private sector, where he could finally practice law and probably earn more money than he did at NPS, even with Mather's supplement. But once again Mather stepped in and offered Albright the superintendency of Yellowstone National Park combined with a position as field assistant to the director. Albright accepted it and moved his family—his wife, Grace, and young children Robert and Marian—to Yellowstone. They remained there for ten years.

Mather died in 1929, and Albright was invited to succeed him as National Park Service director. Albright could not boast the wealth, charisma, or sheer physical energy of Mather, but his time in Washington, D.C., had garnered him the personal acquaintance of 200 congressmen. During the four years that he served as director, he established three new national parks (Grand Teton, Carlsbad Cavern, Great Smoky Mountains) and several national monuments, including Death Valley and Canyon de Chelly. He was able to enlarge nine national parks, some of them significantly, in a way that would make their borders follow natural frontiers such as rivers or watersheds.

When FRANKLIN D. ROOSEVELT was elected president in 1932, he installed HAROLD ICKES as secretary of the interior. Ickes and Albright collaborated to find work in the national parks for the thousands of young men who formed Roosevelt's Civilian Conservation Corps. They built roads, trails, campsites, and bathrooms, strung phone lines, and fought forest fires.

By 1933, Albright had decided to leave the public sector, and he resigned his post with NPS to become president of the U.S. Potash mining company. For the rest of his life, Albright served as adviser to NPS directors. With philanthropist and conservationist JOHN D. ROCKEFELLER, JR., Albright lobbied to make Jackson Hole a national park and colonial Williamsburg a national monument. Albright was awarded the Sierra Club's John Muir Award, the Interior Department's Conservation Service Award in 1953, and the Presidential Medal of Freedom in 1980.

Albright died at the age of 97 in a nursing home in Los Angeles, California, on March 28, 1987.

BIBLIOGRAPHY

Albright, Horace, and Robert Cahn, *The Birth of the National Park Service*, 1985; Albright, Horace, and Marian Albright Schenck, *Creating the National Park Service: The Missing Years*, 1999; McPherson, Stephen Mather, "Horace Albright," *National Parks*, 1987; Shankland, Robert, *Steve Mather of the National Parks*, 1970; Sidey, Hugh, "Present at the Preservation," *Time*, 1985.

Alston, Dana
(December 18, 1951–August 7, 1999)
Environmental Justice Funder and Activist

As one of the founders of the environmental justice movement, Dana Alston coconvened the First National People of Color Environmental Leadership Summit in 1991, which brought 600 environmental justice activists of color together for the first time and at which the influential Principles of Environmental Justice were formulated. Alston's particular niche in the movement was to help grassroots environmental justice groups attain the funding they needed, and she spent the last years of her life working to assure their continued financial support.

Dana Ann Alston was born in New York on December 18, 1951, to Garlan and Betty Alston. She attended Wheelock College in Boston, graduating with a B.S. in 1973. At Wheelock, Alston served as president of the Black Student Organization and led fellow Black students to demand more African American courses and faculty members. She completed a master's degree from the School of Public Health at Columbia University in 1979.

During the 1970s and 1980s Alston worked with organizations devoted to improving the standard and quality of life for poor, rural people of color. She was a founding board member of the Southern Rural Women's Network and worked with farm workers on pesticide issues for Rural America. She aided the solidarity campaign for the South African anti-apartheid movement and helped organize the U.S. visit of South African president and former political prisoner Nelson Mandela.

Committed to increasing funding for people of color and grassroots organizing for social justice, Alston became president of the National Black United Fund, where she oversaw completion of a lawsuit that resulted in workers, for the first time, being able to contribute to Black-led and organized charitable funds. Alston also worked on development and grant making with the National Committee for Responsive Philanthropy and worked for TransAfrica Forum.

In 1990, Alston developed the Environment, Community Development, and Race project for the Panos Institute, an independent policy studies organization that works to raise public understanding of sustainable development. One of her first tasks was to edit *We Speak for Ourselves: Social Justice, Race And Environment*, a collection of articles and interviews about the environmental justice movement. In her introduction to the book, Alston contrasted the environmental justice movement with the better-known, conservation-oriented mainstream environmental movement: "Communities of color have often taken a more holistic approach than the mainstream environmental movement, integrating 'environmental' concerns into a broader agenda that emphasizes social, racial and economic justice."

Alston and other environmental justice leaders, including Patrick Bryant, ROBERT

Bullard, Benjamin Chavis, Donna Chavis, Charles Lee, and Richard Moore, convened the First National People of Color Environmental Leadership Summit, a four-day conference held in Washington, D.C., in October 1991. This event, which attracted 600 representatives of environmental justice organizations led by people of color to address the environmental problems faced by people of color, allowed participants to share experiences and network among themselves. The attendees adopted seventeen Principles of Environmental Justice, which have endured as a reminder of the ultimate goals of the environmental justice movement.

Representatives of mainstream environmental organizations had been invited to attend the second half of the Summit, and Alston was chosen to deliver a welcome and explain the environmental justice movement to them. Her speech continues to be widely quoted because of its directness and its eloquence.

> Our vision of the environment is woven into an overall framework of social, racial and economic justice. It is deeply rooted in our cultures and our spirituality. It is based in a long tradition and understanding and respect for the natural world… The environment affords us the platform to address the critical issues of our time: questions of militarism and defense policy; religious freedom; cultural survival; energy and sustainable development; the future of our cities; transportation; housing; land and sovereignty rights; self-determination; and employment.

Alston led a delegation of environmental justice activists to the Earth Summit in Río de Janeiro in 1992 and made an international call against racism and its effects on the public health in communities of color. That year, she was awarded the Charles Bannerman Memorial Fellowship, a sabbatical given to social justice activists and organizers in recognition of their outstanding activist work. She spent her sabbatical visiting South Africa and resting and reflecting on her work.

In late 1992, Alston joined the staff of the Public Welfare Foundation (PWF), whose mission is to help organizations that seek to remove the barriers that disadvantaged people face to full participation in society. She was senior program officer for PWF's Environmental Initiative, a premier environmental justice grant-making program that prioritized projects focused on the impact of environmental degradation and pollution on public health, particularly in poor communities lacking resources from other funding sources. She encouraged other foundations to take a greater interest in and support the environmental justice movement. She contributed to an influential 1994 open letter to funders that defined the movement, explained its origins and significance, and described various activists and groups and the concrete work they were engaged in.

Alston died on August 7, 1999, in San Francisco, California, while being treated for kidney disease and the consequences of a stroke she had suffered two years earlier. She left a young son, Khalil. Alston's friends and family honored her memory by establishing the Dana A. Alston Fund for the Bannerman Memorial Fellowship. Recognizing that working for social change usually means long hours at low pay, with few tangible rewards and few escapes from the day-to-day pressures, the fund provides outstanding activists of color with sabbaticals for reflection and renewal.

BIBLIOGRAPHY

Alston, Dana, "Black, Brown, Poor and Poisoned: Minority Grassroots Environmentalism and the Quest for Eco-Justice," *Kansas Journal of Law & Public Policy*, 1991; Alston, Dana, *Taking Back Our Lives: Environment, Community Development and Race in the U.S.*, 1990; Alston, Dana, and Nicole Brown, "Global Threats to People of Color," *Confronting Environmental Racism: Voices from the Grassroots*, Robert Bullard, ed., 1993; Douglas, Adisa, "A Tribute… Dana Ann Alston: Sister-Friend," *Sister Ink, National Black Women's Health Project*, 1999; Douglas, Adisa, "Dana A. Alston: Activist and Funder," *Networker News, National Network of Grantmakers*, 1999;

"Environmental Justice Resource Center at Clark Atlanta University," www.ejrc.cau.edu;

"Public Welfare Foundation," www.publicwelfare.org.

Amidon, Elias, and Elizabeth Roberts
(September 12, 1944– ; March 29, 1944–)
Editors, Educators

Elias Amidon and Elizabeth Roberts are environmental activists guided by a global environmental ethic. In their international efforts in support of the environment, women's health, and indigenous peoples, they helped found four schools for spiritually oriented environmental activism: The Institute for Deep Ecology in Occidental, California; the Spirit in Education Movement in Bangkok, Thailand; the Boulder Institute for Nature and the Human Spirit in Boulder, Colorado; and the graduate program in Environmental Leadership at Naropa University, Boulder. Amidon and Roberts have also edited three anthologies of prayers that revere planet earth, *Prayers for a Thousand Years*, *Life Prayers Celebrating the Human Journey*, and *Earth Prayers*, which collectively have reached more than a million readers.

Elias Velonis Amidon was born in Denver, Colorado, on September 12, 1944. His summers in upstate New York's Columbia County were formative. There, in the early 1960s, he witnessed what he later described as "the suburbanization of a beloved landscape." After graduating from Antioch College in 1967 with a degree in literature, Amidon first sought to homestead on an island in British Columbia, living off the land as self-sufficiently as possible. But he soon realized he had more to learn in the human world, and he began a ten-year spiritual journey, studying with Sufis in Europe and India. This apprenticeship deepened both his skills in experiential education and his understanding of the spiritual roots of the environmental crisis. Convinced that one of the most crucial "front lines" of human-earth relations lies in the sustainable and human-scale design of the built environment, in 1978 Amidon founded Heartwood School in Massachusetts. The school was dedicated to teaching energy-efficient home design and construction. At Heartwood, Elias met Elizabeth Roberts.

Elizabeth Roberts was born in St. Louis on March 29, 1944. She began as an academically gifted student who went on to excel at Marquette University, earning a B.A. in philosophy and theology in 1966 and a Master's degree in philosophy in 1969. During the early 1960s she worked with Dr. Martin Luther King Jr. on civil rights marches and voter registration drives in Alabama. At the age of 25 she left Marquette to coordinate the White House Conference on Children and Youth, then went on to National Public Radio to develop the program *All Things Considered*, which, incidentally, she named. For the next five years—starting in 1974—she worked as a special assistant to John D. Rockefeller III, designing and implementing international programs for women in development, as well as leading national studies in the United States on population and sexuality. Roberts also served as a consultant and board member for a broad range of institutions, including the National Institute for Mental Health, the Public Broadcasting Service, and the U.S. Forest Service.

In 1984, when she turned 40, Roberts took a step back from her professional successes and began a two-year retreat. She spent time in nature, with her family and alone, and emerged dedicated to deep ecology (a movement that maintains that extended periods with nature are fundamental to experiencing balance and clarity, vision and morality), engaged Buddhism, environmental action, and prayer.

Roberts and Amidon began their first professional collaboration in 1986. It was a five-year consultancy with the Environmental Research Laboratory at the University of Arizona, researching ecologically sustainable and human-scale design patterns for desert cities. This work took them several times to Saudi Arabia, where they consulted on long-term ecological planning for the capital city of Riyadh. They were awarded a major National Endowment for the Arts grant to write a book on the design of desert cities, *The Soul of the Oasis*. For spiritual nourishment during this project, Amidon and Roberts started taking groups into the desert on wilderness rites of passage, in which people from ages 18 to 80 participate in three- or four-day periods of solitude and fasting to discover or renew their life's purpose and direction.

In 1992 Roberts and Amidon were asked by Buddhist activist and writer Joanna Macy to help in the launching of a national school for environmental activists and educators, the Institute for Deep Ecology. The Institute would bring together many of the nation's leading deep ecology activists and educators who would begin to articulate the principles of deep ecology in environmental curricula throughout the world.

Beginning in 1994 they began administering the Boulder Institute for Nature and the Human Spirit, a nonprofit organization in Boulder, Colorado, dedicated to strengthening interfaith and intercultural understanding, cooperation, and action. Among the Boulder Institute's several projects is the Spirit in Action program in Southeast Asia. One aspect of the Spirit in Action program is the Interfaith Solidarity Walks that Roberts and Amidon lead in support of the indigenous peoples of northern Thailand who are threatened with relocation, racism, and cultural assimilation. The Solidarity Walks—part pilgrimage, part seminar, and part direct political action—bear witness to the wisdom of native cultures and the struggles they face for survival. Other Spirit in Action projects include training for indigenous leaders in bioregional mapping of ancestral lands, environmental education programs for activist Thai Buddhist monks and community leaders in northern Burma, and a microgrant program that supports projects in community self-reliance and sustainability. Exemplary of the spiritual activism that Amidon and Roberts espouse, Spirit in Action has helped facilitate the ordaining of trees in forests threatened by logging companies. Local beliefs hold that it is a grave sin for anyone to kill an ordained priest. So, a local shaman or Buddhist or Christian priest is called upon to ordain the oldest trees as priests. The trees are wrapped with a bright sash to make this designation visible to the peasants hired to fell a forest. Where this has happened, the forests remained standing.

Both Amidon and Roberts have long had an affinity with eastern mysticism and were attracted to the only Buddhist university in the Americas, Naropa University in Boulder, Colorado, where they became adjunct professors and were instrumental in establishing the graduate program in Environmental Leadership. While at Naropa, they compiled their unique and poignant articulations of the earth ethic, *Earth Prayers*, *Life Prayers: Celebrating the Human Journey*, and *Prayers for a Thousand Years*. Used by Christians and Jews, Muslims and Buddhists, mainstream professionals and front-line activists, at weddings and workshops, festivals and funerals, demonstrations and dedications, these collections have become standard sourcebooks for prayers and expressions of interfaith spiritual values. In the introduction to *Earth Prayers*, they write: "Over and over the prayers in this book remind us of a universal marriage of matter and spirit. They call on us to rethink the dualism of our culture that separates the sacred and the secular, the natural and the supernatural, body and mind. They make it clear that we humans are not here simply as transients waiting for a ticket to somewhere else. The earth itself is Christos, is Buddha, is Allah, is Gaia."

Amidon and Roberts have continually renewed themselves and their commitment to nature through retreats to the deserts west of the Rocky Mountains and to the jungles of northern Thailand and Burma. In 1999 they left home and teaching positions in Colorado and began a open-ended pilgrimage as "itinerant activist-teachers" in an effort "to reduce the time spent administering programs and increase the time we spend in the field teaching and putting spirit into action."

They continued their pilgrimage for 6 years, training activists, Christian ministers, and Buddhist monks in the spiritual basis of environmental activism in Thailand, Burma, and Indonesia. During this time they became increasingly aware of the inseparability of the three central activist movements: social, environmental, and peace action. Recognizing the worsening division between Western and Muslim cultures following 9/11, and its potential for destroying societies and the environment, they began a series of citizen-to-citizen "Pilgrimages of Peace" to Syria, bringing groups of 20-25 people to Syria to meet and befriend Syrians from all walks of life. During this time they also worked to establish the Nonviolent Peaceforce, a citizen monitoring and accompaniment project for areas in conflict (their focus was in Southeast Asia and the Middle East.)

Towards the end of 2002, with the United States planning to invade Iraq, they joined the Iraq Peace team and spent the months leading up to the invasion in Iraq, working to make known to western media the plight of ordinary Iraqis with the war approaching.

In 2004 they helped to establish the Abraham Path Initiative, an international project to open a network of walking trails through the Middle East in the legendary footsteps of Abraham, the forefather of Judaism, Christianity, and Islam. Elias continues this work on the Abraham Path as a member of the board, seeing it as a weaving of all three modes of activism for social justice, environmental awareness, and peace.

BIBLIOGRAPHY
"Abraham Path Initiative," www.abrahampath.org; "Nonviolent Peaceforce," www.nonviolentpeaceforce.com; Roberts, Elizabeth J., and Elias Amidon, *Earth Prayers*, 1991; Roberts, Elizabeth J., and Elias Amidon, *Life Prayers: Celebrating the Human Journey*, 1996; Roberts, Elizabeth J., and Elias Amidon, *Prayers for a Thousand Years*, 1999.

Anderson, Adrienne
(February 10, 1952–)
Grassroots Public Health Organizer and Educator

Grassroots community organizer Adrienne Anderson has been a leader in toxic contamination struggles throughout the western United States since she became involved with the issue in 1983. From 1992 till 2005 she worked as an instructor at the University of Colorado–Boulder (CU), sharing her knowledge and research methods with students as they investigated contaminated site histories and how regulatory agencies respond to the problems; her abrupt and controversial termination in 2005 was widely perceived as the University's capitulation to political and corporate in-

Adrienne Anderson (Photograph courtesy of Adrienne Anderson)

terests threatened by her investigations and those of her students. Currently, Anderson coordinates the Nuclear Nexus and Safe Water projects of the Rocky Mountain Peace and Justice Center.

Adrienne Anderson was born February 10, 1952, in Dallas, Texas. From a young age she was concerned about justice; as a child she defended black children's rights to ride their bikes through her tree-lined neighborhood. Then as a student at Southern Methodist University (SMU), she challenged her sorority's practices which favored white students. Anderson earned a B.A. from SMU in 1974 and worked for one year for the Texas Department of Public Welfare in Dallas. Although welfare casework was frustrating because Anderson realized that the system, for all its good intentions, tended to control and harass its clients, Anderson gained a respect for poor people's ability to organize and help one another.

Anderson began work in a doctoral program in sociology at the University of Oregon in 1975, where she concentrated on social policy, political economy, and field research methods. While studying there, she helped to organize one of the first university unions in the country for graduate teaching fellows, and also worked for Lane County, Oregon, to design and implement an outreach program to assist the county's rural poor. Anderson took a leave of absence from her studies in 1979 to pursue her career in social change, organizing full-time in Denver, Colorado. From 1977 to 1983 she served as executive director of the Mountain Plains Congress of Senior Organizations, which advocated for the rights of low-income elderly people living in the Rocky Mountain region.

By 1983 Anderson had focused her attention on energy and the environment and how these issues affected poor people. She became regional director of the national Citizen/Labor Energy Coalition and then organized and became director of the Colorado Citizen Action Network (CCAN). CCAN, which was affiliated with the national coalition Citizen Action (CA), was a statewide coalition of grassroots antitoxics groups and labor, farm, and senior citizen groups devoted to energy, environment, and health care issues. When CA increased its commitment to hazardous waste and public health issues in 1984, Anderson sent her staff on a canvass to garner support for stronger federal legislation to clean up the nation's Superfund sites—the most contaminated areas of the country that the government has committed to clean up. Canvassers returned with disturbing stories about birth defects and children's health problems in the Friendly Hills neighborhood southwest of Denver. Anderson assisted in forming a local citizens' group affiliated with CCAN, the Friendly Hills Health Action Group, to investigate the neighborhood's problems.

The investigation revealed that the Denver Water Board, the county and state health departments, and the Environmental Protection Agency all were aware that Titan missile manufacturer Martin Marietta was routinely violating the Clean Water Act. It was discharging scores of toxic chemicals, including the highly carcinogenic rocket fuel propellant hydrazine, into waterways that ran through the site and into a neighboring Denver water supply treatment plant. The plant treated the water for bacteria but not for the toxic chemicals it contained and then piped it to Friendly Hills and other neighboring areas.

Anderson's work with the Friendly Hills Health Action Group forced the water board to close the contaminated water treatment plant in 1985 and convinced the governor to order a criminal investigation of the cover-up conspiracy between Martin Marietta and the Denver Water Board.

In the midst of this campaign, Anderson became western director for the National Toxics Campaign (NTC). In addition to her work on Denver's interlocking toxic sites, such as Martin Marietta, the Rocky Mountain Arsenal, Lowry Landfill, the Rocky Flats nuclear weapons plants, and the Coors brewery, Anderson also organized and assisted community toxics campaigns in other western states, including Wyoming, Oklahoma, and Alaska. She participated in a three-year campaign in Ponca City, Oklahoma, that eventually forced an evacuation of the entire south half of the town, where benzene poisoning from a Conoco refinery's contaminated groundwater swamped 400 neighboring homes. As part of the successful campaign for evacuation, Anderson helped form a local citizens' group, the Ponca City Toxic Concerned Citizens, and accompanied the group to Oklahoma City, 100 miles away, where they camped out on the grounds of the state capitol for months to protest the governor's failure to respond to the problem. Finally taking Conoco to court while continuing their public protests, the residents in 1990 won the largest private buyout of a contaminated community in the nation.

Over the years, working for various organizations, Anderson has helped some 20 to 30 communities organize citizens' groups to respond to local environmental disasters. She currently concentrates her work in the Denver area, a city ringed by Superfund sites whose owners, she found, have trucked toxic wastes to and between various sites for several decades. A complicated, interlocking set of relationships among corporations, the corporate law firms that defend them, their public relations firms, and municipal and federal government agencies has made it difficult to address the problems. When Anderson, appointed in 1996 by the mayor of Denver to the Metro Wastewater Reclamation District Board to represent the sewage plant's workers, uncovered documents about a plan to treat plutonium-contaminated groundwater from the Lowry Landfill Superfund Site east of Denver, she alerted sewage workers and farmers who worked land close to where the sludge would be spread, who protested the plan. Anderson's and her students' investigations of federal files revealed that the Lowry Landfill was contaminated with plutonium and had been used as a dump for years by the Rocky Flats Nuclear Weapons Plant. This resulted in threatening letters from the sewage plant's management. Anderson fought back, invoking the whistle-blowing protection statutes of several national environmental laws. For her work on this case, Anderson was given the Brown-Silkwood Health and Safety award for 1998 from the Oil, Chemical, and Atomic Workers Local 2-477. In 2001, a senior federal whistleblower judge ruled against the sewage agency for its threats and efforts to silence her. Anderson was awarded nearly half a million dollars in damages, including one of the largest punitive damage awards ever issued. However, just after this victory, the incoming Bush administration—which had put its own appointees into the Department of Labor—reversed the judge and overturned the ruling, instead of implementing the judgement.

From 1992 until her controversial termination in 2005, Anderson taught at the University of Colorado–Boulder, offering such courses as Environmental Ethics: Race, Class and Pollution Politics; Advanced Environmental Investigations; and The War Environment. She emphasized research techniques and assigned her students to investigate local polluters and how the appropriate regulatory agencies responded to their violations. Anderson invited regulatory officials to visit the class at the end of each semester; they were met by well-prepared students demanding explanations for the problems they uncovered. Although Anderson's courses received consistently high scores in student evaluations, and the University's large Environmental Studies program depended upon her to teach required courses for the program, her presence at CU was officially protested by one of the targets of her investigations, the ASARCO mining company. (An Anderson investigation revealed that ASARCO had contaminated a Denver neighborhood, and the company was fined $38 million.) The public relations firm representing ASARCO, Coors, Shell, Martin Marietta, and others—all of which pollute the Lowry Landfill—also complained to the University about Anderson and her courses. Although students successfully rallied for many years to assure that Anderson teach, the Environmental Studies department did not renew her contract in 2005. Students, using the skills Anderson had taught them, investigated University records and found a barrage of communications from polluters and political appointees of governor Bill Owens. The records showed that these corporate and government interests sought to undermine Anderson's faculty position over the pollution research she and her students had discovered, along with evidence of lax enforcement actions by the state. After Anderson filed a grievance, two investigating faculty committees found that her rights had been violated and recommended her reinstatement. The American Association of University Professors-CU Chapter also investigated her case, concluded that her termination had serious implications for the University's academic integrity and its role in protecting public health, and called for her reinstatement. The University, however, refused to reinstate her.

Anderson's current position with the Rocky Mountain Peace and Justice Center allows her to continue researching and organizing around the various toxic and nuclear contamination threats plaguing the region. In one case, she assists Native Americans, in another, ranchers and farmers, and in yet another, residents whose homes abut a radioactive waste site the military has refused to clean up. Anderson's articles and reports are available on-line at the Rocky Mountain Peace and Justice Center's website: www.rmpjc.org.

BIBLIOGRAPHY

"AAUP University of Colorado," www.aaup-cu.org; Cowan, Jessica, *Good Works: Jobs that Make a Difference*, 1991; Obmascik, Mark, "Listen! Money's Talking," *Denver Post*, 1996; "Rocky Mountain Peace and Justice Center," www.rmpjc.org; White, Nadia, "Environmental Studies Made Demands at Campus Rally," *Boulder Daily Camera*, 1998.

Anderson, Ray
(July 28, 1934–)
Entrepreneur

Ray Anderson, chairman of the board and chief executive officer of Interface, Inc., the largest commercial carpet tile and interior fabrics manufacturer in the world, challenged his employees in 1994 to transform their company into a model of environmental responsibility and sustainability. Interface, Inc., is now a widely recognized model for what an industry can accomplish if its priorities are to work toward sustainability.

Raymond Christy Anderson was born on July 28, 1934, in the small town of West Point, Georgia, the youngest of three boys. His father had been forced to quit school in the eighth grade to help support his six siblings and had resented this during the remainder of his life, so he and Anderson's mother, a teacher, provided each of their sons with all the educational opportunities they could. Anderson believes that playing football through secondary school and college gave him the "never say die" attitude that would eventually serve him as he worked in the competitive world of business. Anderson graduated from Georgia Tech in 1956 with high honors and a degree in industrial engineering.

After a couple of years in unsatisfactory jobs immediately after graduating, Anderson joined Callaway Mills Co., a textile manufacturer, where he stayed for 17 years. That company was sold in 1968 to Deering Milliken, and Anderson assumed the directorship for the development of its floor-covering branch. He was responsible for importing carpet tile technology from Europe, and Milliken became the leading carpet tile company in the United States. As a floor-covering expert, Anderson became enamored with these European carpet tiles, 18-inch by 18-inch squares of free-lay carpet, which were practical for office floor coverings because they allowed easy access to subfloor electrical wiring. Anderson recognized the opportunity to found a new company specializing in carpet tiles, and he left Milliken in 1973. He recruited 20 investors to raise $1,250,000 in equity for his new company and joined an English supplier of carpet tiles, Carpets International, to found Carpets International–Georgia in April 1973.

Renamed Interface Flooring Systems, Inc., in 1983, Anderson's company acquired several competitors and related businesses during the mid-1980s and by 1988 had become the world's largest global producer of carpet tiles. Listed in 1988 as a Fortune 500 company, Interface enjoyed spectacular success, from a business point of view. Anderson also believed that the company was on the forefront of the environmental movement; in 1984 it had responded to the problem of indoor air quality–related illness and had developed an antimicrobial agent called Intersept to incorporate into its carpets. This reduced the so-called sick building syndrome that affected many office buildings.

By 1994, however, thanks to a growing popular interest in the environment, clients were frequently asking Interface about its contributions to the environment. Interface Research Corporation—the branch of the company devoted to research and development—decided to organize a task force to formulate the company's official environmental position. Anderson was asked to give the keynote speech, and he was at a total loss for words. Serendipitously, someone sent him a copy of PAUL HAWKEN's *The Ecology of Commerce* while he was trying to formulate his speech. In this book, Hawken describes a long series of ecological disasters over recent history, all caused by human overuse of nature's fragile and limited resources. Hawken accuses business and industry together of being the perpetrators of most of the destruction, but he believes that they are also the forces that can most effectively turn it around. Hawken's ideas resonated with Anderson, whose company was completely dependent upon nonrenewable petroleum-based products. Anderson was thus inspired to issue a dramatic challenge to Interface employees to make their company one that would exemplify how industry could help solve the world's environmental crisis.

Interface employees were surprised at Anderson's challenge, but they did accept it and chose 2000 as the year by which Interface would achieve sustainability. The effort's first focus was on eliminating waste at its 29 factories. At each factory, employee suggestions for eliminating waste were solicited. Anderson assembled what he calls his Dream Team, 11 sustainability experts including HUNTER AND AMORY LOVINS, Paul Hawken, DAVID BROWER, BILL MCDONOUGH, and others, to consult with Interface and help map its path toward sustainability. With their help, Interface formulated six goals in addition to its original waste-reduction effort. They are as follows: to work toward having its factories emit only benign air and water emissions; to consume less energy and shift to alternative energy sources; to use organic, renewable, and closed-loop recycled raw materials to make the carpet tiles; to transport employees, information, and products more efficiently; to educate its suppliers, customers, competitors, and communities about the importance of seeking sustainability; and to "redesign commerce," which includes providing flooring services rather than just selling carpet tiles, allowing Interface to selectively replace tiles as they wear out, and recycle them when they do.

Interface began keeping track of "ecometrics" in 1996, as a way to measure its progress towards sustainability. By 2008, some of its achievements were as follows: 75 percent less water was used in manufacturing than in 1996; 66 percent less waste was sent to landfills thanks to more fiber and carpet backing from used carpet being recycled; and 25 percent of materials used in manufacturing was from recycled or biological sources. In addition, the company purchases carbon credits to offset carbon emissions produced by manufacturing of its carpet, employee commuting, and shipping of product in company vehicles, The company's current goal is to eliminate "any negative impact our flooring and fabric companies may have on the environment by the year 2020."

For his commitment to sustainability and his progress toward it, Anderson was appointed to the President's Council on Sustainable Development in 1996 and served as cochair with Jonathon Lash. He has received a host of recognitions and awards for his commitment to and achievements in sustainability, including being named Entrepreneur of the Year by *Forbes Magazine* and Ernst & Young in 2001 and a *Time* magazine Hero of the Environment in 2007. In 2006, Interface was listed in Sustainablebusiness.com's SB20 list of Companies Changing the World, and the same year was ranked Number One in the world for corporate sustainability by GlobeScan.

Anderson resides in Atlanta, Georgia, with his wife, Pat. Anderson has two grown daughters, Mary Anne and Harriet, and five grandchildren.

BIBLIOGRAPHY
Anderson, Ray, *Mid-Course Correction*, 1998; "Interface," www.interfaceinc.com; McDonough, William, "Heroes of the Environment, Ray Anderson," *Time*, 2007

Andrus, Cecil

(August 25, 1931–)
United States Secretary of the Interior, Governor of Idaho

As secretary of the interior from 1977 to 1981, Cecil Andrus worked for the protection of the environment by attempting to eliminate the control of economic interests over the public domain and by concentrating decision-making power in the hands of a small group of staff members to create a unified conservation mission in a department that until that point had had none. He is a believer in the idea that environmental protection can and must coexist with economic development. "Protection," he once told *Newsweek*, "is no longer a pious sentiment. It is an element of survival of this race."

Cecil Dale Andrus was born on August 25, 1931, to Hal Stephen and Dorothy John Andrus in Hood River, Oregon. His father was a sawmill operator, and Andrus's own first jobs were in the forests and lumber mills of northern Oregon. He developed an early appreciation for the wilderness of the Pacific Northwest, hiking, camping, hunting, and fishing throughout his childhood. His memories of some of the region's wild rivers before and after the erosive effects of indiscriminate logging practices contribute to his conservationist sensibilities.

Andrus attended Oregon State University at Corvallis for a year in 1948 and 1949. He did not graduate. He served in the United States Navy in the Korean War from 1951 to 1955 and was discharged after his tour of duty in the Pacific theater of operations with the rank of aviation electronic technician second class. He began work as a lumberjack for the Tru-Cut Lumber Corporation in Orfino, Idaho, in 1955, eventually working his way up to the position of production manager.

His political career began in 1961, when he was elected to the Idaho state senate from the Clearwater County district. At just 30 years old, he was the youngest senator in the history of Idaho. He was elected to a second term, and he served until 1966, working during his tenure for legislation in the areas of education, conservation, agriculture, social services, and business. He also worked as assistant manager of the Workman's Compensation Exchange from 1963 to 1966. Andrus made a bid for governor in 1966 but was defeated. Andrus served in the state senate again from 1968 to 1970 and became an agent with the Idaho offices of the Paul Revere Life Insurance Company. By 1970, he had been promoted to state general manager.

Andrus ran for governor once again in 1970. One of the major issues in his campaign against the incumbent, Dan Samuelson, was the American Smelting and Refining Company's proposal to operate an open-pit molybdenum mine at the base of Castle Peak in Idaho's White Cloud Mountains in the Challis National Forest. Governor Samuelson supported the project, citing its benefits to Idaho's agricultural economy. Andrus, however, made it clear to the people of Idaho that he felt that temporary economic gain was not reason enough to destroy their irreplaceable natural resources. Andrus's position was popular among environmentalists but not well supported in the areas around Challis that would have reaped the economic benefits from the mine. Andrus won the election by a narrow margin and became governor of Idaho in 1971.

As governor, Andrus increased state aid to public schools, added $1,000,000 a year to state revenues through a revision of the state's income tax law, and reduced the number of state agencies from 268 to 19. He also was a vigorous supporter of conservation legislation, endorsing the 1972 federal legislation that established the Sawtooth National Recreation Area and opposing the construction of two dams in Hells Canyon on the Snake River. He did, however, support the construction of a dam on the Teton River that was considered by both engineers and environmentalists a dangerous dam site. They were proved correct when the dam collapsed in June 1976. Andrus's seemingly contradictory stands on these issues can be explained by his philosophy that conservation does not negate the possibility for development, nor does development negate the responsibility to conserve. He described his basic philosophy to *Reader's Digest* in this way: "If I am faced with a decision of development with adequate safeguards for the environment, I'll come down on the side of development. If I am faced with development without adequate safeguards, I'll come down on the side of the environment."

Andrus was reelected in 1974. During his second term, the Idaho Land Use Planning Act of 1975 was passed, providing for local land-use decision making with the help and support of state agencies. In December 1976, Andrus was nominated by President-elect JIMMY CARTER as secretary of the interior. Andrus brought with him a much deeper concern for conservation and the environment than had previously been found in the Department of the Interior. He saw his job as being to eliminate the department's "three Rs" (rape, ruin, and run). He totally rewrote the organizational chart, taking decision-making capability away from the heads of the 16 separate, specialized bureaus, services, and administrations that make up the Interior Department and concentrating that power at the top of the hierarchy, with a staff that he himself appointed. In doing this he eliminated the disunity and lack of communication that had been the standard mode of operation and created an agency with a unified conservation philosophy and the decision-making structure to act on that philosophy.

During his four-year term, Andrus delighted environmentalists with his strong support of conservation legislation that curbed offshore drilling and strip mining and expanded natural parks. The accomplishment of which he was most proud was the Alaska Lands Conservation Act of 1980, which protected 100 million acres from industrial exploitation and created the largest wilderness area in U.S. history. In accordance with Andrus's views on the appropriate marriage between conservation and development, the act opened another 254 million Alaskan acres to development as well. As secretary, Andrus also concerned himself with breaking the ties of economic interest to decision making in the public domain, stating that public lands should be managed in the interest of all of the people, simply because they belong to all of the people. "The initials B.L.M. [Bureau of Land Management]," he quipped at one point, "no longer stand for the Bureau of Livestock and Mining."

In 1981, after Carter lost the presidential election for a second term and the newly elected Ronald Reagan appointed the decidedly promining and protimber industry James Watt to the post, Andrus joined three former Environmental Protection Agency officials in creating a New Jersey–based corporation that tests the toxicity of industrial and chemical wastes to assist companies in complying with federal and state environmental regulations. In Idaho, he also worked for the federal protection of a part of the Snake River that is a nesting ground for one of the most dense populations of raptors in the world, an endeavor for which he received the Audubon Medal in 1985.

Andrus began to devote himself full-time to environmental issues through the Andrus Center for Public Policy at Boise State University in 1995. His priorities at the Andrus Center have been on the Snake River Birds of Prey Area, Wild and Scenic Rivers, and nuclear waste disposal. He has been married to Carol Mae May since 1949. They have three daughters, Tana Lee, Tracy Sue, and Kelly Kay.

BIBLIOGRAPHY

Andrus, Cecil, *Cecil Andrus, Politics Western Style*, 1998; Andrus, Cecil, "Committed to Conservation," *National Parks*, 2000; Boeth, Richard, William J. Cook, and John Walcott,

"Environment; Interior Redesign," *Newsweek*, 1977; Carter, Luther J., "Interior Department: Andrus Promises 'Sweeping Changes,'" *Science*, 1977; Maxwell, Jessica, "Q and A Interview," *Audubon*, 1995; Miller, James Nathan, "Secretary Andrus Makes His Stand," *Reader's Digest*, 1977; Seligman, Jean, Mark Kirchmeier, and John Accola, "Andrus: A Booster for the Way of the West," *Newsweek*, 1983.

Anthony, Carl
(February 8, 1939–)
Architect, Executive Director of Urban Habitat

Carl Anthony founded and served as first executive director of Urban Habitat, a San Francisco-based environmental justice organization that works toward a socially just and environmentally sustainable economy and builds multicultural urban, environmental leadership. Throughout his career, Anthony has worked to join the environmental and social justice movements, promoting the restoration and revitalization of urban environments as an alternative to suburban sprawl and the social and environmental destruction that it entails.

Carl Anthony was born on February 8, 1939, in Philadelphia. His working-class parents sent him to a racially integrated elementary school—a rarity at that time—in hopes of providing him with the best possible education. After receiving a graduate degree in architecture from Columbia University in 1969, Anthony journeyed to Africa, where he spent more than a year traveling the continent in a Volkswagen van. He became especially fascinated with how well African traditional cultures had adapted, over generations, to climate and other aspects of the environment. This trip inspired Anthony to dedicate himself to ecological architecture.

Upon his return to the United States in 1971, Anthony moved to the San Francisco Bay Area and taught architecture at the University of California, Berkeley (UCB) College of Environmental Design. He continued this until 1978, at which point he opened his own architecture studio and began designing affordable housing in Berkeley and Oakland. Anthony has long felt that the lifestyle and housing option that middle-class white Americans have been choosing since the 1950s—living in the suburbs and becoming increasingly dependent upon automobiles to travel to stores and their workplaces—has had devastating effects on society at large. Low-income people of color, who have remained in urban centers as wealthier whites have poured out, have borne a disproportionate share of the costs of this suburbanization. They have suffered increased air and noise pollution as new highways to the suburbs have bisected their neighborhoods; lack of interest in their inner-city communities as private investment and public infrastructure investment have flowed to the new suburbs; and declining job opportunities and access to jobs as employment centers have moved to the suburban rim. Institutional racism in zoning and land use, such as racial covenants that excluded African American homeowners in suburban developments and redlining within communities of color, have combined to confine many of these same communities to less desirable and older neighborhoods adjacent to industrial and manufacturing facilities.

In addition to experiencing increased exposure to toxics from nearby manufacturing plants, the neighborhoods of low-income people of color are often more likely to be locations for other undesirable land uses, such as solid waste recycling, truck transfer stations, or medical waste incinerators. The inordinate environmental burden that many communities of color face in both urban and rural settings gave rise to the national movement for environmental justice.

To the new environmental justice movement, Anthony brought his expertise in urbanism and commitment to making cities more livable. As a consultant to the Berkeley Redevelopment Agency in the early 1980s, he was able to resolve a conflict between interests fighting for affordable housing, historic preservation, and economic development, by designing plans that integrated all three. In 1989, he was a protagonist in the defeat of a proposal to build a huge shopping development on the Berkeley waterfront. Although the proposal was supported by the area's African American community for the jobs it would offer, Anthony worked against it because he knew the jobs would be only temporary, and he worried about its effects on Berkeley's already declining downtown area. While serving as president of the Berkeley Planning Commission from 1990 to 1992, Anthony worked on a successful downtown revitalization effort that now serves as a model for other urban areas.

During the 1990s Anthony also chaired The East Bay Conversion and Reinvestment Commission, which oversaw the closure of five Bay Area military bases and 500 more throughout the U.S. For the Alameda Naval Air Station, Anthony successfully advocated such environmentally sustainable alternatives as recycling building materials from the structures that are torn down, building housing in a way that preserves open space along the water front, and encouraging environmentally-friendly industry (an electric car factory was built).

Anthony began working with the San Francisco-based Earth Island Institute (EII) in 1989, and eventually became its president. At EII, which nurtures projects that work on specific environmental issues and then helps them spin off into independent organizations, Anthony headed the Urban Habitat Program, which promotes the cultural and economic restoration of inner cities through its conferences, publications, educational programs, and advocacy. It networks environmental activists of color; by 1997 it had assisted more than 100 organizations working on environmental justice issues, including health, food security, recycling, energy, transportation, arts and culture, education, immigration and population, and parks and open space. Urban Habitat spun off from EII in 1997. Anthony worked with Urban Habitat until 2001. Some of the foci of his work included: diversification of the U.S. Forest Service, which had been under court order to increase the ethnic and racial diversity of its staff; prioritizing urban transit over suburban highway development; reclamation of "brownfields" (vacant, blighted, or contaminated land); and empowerment and training of community activists. He also co-founded and served as co-editor with Luke Cole of Urban Habitat's quarterly journal *Race, Poverty and the Environment*.

In a 1999 interview for *Yes!*, Anthony outlined his vision of more sustainable urban areas. He included:

- a growth boundary dividing built-up land from openspace and farmland;
- transit-oriented development, with homes, workplaces, and retail/commercial activity around public transit stations;
- nature reemerging in cities, with creeks and waterways being allowed to run uncovered, and reinvestment in parks and open spaces;
- higher density housing with diversified forms (granny-units, offices within houses, etc.); and
- brownfields cleaned up and converted into parks, urban farms, housing sites, and commercial activities.

Anthony has further described and developed these characteristics of livable cities in his many publications. Since 2001, Anthony has directed the Ford Foundation's Sustainable Metropolitan Communities Initiative and has been a Fellow at Harvard University's John F. Kennedy School of Government, an Advisor to the Stanford University Law School on environmental justice issues, and Professor at Columbia University's Graduate School of Architecture and Planning and at the University of California's College of Environmental Design and Natural Resources. He currently is a Senior Ford Foundation Fellow at the University of California, Berkeley.

BIBLIOGRAPHY
Anthony, Carl, "Livable Communities," *Race, Poverty and the Environment, 2008*; Gilliam, Harold, "Carl Anthony," *San Francisco Chronicle*, 1996; Inman, Bradley, "The Battle Against Environmental Racism," *San Francisco Examiner*, 1993; Kay, Jane, "Community Hero at Helm of Change," *San Francisco Examiner*, 1995; "Urban Habitat," www.urbanhabitat.org; van Gelder, Sarah Ruth, "Diverse, Green, Beautiful Cities: an interview with Carl Anthony," *Yes!, 1999*.

Audubon, John James
(April 26, 1785–January 27, 1851)
Artist, Ornithologist

John James Audubon is easily the best known and best remembered among nineteenth-century naturalists and ornithologists. The artwork of this skilled painter of wildlife first introduced the images of many bird species to the widespread public. Audubon's paintings and simple manner of writing made birding and ornithology accessible to the nonscientist, thereby contributing to their popularity as leisure activities. Audubon's name continues to pervade modern conservationist activity; Audubon societies exist worldwide and have become synonymous with the protection of wild birds.

Jean Jacques Fougère Audubon was born April 26, 1785, on his father's plantation at Les Cayes, Santo Domingo (now Haiti). He was the illegitimate son of Jean Audubon, a sea merchant, and a Creole woman of Santo Domingo, known only as Mlle. Rabin, who probably died within a year after his birth. Audubon, who was called Fougère, or sometimes Jean Rabin, and his younger half-sister Muguet, the daughter of another Creole woman, went to Nantes, France, with their father in 1789. They were warmly received by Jean Audubon's wife, Anne Moynet Audubon, who took charge of their upbringing as her husband became occupied with the brewing French Revolution.

Audubon received the standard bourgeois education; he was instructed in mathematics, geography, music, and fencing, though his lessons were sometimes neglected by his indulgent stepmother. Years later, Audubon regretted not having been drilled in writing in French. He did, however, become influenced by the revival of interest in nature that Rousseau, Buffon, and Lamarck had made popular; by the age of 15, he had already begun a collection of his original drawings of French birds. Recognizing his son's lack of discipline, Jean Audubon put him in military school for a year, but the experience had little effect. Having always encouraged his son's taste in natural history and drawing, Jean Audubon arranged for him to study drawing in Paris under the great French artist, David.

In the autumn of 1803, Audubon left France for America. Early in 1804, he arrived at Mill

John James Audubon (Library of Congress, Prints & Photographs Division, LC-USZ62-11250)

Grove, an estate near Philadelphia that his father had purchased in 1789. Living the life of a country gentleman, free of financial concerns, Audubon became an enthusiastic observer of nature. While the bird protection societies across the United States that carry his name have promoted Audubon as a passionate protector of wildlife, Audubon in reality enjoyed hunting with dog and gun and was an avid sportsman at this stage of his life, killing for amusement as well as for food. Nevertheless, Audubon did have a spirit of scientific inquiry, and it was during this period that Audubon conducted the first banding experiment on wild birds in America. He discovered a nest of pewees in a cave and fastened light silver threads to the legs of some of the baby pewees. The next spring, Audubon found that two of them had returned to the region and were nesting a little way up the creek from their place of birth.

The next few years saw Audubon return to France for a year before returning to the United States, selling Mill Grove and moving to Louisville, Kentucky, where he opened a general store with Ferdinand Rozier, the son of one of his father's business associates. The store suffered considerably because of the Embargo Act, which prohibited the importation of some goods the store would have sold, but all the same, in 1808 he went to Philadelphia to marry Lucy Bakewell, to whom he had been engaged since 1804, and brought her back to Louisville.

At the beginning of the nineteenth century, Kentucky was still almost a wilderness, which strengthened Audubon's passion for natural history. Out of touch with other ornithologists, Audubon worked as an artist and a lover of nature more than as a scientist as he continued to paint birds. Indeed, a seeming lack of interest in science pervades much of his bird paintings from this period. Much criticism has subsequently been directed at Audubon's carelessness in his paintings that has hurt his reputation as a naturalist. The criticism is generally the same, from publishers, ornithologists, and other scientists, who claim that Audubon's birds lack the veracity that science demands. Even his most loyal supporters, such as Elliott Coues, concede that many of his paintings show birds that are posed in anatomically impossible stances.

Audubon's consuming interest in painting birds resulted in his neglect of his business in Louisville and its eventual failure. As the town and business competition grew, Audubon and Rozier moved their business 125 miles down the Ohio River to Henderson, Kentucky, in 1810. There, the same pattern emerged: As Rozier tended to the store, Audubon roamed the country in search of rare birds; his fishing and hunting were often the only means of subsistence for both partners. Ultimately, the partnership was doomed to collapse, which it did, in 1818, though the two remained friends.

Subsequent business ventures also failed, and in 1819, Audubon was jailed for debt. He was released on the plea of bankruptcy with only the clothes he wore, his gun, and his original drawings. This disaster ended his business career, and he spent the winter doing crayon portraits before moving his family to Cincinnati, where he became a taxidermist in the new Western Museum. It was around this time that the idea of publishing his bird drawings came to Audubon. In October 1820, Audubon traveled down the Ohio and Mississippi Rivers, looking for birds to draw and paint. After some time in New Orleans, where Audubon worked as a tutor and a drawing teacher, Mrs. Audubon took a job as a governess and assumed the financial responsibilities of looking after the hungry family; for 12 years, she was the primary wage earner for the household.

Unable to publish his works in the United States, Audubon traveled to England, on funds saved from his wife's wages, where *Birds of America* was published in 1827. He was especially well received in Scotland, where he was elected to the Royal Society of Scotland in March 1827. In 1830, he and his wife bought a home in Edinburgh, where he began to write the text portion of *Birds in America*. The text was published separately in 1838 as *Ornithological Biography*.

Returning to the United States, Audubon purchased a large estate on the Hudson River, called Minnies' Land; this estate in New York is known today as Audubon Park. Audubon returned to the United States to work on a miniature edition of *Birds in America* but almost immediately began collaborating with the naturalist John Bachman on their three-volume *Viviparous Quadrupeds of North America*. Their friendship was cemented by the marriages of two of Audubon's sons to two of Bachman's daughters.

In his final years, Audubon continued to work on color plates for his work with Bachman and tutored several young ornithologists. Audubon suffered a debilitating stroke in early January 1851, leaving his son, John W. Audubon, to finish his work on *Viviparous Quadrupeds of North America*. Audubon died before the month was out, on January 27, at the age of 65. In 1896, the first Audubon Society was formed by a group of conservation-minded bird-watchers, headed by the ornithologist William Brewster, in Massachusetts.

BIBLIOGRAPHY

Audubon, John James and Richard Rhodes, *The Audubon Reader*, 2006; Audubon, M. R., *Audubon and His Journals, with Notes by Elliott Coues*, 2 vols., 1897; Foshay, Ella M., *John James Audubon*, 1997; Herrick, Francis Hobart, *Audubon the Naturalist: A History of His Life and Time*, 2 vols., 1968.

Austin, Mary
(September 9, 1868–August 13, 1934)
Nature Writer

Mary Austin authored fiction, autobiography, and nature-inspired writings, addressing such issues as ecology, mysticism, spirituality, bioregionalism, and feminism. She is known for her commitment to and her portrayal of the land and people of the American Southwest. Her books laid the foundation for science and nature writing as it is practiced today and helped to influence the deep ecology movement.

Born on September 9, 1868, in Carlinville, Illinois, Mary Hunter Austin was the third of four children born to George and Susanna Sa-

Mary Austin (Library of Congress, Prints & Photographs Division, LC-DIG-ggbain-05744)

villa Hunter. Her relationship with her mother was a strained one, as were her relationships with her other family members (they would continue to be so throughout her life), except for those with her father and her younger sister, Jennie. Her father was a successful lawyer, and he encouraged Austin's literary interests. He had fought on the Union side of the Civil War. In 1878, when Austin was ten years old, he died of a malarial illness that he had contracted in his years as a soldier. Two months later, Austin's younger sister died of diphtheria. Of Jennie, Austin would later write, "She was the only one who ever unselfishly loved me."

In 1884, Austin enrolled in Blackburn College in her hometown, where she was editor of the college journal and was elected class poet. Mathematics and science, however, stimulated her imagination as well, and she sought to include both the sciences and the humanities in her studies. Years later, in 1922, in an essay entitled "Science for the Unscientific," Austin would argue that gifted writers should "immerse themselves in the data of science to the point of saturation." In this, she was a precursor to such scientist-writers as ALDO LEOPOLD, RACHEL CARSON, and Ann Zwinger.

Shortly after graduating from Blackburn in 1888, Austin moved with her family to the San Joaquin Valley in California, where her brother Jim wanted to homestead a parcel of land. The train ride west left a deep impression on Austin. She felt drawn to the vast space of the Mojave Desert. The arid lands of the western landscape were to have a profound impact on Austin's life and on her career as a writer. The Hunter family lived in a cabin consisting of a single room with bunk beds and the bare minimum of essential furnishings. Austin spent much of her time outdoors, studying unfamiliar native animals and plants. She slept little, often sitting for hours in the moonlight, watching the nighttime goings on of the San Joaquin Valley wilderness. In 1889, she had an essay published in her alma mater's magazine, *The Blackburnian*. Entitled "One Hundred Miles on Horseback," it is an account of her trip west with her family and contains vivid descriptive passages of a California that no longer exists.

The Hunter family, unfortunately, arrived in the midst of one of California's not uncommon periods of drought and found itself in a constant struggle to survive on the land. Austin took a teaching position away from her family with the Kern County School District in order to provide some income for herself and her struggling kin. During this time, she made the acquaintance of Gen. Edward Beale, owner of the vast Tejon Ranch and early California pioneer. He was an inexhaustible source of information about California and the West. Beale shared stories of the region, of its Indians and early settlers, that provided a substantial amount of material that later appeared in Austin's first books.

In the summer of 1890, after a monetary dispute with her mother that led to Austin's ostracism from her family, she met Stafford Wallace Austin, who was attempting to develop a 20-acre fruit farm. They married a year later, in 1891. When the farm failed, the couple left the San Joaquin Valley, and together they lived in various towns of the Owens Valley in California. Austin taught school, wrote, and observed nature, while Wallace failed at one agricultural endeavor after another and generally failed to provide for his new family. Austin would later refer to this time as "the desert years." This period provided much in the way of literary inspiration, but it was also a time of loneliness and frustration for Austin. Her marriage was deteriorating, and in 1892, Austin gave birth to a child, Ruth, who was mentally disabled. Austin had her daughter institutionalized until her death in 1918 at the age of 26. In 1903, Austin published *The Land of Little Rain*. Her best-known work, it is a collection of essays addressing her experiences with nature, the people of the southwest, and their religion.

In 1906, having visited Carmel two years earlier while researching her novel *Isidro*, Austin sold the house that she and Wallace had lived in since 1900 and bought land in Carmel, joining an artist colony centered around the poet George Sterling. Wallace did not follow her to Carmel. He charged her with desertion. Their divorce was finalized in 1914. While in Carmel, Austin completed two more novels, *Santa Lucia* (1908) and *Outland* (1910), and wrote stories that would be collected in *Lost Borders* (1909). Austin was diagnosed with breast cancer in 1907 and was given only nine months to live. She went to Italy, where she studied prayer and mysticism. While in Rome the pains she had been experiencing suddenly disappeared. She stayed in Europe, spending her time primarily in England and Italy for the next two years, returning to the United States in 1910.

Between 1911 and 1923, Austin divided her time between Carmel and New York. She continued writing, publishing many books during this time, including a novel *A Woman of Genius* (1912), which is considered by many to be her best fiction. In 1924, she moved to Santa Fe, New Mexico, where she had been named an associate in Native American literature at the School of Native American Research. Here, she published *The Land of Journey's End* in 1924 in a return to the subject matter (the landscape of the Southwest) and style of her earliest nature writings. In this book, she presents her perspective that "not the law but the land sets the limit." This has been interpreted as a forerunner of the modern day "deep ecology" philosophy, which attempts to create a nonanthropocentric vision of reality and nature. Austin believed, however, that humans do have a place in nature and that this place was to be created through the creation of working relationships and connections with the land.

While in Santa Fe, Austin also became heavily involved in the water rights battle over the Colorado River. She was appointed a delegate to the Second Colorado River Conference in 1927, where she argued against building a dam in Boulder Canyon (a dam was eventually built here—Hoover Dam was completed in 1936). She objected to the fact that the water from this dam would go to California, a state already beginning to sprawl, rather than to Arizona and New Mexico, states whose legitimate claims to the water would be ignored and lost.

In her autobiography, *Earth Horizon* (1932), Austin wrote that she "wanted to write books that you could walk around in." She considered herself a "naturist," not a naturalist. Her definition of natural history was that it concerns itself with facts and rationalization, two concerns that she most definitely did not have. In her books, the land is always something more than a series of physical, sensual, or intellectual features. Rather, all of its physical aspects (plants, animals, humans, climate, geology) are manifestations of what Austin considers to be "spirit." In her books she addressed issues such as feminism, ecology, and bioregionalism. Mary Austin died in her sleep, on August 13, 1934, in Santa Fe,

New Mexico, after a heart attack the day before.

BIBLIOGRAPHY
Fink, Augusta, *I—Mary, A Biography Of Mary Austin*, 1983; Lanigan, Esther F., Mary Austin: song of a maverick, 1989; O'Grady, John P., "Mary Hunter Austin," *American Nature Writers*, John Elder, ed., 1996; Pearce, T. M., *Mary Hunter Austin*, 1965.

Ausubel, Kenny
(April 20, 1949–)
Social Entrepreneur, Founder of Bioneers

Kenny Ausubel is an investigative journalist, award-winning filmmaker, writer and social entrepreneur working on issues of biological and cultural diversity. In 1989 he co-founded Seeds of Change, an heirloom, organic seed company, to preserve plant diversity. He is best known within the environmental movement as the co-founder (with his producing partner and wife Nina Simons) of the influential national Bioneers Conferences, held annually since 1990 in California as well as in many satellite cities. Ausubel believes that through an awareness of the interdependence of all things, founded on nature's principles of diversity, kinship, community, cooperation and reciprocity, the necessary solutions to environmental and human crises will be found.

Ausubel was born on April 20, 1949, in Brooklyn, New York. His birth was announced in the show business paper *Variety*, where his mother Anne worked. His father, Herman Ausubel, was a Columbia University English professor. Ausubel attended Yale University, and graduated Phi Beta Kappa in 1972 with a B.A. in Psychology and Urban Studies from Columbia University.

Ausubel has published articles since the 1970s on a wide range of topics including environmental health, social justice, politics and alternative medicine. An early investigative piece concerned a controversial alternative cancer therapy. Ausubel came across the story at 19 years of age, when he had a personal health crisis that was not helped by conventional medicine. In 1990 his story of Harry Hoxsey's struggle to practice an alternative treatment for cancer was selected as one of the "Best Censored Stories" of the year. In 1987 this project became Ausubel's first non-fiction film, *Hoxsey: How Healing Becomes a*

Kenny Ausubel (Photograph by Jennifer Esperanza)

Crime, and was released as a book in 2000, *When Healing Becomes a Crime: The Amazing Story of the Hoxsey Cancer Clinics and the Return of Alternative Therapies.* The award-winning film played theatrically and generated tremendous viewer response when it aired on HBO and Bravo. The film was screened for members of Congress at the Kennedy Center, and is credited with influencing the creation of the federal Office of Alternative Medicine (now called the National Center for Complementary and Alternative Medicine).

While working on the Hoxsey project, Ausubel was asked to make a film about master gardener Gabriel Howearth's garden in the San Juan Pueblo. Gabriel had studied traditional indigenous farming and had been gifted with seeds from people with whom he apprenticed. Ausubel saw the benefits of Howearth's approach, and in 1989 he co-founded Seeds of Change with Howearth, Bolivian Quechua Indian agronomist Emigdio Ballon and molecular biologist Alan Kapuler. Seeds of Change's mission: to preserve biodiversity by growing heirloom and traditional open-pollinated, organically grown seed stock, and to promote sustainable, organic agriculture. Ausubel served as CEO of this early social venture project through 1994. He wrote about the effort to restore what he calls "backyard biodiversity" into the food web on a garden-by-garden level in *Seeds of Change: The Living Treasure.* At the time of writing this article, Seeds of Change offers 600 distinct varieties of 100 percent organically grown seeds for the home gardener, and over a hundred varieties in bulk quantities for market growers.

At Seeds of Change, Ausubel actively sought out environmentalists and systems thinkers like John Todd of the New Alchemy Institute in Woods Hole, Massachusetts. In 1990 Ausubel and Simons, who was working at Seeds of Change, co-founded The Bioneers as a project of their nonprofit Collective Heritage Institute (CHI), to bring cutting-edge thinkers together. The Bioneers Conference was held for the first three years in Santa Fe, New Mexico, and from then on in California. It was conceived as a way to disseminate practical and visionary solutions for damaged ecosystems and human communities as well as to conduct programs in the conservation of diversity, traditional farming practices, and environmental restoration. Bioneers attracts over 3,000 people annually to the national conference, with a satellite simulcast now reaching over 10,000 additional remote conference attendees. Ausubel has produced an award-winning weekly radio series about the conference that airs on over 200 channels nationally, and he produces television series from the conferences that air nationally on Free Speech TV and on LINK TV. He has authored many articles and books addressing issues raised at the Bioneers Conferences, like Restoring the Earth: Visionary Solutions from the Bioneers.

"Bioneers" is a neologism for biological pioneers, and for Ausubel, bioneers can come from many cultures and perspectives. They include scientists, artists, economists, activists, farmers, shamans, policymakers and citizens. They represent a culture of solutions, sharing stories that demonstrate how real people, partnering with nature, can make a difference. The Bioneers have an occasional tag-line: "It's All Alive, It's All Intelligent, It's All Connected."

In 2006 Ausubel collaborated with LEONARDO DICAPRIO on the feature documentary *The 11th Hour,* for which he served as central advisor in addition to appearing in the film. Ausubel has his own feature development company, Inner Tan Productions, which is developing the Hoxsey story as a narrative feature.

Kenny Ausubel's work in radio, film, television, books and conferences is focused on solutions and on finding the path to a positive future, combining the natural and the human. His writing is currently published online at Alternet, the Huffington Post and Orion, and in magazines like *Utne, Alternative Therapies* and *Tikkun.* His many awards include the Robert Rodale Award from the Campaign for

Better Health, 2003, with Nina Simons; Global Green Cross Millennium Award for Community Environmental Leadership, 2006, with Nina Simons; WorldMedal, New York Festivals International Radio Programming Competition; UN Department of Information Award, 2003; Utne Visionary Award, 1996, with Nina Simons. When asked what he hopes the outcome of this work will be, Ausubel is quoted as saying, "We like to think of Bioneers as a declaration of interdependence, recognizing that all life is connected."

BIBLIOGRAPHY
"The Empire Strikes Out," Kenny Ausubel, www.oriononline.org/pages/oo/sidebars/Patriotism/index_Ausubel.html; "Restoring the Earth: Visionary Solutions from the Bioneers," Kenny Ausubel, HJ Kramer, Tiburon, California, 1997; "When Healing Becomes a Crime," Kenny Ausubel, www.whale.to/m/ausubel.html; www.greenmoneyjournal.com/article.mpl?newsletterid=29&articleid=308; www.bioneers.org.

Ayres, Richard
(February 2, 1942–)
Attorney, Co-founder of the Natural Resources Defense Council

Cofounder of the Natural Resources Defense Council (NRDC), Richard Ayres is one of the nation's leading experts on the Clean Air Act. Ayres has shaped the nation's clean air program and laws since the passage of the Clean Air Act of 1970 and has litigated many of the key Clean Air Act cases. He has influenced many of the most important Environmental Protection Agency (EPA) rules interpreting the Clean Air Act and has played a leading role in congressional consideration of amendments to the Clean Air Act in 1977, 1980, and 1990.

Richard Edward Ayres was born on February 2, 1942, in Salem, New Jersey. In 1949, his family moved to Beaverton, Oregon, then a quiet Pacific Northwest town outside of Portland. The family spent weekends boating and fishing. Ayres credits his early experience of the beauty of nature in the Pacific Northwest as a formative influence in his later career, along with his father's interest in politics and public policy, sense of stewardship for the natural world, and his personal integrity.

Ayres graduated with honors in 1964 from Princeton University's undergraduate program in the Woodrow Wilson School of Public and International Affairs. In 1969 he received his LL.B. from Yale Law School, together with an advanced degree in political science from Yale University. He was an editor of the *Yale Law Journal* and received the Perez Prize, given for the best student-authored article of the year, for an empirical investigation of police interrogations, "Interrogations in New Haven: The Impact of *Miranda*" (1967).

Along with JOHN H. ADAMS and several other environmentalist attornies, Ayres cofounded the NRDC in 1970. He was instrumental in making it one of the nation's most influential environmental organizations, with a membership today of 475,000. NRDC seeks to safeguard the health of humans and the natural world. With a staff of lawyers, scientists, and others, it attempts to persuade governments, business, and other institutions to adopt more environmentally friendly policies. NRDC is credited with having major impacts on national and international policies in many areas, including air and water pollution, toxic chemicals, energy, transportation and urban development, protection of old-growth forests and other terrestrial and marine habitat, limitation of nuclear proliferation, and global warming. At NRDC, where he worked until 1991, Ayres became one of the most influential voices shaping the nation's clean air policies in all three branches of the federal government.

Ayres has handled nearly three dozen cases in the federal courts, including the Supreme Court of the United States, involving the interpretation and enforcement of the Clean Air Act and the National Environmental Policy Act. Ayres achieved the largest single reduction in pollution in American history in litigation with the Tennessee Valley Authority (TVA), then the nation's largest emitter of sulfur oxides. In settlements in seven federal district courts located in three different states, TVA agreed to cut sulfur oxides emissions by over one million tons per year, at the time approximately 5 percent of the total national emissions of sulfur oxides. Ayres also argued *Train v. NRDC* (1975) and *Vermont Yankee Nuclear Power Corporation v. NRDC* (1977) before the Supreme Court.

Ayres has participated in most of the important EPA rule-making proceedings under the Clean Air Act since 1971. Among the more notable are development of all 50 of the original State Implementation Plans, revisions to the National Ambient Air Quality Standards in 1972 and 1980, regulation of the use of tall smokestacks by large electric power generating plants, emission standards for new coal-fired electric generating plants, development of standards for hazardous air pollutants for several industries, standards for "reformulated" gasoline, adoption of emission trading guidance for states, standards for sulfur content of gasoline, and development of open Market Emission Trading guidance.

During congressional consideration of amendments to the Clean Air Act in 1977, 1980, and 1990, Ayres led the National Clean Air Coalition, which included the major environmental and public health organizations and labor unions, churches, and civic organizations. The Coalition successfully sought important additions to the national clean air program enacted by Congress in the 1970 Clean Air Amendments.

In 1977, the Coalition proposed what became the Prevention of Significant Deterioration program, designed to manage emissions growth in the interests of preserving high quality air and maximizing the potential for economic growth. As a means of achieving these goals, the Coalition successfully advocated requirements that new emissions units be required to install state-of-the-art pollution control technology.

In 1990, the Coalition successfully urged President Bush and the Congress to adopt programs to control acid rain, reduce emissions of toxic chemicals, and cut emissions from new motor vehicles. The acid rain control program requires major reductions in sulfur oxides emissions from electric power plants. It includes the most ambitious and successful emission trading program ever adopted, which has cut costs to about one-fourth of what was predicted when the legislation was being considered. The hazardous emissions control program replaced a previously ineffective section of the Clean Air Act with a list of 190 toxic chemicals and instructions for EPA on how to control them. Motor vehicle standards enacted in 1990 have cut allowable emissions from new cars by 75 percent.

In 1991, Ayres left NRDC for private practice, becoming a partner in the Washington office of O'Melveny and Myers, where he headed its environmental department. He worked as a Parner in the Howrey Simon Arnold and White Firm of Washington, D.C., from 1996 to 2000. In 1998, Ayres participated in settling the largest mobile source air enforcement case in history, brought by the federal government against the manufacturers of diesel engines. Ayres founded the Ayres Law Group in 2001.

Ayres has served on a number of blue ribbon panels dealing with the nation's clean air policy. He was appointed by President Carter to the National Commission on Air Quality in 1978 and served as a Commissioner until

1981; he was a member of the Carnegie Commission on Science, Technology, and Regulatory Decision Making from 1991 to 1994; served on the Environmental Protection Agency's Clean Air Act Advisory Committee from 1993 until 2005; and is currently a member of the Mayor's Environmental Advisory Council for the District of Columbia. In 1988, Ayres was recognized by the Yale Law School Association of Washington for his outstanding service to the public interest. In 1989, he was honored by the Yale Law School Environmental Law Association for his role in creating the public interest law movement.

Ayres also serves on several boards of directors of educational, environmental and energy-oriented organizations, including the Natural Resources Defense Council, the Vermont Law School, Breakthrough Technologies Institute.

Ayres lives in Washington, D.C., with his wife, Merribel, and children, Alice and Richard.

BIBLIOGRAPHY

"Ayres Law Group," www.ayreslawgroup.com; Ayres, Richard, "Setting National Ambient Air Quality Standards, *Clean Air Act Handbook*, 2nd edition. Martineau, Robert J. Jr. and David Novello, 2004; Ayres, Richard, "The Clean Air Act: Performance and Prospects," American Bar Association *Natural Resources and Environment*, 1998; Ayres, Richard, "Developing a Market in Emission Credits Incrementally: An 'Open Market' Paradigm for Market-Based Pollution Control," *BNA Environment Reporter*, 1997.

American Environmental Leaders

From Colonial Times to the Present

B

Babbitt, Bruce

(June 27, 1938–)
Secretary of the Department of the Interior, Governor of Arizona

Bruce Babbitt served as Secretary of the Department of the Interior under President Bill Clinton from 1993 until 2001. He brought a strong conservation ethic to this position, encouraging cooperation between environmental and commercial interests and founding the National Landscape Conservation System, administered by the Bureau of Land Management. Currently, Babbit chairs the Board of the Worldwide Wildlife Federation.

Bruce Edward Babbitt, the second of six children, was born on June 27, 1938, to Paul J. and Francis Babbitt. He grew up in Flagstaff, Arizona, where his family had originally settled in the 1880s and had ranched and operated trading posts. From his early childhood on, Babbitt was exposed to the type of outdoor activities that go along with a ranching heritage. He was an avid hiker and horseback rider. He attended the University of Notre Dame, where he studied geology, graduating with honors in 1960 with a B.S. He continued his education at the University of Newcastle-upon-Tyne in England, receiving an M.S. in geophysics in 1963.

After completing his M.S. degree, he reevaluated the direction of his career and decided to pursue politics rather than geology. To this end he enrolled in law school at Harvard University, graduating in 1965. During his time at law school he became active in the civil rights movement. He joined marches in Selma, Alabama, and upon graduating from Harvard he worked in the federal antipoverty program as a civil rights lawyer. From 1965 to 1967 he served as special assistant to the director of Volunteer Service to America (VISTA), after which he left government service and returned to Arizona, where he joined a private law firm in Phoenix.

In 1974, Babbitt was elected attorney general of Arizona. In this capacity he fought for consumer protection, cracking down on land sale frauds, price-fixing, and insurance irregularities. He published two books on the American Southwest: *Color and Light: The Southwest Canvases of Louis Akin*, 1973, and *Grand Canyon: An Anthology*, 1978. In 1978, after the sitting governor resigned to become an ambassador, Babbitt, being next in line, became the governor of Arizona. He served the remainder of the term and was elected to two more full terms in office, serving 9 years until 1987. As governor, Babbitt's philosophy was that government should be streamlined and show fiscal restraint. He also believed that government should act as a protector of the environment and civil rights. He pushed for environmental controls and water management, and he supported education and child welfare programs. He is known for his leadership in the passage of the Arizona Groundwater Management Act of 1980, which remains the nation's strongest water regulatory system.

After stepping down as Governor, Babbitt practiced law in Arizona and was president the League of Conservation Voters.

From 1993 to 2001, Babbitt served as Secretary of the Department of the Interior under Pres. Bill Clinton. The Secretary of the Interior is responsible for managing the federal government's land holdings and natural resources. Babbitt's views on conservation distinguished him from previous secretaries of the interior. His predecessor, Manuel Lujan, referred to Bureau of Land Management (BLM) land as "a place with lots of grass for cows." Babbitt employed a drastically different perspective in managing the government's resources, believing in the concept of "public use" and basing his management practices on the idea that lands must be shared by accommodating environmental, recreational, and commercial interests.

Babbitt's strong emphasis in coalition building and cooperation were clear in his efforts in the Everglades National Park in Florida, where, in 1995, he and Environmental Protection Agency administrator CAROL BROWNER worked together to negotiate a settlement that would result in the largest environmental restoration project in history, a $700 million cleanup, half of which was to be paid for by the sugarcane farmers, who were also required to cut back on dumping phosphorus into the watersheds that feed the park. The other half was to be paid for by the taxpayers of Florida. According to Babbitt, this type of settlement was ideal because it would lead to the restoration of an entire ecosystem, not just scattered pieces, and because it would put an end to the expensive, time-consuming legal warfare that leads to "environmental train wrecks." Neither the farmers nor the environmentalists were entirely happy with the deal. The farmers felt that they were forced to shoulder an excessive share of the financial burden, and some environmentalists thought that Babbitt had sold out to agricultural interests and had "sounded the death knell for the Everglades." Observers say that any multiple-use resource manager who draws such heavy criticism from two diametrically opposed interest groups must surely be doing his job.

Near the end of his tenure as Secretary of Interior, in 2000, Babbitt created the National Landscape Conservation System, and assigned its administration to the BLM. While serving as Secretary, Babbitt placed 15 National Monuments—including the Grand Staircase-Escalante National Monument, which he helped create in 1996—and 13 National Conservation Areas into the new System and mandated that the BLM keep them "healthy, open and wild." Currently the system includes hundreds of Wilderness Areas and Wilderness Study Areas, almost 40 Wild and Scenic Rivers, and 13 National Trails.

Since 2001, Babbitt has worked as chief counsel of the law firm Latham & Watkins. He currently serves as Chair of the Board of the World Wildlife Fund-U.S. His 2005 book, *Cities in the Wilderness* presents an argument for the creation of a national vision of land use, based on public-private partnerships and use of laws and institutions already in existence.

Babbitt is married to Harriet Coons. They have two sons, Christopher and Thomas Jeffery.

BIBLIOGRAPHY

Babbitt, Bruce, *Cities in the Wilderness: a new vision of land use in America*, 2005; Hines, Susan, "Ground Plan," *Landscape Architecture*, 2006; "Terrain.org interviews Bruce Babbitt," www.terrain.org/interview/18; "U.S. Department of the Interior," www.doi.gov; Williams, Ted, "On The Fire Line for Conservation," *Outdoor Life*, 1996; Wuerthner, George, "The Science Stalemate," *National Parks*, 1995.

Bahouth, Peter

(August 26, 1953–)
Former Executive Director of Turner Foundation and Greenpeace U.S.A.

Known for his refusal to compromise, Peter Bahouth has headed two of the largest environmental organizations in the country. He served as executive director of Greenpeace U.S.A., which evolved from a scrappy, disorganized advocacy group into a powerful environmental organization with 2.2 million members during his leadership. While at Greenpeace, he planned direct action campaigns, marketed the organization to the nation's youth through television ads and a record album, and strove to maintain Greenpeace's integrity in an era of increasing compromises between environmental concerns and corporate interests. Bahouth headed the Turner Foundation from 1993 till 2000, where he helped channel millions of dollars into environmental causes.

Peter Bahouth was born on August 26, 1953, in Syracuse, New York, to Frank and Anne Marie (Pietrafesa) Bahouth. He earned a B.A. in history from the University of Rochester in 1975 and a degree in law from the New England School of Law in 1978; he established a law practice in Boston that same year.

In 1979 he began volunteering his legal services for Greenpeace, an environmental organization known for its confrontational direct action campaigns, such as voyaging to sea to interfere with whaling, nuclear testing, and the killing of seal pups. He became increasingly involved with the organization; he was elected to the board of directors in 1982 and then two years later was named national chairman. In 1985, Greenpeace International sent its flagship, the *Rainbow Warrior*, on a mission to protest French nuclear testing in the South Pacific. While making preparations in a New Zealand port, the ship was sunk by French secret service agents, killing a photographer on board and resulting in an international scandal. The incident prompted an outpouring of sympathy for Greenpeace in the form of new members and contributions. In the aftermath, Bahouth negotiated for compensatory damages; France agreed to pay Greenpeace $8 million.

In 1987 Bahouth coordinated the production of a Greenpeace-sponsored album called "Rainbow Warriors." Among the performers who donated songs were U2, R.E.M., Sting, Peter Gabriel, the Talking Heads, Dire Straits, and many other rock musicians, all of whom gave Greenpeace instant credibility to millions of young people. At this point Bahouth had given up his law practice and had begun working to consolidate Greenpeace's seven regional chapters into Greenpeace U.S.A., of which he became executive director in 1988. He was responsible for planning campaigns, managing personnel, and handling the budget and the media. He participated in many of the direct action campaigns himself, including chaining himself to railroad tracks near the DuPont Company's headquarters to protest shipments of toxic pollutants.

Bahouth also continued helping Greenpeace recruit the nation's youth. Capitalizing on its radical reputation, Greenpeace marketed its environmental activism through a series of "World Alert" commercials on the cable music channel VH-1, featuring celebrities and the quick cuts and hypnotizing graphics used in the channel's music videos. The response from the ads, which ran in 1989 and 1990, was highly enthusiastic, with up to 7,000 phone calls a month coming in from interested viewers, and Greenpeace U.S.A.'s membership reached an all-time high of 2.2 million.

With the influx of money and status, Bahouth had to struggle to resist the pressure to join with the more mainstream environmental groups in forging alliances with what he called the "regulatory-industrial-negotiating complex." When invited to join the Group of Ten, a coalition of mainstream environmental organizations, Bahouth balked, saying he wouldn't join unless LOIS GIBBS (a grassroots hazardous wastes activist) was invited too. As Greenpeace grew, many felt it was losing its vision, and in 1991 Bahouth left the organization and spent a year campaigning in Montana to save over four million acres of publicly owned wilderness from development and logging.

In the spring of 1993, Bahouth became executive director of the Turner Foundation, a private conservation organization founded by billionaire media mogul TED TURNER and his family in 1990. The Turner Foundation, which is endowed with earnings from Turner's Cable News Network and its acquisition by Time Warner, directs funds toward local, national, and international groups that work to protect water quality and wildlife habitat, control world population through family planning, reduce consumption, and conserve natural resources. In 1996, the Turner Foundation gave away $8.9 million in grants. In 1997 this amount doubled to $18 million, and then nearly tripled in 1998 to $25 million. The foundation generally favors grassroots organizations and watchdog groups over the larger national organizations and while Bahouth was at the fore, it instructed its 1,500 applicants per year to limit their grant requests to three pages so as not to waste paper. The Foundation now accepts grant applications by invitation only.

Bahouth stepped down from his position as Executive Director of the Turner Foundation in 2000 but continued to work with it as a consultant. Bahouth promotes environmentally-sensitive "smart-growth" building and development projects in his hometown of Atlanta and beyond.

BIBLIOGRAPHY
Dowie, Mark, *Losing Ground: American Environmentalism at the Close of the Twentieth Century*, 1995; Goldberg, David, "Turner Foundation Funds Efforts to Study, Curb Urban Sprawl," *Atlanta Constitution*, 1997; "Greenpeace: An Antidote to Corporate Environmentalism," *Multinational Monitor*, 1990; Kowet, Don, "A Natural Made-for-TV Movement," *Insight on the News*, 1990; Ploetz, Kristen and Peter Manus, "Conversation with an Environmental Adventurer," New England School of Law—Center for Law and Social Responsibility, www.nesl.edu/clsr/projects/eap/EAPonlineGD.cfm?show=bahouth; Saporta, Maria, "Atlanta Rejects Turner Funds for Energy Conservation Plan," *Atlanta Constitution*, 1998.

Bailey, Florence Augusta Merriam
(August 8, 1863—September 22, 1948)
Ornithologist, Author

Prominent and prolific ornithologist, Florence Augusta Merriam Bailey wrote, taught, and performed extensive fieldwork on birds. Into her 70s, Bailey led numerous bird walks for the general public. She published 10 books and about 100 articles in her lifetime. She was one of the founders and lead instructors of the Audubon Society chapter of Washington, D.C., where she lived on and off her entire adult life mostly in her home on Kalorama Road. In 1885 she became the first woman associate member of the American Ornithologists' Union; in 1929 she was their first woman fellow; and in 1931 she was the first woman to receive the AOU Brewster Medal for her more than 800-page book *Birds of New Mexico* published in 1928. In 1933 she received an honorary LL.D. from the University of New Mexico.

Florence Augusta Merriam Bailey was born in her family's 100-acre estate, "Homewood," in Locust Grove, New York on August 8, 1863. She was the youngest of three children. Her immediate and extended family had a great interest in the natural world and instilled it in Bailey from an early age. Her mother, Caroline Hart Merriam, was a graduate of Rutgers Female Institute in New York and an avid astronomer. Her father, Clinton Levi Merriam, a businessman and later a Member of Congress (1871-1875), visited and corresponded with JOHN MUIR during his years at Yosemite, particularly in regard to Muir's now accepted, but then controversial, theory of glaciation. Bailey's paternal aunt, Helen Merriam Bagg, who lived in close proximity, was the family plant specialist, having a herbarium to which she encouraged all to contribute. No one was to have as profound an influence over Bailey's life and career as her older brother, Clinton Hart Merriam, known as Hart, one of the founders of the American Ornithologists' Union, AOU, and the first chief of the U.S. Biological Survey, USBS, (1885-1910), now U.S. Fish and Wildlife, and one of the founders of the National Geographic Society in 1888. He made expeditions to the West and, as a teenager, developed and published a theory of biological life zones based largely on temperature. He was to pen more than five hundred publications in his lifetime, review all of his sister's early manuscripts, and later be referred to affectionately by her as the GLN (Greatest Living Naturalist).

Bailey attended Smith College from 1882 to 1886 as a special student, receiving an honorary B.A. in 1921. She was very active from the start in leading classmates on bird walks. In 1886 she helped to found the Smith College Audubon Society in large part to heed AOU's William Brewster's calls to protect North American birds from extinction due to the millinery fashion at the time of having feathers and stuffed birds on women's hats. A third of her classmates had joined within three months and they literally changed the course of fashion as their movement spread from campus to town and elsewhere, eventually resulting in a Congressional ban on interstate commerce in birds. That year, through Bailey's efforts, the renowned naturalist JOHN BURROUGHS made the first of many visits to campus.

During her last year at Smith, Bailey began writing articles about her observations and descriptions of birds while in the field. These and subsequent articles formed the basis of her first published book at the age of 26, *Birds Through an Opera Glass* (1889). She advocated the study of live birds, as opposed to only killing and studying dead specimens.

During a bout of tuberculosis, she took several trips to the West. One trip to Utah yielded *My Summer in a Mormon Village* (1895). Her many visits to "Twin Oaks," her paternal uncle Gustav Merriam's homestead in San Diego County, California, resulted in *A-Birding on a Bronco* (1896), about the birds she observed in the area as she traveled on horseback. It was the first book illustrated by the famous bird artist Louis Agassiz Fuertes, who was then only a junior in college. Her next project was a beginner's guidebook named *Birds of Village and Field* (1899).

A naturalist hired by Hart Merriam named Vernon Bailey, who worked for the Survey for 46 years, became Florence Merriam's husband in December of 1899. They were constant travel companions and collaborators in the field and publications for decades. Their travels were extensive and quite rugged by the standards of any day, including extended hiking and camping in elevations at and above tree-line in the mountains of New Mexico, Arizona, Wyoming, Montana, California, Oregon, and the state of Washington, as well as other wild places in North Dakota, Michigan, and elsewhere.

In 1902 Florence Bailey published *A Handbook on Birds of the Western United States*. In 1903, at the request of the USBS and president THEODORE ROOSEVELT, Vernon Bailey undertook a detailed biological survey of what was then the Territory of New Mexico. His wife accompanied him on the almost five months of fieldwork, and contributed to the survey her own personal studies of birds in the territory. These early observations were to form part of the award-winning book she was to complete more than 20 years later on the birds of that state. In 1908 Bailey was honored by GEORGE BIRD GRINNELL, founder of the first Audubon Society, with having a variety of California Mountain Chickadee named after her: *Parus gambeli baileyae*.

In 1918, the Baileys jointly published *Wild Animals of Glacier National Park*.

In between their excursions for work and pleasure to the West, which included leading trips for the Sierra Club, the Baileys were always active in Washington, welcoming many naturalists to their home. Florence Bailey always remained active in the D.C. Audubon Society teaching ornithology and in lobbying Congress for the protection of birds. Although the Baileys remained childless, they were devoted to other members of their families, especially those of the younger generations.

In 1936 Florence and Vernon Bailey set out on their last joint assignment in the American West, to test Vernon's new, humane traps for foxes, beavers and other animals. *Among the Birds in the Grand Canyon National Park* (1939) was Florence Bailey's last major published work. In 1942 both C. Hart Merriam and Vernon Bailey died. Florence Bailey died in Washington, D.C. on September 22, 1948.

BIBLIOGRAPHY
Kofaulk, Harriet, *No Woman Tenderfoot*, 1989; Oehser, Paul H., "In Memoriam: Florence Merriam Bailey," *Auk*, Vol 69, 1952; AAUW St. Lawrence, NY branch, Woman of Courage profile of Florence Merriam Bailey, Pioneer Naturalist.

Ball, Betty, and Gary Ball
(December 26, 1941– ; December 15, 1948–)
Community Organizer, Environmental Activist; Environmental Activist and Analyst

Betty and Gary Ball cofounded the Mendocino Environmental Center (MEC) in Ukiah, California in March, 1987, and codirected it as it became the hub for many of the activists working on a range of environmental issues in northern California, including redwood forest clear-cutting.

Betty Ball was born Elizabeth Louise Johnston on December 26, 1941, in Milwaukee. Ball's father, a YMCA director, was transferred to Scottsbluff, Nebraska, to establish a new YMCA when Betty was six years old and again to do the same in Lubbock, Texas, when she was ten. Ball followed in her father's footsteps by graduating from the YMCA's George Williams College in Chicago in 1967 with a B.A. in group work and psychology. Her first job out of college was as program coordinator for a branch of Jane Addams's Hull House, where she organized recreational programs for disadvantaged children.

In the summer of 1969 she moved back to Boulder, Colorado, where she had spent many childhood summers visiting her grandparents. Ball worked at a home for developmentally disabled adults in Boulder and for the Colorado Department of Social Services in Nucla, in western Colorado. She briefly attended the Jane Addams School of Social Work in Chicago in 1971 but became disenchanted with the program after a professor of a class about the history of social welfare reform refused to allow his class to discuss the U.S. bombing of Cambodia the day after it happened.

Gary Ball was born on December 15, 1948, in Denver, Colorado. At the age of two, he was stricken with polio. Isolated from other children by his disability, Ball found a refuge in music and his intellect. He attended the Boettcher school for disabled children and despite its lack of a precollege curriculum, went on to graduate from the University of Colorado in 1970 with a degree in psychology.

The Balls met in 1970, and together they worked with various community organizations in Boulder, Colorado. They helped run the Boulder Communication Center, an alternative social service center for the town's nu-

Gary and Betty Ball (Photograph courtesy of Dean Pajevic)

merous hippies and transients. A local ecumenical religious center donated space for the Center, and the transients had a place to hang out, leave their backpacks, get messages and mail, receive counseling, find temporary work, catch a free nightly bus to camp in the mountains, eat for free, and so on. Gary Ball's paid job during most of the 1970s was with a team that conducted early studies on biofeedback, a therapeutic technique in which a patient is given information about his or her physiological functions that he or she is not able to perceive otherwise, with the object of trying to gain control over them. Biofeedback is done with modified polygraph equipment; Gary Ball became a computer data analyst during his work on the studies. After these projects were finished, he went on to help analyze data for the National Oceanic and Atmospheric Administration from studies having to do with forecasting hail storms. He left once he discovered that one ulterior motive of this study was to learn if it would be possible to use severe storms as weapons. Betty Ball worked for the National Conference of Christians and Jews from 1973 until 1977. The Balls moved to the mountain town of Nederland, Colorado, where she became town clerk. She also worked with IDEAS, a program based on the "Foxfire" concept, which engaged various groups of children and adults from different cultural groups in collecting and publishing the oral histories of elders in their communities.

In 1984, the couple moved together to California. They spent their first year there as nomads, selling environmental T-shirts at different fairs every weekend. In each destination they learned as much as possible about the area's environmental problems and grassroots environmental organizations. They were invited to work in Ukiah, California, at Between the Worlds, a unique store that sold comic books, science fiction literature, and educational materials and provided desktop publishing services as well. There they became acquainted with the local activist community and learned about the serious environmental problems facing the area. Clear-cutting of the old-growth redwood forests was devastating ecosystems and waterways. The salmon were no longer able to spawn, which ruined the fishing industry. Siltation ruined riverine habitat for many other aquatic species as well. Gary Ball became involved in the Redwood chapter of the Sierra Club and served as its chair for a term and a half.

A year after moving to Ukiah, the Balls were approached by a local environmentalist who had recently inherited a storefront building in downtown Ukiah, across the street from the courthouse, which he wanted to establish as an environmental center. The Balls offered to help create and staff the center, and owner John McCowen readily agreed. The Mendocino Environmental Center (MEC) opened in March 1987, and it soon became a center for the region's grassroots environmentalist and social justice efforts. Previously, groups were working independently from activists' homes; MEC provided space and resources and allowed the groups to collaborate and avoid duplication of efforts. Such organizations as the Redwood Coast Watershed Alliance, Earth First!, and the Sierra Club came to use MEC. What had been a disparate group of environmentalists eventually became one of the best-known and most effective regional environmental movements in the country. Well-known environmentalists like JUDI BARI worked out of the center, organizing the mass protests of the annual Redwood Summers.

When the Wise Use Movement emerged with its assault on environmentalism, Gary Ball authored an extensive article about it in the summer/fall 1992 MEC newsletter. "World War III: Meet the Wise Use Movement" was an exposé of the Wise Use Movement's agenda to disable environmental protection laws and regulations and chill environmental activism. The article identified major Wise Use activists and the movement's main organizations and their financiers and summarized the texts that provide the Wise Use Movement with its ideology. The article is still useful for activists and students of environmental movements and history; re-prints are available from MEC.

Once MEC became enough of an institution to sustain itself, the Balls returned to Colorado. Betty Ball currently works at the Rocky Mountain Peace and Justice Center in Boulder, coordinating the nonviolence education collective that seeks to deescalate tensions that could lead to continued violent conflicts between University of Colorado students, community residents and merchants, and local police; she also works collaboratively with other social justice groups in the area to reduce violence against women, people of color and the GLTBI population. She is engaged in concerted efforts with Boulder Community United and the Bias Incident Hotline to make Boulder a more inclusive and welcoming community for all people. Both Balls work with the Center's Environmental Collective, Boulder Environmental Activists' Resource (BEAR), which seeks to draw the connections between the devastation of the earth, human rights violations, and the structural violence and oppression in our society and to provide support for environmental efforts being undertaken by other groups and individuals. BEAR also serves as the clearinghouse for RAID (Ridding Activism of Intimidation and Disruption), a national group that works to reduce violent attacks on environmental activists and disruption of their work by harassment. BEAR works to increase awareness of these attacks and to elicit support for the activists experiencing attacks and harassment. Betty Ball says that her ability to enthusiastically continue her environmental and social justice work despite the odds against winning every struggle is due to her understanding that "tangible results may not be visible for years, so it's important to do the work because it is the right thing to do, and not to be attached to an immediate or specific outcome."

Gary Ball currently works for Jim Morris Environmental T-Shirt Company.

BIBLIOGRAPHY
Ball, Betty, "Oh What a Tangled Web We Weave, or Stop Me before I Email Again," *Mendocino Environmental Center Newsletter*, 1996; Ball, Gary, "World War III: Meet the Wise Use Movement," *Mendocino Environmental Center Newsletter*, 1992; "Mendocino Environmental Center," www.mecgrassroots.org; "Rocky Mountain Peace and Justice Center," www.rmpjc.org.

Balog, James D.
(July 15, 1952–)
Photographer, Founder and Director of the Extreme Ice Survey

Groundbreaking photographer and geomorphologist James Balog directs the Extreme Ice Survey, a photographic chronicle of retreating glaciers in the Rocky Mountains, Alaska, British Columbia, Greenland, and Iceland. His nature photography, especially the collections found in *Tree: A New Vision of the American Forest* (2004) and *Survivors: A New Vision of Endangered Wildlife* (1990), present a fresh and dramatic take on vanishing flora and fauna. James Balog has photographed endangered species for U.S. stamps, the first time a photographer had ever been commissioned by the U.S. Postal Service to create an entire series of stamps.

Born in Danville, Pennsylvania on July 15, 1952 to James Balog and Alvina Bartos, James Balog Jr. spent his youth in the eastern United States. He attended college in Massachusetts (Boston College, class of 1974). He spent 1975-1977, in Boulder, Colorado, where he earned an M.A. in geomorphology, and where he scampered up mountain peaks. From his climbs, he gained experiential knowledge and an appetite for photography and places beyond the reach of most humans. He worked as an Outward Bound instructor from 1976 until 1980, photographing along the way, and finally launching James Balog Photography.

His early photojournalism assignments took him to the savannas of Africa, the Himalayas, and Eastern and Western Europe. His series in *National Geographic*, "A Day in the Life of the Soviet Union" and "A Day in the Life of Spain," each yielded awards. He also began covering the aftermaths of natural disasters when he first shot the fallout from the eruption of Mount Saint Helens in 1980. His photographs began to appear in exhibits: the International Center for Photography (New York),Centre Nacionale de la Photographie (Paris), and other national and international galleries.

Critics admire Balog's placement– amidst the clash and rub between man and nature. He articulates visually, and accompanies his photographs with essays and extended captions, elegies to the natural world, not as we know it, but as Balog sees it from 'the contact zone between man and nature.' In *Tree: A New Vision of the American Forest*, Balog photographs the oldest Americans, our trees. In *Survivors: A New Vision of American Wildlife*, *Anima* (Arts Alternative), and *James Balog's Animals A to Z* (Chronicle), he creates portraits of fauna in surreal and unnatural environments.

He remains on-call for photojournalism assignments, specializing in dramatic disruptions. He shot the wake of December 2004's tsunami and the flotsam behind Hurricane Katrina in 2005.

The June 2007 cover story for *National Geographic* showcased Balog's work on melting glaciers. [See photo-essay, "The Big Thaw," *National Geographic*, July 2007.] . The experience led him to organize the Extreme Ice Survey, an unprecedented documentation of fast-changing glaciers around the world. He decided to dedicate his photography to the task of influencing environmental policy makers to the real and present dangers of human-generated global warming.

To chronicle the inevitable momentous geomorphical events, Balog has set up twenty-six time-lapse cameras at fifteen locations to shoot once an hour, every hour of daylight, approximately eight photographs a day over two years, through 2009. The Extreme Ice Survey seeks to create a photographic record of the dramatic changes brought on by global warming temperatures.

"The argument that we're not involved in climate change is immoral. It reminds me of the Medieval Era when people dumped garbage and human waste on the street, with no thought that it might cause disease."

Balog's work is widely acclaimed. It won the 2007 Rowell Award for the Art of Adventure and the North American Nature Photography Association named Balog the Nature Photographer of the Year in 2008. When he's not in the Arctic Circle, he lives in the hot, dry foothills of the Rocky Mountains, west of Boulder, Colorado with his wife, Suzanne, and two daughters, Simone and Emily.

BIBLIOGRAPHY

Rainforest Action Network, The Panther, Winter, 2008; Shulgold, Marc, "Cold Reality," *Rocky Mountain News*, April 12, 2008; Holbrooke, David, director, a 16-minute film about James Balog's work, *A Redwood Grows in Brooklyn*, 2006; Michael Shnayerson, "Portrait of a Meltdown," *National Geographic Adventure*, October 2007; "How Photography Can Help Save the Planet," *American Photo*, September/October, 2007; www.jamesbalog.com; www.extremeicesurvey.org.

Bari, Judi
(November 7, 1949–March 2, 1997)
Revolutionary, Labor and Earth First! Organizer

Earth First! activist Judi Bari organized nonviolent mass actions to stop what she and her allies called "the corporate liquidation of Northern California's" redwood forest. Identifying the enemy as the corporate interests that sought to cut the area's forests as quickly as possible without regard for the long-term interests of workers or environmental concerns, Bari used her experience as a labor organizer to help workers and environmentalists find common cause. Bari spent the last seven years of her life severely disabled and in pain as a result of a car-bombing attempt on her life. She dedicated this time to continuing the struggle against clear-cutting as well as to suing the Federal Bureau of Investigation (FBI) for illegally arresting her and fellow victim Darryl Cherney and for improperly investigating the bombing.

Judith Beatrice Bari was born on November 7, 1949, in Baltimore, Maryland. Bari was an enthusiastic activist and organizer from adolescence, participating in student government and the "school spirit" club. Politics caught up with Bari while she was studying at the University of Maryland. She transferred her organizing abilities to the anti–Vietnam War struggle, coordinating mass actions to close major highways to protest the war. The war, as well as her growing interest in the labor union movement, drew Bari away from her studies and toward a life dedicated to activism.

Bari dropped out of college as a senior in 1972, in order to join the labor union movement. She got a job as a checker at a local Grand Union grocery store and was soon elected vice president of her local. When the demand that she put forward for a $1/hour wage raise was supported by her union but denied by store officials, she led 12,000 workers on strike. Fired for her union activity several times, Bari was transferred to the same company's Korvette stores and assigned to the cosmetics counter, a real oxymoron, as anyone who knew her would attest. She was fired after she was not able to assist cosmetics customers in an appropriate manner. Bari then began working for the U.S. Postal Service (USPS) at a Bulk Mail Center and became active in its union. Her cause there was mandatory overtime, which exhausted workers and left them vulnerable to injury while working with dangerous mail-sorting machinery. She helped a researcher for Jack Anderson's investigative column sneak into the plant to witness the problem, and she edited and surreptitiously distributed an underground publication, *Postal Strife*, a take-off on the official USPS publication *Postal Life*. *Postal Strife* rallied workers to resist mandatory overtime and sported a cigarette-smoking buzzard instead of the USPS golden eagle.

In 1979, Bari married union organizer Mike Sweeney and moved with him to northern California. She was active in the antinuclear, prochoice, and Central America solidarity movements of the 1980s; she had two daughters. When her marriage dissolved in 1988, she began to work as a carpenter to support herself. Soon she made the connection between the magnificent redwood lumber her clients demanded and the clear-cuts that were denuding the mountains throughout the area. Ever bold, when Bari was invited to the posh housewarming party of one wealthy client, her gift was a photograph of the clear-cut that his house had been built from.

Attracted by the no-compromise position, impetuous antics, and creative music of Earth First!, Bari became involved in that burgeoning environmentalist movement of northern California in 1988. Clear-cutting had been accelerated as such large corporations as Louisiana Pacific, Georgia Pacific, and Pacific Lumber were cutting the last remaining ancient rain forests of California, some on private lands and others in national forests. Earth First! and other local environmental groups responded with a variety of tactics, including direct action protests, preventing workers from entering, or blocking roads so that timber trucks could not leave sites. Throughout these potentially incendiary conflicts, Bari and other environmental leaders insisted on a policy of nonviolent resistance and in 1990 signed a moratorium on tree-spiking (driving spikes into trees to discourage loggers from cutting them) and other acts of "ecotage."

Bari always encouraged fellow environmentalists to blame corporate management of logging companies rather than the workers. She was one of the first to make the connection between the safety and stability of lumber industry workers' jobs and the concerns of environmentalists. In 1989, when she and activists Anna Marie Stenberg and Darryl Cherney learned of a serious polychlorinated biphenyl (PCB) spill at the Georgia Pacific mill, they reported the incident to the Occupational Safety and Health Administration. The workers were never compensated for their exposure to the chemicals. When Louisiana Pacific laid off 1,000 workers in six mills throughout northern California, forced its remaining workers to work overtime despite the dangers of operating heavy machinery when overtired, and then opened up a new mill in Baja California, Mexico, it became even more evident that the real rift was between management and workers, not environmentalists and workers.

Still, Bari and the environmentalists were subject to the powerful public relations departments of timber corporations, which whipped up hatred for environmentalists by blaming them for the dwindling timber supply. There were a few violent face-to-face incidents in which environmentalists were hurt by loggers during protests, and in 1989, after leaving one event, Bari's car was intentionally rammed from the rear and forced off the road by one of the logging trucks that had been blockaded during the protest. In the spring of 1990, Bari began to receive regular death threats, and false Earth First! press releases were being distributed to local newspapers. At this time, Bari and Darryl Cherney were organizing "Redwood Summer," a series of mass protests through the region that would attract environmentalists and attention from around the country. On May 24, 1990, as Bari and Cherney were driving from Oakland, California, to Santa Cruz to recruit Redwood Summer participants, their car blew up. A bomb under Bari's seat, which was triggered to explode when the car began moving, almost killed Bari and injured Cherney. As soon as the FBI and the Oakland Police Department arrived at the scene, and in defiance of all the physical evidence, they falsely concluded that Bari and Cherney had planted the bomb themselves and blown themselves up and arrested them. Bari was hospitalized for six weeks and underwent a long and painful rehabilitation before she could walk again.

During the next seven years, despite severe pain and disability, Bari remained a key organizer in the Earth First! movement, investigated the bombing, and worked diligently and meticulously on a law suit against the FBI and the Oakland Police Department. Her research led her to think that Earth First! was being infiltrated by the FBI just as the Black Panthers and the American Indian Movement had been during the 1960s and 1970s. Bari's work led her to documents proving that the FBI had illegally infiltrated and actually instigated the power-line downing attempt in Arizona that ended with the arrests of Arizona Earth First! activists, including DAVE FOREMAN, in 1989.

Bari discovered a lump in her breast in July 1996 and learned that she had breast cancer that had already metastasized to her liver in September of that year. She died on March 2, 1997. More than five years later, in June of 2002, a jury ruled unanimously that Bari's and Cherney's first and fourth amendment rights had been violated by the FBI and awarded Cherney and Judi Bari's estate four million dollars in damages. With a portion of these damages, the Redwood Justice Fund and Willits Environmental Center now make biennial "Judi Bari Activist Grants" to environmental activists working in the "Judi Bari tradition."

BIBLIOGRAPHY

Bari, Judi, *Revolutionary Ecology: Biocentrism and Deep Ecology*, 1998; Bari, Judi, *Timber Wars*, 1994; Breton, Mary Joy, *Women Pioneers for the Environment*, 1998; Coleman, Kate, The Secret Wars of Judi Bari: a Car Bomb, the Fight for the Redwoods, and the End of Earth First!, 2005; Faber, Daniel J. "The Struggle for Ecological Democracy: Environmental Justice Movements in the United States", 1998; "Judy Bari Website," www.judibari.org; Zakin, Susan, *Coyotes and Town Dogs: Earth First! and the Environmental Movement*, 1993.

Bartlett, Albert

(March 21, 1923–)
Nuclear Physicist, Educator

Since 1969, nuclear physicist Albert Bartlett has dedicated himself to educating the public about exponential growth of the human population. In his well-known speech "Sustainability 101: Arithmetic, Population, and Energy," which by mid-2008 he had presented more than 1,600 times, Bartlett uses simple arithmetic to demonstrate how quickly even a so-called moderate rate of population growth will lead to overpopulation. He also deconstructs such catchphrases as "sustainable growth," which he identifies as an oxymoron, and explicates the economic, social, and environmental consequences of population growth.

Albert Allen Bartlett was born on March 21, 1923, in Shanghai, China, where his father was principal of the Shanghai American School, a private school for American children. He came to the United States at three months of age and grew up in Ohio. Bartlett began college at Ohio's Otterbein College. After his freshman year, he dropped out of school to wash dishes and cook on two Great Lakes freighters. When he decided to return to his studies, he applied to Colgate University in Hamilton, New York. He earned a B.A. in physics there, graduating summa cum laude in 1944. As Bartlett recounts, "I then hitchhiked, drove trucks, and hopped freights to get to a job at P.O. Box 1663 in Santa Fe where they were hiring physicists for war work. This turned out to be Los Alamos Scientific Laboratory where I worked for the rest of the war." Bartlett spent some time also at Bikini, taking high-speed photos of atomic bomb test explosions. After the war, Bartlett moved on to Harvard University for his M.A. and Ph.D. in physics (1948 and 1951, respectively). Bartlett and Eleanor Roberts were married in 1946, and they had four daughters, Carol, Jane, Lois, and Nancy.

Bartlett was recruited by the Department of Physics of the University of Colorado–Boulder (CU) in 1950, where he developed CU's first teaching laboratories for modern physics and worked in the rapidly expanding field of nuclear physics. While at CU, Bartlett was awarded several National Science Foundation grants for his work on radioactive isotopes and beta-ray spectroscopy. He also received many teaching prizes from the University of Colorado, including the 1972 Thomas Jefferson award for outstanding service to the educational community, the 1974 Robert L. Stearns Award for outstanding achievement, and a University Medal from the University's Board of Regents in 1978. He served as chair of the four-campus Faculty Council of the University of Colorado for two years (1969–1971) and in 1978 was elected national president of the American Association of Physics Teachers. Despite his retirement from full-time teaching in 1988, Bartlett remained active on faculty committees for several years at the university.

After nearly a decade of living in Boulder, which was then a small town nestled at the foot of the Front Range of the Rocky Mountains, Bartlett and other Boulder residents began to worry that Boulder would suffer the same ugly sprawl as a growing number of U.S. communities. In 1959, Bartlett and Robert McKelvey and a small group of activists proposed a City Charter Amendment which established a Blue Line that limited development in the foothills west of Boulder. The Charter Amendment was approved by Boulder voters in July of 1959. Bartlett served on the City of Boulder's Parks and Recreation Advisory Board for five years in the mid-1960s, chairing it in 1967. In 1967 the people of Boulder approved a sales tax measure that allowed Boulder to purchase open space around the city's perimeter. As of 2008, the

Albert Bartlett (Photograph by Casey Cass)

Boulder Open Space Program had allocated over $100 million for 26,000 acres of mountain and plains parks. Bartlett and other members of the local environmental group PLAN–Boulder County also inspired Boulder's unique system of bikeways, which have made Boulder one of the most bike-friendly cities in the nation.

In 1969, Bartlett developed a speech on the hazards of growth that he would give, by mid-2008, over 1,600 times, to an estimated 160,000 interested Americans, including members of Congress and their staff and regulatory, environmental, professional, and educational groups. The speech, which the University of Colorado also sells on videotape, shows the actual numerical increases that result from various growth rates and the effects of growth on a community's resources. For example, the world's 1999 growth rate was 1.3 percent. Its population, estimated in 1999 to be six billion, was increasing at the rate of 80 million/year, and at this rate will double to 12 billion in 51 years. Bartlett deftly exposes the blithe claims of optimists such as the late economist Julian Simon, who wrote, "We have in our hands now… the technology to feed, clothe and supply energy to an ever-growing population for the next seven billion years." After Simon admitted that he had meant seven million—not billion—years, Bartlett did the arithmetic. He found that if Simon assumed that the population could grow at the modest rate of 1 percent per year for seven million years, the size of the population would be 2.3×10 to the 30,410th power.

Bartlett's message incorporates the quantitative analysis of Thomas Malthus, who in the eighteenth century warned that population had the potential to grow much more rapidly than food production could increase and that famine and starvation would inevitably curb population growth. This may still turn out to be the case, although it has not happened on a global scale as quickly as Malthus predicted. Bartlett reminds his audience of Malthus's premise that a population was doomed if it exceeded its environment's ability to provide for its human inhabitants. Modern environmental thinkers often warn people that it's vital not to exceed the "carrying capacity."

Bartlett avoids the frequent conclusion that the problem is most serious in less developed countries where population is growing at the fastest rates. He offers the observation that although the United States' population is growing at about the same rate as the earth's population, the U.S. has the world's most serious population problem because of its enormous per capita annual consumption of resources. An average American uses 10 to 30 times more resources in his or her lifetime than a person from a less developed country. Bartlett uses the following equation: $I = P\,A\,T$, where I is the impact on an area's environment of any group of people, P is the size of the population, A is the per capita affluence, and T is the environmental damage caused by the technologies in place.

The damage done by continuous population growth is wide-ranging. It includes social disorganization, increased economic gaps between the poor and the wealthy, and the following environmental problems: the ozone hole, global climate change, the drop in food grain production per capita, the decline in oceanic fish catch and possible collapse of world fish stocks, and the availability of fresh, potable water. The solution? Most important: STOP population growth worldwide and reduce the overall annual consumption of nonrenewable resources. Alternative, nonpolluting technologies, development of renewable fuels and other resources, and work on social injustice are all important, but gains in those areas can be canceled out by continued population growth. Bartlett insists that Americans concerned about population growth should start their work in the United States but that U.S. foreign assistance should be contingent on recipient countries having effective family planning policies.

Bartlett is not optimistic that humans will be able to curb growth ourselves, and he warned in a 1993 Boulder *Daily Camera* article, "If we don't take care of the problem, Nature will!" Unfortunately, there is little evidence that we have the understanding or the will to solve the problem Still, he perseveres with his message. "Wouldn't you like to believe there's intelligent life on earth? We just have to keep trying to educate people."

BIBLIOGRAPHY

Bartlett, Albert, "Sustainability 101: Arithmetic, Population, and Energy," and reprint book *The Essential Exponential* (available from the University of Colorado Bookstore, UCB 36, Boulder, CO 80309-0036); Bartlett, Albert, "Is There a Population Problem?" *Wild Earth*, 1997; Bartlett, Albert, "Reflections on Sustainability," *The Future of Sustainability*, edited by Marco Keiner, 2006; Havig, Sara, "Sustainability series begins," *Boulder Daily Camera*, 2008.

Bartram, John, and William Bartram

(May 23, 1699–September 22, 1777; April 9, 1739–July 22, 1823)
Botanist; Botanist, Artist

The father-son botanical team of John and William Bartram was among the first to collect and describe indigenous American plants. Their work raised awareness in America and abroad of the rich flora that blanketed the North American continent and inspired naturalists, poets, and artists of their time and in the centuries to come.

John Bartram was born on May 23, 1699, in Marple, Pennsylvania, to William Bartram and Elizabeth Hunt Bartram. His mother died when he was two, and when his father and stepmother moved to North Carolina, he stayed in Pennsylvania with relatives. His only formal education was a few years' study at a local country elementary school. He inherited a farm from an uncle and did well as a farmer. He had two children with his first wife, who died in 1725, and with his second wife, Ann Mendinghall, Bartram had seven more. During the 1720s, Bartram bought a 100-acre farm along the Schuylkill River near the town of Kingsessing, on which he experimented with methods for increasing agricultural productivity, including crop rotation and the use of fertilizer. Part of the plot became Bartram's famous botanical garden, which survives today as part of the Philadelphia park system.

Bartram developed an interest in native flora early in life. His admiration of it was documented by Hector St. John de Crèvecoeur in his 1782 book, *Letters from an American Farmer*. Bartram was said to have sat down for a rest from plowing, plucked a daisy, looked at it carefully, and reflected, "What a shame, said my mind, that thee shouldst have employed so many years in tilling the earth and destroying so many flowers and plants without being acquainted with their structures and uses!" While this "quotation" was most likely imagined by de Crèvecoeur, it describes a man who, despite his lack of formal education, was constantly seeking information from the natural world.

Bartram's career as a botanist began about 1733, when he began to correspond with London merchant and botanist Peter Collinson. Collinson and other correspondents, with whom Bartram came into contact through Collinson, recognized Bartram's gift and sent him the most important botanical texts of that time. Bartram hired a Latin tutor in order to understand these books and to be able to correspond with their authors and other botanists. Collinson offered to hire Bartram to collect American botanical specimens and ship them to him. He was the first of many "subscribers" who funded Bartram's research. Bartram scoured the Pennsylvania countryside for unusual plants and made long excursions, the first with a group of scientists to Lake Ontario in 1743. When his son William grew old enough, Bartram included him on his expeditions. Over John Bartram's lifetime, they traveled as far south as Georgia, north through New England, and west to Ontario.

William Bartram was born to John Bartram and Ann Mendinghall Bartram on April 9, 1739, on their farm in Kingsessing, Pennsylvania. He was given a more complete education than his father had had; he attended the Academy of Philadelphia (which later became the University of Pennsylvania), graduating in 1756, and apprenticed with a Philadelphia merchant for four years after that. Both his schooling and his apprenticeship were broken by frequent trips with his father. Beginning in 1755, with an expedition to the Catskills, his father included him on his botanical expeditions, and young William avidly sketched the plants and animals they found. In 1760, they journeyed to the Carolinas, in 1761 to the forks of the Ohio River, and in 1765, to Florida. William Bartram made his own four-year expedition starting in 1773 to Florida, Georgia, and the western Carolinas.

Both William and John Bartram kept detailed notes during their expeditions, and these notes formed the body of the books, letters, and reports for which they became famous. John Bartram's prose was dense and difficult to penetrate, since his abbreviated education did not include conventional spelling of the time, nor accepted sentence structure. He defended his style by claiming that he preferred to write not by the rules of grammar but rather by "nature." The only book he published was *Observations on the Inhabitants, Climate, Soil, Rivers, Productions, Animals, and Other Matters... From Pennsylvania to Onondago, Oswego and the Lake Ontario in Canada*, which described his first expedition in 1743 and came out in 1751. Otherwise, he wrote reports and long letters, primarily for his patrons, including Collinson and such other seventeenth-century luminaries as American naturalist Mark Catesby, American physician William Byrd II, American inventor and politician Benjamin Franklin, Dutch physician John Frederic Gronovius, Finnish-Swedish naturalist Peter Kalm, Swedish taxonomist Carolus Linnaeus, and many others. Other professional and amateur botanists eagerly read reprints of his papers, since they knew that he was, as Linnaeus called him, the "greatest contemporary 'natural botanist' in the world." His work contained not only elaborate descriptions of climate, landscape, soil conditions, and flora and fauna, but also observations about the indigenous people he encountered: particularly which plants they used for food and supplies.

William Bartram's writings were disseminated to a broader readership and were illustrated with exacting drawings of flora and fauna. Historians now recognize him as the most important natural history artist before JOHN JAMES AUDUBON. William Bartram's journal from his four-year expedition, entitled *Travels through North and South Carolina, Georgia, East and West Florida, the Cherokee Country, the Extensive Territories of the Muscogulges, or Creek Confederacy, and the Country of the Choctaws*, published in 1791, identifies 215 native birds of the Southeast, the most complete list of the day. He described the complexity of ecosystems, marveling at the perfect bodies of even the tiniest insects and at how their great numbers served to nourish fish and other predators on up the food chain. In addition to this book's usefulness for naturalists, it inspired the growing Romantic literary movement, which celebrated wilderness as an expression of the beneficence, rationality, and perfect organization of God's creation. William Bartram wrote of his awe at the spectacular wild landscapes of Appalachia and his feeling of solitude within such places. He was at once exhilarated and terror-struck while alone in the wilderness. Poets Samuel Coleridge and William Wordsworth were said to have been especially inspired by Bartram's work.

Both of the Bartrams made their base at the Bartram botanical garden in Schuylkill. Thanks to generous patronage from King George III, who named John Bartram the king's botanist, and wealthy English physician John Fothergill, who was a correspondent of John Bartram and sponsor of William Bartram, the Bartrams were able to dedicate themselves full-time to botany. Although they sent many specimens to their patrons abroad, they kept many for their own botanical garden, which William and his brother John converted into a nursery after their father's death.

John Bartram died on September 22, 1777, in Kingsessing, Pennsylvania. William Bartram returned to Kingsessing from his last expedition shortly after his father's death, in January 1778. From that point on, William Bartram remained at Kingsessing. He prepared his travel notes for publication; *Travels...* saw several editions in English and was translated into Dutch, German, and French before 1800. William Bartram spent the remainder of his life writing and drawing and receiving famous visitors to Kingsessing. He died on July 22, 1823, while walking in his garden.

BIBLIOGRAPHY

Hoffman, Nancy E. and John C. Van Horne, *America's Curious Botanist: A Tercentennial Reappraisal of John Bartram, 1699-1777*, 2004; Magee, Judith, *The Art and Science of William Bartram*, 2007; Nash, Roderick, *Wilderness and the American Mind*, 1967; Scheick, William J., "John Bartram," in *Dictionary of Literary Biography, American Colonial Writers*, Emory Elliott, ed., 1984; Terrie, Philip G., "William Bartram," in *American Nature Writers*, John Elder, ed., 1996.

Bates, Marston
(July 23, 1906–April 3, 1974)
Zoologist, Writer

One of the foremost zoologists in the United States, Marston Bates insisted that scientists should address a larger audience in their writings. Following his own decree, Bates wrote a series of popular volumes that made the problems of environmental science accessible to a wide audience. Though criticized by his peers for his offering little to students of ecology, Bates found a broader audience; his engaging writing style helped spread awareness and understanding of global ecological problems.

The only son of Glenn, a farmer and horticulturist in Florida, and Amy Mabel (Button) Bates, Marston Bates was born in Grand Rapids, Michigan, on July 23, 1906. Bates attended public schools in Fort Lauderdale, Florida, and then majored in biology at the University of Florida, Gainesville, receiving his B.S. degree in 1927. Before continuing his studies, Bates spent three years, from 1928 to 1931, working for Servicio Técnico de Cooperación Agrícola of the United Fruit Company in Honduras and Guatemala. He started as a research assistant in entomology, working his way up to director. Bates did his graduate studies at Harvard University, receiving his A.M. degree in 1933 and his Ph.D. a year later. His dissertation was entitled "The Butterflies of Cuba."

Bates joined the staff of the Harvard Museum of Comparative Zoology in 1935 but spent most of his two years there on leave with the Rockefeller Foundation, looking into the biology of mosquitoes in Albania. He resigned from the Museum of Comparative Zoology in 1937 and continued his work in Albania until 1939. Bates also studied malaria in Egypt and then, at the onset of World War II, studied yellow fever in Colombia. He remained employed by the Rockefeller Foundation until 1952, except for one year of postdoctoral study at Johns Hopkins University (1948–1949). During this year, Bates wrote *The Natural History of Mosquitoes*, which was widely recognized as a masterpiece and of immense value, especially to scientists but also to the lay public. Understanding the entomology of mosquitoes was essential before control of mosquito-borne diseases could be possible. Bates left the Rockefeller Foundation in 1952 to join the zoology faculty of the University of Michigan.

Bates saw little value in not making scientific findings widely accessible. Writing for a small number of scientists would not help solve the many environmental problems the world faced and that needed a massive popular response to solve. As a faculty member at the University of Michigan, Bates wrote 12 books aimed for a popular audience. The topics of his books ranged from a study of populations and problems in demography in *The Prevalence of People* (1955), to his own observations about the problems of coexistence of several species in *A Jungle in the House: Essays in Natural and Unnatural History* (1970). This last book describes the greenhouse attached to Bates's home in Ann Arbor, Michigan, which he stocked with tropical plants, birds, and animals. His observations about problems of coexistence in his "jungle" led to discussions about the larger environment in which humans, plants, and animals coexist. Opinions of Bates's books were mixed. Scientists often criticized his work, citing that he was too prone to accept the conclusions of authorities in fields where he himself had not specialized. Moreover, his books generally had little to offer professional scientists or their students. Nonetheless, they were praised outside of academia; for many lay readers they were a first, compelling introduction to the natural world.

During his twenty years as a member of the zoology faculty at the University Michigan, Bates continued to travel extensively. In 1954, he was Timothy Hopkins Lecturer at Stanford University, and between 1956 and 1957, the director of research at the University of Puerto Rico. He also spent two years (1956–1958) as chairman of the National Science Foundation's division of comparative biology and medical sciences, three years (1955–1958) on the advisory board of the Guggenheim Foundation, and seven years (1955–1962) as a trustee at the Cranbrook Institute of Science. In 1967, Bates was the recipient of the Daly Medal of the American Geographical Society. The following year, the University of Michigan gave him its Distinguished Faculty Achievement Award.

Bates married Nancy Bell Fairchild, the daughter of botanist David Fairchild, in 1939. She went with him to Colombia and shared their experiences in a *National Geographic Magazine* article, "Keeping House for a Biologist in Colombia," in 1948. Together they had four children, one son and three daughters. Bates died April 3, 1974, in Ann Arbor, Michigan.

BIBLIOGRAPHY

Bates, Marston, *The Forest and the Sea: A Look at the Economy of Nature and Ecology of Man*, 1960; Bates, Marston, *Gluttons and Libertines*, 1968; Bates, Marston, *The Nature of Natural History*, 1950; Bates, Nancy Bell Fairchild, *East of the Andes and West of Nowhere*, 1948.

Bauer, Catherine

(May 11, 1905–November 22, 1964)
Urban Planner, Houser

Catherine Bauer was a leading voice in the development of the fields of housing and urban planning. She wrote many influential articles and a 1934 book, *Modern Housing*, which laid out many of the principles by which federal housing programs were developed. During the 1930s and 1940s she served in executive positions in labor organizations and in federal housing programs. She lobbied successfully for the passage of the United States Housing Act of 1937, an important milestone in the history of the development of national housing policy, leading eventually to the establishment of the Department of Housing and Urban Development (HUD). As administrator, policy advocate, and academic, Bauer successfully championed a new, integrated approach to urban planning that was attentive to the whole environment, including poverty, aesthetics, land use, transportation, and open space issues.

Catherine Krouse Bauer was born in Elizabeth, New Jersey, on May 11, 1905. The oldest of three children, Bauer was raised in an affluent family. Her father, Jacob, was a well-regarded highway engineer; her mother, Alberta, a self-taught biologist and botanist who passed her love of nature on to her children. Bauer graduated at the top of her high school class in 1922 and went to Vassar College. She studied at the Cornell University College of Architecture for one year in 1924 and eventually graduated from Vassar in 1926. Bauer spent the year following graduation in Europe, where her interest in architecture grew into an expertise on developments in European modernism and urban planning. On her return to New York she took a job at the prestigious publishing house Harcourt, Brace, where she first met the architectural critic and social philosopher LEWIS MUMFORD. Mumford and Bauer had a long affair, which played a vital role in shaping Bauer's ideas about urban and regional planning. Both Mumford and Bauer were involved in the Regional Planning Association of America (RPAA), an influential group that advocated for community-based planning and "garden cities," modeled after the ideas of British theorist Ebenezer Howard.

In 1933 Bauer took a job in Philadelphia with the Labor Housing Conference (LHC), a lobbying arm of the Pennsylvania Federation of Labor. Here Bauer's role as "houser" became increasingly political. The term *houser* was used in this period to describe those committed to improving housing for the urban poor. Bauer was involved in the effort to pass comprehensive housing legislation to address the housing crisis facing poor Americans. She fought for federal support of local initiatives that would provide decent living space, with light and open space, parks, and integration of land and water use planning. She eventually moved to Washington, D.C., where she lived until 1939. While in Washington she developed friendships with a number of influential planners and environmentalists, including Ernest Bohn, president of the National Association of Housing Officials, and ROBERT MARSHALL, founder of the Wilderness Society.

Growing weary of the demands of Washington politics, Bauer took a position at the University of California in Berkeley in 1939. She taught classes in housing policy and became involved in California regional planning. In 1941 she helped the California Housing Association expand into the California Housing and Planning Association, a group she served as vice president for three years. In 1942 she married leading Bay Area architect William Wurster; the couple had one daughter, Sarah Louise, born in 1945. In 1943 Bauer moved with her husband to Cambridge, Massachusetts, where he worked on a graduate degree and she continued her advocacy work. In 1950 they returned to California, where Bauer lived for the rest of her life. She taught in the University of California's Department of City and Regional Planning, winning a number of grants to study the effects of California's rapid growth, including a 1956 grant to study the effects of urban development on California's wild places. In 1960 she founded, along with William Matson Roth and Alfred Heller, California Tomorrow, a group dedicated to including conservation in state planning. In 1962 she and Clark Kerr staged a conference on "The Metropolitan Future," which brought together a wide range of experts, including business leaders, planners, social scientists, and politicians.

Bauer died on November 22, 1964, of exposure, after falling on California's Mount Tamalpais.

BIBLIOGRAPHY

Frieden, Bernard, and William Nash, *Shaping an Urban Future: Essays in Memory of Catherine Bauer Wurster*, 1969; Newbrun, Eva, and H. Peter Oberlander, *Houser: The Life and Work of Catherine Bauer*, 1999; Oberlander, Peter,

"Houser: the legacy of Catherine Bauer," *Journal of Housing and Community Development*, 2000; Sussman, Carl, *Planning the Fourth Migration: The Neglected Vision of the Regional Planning Association of America*, 1976.

Bavaria, Joan

Socially Responsible Investment Manager, Co-founder of the Social Investment Forum and the Coalition for Environmentally Responsible Economies

Joan Bavaria is a pioneer in the worldwide movement for sustainable business, demonstrating that business objectives are served by ethical commitments. Founder of one of the first, and now the oldest, socially responsible investment groups, Bavaria has gone on to create best standards and practices that corporations use to measure social and environmental impacts as well as their fiscal performance. Bavaria's critics have claimed that certain clients of her investment advisory company have benefited from a "greenwashing" of some of their corporate practices.

Bavaria attended Massachusetts College of Arts in 1961-1963. Raising two young sons as a single mother brought her to investment. She worked as an investment officer for the Bank of Boston from 1969 to 1975. Her interest in the conditions of workplaces, and the effects of those conditions on workers, surfaced at the bank when Bavaria, in spite of resistance from management, started a lunchtime exercise program.

In 1981 she co-founded the Social Investment Forum, one of the earliest socially responsible investment groups. She served as president for four years and as a board member for eight years.

A year later, she formed the employee-owned investment advisory firm Trillium Asset Management Corporation, for clients wanting to know about the social and environmental impacts of their investments. One of the founding missions has been to create a more scientific, powerful industry around socially responsible investing. This 40-plus person company, as of 2008, manages more than $1 billion dollars, and serves over 600 individual and institutional clients. Bavaria has said that the name "Trillium" embodies three characteristics of sustainability: ecology, economy, and equity. Her understanding of "growth" runs counter to traditional economic theory. Bavaria does not believe that constant growth is necessary or desirable. A sustainable company, Bavaria believes, thinks about the environmental and social costs of economic activity. Trillium publishes research on social issues and investments, works with clients and companies on their social and environmental management issues, contributes significant resources to social activism and community work, and donates five percent of its pre-tax profits to charitable causes.

To widen the impact of her work, in 1989 she co-founded CERES (Coalition for Environmentally Responsible Economies—an acronym for the Roman goddess of agriculture), a national network of investment funds; environmental organizations like the Sierra Club, Friends of the Earth, and Union of Concerned Scientists; and public interest groups to bring measurable concepts of environmental stewardship into the business sector. One outcome has been the development of the CERES Principles (formerly the Valdez Principles, after the Exxon Valdez spill), ten guidelines for sustainable management that include protection of the biosphere, use of natural resources, waste reduction, energy conservation, as well as certain accountability indicators like providing the public with information as well as management audits and reports. Those reports became a national model: the Global Reporting Initiative. Over 100 companies are now reporting. Bavaria served as CERES chair from 1989—2001, and was reelected co-chair in 2005. CERES works with companies like Timberland, Ben & Jerry's, GM, BankAmerica, IT&T Industries, and Sunoco—all companies interested to some degree in environmental reporting, community outreach, and environmental justice issues. Companies pay annual dues of as much as $35,000 and disclose their sustainability efforts.

In the 1990s, General Motors' collaboration with CERES was critiqued by environmentalists who claimed GM was taking advantage of CERES and would not accept changes in practice that would result in lower profits, while retaining a green reputation by continuing the affiliation with CERES. GM had signed on to CERES during a time when it was worried about its image and interested in reaching out to unions, suppliers, and environmentalists. When CERES demanded GM commit to improvements in fuel economy, tension developed in the relationship. Although GM cleaned up plants and reduced energy usage in production, it resists the higher fuel economy standards that CERES has requested.

Bavaria has received significant recognition for her work, including the 2005 Botwinick Prize in Business Ethics; co-recipient of the City of Gothenburg's International Environment Prize 2004; *Investment Advisor* magazine named her one of the 25 most influential people in the planning business in 2004; the Millennium Award for Corporate Environmental Leadership by Green Cross International and Global Green USA in 2000; *Time Magazine* named her a "Hero of the Planet" in 1999. She is on the Dean's Committee for International Development at Harvard University's John F. Kennedy School of Government. She has also served as Chair of the National Advisory Committee for Policy & Technology's subcommittee, Community Based Environmental Policy, which advises the EPA. She is on the advisory boards of the Union of Concerned Scientists and the Greening of Industry Network. She has served for fifteen years as a board of director for Lighthawk, the Council on Economic Priorities for twelve years, the Industrial Cooperative Association Loan Fund for ten years, and several others. Joan is married to Jesse Collins and has two grown sons. She divides her time between Marblehead, Massachusetts; Tiburon, California; and work travel.

BIBLIOGRAPHY

www.aspenscale.org/boston/3overview.htm; www.mindfully.org/Industry/GM-CERES-Impass30jul02.htm; www6.gsb.columbia.edu/cfmx/web/alumni/news/article.cfm?legacy=0511/bavaria; www.trilliuminvest.com.

Bean, Michael
(July 3, 1949–)
Wildlife Lawyer

Michael J. Bean has been a leader in wildlife law and endangered species protection since 1977, when he joined the staff at the Environmental Defense Fund (EDF) as chairman of its Wildlife Program.

Michael Bean was born on July 3, 1949, in Fort Madison, Iowa, a small town of 12,000 along the Mississippi River where he first became interested in the natural world. Bean spent as much time as possible exploring the Mississippi riverbanks and an intermittent stream in his backyard. As a child, Bean caught and raised snakes and collected insects. His grandmother shared his interest in insects and helped him amass his bug collection. Bean decided to pursue a degree in entomology when he entered Iowa State University in 1966 but reevaluated his decision after realizing that this field concentrated on controlling insects in the state's croplands. His decision was solidified in 1967 when Bean discovered a robin suffering from what he suspected were the effects of dichlordiphenyltrichlor (DDT) poisoning near the campus. Coincidentally, scientists in Stoney Brook, New York, at just that time were forming the EDF to combat the use of DDT in the United States. EDF's efforts to ban DDT played a significant role in Bean's eventual acceptance of a position at EDF. Certain that he did not want to major in entomology, Bean transferred to the University of Iowa in 1968 and studied political science. Having earned a Phi Beta Kappa key and graduated summa cum laude from the university in 1970, Bean entered Yale Law School later that year.

Bean received his J.D. in 1973 and began work in antitrust law with a well-respected Washington, D.C., firm, Covington & Burling. Finding the work unsatisfying, Bean considered combining his interests in the natural world with his legal education. While working for Covington & Burling, Bean wrote an article about the "impending extinction of the desert-dwelling pupfish of Devil's Hole National Monument" that was published in the *Washington Post* and a review of a book on endangered species in *Natural History Magazine* in 1976.

These articles proved to be well-timed, because to celebrate the bicentennial in 1976, the President's Council on Environmental Quality commissioned a book on wildlife conservation law in the United States. The Environmental Law Institute was selected to write the book, but it determined that no one on its staff was qualified. Bean later told an EDF reporter that "in 1976, there weren't any experts in wildlife law; indeed, the very term 'wildlife law' was a novelty. There were environmental lawyers then, including some who had handled cases pertaining to wildlife, but no one

Michael Bean (Photograph courtesy of the Environmental Defense Fund)

who had developed that expertise as a specialty. The Institute concluded that there weren't any qualified candidates, so they hired me instead." Nine months after he started the book, he had finished the first edition of *The Evolution of National Wildlife Law*. As Bean says, "It was instantly recognized as the leading book on the subject (because there weren't any others), and it suddenly opened a lot of doors for me." The Environmental Defense Fund offered Bean a position, which he accepted and has never regretted. Not only was EDF working on endangered species recovery, the group had succeeded in ensuring a ban on DDT in the United States—two issues about which Bean cared deeply.

Over the past 30 years at EDF, Bean's work has focused extensively on endangered species conservation. His work has included lobbying, litigating, and brokering novel conservation agreements with private landowners. Bean has made significant headway in furthering endangered species recovery. Owing in part to his work on sea turtle protection, regulations are in place that protect six threatened species. Bean also worked to protect wildlife refuges from oil and gas exploration under Secretary of the Interior James Watt. Watt's proposal would have opened up to oil and gas leasing nearly all the wildlife refuges that were created for endangered species protection and almost all the refuges east of the Rocky Mountains. From 1977 to 1987, Bean influenced the initial implementation of the Convention on International Trade in Endangered Species (CITES) that was signed in 1972 and enforced in 1973.

Recently, Bean's work has centered around protecting rare species on private land. In describing his work, Bean recalls ALDO LEOPOLD's words, "the only progress that counts is that on the actual landscape." That is, the number of lawsuits won is ultimately less important than what actually happens to the species themselves. To encourage beneficial changes in land management by private landowners, Bean pioneered the concept of "Safe Harbor Agreements." Under these, landowners implement management activities to help endangered species, but are shielded from the imposition of new regulatory restrictions as a result of their voluntary actions. More than three million acres of private land are currently enrolled in such agreements.

As another means of working with private landowners, Bean helped create the Center for Conservation Incentives at Environmental Defense, a group of scientists, lawyers and economists that works with farmers and other landowners to promote conservation of natural resources on their land. For example, the Western Lake Erie Basin Conservation Program pays farmers to take areas along streams and rivers or in areas prone to flooding out of cultivation and instead to plant grass or tree buffers, or create wetlands. Farmers who did this escaped the damage that devastated their neighbors not enrolled in the program during the 2008 flooding in Northwest Ohio.

Along with his on-the-ground success, Bean is a prolific author and speaker. He has written over 75 articles on endangered and rare species issues and has been a panelist in numerous wildlife events and an adviser to wildlife conservation organizations. His book, *The Evolution of National Wildlife Law*, published in 1977, has been twice revised, most recently as *The Evolution of National Wildlife Law: Revised and Expanded Edition* (1997) with Melanie Rowland. This book is still considered the leading source of information for wildlife law.

Bean has received several awards, including Pew Charitable Trusts Conservation and the Environment Scholar (1990), the Society for Conservation Biology's Distinguished Achievement Award for the legal defense of endangered species (1988), and the Desert Tortoise Preserve Committee's "Golden Tortoise" Award for securing legal protection for the desert tortoise (1990).

Although Bean no longer collects insects, he spends much of his free time in the field, identifying and observing dragonflies and butterflies. He lives in the Washington, D.C., area, with his wife, Sandy, and has two adult daughters, Amanda and Emily.

BIBLIOGRAPHY

Bean, Michael F., "The Endangered Species Act and Private Land: Four Lessons Learned from the Past Quarter Century," *Environmental Law Reporter: News and Analysis*, 1998; Bean, Michael F., "Endangered Species, Endangered Act?" *Environment*, 1999; Bean, Michael F., with Melanie Rowland, *The Evolution of National Wildlife Law: Revised and Expanded Edition*, 1997; Bean, Michael F., "The Private Land Problem," *Conservation Biology*, 1997; Bean, Michael F., "A Tool Kit for Conservation Issues, a Review of Private Property and the Endangered Species Act," *Bioscience*, Josen F. Shogren, ed., 1999; Geniesse, Jane, "Environmental Defense Fund," www.edf.org.

Beattie, Mollie
(April 27, 1947–June 27, 1996)
Director of the U.S. Fish and Wildlife Service, Forester

As director of the U.S. Fish and Wildlife Service (USFWS) from 1993 to 1996, Mollie Beattie presided over the agency in a time of shrinking budgets and an often hostile Republican Congress. The first woman and nonhunter ever to hold the position, Beattie successfully defended the Endangered Species Act, oversaw the reintroduction of wolves into the northern Rockies, and developed successful public/private partnerships to protect wildlife and wilderness. Beattie pushed the agency to put the issue of endangered species into a larger context and moved policy from a crisis-oriented, species-centered approach to a more forward-thinking, ecosystems approach to preservation.

Mollie Hanna Beattie was born on April 27, 1947, in Glen Cove, New York. She was raised in Connecticut and later attributed her love of nature to her grandmother, Harriet Hanna, who lived on a farm in upstate New York. Hanna was a self-taught botanist who knew the scientific names of all the local plants and kept a number of wild animals, including raccoons, a crow, and a deer with an artificial hip. Beattie said that she learned an important lesson from her grandmother: "If it moves, feed it." After graduating from Marymount College with a B.A. in philosophy in 1968, Beattie worked for several years as a journalist.

In 1973 she was offered a job writing for *Country Journal*. In order to gain the outdoor skills she needed for the job, Beattie enrolled in an Outward Bound course in the Colorado Rockies. She had little wilderness experience and arrived with luggage that included electric curlers, a hair dryer, clean sheets, and stiff new hiking boots with their tags still on. At the end of the course, after first swearing the brutal final hike would be her last for life, Beattie signed on to be an instructor, and she began a new career in wilderness pursuits. In 1979 she earned a master's degree in forestry from the University of Vermont. During her studies, Beattie chose wildlife management pioneer ALDO LEOPOLD as a role model for her approach to wildlife conservation. Leopold saw the forest not as timber but as an ecosystem, considering it, in Beattie's words, as "all that it produces and all the things that are seen and heard there." From 1980 to 1982 she worked for the University of Vermont Extension Service, teaching forestry and wildlife management to private landowners and coordinating federal, state, and private land management efforts. From 1983 to 1985 Beattie was the program director and lands manager for the Windham Foundation in Grafton, Vermont, where she gained more experience directing public/private cooperative conservation efforts. While living in Grafton she and her husband, builder Richard Schwolsky, built a solar house, a mile away from the nearest utility pole. (Schwolsky once installed solar panels on the White House, during JIMMY CARTER's presidency, though Ronald Reagan ordered their removal.)

In 1985 Beattie was appointed by Madeleine Kunin, Vermont's first female governor, as commissioner of the Department of Forests, Parks, and Recreation for the state of Vermont. This position prepared her for the USFWS in a number of ways, one of them being the fact that she was the first woman to hold the post. During her tenure Beattie addressed a number of pressing environmental issues, including clear-cutting, resort development, overuse of pesticides, and air and water quality concerns. Beattie pushed for local control over development decisions and initiated a task force that eventually became the federally funded Northern Forest Council, an alliance of conservation efforts in Maine, New Hampshire, New York, and Vermont. She also oversaw the acquisition of several thousand acres of land for state parks and forests. From 1989 to 1990, she continued her work for Vermont as deputy secretary for the Agency of Natural Resources. In 1991 she earned an M.P.A. from Harvard University's Kennedy School of Government.

In 1993 she became President Clinton's USFWS director. Much of the confirmation hearing addressed her view of the Endangered Species Act, and she signaled in the hearing her commitment to working with private landholders to protect species and habitat before species become officially listed as endangered. Too often, she said, the act is used as an emergency measure when it should be seen as an ethical principle to protect whole ecosystems as wildlife habitat. She followed through on this principle throughout her years at the USFWS, developing regulations to encourage landholders to contribute to the preservation of species as a whole, while allowing flexibility for farmers and ranchers to kill single, troublesome members of those species. Beattie came under fire for allowing fishing and hunting in about half the National Wildlife Refuges, which she permitted as long as scientists determined these uses were compatible with wildlife preservation goals. Beattie oversaw the return of wolves to Yellowstone National Park and was effective in preserving wilderness in Alaska, where she negotiated the competing interests of Alaska natives, sportsmen, industry, and habitat preservation. In addition, Beattie presided over the addition of 15 national wildlife refuges to the existing system.

Mollie Beattie died in Townshend, Vermont, on June 27, 1996, from brain cancer. Since her death, portions of the Arctic National Wildlife Refuge in Alaska and 76 acres of forest and bog near Island Pond, Vermont, have been named in her honor.

BIBLIOGRAPHY

Dicke, William, "Mollie Beattie," *New York Times*, 1996; Gup, Ted, "Beattie's Battle," *Audubon*, 1994; Holmes, Madelyn, *American Women Conservationists: Twelve Profiles*, 2004; "Mollie Beattie," *Time*, 1996; Walsh, Barry Walden, "The Ecosystem Thinking of Mollie Hanna Beattie," *American Forests*, 1994.

Beebe, C. William

(July 29, 1877–June 4, 1962)
Marine Biologist, Ornithologist, Nature Writer

William Beebe, director of tropical research with the New York Zoological Society for nearly 63 years, was a professional field biologist who started his career studying jungle birds and later became famous for his deep sea dives to study ocean life. In addition, he was a skillful writer, and with a cordial and entertaining style he wrote popular accounts of his fieldwork; in the process becoming the best known American nature writer of his time. His writings demonstrate his strong interest in conservation; he wrote of his distress at the devastation already occurring in the tropical forests, predicted a time when hu-man destruction would wipe out whole populations of birds, and spoke of nature's most terrible enemy—humans. His vivid presentation made his message especially compelling, and he is credited with popularizing the study of zoology and giving many people a new concern for threatened species and habitats.

Charles William Beebe was born on July 29, 1877, in Brooklyn, New York, the only child of Charles and Henrietta Marie (Younglove) Beebe. He was raised in East Orange, New Jersey. As a boy he enjoyed reading the scientific adventure stories of Jules Verne and others, and he cultivated a taste for excitement and exploration. In 1891 he entered East Orange High School, where he would achieve highest marks in geology, botany, physiology, and zoology. He attended Columbia University for three years as a zoology student, and although he subsequently claimed a B.S., he never actually completed the classes required for a degree. One of his teachers, Henry Fairfield Osborn, encouraged and inspired Beebe's curiosity and helped Beebe get a job as assistant curator of birds at the New York Zoological Park (later known as the Bronx Zoo) in 1899. Three years later he became full curator, but he was becoming more interested in field studies and began taking expeditions to study birds. In 1902 he married Mary Blair Rice, and the two of them traveled to Mexico and collaborated on a book for the general public called *Two Bird Lovers in Mexico* (1905). They later wrote another book together, *Our Search for a Wilderness* (1910), about the natural history of the jungles of Venezuela and British Guiana (now Guyana). Mary eventually divorced him in 1913 and made a name for herself writing novels and travel books.

In order to continue his studies in the tropics, Beebe established the New York Zoological Society's department of tropical research in British Guiana in the mid-1910s. The results of his first year of fieldwork in ornithology and entomology there yielded a technical work titled *Tropical Wild Life in British Guiana* (1917), written in collaboration with his chief assistants, C. I. Hartley and P. G. Howes.

In 1917 and 1918, Beebe served as an aviator in World War I, an experience that left him agitated and unhappy. He returned to the jungles of British Guiana for healing and solace and compiled a series of essays originally published in the *Atlantic Monthly* and later collected in *Jungle Peace* (1918). Another work published around this time was the result of years of studying pheasants in southeast Asia and other parts of the world. The beautifully illustrated four-volume series was later abridged to a one-volume version, *Pheasants: Their Lives and Homes* (1926), which was more accessible to the general public.

Beebe's works endure largely because of their appeal to a large audience. Although he was a detail-oriented researcher, he was not so taken with science as to be obsessed and instead brightened his observations with humor and enjoyment of life. He conveyed a contagious excitement over his discoveries and observations of the natural world and offered readers a stimulating introduction to science in general and the tropical jungles in particular. His concern for the future of the jungles is also contagious, and often his books reveal these conservation ideals. Even though it was early in the twentieth century, he wondered if there was any place on earth left untrampled by people and lamented the tragic succession of chopping, overcultivation, and overgrazing in the tropics where he worked. Proclaiming humans to be the worst enemy of the natural world, he pointed out that everywhere they have gone, they have worked havoc on the wild plants and animals. Beebe's writings describe the interrelationships that bind different organisms together, creating a web of life that is in constant danger of being upset by environmental degradation—a concept that he articulated far earlier than the rest of the scientific community. He frequently details how particular organisms interact with their larger habitat, providing many of his readers with their first taste of the principles of ecology. Among his many admirers was RACHEL CARSON, who acknowledged Beebe as an inspiration.

In 1927 Beebe was married to the novelist Elswyth Thane and the following year set up a six-acre tropical research laboratory on Nonsuch, an island in Bermuda. His career as a marine biologist had begun three years earlier on a trip to the Galapagos Islands where he became interested in collecting ocean specimens. From then on he shifted his focus from birds to undersea life and began a series of deep-sea exploratory expeditions. Several of his close studies of Bermuda sea life were documented in *Nonsuch: Land of Water* (1932), a book that demonstrated the links between land and sea and the interrelationships of life on the shore. His studies led him deeper and deeper underwater as well, and he became famous for a dive he made with Otis Barton on August 15, 1934, in a bathysphere. Barton and Beebe had designed this contraption—a spherical chamber made of a single casting of finest grade open-hearth steel, just large enough for two men to fit inside. Oxygen tanks were fixed to the sides, along with trays of powdered chemicals for absorbing carbon dioxide and water vapor. Curled into the bathysphere, Barton and Beebe descended to 3,028 feet, deeper than any human had ever dived beneath the ocean's surface.

Beebe chronicled the experience in *Half Mile Down* (1934) and continued oceanographic studies through the 1930s in the Pacific and Central America. By the early 1940s, he was ready to return to his studies of tropical land, and he began a series of expeditions to the Venezuelan Andes. In 1949 he established another New York Zoological Society research station, this time at Simla, Trinidad, where he worked until his death. *High Jungle*, the last of his full-length books, was published that same year. In the latter part of 1955, Beebe took his last major expedition, a 144-day trip that included visits to Naples, India, and Singapore. After three years of slowly failing health, William Beebe died of pneumonia on June 4, 1962, at his Simla station.

BIBLIOGRAPHY

Beebe, Mary Blair, and C. William Beebe, *Our Search for a Wilderness*, 1910; Beebe, William, *High Jungle*, 1949; Gould, Carol Grant, *The Remarkable Life of William Beebe: Explorer and Naturalist*, 2004; Matsen, Bradford, *Descent: the heroic discovery of the abyss*, 2005; Pollard, Jean Ann, "Beebe Takes the Bathysphere," *Sea Frontiers*, 1994; Tracy, Henry Chester, *American Naturists*, 1930; Welker, Robert H., *Natural Man: The Life of William Beebe*, 1975.

Begley, Ed, Jr.
(September 16, 1949–)
Actor

Ed Begley Jr. may be best known as the actor who portrayed of Dr. Victor Ehrlich on the long-running television series *St. Elsewhere*, but he is also highly respected as a passionate and dedicated environmentalist. He and his wife Rachelle Carson produce and star in "Living with Ed," a TV series all about living green. Begley gives about 90 percent of his time to environmental causes, serving on the boards of several environmental organizations. He is also well known for putting his principles into practice with an ecologically sound lifestyle that includes alternative transportation, a solar home, a vegetarian diet, and intelligently informed activism.

Edward James Begley Jr. was born on September 16, 1949, in Hollywood, California. His father, Ed Begley Sr., worked as a factory laborer in Hartford, Connecticut, before finding later success as a radio personality and actor. In 1962, at the age of 62, Ed Begley Sr. won an Oscar for best supporting actor for his role in *Sweet Bird of Youth*. Following in his father's creative footsteps, Ed Begley Jr. decided at the age of five that he wanted to be an actor and began auditioning. His first role was as a friend of Chip's on an episode of the famous 1960s situation comedy *My Three Sons*.

Begley grew up attending private Catholic and military schools until his senior year. Then he attended Van Nuys High School, the alma mater of several well-known Hollywood actors, including Marilyn Monroe, Robert Redford, and Natalie Wood. After high school, Begley attended Los Angeles Valley College, where he became friends with actor Michael Richards. The chemistry between the two was magnetic, and soon they were doing improvisations on stage at the Troubadour nightclub in West Hollywood. After they went their separate ways, Begley decided to pursue work as a cameraman, which he did for several years until moving to Boulder, Colorado, in 1971. In Boulder, where he lived for only six months, Begley had his first solo nightclub performance as a stand-up comedian. His comedy routine landed Begley work opening for singers and musicians from Don McLean to Barry Manilow at venues from New York City to Kansas City.

Returning to Hollywood, Begley began acting again with a part in *Stay Hungry*, a film starring Jeff Bridges and Sally Field. His career included many cameos in movies such as *This Is Spinal Tap*, *Streets of Fire*, *Eating Raoul*, *Cat People*, *The Accidental Tourist*, and *Protocol*. Begley has also guest starred in many television shows, including *Happy Days*; *Mary Hartman, Mary Hartman*; *MASH*; *Roseanne*; *The Simpsons*; *The Drew Carey Show*; *Star Trek Voyager*; and *Providence*. His most recent large-scale success was as Dr. Victor Ehrlich on the television series *St. Elsewhere*, a role for which Begley was nominated twice for an Emmy.

Begley's personal life in his teens and twenties was often filled with turmoil, and Begley admits to having an addictive, obsessive personality. He has struggled with alcoholism and gambling and has even been known to clean obsessively. Begley told Mark Morrison in *Rolling Stone* that in 1976, he was drinking a quart of vodka a day. Begley married Ingrid Taylor in 1977, and they had their first child, Amanda. The following year, at the age of 29, Begley stopped drinking alcohol for good. Married for 13 years, Begley and Ingrid had their second child, Nick, before divorcing in 1989.

Begley has said that his "passion for preserving this beautiful planet" began when he was a child in the late 1950s living with his family in rural Long Island, New York: "Anyone camping in those wild and beautiful areas couldn't help but grow up with a profound respect for natural systems." Begley also says that in 1969, when he saw the first photographs of Earth from the moon, he was deeply moved. "It had a profound effect upon me because I saw that, for better or worse, we have nowhere else to go.... And I don't think it's any coincidence that not too long after, we had the first Earth Day." According to Begley, that was the beginning of his activism on behalf of the environment; he became a vegetarian, started recycling and composting, and bought his first electric car.

Begley receives praise for his ecologically sound lifestyle and activism from all ranks of the Hollywood and environmental communities. "Ed is a very political guy in the best sense of the word," says Lucy Blake of the California League of Conservation Voters. "He understands the relationship between political leadership and environmental quality, and he's been very powerful in getting that message across to the public." Sandra Jerabek, executive director of Californians Against Waste, says, "No doubt about it, Ed's a fully committed environmentalist.... He drives an electric car, he rides his bike, he takes the bus and the train. When he renovated his garage, he found a way to recycle the broken concrete they ripped out. I mean, how many people take their commitment that far?"

Begley and his wife, Rachelle Carson, produce and co-star in "Living with Ed," a television series broadcast on the HGTV channel in which they show off green home technologies and tour and sometimes audit the homes of their friends. In addition to the earnest exploration of living green, Rachelle occasionally—yet goodnaturedly—complains about living with her eco-obsessed husband.

Begley himself is unabashedly enthusiastic when he talks about what he has done, and what he encourages others to do as well, to make life more ecologically sustainable. His official website (www.edbegley.com) and the website for his television show "Living with Ed" (www.livingwithed.net) are virtual environmental education centers where readers can log on and find out almost anything they want to know about how to live more lightly on the planet. In 2008, Begley published *Living like Ed: A guide to the eco-friendly life* with chic yet practical pointers for living green. Begley talks about everything from biodegradable soap and recycled toilet paper, to compact fluorescent light bulbs and energy-saving thermostats, to how he retrofitted his existing house to be off the power grid, using thermal collectors for hot water and solar energy for electricity. He sells a line of natural cleaning products, Begley's Best, through his websites. Begley's most ardent advice for anyone interested in doing something that will help to protect the natural environment is to avoid automobiles and use alternative transportation as much as possible. He is well known for riding his bike, taking the bus, and driving his electric car. Even his exercise bike has a generator that returns power to the same battery array that stores the solar energy for the house.

Begley serves on the boards of the Environmental Media Association, Earth Communications Office, the Santa Monica Mountains Conservancy, the Thoreau Institute, Tree People, Friends of the Earth, and many others. He is often asked to speak at events, including the 2000 Earth Day celebration in Washington, D.C. Currently, Begley lives in Los Angeles with Rachelle Carson and their child, Hayden Carson Begley.

BIBLIOGRAPHY

"Ed Begley Jr.—Actor & Activist," www.edbegley.com; Esrey, Susan, "Living with Ed," *Delicious Living*, 2007; Lewine, Edward, "Hollywood and Green," *The New York Times Magazine*, 2007; "Living with Ed—Hit TV Series," www.livingwithed.net; Morrison, Mark, "The Trivial Pursuits of Ed Begley Jr.," *Rolling Stone*, 1984; Russell, Dick, "Ed Begley, Jr." *E: the Environmental Magazine*, 1996; Stark, John, "No High-Pollutin' Actor, Ed Begley Jr. Successfully Recycles His Love Life and Career," *People Magazine*, 1990.

Bennett, Hugh Hammond

(April 15, 1881–July 7, 1960)
Soil Scientist, Director of U.S. Soil Conservation Service

Soil scientist Hugh Hammond Bennett is known as the father of soil conservation. He discovered the connection between soil erosion and loss of agricultural productivity in 1903 and worked for 50 years through the U.S. Department of Agriculture to educate farmers on how to prevent it. Bennett was the first director of the Soil Erosion Service, which later became the Soil Conservation Service.

Hugh Hammond Bennett was born on a farm near the town of Wadesboro, North Carolina, on April 15, 1881. His family cultivated cotton on poor, tree-stripped land; Bennett was later to realize that his family had broken the soil conservation rules that would have conserved its productivity. Despite his family's financial hardship, Bennett studied chemistry at the University of North Carolina. To pay for his studies, he took time off to work clearing trees from future cotton fields.

After graduating with a B.S. in 1903, Bennett joined the Bureau of Soils of the U.S. Department of Agriculture. His first assignment was to learn why crop yield was so poor on the farms of Louisa County, Virginia. He compared the rich loam in virgin hardwood forests to the hardpan of the sloping cotton fields that bordered them. Bennett discovered that rain falling on cultivated hillsides gradually washed away layer after layer of topsoil—he called this process "sheet erosion." When three years later Bennett was promoted to soil scientist at the Bureau of Soils and took charge of soil surveys throughout the eastern half of the country, he began to compile a list of farming practices that led to loss of topsoil and, hence, productivity. For each problem he developed an alternative practice. Cultivation of steep land in vertical rows was common; Bennett recommended plowing along the contours of the land and terracing so that rainwater draining downhill would be caught in trenches along each terrace. Farmers often left the soil surface bare after the harvest, which facilitated erosion by rain or wind; Bennett instructed farmers to "stubble-mulch," or leave the roots and part of the plants in the ground over the winter, in order to hold the soil more effectively.

Bennett decided that soil conservation was the nation's major agricultural issue. During the almost 20 years he was in charge of soil surveys, he became an effective, charismatic educator about soil erosion. His demonstrations included one in which he poured a glass of water (representing rain) onto a towel (vegetation) on a table (soil). Of course the towel absorbed the precipitation. But then when he removed it and the water was poured right onto the table, a miniflood ensued. He used drama again when lobbying Congress in 1928 for a national erosion control program. The dust bowl was in its peak, and Bennett timed his testimony to coincide with the arrival over Washington, D.C., of a huge dark cloud of wind-eroded topsoil that was blowing east from New Mexico. Congress readily passed the 1929 Buchanan Amendment to the Agricultural Appropriations Bill that established a fund to study and control erosion. This program became the Soil Erosion Service, later renamed the Soil Conservation Service, which Bennett directed for the duration of his career.

Under Pres. FRANKLIN D. ROOSEVELT, who recognized the importance of conservation and promoted it during his four terms in office, Bennett's Soil Conservation Service reached thousands of farmers. In its first year of full operation, 1935, 147 erosion control demonstration projects were set up, each 25,000 to 30,000 acres in size. Fifty thousand farmers were trained in erosion control techniques every year. They were taught such techniques as terracing and contour plowing, crop rotation, fertilization, soil strengthening through planting of grasses and legumes, planting trees as windbreaks, and strip cropping. Farmers found the program so worthwhile—it was said to improve farmers' incomes by up to 20 percent—that in 1937 states began to organize "soil conservation districts." The federal government was proud of these because they were so economical; all the federal government had to provide was technical assistance. There are now over 3,000 soil conservation districts nationwide.

Bennett's influence extended even beyond the borders of the United States. During the 1920s he studied soils on sugar and rubber plantations in Cuba and South America. Eighty-eight countries sent over 1,100 technicians to study Bennett's methods in the United States, establishing similar erosion control programs in their own countries.

Bennett directed the Soil Conservation Service until 1951, when age forced him into mandatory retirement. A *New York Times* editorial celebrating his 50 years at the U.S. Department of Agriculture claimed that "this 'father of soil conservation' stands among the nation's most useful citizens."

Bennett died of cancer in Burlington, North Carolina, on July 7, 1960. He left his second wife, Betty Brown Bennett, to whom he had been married since 1921, and two children, Sarah and Hugh.

BIBLIOGRAPHY
Bennett, Hugh Hammond, and William R. Chapline, "Soil Erosion, a National Menace," USDA Circular No. 33, 1928; Brink, Wellington, *Big Hugh: The Father of Soil Conservation*, 1951; Lehman, Tim, *The National Interest in Farmland Preservation: a History of Federal Policy in the Twentieth Century*, 1988; "Hugh Hammond Bennett Dead; 'Father of Soil Conservation,' 79," *New York Times*, 1960; Petulla, Joseph M., *American Environmental History*, 1977.

Berg, Peter
(October 1, 1937–)
Bioregionalism Philosopher, Founder and Director of Planet Drum Foundation

One of the leading advocates of bioregionalism, Peter Berg is the founder and director of Planet Drum Foundation, a noted ecologist, and a popular public speaker on several continents. He is widely acknowledged as an originator of the use of the terms *bioregion* and *reinhabitation* to describe land areas in terms of their interdependent plant, animal, and human life. Berg believes that the relationships between humans and the rest of nature point to the importance of supporting cultural diversity as a component of biodiversity.

Peter Stephen Berg was born October 1, 1937, in Jamaica, Long Island, New York. When he was six, his family moved to Florida. At the University of Florida in Gainesville, Berg discovered beat poetry and was introduced to the emerging revolution that it expressed. Berg joined an underground minority at the overwhelmingly conservative institution and became involved in the civil rights movement. Leaving the University of Florida while still a teenager, Berg hitchhiked across the United States, at which time he first visited San Francisco. In 1964, he settled in the city, where he joined the San Francisco Mime Troupe. He later helped create the Diggers in San Francisco, who served free food at the

Peter Berg (Photograph by Philip Woodard)

Be-In and began, as he puts it, "ecologizing the left."

As the revolution died down at Haight-Ashbury, Berg and a caravan of former Diggers set out on a cross-country tour in the summer of 1971 to determine what common threads existed in the nation's land-based communities. By winter, he had reached Nova Scotia and visited the expatriate American poet, Allen Van Newkirk, who also studied the connections between society and ecology. Interested in the research, classification, and preservation of the natural features within a given geographic area, Van Newkirk—along with Berg, Raymond Dasmann, and others—began promoting the idea of the bioregion. Berg and Van Newkirk both felt that the environmental movement was incapable of dealing with the underlying problems that industrial society posed for the biosphere. Rather than cleaning up after disasters, both felt the disasters needed to be prevented. Whereas Van Newkirk had explored the possibility of the bioregion as an arena for wildlife conservation, Berg proposed the inclusion of humans into the bioregion as an active—not dominant—species in that habitat. In essence, this was an exercise in reinhabitation; humans had to learn how to live in nature, not with dominion over it. As Berg states in his essay, "Beating the Drum with Gary," the only way to succeed at preventing further environmental disasters "was to restructure the way people satisfied basic material needs and related to the natural systems upon which their own survival ultimately depended." Pushing ecological concerns to the center of society was the only tangible approach that might successfully broach this problem. As a movement, bioregionalism was born.

Berg and others took these new ideas to the 1972 United Nations (UN) Conference on the Environment in Stockholm. In the company of thousands of activists and demonstrators from all over the world, Berg discovered that ecology was not just a North Atlantic cause. Berg mixed with groups of Japanese mercury-poisoning victims, Eritrean rebels, Laplanders from the Arctic Circle, Native Americans, and countless others, who made up what Berg called "the planetariat." For most of "the planetariat," no real answers to their issues emerged from the official gathering. Instead, their experience at the conference left them with increased frustration about the inability of any established institution to deal with planetary problems.

Returning to the United States with these frustrations, Berg was determined to find a method for constructing a forum for human and ecological sustainability in the biosphere. His focus naturally shifted from the global to the local or regional and resulted in the founding of the Planet Drum Foundation in San Francisco in 1973.

Planet Drum's mission is to determine the cultural and ecological dimensions of a human-scale geographical region. Given the relative failure of the 1972 UN conference, Berg became convinced that breaking down the world into separate biotic provinces or bioregions would help find plausible routes toward sustainable living for the earth as a whole.

In 1979, Berg introduced the Planet Drum Foundation review, *Raise the Stakes*. A radical review that argues that environmentalism is not demanding enough from the corporate government, Berg suggests that bioregionalism is postenvironmentalist in that it pushes the limits of the environmental movement; that it "raises the stakes." Modern environmentalism does not deal sufficiently with the currently important issues of ecosystem restoration and urban sustainability. Bioregionalism proposes a whole new philosophy necessary if these goals are to be reached. *Raise the Stakes* helped popularize the notion that health, food, and culture are all bioregional issues, profoundly affected by the place in which they are situated.

Unlike many environmentalists and ecologists, Berg looks to the future with a certain degree of optimism. He believes that the localization of politics will eventually take a bioregional turn. While there is concern that globalization appears to be a dominant force that even threatens the nation state, Berg insists that localization, the forwarding of ethnic autonomy and home rule, for example, is playing an equally influential role in this movement away from the nation state and toward regional ecology.

One of Berg's current projects is in the town of Bahía de Caráquez, on the central coast of Ecuador. The town legally committed itself to becoming ecological and sustainable in 1999. Planet Drum has helped by establishing a field office in the town and revegetating with native trees for erosion control and the creation of an urban "wild corridor," conducting after-school bioregional education classes for junior-high age students, and assisting other groups. There are many reports and dispatches about their work in Bahía de Caráquez on the Planet Drum website.

In 1998, Berg was awarded the Gerbode Professional Development Program Fellowship for outstanding nonprofit organization executives. He was a presenter at the 2005 United Nations World Environment Day Conference, and at the 2008 Ecocity World Summit. He lives and works in Shasta Bioregion in northern California. Berg and Judy Goldhaft have two children, Aaron and Ocean, and two granddaughters, Florence Amelia and Estelle Rose.

BIBLIOGRAPHY

Berg, Peter, "Beating the Drum with Gary," in *Gary Snyder: Dimensions of a Life*, John Halper, ed., 1991; Berg, Peter, *Discovering Your Life-Place: A First Bioregional Workbook*, 1995; Berg, Peter, *Figures of Regulation: Guides for Re-Balancing Society with the Biosphere*, 1981; Berg, Peter, *A Green City Program for the San Francisco Bay Area and Beyond*, 1990; Berg, Peter, ed., *Reinhabiting a Separate Country: A Bioregional Anthology of Northern California*, 1978, "Planet Drum Foundation," www.planetdrum.org.

Benyus, Janine
(1958–)
Writer, Natural Scientist, President of the Biomimicry Institute

As a writer and scientist, Janine Benyus goes beyond sharing information about the natural world; she focuses on what we can learn *from* the natural world. Her work with biomimicry teaches people to learn from naturally occurring processes to create sustainable products and solutions. She is the author of six books and lectures widely on biomimicry. Such work has led to many honors, including recognition as one of Time Magazine's 43 Heroes of the Environment in 2007.

Janine Benyus was born in New Jersey in 1958. She holds two degrees in Natural Resource Management and English Literature and Writing from Rutgers University, where she graduated *summa cum laude*. She spent her early career translating science-speak for research labs. Her interest in ecosystems led her to write three field guides, *Northwoods Wildlife: a Watcher's Guide to Habitats*; *Field Guide to Wildlife Habitats of the Western United States*; and *Field Guide to Wildlife Habitats of the Eastern United States*, all published in 1989.

After immersing herself in animal behavior and wildlife habitats, Benyus began to see how nature had already found solutions for many of the problems that designers, manufacturers and engineers try to solve. She coined the term "biomimicry" to describe this phenomenon.

Benyus's *Biomimicry: Innovation Inspired by Nature* marks the genesis of the biomimicry movement. Published in 1997, the book poses a series of open-ended questions such as "How will we harness energy?" and "How will we heal ourselves?" to introduce chapters describing possible biomimetic ideas for business, industry, and sustainable ways to make our way in the world.

Benyus is not satisfied with stopping at nature-inspired product design; she believes that ethical biomimicry involves finding sustainable ways to transport these products and finding responsible ways to create and do business within our ecosystem. Her book addresses various stages of commerce, from the question of "How will we make things?" to the idea of "running a business like a redwood forest."

One year after publishing *Biomimicry: Innovation Inspired by Nature*, Benyus founded the Biomimicry Guild. Through workshops, field excursions, and biological consulting, The Biomimicry Guild provides research and strategic advice to designers, engineers, architects and business leaders. They place biologists at design tables to assist clients with accessing and interpreting technical scientific information in order to emulate natural models. Their extensive client list includes universities, cities, trade associations and corporations, illustrating the widespread applications of biomimetic work.

Benyus is also the president of The Biomimicry Institute, a nonprofit organization that promotes the concept of biomimicry and provides educational resources to K-12 schools, colleges, and universities. The Biomimicry Institute is also developing a sustainable design challenge as well as other programs intended to encourage Benyus's four steps of the biomimetic path: quieting human cleverness, listening to life's genius, echoing what we learn, and giving thanks.

Benyus is an engaging, dynamic writer and speaker. She has given lectures and keynote addresses to several groups, including Cambridge University's Centre of International Studies and the Environment, Design Futures Council, the Prince of Wales' Business and the Environment Programme, and the President's Council on Sustainable Development. Her presentation "Twelve Sustainable Design Ideas From Nature" is featured on the TED Conference archive website, a resource of conference presentations from the Technology, Entertainment, Design conference. Benyus also co-wrote and hosted a two-hour public television special for *The Nature of Things with David Suzuki* which aired in 71 countries.

Among the awards Benyus has received are the RACHEL CARSON Environmental Ethics Award, the Lud Browman Award for Science Writing, the Science Writing in Society Journalism Award, and the Barrows and Heinz Distinguished Lectureships.

Benyus lives in Stevensville, Montana, where she lectures at the University of Montana, teaches interpretive writing, and works toward restoring and protecting wild lands. She also serves as president of Living Education, a nonprofit organization focused on place-based living and learning. She is currently working on the Biomimicry Design Portal, a public research database which aims to connect designers and engineers with an extensive array of biological literature.

BIBLIOGRAPHY

Benyus, Janine. *Biomimicry: Innovation Inspired by Nature*, 1997; TED, www.ted.com/index.php/talks/view/id/18; *TIME Magazine*, www.time.com/time/specials/2007/article/0,28804,1663317_1663319_1669888,00.html.

Berle, Peter

(December 8, 1937–November 2, 2007)
Attorney, Chief Executive Officer of the National Audubon Society, Radio Show Director and Host

Peter Berle was an environmental lawyer, legislator, administrator, and educator. As a lawyer he won many environmental cases of national significance. As legislator and administrator, he helped to write and enact much of New York State's early environmental legislation. He was chief executive officer of the National Audubon Society from 1985 to 1995. From 1995 to 2001, he directed and hosted the "Environment Show" on public radio station WAMC, and after that provided weekly public commentary for the station.

Peter Adolf Augustus Berle was born on December 8, 1937, in New York City. His father, Adolf A. Berle Jr., was a lawyer and a professor of law, and his mother, Beatrice Bishop Berle, a medical doctor. Growing up, Berle spent his weekends and summers on the family farm in Massachusetts. The farm, still operated by the Berle family, occupies land adjacent to the Appalachian Trail, and Berle and his father would go on backpacking trips along this trail together, hiking all the way up the trail to Maine.

Berle attended Harvard University, where he earned a B.A. degree in 1958 and an LL.B. degree in 1964. In the time between these degrees, from 1959 to 1961, he married his wife Lila and served as an Air Force officer and parachutist in Southeast Asia. Upon graduating from Harvard Law School, Berle accepted a position with the large New York law firm, Paul, Weiss, Rifkind, Wharton and Garrison. One of his first assignments was to the legal team representing an environmental group that challenged the Federal Power Commission. The issue was the Commission's issuance of a permit to the Consolidated Edison Company to construct a pump storage plant on Storm King Mountain on the scenic Hudson River. The federal court invalidated the permit, accepting the legal team's argument that the Federal Power Commission could not make a decision simply by calling "balls and strikes" at a hearing when the public interest was not represented. The court held that it was the responsibility of the Power Commission to see that a full record was developed. This was a landmark case in environmental law. It provided direction and set precedent for government regulatory agencies. It set the forces in motion that would eventually result in the passage of such national legislation as the National Environmental Policy Act (NEPA). Berle was also heavily involved in preparing and presenting witnesses for the congressional hearings that would lead to the Alaska Native Lands Claims Settlement Act of 1971. He spent much of 1967 and 1968 commuting to Alaska to assist in organizing the effort. The act dealt with long unsettled claims of native Alaskans. It provided $962 million and 40 million acres of land and established 12 native regional corporations to manage the acquired resources.

Berle left Paul, Weiss, Rifkind, Wharton and Garrison in 1971 to start his own firm, Berle, Butzel and Kass. He continued practicing law until 1976, concentrating, whenever possible, on environmental issues. One significant case he was involved with during this time centered on the United States Postal Service, which, being only a quasi-government agency, claimed not to be subject to NEPA. The Postal Service was making plans to build a facility that was to run diesel trucks continuously in a densely populated area of Manhattan. The court found that the Postal Service was responsible for adhering to the requirements of NEPA, and the shipping facility was not constructed. In another case, representing Long Island homeowners in a class action suit, Berle successfully sued Union Carbide over groundwater contamination caused by Aldicarb, a pesticide the company manufactured.

In 1968, Berle was elected to the New York state legislature from the east side of Manhattan. He served for three terms, until 1974. While in the legislature he became the ranking member of the Environmental Conservation Committee and managed the floor fight to pass the Adirondack Park Act of 1971, which established a zoning, land use agency to oversee management of Adirondack Park, the largest state park in the lower 48 states. Berle also introduced the first New York legislation to require projects to be subject to environmental impact assessment.

In 1976, Berle became commissioner of the New York Department of Environmental Conservation, one of the most comprehensive state environmental agencies in the nation. As commissioner, Berle was responsible for bringing the state of New York into compliance with many of the laws he had proposed while in the legislature. He was also a key player in the infamous Love Canal toxic waste crisis in 1979. He and his agency were the first public authorities to recognize the impact of the contamination and take action. He and the local regional administrator of the federal Environmental Protection Agency convinced Pres. JIMMY CARTER to designate Love Canal a disaster area. This marked the first time a crisis created by the acts of humans was named a disaster area under federal law, a designation until then reserved for natural disasters such as floods and earthquakes. As commissioner, Berle was also able to free up state funding for land acquisition. On behalf of the state, he purchased the last 11 high peaks in the Adirondack Park that were in private ownership, as well as substantial lake and forest properties.

Berle returned to private law practice for six years in 1979, before becoming president and chief executive officer of the National Audubon Society in 1985. One of his main goals in this position was to combine the Audubon Society's traditional interests with an increased degree of activism. He wanted people to see birds as indicators of environmental health and thus expanded the scope of the Society and its members to include such issues as toxic waste and pesticides. Berle orchestrated an increase in grassroots activism through the 500 local chapters of the Audubon Society and continued to emphasize the importance of education. He increased the Audubon Society's presence in Washington, D.C., and brought about the creation of the Audubon House, the organization's new headquarters in New York City. When the renovation of this historic building was completed in 1992, the structure was heralded as one of the most environmentally benign and energy-efficient structures in the United States. Under Berle's leadership the National Audubon Society's budget increased from $23 million to $46 million per year. By the time his 10-year stint as president was completed in 1995, Audubon had been involved in many high-profile environmental battles, including the fight to protect the Arctic Wildlife Refuge from oil development in 1987.

After leaving the Audubon Society in 1995, Berle considered returning to his environmental law practice but instead decided to pursue a path that he hoped would lead to a greater public understanding of environmental issues. He became director and host of the "Environment Show," which aired on National Public Radio and ABC stations nationwide and abroad on Voice of America and Armed Forces Radio. The show addressed a diverse array of environmental issues from genetically modified foods to urban sprawl. The show sought to educate and to help stimulate thought on the idea that everything is interconnected. It included short segments that reflected on the importance of place, debates between opposing viewpoints, and a highlight of local activism. The show also included Berle's interviews with prominent activists, politicians, and scientists about pressing environmental issues and potential solutions. Berle's show tackled moral and ethical issues, addressed the importance of urban spaces, portrayed humans as a part of a biologically diverse system, and attempted to deliver the message that everyone can make a difference. In 2001, Berle shifted gears and began providing weekly commentary on environmental topics to WAMC—all of the transcripts are still archived at www.wamc.org/commentators-berle.html.

Berle was a presidential appointee on the Joint Public Advisory Committee on Environmental Cooperation (JPAC), which was created under the North American Free Trade Agreement (NAFTA) environmental side agreement, negotiated by President Clinton. He also served as a board member of the New York Independent System Operator (NYISO), an entity set up to manage the sale and distribution of electricity in New York's deregulated market. Berle also taught as a lecturer and adjunct professor at various academic institutions, including Syracuse University, the Century Foundation, and New York State University.

On November 2, 2007, Berle died of injuries sustained during an accident on his farm two months earlier. He is survived by his wife, Lila Berle, and their four grown children.

BIBLIOGRAPHY

Begley, Sharon, "Audubon's Empty Nest," *Newsweek*, 1991; Berle, Peter, "Building for a Sustainable Future," *Audubon*, 1995; DePalma, Anthony, "Peter A.A. Berle, Lawmaker and Conservationist, Dies at 69," *New York Times*, 2007; Raver, Anne, "Audubon Society Pursues an Identity Beyond Birds," *New York Times*, 1991; "WAMC Public Radio—Commentators: Peter Berle," www.wamc.org/commentators-berle.html.

Berry, Friar Thomas

(November 9, 1914–)
Philosopher, Passionate Order, Author

Contemporary philosopher, cultural historian, theologian, and "geologian," Friar Thomas Berry merges religion and modern science toward a new understanding of the human relation to the universe and the world. Fr. Berry's eco-theology maintains that the universe is a communion of subjects rather than a collection of objects; therefore, the human connection to the whole universe is imperative. Within this framework, the responsibility of humans to care for and nurture the planet is a spiritual responsibility, and our current state of environmental damage and social upheaval is ultimately a crisis of spirituality.

Born November 9, 1914, William Nathan Berry grew up in a large family exploring the woods and hills of Greensboro, North Carolina. At the age of eleven, the young boy enjoyed an early epiphany in a field of lilies near his family's new house. That moment, the lilies, the crickets, and the clouds in the summer sky invoked a sense of awe and a recognition of the holistic divinity of the universe. This experience informed his life and philosophy: that what does harm to that field of flowers is unhealthy; and, what serves to preserve and enhance that natural beauty is good. From that basic tenet developed his cosmological theory encompassing economics, politics, education, and religion.

To escape the "crass commerciality" of the world, Berry entered the novitiate of the Passionist order in 1934. Taking the name Thomas for the Christian scholar Thomas Aquinas, Berry was ordained in 1942. After earning his doctoral degree in European Intellectual History from The Catholic University of America, Berry studied Asian history, language, and religion, traveling to China in 1948 to study Chinese philosophy and language. Shipping out of San Francisco, he met the now premier Asian scholar William Theodore De Bary, who became a lifelong friend and collaborator.

Berry was forced to leave China early due to the Maoist uprising in 1949. Upon returning to the States, Berry and De Bary founded the Asian Thought and Religion Seminar at Columbia University. In his late-thirties, Berry served as a U.S. Army chaplain in Europe. He went on to teach at the Institute for Asian Studies at Seton Hall University, the Center for Asian Studies at St. John's University, Columbia University, Drew University, and the University of San Diego, before settling in at Fordham, where from 1966 to 1979, he was director of the graduate program in the history of religions. In 1970 he founded the Riverdale Center of Religious Research in Riverdale, New York, which he directed for seventeen years until 1987.

In the 1970s Berry wrote and lectured widely on both Asian studies and the relationships between spiritual, social, and ecological issues. He wrote *Buddhism* in 1966 and *Religions of India* in 1971. In 1988 he published *Dream of the Earth*, and *Befriending the Earth* in 1991, and in 1992 collaborated with physicist Brian Swimme on *The Universe Story: From the Primordial Flaring Forth to the Ecozoic Era, A Celebration of the Unfolding of the Cosmos*. In 1999 he wrote *The Great Work: Our Way Into the Future*, and his latest book, a collection of essays entitled *Evening Thoughts: Reflecting on Earth as Sacred Community*, was published in 2006.

Friar Berry addresses the disconnect between traditional Western religious settings and people's relationship with their physical world and the universe. Like Martin Luther, he encourages people to see the natural world and social constructs as equally sacred as the settings of the church.

One of Berry's most revolutionary concepts is the marriage of science and religion, incorporating evolution and the scientific dating of time and creation into religious theory. In *Befriending the Earth*, he writes, "That is why Christians are alienated people in their relationship to the present world. We cannot accept the story of an evolutionary universe as our sacred story.... This is possibly the most significant change in human consciousness since the beginning of human consciousness, the change in perception of the world as cosmos to its perception as cosmogenesis, from being to becoming."

Berry believes that a re-awakening to the divinity of the universe is achieved not solely through respectful study of written religious texts. Through studying and respecting nature, we enter a complex framework where "the human is derivative; the planet is primary." Traditional anthropocentric roles for humanity are diminished. The struggle for environmental justice and social justice becomes spiritual activity in Berry's eco-theology.

Friar Berry lives in Greensboro, North Carolina.

BIBLIOGRAPHY

Berry, Thomas, and Thomas Clarke, *Befriending the Earth: A Theology of Reconciliation Between Humans and the Earth*, Mystic, 1991; Berry, Thomas, *The Dream of Earth*, 1988; Berry, Thomas, *The Great Work: Our Way into the Future*, 1999; In his paper, 'The Spirituality of the Earth,' published in *The Riverdale Papers*, vol. V, and *Liberating Life: Contemporary Approaches in Ecological Theology*, Charles Birch, William Eaken and Jay B. McDaniel (eds.),1990; Heffern, Rich, "Thomas Berry," *National Catholic Reporter*, August 10, 2001, www.natcath.com/NCR_Online/archives/081001/081001a.htm; www.earth-is-community.org.uk/aboutthomasberry.htm; www.greenspirit.org.uk/resources/TBerry.htm; Colebrook, Michael, "Thomas Berry: Geologian," presentation to a seminar held at the College of St Mark & St John, Plymouth, February 2001, www.thomasberry.org/; Tucker, Mary Evelyn, "Biography of Thomas Berry," www.thomasberry.org/Biography/tucker-bio.html.

Berry, Wendell
(August 5, 1934–)
Poet, Farmer

Wendell Berry has carefully tended a farm in north-central Kentucky that his family has tilled since 1803, while simultaneously conducting a formidable literary and academic career. His many novels, short stories, poetry, and essays on rural life, land use, conservation, and forestry have encouraged and inspired the modern environmental movement in the United States. Berry's principal preoccupation as a writer derives from his work as a farmer: transforming the man *versus* nature paradigm into the more appropriate man *with* nature.

Wendell Erdman Berry was born on August 5, 1934, in Henry County, Kentucky, and grew up a studious and hardworking child on land that had provided for over a hundred years of Berrys before him. In Port Royal, Kentucky, along the Kentucky River, at a riverside cabin on stilts built by his great-uncle, young Wendell Berry discovered his peace with nature and his facility for contemplation and writing. There he learned to use the hand tools of his life work: vice grips, hatchets, pens, and notebooks. At 18 years of age his formal education took him to the University of Kentucky at Lexington, where he attained a B.A. in English in 1956, staying on to complete an M.A. in 1957. Upon graduation Wendell Berry married Tanya Amyx and took up residence at the "long-legged house" by the river.

At this point in his life Berry committed himself deeply not only to what would be a long and happy marriage to his wife, but also to the land that had nurtured his forebears. He accepted a teaching position nearby at Georgetown College and laid down the groundwork for his first novel. However, in 1958 Berry was awarded a Wallace Stegner Writing Fellowship and moved to California to study creative writing at Stanford University. In 1961, a Guggenheim Fellowship sent him to Europe for a year, and the next year he joined the English Department at New York University. But, as he wrote in his autobiographical essay, "The Long-Legged House," "for reasons that could perhaps be explained, I never lost affection for this place, as American writers have almost traditionally lost affection for their rural birthplaces. I have loved this country from the beginning." He decided to move back to Kentucky after the release of his first book of poems, *The Broken Ground*, in 1964. He took a position teaching English at his alma mater, settling first in Lexington and slowly retreating back to his farm in Port Royal and the long-legged house.

Berry's fiction writing found fertile ground in Port Royal. Beginning with his first novel, *Nathan Coulter* (1960), Berry introduces characters who inhabit Port William, a thinly disguised Port Royal. Over the course of four novels, Nathan Coulter, Jack Beechum, Mat Feltner, and their progeny moved over the same land that Berry still cultivated.

Wendell Berry's writing is largely autobiographical. He uses family history to chart the evolution of characters who are wedded to the Port Royal setting. By describing his own life, through a humble farmer's-eye view, his fiction gains the detail necessary to be authentic. In his essays the sincerity of the first person voice aids his arguments. Berry's first five books of essays are compiled in *Recollected Essays: 1965–1980* (1981). He diagnoses the havoc wreaked by white man's mistreatment of the land and white society's lack of discipline in politics, production, and consumption, and he prescribes approaches to the necessary healing: going local (living responsibly in one small part of the planet), getting personal (reforming lifestyle; learning to treat our bodies as we should treat the earth), and getting away from a bottom-line-driven, industrial capitalist culture. His polemic book *The Unsettling of America* (1977) depicts modern agriculture as a practice that is as predatory to communities as the industrial economics behind it.

Berry asks broad questions in the essay "Preserving Wildness" in *Home Economics*:

> What is the proper amount of power for a human to use? What are the proper limits of human enterprise? ... Such questions may seem inordinately difficult, but that is because we have gone too long without asking them. One of the fundamental assumptions of industrial economics has been that such questions are outmoded and that we need never to ask them again. The failure of that assumption now requires us to reconsider the claims of wildness and to renew our understanding of the old ideas of propriety and harmony.

Wendell Berry's poetry could also be called autobiographical, even as its focus strays to nonhuman elements—the sparrows, the soil, the river, the locusts, the lilies, the minute particulars of his own locale. His method is simple. He carries a small notebook in his workshirt pocket for jotting down his epiphanies and observations. Berry has always been taken by HENRY DAVID THOREAU's notion of the "hypaethral," or roofless book, written out of doors under the open sky. The circle of life is the chief concern of his early books of verse, *The Broken Ground* (1964), *Openings* (1968), and *Farming: A Handbook* (1970).

In a later collection of essays that recounts his own ecological creed, *The Gift of Good Land: Further Essays on Culture and Agriculture* (1981), Wendell Berry joins RALPH WALDO EMERSON in his insistence on a religious understanding of ecology and repeats Emerson's notion of the Chain of Being. His message is that the dead coinhabit the land of the living, that all things—dead and alive—are interconnected. In "The Man Born to Farming" in *Farming: A Handbook*, he wrote:

> The grower of trees, the gardener, the man born to farming,
> Whose hands reach into the ground and sprout,
> To him the soil is a divine drug. He enters into death
> Yearly, and comes back rejoicing. He has seen the light lie down
> In the dung heap, and rise again in the corn.

Religious implications aside, the poetry of Wendell Berry is essentially bucolic. Some critics complain that Berry writes too much in the shadow of Thoreau and that his work represents pastoral works of withdrawal rather than the engagement to which he seems to aspire. But Berry is a writer with an ear not so much for what critics say as for what his experience on the land has told him. His unique nonindustrial means of farming and creative production (he still writes with a pencil and paper tucked in his workshirt pocket) bring an integrity to his voice and to the second half of twentieth-century American literature.

Few American writers have delivered their convictions in as many varied forms as Berry. His contribution of fiction, nonfiction, and poetry continues to grow and evolve each year. Berry's essay "A Citizen's Response to the National Security Strategy" (2003), decrying President Bush's plan for a preemptive strike against Iraq, was compared by *Sojourners Magazine* to Thomas Paine's *Common Sense*, and was published as a full-page advertisement in the *New York Times* a month before the U.S. invasion of Iraq.

Berry has been awarded the O. Henry Prize for his story "The Hurt Man" (2005), the *Writer* award (2004), the T.S. Eliot Award from the Ingersoll Foundation (1994), the Lannan Foundation Award for nonfiction (1989), the Jean Stein Award from the American Academy of Arts and Letters (1977), the Vachel Lindsay Prize (1962), and numerous honorary doctorates and accolades. He still lives at Lanes Landing Farm in Port Royal, Kentucky, with his wife, Tanya. They have two children, Mary Dee and Pryor Clifford.

BIBLIOGRAPHY

Angyal, Andrew J., *Wendell Berry*, 1995; Berger, Rose Marie, "One Citizen's Shining Light," *Sojourners Magazine*, 2003; Berry, Wendell, *Collected Poems: 1957–1982*, 1985; Berry, Wendell, *A Continuous Harmony: Essays Cultural and Agricultural*, 1981; Berry, Wendell, *The Hidden Wound*, 1970; Berry, Wendell, *The Memory of Old Jack*, 1974; Berry, Wendell, *What Are People For?* 1990; Berry, Wendell, *The Wild Birds: Six Stories of the Port William Membership*, 1986; "Mr Wendell Berry of Kentucky," www.brtom.org/wb/berry.html; Nibellink, Herman, "Wendell Berry," *American Nature Writers*, John Elder, ed., 1996.

Bertell, Rosalie

(April 4, 1929—)
Mathematician, Biochemist, member of the Grey Nuns of the Sacred Heart

Armed with a Ph.D. and the moral conviction of her vocation as a member of the Grey Nuns of the Sacred Heart, Dr. Rosalie Bertell has spent the best part of the last forty years of her life in cancer research, and in raising awareness about the dangers to the public health from the proliferation of chemical and radioactive pollutants.

Rosalie Bertell was born on April 4, 1929, in Buffalo, New York, to Helen Towhey Bertell, an Irish-Canadian, and Paul Bertell, an American from New Jersey, giving her American and Canadian citizenship.

A frail child, Rosalie was often ill and absent from school in the early years. Her doctors recommended subdued recess times, when she was able to attend, and quiet and restful pursuits when she was at home. Rosalie read a great deal and taught herself to play chess. She had a natural talent for music and excelled at mathematics. She grew up quietly as a much loved middle child, close to her older sister, Mary Katherine, who became an art teacher, and her younger brother, John, who became a lawyer. As adults, Mary Katherine and John were able to offer Rosalie great moral and legal support during her many confrontations with the powerful nuclear industry.

In high school, Rosalie showed a keen interest in liturgical music and felt the beginnings of a religious calling. Upon graduation, she won a scholarship to D'Youville College in Buffalo, which was named after a Canadian-born saint and the founder of the Order of the Grey Nuns of the Sacred Heart. Rosalie attended D'Youville and graduated *magna cum laude* in 1950. She then joined the Carmelites, a Roman Catholic religious community and contemplative order for women, in Vermont. Rosalie left the order in 1956 to attend graduate school at The Catholic University of America in Washington, D.C., where she received an M.A. in Mathematics. Two years later, she joined the Grey Nuns of the Sacred Heart. The Grey Nuns was not a secluded, contemplative order, as was the Carmelites, but one that had a tradition of social work and teaching, which better suited Rosalie's temperament for scholarship and reaching out to people. She continued her academic studies, and in 1966, earned a Ph.D. in Mathematics, with a minor in Biology and Biochemistry.

Dr. Bertell won a postdoctoral grant and became a cancer research scientist at Roswell Memorial Park Institute, in Buffalo, New York, one of the world's first cancer research facilities. There, she studied the harm of overexposure to X-rays and the rising incidence of leukemia. She soon became a pioneer in the study of X-rays and cancer, and began to understand the dangers of nuclear power plants releasing radioactive materials into the air, indiscriminately exposing the public to their lethal effects.

Dr. Bertell joined members of the scientific community who were concerned about radiation safety and, with her colleagues, challenged the Atomic Energy Commission by raising awareness of public health issues. She spoke out against the development of nuclear reactors, and became a leader as an anti-nuclear activist.

In the Preface to *Rosalie Bertell: Scientist, Eco-Feminist, Visionary*, by Mary-Louise Engels (Women's Press, Toronto, 2005), Engels begins this fascinating biography by describing how Bertell's 1973 speech to a gathering near Buffalo, New York, encouraged residents to vote down a proposal to build a nuclear reactor nearby. This was viewed as the beginning of her life as an anti-nuclear activist.

In an interview published in 1998 in the *Toronto Star*, Staff Reporter Donna Jean MacKinnon describes Dr. Bertell as "... neither a recluse nor a denizen of the ivory Tower. She is an activist and self-confessed whistle blower." MacKinnon reports that after the Bhopal disaster in India in 1984, Bertell directed the International Medical Commission investigating the effects of the Union Carbide chemical spill. And, after the Chernobyl nuclear disaster in the then USSR, in 1986, Bertell helped convene a tribunal to fight for the rights of its victims.

Dr. Rosalie Bertell has devoted her long professional life to teaching, lecturing, consulting, and public speaking. She has held positions at Sacred Heart Junior College, Pennsylvania; D'Youville Academy, Atlanta; D'Youville College, Buffalo; State University of New York, Buffalo; Graduate School of the State University of New York, Buffalo; Ministry of Concern for Public Health, Buffalo; Jesuit Center for Social Faith and Justice, Toronto; and Ovum Pacis: The Women's University, USA and Canada.

She has served as a consultant to the British Columbia Medical Association, the Environmental Protection Agency, the National Council of Churches, the New York State Medical Society, the Japanese Association of Scientists, Native Americans for a Clean Environment, African National Congress, Interchurch Coordination Committee in the Netherlands, and many other environmentally concerned organizations around the world. She has received numerous honors and awards for her work, and has been cited in more than one hundred publications.

In 1984, she was a co-founder of the International Institute of Concern for Public Health (IICPH), and served as its president from 1987 to 1994, and Editor in Chief of *International Perspectives in Public Health.* Dr. Bertell is the author of *Handbook for Estimating the Health Effect of Ionizing Radiation* (1984-1986); *No Immediate Danger: Prognosis for a Radioactive Earth* (Toronto: Women's Press, 1985); and *Planet Earth: The Latest Weapon of War: A Critical Study into the Military and the Environment* (Montreal: Black Rose Books, 2001). Dr. Bertell won The World Federalist Peace Award in 1988, and the Ontario Premier's Council on Health's Health Innovator Award in 1991. She retired from IICPH in 1994, but grants interviews and accepts limited speaking engagements. Dr. Rosalie Bertell, Grey Nun of the Sacred Heart, was a Nobel Peace Prize nominee in 2005.

BIBLIOGRAPHY

Donnelly, Mary Rose and Louisa Blair, "Option for Life and Health," *Compass*, 1995; Engels, Mary-Louise, *Rosalie Bertell, Scientist, Eco-Feminist, Visionary*, 2005; Jewell, Wendy, "Science Hero: Dr. Rosalie Bertell Anti-Nuclear Nun," *My Hero: Directory of Heroes*, 2007, The My Hero Project, and interactive Web project; MacKinnon, Donna Jean, "Anti-Nuclear Nun" *Toronto Star*, 1998; Wolfwood, Theresa, "Planet Earth," *The Ecologist* Book Review, 2001; YouTube Video "Depleted Uranium in the Human Body: Sr Rosalie Bertell, PhD," from Yoryvrah, 2007, www.youtube.com/watch?v=WgQ79-oDX2o.

Bien, Amos
(February 12, 1951-)
Biologist, Ecotourism Pioneer, Entrepreneur

Tropical biologist Amos Bien is a pioneer of ecotourism, establishing Rara Avis, Costa Rica's first rain forest reserve devoted to conservation, sustainable development, and education, in 1983. During the 1990s, Bien helped found and has served as president of the Costa Rican Natural Reserve Network, an association of private reserve owners that promotes conservation on privately held land of ecological value. In recent years he has worked internationally to develop global baseline criteria for sustainable tourism, a major international effort for certification programs and government policy.

Bien was born on February 12, 1951, in New York City and grew up in Lynbrook, New York. He spent formative years studying nature and learning about civic responsibility with the Boy Scouts. While attending the University of Chicago, Bien and three friends helped found the Midwest's first recycling program, which is still in operation and is now the largest in the region. The same group of friends also used the equipment in the university's chemistry lab to test brand-name clothing detergents for their phosphorous content. Once they found that the detergents contained far more phosphorous than the labels claimed, they called the press. Soon the City of Chicago was demanding that the companies change their recipes. After graduating from the University of Chicago in 1973 with a degree in biology, Bien went on to State University of New York–Stony Brook for master's and doctoral work in ecology, specializing in sea slugs and tropical forest structure.

Bien moved to Costa Rica in 1979 to carry out doctoral dissertation research at La Selva Biological Station. Within six months, he was invited to coordinate the Station. While there,

Amos Bien (Photograph by Steve Martindale, courtesy of Rara Avis)

he began to hear frightening predictions about the disappearance of rain forests. He was pained by the irony that he and his colleagues were studying the forest's secrets just as massive deforestation was coming to claim them. So he began to visit La Selva's neighbors, the men armed with chainsaws and machetes, to find out why they were cutting down trees. He learned that far from being ill-intentioned forest-haters, they were just trying to make a living the best way they knew how.

Bien decided to see if he could beat that. He made some calculations and found that cutting trees, leaving them to rot on the ground, and setting cows out to pasture was one of the most inefficient ways of making money off of the land; annual profit was rarely more than $20 per hectare. Harvesting and selling one tree from one hectare of land per year was more profitable than grazing cattle on that hectare, in fact. And even more profitable than cutting the trees at all, Bien imagined, was leaving them there and inviting tourists to come admire the rainforest.

In 1983, Bien put his ideas into practice and founded his mountainous rain forest reserve, Rara Avis. The first tourist accommodations at Rara Avis were in an old building that had been a penal colony guardhouse. The bunk-style accommodations there were rustic but comfortable for the curious tourists who braved the four-hour ride by horse or tractor through the foothills to Rara Avis. Through the 1980s, Bien added what was needed to make Rara Avis the model ecotourism development it has become. Nature trails crisscross the forest, and for cooling down after the day's hike there is a swimming hole at the foot of a spectacular waterfall. Bien offers a variety of accommodations ranging from a luxurious lodge, to a treehouse, to riverside cabins. In his on-going experiments with making a living from the rain forest without destroying it, Bien and his associates have established a butterfly research and production project and a nursery for endangered rain forest trees and orchids. Bien is now internationally recognized as a pioneer in the world's growing ecotourism industry.

In addition to managing his successful rain forest resort, Bien was the founding president of the Costa Rican Private Nature Reserves Association, an association of owners of private nature reserves. As government and international resources for conservation shrink, Bien and his fellow reserve owners are showing that private landholders can be important collaborators in national conservation strategies, because they conserve habitat and watersheds that the government alone could not afford to protect. The private reserve owners can also contribute to the national economy by allowing bioprospectors to survey their land for pharmaceuticals or other substances of value to industry. Bien and his colleagues lobby for economic credits for landholders who commit to conserving their land in a natural state and for more input into government conservation policies, and at an international level, for support for reducing the carbon emissions caused by tropical deforestation.

Bien has collaborated internationally with The International Ecotourism Society, the Rainforest Alliance, and other organizations to establish formal operational criteria for sustainable tourism—these criteria are becoming the backbone of certification programs and government policy. He has written many reports and studies on issues related to sustainable tourism, including a 2007 study for the Inter-American Development Bank on the impacts of cruiseship tourism in Central America. Bien also directs the on-line masters' degree program at the Universidad de Cooperación Internacional in Costa Rica, and at Tulane University he teaches a yearly course on Climate Change, Tropical Forests, and Biodiversity. He makes frequent appearances on international television and radio programs devoted to nature and conservation, and is an active participant in the public debate on conservation in the Costa Rican media. Bien has been honored with the Costa Rica Tourism Professionals Association's 1996 Amigo de la Naturaleza award, given annually to a prominent "Friend of Nature" and he has represented Costa Rica at the United Nations Convention on Biological Diversity and the Johannesburg Summit on Sustainable Development.

Bien resides in Costa Rica and has three grown children.

BIBLIOGRAPHY

Auerbach, Jonathon, "Journey Deep into a Rainforest," *Christian Science Monitor*, 1991; Bien, Amos, "Indicators and Certification/Standards Programs," in *Indicators of Sustainable Development for Tourism Destinations: A Guidebook*, World Tourism Organization, 2004; Honey, Martha, *Ecotourism and Sustainable Development: Who Owns Paradise*, 1999; "Rara Avis Rainforest Lodge," www.rara-avis.com; "The International Ecotourism Society," www.ecotourism.org; Tripoli, Steve, "Tramway in the Treetops, Bird's Eye View," *Christian Science Monitor*, 1989.

Bierstadt, Albert
(January 7, 1830–February 18, 1902)
Landscape Painter

Landscape painter Albert Bierstadt produced some of the first images of the vast, breathtaking topography of the American West. His paintings resonated with Americans of the nineteenth century because they called attention to the beauty of the briskly disappearing wilderness of the American West and because they reinforced a sense of national identity.

Albert Bierstadt was born on January 7, 1830, in Solingen, Germany, near Düsseldorf on the Rhine River. He was the youngest of six children born to Henry and Christina Bierstadt. The Bierstadt family emigrated to the United States in 1832, settling in New Bedford, Massachusetts. Little is known about Bierstadt's childhood. He attended the local public schools. His formal education, though, never extended past this rudimentary level. His artistic career began in May 1850 when he published a flyer offering to teach "Monochromatic Painting at Liberty Hall," 24 hours of instruction for just three dollars, promising "every picture the scholars make worthy of a frame."

Bierstadt traveled to Düsseldorf in 1853 to study art. He never formally enrolled at the academy in Düsseldorf, but instead gained knowledge of color and compositional techniques through his friendships with artists such as Emanuel Lenze, Worthington Whittridge, and Sanford S. Gifford, who were formal students at the Düsseldorf Academy. It was here that Bierstadt began to master techniques that would make his later landscape paintings so powerful. He remained in Europe for four years, traveling the countryside and sending home his Düsseldorf-influenced landscapes with their volatile skies, sharply contrasted lighting, and minute brush strokes. When he returned home in 1857, he unveiled several new paintings, all of which were praised by the New Bedford newspaper. Significant among his paintings of this time period are his *Westphalian Landscape* (1854), *Gosnold at Cuttyhunk* (1858), and *Lake Lucern* (1858), which he submitted to the National Academy of Design exhibition in New York.

In 1859, Bierstadt joined Col. Frederick Lander's South Pass Wagon Road Expedition in its search for an overland route from St. Louis, Missouri, to the Pacific. He left the expedition to explore the Wind River country of the Rocky Mountains, where he found scenes that lent themselves perfectly to his ambitious and dramatic style of painting. The sketches he made on this trip would supply him with subjects for the rest of his life. In one letter, he wrote "such beautiful cloud formations, such fine effects of light and shade, and play of cloud shadows across the hills, such golden sunsets, I have never before seen. Our own country has the best material for artists in the world." When Bierstadt returned from his journey, he settled in New York City and began painting huge landscapes (up to 9 feet by 15 feet), tremendous in scale yet containing the minutest of details. His paintings provided many Americans with their first view of the West. Bierstadt's reputation soared, and collectors enthusiastically purchased his paintings. In 1860, he was elected to the National Academy of Design. Of one of his most famous works, *The Rocky Mountains, Lander's Peak* (1863), critic and historian Henry T. Ackerman wrote, and is quoted by Tom Robotham in his book about Bierstadt, "No more genuine and grand American work has been produced in landscape art."

After the outbreak of the Civil War in 1861, Bierstadt was granted permission to visit the country around Washington, D.C., in search of material. *Guerrilla Warfare* (1876) and *The Ambush* (1876) were likely products of this excursion. Another Civil War painting of his,

Bombardment of Fort Sumter (1863?), was purely a product of his imagination. At the time the painting was done, there is no way Bierstadt could have accessed Charleston. He likely created the painting based on a series of eyewitness accounts of the bombardment, which were published in the New York newspapers.

Bierstadt once again traveled west in the spring of 1863, this time in the company of Fitz Hugh Ludlow. Ludlow, a journalist, published an account of their journey, entitled *The Heart of the Continent* (1870). They passed through Kansas and Nebraska, visited Denver and Salt Lake City (where they met Brigham Young), and made their way to California. Bierstadt sketched for six weeks in the areas in and around Yosemite Valley. With these sketches he would produce, among others, *Yosemite* (1863), *Looking Down Yosemite Valley* (1865), and *The Yosemite Valley* (1868). After venturing into Oregon, the pair returned to New York via San Francisco and the Isthmus of Panama in late 1863.

The period of 1864 to 1873 brought Bierstadt growing critical acclaim as well as growing financial success. His paintings were some of the highest priced of nineteenth-century America. *The Rocky Mountains, Lander's Peak* sold for $25,000, and *Storm in the Rocky Mountains, Mount Rosalie* sold for $35,000. In 1866, he married Rosalie Osborne, the ex-wife of his friend Fitz Hugh Ludlow, and began plans for a large estate on the Hudson River. The house was completed in the next year and was, according to the *Home Journal*, one of the most "commanding and noticeable" on the Hudson. It would burn to its shell in 1882. In 1867, Bierstadt and his new wife sailed for Europe. Over the course of the next two years they visited London, Düsseldorf, Paris, Rome, Munich, Dresden, Berlin, Vienna, Switzerland, and Spain. They returned to their home on the Hudson in 1869.

In 1871, Bierstadt made his third trip west. This time he took his wife along and rode the newly completed transcontinental railroad. They stayed on the Pacific coast until 1873, sketching in the High Sierras and in Yosemite and occupying a studio in San Francisco for a time. During this period, he produced at least four paintings of coastal seal rocks, including *Seal Rocks, San Francisco* (1872) and *Seal Rocks, Farallon Islands* (1873). After two years on the Pacific Coast, the Bierstadts returned to the East. At this point in his career, his popularity began to wane. It became difficult for him to sell his paintings, for the tastes of critics and collectors had changed. They were no longer enamored with Bierstadt's sweeping and sublime interpretations of the American West and were turning their attention more toward the French impressionist painting style that was coming into vogue. In 1889, when Bierstadt submitted *The Last Buffalo* (1888) to the American Selection Committee for the Paris Exposition, it was rejected. It was, according to one committee member, "too big and not representative of his style." His later years would, in fact, be marked by a departure from his earlier style. He turned toward a greater diversity of subjects, including paintings tranquil and less dramatic in scope. In 1893, his wife died after a long battle with consumption. Bierstadt remarried in 1894, wedding a widow, Mrs. David Stewart.

Bierstadt's last years were busy ones. He became involved in a project to establish a National Academy of Art in Washington, D.C., continued painting, and applied for a series of patents concerned with improvements to railway cars. He also spent time promoting a gun that had been invented by Henry Schulhof and became interested in the gas and electrical projects of Charles Sanders Pierce. Bierstadt died on the morning of February 18, 1902.

BIBLIOGRAPHY

Anderson, Nancy K. and Linda S, Ferber, *Albert Bierstadt: Art and Enterprise*, 1990; Baigell, Matthew, *Albert Bierstadt*, 1981; Carr, Gerald L. and Dan Morse, *Albert Bierstadt's West*, 1997; Hendricks, Gordon, *Albert Bierstadt, Painter of the American West*, 1974; Lewison, Florence, "The Uniqueness of Albert Bierstadt," *American Artist*, 1964; Robotham, Tom, *Albert Bierstadt*, 1993.

Bingham, Eula

(July 9, 1929–)
Director of the Occupational Safety and Health Administration, Toxicologist

The first woman director of the Occupational Safety and Health Administration (OSHA), Eula Bingham led the agency to focus on health concerns raised by worker exposure to chemical toxins. Trained as a toxicologist, Bingham pushed for recognition of the cancer-causing properties of a broad range of chemicals, making it easier to enforce stricter exposure regulations. In 1977, when Bingham was appointed assistant secretary of labor for occupational safety and health, she inherited an agency with a reputation for arbitrary rules and unnecessary paperwork. During her three years as OSHA director, she worked to ease the regulatory burden on industry and improve the agency's image, while ensuring that OSHA stayed true to its role as advocate for worker health and safety. As professor in the Department of Environmental Health at the University of Cincinnati, Bingham has conducted scientific studies on numerous environmental toxins, labored for government accountability for protecting citizens from the effects of chemical agents, and connected community activists with scientific investigators to work for safer environments.

Eula Lee Bingham was born in Covington, Kentucky, on July 9, 1929. Bingham was an only child, her father a railroad worker who became a farmer after losing his job during the Great Depression. Bingham lived in Covington until she went to Eastern Kentucky University in Richmond. She graduated in 1951 with a B.S. in chemistry and worked for one year at the Hilton Davis Chemical Company in Cincinnati, Ohio. Interested in pursuing a career as a research scientist, Bingham studied zoology at the University of Cincinnati, receiving an M.S. in 1954 and a Ph.D. in 1958. She was hired by the University of Cincinnati's College of Medicine, where she began conducting research into the carcinogenic properties of a variety of agents and eventually was recognized as one of the leading national experts on environmental health.

In the early 1970s, Bingham served on a series of national committees investigating and recommending policy on environmental hazards. During 1974–1975 she served as chair of the Department of Labor's Standards Advisory Committee on Coke Oven Emissions, where she came to the attention of Ray Marshall, who was to become Pres. JIMMY CARTER's secretary of labor. Bingham was nominated as assistant secretary of labor for occupational safety and health in 1977. The late 1970s were a time of high inflation and growing conservatism, and Bingham inherited an agency that had come under very public attack, as a symbol of the government overregulation perceived to be crippling the economy. In her nomination hearing she promised to rescind unnecessary and unproductive regulations and to concentrate OSHA's resources on addressing genuinely life-threatening workplace hazards. She also promised to turn the agency's attention more fully to health issues in addition to its traditional concern with safety.

Bingham was sympathetic to the concerns of labor unions and environmental activists and led OSHA to support a number of grassroots, local, and union-based environmental health initiatives, through the New Directions Grant Program. She also pushed for a more aggressive approach to setting permissible exposure limits for carcinogens. Prior to Bingham's term in office, OSHA set standards on a case-by-case basis, only after definitive scientific evidence proved the substance was harmful to humans. Bingham proposed to treat chemical agents in broad categories of known and suspected carcinogens and to set exposure limits at minimum feasible levels. This, it was hoped, would speed and simplify the regulatory process and protect the greatest number of workers. A case in point is that of regulating worker exposure to cotton dust. The scientific evidence demonstrating a link between cotton dust and brown lung disease was irrefutable, and Pres. Carter supported Bingham's proposed exposure limits despite economists' and industry's position that meeting the new standard would be too costly and inflationary. Bingham was also successful in setting tough standards in other cases, including benzene, lead, and arsenic, establishing exposure limits at the lowest feasible levels. Bingham achieved an impressive inspection and enforcement record, decreasing the inspection rate for minor violations while increasing inspections and penalties for the most serious violations.

After Ronald Reagan's election in 1980 ended her tenure at OSHA, Bingham helped spearhead organizations to press for environmental safety and health. These organizations included the Occupational Safety and Health Political Action Committee, which Bingham chaired in 1982, and the Regulatory Audit Project, a group of former environmental and consumer administrators who joined together in 1983 to educate the public about the costs of failing to enforce health and safety regulations. Bingham also chaired the Department of Veterans Affairs' Persian Gulf Expert Scientific Committee in 1996 and pushed for full scientific investigation into and government accountability for the effects of exposure to low levels of chemical weapons and other agents present during the Gulf war. Bingham has continued her work at the University of Cincinnati, which has included directing the Community Outreach and Education Project for the Center for Environmental Genetics.

Bingham has won a number of awards and recognitions for her work, including a Rockefeller Foundation Public Service Award in 1980, and her induction into the National Academy of Sciences Institute of Medicine in 1989 and the Ohio Women's Hall of Fame in 1983. She lives in Ohio.

BIBLIOGRAPHY

"National Institute of Environmental Health Sciences—National Institutes of Health Research Centers," www.niehs.nih.gov/research/supported/centers/; Noble, Charles, *Liberalism at Work: The Rise and Fall of OSHA*, 1984; Shenon, Philip, "Panel Disputes Studies on Gulf War Illness," *New York Times*, 1996.

Bixby, Kevin
(1956–)
Natural Resources Policy Advocate, Founder and Executive Director of Southwest Environmental Center

Kevin Bixby is founder and executive director of the Southwest Environmental Center (SWEC). He works to preserve New Mexico's state parks and wildlife areas from oil drilling and development, and campaigns for restoration of the Rio Grande corridor.

Born in San Diego, California, in 1956, Bixby spent his childhood in the outdoors. As a boy he was in the Boy Scouts and would often go to national parks with his family. High school back packing trips into the California mountains with the Berkeley Ecology Center lead to a long interest in environmentalism and wildlife.

In 1978, Bixby got a B.A. in Biology from Dartmouth College, focusing on fieldwork and taxonomy. A westerner at heart, Bixby returned to the Bay area after college. He worked briefly for the Environmental Protection Agency as an environmental regulator, but did not like the bureaucratic atmosphere and took to the highway. He traveled for several months through Mexico, Ecuador and Alaska. When he returned to San Francisco after his travels, he drove a taxi at night and by day he volunteered with Friends of the Earth. There, he was influenced by the work of environmentalists Dave Phillips and DAVID R. BROWER. But when he heard the founder of Earth First! DAVE FOREMAN speak in San Francisco in the early 1980s, he decided to make a career out of wildlife conservation.

In 1985 Bixby entered the University of Michigan's School of Natural Resources and Environment, where he earned an M.S. in natural resources policy, working under the tutelage of MICHAEL E. SOULÉ. Professor Soulé had only just begun articulating a new definition of conservation biology, "Deep Ecology" an emerging field that addresses the maintenance, loss and restoration of biological diversity. After graduate school, Bixby moved to Las Cruces, New Mexico, with his wife, Lisa LaRocque, an environmental educator and consultant. And from Las Cruces, Bixby would dedicate his expertise.

Bixby started the Southwest Environmental Center after realizing that the environmental activism in Las Cruces was disjointed. There were several national groups meeting in the area, such as the Sierra Club and the Audubon Society, but says Bixby, they were meeting in people's homes and not speaking to one another. Bixby thought that if there were one physical location for the various groups to meet, share resources, and provide an easy place for the public and the media to seek out environmental groups, it would give a boost to the activism in the area. The SWEC was started in 1991. It provided a meeting and working space for different groups, built an environmental library, and offered lectures and guided natural history outings.

But the organization eventually began to have a new identity and agenda. The main priorities of the SWEC have been the restoration of the Rio Grande ecosystem, focusing on streamside woodlands and wetlands, and keeping water in the river year round; protecting state lands from uncontrolled livestock grazing; and the protection of threatened species including Mexican wolves, prairie chickens, prairie dogs, jaguars, native fishes and mountain lions. Bixby and the SWEC led public education campaigns, advocated for environmental legislation and helped prepare litigation to sue energy companies in order to protect wildlife. His efforts helped keep the Otero Mesa, one of the last Chihuahuan grasslands, safe from oil and gas drilling, bringing in wetland restoration projects instead. Bixby was also instrumental in establishing Mesilla Valley Bosque State Park, the thirty-fourth state park in New Mexico.

Bixby is especially proud of the collaboration between the SWEC and local farmers in the Las Cruces irrigation district on wetland projects, overcoming the usual enmity between environmental groups and farmers and ranchers around the necessity of clean water and healthy ecosystems. Bixby says that one area where they have yet to find a common ground has been the reintroduction of the Mexican wolf.

When the U.S. Congress gave the Department of Homeland Security the authority to waive environmental laws in order to construct a border fence between Mexico and the U.S., Bixby and the SWEC voiced concerns about the environmental impact to the migration patterns of jaguars, free-roaming herds of bison, deer and antelope.

Bixby believes that the loss of biodiversity is the most important environmental problem to date, more important than climate change, which he believes can be reversed. "We can get back to healthy CO_2 levels, but when we lose species, they're gone forever. Evolution can fill that niche again, but it won't be the same. This is a very serious matter that deserves our attention; that's what gets me out of bed in the morning."

Kevin Bixby continues to live and work in Las Cruces with his wife Lisa LaRocque.

BIBLIOGRAPHY

www.tpl.org/tier3_cd.cfm?content_item_id= 20296&folder_id=674, personal interview, 01/26/08; www.wt.org/magnoliatrust/grants.htm.

Blackgoat, Roberta
(1917-April 23, 2002)
Dineh (Navajo) Relocation Resistance Leader

Roberta Blackgoat was a leader of her Dineh (Navajo) people's resistance movement to a government relocation order following the passage of the Navajo-Hopi Land Settlement Act in 1974. She and the 200 Dineh families who refused to leave their ancestral lands believed that they were "planted" by the Creator on their land and charged with taking care of it and that to leave would be to abandon the wishes of the Creator.

Born in 1917 on Thin Rock Mesa, Arizona, where her family had lived for at least ten generations, Roberta Blackgoat had a traditional Dineh childhood during which she was taught how to survive in her people's dry, rugged homeland. The land her people claim as home is defined by four peaks spanning the Four Corners region of the Southwest: Mount Blanca in Colorado to the northeast, Mount Taylor in New Mexico to the southeast, the San Francisco Peaks in Arizona to the southwest, and Mount Hesperus in Colorado to the northwest. The Dineh people consider these mountains sacred, and the land between them their church. Their hogans, built in the western area of the quadrant, are considered an altar.

Historians say the Dineh people migrated from northern Canada to what is now the southwestern United States in about 1400 A.D. They herded sheep and lived relatively peacefully with their Hopi neighbors for hundreds of years. Both peoples resisted Spanish and Anglo invaders of their lands, but the Dineh, because their shepherding culture required larger expanses of land, encountered more violence from the invaders. In 1864, 8,000 Dineh people, among them Blackgoat's grandparents, were herded by Kit Carson's soldiers on the "Long Walk"—a forced journey by foot from their homeland to Fort Sumner, New

Mexico. It resulted in the death by exhaustion, famine, disease, beating, and bayoneting of about 4,000 Dineh people, before the government signed a treaty with Dineh representatives to establish a Navajo reservation straddling northeastern Arizona and northwestern New Mexico in 1868. Blackgoat's grandmother and her family returned to Thin Rock Mesa.

In 1882, boundaries for a Hopi reservation were drawn by the government, quickly and rather arbitrarily. Hundreds of Dineh people, scattered in family groups, were living on the land designated as the Hopi reservation, and a few Hopi people were living on Navajo reservation land. One Hopi village was totally left out of the reservation. Later additions to the Navajo reservation left the Hopi reservation totally encircled by the Navajo reservation. The Dineh and Hopi peoples lived with this ambiguity for almost a century. There were some territorial problems, but their coexistence was relatively peaceful. But in the mid-1960s, Peabody Coal announced its intention to mine the rich 100-square-mile coal deposit at Black Mesa, which was officially Hopi land but was inhabited principally by the Dineh. The Peabody negotiator, lawyer John Boyden, understood that Peabody could not sign leases unless land ownership was official and boundaries were clear, so he wrote legislation that divided the disputed parts of the Hopi reservation evenly between the Navajo and the Hopi. Sen. Barry Goldwater pushed this Navajo-Hopi Land Settlement Act through Congress in 1974. Ten thousand Dineh people were determined to be living on what were referred to as Hopi Partitioned Lands and were told to leave, the largest relocation effort in the United States since the World War II internment of Japanese Americans. Most of the people did leave, but a few hundred Dineh families defied the order. Within three years, one-third of those who had accepted relocation benefits and moved off the reservation had lost their new homes due to exploitation and inexperience with the Anglo economic system; unemployment, alcoholism, and suicide rates among relocated Dineh people remain much higher than other Dineh populations.

Although most of her six children agreed to relocate, Blackgoat, who was widowed during the 1960s, remained in her hogan on Hopi Partitioned Land. She lived 30 miles from the nearest paved road and had neither running water nor electricity. At first, Blackgoat did not take the relocation order seriously, but once the government erected a fence in 1977 to keep the Dineh people and their sheep out of the Hopi Partitioned Lands, she understood the act's threat to her livelihood. In 1979, Blackgoat chaired a council of 64 members of the Independent Dineh Nation at Big Mountain. They wrote a declaration of independence, claiming that the U.S. government and the Navajo Tribal Council (which had signed coal leases with Peabody) had "violated the sacred laws of the Dineh nation" and had allowed Mother Earth to be "raped by the exploitation of coal, uranium, oil, natural gas and helium." They declared that they "speak for the winged beings, the four-legged beings, and those who have gone before us and the coming generation. We seek no changes in our livelihood because this natural life is our only known survival and it's our sacred law."

Deadlines for relocation have come and gone over the decades, yet Blackgoat and the remaining 200 Dineh families on Hopi Partitioned Land refused to leave. After the original relocation during the 1970s, there have been several renewed offers by the U.S. government of relocation benefits or accommodations to stay on the land. The most recent offer, authorized by Congress in 1996, allowed Dineh relocation resisters to stay on their land for 75 years if they reduced their herds of livestock, built no more dwellings, cut no more wood, and did not bury their dead on the land. Blackgoat and other resisters saw these restrictions as unacceptable and did not sign on to them.

Blackgoat said that by remaining on the land she was following Dineh spiritual laws; the Creator charged the Dineh with the care for their given area of Mother Earth. She was deeply disturbed by the mining, which she believed was killing Mother Earth. Coal, she was told by her grandfather, is Mother Earth's liver, crucial to Mother Earth's functioning and survival. Cutting the liver out of Mother Earth without putting anything back inside or allowing her to heal hurts her seriously. A direct effect is the air and water pollution caused by the mining activity, but Blackgoat also saw a relation between the mining and increased tornadoes, floods, earthquakes, loss of biodiversity, and other disasters.

Blackgoat led the Dineh resistance movement, along with other grandmothers, including Pauline Whitesinger and Katherine Smith. Being elderly women, they knew that they are less likely targets of police violence than young men, so they were usually at the front of marches and protests. Blackgoat spoke worldwide about the plight of the Dineh relocation resistors; she is an international symbol of indigenous people struggling to maintain a traditional relationship with the Earth. Younger generations of Dineh resisters, led by such activists as Louise Benally who accompanied Blackgoat on her speaking tours, have vowed to continue the resistance of their elders.

Roberta Blackgoat died on April 23, 2002. Following her death, the Arizona House of Representatives passed a resolution praising her: "Roberta Blackgoat could be stopped by the passage of time, but not by any government…. She walked in beauty through her life. We praise her life." The Dineh resistance movement remains in full force, with support organizations organizing letter-writing campaigns to fend off Peabody's continued attempts to mine Black Mesa coal and support the Diné people's continued presence at Black Mesa.

BIBLIOGRAPHY

Benedek, Emily, *The Wind Won't Know Me: A History of the Navajo-Hopi Land Dispute*, 1992; Bergman, B.J., "Wrong Side of the Fence," *Mother Jones*, 2000; "Black Mesa Latest Information," www.blackmesais.org; Cockburn, Alexander, "Indian Rights: The Forced Relocation of Navajo families Is a Triumph of Greed," *Los Angeles Times*, 1997; "Death resolution; Roberta Blackgoat," State of Arizona House of Representatives, 2002; Draper, Electa, "Forced Relocation Tears at Tribal Soul," *Denver Post*, 1999; Isay, David, and Harvey Wang, *Holding On*, 1996; as told to Johnson, Sandy, *The Book of Elders*, 1994; Kammer, Jerry, "Dividing the Sky," *The Arizona Republic*, 2000; "Roberta Blackgoat's Page," www.angelfire.com/art/hoganview/RBPage/Rblackgoat.htm.

Blaeloch, Janine
(1957–)
Public Interest Environmentalist, Founder and Director of Western Lands Project

Since 1985, Janine Blaeloch has worked as a forest activist and advocate for public lands. She is the founder and director of the Western Lands Project, an organization that monitors attempts to privatize federal land. She started the organization in 1997 as the Western Land Exchange Project with a mission to monitor exchanges of land between the federal government and private parties. Over time, the organization expanded its purpose to include monitoring not only exchanges, but also attempts by Congress and land agencies to privatize federal land through land sales and congressional give-

Janine Blaeloch (Photograph courtesy of Western Lands Project)

aways. The Western Lands Project also works toward helping citizens to involve themselves in the decisions that affect their federal lands.

Born in 1957, Janine Blaeloch was interested in politics and issues of truth and fairness since an early age, but she developed a concern for public lands when she began hiking with her father in her teens. Other influences on her commitment to public land activism included discoveries about the importance and the vulnerability of old-growth forest in the Northwest and her involvement with the organization Earth First! in the mid-1980s. She went on to earn her B.A. in Environmental Studies at the University of Washington in 1989 with a self-designed program focusing on Public Lands Management and Policy, which led her to work as an environmental planner in the public and private sectors for eight years.

In 1997 she became involved with contesting the Huckleberry Land Exchange between the U.S. Forest Service and the Weyerhaeuser Corporation. Over 4,000 acres of public land on Huckleberry Mountain were traded for 30,000 acres of Weyerhaeuser land, which consisted of mostly clear-cut land. The stated justification was to improve land management by eliminating a checkerboard pattern of ownership, but the Western Land Exchange Project was concerned about the quality of land being traded to the public. A large portion of the Weyerhaeuser acres was given the timber industry's lowest rating for its ability to grow trees. After working with the Pilchuck Audubon Society to challenge the land trade, Blaeloch did further research and discovered that 300 federal land exchanges were occurring each year, primarily in the western states. After realizing the scope of the issue, Blaeloch founded the Western Lands Exchange Project to address the privatization of this valuable land.

The Western Lands Project helps citizens and other organizations stop proposed land exchanges or improve the terms of the exchange.

In addition to this direct involvement, Janine Blaeloch has co-written reports to raise awareness of land trades, the policies that govern them, flaws in the process and suggestions for reform. Publications include "Commons or Commodity? The Dilemma of Federal Land Exchanges," co-written with historian George Draffan, and "Quid Pro Quo Wilderness: A New Threat to Public Lands," co-written with Katie Fite of the Western Watersheds Project. In 2001 The Western Lands Exchange Project published the "Citizens' Guide to Federal Land Exchanges," offering advice on how any citizen can work to stop or improve a land trade.

In addition to her work as Director of the Western Lands Project, Janine Blaeloch serves on the Board of Directors of the Railroads & Clearcuts Campaign and on the Board of Directors at Greenlaw, an association aimed at providing environmental litigation experience to law students at the University of Washington. She lives in Seattle, Washington.

BIBLIOGRAPHY

Blaeloch, Janine and Katie Fite, "Quid Pro Quo Wilderness," May 2006, www.westlx.org/quid-pro-quo.pdf; McClure, Robert. "Huge Land Swap Ok'd." *Seattle Post-Intelligencer Reporter*, November 21, 2001; Western Lands Project "In the Media" Resources, www.westlx.org/html/in_the_media.html.

Bloomberg, Michael
(February 14, 1942-)
Financier, Mayor of New York City

As the 108th mayor of New York City, Bloomberg proposed "PlaNYC: A Greener, Greater New York," a revolutionary, comprehensive plan to fight global warming, to encourage environmental protection, and to prepare the city for a projected influx of an additional one million residents by 2030. Bloomberg announced the plan on Earth Day (April 22) in 2007. As part of the plan, Bloomberg set a goal for his administration of reducing global warming emissions by 30 percent by 2030. Bloomberg has also taken an active role in encouraging other cities to take similar steps. He led New York City to become the first American city to join C40 Cities—Climate Leadership Group and to host the second C40 Large Cities Climate Summit in Manhattan on May 15, 2007.

Michael Bloomberg was born on February 14, 1942 to William Henry Bloomberg and Charlotte Rubens Bloomberg in the Brighton neighborhood of Boston. The family later moved to the Allston neighborhood of Boston, and finally settled in the Boston suburb of Medford, where Bloomberg lived until he graduated college. As a child, Bloomberg had a fondness for rescuing snakes from a wooded thicket near the family home. He would smuggle the snakes upstairs to his bedroom in knotted socks. He would become an Eagle Scout, a horseman, and active in the school debate team. Bloomberg received an undergraduate degree from John Hopkins University in electrical engineering, and later an M.B.A. from Harvard Business School.

In 1966, Bloomberg was hired by Salomon Brothers to work on Wall Street. He eventually became a general partner with Salomon, and headed equity trading, sales, and eventually systems development. Bloomberg was fired from Salomon on August 1, 1981 as the company merged with Philbro. He founded Bloomberg L.P., a financial software company, later that year. The company eventually blossomed to include a radio network. Today, more than 250,000 people around the word subscribe to Bloomberg's financial and information services. In 2007, Forbes reported his net worth at $11.5 billion.

Accustomed to changing his horses midstream, Bloomberg was a lifelong Democrat who switched parties to run for New York mayor. He was elected as New York's 108th mayor in 2001 and took office on January 2, 2002. He was re-elected in 2005 with a 20 percent margin of victory—the largest margin ever for a New York mayoral re-election campaign. On January 19, 2007 he renounced his affiliation with the Republican Party and was quickly mentioned as a potential independent candidate for president of the Untied States.

One of his major foci during his second term as mayor was his comprehensive plan (PlaNYC) for the city's environment. PlaNYC is a made up of three major components. MaintaiNYC, one component of the plan, focuses on repairing aging infrastructure such as city bridges and water mains, as well as mass transit and power generation facilities. Another aspect of the plan, GreeNYC, sets the goal of reducing the city's carbon emissions by thirty percent. Part of this would be as a result of the expansion of public transportation, such as the subway, through state and city funding. The plan also called for a $2.50 fee assessed to electrical power customers to be used to finance grants and similar incentives for property owners to retrofit buildings.

The plan also called for a "re-greening" of the city in the form of planting one million trees in the next ten years. The plan further promises that every New York City resident would live within a ten minute walk from a park.

The final tier of the plan, OpeNYC, is the preparation for the city's population expansion, which is expected to increase by one million by 2030. Under the plan, the city would encourage the construction of platforms over highways and railway yards to create additional land for housing. The plan also calls for changes in zoning in a number of neighborhoods central to public transportation to facilitate larger homes and a higher density of housing.

PlaNYC was controversial. Part of the plan has called for "congestion pricing," which would entail an $8.00 fee assessment on all cars entering midtown Manhattan during peak hours on weekdays. The proposal has met with significant opposition in the New York State Legislature and Mayor Bloomberg continues to push for its passage.

Bloomberg married Susan Brown in 1975. The couple had two daughters, Emma in 1979 and Georgina in 1983. They divorced in 1993. His career in politics is very much "in-play" as he continues to serve the City of New York as a popular mayor.

BIBLIOGRAPHY

"Bloomberg Leaves Republican Party," Associated Press, June 20, 2007; Bloomberg, Michael, *Bloomberg on Bloomberg*, 1997; Murphy, Dean E., "Bloomberg a Man of Contradictions, but With a Single Focus," *New York Times*, November 26, 2001; Lueck, Thomas, J., "Bloomberg Draws Blueprint For A Greener City," *New York Times*, April 23, 2008; nyc.gov/portal/site/nycgov/menuitem.e985cf5219821bc3f7393cd401c789a0/; www.mikebloomberg.com/en/issues/environment_sustainability/mayor_michael_bloomberg_delivers_keynote_address_at_the_c40_large_cities_climate_summit.htm; www.nyc.gov/html/planyc2030/html/home/home.shtml.

Bookchin, Murray
(January 14, 1921–July 30, 2006)
Philosopher, Writer

Anarchist philosopher Murray Bookchin founded the field of social ecology, a school of thought that holds that human destruction of the environment has its roots in social hierarchy in which elites dominate and exploit the great mass of humanity and that humanity's relationship with nature will improve only if such hierarchies are dissolved. He was credited for introducing ecology into the agenda of the radical political movements of the 1960s and, in later decades, for inspiring the emergence of Green parties throughout the United States.

Murray Bookchin was born on January 14, 1921, in New York City to Nathan and Rose Bookchin, Russian-Jewish immigrants who had been active in the revolutionary movement under tsarism. As a child he joined communist youth groups but became disillusioned with their authoritarian leaders and with the Stalinist betrayal of the workers' and peasants' revolution during the Spanish civil war in the late 1930s. He was expelled from the Young Communist League in 1939 for his "Trotskyist-anarchist deviations" and joined the American Trotskyists, but he left that group too, disappointed by its authoritarian leadership. He worked as a foundryman in northern New Jersey during the late 1930s and early 1940s, organizing unions for the Congress of Industrial Organizations (CIO). He served in the U.S. Army during World War II, and after the war, he became an autoworker, actively involved in the United Auto Workers (UAW), participating in the massive General Motors strike of 1946. When the resolution of that labor conflict converted the UAW into what he considered a proponent of the status quo, Bookchin left the traditional U.S. labor movement and began working with a group of German immigrant Trotskyists who were developing a libertarian socialist movement in New York City. It was during this period, the early 1950s, that Bookchin's articles began appearing in that group's periodical, *Contemporary Issues*. Because Sen. Joseph McCarthy was persecuting the Left at this time, Bookchin used several pseudonyms to sign his articles: M. S. Shiloh, Lewis Herber, Robert Keller, and Harry Ludd.

Bookchin had always been concerned about improving the quality of life for his fellow human beings, but his first major work to explicitly address environmental quality was a 1952 article in *Contemporary Issues* entitled "The Problem of Chemicals in Food" (written under the name of Lewis Herber). It was inspired by congressional hearings on new chemical inputs that had been developed by the same postwar chemical industrial boom that created new pesticides, later decried by RACHEL CARSON in *Silent Spring*. Herber's article was published in booklet form in Germany in 1954 and was expanded into a full-length book in the United States in 1962 under the title *Our Synthetic Environment*, published six months before Carson's bestseller. Bookchin's scope in this volume was wider than food safety: he covered agriculture, various environmental carcinogens, and social health questions. In the 1950s Bookchin came out as an early opponent of nuclear power plants, because of the dangers of radioactive fallout were so great. He founded the Citizens Committee on Radiation Information in 1963, which successfully opposed the construction of the Ravenswood Reactor in New York City.

During the 1950s and 1960s, Bookchin developed the historical and philosophical framework for social ecology. According to Bookchin's historical analysis, human society originally was cooperative, with men and women, old and young, working together within the same community, without significantly harming the natural world. As males came to dominate females, the young, and other males, they also began to develop the idea of dominating nature. At their root, the environmental ills society faces today have emerged from society's domination and exploitation of human beings, as well as the natural environment, according to social ecology proponents.

Social ecology calls for the dissolution of the hierarchical and class institutions that allow people to dominate one another and nature. A society whose citizens do not allow themselves to be dominated and exploited, Bookchin believed, must be based on directly democratic and confederated local governments, a design he called libertarian municipalism. People would organize on the most local level possible, for example, in their own neighborhoods or townships, and send delegates to free confederations to adjust differences in a democratic manner. This concept is based on the political institutions of the Athenian *polis* or city-state, in which citizens resolved differences and formulated policies in a manner later adopted in New England town meetings. Bookchin believed that technological advances would provide working people with ample free time to participate in such self-government.

Bookchin introduced social ecology to radical students during the social upheaval of the 1960s, in the hopes that their youth would give them the energy to hoist off the restraints of dominant hierarchies. His numerous speeches and publications during the 1960s resulted in the acceptance of an environmental agenda by the radical and progressive movements of that time. He was an active participant in the civil rights movement and in various groups for human freedom in New York City and taught in the late 1960s at the Alternative University in New York, a free university at the City University of New York.

Once a true environmental movement blossomed in the United States, following the blast of publicity on Earth Day, 1970, Bookchin wrote extensively, developing an ethic of ecology based on anarchist and libertarian political ideals and promoted a nonhierarchical, decentralized approach to decision making. His ideas from this period appear in several books, including *Toward an Ecological Society* and *The Ecology of Freedom*. In the 1970s, many radical Greens drew their ideas from his writings, speeches, and lectures, initially basing their politics and practice on Bookchin's articulation of social ecology. Bookchin was considered dangerous enough by the U.S. government in 1973 that his apartment in the East Village of Manhattan was broken into by an FBI agent later revealed to be the Number 2 man in the Bureau and Watergate informant Deep Throat.

During the 1980s Bookchin became concerned about certain tendencies adopted and publicized by some of the founders of Earth First!, a loosely organized environmentalist group known mainly for its acts of civil disobedience to stop logging, mining, and road building in undeveloped wilderness areas. These founders, including DAVE FOREMAN, often tied criticism of environmental abuses to calls for population reduction, which Bookchin found reactionary and potentially racist. In 1987, an article in *Earth First! Journal* by one Miss Ann Thropy, a.k.a. Christopher Hanes, an *Earth First! Journal* writer, welcomed the acquired immunodeficiency syndrome (AIDS) epidemic as a means of population reduction. In an interview, Foreman seemed to agree with this view, and advocated letting "nature taking its course" in Third World countries, where starvation was claiming the lives of thousands of people. Bookchin wrote an extensive response, criticizing the deep ecology movement—the philosophical basis for Earth First!—for its antihumanism. Bookchin published the article as "Social Ecology vs. 'Deep Ecology'" in his own newsletter, *Green Perspectives*, in 1987. He challenged the deep ecology position that humanity is a hindrance to nature; he insisted that people as such do fit into a natural evolution and that they can even be beneficial to the natural world. Bookchin engaged Foreman in a debate between social ecology and deep ecology transcribed and published in 1991 as *Defending the Earth, A Dialogue between Murray Bookchin and Dave Foreman.*

In addition to his work as a teacher in New York during the 1960s, Bookchin taught at Goddard College during the 1970s and was professor of social theory in the School of Environmental Studies at Ramapo College in New Jersey from 1974 to 1983. He established and directed the Institute for Social Ecology in Plainfield, Vermont, in 1974. It offered advanced courses in ecophilosophy, social theories, and alternative technologies.

Bookchin retired from his political activity in 1990, and spent the next 16 years lecturing and writing. His writing during those years included the *Philosophy of Social Ecology* (1990, revised in 1994) and a four-volume history of popular revolutionary movements. Bookchin lived, with companion Janet Biehl, in Burlington, Vermont, until his death on July 30, 2006.

BIBLIOGRAPHY

Biehl, Janet, ed., *The Murray Bookchin Reader*, 1997; Biehl, Janet, "A Short Biography of Murray Bookchin," dwardmac.pitzer.edu/anarchist_archives/bookchin/bio1.html; DeLeon, David, ed., *Leaders from the 1960s: A Biographical Sourcebook of American Activism*, 1994; Martin, Douglas, "Murray Bookchin, 1921-2006," *New York Times*, 2006; Plant, Christopher, and Judith Plant, *Turtle Talk: Voices for a Sustainable Future*, 1990.

Boulding, Kenneth
(January 18, 1910–March 19, 1993)
Economist

Kenneth Boulding was an economist known for his integration of insights from many social sciences, humanities fields, and ecology into his analyses of the "social system," the organization and inner workings of society. He was an early voice for a new ethic for life on "Spaceship Earth," declaring in 1965 that in order to solve the problems of a growing population, a rapidly depleting supply of fossil fuels, and increasingly polluted air and water, humanity should redefine the planet as a "closed-cycle" system that has no sewer and upon which "unrestrained conflict" would no longer be viable.

Kenneth Ewart Boulding was born on January 18, 1910, in Liverpool, England. He grew up in what he characterized later as a slum—"really rather an exciting neighborhood"—and at the age of nine he began to publish a neighborhood newspaper, which he typed with several carbon copies and distributed to his friends. He was the first in his family to continue his formal education beyond elementary school; his father was a plumber by trade and a lay preacher in the Methodist church, and his mother had been a maid before having children. Boulding attended high school on scholarship and received another scholarship to study chemistry at New College, Oxford. He shifted his emphasis to politics, philosophy, and economics after his first year and graduated with honors in 1931. Shortly after graduation his first paper was accepted for publication by John Maynard Keynes's *Economic Journal*. This paper, which challenged the concept of displacement costs—accepted without question at that time by nearly all working economists—was bold and controversial and established Boulding as an important economist with fresh ideas and a cogent writing style.

In 1932, Boulding received a two-year Commonwealth Fellowship to study at the University of Chicago and Harvard University, where he got a first-hand view of the Great Depression. The United States exhilarated Boulding, in part because his working-class background did not subject him to discrimination, as it had in England.

After returning to England in 1934 and teaching at the University of Edinburgh until 1937, Boulding returned to the United States, this time permanently. His first post was at Colgate University, where he stayed until 1941, and after that, he spent time at Princeton University, Fisk University, Iowa State College, University of Michigan, Stanford, University of the West Indies in Jamaica, International Christian University in Tokyo, Japan, and finally, University of Colorado–Boulder, where he was hired in 1967 and stayed for the remainder of his career.

At each post, Boulding absorbed whatever he could from his colleagues—economists and other social scientists—and early in his career he began to realize that economics as a social science must integrate observations from other social science perspectives to become a more accurate science. He felt that sociology, anthropology, political science, and psychology (and even the humanities fields of philosophy and theology) each approached the social system from a particular vantage point but that the social system could only be understood completely through an integration of all of these approaches. Later, Boulding realized that biology too shed light on social systems and he advocated that research on biological ecosystems be taken into consideration when trying to understand the social system. For example, he drew a parallel between the ecological niches of an ecosystem (physical locations or survival strategies for various organisms) and the niches of an economic system (strategies human beings use to earn a living). Boulding believed that social systems evolved just as ecosystems did, with niches opening and being filled by opportunistic species. "Human artifacts" such as the automobile, for example, competed with horses and reduced the number of horses in the social system. These ideas were articulated in his 1978 book *Ecodynamics*.

At the same time that he urged economics to adopt some insights about the social system from ecology, he criticized one of ecology's sacred tenets, that of Darwin's principle of survival of the fittest. In *Ecodynamics*, he recommended restating this principle as "survival of the fitting… fitting being what fits into a niche in an ecosystem."

Boulding's intellect spanned many fields and he rejected the boundaries that more orthodox scholars had erected between fields. His 1956 book *The Image: Knowledge and Life in Society* suggested that human behavior was not dictated as much by immediate stimulus, as economists and other social scientists influenced by behaviorism generally believed, but rather that people used their consciousness to form images of the world that influenced how they behaved. In 1965, he presented a paper at Washington State University entitled "Earth as a Spaceship" that warned that increased knowledge about space and how tiny planet earth was in comparison to other possible worlds, along with an ever-expanding human population, would require society to change its practices and develop "symbiotic relationships of a closed-cycle character with all the other elements and populations of the world of ecological systems." He hoped that a new image of the planet's plight would allow society to realize that "unrestrained conflict" was no longer viable and that "in a spaceship there are no sewers." Although he admitted that "once we begin to look at earth as a space ship, the appalling extent of our ignorance about it is almost frightening," Boulding often expressed the hope that human intelligence would help society evolve to become more ecologically harmonious and peaceful.

Boulding received several prestigious awards for his work in economics, including the 1949 John Bates Clark medal, given biannually to an economist under the age of 40 who shows exceptional promise. He served as president of the American Economics Association in 1969, and in 1973–1974 presided over both the American Academy for the Advancement of Science and the International Studies Association. He is known as a forefather of a diverse group of publications and institutions, including the *Journal of Conflict Resolution*, International Society for General Systems Theory, Association for the Study of the Grants Economy, and the fields of evolutionary economics and ecological economics. In addition to his more than 1,000 scholarly publications, including 40 books, Boulding published several volumes of rhymed poetry.

Kenneth Boulding died on March 19, 1993, in Boulder, Colorado, after a long struggle with cancer. He was survived by his wife, Elise Boulding, and their five children.

BIBLIOGRAPHY

Boulding, Kenneth E., "My Life Philosophy," *American Economist*, 1985; Boulding, Kenneth E. and David McComb, *Oral History Interview of Kenneth Boulding*, 2005; Keyfitz, Nathan, "Kenneth Ewart Boulding", www.nap.edu/html/biomems/kboulding.html; Kerman, Cynthia Earl, *Creative Tension: the Life and Thought of Kenneth Boulding*, 1974; Latzko, David A., "Kenneth E. Boulding," *Proceedings of the American Philosophical Society*, 1995; Nasar, Sylvia, "Kenneth Boulding, an Economist, Philosopher, and Poet, Dies at 83," *New York Times*, 1993; Solo, Robert A., "Kenneth Ewart Boulding: 1910–1993. An Appreciation," *Journal of Economic Issues*, 1994.

Bramble, Barbara

(February 27, 1947–)
International Program Director and Vice-president of Strategic Programs Initiative at National Wildlife Federation

Barbara Bramble has played a leading role in ensuring that sustainable development be a central goal of environmentalists and developers domestically and abroad. Her efforts to link the goals of environmental protection with economic and social realities in domestic and international issues have been invaluable to the environmental movement.

Barbara Janet Bramble was born in Washington, D.C., on February 27, 1947, and spent much of her childhood in the nation's capital. Her parents, though from impoverished backgrounds, both worked their way through college to become economists and then joined Pres. FRANKLIN D. ROOSEVELT's New Deal administration in the 1930s. They took the family abroad to Latin America for several years at a time. The disparity between the standard of living of the rich and poor concerned Bramble and played a critical role in her decision to pursue a career as an environmental and social activist. Bramble's father, while a western pioneer at heart who built the family's home and loved urban subsistence gardening, was the U.S. economic counselor to embassies in Mexico, Venezuela, and the Dominican Republic. In Venezuela, at age nine, Bramble became aware of the oppressive reality of quality of life for the poor in developing countries. Later, as a teenager, Bramble lived in the Dominican Republic, a society yearning for democracy. In both countries, she observed deforestation, repression, miserable living conditions of the poor, and political revolution. At the same time that Bramble dealt with the reality of life in developing countries, she explored each country's unspoiled beauty with her family and learned first hand the value of natural environments. Her father, ahead of his time in the 1950s, suggested what is now called "ecotourism" as an option to resource extraction to provide jobs and increased income for indigenous people. The family once traveled to a jungle area of Venezuela where they stayed with an Indian tribe and delighted in the timeless landscape.

Bramble attended the University of the Americas in Mexico for her first year of college. She graduated with a B.A. in history from George Mason University in 1969. Inspired by colleagues involved in public interest law, Bramble attended George Washington University (GWU) Law School, and graduated with a J.D. in 1973. During Bramble's first fall in school, the law school expanded its environmental law program and provided the most extensive clinical program in the country at the time. Not only was the first Earth Day celebrated the spring before she began school, but GWU was in the middle of Washington, D.C., where the first environmental legislation was being passed. Bramble says environmental law fascinated her from the start, and she has never looked back.

After law school, Bramble worked as an environmental lawyer on domestic energy cases with a small firm, Wilson and Graham. While there, Bramble was introduced to the importance of linking economic viability of potential projects with environmental protection. Along with her partner, Ronald J. Wilson, she successfully stopped a gas pipeline from being built through the Arctic National Wildlife Refuge (ANWR) in Alaska and a hydro-electric "pumped storage" project in West Virginia. Bramble realized that touting the environmental value of ANWR and West Virginia's Canaan Valley would not have been sufficient to stop the projects. Instead, she brought in supply-and-demand economics to explain that the deals were not economically viable. Through litigation she held up the projects long enough to allow the financial backers to pull out of the projects. An important tactic in all of Bramble's work is to seek out the economic arguments for protecting the environment, which often prove the folly of imprudent development.

After working with Wilson and Graham, Bramble served as legal counsel to the Council on Environmental Quality (CEQ) from 1979 to 1981, in the Executive Office of the President, where she mediated environmental disputes among federal agencies and handled international legal matters for the Council. She also wrote the CEQ procedures directing federal agencies how to comply with National Environmental Policy Act regulations.

In 1982 Bramble moved to the National Wildlife Federation (NWF) to begin and direct an international program, a position she held for 16 years. NWF's International Program focuses on global environmental issues in which the U.S. government plays an influential role and in which NWF's large membership can impact government positions. Its goal is to encourage the U.S. government to make socially and environmentally responsible decisions, particularly to protect biological diversity. During Bramble's time as director, issues ranged from reducing the export of pesticides banned in the United States to supporting increased U.S. contributions for international family planning to reforming international trade rules. She cofounded the worldwide citizens campaign to reform the World Bank and other multilateral development banks and advanced the campaign's evolution from simplistic reforms within the World Bank (such as pushing for Bank-funded projects to have environmental impact assessments) to more complex goals (such as the involvement of local, and particularly minority, people in development decisions). Bramble's strategy was to explain the real-life damages to both people and ecosystems in developing countries and to argue that large-scale government-supported development is not necessarily the best option. For example, she helped form alliances between U.S. environmental groups and Brazilian nongovernmental organizations (NGOs), the National Council of Rubbertappers and its founder, Chico Mendes, and several indigenous tribal leaders. Together, they provided evidence of the value of "extractive reserves" (preserved forests where local people may harvest nontimber resources, such as rubber and Brazil nuts) over government projects (such as dams, mines, and inappropriate agriculture) that would lead to the destruction of tropical forests. As a result, millions of acres of extractive reserves are conserving a significant fraction of the Amazon rain forest.

In the 1980s, when many developing countries faced enormous debt, Bramble was an architect of the concept of "debt for nature" swaps that are carried out by groups such as The Nature Conservancy and World Wildlife Fund. The successful concept has spread to dozens of countries; its benefits include debt relief and increased funding of sustainable development projects.

Bramble worked effectively with other NGOs as well as with local people, political leaders, and international development banks. As an elected member to the steering committee for the International NGO Forum at the 1992 Earth Summit in Rio, Bramble helped organize 3,200 NGO representatives—the largest conference of NGOs at that enormous event. The conference produced alternative NGO "treaties" that many called the most concrete outcome of the United Nations Conference on the Environment and Development (UNCED). Through the UNCED process, members of NGOs recognized that environmental democracy and finding economic solutions to development issues challenged all countries, rich and poor. In fact, Bramble and other NGO participants from industrialized countries took lessons from international development dilemmas and returned home to make sustainable development a focal point in Europe and North America. In the United States, NWF helped push through the formation of the President's Council on Sustainable Development. NWF now has programs in urban areas to advocate smart growth, restoring center city cores, greenbelts, and urban wildlife habitat as a strategy for conserving biological diversity. The experiences of the International Program are benefiting Americans at home.

After UNCED, in 1992, Bramble worked with Friends of the Earth and the Sierra Club to form the Global Forest Policy Project, which soon resulted in the formation of the Forest Stewardship Council (FSC). From the beginning, Bramble helped ensure the success of the FSC's efforts to set principles and standards for sustainable forest management. She has worked with the different interests involved to make sure that the environmental arm was represented and that environmentalists understood the challenges faced by the other two interests—industry and the "social chamber" (i.e. the public relations or marketing arm). In 2006 Bramble was elected Chair of the Board of U.S. Board of Directors of FSC.

After 16 years as the director of the International Program, Bramble became a Senior Program Advisor in International Affairs at the NWF. Her position allows her to bring the concepts of sustainable development from the International Program into NWF's domestic agenda. Specifically, she has run a project through which the NWF collaborates with Mexican environmental groups and trains them in advocacy techniques, and she has promoted the environmental benefits of shade-grown coffee and pesticide-free flowers, among other sustainably-grown international products.

Bramble lives in Washington, D.C.

BIBLIOGRAPHY

Bramble, Barbara, "Financial Resources for the Transition to Sustainable Development," in *The Way Forward: Beyond Agenda 21*, Felix Dodds, ed., 1997; Bramble, Barbara, "Non-Governmental Organizations and the Making of U.S. International Environmental Policy," in *The International Politics of the Environment*, Andrew Hurrell and Benedict Kingsbury, eds.,

1992; Bramble, Barbara, "Swapping Debt for Nature?" *Hemisphere*, 1998; "Buyer Be Fair—The Promise of Product Certification," www.buyerbefair.org/interview_bramble.html"; "Forest Stewardship Council," www.fscus.org; "National Wildlife Federation," www.nwf.org.

Brand, Stewart

(December 14, 1938–)
Publisher, Editor, Technology Consultant

Stewart Brand, author, publisher, business consultant, and proponent of computers and communications technology, shaped the counterculture environmental movement in the late 1960s with the publication of his *Whole Earth Catalog: Access to Tools and Ideas* (1968 to 1971). This highly original catalog empowered the country with information—presenting books, tools, and advice on community, self-reliance, and ecological living. Following the catalog, Brand published the magazine *Co-Evolution Quarterly*, which later evolved into *Whole Earth Review* (now known as *Whole Earth*), continuing his mission to educate people about the power of ideas and the importance of putting the right tools in the right hands. Dismissing the commonly held concept that advancements in technology must be at odds with conservation, Brand believes that computer technology has the potential to create innovative and efficient solutions to many environmental problems.

Stewart Brand was born on December 14, 1938, in Rockford, Illinois, to Arthur Barnard and Julia (Morley) Brand. From early childhood Brand was driven by an insatiable curiosity and restlessness that would stimulate all his future endeavors. At the age of 16 he borrowed his parents' car so that he and his high school friends could leave Rockford and head to California to pan for gold. He cultivated quirkiness and began wearing a beret, to the chagrin of his father and to the amusement of his somewhat offbeat mother. Yet he possessed a conservative streak as well, and from 1954 to 1956 he went to high school at Phillips Exeter Academy, a boarding prep school. He then attended Stanford University and received his B.S. in biology there in 1960. He also studied design and photography at San Francisco Art Institute College and San Francisco State College (now University). On completing his studies, he served in the United States Army from 1960 to 1962, teaching basic infantry training and working as a photojournalist out of the Pentagon. During these years Brand began getting involved in the performance art scene in New York, and when his Army stint ended he moved to San Francisco and became a multimedia performance artist. He was the founding artist of the performance piece "America Needs Indians," in which he performed until 1966. In the meantime, he had joined up with novelist Ken Kesey's band of Merry Pranksters in 1964 and went along on the psychedelic bus journey chronicled in Tom Wolfe's *The Electric Kool-Aid Acid Test* (1968). In December 1966, he and Lois Jennings were married (the marriage ended in divorce in 1976).

Brand's interest in technology and its tools began infiltrating his work, and he was especially intrigued by the possible connections between ecology and technology. During his travels he had conceived and sold buttons that read "Why haven't we seen a photograph of the whole Earth yet?" Eventually NASA did succeed in producing a photograph of the world during the Apollo program in 1969, and

Brand contends that this helped to create an awareness of the global environment and that it was no accident that the first Earth Day came one year later. His preoccupation with the earth, information, and using appropriate tools led to the creation of one of his most famous endeavors, *The Whole Earth Catalog*, which was first published in 1968. The catalog, which swiftly became a mainstream hit, was a wide-ranging guide to tools and books, providing unorthodox advice and philosophical commentary on returning to nature and being self-reliant. It promoted select high-tech items—such as computers, ham radios, and solar electric systems—as well as low-tech approaches—such as hand grain-grinders, adobe buildings, and organic gardening. The book became the bible of the counterculture and spawned a trend toward more earth-friendly thinking. It was updated continually and issued for three years, and in 1972 its final edition, *The Last Whole Earth Catalog*, won a National Book Award.

In 1972 Brand founded the nonprofit Point Foundation to run activities related to the catalog and other subsequent Whole Earth projects. During its first few years it gave away $1 million to various ecology groups. Following the success of *The Whole Earth Catalog*, Brand went on to write other titles concerning topics such as environmental restoration and communication technologies. Then in 1974 he started a new periodical titled *Co-Evolution Quarterly*, a practical magazine that encouraged social change and new ideas. It introduced concepts such as the Gaia hypothesis and watershed consciousness and continued where *The Last Whole Earth Catalog* left off by providing book and tool reviews and promoting access to information. Also in 1974, Brand published *Two Cybernetic Frontiers*, a book on new trends in computer science, and the first ever to use the term *personal computer*. Along with his writing and editing at the magazine, Brand served as special adviser to California governor Jerry Brown for two years, until 1979, and continued exploring communications technology and the use of the computer as a personal tool. In 1984 he helped found the WELL (Whole Earth 'Lectronic Link), an experimental computer networking system that became a pioneer of electronic discussion and now has over 11,000 active users worldwide.

In 1985 *CoEvolution Quarterly* changed its name to *Whole Earth Review* and in the years since has hosted discourse on such topics as cyberspace, community building, and ecosystem restoration. Over the next few years, Brand also worked as a business consultant for Royal Dutch/Shell Group, an oil giant that wanted Brand to help them strategize ways to stay up to date and competitive. Brand's technological knowledge and his ability to think outside of the box made this endeavor particularly successful, and in 1988 he helped found the Global Business Network (GBN), a management consulting firm that explores strategic development and global futures for large institutions. GBN's client list has since swelled to 90 multinational corporations, including Xerox, IBM, Monsanto, Disney/ABC, and Texaco.

Since GBN was started, most of Brand's time is devoted to his consulting work. His perspective on the global environment has evolved since the years of *The Whole Earth Catalog*. Immersed in the world of technology, Brand sees computer hackers as the new grassroots contingent. He senses that the environmental movement these days has an antitechnology bias, which he condemns, saying that computer and communications technology can help lighten the load on the environment and increase efficiency—through telecommuting, for example.

As the new millennium approached, Brand and a few colleagues established The Long Now Foundation as the seed of a very long-term cultural foundation, one that would foster long-term thinking and responsibility. The Long Now Foundation—named by Board member and artist Brian Eno—initially supported two projects: the invention of the world's largest and slowest mechanical clock which inventor Danny Hillis envisioned as a monument to long-term thinking; and the Rosetta Project, an on-line archive of all documented human languages. A prototype of the clock was completed by Hillis just in time for New Year's Eve, 1999. It is now on exhibit at the London Science Museum. Brand wrote a book about the clock project called *The Clock of the Long Now: Time and Responsibility* (1999).

Brand and his second wife, Patricia, a software agent and director of a medical resource center, live in a renovated 83-year-old tugboat docked on the waterfront in Sausalito, California. Brand currently spends about half his time working with GBN and half with Long Now.

BIBLIOGRAPHY

Betts, Kellyn S., "Stewart Brand: Whole Earth Vision for the 21st Century," *E*, 1996; Kleiner, Art, and Stewart Brand, eds., *Ten Years of CoEvolution Quarterly: News That Stayed News*, 1986; "The Long Now Foundation," www.longnow.org; "Stewart Brand," .sb.longnow.org; Stipp, David, "Stewart Brand: The Electric Kool-Aid Management Consultant," *Fortune*, 1995; Sussman, Vic, "A Born-Again Whole Earth Catalog: Looking toward the Millennium, The Editors Show How New Technologies Can Perk Folks Up," *U.S. News & World Report*, 1994; Turner, Fred, *From Counterculture to Cyberculture: Stewart Brand, the Whole Earth Network, and the rise of Digital Utopianism*, 2006.

Brandborg, Stewart

(February 2, 1925–)
Conservation Activist, Executive Director of the Wilderness Society

Stewart Brandborg was a key player in assuring the passage of the Wilderness Act in 1964 and devoted the next 12 years, during which he served as executive director of the Wilderness Society (TWS), to the expansion of the newly established National Wilderness Preservation System. Through Brandborg's efforts, millions of acres of wilderness were added to the National Wilderness Preservation System, and more than 100 million acres in Alaska were preserved in the National Park, National Forest, Wildlife Refuge, and Wilderness systems. Brandborg's specialty was in training concerned citizens to become environmental activists and participate in the designation process. Over the years, hundreds of grassroots leaders attended the training seminars that he designed and oversaw.

Stewart Monroe Brandborg was born in Lewiston, Idaho, on February 2, 1925, son of Edna Stevenson Brandborg and Guy Mathew Brandborg. His father, who spent his entire forty-year career with the U.S. Forest Service (USFS), was supervisor of the Bitterroot National Forest for 20 years. As a strong wilderness advocate, he passed down to his son a love of nature and commitment to responsible stewardship. It was through his father that Brandborg as a young man had known GIFFORD PINCHOT, founder of the USFS, and ROBERT MARSHALL, pioneer wilderness advocate and founder of the Wilderness Society. Starting at the age of 17, Stewart Brandborg worked seasonally in various national forests throughout Montana, Idaho, and Oregon, on range and forest surveys, trail maintenance, and as a lookout fireman. By 1944, when he was 19 years old, he had risen through the ranks to train other lookout firemen in fire suppression. Brandborg graduated from the University of Montana in 1948 with a B.S. in

Stewart Brandborg (Photograph courtesy of Becky Brandborg)

wildlife technology; in 1951 he earned his M.S. in wildlife management from the University of Idaho.

As a research fellow for the Idaho Cooperative Wildlife Research Unit at the University of Idaho, Brandborg completed seven years of field research on the life history of the mountain goat and wrote the first (and thus far only) monograph about this species. He performed population, range, and management studies of other major big game species of the region for the Montana and Idaho Departments of Fish and Game from 1947 to 1954.

Brandborg left the Northern Rockies for Washington, D.C., in 1954, when he was appointed assistant conservation director of the National Wildlife Federation (NWF). With a background in public lands and wildlife ecology, his duties included planning and overseeing conservation education programs and editing NWF's weekly "Conservation Report," a digest of all the legislation on natural resource and conservation issues before the U.S. Congress. It was with NWF that he developed many useful skills; for example public interest advocacy—lobbying and testifying before Congress on behalf of wildlife, public lands, and a broad range of environmental issues—and mobilizing conservationists throughout the nation in support of these measures.

In 1956, TWS elected him to its council, where he worked closely with TWS director HOWARD ZANHISER on an issue of concern to both TWS and NWF. The Wilderness Bill, drafted by Zanhiser in 1956, was the first legislation to propose a system to designate federally owned wild lands as wilderness, giving them protection within a National Wilderness Preservation System. TWS offered Brandborg the position as director of special projects in 1960. He was the closest collaborator with Zanhiser in gaining passage of the Wilderness Bill. When Zanhiser died suddenly in May 1964, Brandborg was appointed to succeed him as executive director. He escorted the Wilderness Bill through its last crucial steps in Congress and final passage in September 1964.

The Wilderness Act initially provided for the protection of some nine million acres of wilderness. Conservationists set what was then the ambitious goal of adding at least 50 million more acres of wilderness to the system, and TWS, under Brandborg's leadership, worked hard to achieve this. One of the stipulations of the Wilderness Act was that, for each proposed new wilderness area, there would be a public hearing and review by the wilderness agencies and Congress. Drawing on his experience with Congress and with local and state environmental groups and leaders, Brandborg initiated training programs for citizen activists. These programs taught them to carry out field studies of the areas in question, work with the agencies charged with managing the areas, testify effectively, and carry out grassroots publicity campaigns to congressional designation of the areas. TWS brought selected state activist leaders to Washington for week-long seminars on how Congress and government agencies work, while providing assistance and advice for formation and funding of local groups. Between 1964 and 1974, 150 new areas in 40 states were reviewed for protection under the Wilderness Act. A total of more than 103 million acres have now been designated as wilderness in Alaska and in the lower 48 states, many of them as a result of the dedication of TWS-trained volunteers.

While with TWS, Brandborg made other notable contributions to preservation of wilderness and the nation's public lands as well. He led a legal fight against the Trans-Alaska Pipeline, which was found by the courts to violate the 1969 National Environmental Policy Act (NEPA). This landmark, precedent-setting case strengthened the environmental impact assessment procedures of NEPA. Brandborg also directed a two-year lobbying campaign that eventually resulted in the designation of more than 100 million acres of public lands in Alaska as wilderness, national parks, and wildlife refuges. He enlisted Congressman

John P. Saylor of Pennsylvania (the original House of Representatives sponsor of the Wilderness Act) in sponsorship of the Wild and Scenic Rivers Act, drafted by JOHN AND FRANK CRAIGHEAD. This measure, with TWS's support, was enacted in 1968, establishing the National System of Wild and Scenic Rivers.

Brandborg worked on other environmental issues in addition to wilderness preservation. Prior to the first Earth Day in April 1970, he gave strong backing to Earth Day organizers, providing start-up funding for the celebration. From 1971 to 1975, he served as cochair of the Urban Environmental Conference, one of the nation's first groups to focus on the joint concerns of environmentalists, urban reform groups, and organized labor. Members of its board included senior staff of such national organizations as TWS, United Auto Workers, and the National Urban League. The issues it addressed in its congressional lobbying work included lead poisoning, occupational health, clean air and water, energy conservation, urban transit, and land use planning.

When Brandborg left TWS in 1976—he was dismissed by the governing council, some of whose members believed that he had devoted too much time to wilderness preservation in Alaska—the organization's membership had grown to 130,000, five times larger than when he had become executive director 12 years earlier. The organization's budget was $1.8 million per year, and there was a full-time staff of 43, plus 12 part-time regional organizers. Environmental movement historian MARK DOWIE called Brandborg a "committed warrior" and "the last true activist to lead" TWS. TWS honored Brandborg in 2000 with its highest honor, the Robert Marshall Award, which in other years has been given to such environmental luminaries as MARDY MURIE, WALLACE STEGNER, DAVID BROWER, JOHN H. ADAMS, and TERRY TEMPEST WILLIAMS.

Brandborg spent the remainder of the 1970s working for the government, first as special assistant to the assistant secretary of the interior and later as special assistant to the director of the National Park Service. In these posts he worked with parks personnel, teaching them how to work more effectively with citizen activists in building support for the National Park System. From 1982 to 1986, he was the national coordinator of the Regional Environment Leadership Conference Series, a collaboration of the ten largest national environmental organizations. This was a series of nine regional activist training seminars for environmentalists and representatives of labor, ethnic minorities', women's, and urban groups.

In 1986, Brandborg moved back to western Montana's Bitterroot Valley, where he quickly became involved in public land and other environmental issues in the Northern Rockies. He was founder and president of Friends of the Bitterroot from 1988 to 1990 and serves on the boards of Wilderness Watch and several state and regional environmental groups. Long active in land planning, he is currently president of Bitterrooters for Planning, working to develop a growth plan in his home valley. He lives near Darby, a small town in western Montana, with Anna Vee, his wife of more than 50 years. They have five grown children.

BIBLIOGRAPHY

Dowie, Mark, *Losing Ground: American Environmentalism at the Close of the Twentieth Century*, 1995; Frome, Michael, "Stewart M. Brandborg: Wilderness Champion," *Wilderness Watch*, 1999; Stroud, Richard, ed., *National Leaders of American Conservation*, 1985.

Bresette, Walt

(July 4, 1947–February 21, 1999)
Native American Treaty Rights and Environmental Activist

Walt Bresette led grassroots Native American treaty rights and environmental movements in the Lake Superior region during the 1980s and 1990s. He defended the Lake Superior Chippewa people's treaty rights to harvest fish, game, and plants from public lands and fought successfully for a moratorium on mining in the state of Wisconsin. He was known for his skill in empowering activists and for unifying Native and nonnative people committed to environmental justice. One of his last efforts was to author and promote a visionary Seventh Generation or Common Property constitutional amendment proposal, which would force lawmakers to think seven generations into the future when making decisions about common property such as water, air, and public lands.

Walter Albert Bresette was born on July 4, 1947, in Reserve, Wisconsin, to Henry and Blanche Bresette. His father was a lumberjack and gardener; his mother raised seven sons. The family lived on the Red Cliff reservation, located on the southern shore of Lake Superior. Blanche Bresette's sister, Victoria Gokee, was one of the first female tribal chairs in the United States, and she recruited young Walt and his brothers and cousins to help research issues affecting the Red Cliff Band of the Lake Superior Chippewa. As a teenager, Bresette and his cousins held their first nonviolent environmental protest and succeeded in stopping loggers from illegally cutting a pine grove on Madeline Island, a sacred place for the Lake Superior Chippewa.

Bresette was drafted by the United States Army in 1964 and served four years as a noncombatant with an electronic intelligence unit, mostly in Japan. When he returned in 1968, he received a Bureau of Indian Affairs grant to study advertising art in Chicago. Bresette became a graphic artist, working freelance during the 1970s in Madison and Red Cliff. From 1978 to 1980, Bresette served as a public information officer of the Great Lakes Intertribal Council, a statewide organization that provides social and economic services to ten Indian tribes in Wisconsin. In an attempt to unify scattered Chippewa (who also call themselves by their own names: Anishinaabe or Ojibwe), Bresette organized an event to commemorate the 125th anniversary of the final treaty that the Chippewa had signed with the U.S. government. The three treaties that the Chippewas signed under pressure during the mid-nineteenth century ceded their rich territory in what is now Wisconsin, Michigan, and Minnesota to the U.S. government. The Chippewa people agreed to live on several reservations, including the six that dot northern Wisconsin. The 1979 treaty commemoration held in Red Cliff and Madeline Island was the first of its kind; it celebrated tribal history, language, and culture. Bresette and the Chippewa attendees hoped that it would mark the beginning of a reunification of the Chippewa.

In 1982, Bresette became news and public affairs director at the northwestern Wisconsin WOJB public radio station. As he was preparing for his nightly news broadcast on January 25, 1983, a story came over the wire that Lake Superior Chippewa Indians had just been granted "unlimited hunting and fishing rights" by a panel of three federal judges. The so-called Voigt decision, named after Lester Voigt, head of the Wisconsin Department of Natural Resources (WDNR), came after a nine-year legal battle by Chippewa spearfishers to reaffirm their treaty rights to hunt and fish on treaty-ceded territory. Bresette was outraged at the report; he knew that the spearfishers neither desired to nor would be able to fish to an "unlimited" extent. Soon, a virulent antispearfishing, anti-Indian movement emerged in northern Wisconsin.

Spearfishing for walleyed pike is traditionally done at night during the spring. When native spearfishers set their boats out in northern Wisconsin's small lakes after the Voigt decision, they were harassed by mobs of racist white sportsmen who sometimes physically endangered the Indians by rocking their boats, blinding them with spotlights, or threatening to shoot them. Bresette later recalled that "the only people fishing in Northern Wisconsin during that time were those willing to risk their lives."

In an attempt to protect spearfishers, Bresette appealed to a statewide network of environmentalists, civil rights and church activists, and concerned citizens from throughout Wisconsin to come to the boat landings in the spring as peaceful observers. This "witness" provided important support as the antispearfishing protests grew larger and the protesters more violent. The Native-nonnative collaboration that Bresette nurtured during the worst years of spearfishing protests has become a model for nonnatives doing solidarity work with Native peoples. It is described in *Walleye Warriors*, which Bresette coauthored with Green activist Rick Whaley.

Bresette himself became a protagonist in the definitions of treaty rights. As an artisan, Bresette earned a living by making and selling dream catchers containing bird feathers, some of them from migratory birds. This was illegal under the Migratory Bird Act. He and fellow artisan, Chippewa elder Esther Nahgahnub, were arrested in 1989. "Feathergate," as it came to be called, yielded a landmark decision on Chippewa harvesting rights. In 1991, a U.S. District Court ruled that Bresette and Nahgahnub were not causing severe impact on endangered migratory bird populations with their activity and that, furthermore, feather gathering on treaty-ceded land was allowed under Chippewa treaty rights.

After the spearfishing problems subsided, Bresette turned his attention to other serious environmental problems in northern Wisconsin. In 1990, he cofounded Anishinaabe Niijii, an Ojibwe mining watchdog group. Throughout the 1990s, Bresette led and participated in grassroots protests against northern Wisconsin's copper mines, adding his signature charisma and humor to them. One story often retold is of a protest at the Ladysmith open pit copper mine site in 1992, during which he scaled a fence, jumped into the site holding a war club that had once belonged to Sauk and Fox war chief Black Hawk, and "counted coup" (symbolically claiming victory over enemies) on a giant bulldozer. Bresette participated in a 28-day encampment in 1996 with the Bad River Ogitchida (Anishinaabe word for "Protectors of the People") on the Wisconsin Central Railroad tracks. They blocked a train carrying 64,000 gallons of sulfuric acid to be mixed with water and poured into the tunnels of a copper mine at White Pine, Michigan, only five miles from Lake Superior. Bresette had been a member of the Environmental Justice Committee of the Environmental Protection Agency (EPA) but had quit when the EPA approved this project without a hearing or clean-up plan. The EPA did do another review of the project, but while it was in process, the mining company withdrew its project. In 1998, thanks in part to efforts of Anishinaabe Niijii, the Wisconsin legislature passed a moratorium on mining in the state.

Convinced that the government should be obligated to protect common property at least to the same extent that it protects private property, Bresette authored the Common Property or Seventh Generation constitutional amendment, which would require lawmakers to think seven generations (or 150 years) ahead when considering laws that pertained to public lands, air, and water. During the summer of 1998, Bresette led a month-long walk from Red Cliff to Madison to promote the amendment.

Bresette received many awards for his activism, including the Eagle Feather Award from the Red Cliff Cultural Institute in 1985, the Wisconsin Labor Farm Party's Antinuclear Waste Organizing award in 1986, and the Progressive Social Change Award in 1987 from the Wisconsin Community Fund. *Walleye*

Warriors received the Council for Wisconsin Writers book-length nonfiction award in 1993. Bresette worked on the All My Relations public radio project, which included conversations with people from Canada and the United States on the value of life and land, and appeared in the film "Wisconsin Powwow." He cofounded and served on the boards of directors of many organizations, including the Indigenous Environmental Network; the Midwest Treaty Network; Project Underground; the Anishinaabeg Millennium Project, which reclaims and redefines a vision for the future of the Anishinaabe nation; and many more.

Bresette died of a heart attack in Duluth, on February 21, 1999, while visiting friends. He left four children, Nicholas, Claudia, Katy, and Robin.

Bibliography

Brain-Box Digital Archives, *Maawanji'iding: Ojibwe Histories and Narratives from Wisconsin* (multimedia CD), 1999; Bresette, Walt, "'We Are All Mohawks,'" *Green Letter*, 1990; Bullard, Robert and Maxine Waters, eds., *The Quest for Environmental Justice: Human Rights and the Politics of Pollution*, 2005; Gedicks, Al, *The New Resource Wars, Native and Environmental Struggles against Multinational Corporations*, 1993; Whaley, Rick, and Walt Bresette, *Walleye Warriors: The Chippewa Treaty Rights Story*, 1999.

Brower, David

(July 1, 1912– November 5, 2000)
Director of the Sierra Club, Founder of Friends of the Earth, League of Conservation Voters, and Earth Island Institute

David Brower, proclaimed "archdruid" of conservation by his biographer, JOHN MCPHEE, was perhaps the most famous environmentalist of the twentieth-century United States. An intrepid mountaineer credited with over 70 first ascents, Brower headed several of the country's most effective environmental groups. He directed the Sierra Club from 1952 to 1969, transforming it from a group of 2,000 mountaineers to a powerful political lobby representing 77,000 members, and then went on to found several more environmental groups, including the John Muir Institute, Friends of the Earth (FOE), the League of Conservation Voters, and Earth Island Institute. Brower can be credited for keeping Dinosaur National Monument and the Grand Canyon free of dams and for helping establish Kings Canyon, North Cascades, and Redwood National Parks, as well as the Point Reyes National Seashore. His credo is now inscribed on the National Aquarium in Washington, D.C.: "We do not inherit the Earth from our fathers, we are borrowing it from our children."

David Ross Brower was born in Berkeley, California, on July 1, 1912. His parents took their four children on frequent trips to Lake Tahoe and on hikes in Berkeley's hilly backdrop. As a child, Brower once broke open a chrysallis and discovered that the wings of the butterfly inside had not yet developed. Immediately he realized that his interference in its life cycle had doomed it, and this revelation transformed him into a conservationist. Brower began studying forestry and biology at the University of California at Berkeley in 1929 but dropped out during his sophomore year in 1931. In a 1994 interview, Brower claimed that his later success was due to this early escape from academia. "I hadn't been educated to know what you couldn't do," he

David Brower (AP Images)

told *Progressive* writer David Kupfer. After quitting school, Brower worked as a clerk at a candy company during the year and spent all his free time in Califonia's Sierra Nevada.

In 1933, Brower joined the Sierra Club and in 1935 published his first article in the Sierra Club *Bulletin*. Brower joined Sierra Club activists on a campaign to have Kings Canyon signed into the National Park System in 1940. He produced a publicity film about Kings Canyon and worked with the Sierra Club Press to publish ANSEL ADAMS's book *The Sierra Nevada: The John Muir Trail*. With this publications experience, Brower took a job as an editor at the University of California Press. He met his wife, editor Anne Hus, at the Press and married her in 1943. Their marriage was life-long and together they had four children.

When World War II broke out, Brower enlisted in the 10th Mountain Division and taught U.S. troops mountaineering skills in the Italian Apennines. His commitment to conservation was reinforced after witnessing the war's environmental devastation of that scenic area.

Brower returned home after the war to become a vocal protagonist in several conservation struggles, including a drive against logging in Olympic National Park and a controversial plan to build roads through Kings Canyon. The Sierra Club was divided on the latter issue: some members felt that accessibility to the beauty of Kings Canyon should not be a privilege of only those fit enough to hike in while others believed that more roads through Kings Canyon would lead to overuse. Brower's side, against road construction, prevailed. He was chosen in 1952 to serve as executive director of the Sierra Club, because club members were realizing that political action would become increasingly necessary to save the natural wonders of the West.

Brower's first major political fight, in which he successfully convinced the federal government to scrap a dam project in Dinosaur National Monument in exchange for a promise not to oppose a dam at Glen Canyon, is one that has marked his work ever since. He favored the Glen Canyon dam simply because Dinosaur was so beautiful and he had never seen Glen Canyon. But later, once he visited Glen Canyon, he was convinced he had made a terrible mistake. After that he decried compromise, and near the end of his life joined a coalition lobbying for the destruction of Glen Canyon dam.

Working together with HOWARD ZAHNISER of the Wilderness Society, Brower's Sierra Club was instrumental in the passage of the 1964 Wilderness Act, which designated nine million acres of wild country in the United States as unexploitable wilderness. During the mid-1960s, Brower coordinated publicity campaigns to keep dams out of the Grand Canyon. His full-page newspaper ads, designed by JERRY MANDER's ad agency Freeman, Mander, and Gossage, were sufficiently political that the Sierra Club lost its tax-exempt status. This angered more conservative elements of the Sierra Club, who deposed Brower in 1969 after a bitter internal struggle over the siting of a California nuclear power plant. The PG&E power company intended to build its plant in the coastal Nipomo Dunes area. Since this was an ecologically rich site, the club's board of directors negotiated with PG&E for an alternative site. If PG&E would make Nipomo Dunes available for purchase as a state park, the Sierra Club would not protest the siting at the Diablo Canyon area. Brower reared at this compromise, similar to the compromise he considered the most serious mistake he had ever made. He published a "half-bulletin" about the controversy, including only his own opinion since the opposition did not submit its opinion in time for publication. A major conflict erupted, and Brower was ousted as director.

In 1968, Brower founded the John Muir Institute, which promoted environmental research and education, and in 1969 he founded the lobbying group Friends of the Earth along with its partner organization, the League of Conservation Voters. Brower served as president of FOE for 10 years, before founding Earth Island Institute in 1982. Earth Island Institute provides institutional support and networking for some 30 projects that focus on environmental and social problems throughout the world. Certain projects, such as the Rainforest Action Network and Urban Habitat, have bloomed into independent organizations.

Brower wrote a two-volume autobiography and wrote or edited dozens of volumes on the nation's wild places. His last book, cowritten with Steve Chapple, *Let the Mountains Talk, Let the Rivers Run* (1995), calls for emergency CPR therapy for a stricken earth: Conservation, Preservation, and Restoration in massive doses. Among Brower's and Chapple's prescriptions were to limit development and ring cities with green belts, link protected areas with wildlife corridors and expand them with buffer zones, and use alternative natural resources (for example, expand the production of electric cars, develop more ways to cook with solar energy, and use tree-free paper such as kenaf paper for publishing—the book was printed on this paper, as is *Earth Island Journal*).

Brower received many conservation and publications awards during his life, including three nominations for the Nobel Peace Prize. He died on November 5, 2000. The Earth Island Institute maintains the Brower Legacy, which includes annual Brower Youth Awards for effective leaders between the ages of 13 and 22 years old, the Brower Center, a green-built four-story, 50,000-square-foot home for environmental groups in Berkeley, and the Brower Legacy Campaign, which provides small grants for environmental initiatives.

BIBLIOGRAPHY

Brower, David, *For Earth's Sake, the Life and Times of David Brower*, 1990; Brower, David, *Visions of the Environmental Movement*, 1993; Brower, David, *Work in Progress*, 1991; "Browerweb," www.earthisland.org/brower/index.cfm; McPhee, John, *Encounters with the Archdruid*, 1971; Scarce, Rick, *Eco-warriors: Understanding the Radical Environmental Movement*, 1990; Strong, Douglas H., *Dreamers & Defenders: American Conservationists*, 1988.

Brown, Janet

(September 20, 1931–)
Director of Environmental Defense Fund, Political Scientist

Director of the Environmental Defense Fund (EDF) from 1979 to 1984, Janet Welsh Brown is an environmental policy advocate and expert on global environmental politics. She is the coauthor of two important books on global politics: *Bordering on Trouble* (1986), with Andrew Maguire, and *Global Environmental Politics* (1996), with Gareth Porter. She has served in a number of executive positions in policy and political organizations and continues to be an influential voice in Washington, D.C., environmental circles.

Janet Welsh Brown was born on September 20, 1931, in Albany, New York. She attended Smith College, earning a B.A. in government in 1953. She received an M.A. in 1955 from Yale University in Southeast Asian studies and a Ph.D. in international relations from American University in 1964. She taught at Sarah Lawrence College from 1956 to 1958, at Howard University from 1964 to 1968, and at the University of the District of Columbia from 1968 to 1973. In 1973 Brown became director of the Office of Opportunities in Science for the American Association for the Advancement of Science, where she developed a program to increase opportunities in the natural and social sciences for women, minorities, and the physically handicapped. She also served as president of the Federation of Organizations for Professional Women. From 1975 to 1976, she was president of the Scientific Manpower Commission. During this period Brown earned a reputation as an expert on science education. She served as consultant to the National Science Foundation, the Department of Health and Human Services, and other federal agencies.

In 1979, Brown was hired as executive director of the EDF. She inherited the organization during a period of antienvironmental backlash. The energy crisis of the 1970s had led to high inflation and economic recession, and environmental regulation became a scapegoat for the economic crisis. In her first message as director in EDF's annual report, she emphasized the importance of the energy crunch: "All of us, in 1979, have felt the powerful pressures of inflation and the drive to develop new energy sources, however dangerous." Ronald Reagan's election in 1980 accelerated the fear of environmental rollbacks. EDF was preoccupied with protecting the Clean Air Act, the Marine Mammal Protection Act, the Clean Water Act, and other landmark legislation under threat of repeal by the Reagan administration. It was in this atmosphere that the "Group of Ten" environmental leaders first met at the Iron Grill in Washington, D.C., in January 1981, in an effort to combine forces to face attacks on established environmental policy. Brown was at that meeting, representing EDF. The organization developed into one of a new breed of professional, staff-based environmental agencies, distinct from and sometimes opposed to grassroots, activist-based groups. Brown's leadership took this professional, corporate mode. Brown celebrated the teams of scientists and lawyers who did much of EDF's work. These experts were consulted by elected officials, policy makers, and the media, and Brown nurtured the image of a knowledgeable, professional staff. During Brown's tenure as director, EDF focused broadly on energy, toxic chemicals, water resources, and wildlife issues, using both research and litigation to bring about policy changes. Brown also emphasized the importance of economics in formulating sound environmental policy, saying in her 1982 annual message to members, "EDF understands what the President doesn't—that good environmental practices are good business, and that there are at least as many jobs in caring for the environment as in destroying it." Brown resigned from EDF in 1984.

In 1985 Brown became a senior associate of the World Resources Institute, an organization devoted to research about global resources and environmental politics. As a research fellow Brown authored several studies of global environmental politics. *Bordering on Trouble: Resources and Politics in Latin America*, an anthology of essays by economic and political analysts coedited with Andrew Maguire, was published in the midst of the 1980s crises in Nicaragua and El Salvador. The authors of the essays attempt to shift debates about Latin America away from the old paradigm of "communist" versus the "free world" to an understanding of the way resource management and distribution shape political change. In their introduction to the collection, Brown and Maguire outline four major themes running through the essays: longstanding U.S. involvement in resource exploitation in Latin America, closeness of cultural ties between the United States and Latin America, damaging effects of U.S. support of repressive Latin American regimes, and the tendency of U.S. policy to focus on short-term economic and security interests rather than the long-term health of the economy and environment at home and abroad. *Global Environmental Politics* looks at the state of environmental politics across the world. Brown and Porter describe major trends in environmental policy, important actors in the arena (from governments and international state organizations to nongovernmental organizations and corporations), a broad array of case studies, and the politics of international development. The book serves as a primer to the current state of global environmental politics and is often used as such in college classrooms.

Brown has published a number of other works, including *In the U.S. Interest: Resources, Growth, and Security in the Developing World* (1990). *Global Environmental Politics*, which is frequently updated, continues to be a definitive textbook for international relations and environmental politics courses. Brown has served on a number of boards and committees, including the editorial board of *Society and Natural Resources*, the CARE Advisory Committee on Population and Development, and a term as president of the board of Friends of the Earth.

BIBLIOGRAPHY
"Environmental Defense Fund," www.edf.org; Gottlieb, Robert, *Forcing the Spring*, 1993; Lerner, Steve, "Janet Brown; on global environmental issues, the people are leading and the leaders are following," *Commonweal*, 1991; "World Resources Institute," www.wri.org.

Brown, Lester
(March 28, 1934–)
Founder of Worldwatch Institute and Earth Policy Institute, Economist

Lester Brown founded and served as President for 26 years of the Worldwatch Institute, an interdisciplinary, global think tank that publishes the annual *State of the World* reports. In 2001, he founded the Earth Policy Institute, which maps out plans for an "eco-economy," through which the environment is sustained—not destroyed—by economic activity. Brown is an internationally influential agricultural economist and author, who sees food production and population growth as two of the most urgent environmental issues facing society today.

Lester Russell Brown, the oldest child of Calvin C. Brown and Delia Smith Brown, was born on March 28, 1934, in Bridgeton, New Jersey. He was raised on a farm in Bridgeton where his parents grew tomatoes. He was an active member of the local 4-H club and, later, the Future Farmers of America. When Brown was 14, he and his brother Carl bought a small plot of land and an old tractor and began farming tomatoes themselves. Their farming operation was producing 1.5 million pounds of tomatoes per year by the time Brown received his B.S. degree in agricultural science from Rutgers University in 1955, a yield that put the Browns in the most productive 2 percent of East Coast tomato farmers.

Upon graduation Brown had every intention of farming for the rest of his life. However, the year after he graduated, he was given the opportunity to live and work for six months in a small farming community in India, through the International Farm Youth Exchange program of the National 4-H Club Foundation. His experiences in India opened his eyes to the pervasive problem of world hunger, and suddenly "the idea of just growing tomatoes for the next forty years no longer seemed very challenging," he told Jim Patrico in *Top Producer* in 1987. In 1959, after completing an M.A. degree in agricultural economics at the University of Maryland, Brown became an agricultural analyst with the Foreign Agricultural Service, a branch of the U.S. Department of Agriculture (USDA). At the USDA, Brown produced a study that was the first to link the issue of food supply to rapid population growth. It received quite a bit of attention and was even featured on the cover of the January 6, 1964, issue of *US News and World Report*. This study led to Brown's first book, *Man Land and Food: Looking Ahead at the World's Food Needs*, published in 1963.

In 1963, Brown left the USDA and earned a master's degree in public administration from Harvard University. Orville L. Freeman, who was at that time secretary of agriculture, appointed Brown adviser on foreign agricultural policy in 1964. In this post, Brown was able to convince U.S. government officials to demand dramatic changes in India's agricultural policies in exchange for food shipments from the United States. These policy changes helped to avert large-scale famine. In 1966, Brown was named administrator of the USDA's International Agricultural Development Service, where he was responsible for overseeing projects being conducted in more than 40 countries. Brown stayed in this position for three years, until 1969, when he left government service altogether. At that time, along with James Grant, Brown formed the Overseas Development Council, a private, nonprofit organization whose purpose was to analyze economic and political issues affecting relations between the United States and developing countries.

In 1973, at a chance meeting with William Dietel, then executive vice president of the Rockefeller Brothers Fund, Brown learned that Dietel shared many of his concerns about the environment and was willing to support the formation of a research institute. In 1974, with a startup grant of $500,000 from the Rockefeller Brothers Fund, Brown founded the Worldwatch Institute, whose purpose is is "to raise public awareness of environmental threats to the level where it will support an effective public policy response." Until 2000, Brown served as president and as one of the Institute's senior researchers. The Institute conducts interdisciplinary, global research on everything from air pollution to biodiversity to "jobs in a sustainable society." It publishes two yearly reports, *Vital Signs: The Trends that Are Shaping Our Future* and *State of the World*, and a bimonthly magazine, *World Watch*.

The State of the World reports are broad in scope, and they differ from the reports of other think tanks in that they are sold (all of Worldwatch's publications are sold, rather than given away). The fact that the reports are purchased is proof of their usefulness and value; in addition, their sale helps pay the Institute's operating expenses. The reports are translated into many different languages and address agricultural and economic trends as well as population growth in developing countries. They provide up-to-date statistical information to the public, especially to policy makers.

In 2001, Brown co-founded the Earth Policy Institute with Reah Janise Kauffman "to provide a vision of a sustainable future and a plan for how to get from here to there," according to the Institute's website. Its small staff publishes on-line "Eco-Economy" updates and indicators on its website, and distributes them via email. Updates "focus on trends affecting progress toward an eco-economy" and there are 12 Indicators—among them population, economic growth, carbon emissions, grain harvest, and ice melting—that "measure progress in building an eco-economy."

Brown has written many influential books, including among others *World Without Borders* (1972), *In the Human Interest: A Strategy to Stabilize World Population* (1974), *Building a Sustainable Society* (1981), and most recently, *The Earth Policy Reader* (2002), *Outgrowing the Earth* (2004), and three editions of *Plan B*, (2003, 2006, 2008). In his books, Brown addresses problems that threaten life on earth as we know it. He calls for a greater degree of international cooperation between scientists and governments, and he challenges people to change their consumptive habits and attitudes toward the environment.

In an article published in *E Magazine* in 2003, Brown acknowledged that lifestyle changes are very common, "Lifestyle changes are fine—shifting from a car to a bike, recycling, switching to compact fluorescent lights. These are all useful and important things..." But the most important thing we can do is to "become politically active...we got to change the system. And we've got to do it fast."

Brown has received numerous service and literary awards over the course of his career, including the National Wildlife Federation Special Conservation Award in 1982, the Lorax Award, Global Tomorrow Coalition in 1985, and a Gold Medal from the Worldwide Fund for Nature, 1989. He was named one of "100 who made a difference" by *Earth Times* in 1995, and he is one of the Audubon Society's 1998 "100 Champions of Conservation." He was named a Heifer Hero by Heifer International in 2008. Brown lives in Washington, D.C. He and his ex-wife, Shirley Ann Woolington, have two grown children, Brian and Brenda Ann.

BIBLIOGRAPHY

"Earth Policy Institute," www.earth-policy.org; Lawson, Trevor, "The Voice of Reason," *The Geographical Magazine*, May 1995; "Lester Brown," *Current Biography Yearbook*, 1993; Luh, Corene, "A Taxing State of Affairs," *E: the Environmental Magazine*, 2003; "Worldwatch Institute," www.worldwatch.org.

Brown, Michael
(March 5, 1952–)
Journalist

Journalist Michael Brown has contributed to the nation's environmental awareness through his investigative reporting on industrial pollution and toxic waste disposal. While working as a reporter at the *Niagara Gazette*, he tackled the issue of toxic contamination at Love Canal and helped bring it to national attention. He was nominated four times for a Pulitzer Prize for his coverage of the story, which he later chronicled in a book called *Laying Waste: The Poisoning of America by Toxic Chemicals* (1980). He also wrote *The Toxic Cloud: The Poisoning of America's Air* (1987), in which he examined the sources of pollutants in the air over the United States and the potentially disastrous health consequences of allowing industries to ignore their responsibility to those who live downwind.

Michael Harold Brown was born on March 5, 1952, in Niagara Falls, New York. His father, Harold Brown, was an accountant, and his mother Rose (Mento) Brown was a teacher. He attended Fordham University, where he graduated with a bachelor's degree in 1974. Having always wanted to be a writer, he began working three years later for the *Niagara Gazette* as a reporter. Soon after starting his job, he learned about the toxic waste leakage problems in the Love Canal neighborhood of Niagara Falls and began reporting on it for the *Gazette*. Residents of the neighborhood had first begun noticing something was wrong in 1976, when heavy rains were causing foul-smelling chemicals to seep into the local schoolyard and the basements of homes in the area. They discovered that the school had been built over an old, dry canal, which had been used by the Hooker Chemicals and Plastics Corporation to bury 20,000 tons of chemical wastes in the 1940s and 1950s.

Brown undertook an uncompromising investigation of the leak, which eventually led to more than 100 articles for the *Niagara Gazette*. The municipal government and Hooker Chemical attempted to downplay the issue, and at no time tried to warn the people who lived in the area about the waste dump or any health risks it could pose. Brown, dissatisfied with the way things were being handled, continued his investigations. Along with LOIS GIBBS, a resident who was quickly becoming an impassioned toxic wastes activist, Brown conducted informal health surveys of area residents that turned up abnormally high rates of cancer, miscarriages, birth defects, and nerve damage. Partly as a result of people like Brown and Gibbs urging officials to take responsibility—and Brown's refusal to let the issue die down in the press—governmental agencies began a detailed chemical analysis of the leak. They eventually isolated over 180 compounds, many of which were carcinogenic or capable of damaging the nervous system—this included dioxin, which is so toxic that its potency is measured in parts per trillion.

Besides exposing the problem through the newspaper, Brown took further action by continually pressuring Hooker Chemical and the federal Environmental Protection Agency to remedy the situation by cleaning up the leak and compensating the victims. Hooker Chemical refused to accept responsibility for what happened, claiming that it had followed standard procedures back in the 1940s and 1950s when it buried the waste. Finally, Pres. JIMMY CARTER declared Love Canal a national emergency and more than 900 families were evacuated from the area. State and federal authorities filed $760 million in damage suits against Hooker Chemical to recover costs and compensate displaced residents. Some of the lawsuits were settled when Hooker Chemical agreed to take some remedial steps and pay a portion of the cleanup costs. One result of the

Love Canal incident is that the Environmental Protection Agency began to pay more attention to waste disposal sites. In 1978 the agency began surveying other hazardous waste sites; it found 32,000 that were deemed a risk to human health and the environment and at least 18,000 other sites that were unregulated.

For his reporting work on the Love Canal toxic waste leak, Brown earned four Pulitzer Prize nominations. In 1979 he received an award from the Environmental Protection Agency; in that same year he left the *Niagara Gazette* and began work on a book that would chronicle the entire Love Canal story. In *Laying Waste: The Poisoning of America by Toxic Chemicals*, published in 1980, Brown also looks beyond Love Canal to give an account of some of the other known toxic chemical dumps around the country. He discovered that only a small fraction of hazardous wastes are disposed of properly—even the Environmental Protection Agency estimated that as of 1979, less than 7 percent of the millions of tons of toxic wastes produced in the United States were legally disposed of. Brown concludes that the corporate irresponsibility behind this neglect leaves the rest of the population to pay the price and that federal, state, and local regulatory agencies have not provided adequate protection against the problem.

Continuing his mission to uncover the causes of environmental contamination, Brown wrote a book about airborne pollutants, *The Toxic Cloud: The Poisoning of America's Air* (1987). He found that pollution could travel great distances from its point of origin. In the 1970s, impurities were detected in an isolated lake ecosystem in Isle Royale in the northern part of Lake Superior, which was completely cut off from all other water sources except rain. Scientists found pesticide residues there that were traced back to cotton fields in the southern United States. Brown also describes the smothering petrochemical pollution along the Gulf coast and how the chances of contracting cancer there are one in three. In *The Toxic Cloud*, Brown reveals that no place in the country is free from unseen toxic particles blown by winds, causing potential health risks. He emphasizes that much of the emissions from industrial sources are unregulated, and many of the gases and chemicals that are released are untested—especially for long-term effects or for how they interact when combined. Once again Brown blames governmental agencies for policies that seem to favor industry over clean air and challenges them to take responsibility.

In addition to his books, Brown has written articles for various magazines such as *Atlantic Monthly*, *Science Digest*, *New York Times Magazine*, and *Reader's Digest*. In 1990, he published *The Search for Eve*, a look at paleoanthropology and the evolutionary origin of humans. The focus of his most recent books, including *The Best of Spirit Daily* (2002) and *The Bridge to Heaven* (2003), is on spirituality and prophecy.

BIBLIOGRAPHY

Brown, Michael, *Laying Waste: The Poisoning of America by Toxic Chemicals*, 1980; Brown, Michael, *The Toxic Cloud: The Poisoning of America's Air*, 1987; Cohen, Richard, "Laying Waste: The Poisoning of America by Toxic Chemicals," *New Republic*, 1980; Kaiser, Charles, "Hell Holes," *Newsweek*, 1980.

Browner, Carol

(December 16, 1955–)
Administrator of the Environmental Protection Agency

Attorney and natural resources expert Carol Browner was nominated by Pres. Bill Clinton as administrator of the Environmental Protection Agency (EPA) in 1992 and has served longer in her position than any other EPA administrator. Browner has worked to reform a notoriously bureaucratic and corrupt agency and has attempted to work out solutions to environmental problems through compromise among business, consumer, and environmental protection interests. At the same time that she has collected the largest fines from major polluters in the EPA's history, she has tried to reward compliant industries by streamlining the regulatory process in a way that has saved them time and money.

Carol Browner was born on December 16, 1955, in Miami, Florida, to Isabella Harty-Hughes and Michael Browner, the first of their three daughters. As a child, she would often bicycle into the wilderness of the Everglades very near her south Florida home, an activity that she now believes was a source of motivation for her career choice. Both of Browner's parents were university professors; her father taught English and her mother social sciences. Browner graduated from the University of Florida at Gainesville in 1977 with a B.A. in English, enrolled directly in the University's law school, and earned her law degree in 1979.

Browner began her legal career in 1980, working for a year as general counsel for the Committee on Governmental Operation of the Florida House of Representatives. In 1983 she became the associate director of the Washington environmental lobbying group Citizen Action. Browner held that position until 1986, when Florida senator Lawton Chiles named her his senior legislative aide for environmental issues. During her tenure at that post, Browner performed her official duties with uncommon vigor. In 1987, while pregnant, she dived into Florida coastal waters to view the environmental effects of oil drilling firsthand. That experience later drove her to help negotiate a ban on drilling for oil and gas off the Florida Keys. Her nonconventional approach earned her notoriety and eventually a place as counsel for the U.S. Senate Committee on Energy and Natural Resources, a position that she accepted in 1989. That same year Browner left her charge with Chiles to join the staff of Tennessee senator AL GORE, JR. as a senior legislative aide. Browner worked with Senator Gore until 1991, at which time she left Washington at the request of then-governor Chiles to become secretary of Florida's Department of Environmental Regulation, the third-largest environmental agency in the country.

Exemplary of her desire to accommodate the interests of business while protecting the environment, one of Browner's first official acts as secretary was to help win passage of Florida's Clean Air Act, which streamlined the process by which businesses obtain permits to develop wetlands and expand manufacturing plants, thereby reducing the amount of money and time that the process was costing both business and the department. Browner's practical yet controversial approach earned her more praise than criticism, however, in a land-preservation compromise agreement with the Walt Disney Company in 1992. When Disney filed for the permits it needed to build on 400 acres of wetlands that it already owned, Browner brokered a deal that provided Walt Disney with the necessary means to proceed with its development plans in return for a $40 million commitment by the company to buy and restore 8,500 acres of endangered wetlands south of Orlando.

As secretary, Browner was also the primary negotiator in the settlement of a federal lawsuit brought against the state of Florida in 1988 for violating its own environmental laws. The suit alleged that the state allowed sugarcane growers and other farmers to siphon water from the Everglades for agricultural use, harming the ecosystem, and that it did not require them to filter the contaminated runoff water that flowed into the swamp. Browner took the side of the federal government and, in so doing, took on the region's wealthy sugarcane families. A settlement reached in 1991 resulted in the largest ecological restoration project ever attempted in the United States. It included the construction of filtering marshes to purify and restore the natural flow of water to the Everglades, the cost of which was shared by the sugarcane farmers and by state and federal governments.

In 1992, Vice President Al Gore asked Browner to join President Clinton's transitional team for environmental issues, and in January 1993, the president appointed Browner EPA administrator. Browner's career at the EPA began precariously. She was thought of as inexperienced and unqualified for such an important position, and many worried that she would unfairly favor the White House because of her connection to Vice President Gore. Browner had to contend with the most antienvironmental Congress in recent history, the 104th Congress, which tried to roll back the major environmental gains of the last quarter century. The 104th Congress undercut the EPA's funding and its regulatory powers and denied the Clinton administration the votes necessary to raise the EPA to cabinet status.

Browner persevered through her first difficult years in the post and has focused on water quality, cleanup of toxic waste sites, children's health, and more efficient regulation of industry during her tenure. Browner lobbied for the Safe Drinking Water Act, which was signed by Clinton in 1996. Under her leadership, more Superfund sites were cleaned up than had been since the Superfund program was established in 1980. Browner prioritized the clean up of "brownfields" (contaminated lots in urban areas) as well, envisioning the conversion of these areas into revitalized places for new urban development. She announced new stringent regulations of future hazardous waste incinerators and increased community involvement in incinerator sitings and has issued new standards for air pollution. Browner made children's health a focal point, introducing new policies that would always take children's health risks into consideration in the permit process. She introduced what she called a Common Sense Initiative, by which regulations were designed for specific industries, and companies were asked to meet and even exceed environmental regulations in ways that are both creative and cost effective.

With the arrival of the G. W. Bush administration in January 2001, Browner left the EPA, after leading the agency longer than any previous chief. She currently works as principal of The Albright Group LLC, where she provides counsel to clients in the areas of environmental protection, climate change, and energy conservation. Browner also chairs the Board of the National Audubon Society, and serves on the Boards of the Center for American Progress, the Alliance for Climate Protection, and the League of Conservation Voters.

Browner is married to Michael Podhorzer, who directs the Political Department of the AFL-CIO. They live in Maryland with their son, Zachary. She received the Mother's Day Committee's 1997 Mother of the Year Award and was recognized by *Working Mother* magazine in 1998 as one of the 25 most influential working mothers.

BIBLIOGRAPHY

Breton, Mary Joy, *Women Pioneers for the Environment*, 1998; "Carol M. Browner, EPA History, US EPA" www.epa.gov/history/admin/agency/browner.htm; Nixon, Will, "Twenty Minutes with Carol Browner," *E: The Environmental Magazine*, 1993; Wilkinson, Francis, "The Sinkable Carol Browner," *Rolling Stone*, 1993.

Bullard, Robert D.
(December 21, 1946–)
Sociologist, Environmental Justice Movement Activist

Robert Bullard is the nation's foremost scholar specializing in issues of environmental justice, including land use, transportation equity, suburban sprawl, housing, minority health, regional equity, and emergency response and community preparedness. His research on patterns of environmental racism as well as the grassroots groups combating it has provided a solid academic foundation for the environmental justice movement. Through his technical assistance to grassroots environmental justice groups via the Environmental Justice Resource Center that he founded and directs at Clark Atlanta University and its *People of Color Environmental Groups Directory* networking tool Bullard has been as much an actor in the movement as a student of it.

Robert Doyle Bullard was born on December 21, 1946, in Elba, Alabama, to Nehemiah and Myrtle Bullard. As a youth in the segregated South, reminders of racism were everywhere, and he found inspiration in such African American leaders as W.E.B. Dubois, Sojourner Truth, and Malcom X. Bullard attended Alabama A & M University in Huntsville, Alabama, graduating with a B.S. in government in 1968. He spent two years with the United States Marine Corps as a communication specialist immediately following graduation, and after his honorable discharge in 1970, he resumed his studies, earning an M.A. in sociology in 1972 from Atlanta University (now Clark Atlanta University) and a Ph.D. in sociology in 1976 from Iowa State University. Bullard accepted a position as assistant professor at Texas Southern University in Houston in 1976.

Bullard's research into environmental racism began in Houston in 1979, when his wife, lawyer Linda McKeever Bullard, asked for his help in researching her case *Bean v. Southwestern Waste Management*. She was representing a group of African American homeowners of the Northwood Manor suburb who were suing the city of Houston, the state of Texas, and Browning-Ferris Industries for environmental discrimination in siting a municipal landfill in their neighborhood, whose population was 82 percent Black. This was the first environmentally oriented lawsuit filed under the 1964 Civil Rights Act. Bullard's research revealed that in Houston, all of the city-owned garbage dumps, six of the eight city-owned garbage incinerators, and three of the four privately owned municipal landfills were in Black neighborhoods. Despite the evidence that the city of Houston and private landfill companies were deliberately targeting Black neighborhoods, the homeowners lost

Robert Bullard (Photograph courtesy of Environmental Justice Resource Center, Clark Atlanta University)

their suit and the landfill was built. The publicity surrounding the case did have an effect, however. In 1980 the Houston city council passed a resolution that prohibited city trucks from dumping at the Northwood Manor landfill; the next year it passed an ordinance prohibiting landfill construction near schools and other public facilities. The state Department of Health rewrote its landfill permit applications to require detailed land use, economic, and sociodemographic data for its proposed sites. In the years since the Northwood Manor landfill was built, no new landfill in Houston has been sited in a Black neighborhood.

Bullard's findings drove him to continue his research on the phenomenon of locally unwanted land uses (LULUs) in Black communities. Bullard found that Black communities in the South—regardless of their economic status—were much more likely than White communities to be targeted for LULUs. His case studies of Dallas and Houston, Texas; Emelle, Alabama; Institute, West Virginia; and Alsen, Louisiana, make up *Dumping in Dixie: Race, Class, and Environmental Quality* (1990), a primer on environmental racism. Bullard's later books, *Confronting Environmental Racism: Voices from the Grassroots* (1993) and *Unequal Protection: Environmental Justice and Communities of Color* (1994) examine environmental racism as it manifests itself in different areas of the country against people of color and how grassroots groups have organized to fight it. These two books have joined *Dumping in Dixie* as classics in the field of environmental justice.

Bullard has gone further than simply describing and decrying environmental racism; he has actively served as a networker between the environmental justice groups that he has come into contact with through his research. In 1990 he began to compile a list of grassroots environmental justice organizations run by people of color. In an attempt to help them network, Bullard and a planning committee consisting of DANA ALSTON, Patrick Bryant, BENJAMIN CHAVIS JR., Donna Chavis, Charles Lee, and Richard Moore convoked the First National People of Color Environmental Summit held in Washington, D.C., October 24 to 27, 1991. More than 600 people from virtually every state in the United States as well as Canada, Central America, Puerto Rico, and the Marshall Islands gathered for the very first time to discuss environmental and social justice activism in communities of color. The four-day gathering resulted in the articulation of 17 principles of environmental justice (published in their entirety on the Clark Atlanta University Environmental Justice Resource Center web site www.ejrc.cau.edu/). These principles reaffirmed the strong connection that people of color have with the earth and set up guidelines for how environmental justice groups would collaborate both among themselves and with mainstream environmental organizations.

One result of the publicity surrounding the Summit was the decision of the U.S. Environmental Protection Agency (EPA), under Bush appointee WILLIAM K. REILLY, to create an Office of Environmental Equity. As part of a team of environmental justice experts on the Clinton-Gore transition team in 1992, Bullard cowrote a position paper that convinced Pres. Bill Clinton to expand the Office of Environmental Equity, appoint a National Environmental Justice Advisory Council (NEJAC) to advise the EPA on matters of environmental justice, and sign an executive order on environmental justice in 1994 that ordered every federal agency to identify and address "disproportionately high and adverse human health or environmental effects of its programs, policies, and activities on minority populations and low-income populations." Bullard served on NEJAC from 1994 to 1996, chairing its Health and Research Subcommittee.

During the 1980s and early 1990s, Bullard taught consecutively at Texas Southern University, Rice University, University of Tennessee, and University of California at Berkeley, Riverside, and Los Angeles, respectively. In 1994, he moved to Clark Atlanta University (CAU), where he holds an endowed chair as the Ware Professor of Sociology. In September 1994, he founded CAU's Environmental Justice Research Center (EJRC), a clearinghouse that generates scientific, technical, and legal research on environmental justice issues and provides this information to environmental justice activists.

With support from the EJRC, Bullard has prepared testimony, testified, and served as expert witness for dozens of cases having to do with LULUs and environmental racism. In one of them, Bullard worked with the communities of Forest Grove and Center Springs, Louisiana, to fight the nation's first privately owned uranium enrichment plant. The plant was to be built between these two small, predominantly Black communities, less than a mile from either one. Residents would not benefit from the highly paid jobs, yet they were to bear increased traffic, noise, and threats to their health. They formed Citizens Against Nuclear Trash (CANT) and sued the company, Louisiana Energy Services. Bullard provided expert testimony for CANT, and a federal court ruled in its favor. The 1997 victory was the first major environmental justice lawsuit to be ruled upon favorably.

Bullard has published more than a dozen books on many areas of environmental justice including two on urban sprawl and transportation issues with colleagues GLENN S. JOHNSON and Angel O. Torres: *Sprawl City: Race, Politics, and Planning in Atlanta* (2000), a study of the unrestrained spread outward of Atlanta, one of the nation's fastest-growing cities and *Highway Robbery: Transportation Racism and New Routes to Equity* (2004), a case-by-case, coast-to-coast description of the barriers to reliable transportation faced by poor people and people of color. His latest books are *Growing Smarter: Achieving Livable Communities, Environmental Justice, and Regional Equity* and *The Black Metropolis in the Twenty-First Century: Race,* *Power, and the Politics of Place*, both published in 2007. The devastation wreaked by Hurricane Katrina in 2005, and the negligence apparent in the official response to it, have inspired Bullard's latest focus; he and colleague Beverly Wright are currently finishing two books about Katrina: *Deadly Waiting Game Beyond Katrina: How Government Actions Endanger the Health and Welfare of African Americans* and *The Environment After Katrina: Looking Back to Look Forward.*

Bullard serves on the board of directors for several scholarly and environmental organizations and has won numerous awards, including the Citizens Clearinghouse for Hazardous Waste's Environmental Justice Award in 1993, the National Wildlife Federation's 1990 Environmental Achievement Award, the American Sociological Association William Foote Whyte Distinguished Career Award in 2007, and several awards for his books. He directs the EJRC and is a widely sought speaker on issues of environmental justice. Bullard resides in Atlanta with his wife, Linda, and his children, Robert Jr. and Kai.

BIBLIOGRAPHY
Bullard, Robert, "Overcoming Racism in Environmental Decisionmaking," *Environment*, 1994; Bullard, Robert D., Mohai, Paul, Saha, Robin, and Wright, Beverly. 'Toxic Wastes and Race at Twenty 1987-2007: A Report Prepared for the United Church of Christ Justice Witness Ministries," www.ejrc.cau.edu/TWART-light.pdf; "Clark Atlanta University Environmental Justice Resource Center," www.ejrc.cau.edu/; Fletcher, Kenneth, "Robert Bullard: Environmental Justice Advocate," *Smithsonian*, 2008; Johnson, Glenn S., "Robert D. Bullard: Godfather of Environmental Justice," *Environmental Activists*, John Mongillo and Bibi Booth, eds., 2000; Joseph, Pat, "Race and Poverty are Out of the Closet," *Sierra*, 2005; Motavalli, Jim, "Dr. Robert Bullard," *E Magazine*, 1998.

Burroughs, John
(April 3, 1837–March 29, 1921)
Naturalist, Nature Writer

John Burroughs is a giant among natural historians, the creator of the literary genre of the nature essay as it exists in its modern form. He published many collections of nature essays, popularizing, in the process, natural history and a general interest in the natural world.

John Burroughs was born on April 3, 1837, in the Catskill Mountain town of Roxbury, New York. His parents, Chauncey and Amy Burroughs, were well off. They owned and worked a 300-acre farm, keeping a herd of dairy cows and growing such field crops as hay, oats, buckwheat, and potatoes. Burroughs would later describe his father as a "good farmer, a helpful neighbor, a devoted parent and husband." Of his mother, Burroughs wrote that from her he inherited "my temperament, my love of Nature, my brooding introspective habit of mind." Burroughs was their seventh child. He grew up helping out with chores around the farm and attending the local one-room schoolhouse. He spent Sundays wandering around the countryside, fishing, swimming, and exploring. As a teenager, he earned money for books by making maple sugar and selling cakes of it in town for as much as two cents apiece.

Burroughs left home in 1854, at the age of 17. For three years he held a series of teaching positions in small country schools, interspersing them with writing courses and attempts at writing newspaper articles for a living. After 1857, when he married Ursula North, the daughter of a farmer he had boarded with while teaching in Tongore, New York, he alternated between more temporary schoolteaching posts, half-hearted business ventures, and short stints on his family's farm.

In 1860, Burroughs published an essay entitled "Expression" in the *Atlantic Monthly*. This piece was philosophical and theoretical in nature and borrowed heavily from the writings of RALPH WALDO EMERSON. The publisher even held up its publication in order to compare it with Emerson's work to ensure that it had not been plagiarized. Shortly after its publication, Burroughs realized that such writing was not his strong point, and he began to focus on writing about the rural world he knew best. An occasional column of his called "From the Back Country" began appearing in the *New York Leader* later in 1860. It featured essays about such topics as making butter, maple sugar, and building stone walls.

In 1863, Burroughs and his wife moved to Washington, D.C. Burroughs found employment working as a clerk for the Treasury Department. This job actually inspired many of his nature essays because it was so bland. Later he would write, "During my long peri-

From left to right: Thomas Edison, John Burroughs, and Henry Ford at Thomas Edison's home in Florida. (Library of Congress, Prints & Photographs Division, LC-USZ62-131044).

ods of leisure I took refuge in my pen. How my mind reacted from the iron wall in front of me, and sought solace in memories of the birds and summer fields and woods!" Essays that he wrote during this time include "With the Birds," "The Snow Walkers," and "In the Hemlocks." Also, during this time, Burroughs became friends with the famous poet WALT WHITMAN. They would remain lifelong friends, with Whitman having a significant influence on Burroughs's writing. In 1867, Burroughs published *Notes on Walt Whitman as Poet and Person*, a book for which Whitman himself wrote one chapter and which he helped edit.

In 1871, Burroughs's second book, *Wake-Robin*, was published. It was a collection of nature pieces, mostly about birds, some of which had appeared in slightly different forms in the *Atlantic Monthly*. *Wake-Robin* received positive reviews and sold well. It established Burroughs as a master of the nature essay, a form of essay based on field observations and marked by anecdotes and emotional interactions with the subject matter. At the end of December 1872, Burroughs resigned his post with the U.S. Treasury (he had, by that time, worked his way up to the position of special bank examiner) to take a position with a bank in Middletown, New York, just a few miles from his native Catskills.

Burroughs purchased property on the west bank of the Hudson River, near Poughkeepsie, where he designed and built a house that he dubbed "Riverby." Burroughs and his wife would live here for the rest of their lives. Burroughs worked part-time as a bank receiver. His idle weeks were spent writing essays and exploring the countryside. In 1875, his third book, *Winter Sunshine*, was published. It included such essays as "The Fox," "The Snow Walkers," and "The Apple." *Locusts and Wild Honey* (1879) and *Pepacton* (1881), more collections of his nature essays, appeared soon thereafter. Burroughs would publish, on average, one book every two years for the remainder of his life. In 1878, a son, Julian, arrived in the Burroughs household, an arrival not without some controversy, for Ursula was not the baby's mother. She was, however, convinced to adopt the child and the days at Riverby were brightened. "The baby," Burroughs wrote, "is a refuge."

Though very much a homebody, during his years at Riverby, Burroughs did travel extensively, visiting Canada, California, Hawaii, and Alaska. He made friends in some fairly high places during this time as well, Pres. THEODORE ROOSEVELT, Henry Ford (who in 1913 sent Burroughs a gift of a new Model T), and JOHN MUIR among them. Above all, he continued to write. He published a total of 54 books before his death in 1921. In the process he established and popularized the genre of nature essays and helped to foster a widespread interest in natural history in the American people. He believed that a nature essay should be based upon accurate information about the physical and biological environment. He also believed in the integration of humans into natural processes. He did not "observe" nature so much as he "participated" in it. And through his nature essays he helped his readers to do so as well.

Burroughs died on March 29, 1921, in a rail car on his way home from a trip to California.

BIBLIOGRAPHY

Barrus, Clara, *Our friend John Burroughs*, 2006 Black, Ralph W., *American Nature Writers*, 1996; Burroughs, John, *John Burroughs' America: Selections from the Writings of the Naturalist*, 1997; Burroughs Kelley, Elizabeth, *John Burroughs: Naturalist, the Story of His Work and Family*, 1989; Kanze, Edward, *The World of John Burroughs*, 1999; Renehan, Edward, *John Burroughs: An American Naturalist*, 1992; Walker, Charlotte Zoe, ed., *Sharp Eyes: John Burroughs and American Nature Writing, 2000;* Warren, James Perrin, *John Burroughs and the Place of Nature*, 2006.

Butcher, Devereux

(September 24, 1906–May 22, 1991)
Executive Secretary of National Parks Association, Editor, Photographer, Writer

As executive secretary of the National Parks Association (NPA; now called the National Parks and Conservation Association [NPCA]) at a time in which U.S. national parks were threatened by budgetary problems and wartime needs for timber and mineral resources, Devereux Butcher worked to assure their continued preservation. He held firm throughout his life that national parks must also be defended from commercial development, and he worked to establish standards for different classes of protected land. In addition, Butcher is remembered for his photographs, his paintings, and his series of picture books on national protected areas.

Devereux Butcher was born in Devon, Pennsylvania, on September 24, 1906, to Henry Clay and Constance Devereux Butcher. His parents were wealthy and encouraged their son's interest in art. Butcher studied painting and photography at the Philadelphia Academy of Fine Arts, and upon graduation in 1928, he traveled to California to photograph its Spanish colonial missions. Butcher married Mary Taft in 1935, and the couple built their own stone cabin in the Delaware River valley. This experience deepened Butcher's interest in nature and conservation, and he began to submit articles, art, and photographs to *American Forests*, the publication of the American Forestry Association. He worked as an editorial assistant for *American Forests* from 1941 to 1942.

Butcher's work at *American Forests* caught the notice of ROBERT STERLING YARD, founder of the NPA. Founded in 1919, three years after the creation of the National Park Service (NPS), the NPA supported national parks by lobbying Congress for their protection, raising private funds that the financially strapped NPS could not provide on its own, and promoting parks and conservation to the American public. Butcher was recruited as executive secretary of the NPA in 1942, a time of crisis for the national parks. The wartime effort was making demands on the nation's natural resources, and some members of Congress were pressuring the Department of the Interior to allow the exploitation of timber and minerals within national parks. The NPA worked hard to oppose these forces and was supported by NPS director NEWTON DRURY, who kept the NPA well-informed of challenges to NPS. Because NPS headquarters had been moved to Chicago and its budget reduced at the beginning of World War II, Drury depended upon the NPA, based in Washington, D.C., to maintain a close watch over Congress and lobby on its behalf. At the same time that Butcher was expected to defend national parks from violations of this type, he also led the NPA to demand a clear definition of standards for varying classes of protected land. New national parks, in Butcher's opinion, should be designated only in places of spectacular beauty and particular vulnerability to development. Other areas, in the opinion of Butcher and the NPA, should be designated for other types of protection.

In addition to his administrative duties, Butcher also edited NPA publications. Since the founding of NPA, Yard had served as the editor of *National Parks Bulletin*, a simple newsletter for members. But Yard, who previous to his work with NPA had edited highly popular picture books on the national parks, knew that the publication held great potential. Once Butcher took the reins of the publication, he quickly revamped it. It was renamed *National Parks Magazine*, and it began coming out as a regular quarterly. He recruited well-known contributors, including OLAUS MURIE and SIGURD OLSON. Rather than addressing only NPA-related issues, the magazine became an attractive showcase for the national parks. Its increased printing budget allowed for better reproduction of beautiful photos—many by Butcher himself—of national park scenery. During the 1940s and 1950s, public and school libraries throughout the country subscribed to *National Parks Magazine*, giving many readers their first view of the most beautiful places in the nation. NPA membership under Butcher rose to its highest level in the organization's history.

In 1947, Butcher published *Exploring Our National Parks and Monuments*, a picture book that included reprints of features from the magazine and was republished eight times. The book fulfilled the vision of Yard, who early in his tenure with NPA had proposed such an album. When Butcher decided in 1950 that editing and directing NPA was too much for one person and that his publications work was more fulfilling to him than his administrative work, he requested that the board reassign him as field representative. This allowed him more time to travel the country with his wife and son, Russell, visiting national parks and preparing material for the magazine. Between 1950 and 1957, when he left NPA, Butcher continued to publish *National Parks Magazine* and edited two more books: *Exploring the National Parks of Canada* (1951) and *Seeing America's Wildlife in Our National Refuges* (1955).

During the 1950s, Butcher was a key player in the defense of Dinosaur National Monument against the dams proposed in Echo Park and Split Mountain. He took many of the photographs that revealed the area's beauty and swayed public opinion against the dams. Butcher also was recruited by Wilderness Society's HOWARD ZAHNISER to help draft and lobby for the Wilderness Bill. Yet as the decade wore on, Butcher became increasingly disillusioned by the growing commercialism in national parks. He was disgusted by the "tramways, chair lifts, swimming pools, golf courses and honky-tonks" infiltrating the parks, he wrote in a 1954 edition of *National Parks Magazine*, and he began to criticize the executive committee members of NPA for their refusal to fight this type of development. To censor what he wrote on the issue, the NPA executive committee appointed an editorial advisory board for the magazine. This was too much for Butcher, and he resigned from NPA in 1957.

Butcher and his wife published their own magazine, *National Wildlands News*, for three years, 1959 to 1962. In 1963, Butcher became director of Hawk Mountain Sanctuary Association, the organization that preservationist ROSALIE EDGE had established to administer her Hawk Mountain Reserve in Pennsylvania; he remained at that post until his retirement in 1980. Butcher wrote two more picture books, *Exploring Our National Wildlife Refuges* (1963) and *Our National Parks in Color* (1964), and cowrote the series *Knowing Your Trees*.

Butcher's son, Russell, followed in his father's footsteps, working as a conservation journalist during the 1960s and then becoming the southwestern regional representative for the NPCA in 1980. Devereux Butcher had initially sponsored his son in this position but withdrew his sponsorship shortly after, disagreeing with NPCA leadership about its stand on hunting in Alaska parks.

Devereux Butcher died on May 22, 1991, at his home in Gladwyn, Pennsylvania, of complications following a fall.

BIBLIOGRAPHY

Butcher, Devereux, *Exploring Our National Parks and Monuments*, 8th ed., 1985; "Devereux Butcher, 84, A Park Preservationist," *New York Times*, 1991; Miles, John C., *Guardians of the Parks*, 1995.

C

American Environmental Leaders

From Colonial Times to the Present

Cade, Thomas

(January 10, 1928–)
Ornithologist

Tom Cade has made a career of studying birds and how they are adapted to live within their particular environments; he is especially known as a champion of peregrine falcons. He has conducted field studies in Alaska, Africa, Arabia, Central America, Mauritius, and the southwestern United States and has published numerous articles and scientific papers. His efforts toward reestablishing peregrine falcons, whose numbers were greatly reduced in 1970, have been outstanding and have ranged from documenting their decline due to dichlordiphenyltrichlor (DDT) to establishing The Peregrine Fund, a conservation organization devoted to the preservation of falcons and other birds of prey. Cade's work on peregrine falcons has contributed to one of the first truly successful recovery efforts for an endangered species.

Thomas Joseph Cade was born January 10, 1928, in San Angelo, Texas. He spent some of his early years on a homestead in southern New Mexico and then moved with his father and mother to Glendale, California, in 1943. There he graduated from high school and spent two years at Occidental College. He studied biology at the University of Alaska, receiving his B.A. in 1951. He earned his master's degree in 1955 in zoology at the University of California, Los Angeles, and his Ph.D. in zoology from the same university in 1957. He taught at Syracuse University in the Department of Zoology, then at Cornell University, where he was professor in the Section of Ecology and Systematics and served as research director at the Laboratory of Ornithology. In 1988 he moved to Boise State University, Idaho, where he developed a graduate program in raptor biology.

In 1968 Cade and some colleagues published a paper in the *Condor* entitled "Peregrines and Pesticides in Alaska." At this time, peregrine falcons had begun to show reproductive failures resulting in catastrophic population declines over most of North America and Europe. Working in Alaska, where peregrines were still common and seemed to be unaffected by the decline, the researchers looked at the possibility that pesticides could be responsible for the dwindling numbers elsewhere. In the course of their study, they found residues of organochlorine pesticides such as DDT, dichlordiphenylethylene (DDE, a metabolite of DDT), dichlordiphenyldichlor (DDD), and dieldrin in the tissues of adult peregrines in concentrations 100 times greater than in the prey of these birds. While the Alaskan population appeared to be holding its own despite this contamination, Cade and his colleagues concluded their paper by warning that peregrines could be nearing a threshold level of pesticide poisoning that could lead to reproductive malfunction. Population declines in Alaskan peregrines subsequently occurred in the 1970s.

While researchers were beginning to uncover the link between the increased use of DDT that began just after World War II and the dramatic reductions in peregrine falcons and other species, the actual mechanism was not fully known. The emerging picture became much clearer in 1971 when Cade and others published a paper in *Science*, "DDE Residues and Eggshell Changes in Alaskan Falcons and Hawks." Cade and his coworkers found that the organochlorine pesticide residues in the Alaskan peregrines, which had previously shown little or no declines, were starting to have an effect. They found that eggshell thickness in these falcons was reduced after exposure to DDT, as reported earlier in Great Britain; in fact, there was a highly significant negative correlation between eggshell thickness and DDE content. This meant that a contaminated female would lay eggs that were so fragile that they would break during incubation, leaving the female incapable of producing offspring.

Concerned over what he was finding and what it meant for the future of peregrines and other species, in 1970 Cade founded a conservation organization at Cornell University called The Peregrine Fund. This allowed for a focused effort on the recovery of the peregrine falcon, and Cade felt confident that his group could develop the techniques to do it. In the meantime, a new public awareness was emerging over DDT and its lethal effects on wildlife, and birds of prey such as the peregrine falcon figured prominently in this concern. Thanks in part to scientists like Cade who provided evidence on the threat of organochlorine pesticides, DDT was banned in 1972 by the Environmental Protection Agency.

At the time of The Peregrine Fund's inception, only a very small number of peregrines had ever been bred in captivity. Cade began a project to develop a captive breeding stock of peregrines to release to the wild. In 1973 the first successful hatch occurred, and the first release took place a year later—a breakthrough in endangered species research. Since then The Peregrine Fund has released over 4,000 captive-bred peregrines in 28 states, one of the first successful attempts at reestablishing an endangered species by this method. The recovery of the peregrine has been so complete that in August 1999 the Department of the Interior announced its decision to remove the peregrine falcon from the Endangered Species List. The entire history of this effort has been celebrated in a book Cade co-edited in 2003, entitled *Return of the Peregrine: A North American saga of tenacity and teamwork.*

The organization that Cade founded in 1970 has greatly expanded and is now involved with restoration efforts in over 35 countries on five continents. The Peregrine Fund has moved its headquarters to the World Center for Birds of Prey in Boise, Idaho, where research and conservation projects continue. Cade is currently retired but remains involved with the organization as its founding chairman. While pleased with the continuing increase of peregrine falcons, he is now mainly concerned with solving the problem of lead-poisoning of California Condors by bullet fragrments and shotgun pellets embedded in the carrion they eat.

BIBLIOGRAPHY

Cade, Tom J., "Exposure of California Condors to Lead from Spent Ammunition," *Journal of Wildlife Management*, 2007; Cade, Tom J., *Ecology of Peregrine and Gyrfalcon Populations in Alaska*, 1960; Cade, Tom J., *The Falcons of the World*, 1982; Cade, Tom J. and William Burnham, eds., *Return of the Peregrine: A North American saga of tenacity and teamwork*, 2003; Cade, Tom J., James H. Enderson, Carl G. Thelander, and Clayton M. White, eds., *Peregrine Falcon Populations, Their Management and Recovery*, 1988; Cade, Tom J., Jeffery L. Lincer, Clayton M. White, David G. Roseneau, and L. G. Swartz, "DDE Residues and Eggshell Changes in Alaskan Falcons and Hawks," *Science*, 1971; Cade, Tom J., Clayton M. White, and John R. Haugh, "Peregrines and Pesticides in Alaska," *The Condor*, 1968.

Caldwell, Lynton

(November 21, 1913–August 15, 2006)
Political Scientist

Lynton Caldwell helped to author the National Environmental Policy Act (NEPA) of 1969, one of the best-known and most significant pieces of national environmental legislation and the "inventor" of the Environmental Impact Statement, the teeth of NEPA. He was a political scientist and wrote prolifically on public administration and human-environment relations.

Lynton Keith Caldwell was born on November 21, 1913, in Montezuma, Iowa. He attended the University of Chicago, receiving a B.A. degree in English in 1935. He finished a master's degree in history and government three years later at Harvard, before returning to the University of Chicago, where he earned a Ph.D. in political science in 1943.

Caldwell began his career at Indiana University as an assistant professor of government and as director of the South Bend Center, where he worked from 1938 to 1944. In 1944, he took a position with the Council of State Governments, then in Chicago. He remained in this position until 1947, when he became professor of political science at the Maxwell Graduate School of Citizenship and Public Affairs at Syracuse University. In 1954 he joined the United Nations Technical Assistance Programme for one year as codirector of the Public Administration Institute for Turkey and the Middle East. In 1955 he was visiting professor of political science at the University of California at Berkeley. In 1956 he returned to Indiana University and remained there for the duration of his career as Professor of Public and Environmental Affairs and Arthur F. Bentley Professor of Political Science.

Caldwell began publishing in 1944 with a book entitled *The Administrative Theories of Hamilton and Jefferson*. His early writings did not focus on environmental topics. Over the course of the next 20 years he published books such as *The Government and Administration of New York* (1954) and *Improving the Public Service through Training* (1962), before shifting his focus to environmental issues. It was in 1962 that he had what he describes as an environmental "revelation." He was in Hong Kong for the Chinese New Year, and being that this is a family-oriented holiday and he was there alone, there was not much for him to do. He took a tram ride to the top of Victoria Peak, which overlooks the heavily populated island, and sat there in the early evening thinking about the future. Having traveled extensively in his role as an expert on public administration for the U.S. foreign aid program and the United Nations, Caldwell had become worried about the carelessness with which humans were treating the environment. He decided that he wanted to find a way to combine his expertise on management and public policy with a concern for the environment.

This decision led to a 1963 paper entitled "Environment: A New Focus for Public Policy?" for which he received the William E. Mosher Award from the American Society for Public Administration. This article has been credited for literally creating a new subfield of scholarly inquiry, one that suggests that governments should purposefully act to modify the interactions between humans and their environment. Caldwell was a catalyst for the founding, in 1972, of the School of Public and Environmental Affairs at Indiana University, Bloomington.

Starting in 1964, Caldwell wrote, edited, and contributed to many books focusing on environmental issues. Among them are *Environment: A Challenge to Modern Society* (1970), *Man and His Environment: Policy and Administration* (1975), *International Environmental Policy Emergence and Dimensions* (1984), and *Between Two Worlds:*

Science, the Environmental Movement, and Policy Choice (1992). Caldwell also contributed to such journals as *American Behavioral Scientist, Human Ecology, BioScience, Yale Review, Environmental Conservation, Public Administration Review, National Resources Journal, Unesco Courier, International Review of Administrative Science,* and numerous law reviews.

Caldwell was best known for the role he played in helping to bring about the NEPA, one of the United States' best-known and most significant pieces of national environmental legislation. Acting as a consultant to the Senate Committee on Interior and Insular Affairs in 1968, he composed *A Draft Resolution on a National Policy for the Environment.* The report created a statement of intent and purpose for Congress and examined the constitutional validity for a national environmental policy. Many of the concepts introduced by Caldwell in this draft were incorporated into the final bill, which was passed into law in 1969. NEPA created the Council on Environmental Quality (CEQ) and required environmental impact assessments to be carried out on "all major federal actions significantly affecting the quality of the human environment." These assessments were to be accompanied by environmental impact statements (EISs). NEPA placed responsibility on the federal government to act as an environmental trustee for future generations and to achieve a balance between population and resource use, allowing for a high standard of living. It has been argued, however, that because of the high-minded, sometimes vague wording of the act, it has been difficult to implement without active presidential initiative.

Caldwell was an ardent supporter of NEPA after its enactment, pointing out that its passage marked the first time that any modern state had enacted a comprehensive commitment toward responsible custody of its environment. He saw the Act and its requirement of Environmental Impact Statements as arms for strong environmental protection, and he believed that under the provisions of NEPA, the executive branch of the U.S. government was in possession of great protective powers. In Caldwell's pamphlet, *Population and Environment: Inseparable Policy Issues* (1985), he wrote that the NEPA could bring about a renewed "relationship of understanding and trust between the society-at-large and the government" when it came to environmental issues. He envisioned a situation where the president would work to identify crucial problems, while a network of locally based councils would work toward solving them. Many states and countries have emulated NEPA, establishing their own versions of the Act.

Caldwell was also active in international environmental issues. He acted as co-director of the Public Administration Institute for Turkey and the Middle East for the United Nations and on special assignments provided technical assistance in Colombia, Pakistan, India, the Philippines, Thailand, and Indonesia. He was a strong believer in population control and saw environmental protection and population control as one issue rather than two separate ones. Caldwell received many awards for his writings on public administration and the environment, including: National Science Foundation grants from 1965 to 1976, the Laverne Burchfield Award from the American Society for Public Administration in 1972, the Marshall E. Dimrock Award from the American Society for Public Administration in 1981, the John Gaus Award in 1996 from the American Political Science Association, and the Award of Achievement, Natural Resources Council of America, 1996. He was a United Nations Environment Programme Global 500 Laureate as of 1991.

Caldwell died at home in Bloomington, Indiana, on August 15, 2006, at the age of 96, survived by his wife of 65 years, Helen and their two children, Edwin and Elaine.

BIBLIOGRAPHY

"Caldwell Center for Culture and Ecology," www.thecaldwellcenter.org, Erdman, Karen, "Preventing Catastrophe," *Progressive*, 1985;

Hadley, Donita, 'Founding father' of ecological policy dies at 92," *Bloomington Herald-Times*, 2006; Kareiva, Peter, "A Science with the Answers, but Too Little Influence?" *Ecology*, 1993; "Lynton (Keith) Caldwell," *Contemporary Authors Online*, 2003.

Callicott, J. Baird
(May 9, 1941–)
Environmental Philosopher

J. Baird Callicott is a founder and seminal thinker in the modern field of environmental philosophy. He is best known as one of the leading experts on ALDO LEOPOLD's land ethic and in interpreting and applying Leopold's land ethic in light of recent paradigm shifts in ecology to such modern resource issues as wilderness designation and biodiversity protection. As a trailblazer in environmental philosophy, Callicott has succeeded in communicating his ideas in a way that is both valuable to academics and accessible to the general public.

John Baird Callicott was born May 9, 1941, in Memphis, Tennessee, to Burton (an artist) and Evelyne Baird Callicott. Callicott completed his B.A. in philosophy with honors at Rhodes College in Memphis in 1963. He then went to Syracuse University for graduate studies in philosophy, completing his M.A. in 1966 and his Ph.D. in 1971.

Callicott's interest in the environment did not evolve from any intense childhood experience in or with nature. Rather, his environmental philosophies were born from his participation in the late 1950s and 1960s as a foot soldier in the movement led by Martin Luther King Jr. In 1966, after completing his class work at Syracuse, Callicott returned home to teach at Memphis State University (now the University of Memphis). He served as faculty sponsor/adviser to the Black Students' Association and participated in the civil rights actions in 1968, which brought Martin Luther King Jr. to Memphis for his last and fatal campaign. In the deep reflection brought about by King's assassination, Callicott began to consider that the environment was the ultimate object of oppression. Studying during the Age of Ecology of the 1960s, Callicott became aware that the existing environmental crisis challenged the most fundamental assumptions of Western thought. Whereas the philosophy animating civil rights was centuries old—though still recognizably unrealized in political practice—a philosophy animating a liberation of nature was hitherto nonexistent. The age-old problems of the nature of nature, human natur and the human-nature relationship required reexplanation. As one of the founders of environmental philosophy, Callicott devoted his career to addressing these problems.

In 1971, Callicott accepted an appointment at the University of Wisconsin-Stevens Point. Until 1995, he taught in the UWSP Department of Philosophy where, in 1971, he designed and taught what is widely acknowledged as the nation's first college course in environmental ethics.

In 1979, Callicott contributed an article to the first issue of *Environmental Ethics*, the first academic journal in the fledgling field. His essay, "Elements of an Environmental Ethic: Moral Considerability and the Biotic Community," elaborated Aldo Leopold's argument for an environmental ethic. Two subsequent books on Leopold have made Callicott one of the nation's leading interpreters of *A Sand County Almanac* and Leopold's other

J. Baird Callicott (Photograph by Priscilla Solis Ybarra)

writings. His 1987 volume, *Companion to A Sand County Almanac*, which he edited and to which he contributed, is the first interpretive and critical discussion of Leopold's classic text. In 1991, Callicott coedited, with Susan Flader, *The River of the Mother of God and Other Essays by Aldo Leopold*, a collection of essays written by Aldo Leopold—many unpublished until they appeared in this book—that chart his thought from his time in New Mexico and Arizona as a Forest Service employee to author of one of the great conservation classics of the twentieth century. This chronologically-arranged collection of Leopold's pre-*Almanac* lierary and philosophical essays is especially valuable, as it illustrates the evolution of Leopold's ecological thinking, culminating with his advocation of a land ethic. Callicott's most important essays focused on Leopold's land ethic are collected in his 1989 *In Defense of the Land Ethic: Essays in Environmental Philosophy* and his 1999 *Beyond the Land Ethic: More Essays in Environmental Philosophy*.

Callicott suggests that we live on the verge of a profound paradigm shift concerning human interactions, perceptions, and attitudes toward nature and the natural world. Much of his work has sought to address or discover an ecologically and philosophically valid concept of sustainability. Callicott's concept revolves around dynamic human/nonhuman mutualism; the suggested (or imaginary) dichotomy between culture and nature is only detrimental to the progress of ecosystem conservation and restoration on which rest, ultimately, human wellbeing and human civilization. In a number of his writings he has explored how different cultures—both indigenous and "Western"—consider their environment: he wrote *Earth's Insights: A Survey of Ecological Ethics from the Mediterranean Basin to the Australian Outback* in 1997, and with has completed two books about the Ojibwa people's environmental ethics, *Clothed-in-Fur and Other Tales: an introduction to an Ojibwa world view* (1982, with co-author Thomas Overholt) and *American Indian Environmental Ethics: An Ojibwa Case Study* (with Michael P. Nelson, 2003), an examination of the Ojibwa worldview and relationship with the environment.

In 2004, with Clare Palmer, he edited a five-volume reference work titled *Environmental Philosophy: Critical Concepts in the Environment*, which includes the most important and influential papers relating to the field, written between the late 1960s, when the field was first developing, and the present. He co-edited with Robert Frodeman the two-volume, A-Z *Encyclopedia of Environmental Ethics*, published in 2008. In response to the most urgent environmental concern of the twenty-first century, global climate change, Callicott is engaged in scaling up the land ethic, which is scaled to "biotic communities," to an Earth ethic, which is scaled to the planetary biosphere, based on Leopold's earliest sortie into "conservation as a moral issue."

Callicott left Stevens Point in 1995 to join the Department of Philosophy and Religion Studies at the University of North Texas in Denton, where he now is a Regents Professor. As a Visiting Professor at Yale University in 2004-5, he received the Outstanding Teaching and Leadership Award from Yale's Interdisciplinary Center for Bioethics. Callicott serves on the advisory boards of the major academic journals of his field, including *Common Ground, Conservation Biology*, and the *Journal for the Study of Religion, Nature, and Culture*. He resides in Denton, Texas.

BIBLIOGRAPHY

Callicott, J. Baird, *Beyond the Land Ethic: More Essays in Environmental Philosophy*, 1999; Callicott, J. Baird, *In Defense of the Land Ethic: Essays in Environmental Philosophy*, 1989; Callicott, J. Baird, and Roger T. Ames, eds., *Asian Traditions of Thought: Essays in Environmental Philosophy*, 1989; Callicott, J. Baird, and Eric T. Freyfogle, eds., *For the Health of the Land: Previously Unpublished Essays and Other Writings by Aldo Leopold*, 1999; Callicott, J. Baird, and Michael P. Nelson, eds., *The Great New Wilderness Debate*, 1998, Callicott, J. Baird and Michael P. Nelson, *American Indian Environmental Ethics: An Ojibwa Case Study*, 2003, Callicott, J. Baird and Clare Palmer, *Environmental Philosophy*, 2004.

Carhart, Arthur
(September 18, 1892–November 30, 1978)
Landscape Architect

As a young U.S. Forest Service (USFS) employee in 1919, Arthur Carhart was instrumental in convincing the USFS to preserve a portion of its land for public recreation. Until that time, the USFS had loyally followed the precept of its founder GIFFORD PINCHOT, who held that all public forest land should be available for managed use by the logging, mining, and grazing industries. Carhart went on to write over 5,000 articles and books, many of them promoting the preservation of wilderness for primitive recreational use.

Arthur Hawthorne Carhart was born in Mapleton, Iowa, on September 18, 1892. He gained an appreciation for tree-filled landscapes from his grandfather, who had acquired his Iowa farm under the Tree Claim Act, which gave land to settlers who planted trees on it. Carhart studied at Iowa State College, earning that institution's first degree in landscape design in 1916. Upon graduating, Carhart served as a nurseryman in the United States Army during World War I. After the war, in 1919, he was hired by the U.S. Forest Service for a recently developed recreational engineer position and was dispatched to Denver. His role was scorned by many of the forest rangers, who nicknamed him "Beauty Engineer" or "Beauty Doctor," but Carhart proceeded undaunted.

Carhart's first assignment was to spend the summer of 1919 at Trappers Lake in northwestern Colorado. The largest lake in Colorado, and "one of the three finest mountain lakes in the American West," he later wrote, Carhart was to survey the lake's shore for homesites and for a road that would encircle the lake. He bunked at Scott Teague's fishing camp and spent his evenings talking to guests. One guest, Paul J. Rainey, a well-known big-game hunter, conversed at length with Carhart about the value of the plan to develop such a scenic public area. Eventually Carhart too doubted the ethics of the plan. Constructing private homes there would ruin the area's spectacular natural scenery. When Carhart submitted his report in the fall of 1919, which recommended that the area not be used for homesites, his supervisor, Carl Stahl, suggested he meet with another USFS employee, ALDO LEOPOLD, who was then supervisor of Carson National Forest in New Mexico. Leopold and Carhart no doubt were both encouraged to find that they shared the same hopes for USFS wilderness. (Two years later, in 1921, Leopold published his landmark article, "The Wilderness and Its Place in Forest Recreation Policy" in the *Journal of Forestry* and proposed that a 500,000-acre area of wilderness in Gila National Forest be set aside for recreational use only.) The memorandum that Carhart wrote about his meeting with Leopold outlined four types of USFS land that should be left undeveloped: the most beautiful places; mountain ridges and other areas that cannot support development; areas of use to groups, such as lakeshores, medicinal springs, and streams; and those so spectacular that God must have meant that they never be altered. After three years of consideration by the USFS, Carhart's proposal to scrap the road and shoreline homes at Trappers Lake was accepted. The land surrounding Trappers Lake was preserved in 1932 as the Flat Tops Primitive Area, to be used only for nonmotorized recreation.

During the interim, Carhart worked on two more projects. In 1920, he worked to preserve San Isabel National Forest in southern Colorado and develop the recreational possibilities there. Supported by an enthusiastic group of local public officials and business leaders, Carhart designed the first public campground in a national forest. The San Isabel Public Recreation Association raised funds to finance the improvements that the USFS would not pay for; several more campgrounds and recreational sites were built near the major towns bordering the national forest. Carhart surveyed the Quetico-Superior area of Superior National Forest in northern Minnesota in 1921 and recommended that it be left in as wild a state as possible, since the recreational potential there was immense. Now that area of lakes and streams is the preserved Boundary Waters Canoe Area.

Despite his success in promoting preservation at the USFS, Carhart left in 1922, disenchanted with its lack of greater support for recreation. He established his own landscape architecture firm, one of whose contracts was with the city of Denver. Carhart's plan was to design several large parks for Denver, each devoted to a different type of recreation. He worked especially on mountain parks in the foothills that border Denver to the west.

Carhart is also known for the 5,000 articles and books that he wrote after leaving the USFS. Some of these were popular western novels that he wrote either under his own name or his pen names, Hart Thorn and V. A.

VanSickle. Others were guides to outdoor activities, such as *Hunting North American Deer* (1946) and *Fresh Water Fishing* (1949). Yet others were important contributions to the growing body of conservation scholarship. *Timber in your Life* (1955), for example, was a detailed description of the forestry industry. *National Forests* (1959) was a guide to the geological and anthropological history of land held by the USFS. *Planning for America's Wildlands* (1961), which came out during the long campaign to pass the Wilderness bill, consisted of a clear philosophical basis and concrete recommendations for the protection of wilderness. He delineated the types of protection that were necessary for different categories of wilderness and insisted that extractive industries could not be allowed in lands set aside for primitive (nonmotorized) recreation.

One of Carhart's most prized contributions to conservation was the Conservation Library Center at the Denver Public Library, which he conceived of and helped establish in 1961. This collection of important material relating to conservation includes his own papers, as well as those of Wilderness Society director HOWARD ZAHNISER, the Soil Conservation Service's HUGH BENNETT, and population expert and writer WILLIAM VOGT.

Carhart's wife, Vera VanSickle, died in 1966. They had no children. Carhart died on November 28, 1978.

BIBLIOGRAPHY

Martin, E. J., "A Voice for the Wilderness: Arthur Carhart," *Landscape Architecture*, 1986; Nash, Roderick, "Arthur Carhart: Wildland Advocate," *Living Wilderness*, 1980; Stroud, Richard, *National Leaders of American Conservation*, 1985; Wolf, Tom, *Arthur Carhart: Wilderness Prophet*, 2008.

Carlton, Jasper

(March 16, 1940–)
Attorney, Founder and Director of Biodiversity Legal Foundation

Jasper Carlton co-founded and directed the Biodiversity Legal Foundation (BLF), a science-based nonprofit organization to protect imperiled ecosystems. The BLF differed from other conservation organizations in that it chooses ecosystems that others generally ignored and worked on behalf of all of the species that inhabited them, from the bottom of the food chain on up—not just the so-called charismatic species on which mainstream conservation organizations often focus. Due to its commitment to impeccable science and the skill of its staff, the BLF's litigation to hold federal agencies responsible for upholding environmental legislation such as the Clean Water Act, the National Forest Management Act, the Migratory Birds Treaty Act, the Endangered Species Act, and others was successful about 90 percent of the time. The BLF contributed to the listing of about one-third of the more than a thousand species currently listed as endangered or threatened.

Donald Conrad "Jasper" Carlton was born in Picayune, Mississippi, on March 16, 1940. His father, an adventuresome horticulturist, had worked in Africa before Jasper was born and passed a strong conservation ethic on to his children. When he was four, Carlton moved with his family to the Amazon rain forest for two years, where his father was assigned by the U.S. government to extract rubber from the jungle for the war effort. Spending his formative years in a tropical rain forest awoke what has been a life-long interest in and love for nature. The family moved to the coast of Maine when Carlton was six years old, so that he and his sister could receive what their parents considered a proper education, and he spent the remainder of his youth there, frequently exploring Baxter State Park and the backwoods of Maine with naturalist friends.

Worried that his son was spending too much time in the woods, Carlton's father urged him to study business. Carlton did so at the University of Florida, working his way through college and graduating in 1962. He was hired by the international division of the Genesco Corporation, the world's leader in apparel, and spent the next eight years opening up new export markets all over the world. He had become one of the youngest international trade executives in the country by 1968.

But by 1970, he became dissatisfied with what he came to feel was the "futility and meaninglessness of spending one's life making a living." So he returned to college, studying botany, behavioral psychology, and law at the University of Tennessee and the National Testing Lab Institute for Applied Behavioral Science in Bethel, Maine. He worked for two years as assistant director of a school for autistic children in Nashville and in his free time became increasingly involved in Tennessee conservation movements. Carlton joined the Sierra Club and Friends of the Earth, holding Tennessee state chapter office positions for both organizations. He worked on campaigns in the Tennessee Valley to protect native fisheries, freshwater mollusks, and the valley's last free-flowing rivers.

Carlton moved to Oregon in 1972, where he led a legal fight to defeat an oil platform manufacturing plant at the mouth of Oregon's Columbia River. He then spent several years in Idaho, where he began working in a naturalist's capacity on mountain caribou and grizzly bears in the Selkirk ecosystem. These animals and others were negatively impacted by the Forest Service roads that transected the area, and Carlton eventually sued Interior secretary James Watt to obtain the emergency listing as an endangered species of the woodland caribou and the closure of the Forest Service roads. For these accomplishments, Carlton was awarded the Wildlife Society's Public Service award in 1982. Moving east to Montana, Carlton directed the Montana Woodland Caribou Ecology Project during the mid-1980s, during which time he helped force a court order to end sport hunting of grizzly bears in Montana's wilderness areas.

By the late 1980s, Carlton had become an expert in the integration of biology and law. He had developed his ecosystem approach to conservation, which combines both scientific and legal perspectives, and was well-known for his reliance on only the best science and his objectivity. In 1991, Carlton along with a number of attorneys and conservation biologists founded the Biodiversity Legal Foundation, based in Boulder, Colorado. The BLF was a sleek, efficient organization, with just five full-time employees and between six and a dozen volunteers. Its office space was donated, and its computers and other equipment were not new. Its annual budget was less than $100,000. From its very beginning the BLF chose not to solicit funds from major foundations, in order to protect its freedom to work on the vanguard and choose controversial cases that corporate-funded foundations might not like.

The BLF worked in the following way. First, it chose imperiled ecosystems that were ignored by other conservation organizations. Then the BLF engaged expert scientists (who usually worked pro bono) to share their knowledge about all of the ecosystem's component species, from the bottom of the food chain on up, how they interacted, and what their individual habitat requirements were. The individual species that were most imperiled were identified, and reviews of their status were conducted. The federal agencies charged with protecting these species—the U.S. Fish and Wildlife Service, the U.S. Forest

Service, the National Marine Fisheries Service, the Bureau of Land Management, the Bureau of Reclamation, and many more—were then approached and were forced, through administrative and sometimes legal actions as well, to protect the species in question. Because the science that BLF based its actions on was irrefutable, and the BLF's pro bono attorneys were highly skilled at educating judges about the intricacies of ecosystems, BLF prevailed in about 90 percent of its legal suits.

Carlton traveled the country to teach environmental activists the steps necessary to successfully combine biology and law for conservation of species and their ecosystems. The BLF itself served as a classroom for interns or staff who typically worked for a few years to learn the process, then went on to begin their own similar organizations in other regions of the United States.

The BLF dissolved when Carlton retired in the early part of the 21st century, but many organizations, including the Center for Biological Diversity and the Center for Native Ecosystems continue to do the same type of work.

Carlton was the recipient of the Deep Ecologist of the Year award by the Foundation for Deep Ecology in 1994, and the first Conservation Legacy Award ever presented by the Center for Native Ecosystems, in 2006, which he received for "gonzo law, guerilla lawyering, a deep belief in the importance of good science, and an unwavering commitment to passionately defending and appreciating all forms of life." The Center for Native Ecosystems also presents the annual "Jasper Carlton Activist in the Trenches" Award to an activist who demonstrates exceptional advocacy on behalf of native biological diversity.

BIBLIOGRAPHY

Fantle, Will, "Wildlife defender – Jasper Carlton of the Biodiversity Legal Foundation," *The Progressive*, 1995; Frankowski, Eric, "Defending Animals vs. Mankind Is His Battle," *Longmont Daily Times-Call*, 1999; Noss, Reed, *A Citizen's Guide to Ecosystem Management*, Biodiversity Legal Foundation Special Report, 1999; Worland, Gayle, "He Walks with the Animals," *Westword*, 1999.

Carr, Archie
(June 16, 1909–May 21, 1987)
Zoologist, Writer

Archie Carr, a prominent and dedicated pioneer of conservation biology, is credited for shedding light on the previously unknown life history of sea turtles and stimulating an international demand to protect them and their nesting grounds. Many of his books, including *The Windward Road* (1956) and *So Excellent a Fishe* (1967), have become natural history classics and have won great acclaim both for their high literary quality and for contributing to the awareness of the ecology of sea turtles and their tropical habitats. Carr went beyond the research of these animals and fought for their preservation at a time when turtle hunting was rampant. He convinced the government of Costa Rica to protect the sea turtle nesting site at Tortuguero beach as a national park, and thanks to his efforts, sea turtle populations have shown dramatic increases.

Archie Fairly Carr Jr. was born on June 16, 1909, in Mobile, Alabama, to Archibald Fairly and Louise (Deaderick) Carr. His father, a Presbyterian minister, moved the family away from Alabama, first to Fort Worth, Texas, and later to Savannah, Georgia. Archie Carr Sr. enjoyed duck hunting and had a collection of natural history books, which young Archie pored over. Early on, Archie asserted an interest in snakes and other reptiles, an interest that horrified his mother and especially his grandmother, who forbade anyone to talk about snakes after three o'clock in the afternoon for fear that she would dream about them. Both parents encouraged him to do a lot of reading as a child, and his love of words followed him for the rest of his life.

Carr began attending Davidson College in 1928, intending to study English. But his interest in the natural world won out, and he soon switched to the University of Florida in Gainesville to study biology, earning his B.S. in 1932. He continued studying there and in 1934 received his master's degree. His 1937 Ph.D. was the first granted in zoology by the University of Florida. On January 1, 1937, Carr married MARJORIE HARRIS CARR, who became a well-known conservationist herself, and they eventually raised five children together.

Carr started teaching at the University of Florida in 1938 but spent his summers on a fellowship at Harvard University's Museum of Comparative Zoology, honing his skills in taxonomy and evolutionary biology. Working with another scientist from Harvard, he coauthored a monograph on the turtles of Cuba, Haiti, and the Bahamas, *Antillean Terrapins.* At the time, there was substantial scientific knowledge on freshwater turtles, but information on sea turtles was almost nonexistent and seemed based mainly on rumor and folklore. Carr formulated a goal for himself: to become the world's expert on sea turtles. In order to study sea turtle populations from both the Atlantic and the Pacific, he arranged for a leave of absence from the University of Florida, and in 1945 he and his wife and two children moved to Honduras. He taught biology there for five years at the Escuela Agrícola Panamericana while also studying sea turtles. During those years he filled in some of the gaps of scientific knowledge about sea turtles and began creating an international reputation for himself.

Carr and his family returned to Florida in 1949, and he was made a full professor by the university. They bought a house, near Micanopy on an alligator pond, that became their permanent home. In 1952 Carr published a second monograph called *The Handbook of Turtles: The Turtles of The United States, Canada, and Baja California*, which identified 79 species and subspecies of sea turtles. In addition to this and other scientific papers reporting facts of the sea turtles' natural history, Carr published a book that would become a conservation classic and profoundly affect his career. *The Windward Road: Adventures of a Naturalist on Remote Caribbean Shores* (1956) told stories of exotic Caribbean wildlife and the interactions he had with the local people as he searched for sea turtle nesting areas. Although it reads almost like an adventure book, it also educates readers about the life history of sea turtles and the imminent dangers facing them and their habitat. The book created worldwide concern over the plight of sea turtles and helped to launch a campaign to protect their nesting areas. Part of the popularity and critical acclaim for the book came from Carr's famous and abundant sense of humor and from the high quality of his writing. One chapter of the book, titled "The Black Beach," was published separately in *Mademoiselle* and won an O. Henry Award as one of the best short stories of 1956. Such was Carr's growing fame that the University of Florida relieved him of his teaching duties and made him a graduate research professor in 1959, which allowed him to concentrate on researching and writing books.

One especially avid fan of *The Windward Road*, Joshua Powers, formed an informal organization called the Brotherhood of the Green Turtles. An offshoot of this group was the Caribbean Conservation Corporation

(CCC), which set about to preserve and protect sea turtles and their habitat in the tropics. Carr was the founding scientific director of CCC, a post he held until his death. Many of his research projects were funded by the CCC; he conducted most of them at Tortuguero, a beach on the coast of Costa Rica. His studies also led him on numerous expeditions to other sea turtle habitats, including Brazil, South Africa, West Africa, the Azores, every part of the Gulf of Mexico, Jamaica, Portugal, and Pacific Central America, to name but a few. But the study site at Tortuguero, the last nesting grounds of the green sea turtle in the Americas, was where Carr concentrated most of his efforts—resulting in one of the most intensive and longest-lasting studies of an animal population ever conducted. His studies, almost all of which have implications for conservation, elucidated aspects of sea turtles' migration, nesting behavior, nest physiology, nutrition, demography, and more. During the 1960s, when Tortuguero beach was plagued with turtle hunters, Carr began working on a project called Operation Green Turtle, to distribute green turtle eggs and hatchlings to historical nesting grounds around the Caribbean and the Gulf of Mexico, in an attempt to reestablish hatcheries. He eventually convinced the Costa Rican government to declare the beach at Tortuguero a national park in 1975 and to enforce laws against turtle hunting. Tortuguero National Park also became one of the first successful ecotourism destinations, as thousands of people traveled to witness the turtles that Carr had made famous in his books. Carr's conservation efforts there became evident during the 1980s with dramatic increases in the nesting green turtle population.

Carr's conservationism was not limited to sea turtles. In 1964 he published two books about Africa and its wildlife: *Ulendo: Travels of a Naturalist in and out of Africa* and *Land and Wildlife of Africa*. In both books he repeatedly expresses his concern for the future of these unique animals and ecosystems. By the end of his life, he had written ten books and more than 120 scientific papers and magazine articles on sea turtles and other natural history subjects. He was the recipient of many awards and honors for his conservation work, including the World Wildlife Fund Gold Medal (1973) and the National Audubon Society's first Hal Borland Award (1984) for contributing to the understanding and protection of nature. He continued his research and writing up until his death and also continued to serve as chairman of the Marine Turtle Specialist Group of the International Union for the Conservation of Nature, as he had done since the 1960s. Carr died of cancer on May 21, 1987, at his home on Wewa Pond near the town of Micanopy, Florida.

BIBLIOGRAPHY

"Caribbean Conservation Corporation & Sea Turtle Survival League," www.cccturtle.org; Carr, Archie, *So Excellent a Fishe: A Natural History of Sea Turtles*, 1967; Davis, Frederick Rowe, *The Man Who Saved Sea Turtles: Archie Carr and the Origins of Conservation Biology*, 2007; Ehrenfeld, David, "Archie Carr Tribute", *Conservation Biology*, 1987; Graham, Frank, Jr., "What Matters Most: The Many Worlds of Archie and Marjorie Carr," *Audubon*, 1982; Maslow, Jonathan, *Footsteps in the Jungle: Adventures in the Scientific Exploration of the American Tropics*, 1996.

Carr, Marjorie Harris

(1915–October 10, 1997)
Biologist, Founder of Florida Defenders of the Environment

Marjorie Harris Carr, a biologist and conservationist, was a dominant figure in the protection of Florida's inland waters. She was the founder and longtime president of Florida Defenders of the Environment (FDE), a group she formed to help stop construction on the Cross-Florida Barge Canal, a shipping canal that was being excavated across the entire state to connect the Gulf of Mexico with the Atlantic Ocean. When she and her group were successful in halting the canal before it could be completed, she then worked to undo the environmental damage caused by the ill-advised project, which had included damming of one of Florida's most beautiful rivers, the Ocklawaha. The 110-mile Cross-Florida Greenway, a recreational trail system consisting of governmental lands formerly set aside for the canal, has been named after Carr, whose name will always be synonymous with conservation in Florida.

Marjorie Harris was born in 1915 in Boston, Massachusetts. In 1923, her father, a lawyer and schoolteacher, bought land in Florida as an escape from the bitter winters in New England. The family moved into a house near Bonita Springs, where her father planned to raise oranges in his retirement. Marjorie grew up with few neighbors but surrounded by a fascinating landscape of plants and animals, sparking a lifelong interest in natural history. She also enjoyed having parents who could answer her questions about the natural world and who encouraged her love of knowledge. By the age of nine she could identify more birds and flowers than most people know in a lifetime. Though the death of her father in 1931 and the subsequent years of the Depression had left her and her mother with little money, a bequest of $500 from a maiden aunt allowed Marjorie to begin attending the Florida State College for Women (now Florida State University) in 1932. She began a course of study that was highly unusual for a woman at that time—a major in zoology with a minor in bacteriology.

After graduating with a B.S. in zoology in 1936, she hoped to continue her studies at the University of North Carolina, but her fellowship fell through. So she took a job with the Resettlement Administration, a federal program established during the Depression, and became the state's first female wildlife technician at a fish hatchery in Welaka, Florida. Her supervisor, uncomfortable with a woman biologist, gave her a busywork assignment: to figure out what was wrong with some sick quail. She took the birds and sought advice at the laboratory at the University of Florida, where she met a doctoral student in zoology named ARCHIE CARR. Three months later, in January 1937, they were married.

When her new husband was offered a summer fellowship at Harvard's Museum of Comparative Zoology, the Carrs began a routine of spending winters in Florida and summers in Massachusetts. Marjorie Carr worked at the Museum for several summers but was not assigned the kind of challenging research she wanted. When she applied to Cornell to do graduate work on her first love, ornithology, the director told her that there was no place for a woman in that field. She was finally able to earn her master's degree from the University of Florida in 1942, with her thesis, "The Breeding Habits, Embryology, and Larval Development of the Large-mouthed Bass in Florida." During the course of her graduate research she became the first scientist to discover cases of social parasitism (the type commonly associated with cowbirds, who leave their chicks in the nests of other bird species to raise) in freshwater fish.

During the 1940s and early 1950s, Carr moved to Honduras and assisted her husband with his studies on sea turtles, contributed a paper to the *Wilson Bulletin* on swifts, and had five children. In 1949 the Carrs returned to Florida and bought a house on Wewa Pond near Micanopy. Carr settled into raising a family and teaching biology at nearby Gainesville High School. She was also a charter member of the Alachua Conservation Society and served on the conservation committee of the Alachua Audubon Society. In the early 1960s Carr began investigating a proposal announced by the Army Corps of Engineers to resume construction on the Cross-Florida Barge Canal. The controversial project, intended to connect the Gulf of Mexico with the Atlantic Ocean by way of a 12-foot-deep, 150-foot-wide canal, was initiated in the 1930s but had stalled shortly thereafter, only to be revived in 1964. Carr opposed the shipping canal for many reasons, but her main cause for alarm was that the canal would necessitate damming the Ocklawaha River—flooding a 16-mile section of the free-flowing river, threatening wildlife, converting 9,000 acres of hardwood forest into a shallow weedy reservoir, and ultimately destroying a uniquely beautiful semitropical stream. Carr accumulated documents and scientific information on the river, and in 1965 she began an unwavering lobbying effort to save the river and stop the canal. She besieged members of Congress and state leaders with letters and recruited scientists, lawyers, and economists to help her cause. Nevertheless, the Corps of Engineers continued construction and erected the Rodman Dam on the Ocklawaha in 1968.

By the following year, the Corps of Engineers had completed about a third of the canal, and Carr rallied other conservationists and formed FDE, a nonprofit citizens' group. The organization concentrated on publicizing undisclosed facts about the canal project and educating policy makers about the issue—emphasizing the facts that the canal threatened to contaminate the freshwater aquifer and that many aquatic species were already disappearing as a result of the dam. At Carr's request, attorneys from the Environmental Defense Fund (EDF) joined in legal action to halt the canal, and in 1971 FDE and EDF won a federal court injunction and persuaded President Nixon to issue an executive order halting construction. Though construction on the Cross-Florida Barge Canal ended, it was still an authorized federal project, and Carr spent the next two decades fighting to get the project officially deauthorized. She set other goals as well—to restore the Ocklawaha to its natural meandering course by breaching the Rodman Dam and to have the federal land that was granted to the canal turned over to the state as a conservation area. By 1990 the canal was finally deauthorized with a bill signed by President Bush.

The fight to tear down the dam has been less successful, hampered by a handful of local constituents who claim that the reservoir is a prime bass fishing spot. But the rest of the old canal route was turned over to the state in 1992, and Carr and FDE came up with a management plan for the land as a conservation area. The state legislature endorsed the plan, and the 110-mile-long corridor, named the Marjorie Carr Cross-Florida Greenway, has become a model recreational trail system.

Carr influenced other conservation efforts in the state as well. She was instrumental in establishing the Payne's Prairie State Preserve south of Gainesville and helped with restoration in the Everglades and with protecting the endangered Florida panther. In 1997 she was inducted into the Florida Women's Hall of Fame. Carr died at her home in Micanopy on October 10, 1997, of emphysema, just months before state agencies began considering the permit application of the Florida Department of Environmental Protection to demolish the Rodman Dam.

BIBLIOGRAPHY
Barash, Leah, "People Who Made a Difference: Marjorie Carr/Jack Kaufman," *National Wildlife*, 1992; Breton, Mary Joy, *Women Pioneers for the Environment*, 1998; Carr, Marjorie, "A Florida Scandal," 1996, www.

fladefenders.org/publications/FloridaScandal.html; Graham, Frank, Jr., "What Matters Most: The Many Worlds of Archie and Marjorie Carr," *Audubon*, 1982; Pittman, Craig, "Digging Ourselves into a Hole," *St. Petersburg Times*, 1999.

Carson, Rachel
(May 7, 1907–April 14, 1964)
Biologist, Writer

Biologist and writer Rachel Carson is often credited as the founding mother of today's environmental movement. Her early books, *Under the Sea Wind* (1941), *The Sea around Us* (1951), and *The Edge of the Sea* (1958), opened a world that had previously been unknown to most landbound humans. They established Carson's reputation as an eloquent writer who could explain science both clearly and poetically. Her best-known book is *Silent Spring* (1962), an exposé that revealed the grave dangers posed by synthetic pesticides. These "elixirs of death," as she called them, were first used during World War II and after the war were introduced to civil society to combat insect and weed pests. A best seller, *Silent Spring* raised much public concern in the United States and resulted in the first federal and state laws that regulated pesticide use.

Born on May 7, 1907, in Springdale, Pennsylvania, to Robert Warden and Maria Frazier (McClean) Carson, Rachel Louise Carson was a child fascinated by nature. Her chief pastimes included writing and illustrating stories about the wildlife surrounding her western Pennsylvania home. By the age of 12 she had published several stories in a national children's magazine and had won three prizes for her writing. Although her family was of modest means, and most women in her generation did not pursue a college education, Carson studied English and biology at Pennsylvania College for Women (now called Chatham College). After realizing that the natural world

Best known for writing *Silent Spring*, ecologist and author Rachel Carson spent summers in college studying marine biology. She believed that all life is interconnected and that everyone is responsible for stewardship of the environment. (Photograph courtesy of the National Oceanic and Atmospheric Administration, U.S. Department of Commerce)

could provide great inspiration for her literary work, she opted to major in biology. Carson graduated with a B.A. in 1929. Her biology professor and mentor, Mary Skinker, encouraged Carson to pursue postgraduate studies in biology, and she did, earning an M.A. in marine zoology from Johns Hopkins University in 1932. She probably would have worked toward a doctorate in aquatic biology had the sudden deaths of her father and sister not left her the family's sole breadwinner. To support her mother and young nieces, Carson began to work for the U.S. Bureau of Fisheries, first editing transcripts for radio broadcasts and then, starting in 1936, as an aquatic biologist. Once that bureau merged with the U.S. Biological Survey to become the U.S. Department of Fish and Wildlife in 1940, she became the editor in chief of its publications. Carson published 12 pamphlets with a strong conservationist message, called the Conservation in Action series.

Carson always supplemented her work for the government with independent natural history writing, which was published in magazines and as books. She published an essay entitled "Undersea" in the *Atlantic Monthly* in 1937, which she expanded into her first book, *Under the Sea Wind* (1941). This work provided a scientifically astute and poetic portrait of the sea and its inhabitants, a world most people at that time knew little about. *Under the Sea Wind* was issued shortly before the bombing of Pearl Harbor, and the ensuing national crisis hindered its sales. However, it received favorable reviews and established Carson's literary reputation. It took her 11 more years to publish *The Sea around Us* (1951), a *New York Times* best seller and winner of the National Book Award. The success of this book led to the reissue of *Under the Sea Wind* in 1952. That same year, finally earning enough income solely from her writing, Carson left the Department of Fish and Wildlife to pursue writing, biology, and life with her adopted son, her orphaned grandnephew Roger. Carson next wrote *The Edge of the Sea*, a book about life on the ocean shore, which also met with high acclaim when it came out in 1955. Raising Roger, Carson became aware of the importance of helping children appreciate nature. She wrote a short article for *Women's Home Companion* in 1956, "Help Your Child to Wonder," which she hoped to expand into a full-length book.

In the years following World War II, Carson became increasingly concerned about a newly emerging environmental problem. Chemical companies were developing a host of new synthetic pesticides that on the recommendation of the U.S. Department of Agriculture were being used rashly throughout the United States, on farms, in cities and the suburbs, even in wildlife refuges. When a birdwatcher named Olga Owens Huckins wrote Carson that the government had sprayed dichlordiphenyltrichlor (DDT) in her private wildlife refuge, resulting in the deaths of most of the refuge's bird life, Carson was inspired to begin a new writing project, which was to become her most famous and influential. *Silent Spring* (1962) was the product of painstaking, voluminous research into the problem. There was scientific evidence that such common pesticides as DDT, chlordane, dieldrin, aldrin, and others were harmful to many more organisms than the pests they were designed to kill, but the studies were scattered and published mostly in specialized academic journals. Carson culled the evidence and consolidated it into an eloquent and concise yet horrifying wake-up call to a society becoming increasingly dependent upon these toxic substances. Carson indicted chemical companies and the government for exaggerating the threat of insect pests and withholding information on the dangers posed by overuse of pesticides.

The book had an enormous public impact. Within days of its publication, a U.S. Senate hearing on the dangers of pesticide was convoked, and Pres. John F. Kennedy was compelled to respond to questions of pesticide abuse at press conferences. The chemical industry lashed out against Carson, spending a quarter of a million dollars to defame her. The industry withdrew its sponsorship of a television talk show she appeared on and pulled its advertisements from the *New Yorker* magazine, when it serialized excerpts of *Silent Spring*. Nevertheless, Carson's clarion held the public's attention, and in the years following the book's publication, 42 bills in state legislatures around the country were introduced to curb widespread use of insecticides, many of them becoming law. Carson herself campaigned for many of the bills, and she was awarded the Conservationist of the Year award from the National Wildlife Federation in 1963.

Ironically, during the writing of *Silent Spring*, Carson was struck by breast cancer (which her research revealed to be linked to pesticide exposure). Carson endured frequent trips to the hospital for radiation treatment during her four years' work on the book. Carson made herculean efforts to continue publicizing her cause during her last years and finally succumbed to the cancer on April 14, 1964. Her article "Help Your Child to Wonder" was reprinted in book form as *A Sense of Wonder* in 1965. In that year, the Rachel Carson Council, Inc., was founded by Carson's friends and colleagues to further Carson's research on pesticides. The Coastal Maine Wildlife Refuge was renamed for her in 1969, and she was posthumously awarded the Presidential Medal of Freedom in 1980.

BIBLIOGRAPHY
Brooks, Paul, *The House of Life: Rachel Carson at Work*, 1972; Gartner, Carol B., *Rachel Carson*, 1983; Lear, Linda, *Lost Woods: The Discovered Writing of Rachel Carson*, 1998; Lear, Linda, *Rachel Carson: Witness for Nature*, 1997; Lytle, Mark Hamilton, *The Gentle Subversive: Rachel Carson, Silent Spring, and the Rise of the Environmental Movement*, 1997; McCay, Mary A., *Rachel Carson*, Twayne's United States Authors Series, edited by Frank Day, 1993; Matthiessen, Peter, *Courage for the Earth: Writers, Scientists, and Activists Celebrate the Life and Writing of Rachel Carson*, 2007; "Rachel Carson Council, Inc.,"; www.members.aol.com/rccouncil/ourpage/index.htm; *Rachel Carson's Silent Spring*, PBS Video, 1992; Strong, Douglas H., *Dreamers & Defenders: American Conservationists*, 1988.

Carter, Jimmy
(October 1, 1924–)
Governor of Georgia, President of the United States

As governor of Georgia and president of the United States, Jimmy Carter initiated significant environmental protection. While governor, he created Georgia's Department of Natural Resources and enacted tough regulations on polluters. As president, he enacted the Superfund toxic waste cleanup legislation in the form of the Comprehensive Environmental Response Compensation and Liability Act and signed the Alaska Lands Act, the largest designation of wilderness in the history of the United States.

Born in Plains, Georgia, on October 1, 1924, James Earl Carter was the first child of James Earl and Lillian (Bessie) Carter. His father ran a farm supply store and an office that purchased peanuts from local farmers. He also, eventually, obtained 4,000 acres of farmland in Archery, Georgia, just outside of Plains, where he added the bagging and selling of fertilizer to his other lines of business. Carter followed in his father's footsteps and developed a capacity for hard work and entrepreneurship. As an adolescent, he would go in to town on Saturdays to sell peanuts, ice cream, and hot dogs with a cousin. Carter attended high school in Plains, where he is remembered as a bookworm and an excellent student. He played basketball and participated in debate.

Carter graduated from high school in 1941, at the age of 16. He studied at Georgia Southwestern College in Americus and the Georgia Institute of Technology, before entering the United States Naval Academy in 1943. At the Naval Academy, he continued to earn high grades and graduated in the top 10 percent of his class, in 1946. He spent his next two years working on battleships in the Navy. In 1948, he transferred to submarine service, applying in 1952 for admission to the nuclear submarine program. Carter was assigned to duty in Schenectady, New York, where he studied nuclear physics and engineering at Union College. However, when his father died in 1953, he abandoned his naval aspirations. Carter returned to Plains and took over the floundering family businesses, rebuilding and expanding them.

Carter's political career began in 1962, with a bid for the Georgia state senate. He was narrowly defeated in the primary but was selected as the Democratic candidate after it was discovered that his opponent had stuffed the ballot boxes. Carter won this election and was reelected two years later, serving in the Georgia senate from 1963 to 1966. He sought the Democratic nomination in the Georgia gubernatorial race of 1963 but did not receive it. It was at this point in Carter's life that he was "born again" as a Christian. This did not occur because of any one specific experience but rather emerged as a result of a cumulative period of spiritual growth for Carter. By nearly all accounts, being "born again" had little external effect on Carter's life. He did not go through any dramatic transformation as a politician, and he retained his confident, comfortable style of interacting with his constituents.

In 1970, he again sought the Democratic gubernatorial nomination. This time he was successful. He was elected the 76th governor of Georgia and served from 1971 to 1975. As governor, Carter involved women and minorities in Georgia's government, introduced a merit system for cabinet and judicial appointments, and improved prison rehabilitation programs.

One of his most significant accomplishments was structural in nature. He consolidated the 300 existing state agencies into a total of 22 agencies. He also instituted a system known as zero-base budgeting, which required each department to justify its annual budget from scratch.

Carter's period as governor was marked by significant environmental protection as well. He wrote in his book *Why Not the Best?*, published in 1975 as he was campaigning for the 1976 presidential election, that as governor he spent more time on preserving natural resources than on any other issue. Out of all of the newly reorganized state agencies, the Department of Natural Resources was perhaps the most successful. It gave environmentalists considerably more political clout, as well as a larger share of the annual state budget. In addition, Carter proposed several measures for the prevention of erosion and sedimentation and for the regulation of flood hazard areas. He also signed legislation that strengthened environmental enforcement procedures and provided civil penalties for violations of water, air, and surface mining protection laws. By the end of his term, nearly all industrial air and water polluters in Georgia had met federal and state pollution control regulations.

In December 1974, just before his first and only term as governor was about to end, Carter announced his candidacy for the Democratic presidential nomination. He campaigned across the country for the next two years and won the nomination at the Democratic National Convention in July 1976. He won the presidency with his open, populist style of campaigning, defeating incumbent Gerald Ford by a narrow margin. His first act as president was to sign an executive order granting full and unconditional pardons to Vietnam War draft resisters. His term of presidency was characterized by considerable achievements in foreign policy. Carter established diplomatic relations with China and negotiated a successful agreement between the leaders of Egypt and Israel, virtually ending the strife between these two countries. He signed an agreement to relinquish control of the Panama Canal to Panama in 2000, and arranged for an agreement with the USSR, enacting the Strategic Arms Limitation Talks II arms reduction treaty. Carter had a more difficult time at home, however, suffering poor relations with Congress and being unable to stimulate a U.S. economy that was undergoing a period of both inflation and unemployment.

As in his tenure as governor, though, Carter's presidency had a strong environmental focus. One of his first acts as president elect was to nominate Idaho governor and conservationist, CECIL ANDRUS, for the position of secretary of the interior. Carter was in staunch opposition to the pork-barrel federal dam projects that were then very popular with Congress. And he attempted, with a moderate degree of success, to bring an end to the dam-building frenzy in the western United States. He issued executive orders protecting wetlands, flood plains, and desert ecosystems. He created a Department of Energy. He was a believer in alternative energy sources, and entering office when he did, in the midst of an energy crisis, he advocated the use of natural gas and solar power and coordinated, in his first year in office, a comprehensive long-range energy policy. In response to the Love Canal contamination crisis, Carter initiated Superfund legislation that mandated collection on chemical manufacturers' insurance policies in order to clean up dumping grounds for toxic-waste. He also sent to Congress one of the most sweeping pieces of environmental legislation in U.S. history: the Alaska Lands Act, which in one bill doubled the size of the national parks in the United States and nearly tripled the amount of U.S. land designated as wilderness. The legislation was, according to author Douglas Brinkley, "hailed as a miracle by environmentalists."

Carter was not reelected to office in the 1980 election. He lost in a landslide to Ronald Reagan. Since leaving office, Carter has remained active in international and humanitarian affairs through the Carter Center of Emory University in Atlanta, Georgia, which he founded in 1982. The Center works for better opportunities for health and peace throughout the world, both through working through international policy-makers and at the grassroots level. Carter has also been heavily involved since the mid-1980s with Habitat for Humanity, an organization that provides housing for low-income, needy families in the United States and internationally.

Carter found himself again in the international spotlight in 1994 when he helped North Korea to negotiate a dispute over the production of nuclear weapons; he also journeyed to Bosnia in 1994, where he aided in bringing about a four-month cease-fire in the conflict between Serbia and Kosovo. Carter has recently been most active in attempts to resolve conflicts between Israel and the Palestinians. In 2002 he was awarded the Nobel Peace Prize "for his decades of untiring effort to find peaceful solutions to international conflicts, to advance democracy and human rights, and to promotes economic and social development."

Carter has been married to Rosalynn (Smith) Carter since 1946. They have four grown children, Jack, Chip, Jeff, and Amy Lyn. In his free time, and during breaks from his desk work, Carter makes furniture in his garage woodworking studio. He auctions off the furniture during annual fundraisers for the Carter Center, and has so far raised more than $10 million in this way.

BIBLIOGRAPHY
Brinkley, Douglas, *The Unfinished Presidency*, 1998; "The Carter Center: Advancing Human Rights and Alleviating Suffering," www.cartercenter.org; Carter, Jimmy, *Beyond the White House: waging peace, fighting disease, building hope, 2007;* Glad, Betty, *Jimmy Carter, in Search of the Great White House*, 1980;"Habitat for Humanity Int'l," www.habitat.org; "Jimmy Carter—Biography," www.nobelprize.org/nobel_prizes/peace/laureates/2002.

Carter, Majora
Community Organizer, Founder and Executive Director of Sustainable South Bronx

Founder and executive director of Sustainable South Bronx, Majora Carter is devoted to environmental and economic justice for the disenfranchised community of Hunts Point and the South Bronx, one of the poorest congressional districts in New York and home to the most power plants and waste facilities in the state. Through Carter's initiatives, the SSBX converted several landfills and empty lots into parks, created a "green roofs" initiative, removed an underused expressway, and started one of the first green collar training programs: the Bronx Environmental Stewardship Training Program.

Born and raised in the South Bronx, Carter grew up with a severe disconnection to the environment. The environment was only something to visit in Connecticut or New Jersey, not in the concrete jungle she called home. Opportunities to leave the South Bronx presented themselves through academics. She was accepted into the prestigious Bronx High School of Science, and then went on to receive a degree in film studies at Wesleyan University and an MFA in English and creative writing from New York University. While working on her MFA and going through a divorce, Carter moved back to her parents' house in Hunts Point in order to have a cheap place to live, but spent as little time as possible in the neighborhood.

All this began to change when she joined Writers Corps, a writing program for NYU fellows, and learned about an art-based community center right in her own neighborhood. She joined the organization and volunteered to work on public arts projects starting with the South Bronx Film and Video Festival. When Carter learned that the state was planning yet another landfill in their neighborhood to bring 48 percent of the city's waste to their area, she became an activist. Carter's investigations discovered other planned waste facility plants opening up, plants that released dioxins and other pollutants, contributing to an already high asthma rate in the area. Carter took up the fight against the landfill and eventually defeated the plans for the new landfill.

During this campaign, Carter began relating environmental degradation with social and economic injustice. Carter began visualizing ways to beautify her neighborhood. In 1998, $10,000 in seed money was granted by the New York City Parks Department to support Bronx River restoration projects. Carter then raised an additional $3.2 million to create Hunts Point Riverside Park, the first area park in over 60 years.

Through the SSBX organization, Carter and her team created several city parks, ensured more equitable distribution of New York's City's trash, and worked to reduce the use of long-haul diesel trucks hauling trash with barge and rail transport.

The SSBX developed the Bronx Environmental Stewardship Training Program to train local residents in landscaping, parks maintenance, green roof installation and hazardous waste clean-up. The goal is ecological and economical restoration. SSBX also began the South Bronx Green and Cool Roofs Demonstration Project, planting rooftop gardens to beautify the neighborhood, retain storm water, and provide insulation.

SSBX has fought prison construction in the South Bronx, and, with the Southern Bronx River Watershed Alliance, had 1.25 miles of the Sheridan Expressway that runs through the Bronx decommissioned and replaced with affordable housing, economic development, parks and river access. Carter wrote a successful $1.25 million feasibility study proposal for the South Bronx Greenway Project and has secured $30 million in funding for the community-led plan, which will build a bicycle and pedestrian greenway along the South Bronx waterfront, and provide open space and economic development.

Majora Carter (Photograph courtesy of Sustainable South Bronx)

Other projects of the SSBX include a Bronx Recycling Industrial Park instead of a proposed new power plant, holding current plants and treatment facilities in the South Bronx accountable for their pollution, and a city-wide Zero Waste campaign.

Carter is the recipient of numerous awards and grants including a 2005 MacArthur "Genius" Grant, the 2007 National Audubon Society's Rachel Carson Women in Conservation Award, and New York University's Martin Luther King Jr. Award for Humanitarian Service. She received an honorary doctorate from Mercy College in 2007 and was appointed to the New York Governor's Energy and Environmental Transition team, and the Clinton Global Initiatives Poverty Alleviation panel.

In 2006, Carter married filmmaker and SSBX's director of communications, James Burling Chase, in a ceremony at Hunts Point Riverside Park.

BIBLIOGRAPHY

Piperato, Susan, "Green the Ghetto," *Yoga and Joyful Living Magazine*, March/April 2008; Bello, Marisol, "Cities cultivate 2 types of green," *USA Today*, Dec. 2007; Bright, Adam M., "A tree grows in the Bronx," *Good Magazine*, September 26, 2006; www.goodmagazine.com/section/Portraits/A_Tree_Grows_in_the_Bronx; www.plentymag.com/features/2007/02/a_bronx_tale.php; www.ssbx.org/.

Carver, George Washington

(1860–1864 (?)–January 5, 1943)
Botanist, Agricultural Scientist, Inventor

George Washington Carver developed and promoted conservationist agricultural practices during the 46 years that he worked at the Tuskegee Institute in Alabama. His work focused on the most practical aspects of agricultural science, and he directed his efforts toward the people he most wanted to help, poor rural African American farmers of the Deep South.

George Washington Carver was born in Diamond Grove, Missouri. His exact birthdate is unknown, but his biographers estimate that he was born sometime between 1860 and 1864. His mother, Mary, was a slave owned by Moses and Susan Carver, and his father was most likely a slave too, killed before or shortly after his birth. When George Carver was just a year old, a gang of slave raiders kidnapped him and his mother. Mary was never found, but the Carvers tracked down George and raised him and his older brother, Jim, on their farm. Although he showed a precocious interest in learning and knew so much about plants that even as a child local farmers sought him out to diagnose and cure ailing plants, he was not allowed to attend the local elementary school because it accepted only White children. He left the Carver family when he was 14 years old to attend school in Neosho, Missouri. Once he realized that he knew more than the teacher, he moved with a local family to Fort Scott, Kansas. He fled Fort Scott horrified after witnessing the lynching of a Black man and spent the next decade wandering the Midwest, supporting himself by doing odd jobs and even spending a short period of time homesteading on 160 acres in arid western Kansas.

Carver graduated from high school in Minneapolis, Kansas, in the early 1880s and sought admission to Highland College in northeastern Kansas in 1885. He was prohibited from attending there because of his race but was accepted in 1890 at Simpson College in Indianola, Iowa. He studied art and supported himself by taking in laundry but was dissuaded from completing his degree by a professor who believed that an African American man—even one as artistically gifted as Carver—could not make a living as an artist. Carver moved to Ames, Iowa, to study agriculture at Iowa State College, where he rose to take charge of the school's greenhouse, assist botany professors in their research, and teach freshman botany courses. The school's first African American graduate, he earned a B.S. in 1894 and an M.S. in 1896 from Iowa State.

In 1896, Carver was offered a position as head of the new agricultural experimental station at Booker T. Washington's Tuskegee Normal and Industrial Institute in Alabama, an educational and research institution run by and for African Americans. Carver accepted the offer, replying to Washington that "it has always been the one ideal of my life to be of the greatest good to the greatest number of my people." His duties included running an experimental station, sharing his findings with local farmers, and teaching a variety of disciplines, including botany, chemistry, agricultural science, and mycology.

Upon his arrival in 1896, Carver dove immediately into the serious agricultural problems of the Deep South, which included soil depletion and pest infestation. Farmland had been used for intensive cultivation of cotton and tobacco for many generations, and it was severely eroded. Carver developed and promoted composting techniques, and he discovered that the soil could be nourished by rotating such alternative crops as peanuts, sweet potatoes, and black-eyed peas. Alternating these crops with cotton and tobacco helped discourage plant disease; Carver also experimented with hybridization to increase plant resistance to common pests. Through these techniques, he was able to produce impressive yields without the use of commercial fertilizer.

To disseminate his findings and advice, Carver wrote a series of 44 instructional bulletins on different topics over the years. They were notable for their readability and were printed in large quantities to be distributed to small farmers. Some focused on agricultural techniques; No. 6, for example, was entitled *How to Build Up Worn Out Soils* and described how he built up an acre of depleted farmland that initially produced $2.40 per acre, to the point that it yielded a net profit of $94.65 per acre. Others served to convince farmers of the usefulness of the new crops that Carver recommended. No. 5, *Cow Peas*, heralded this legume as a "nutritious and palatable food for man and beast" and provided 25 recipes that featured cow peas; No. 17, *Possibilities of the Sweet Potato in Macon County, Alabama*, covered every aspect of cultivation and use of this tuber and was such a popular edition that it was reprinted several times.

Despite the demand for Carver's bulletins, they did not entirely fulfill Tuskegee's mission to improve the lives of the southern farmer. Because many local farmers were illiterate, Carver traveled through the countryside to give demonstrations and lectures at church after Sunday services or in town squares. Educating farmers in this direct way was formalized in 1906, with the "movable school," a wagon that Tuskegee students equipped with demonstration materials and exhibits. This school on wheels promoted Carver's methods of scientific agriculture to some 2,000 farmers per month during its first summer and served as a model for the U.S. Department of Agriculture extension program.

Carver is best remembered for his promotion of the peanut. Carver had discovered that peanuts effectively added nitrogen to the soil and protected it from erosion, but he understood that farmers would not cultivate them unless there was a market for them. Bulletin No. 31, *How to Grow the Peanut and 105 Ways of Preparing It for Human Consumption*, published in 1916, suggested a tremendous variety of uses for peanuts and their by-products, including peanut butter, peanut oil, peanut flour, shaving cream, face cream, ink, cardboard, dyes, and shoe polish. His later work with the peanut resulted in almost 200 more uses for it. Once a strong peanut industry developed, it adopted Carver as its spokesman and asked him to address Congress in 1921 during its campaign to raise import duties on peanuts raised in the Orient. Carver impressed the congressmen with all of the samples of peanut products that he had brought, and they subsequently voted an import tax of four cents per bushel to save the southern peanut industry.

After this presentation Carver became an instant legend. Articles in national publications extolled his miraculous rise from slavery, his deep religious faith, his humble lifestyle and genuine unpretentiousness. Henry Ford and Thomas Edison both tried to convince Carver to work for them at much higher salaries than Tuskegee could ever offer him, but Carver insisted that he preferred to remain at Tuskegee and serve his own people.

Carver received many awards during his lifetime, including his induction into Great Britain's Royal Society of the Arts in 1916 and the Spingarn Medal from the National Association for the Advancement of Colored People in 1923. There have been many more after his death. Carver died of heart failure at Tuskegee on January 5, 1943.

BIBLIOGRAPHY

Adair, Gene, *George Washington Carver*, 1989; Elliott, Lawrence, *George Washington Carver: The Man Who Overcame*, 1966; Holt, Rackham, *George Washington Carver*, 1943; Kremer, Gary, *George Washington Carver in His Own Words*, 1987; McMurry, Linda, *George Washington Carver, Scientist and Symbol*, 1981.

Castillo, Aurora

(1914–April 30, 1998)
Cofounder and Director of Mothers of East Los Angeles

Aurora Castillo was a community activist who helped found and direct Mothers of East Los Angeles (MELA), a grassroots organization that works to improve the environments of poor, largely Chicano neighborhoods in southern California. Known as "La Doña" of East Los Angeles, Castillo received a 1995 Goldman Environmental Prize for her work.

Born in 1914, along with her twin sister, Bertha, Aurora Castillo was the daughter of Frances and Joaquin Pedro Castillo, both of whom were laundry workers. Aurora Castillo was the great-great-granddaughter of Augustine Pedro Olvera, for whom Los Angeles's famous Olvera Street was named. Castillo credited her father for her fighting spirit, saying she always carried with her his advice: "Put your shoulders back, hold your head high, be proud of your heritage and don't let them buffalo you." When she was in high school, Castillo wanted to study accounting, though she was discouraged by the anti-Latino prejudice of her teachers. Castillo did go to business school, as well as study drama and voice at Los Angeles City College. In 1940 she spent three months as a translator for the movie *Across the Wide Missouri*, starring Clark Gable and the Mexican actress María Elena Márquez. She eventually landed a job as secretary at Douglas Aircraft, after scoring high on a business law test; she worked for Douglas Aircraft for most of her career. Castillo never married or had children of her own, and she remained close to her family, including her many nieces and nephews, throughout her life.

Castillo's career as an activist began in 1984, when John Moretta, the priest of the local East Los Angeles Church of the Resurrection, asked women parishioners to protest the construction of a state prison in the neighborhood. The prison would have been the eighth in the area, and the women united to form MELA. Moretta later said he was surprised at how effective the group was, because its members had no training or experience in political organizing. The women were determined to protect their children, fearing possible escapes from the facility, and were no longer willing to see their neighborhood used as a dumping ground for state problems. Castillo said she decided to "fight like a lioness for the children of East Los Angeles." The group informed the community about the threat, using church crowds to spread the word. For two years, the mothers held protest marches every Monday at noon. The marches grew in size, the largest involving over 3,500 participants. MELA united with other groups in the Coalition Against the Prison in East Los Angeles, and the prison was finally relocated in 1992.

As MELA grew in size and experience, it began to work on a broad range of environmental issues. In 1987 MELA began a successful fight against the Lancer Project, a municipal waste incinerator that was to have been built in East Los Angeles. In 1988 the community organized against another toxic incinerator, this time to be built in Vernon, a small industrial community in the area. MELA developed a phone list of over 400 women who could be mobilized very quickly, and Castillo guarded this list fiercely, refusing to sell or give the names to any other group. In 1989 MELA united with Huntington High School students to stop a chemical treatment plant. The Chem-Clear Plant Project, which was to process cyanide and other hazardous chemicals, would have been located across the street from the high school, the largest in the district. The group also successfully rerouted an oil pipeline, which would have gone directly beneath a middle school. One notable defeat was the failure to stop malathion spraying for the Mediterranean fruit fly, commonly referred to as the Medfly. The group currently participates in the Water Conservation Program, which provides low flush toilets to area residents; leads a Lead Poison Awareness Program, which employs high school students to go door to door to educate the community about the dangers of lead poisoning; sponsors higher education scholarships; and directs a Graffiti Abatement Program.

In 1995 Castillo was awarded a Goldman Environmental Prize, which carried a no-strings-attached award of $75,000, the largest of any environmental award. Castillo was the first Latina and the oldest person ever to win the award, at 81. In an interview with the *Los Angeles Times* on receiving the award, Castillo said, "We may not have a Ph.D. after our names, but we have common sense and logic and we are not a dumping ground. We are not the sleeping giant people think we are. We're wide awake and no way will anything be put over on us." Castillo died of leukemia in Los Angeles on April 30, 1998.

BIBLIOGRAPHY

"Aurora Castillo: Goldman Prize," www.goldmanprize.org/node/89; Berger, Rose Marie, "Women Heroes of Environmental Activism," *Sojourner's Magazine*, 1997; "Madres del Este de Los Angeles Santa Isabel," www.clnet.ucla.edu/community/intercambios/melasi/; "Mothers' Group Fights Back in Los Angeles," *New York Times*, 1989; Quintanilla, Michael, "The Earth Mother," *Los Angeles Times*, 1995; Schwab, Jim, *Deeper Shades of Green*, 1994.

Catlin, George
(July 26, 1796–December 23, 1872)
Painter

George Catlin is best known for his large collection of paintings of Native Americans, pictured at work in their villages or in traditional ceremonies. He is known as a conservationist for his proposal, in 1841, of a "nation's Park" that would preserve wild America—"man and beast, in all the wild and freshness of their nature's beauty!"—as he had witnessed it during his painting expeditions. This call was sounded 30 years before the first national park, Yellowstone, was established by Congress. Although some now complain of the racist tinge to Catlin's call for parks as a place where Indians would be on exhibit for visitors, environmental historians cite Catlin as the first American to move from lamenting the destruction of nature during westward expansion to a plan for preserving wild places.

George Catlin was born on July 26, 1796, in Wilkes Barre, Pennsylvania, the fifth of 14 children. His mother, who had been captured by the Iroquois when she was eight years old, told her children stories about Indian ways of life, and Catlin heard more from the many white visitors who stayed at their home on their way to or from Indian lands. Catlin studied and practiced law professionally and painted as a hobby until 1823, when he decided to paint full time. He painted portraits of the wealthy until about 1830, when he discovered his calling. On a visit to Philadelphia he saw a delegation of a dozen Indians who seemed to him awesome and dignified in their traditional dress, and he was struck by the thought that when their lands were conquered by Whites, their culture and traditions would disappear. Catlin later wrote that seeing the delegation inspired his decision "to use my art… in rescuing from oblivion the looks and customs of the vanishing races of native man in America."

Catlin took off west in approximately 1831 with a fur-trapping expedition to paint Plains Indians. He painted or drew whenever he could, spending sometimes just a few minutes doing a rapid pencil sketch that he later filled in or, if he had more time, painting with oils on canvas. His first expedition was three months long, and for the next eight years, Catlin would travel extensively with explorers and frequently with William Clark, the U.S. Superintendent of Indian Affairs. He, his wife, Clara Gregory, and their son would use Saint Louis as their base, and he did the finishing work on his paintings there.

During his time with the Indians, Catlin developed a familiarity and respect for them. He became convinced that the Plains Indians were superior beings who were able to manage their land well and live comfortably without depleting their main source of meat, the buffalo. Catlin was worried, however, as were other thinkers of his time, most notably author JAMES FENIMORE COOPER, that Indian culture would be destroyed by the droves of Whites to come. Instead of merely bemoaning what he feared was inevitable, however, Catlin proposed the creation of "a nation's Park," which would preserve an area of the Great Plains as it was, complete with buffalo and Indians, and keep out White settlers. Catlin wrote his proposal in "Letter—No. 1," a chapter in his 1841 book *Letters and Notes on the Manners, Customs, and Conditions of the North American Indians*:

> And what a splendid contemplation too, when one (who has traveled these realms, and can duly appreciate them) imagines them as they might in future be seen, (by some great protecting policy of government) preserved in their pristine beauty and wildness, in a *magnificent park*, where the world could see for ages to come, the native Indian in his classic attire, galloping his wild horse, with sinewy bow, and shield and lance, amid the fleeting herds of elks and buffaloes. What a beautiful and thrilling specimen for America to preserve and hold up to the view of her refined citizens and the world, in future ages! A *nation's Park*, containing man and beast, in all the wild and freshness of their nature's beauty!
>
> I would ask no other monument to my memory, nor any other enrollment of my name amongst the famous dead, than the reputation of having been the founder of such an institution.

Catlin was not to be the founder of national parks; he spent the rest of his life painting and exhibiting his work and trying unsuccessfully to make a living from his art. He suffered financial ruin and traded his first 600 paintings in 1852 to Joseph Harrison for the cash he needed to repay his debts. He set out once again for the western United States and to South America as well and by 1870 had completed 600 more paintings. Catlin had made a friend at the Smithsonian Institution and exhibited his work there in 1872, in the hopes of convincing the U.S. Congress to purchase his "Indian Gallery," as he called his collection. While he was in Washington, Congress voted to establish Yellowstone National Park, the first national park in the United States.

Catlin died on December 23, 1872, in Jersey City, New Jersey, after a sudden decline in his health. The heirs of Joseph Harrison donated Catlin's work to the Smithsonian Institution after Harrison's death, and Catlin's later collection of paintings was purchased by the American Museum of Natural History and the New York Historical Society.

BIBLIOGRAPHY

Brutvan, Sheryl A., *George Catlin: An American View*, 1988; Dippie, Brian W., *Catlin and His Contemporaries: The Politics of Patronage*, 1990; Mitchell, Lee Clark, *Witness to a Vanishing America*, 1981; Reich, Susannah, *Painting the Wild Frontier: The Art and Adventures of George Catlin*, 2008 Weber, Ronald, "I Would Ask No Other Monument to My Memory: George Catlin and a Nation's Park," *Journal of the West*, 1998.

Caudill, Harry
(May 3, 1922–November 29, 1990)
Writer, Attorney

Harry Caudill, whose roots trace back to the earliest white settlement of southeast Kentucky's Appalachia region, was an eloquent spokesman for his homeland and its people in their struggle against the exploitations of the coal-mining industry. For years he practiced law in mountain courthouses, and he served three terms in the Kentucky state legislature—striving to loosen the grip of the out-of-state coal companies that have wreaked such destruction in the Appalachian region in their pursuit of coal and huge profits. Eventually Caudill began writing books in an attempt to make the abuses of the industry a national issue and to sound the warning that in disregarding coal mining's cost in human and environmental misery, a precedent is set that the whole country must contend with. His books, *Night Comes to the Cumberlands: A Biography of a Depressed Area* (1963), *My Land Is Dying* (1971), *Watches of the Night* (1976) and others, many of which draw an unyielding portrait of a land rich in resources yet impoverished by neglect and misuse, were extremely influential in bringing attention to the problems in Appalachia.

Harry Monroe Caudill was born in Whitesburg, Kentucky, on May 3, 1922, to Cro Carr and Martha (Blair) Caudill. Cro Carr worked in the coal mines until he lost an arm in an accident in 1917. Caudill and his siblings were raised in Whitesburg on the Cumberland Plateau in southeastern Kentucky, a mountainous region of ridges and hollows, which contains dense forests and rich veins of coal. In 1943 during World War II the U.S. Army sent Caudill to fight in Italy; he eventually sustained a severe leg injury and was posted home. By 1948 he had earned a bachelor of law degree from the University of Kentucky and was admitted to the bar of the State of Kentucky. He began practicing law in a private practice in mountain courthouses in the Appalachian region, which he would continue to do for 28 years. In 1949 he married Anne Frye, with whom he would raise a family of two sons and a daughter. Three times he represented Letcher County in the Kentucky legislature, starting in 1954.

In the spring of 1960, Caudill accepted an invitation to give the commencement speech at an eighth-grade graduation in a coal camp school. Only seven students were graduating from the ramshackle two-room schoolhouse, and only one of the students' parents had steady work. From the window Caudill could see a hill of mining slag and was pained to hear the students singing "America the Beautiful." The irony of that setting inspired him to write his first book, *Night Comes to the Cumberlands: A Biography of a Depressed Area*, which was published in 1963. This book, which would later come to influence the formation of public policy, rendered a harsh indictment of the coal industry's abuses. Caudill articulates the irony he perceived in that two-room coal camp schoolhouse: the Appalachian region, endowed with unmatched deposits of coal, petroleum, and minerals, holds several of the poorest counties in the United States. Coal barons managed to extract vast fortunes out of the coal veins in the hills and left nothing behind but political corruption and a wasted landscape.

In *Night Comes to the Cumberlands* Caudill traces the history of mining in his homeland, highlighting some of the worst atrocities, such as the "broad-form deed," which the earliest coal speculators devised to chisel the coal out from under the landowners without paying a fair price for it. Coal company agents would approach the people living in the hillsides and offer a sum of money in exchange for the right to mine there someday, using whatever methods were "convenient or necessary" to extract the coal. It wasn't until years later that these deeds, many of which had been signed by illiterate farmers, would come back to haunt their descendants. Strip mining had become the mode of choice among coal operators, being the fastest and cheapest way, yet it left the surface land and even the landowners' houses destroyed and left the landowners with no legal recourse or remedy. Those who worked in the mines suffered as well, from rock-bottom wages and negligent safety standards. The lax governmental regulations allowing coal companies to operate in destructive and oppressive ways set a pattern for later industrial ventures everywhere else in the country. *Night Comes to the Cumberlands* eventually stirred things up in the rest of the nation: the general public began to take an aversion to strip mining, and the plight of Appalachian people began to gain publicity. Even President Kennedy took notice and began making an effort to alleviate some of the evils of poverty that plagued the region.

In *My Land Is Dying*, published in 1971 complete with photo illustrations, Caudill focuses on surface mining and the trauma it causes the environment. He writes with pride about the Appalachian woodlands where he grew up and the complex diversity of tree species there—a greater variety of trees than anywhere else in the Northern Hemisphere. Yet by the beginning of 1970, over a million acres in the region had been strip-mined, with operations accelerating every year. In the process, strips of mountainside were peeled away, denuding the area of all vegetation, and the coal was mined out of the cuts. The resultant spoil was dumped down the side of the mountain, filling the hollow below with silt and allowing the creek to turn to acid mud. Anyone who raised concerns for the wrecked land was just plowing straight into heavy seas, writes Caudill, since no politician from a coal state wanted to challenge the power of the coal cabal.

In 1976, *Watches of the Night* was published, perhaps Caudill's angriest book of all. In frustration he writes that in the 13 years since *Night Comes to the Cumberlands* there had been no significant changes in the federal effort to regulate coal strip mining or to finance reclamation efforts. He continues the warnings of earlier books and describes the results of a coal boom in the early 1970s as the "murder of a land."

Caudill's work earned him many rewards, including a Kentucky Statesman award (1968), a Tom Wallace Forestry award (1976), and honorary degrees from Tusculum College (1966), Berea College (1971), and the University of Kentucky (1971). In addition to writing books and attending conferences on public affairs around the country, Caudill taught Appalachian studies at the University of Kentucky from 1977 to 1990.

Suffering from Parkinson's disease, Caudill died of a self-inflicted gunshot wound to the head on November 29, 1990, in Whitesburg, Kentucky.

BIBLIOGRAPHY

Caudill, Harry M., *My Land is Dying*, 1971; Caudill, Harry M., *Night Comes to the Cumberlands: A Biography of a Depressed Area*, 1963; Caudill, Harry, M., *Theirs Be the Power: the Moguls of Eastern Kentucky*, 1983; Caudill, Harry M., *The Watches of the Night*, 1976; Mitchell, John G., "The Mountains, the Miners, and Mister Caudill," *Audubon*, 1988; Mullins, Tylina Jo, *A "Good Angry Man" Harry Caudill: the Formative Years, 1922-1960*, 2002.

Chafee, John
(October 22, 1922–October 24, 1999)
U.S. Senator from Rhode Island

John Chafee was a moderate Republican who served as governor of Rhode Island for 6 years and as a senator for Rhode Island for 22 years. He was a successful statesman, largely due to his consensus-building capabilities. During his tenure in the U.S. Senate, which lasted from 1977 to 1999, he was significantly involved in the passage of nearly every piece of environmental legislation.

John Hubbard Chafee was born in Providence, Rhode Island, on October 22, 1922, to John and Janet (Hunter) Chafee. His father was a tool manufacturer and was descended from a family that had been in Rhode Island since the seventeenth century. On his mother's side he had two relatives who had served as governors of Rhode Island: his great-grandfather and one of his great-uncles. However (as he is quoted in a 1994 *Washington Monthly* article), "in those days you were governor of Rhode Island for a year, so everybody and his brother had served as governor. I never met a politician before I went to college." Chafee attended the Providence public elementary schools, then the Providence Country Day School, and finally Deerfield Academy in Deerfield, Massachusetts, from which he graduated in 1940.

Chafee attended Yale University, where he captained the undefeated freshman wrestling team. During Chafee's sophomore year at Yale, the United States entered World War II. Chafee left school and enlisted in the U.S. Marine Corps as a private. He served from 1942 to 1945, first as a soldier, landing with the first troops at Guadalcanal. He then served in Australia before being ordered back to the United States in 1943 to attend Officers Candidate School. He was commissioned a second lieutenant, U.S. Marine Corps Reserve, in June 1944. At the beginning of 1945, he was sent to Guam, and he served in the battle of Okinawa with the 6th Marine Division. He left active duty in December 1945.

Returning to Yale at the end of the war, Chafee resumed his studies. At Yale, he rubbed elbows with prominent politicians and future statesmen, including George Bush. Like Bush, Chafee was "tapped" into the distinguished Skull and Bones secret society in his junior year. He received his B.A degree in 1947. Chafee then attended Harvard Law School, graduating with an LL.B. in 1950. He was admitted to the Rhode Island bar later that year, and he opened a practice in Providence, only to have his career interrupted by the Korean War. He served as commander with a rifle company in Korea, and then with the Marine Corps legal office at Pearl Harbor for the years 1951 to 1953. A longtime aide of Chaffee's would later observe that he thought the military, with its diverse array of people from different backgrounds gathered for a common purpose, had a profound effect on Chafee's attitude toward people. It made him curious about the lives of others.

When Chafee returned from Korea, he resumed his law practice and became involved in local politics. In 1952, he served as an aid in the unsuccessful Providence mayoral campaign of Christopher Del Sesto. In 1956, Chafee sought and was elected to a seat in the Rhode Island House of Representatives from the third district, Warwick. He was a member of the house from 1957 to 1962 and was minority leader from 1959 on. In 1962, Chafee ran for governor. Being a Republican in a heavily Democratic state, Chafee was not favored to win. However, thanks to his keen political sense and his promises to impose no new taxes and to bring more jobs and higher wages to Rhode Islanders, he defeated the incumbent by the narrow margin of 398 votes. Serving a total of three terms as governor, from 1963 to 1969, Chafee worked successfully with a Democratic legislature, signing a comprehensive medical aid program for the aged and authorizing the acquisition of large tracts of land for seven woodland and waterfront state parks. In 1969, Chafee was defeated in his bid for a fourth term as governor, probably due to his frank advocacy of a new, unattractive tax on Rhode Islanders (which his opponent instituted despite his campaign promises to the contrary). By this time, Chafee had risen to prominence as a leader in the national Republican Party. After he failed to be reelected as governor, Chafee was appointed to the post of secretary of the navy by Richard Nixon in 1969, a position he held until 1972.

During the years 1973 through 1976 Chafee practiced law in Providence, an occupation he found to be not nearly as exciting as public service. In 1976, he was elected to the U.S. Senate. He served in the Senate from 1977 until his death in 1999. Chafee was a moderate Republican who was well respected for his consensus-building skills and for his willingness to compromise. From his post on the Environment and Public Works Committee (which he occupied from his arrival in the Senate; he was its chairman from 1995 to 1999) he was involved in nearly every piece of important environmental legislation that went through the Senate during his 22-year tenure. In 1980, he authored the Superfund program that was created under the Comprehensive Environmental Response Compensation and Liability Act (CERCLA), which funded and directed the cleanup of hazardous-waste dump sites across the country. In 1982, he helped to create the National Estuary Program and the Coastal Barrier Resources Act, a piece of legislation that cataloged shoreline areas to be protected from development. Chafee was also involved in the passage of the Clean Water Act of 1986 and in the Oil Pollution Act of 1990, which demanded that polluters pay for oil cleanup and compensate victims. He also played a central role in 1990 in amending the Clean Air Act, which had first been passed in 1967.

Chafee was a defender of the Environmental Protection Agency, protecting it from the cuts and budget riders with which it was assailed by the conservative Republican Congress throughout the mid-1990s. He carried a lifetime 70 percent rating from the League of Conservation Voters and enjoyed the support of such organizations as Defenders of Wildlife. Chafee received many awards for his environmental efforts. He received a National Environmental Quality award from the Natural Resources Council of America in 1995, and in 1999 the League of Conservation Voters presented him with a Lifetime Achievement Award for his "successful leadership in strengthening the Clean Air and Safe Drinking Water acts and his tireless efforts to preserve open space and conserve America's natural resources."

Chafee died October 24, 1999, from heart failure at Bethesda's National Naval Medical Center at the age of 77. He is survived by his wife of 49 years, Virginia, and by five of their grown children (a sixth died in 1968).

BIBLIOGRAPHY

Benenson, Bob, "Environment and Public Works," *Congressional Quarterly Weekly Report*, 1994; "John Chafee's Rarity", *London Economist*, 1999; Pope, Charles, "In the Lull after Chafee's Death, A Sigh of Uncertainty," *Congressional Quarterly Weekly Report*, 1999; Shenk, Joshua Wolf, "An Endangered Species," *Washington Monthly*, 1995.

Chapman, Frank
(June 12, 1864–November 15, 1945)
Ornithologist, Editor

Frank Chapman was a self-educated ornithologist who rose to curate the Department of Birds at the American Museum of Natural History. He founded and edited the ornithological publication *Bird Lore*, later to become the National Audubon Society's magazine *Audubon*. Chapman's work encouraged both amateur bird-watchers and professional ornithologists. From his position of prestige and influence, he called for strict federal protection of birds and their habitat.

Frank Michler Chapman was born on June 12, 1864, in Englewood, New Jersey. When he graduated from high school in 1880, he immediately began working for the American Exchange National Bank, with which his late father had been associated. Chapman worked there for six years, spending all of his free time bird-watching. He befriended local birders, experimented with taxidermy, and worked with the U.S. Biological Survey on bird counts. By 1886, he reportedly could no longer stand to spend so much time away from birds, and he quit the bank. An inheritance from his father funded a year of independent study in Florida.

When Chapman returned from Florida with a large collection of bird skins, he visited the American Museum of Natural History in New York City and received permission to compare his specimens with those in the museum's laboratories. Within the year his talent and interest became apparent to the staff, and he was offered a position as assistant to the head of the Department of Mammals and Birds, Dr. J. A. Allen. Chapman soon became assistant curator of that department, and when it was divided in 1920, he was named curator of the Department of Birds. He retained that position until his retirement in 1942.

Chapman made several innovations to the way birds had traditionally been exhibited: rows of stuffed specimens on perches. He divided the museum's bird collection by region and designed exhibits that incorporated the birds' natural habitats. His trademark designs included a painted background and a foreground with natural elements such as vegetation and rocks. Because these were far more expensive to mount, Chapman raised the money for them himself. Chapman also encouraged local bird-watchers by providing a special exhibit of birds local to New York City and a rotating New York City "Birds of the Month" exhibit.

A board member of the newly fledged Audubon Society, Chapman founded and edited its official publication *Bird Lore*, again financing it himself. In addition to its studies written for the experienced ornithologist, *Bird Lore* included notes from Audubon Society meetings and editorials calling for more stringent government protection of birds. After the passage of the first law to protect birds, the Lacey Act of 1900 that prohibited interstate commerce of birds killed in violation of state laws, Chapman accompanied the first National Audubon Society president, WILLIAM DUTCHER, on surveys of New York clothing and millinery shops in search of illegal plumes. This vigilance was crucial to the success of the Lacey Act. Chapman reportedly persuaded Pres. THEODORE ROOSEVELT to proclaim Florida's Pelican Island the country's first federal bird reserve in 1904. He also established Audubon's annual Christmas bird count, in which bird-watchers spend a 24-hour period during the Christmas season recording species and numbers of all the birds they see within an area 15 miles in diameter.

Chapman was an important behind-the-scenes actor in the controversies that rocked the Audubon Society during its first few decades. When Society president Gilbert Pearson was challenged by several influential members at annual meetings from 1929 to 1933 for what they felt was inappropriate collaboration with the hunting industry, Chapman excluded any mention of it in his meeting notes for *Bird-Lore*. He likewise published nothing about the Emergency Conservation Committee, formed by Audubon members ROSALIE EDGE, Willard Van Name, and Irving Brant to reform the Audubon Society and oust Pearson. But when Pearson's decision to lease trapping rights to Audubon's Louisiana Paul Rainey Wildlife Refuge and his exorbitant annual salary became public knowledge, Chapman played a critical role in finally deposing Pearson.

Chapman handed the reins of *Bird-Lore* to the National Audubon Society in 1934. The name of the publication was changed to *Audubon* in 1941; it continues to be an influential conservation magazine to this day. Chapman authored 17 books, including bird guides and accounts of his expeditions. For his scientific work he was awarded the Brewster Medal, the John Burroughs Medal, the Roosevelt Medal, and the very first Elliot and Linnaean Society Medals.

Upon his retirement from the Museum in 1942, Chapman moved to Florida where he could study birds year-round. His wife, Fannie Bates, whom he had married in 1898 and of whom he once wrote that "she made it the chief object of her life to advance the aims of mine," died in 1944. Chapman, survived by his son Frank Chapman Jr., died in New York City on November 15, 1945.

BIBLIOGRAPHY

Chapman, Frank, *Autobiography of a Bird Lover*, 1933; "Christmas Bird Count," www.audubon.org/bird/cbc/history.html; Graham, Frank Jr., "National Wildlife Refuge Centennial, Safe Havens: Where Wildlife Rules," *Audubon*, 2003; Griscom, Ludlow, "Frank Michler Chapman, 1864–1945," *Audubon*, 1946; Murphy, Robert Cushman, "Frank Michler Chapman, 1864–1945," *The Auk*, 1950; Zimmer, John T., "Frank Michler Chapman," *American Naturalist*, 1946.

Chappell, Kate, and Tom Chappell

(October 17, 1945– ; February 17, 1943–)
Entrepreneurs

In 1970, Kate and Tom Chappell founded Tom's of Maine in Kennebunk, Maine, for the purpose of selling environmentally safe household products. The company has become one of the most successful and influential players in the "greening" of the American marketplace. The success of Tom's of Maine demonstrated that environmentally and socially responsible business practices are compatible with profit. In 2006, the Chappells announced that they had sold the majority of the company's shares to Colgate-Palmolive, but that Tom's of Maine's products would remain the same, and their company's model of stewardship and sustainable practices continue on under Colgate's control.

Kate Cheney Chappell was born on October 17, 1945. She attended Chatham College, Sarah Lawrence, and the Sorbonne in the 1960s, and then, after a two-decade hiatus from college, graduated from the University of Southern Maine with an A.B. in communications in 1983. Tom Chappell was born on February 17, 1943, and attributes his commitment to the environment to the time he spent during his boyhood in the countryside near

Kate and Tom Chappell (Photograph courtesy of Tom's of Maine)

Pittsfield, Massachusetts, and on the coastal islands of Maine. His father ran an unsuccessful textile company. When the business failed, the family lost its home, an experience that shaped Tom's business acumen and understanding of the need to attend to the bottom line. He graduated from Trinity College in 1966, with a B.A. in English. The Chappells married in 1966 and would go on to have five children together.

In 1968 Kate and Tom Chappell moved from Philadelphia, where Tom was working in the insurance industry, to Kennebunk, Maine. They were ready to leave the pressures of corporate and urban life for a quieter, more rural world. In 1970 they founded Kennebunk Chemical Center, with the aim of combining a business with their ecological concerns. They wanted to develop and market products that would be safe for the consumer and the environment, using natural, nonpolluting ingredients. The first two products were a cleaner for dairy equipment and a phosphate-free detergent, ClearLake. The company really began to grow when the Chappells met PAUL HAWKEN, who owned a chain of natural food stores called Erewhon. Hawken needed natural soap to sell to his customers, so the Chappells developed one and called it "Tom's." By 1981, the company, which had been renamed Tom's of Maine, dominated the personal-care sections of health and natural food stores nationwide and boasted annual revenues of over $1.5 million. In 1983 the Chappells decided to expand the business. They raised new capital, hired experienced business advisers, and began to sell their products in larger, more mainstream drug and grocery stores.

As the business grew, the Chappells maintained a controlling interest in it but began to give themselves the freedom to explore other pursuits. In addition to completing her bachelor's degree, Kate devoted time to her painting and became a successful professional artist. In 1987 Tom enrolled in the Harvard Divinity School and earned a master's degree in theology in 1991. His work at the Divinity School brought new focus to Tom's of Maine. This new sense of mission is outlined in his two books, *The Soul of a Business: Managing for Profit and the Common Good* (1993) and *Managing Upside Down: Seven Intentions for Values-Centered Leadership* (1999). The books offer a vision of a company unified by values, in its relationships to customers, employees, shareholders, and community. The company's mission statement, written collaboratively by the employees and board of directors, offers twelve goals, including: "to respect, value, and serve not only our customers, but also our coworkers, owners, agents, suppliers, and our community"; "to be distinctive in products and policies which honor and sustain our natural world"; and "to be a profitable and successful company while acting in a socially and environmentally responsible manner." In practice, the company fulfills its mission in a variety of ways, including the kinds of ingredients it uses, using recycled packaging materials, refusing to test on animals, providing employees with a $4000 benefit if they choose to purchase a hybrid car, and offsetting all of the electricity used in its plant with independently-certified wind energy. The company tries to use natural ingredients, produced in sustainable ways, and faithfully donates 10 percent of its pre-tax profits to environmental, human need, arts, and education organizations. Some nonprofit organizations supported by the company include the Nature Conservancy and the Trust for Public Land. Tom's of Maine also frees its employees to devote 5 percent of their on-the-job hours to local volunteer projects.

Tom's of Maine is recognized as a leader in the world of "green" commerce and is often compared to Ben and Jerry's, the Body Shop, and Stonyfield Farm, which have succeeded as socially responsible enterprises. These companies have helped create consumers attentive to the environmental consequences of their purchases, by marketing their own commitment to social welfare. Though these companies are not all industry giants, they have influenced larger companies to include the environment as an important factor in decision making. Tom's of Maine created a niche for itself and altered the surrounding commercial climate at the same time. The Chappells have often been honored for their business practices, winning recognition from *Working Mother* and *Child* magazines. In 1992 Tom's of Maine received the Corporate Conscience Award for Charitable Contributions from the Council on Economic Priorities. In 1993, the Chappells were presented with the New England Environmental Leadership Award.

In 1999, Tom Chappell founded The Saltwater Institute to share his experience with socially and environmentally-responsible business, and help executives be more able to run their businesses according to common human values: family and community responsibility, respect and appreciation for the natural world, service and stewardship…work and productivity, [and] an intentional commitment to goodness." The Saltwater Institute is headquartered in Portland, Maine, and offers training programs for executives, helping them lead with their values.

When the Chappells sold a majority ownership of Tom's of Maine to the Colgate-Palmolive company in 2006, they explained that they would remain minority owners, and that Tom would continue to act as CEO and Kate as vice president. They confirmed that even as the company grew, the "character, spirit and values" of Tom's of Maine would be preserved—including making community donations of 10 percent of what it earns, and freeing employees to donate five percent of their work hours to nonprofit organizations of their choosing. The Chappells live in Kennebunk, Maine.

BIBLIOGRAPHY

"Art Website of Kate Cheney Chappell," www.katecheneychappell.com, Barasch, Douglas, "God and Toothpaste," *New York Times*, 1996; Hart, Stuart, "Beyond Greening: Strategies for a Sustainable World," *Harvard Business Review*, 1997; Kontzer, Tony, "The Greening of American Marketing," *E Business Magazine*, 1998; Miller, Samantha, "Maine Squeeze," *People Weekly*, 1999; "The Saltwater Institute," www.saltwater.org; "Tom's of Maine," www.tomsofmaine.com.

Chase, Robin
Transportation entrepreneur, Co-founder of Zipcar, CEO of GoLoco.org and Meadow Networks

Transportation entrepreneur Robin Chase co-founded Zipcar, the largest car-sharing company in the world, to change the way people think about driving. Zipcar, along with Chase's other startups, transportation consulting group Meadow Networks, and ridesharing website GoLoco.org, promotes more sustainable transportation towards a society where less people rely on car ownership for survival. Her work focuses on using wireless technology to reduce dependency on fossil fuel, and promote more efficient transportation with fewer cars and less carbon emissions.

As the daughter of an American diplomat, Chase grew up in Africa and the Middle East. She graduated from Wellesley College in 1980 and earned her M.B.A. in 1986 from the Massachusetts Institute of Technology's Sloan School of Management. She worked as a public health consultant with John Snow, Inc. in Boston, and also served as managing editor of the *Public Health Reports* journal from 1995-1998.

Chase co-founded Zipcar in 2000 with Antje Danielson. The two friends based Zipcar on a German company in Berlin that rented cars by the hour instead of by the day. Zipcar operates by parking cars throughout urban areas for customers to rent when they need them, in place of using their own personal cars. The concept of Zipcar was perfect for Chase, who lived in Cambridge with three children, and shared a car with her husband. Not wanting to buy a second car, car-sharing was a solution that would provide the occasional car mobility her family needed without the responsibilities, costs, and environmental impact buying a second car would bring. This model of transportation allows individuals to pay for only what they need in terms of transportation expenses, and to not have to deal with the hassle of vehicle maintenance, gas, insurance, and parking. Another benefit is that drivers can reserve a specific type of car, from a Mini Cooper, to a Honda Element, to a pickup truck, to meet their needs on a particular day. Zipcar utilizes wireless technology such as Internet billing and a wireless key system (each member has a "Zipcard") for convenience and fast access to vehicles. As of January 2008, Zipcar had nearly 200,000 members sharing 5,000 vehicles in fifty cities in North America and the United Kingdom including New York, Boston, Atlanta, Washington D.C., Seattle, Chicago, San Francisco, Vancouver, and London. Chase served as Zipcar's CEO from 2000-2003. In 2007 Zipcar merged with Washington D.C.-based Flexcar, its biggest competitor.

According to Chase, the element of price is a key factor to changing driving habits in the United States. If the price of driving were higher, people would drive less. Chase advocates pay-per-drive car rental because it encourages drivers to really think about the need for the trips they take and whether a car is the best way to travel. Short trips, such as driving to the store to buy a single item, usually prove to be uneconomical when paying for a car by the hour. Chase's goal in starting Zipcar was to give city dwellers an alternative to owning their own car and car rental. The positive social and environmental side effects of this include helping drivers reduce their negative environmental impact by reducing the number of cars on the road and parking spaces needed, reducing the total amount that people drive, and increasing the use of other modes of transportation such as walking and biking. According to Zipcar, ninety percent of their members drive less than 5,000 miles per year, compared to a national average of around 12,000 for car-owners. The company estimates that every Zipcar takes fifteen personal cars off the road and out of cities, creating less congestion on the roads and less demand for parking.

After stepping down as Zipcar's CEO to explore other avenues, Chase was awarded the Loeb Fellowship from Harvard University Graduate School of Design in 2004. She focused on urban design, city planning and transportation policy. The following year she applied what she had learned to starting Meadow Networks, a consulting group that applies wireless technology to the transportation sector. Meadow Networks consults to national, state, and local governments and organizations on ways to leverage transportation wireless infrastructure investments to support larger economic growth goals. Through Meadow Networks, Chase maintains a blog entitled "Network Musings" that focuses on issues related to sustainable transportation such as wireless technology, road financing, and cars.

While Zipcar helps people who don't need a car to get to work to reduce their car use, Chase turned her mind to the needs of those who were car-dependent. In the United States, seventy-five percent of all car trips are single occupancy, with just one person in the car, and only twelve percent of people carpool to work. To promote ridesharing and decrease the number of single-occupancy trips, Chase started the ridesharing site GoLoco.org. This website allows people to connect to ridesharing opportunities through a social networking experience, providing users a way to share trips with their groups and communities, and includes a Facebook.com application. All expenses, including gas and tolls are settled online in advance to avoid any miscommunication or awkwardness in the car. The site allows friends, neighbors and co-workers to utilize their social networks to share rides, creating a public transportation network that reduces the number of cars on the road. It also tracks the amount of CO_2 saved for each user. Chase promotes the benefits of GoLoco.org as threefold: to help members save money, socialize with friends, and contribute to reducing carbon emissions.

Chase has been recognized worldwide for her contributions to alternative transportation with awards such as the Massachusetts Governor's Award for Entrepreneurial Spirit, and Business Week's top 10 designers. She has also served on the Mayor's Wireless Task Force in Boston, the National Smart Growth Council, and the Governor-elect's Transportation Transition Working Committee.

Currently, Chase serves as CEO of both GoLoco.org and Meadow Networks and remains on the Zipcar Board of Directors. She lives in Cambridge with her husband Roy Russel and their three children. Chase lectures worldwide, advocating for road-pricing plans such as congestion pricing plans, no-fee mesh networks to connect drivers, and inspires audiences reinvent the way we think about transportation.

BIBLIOGRAPHY

www.goloco.org; www.meadownetworks.com; networkmusings.blogspot.com; www.zipcar.com.

Chávez, César
(March 31, 1927–April 23, 1993)
Cofounder of United Farm Workers

As a labor leader whose constituency was endangered by exposure to carcinogenic chemical pesticides and fertilizers, César Chávez and his organizing team at United Farm Workers (UFW) fought California's powerful agribusiness interests for healthier working conditions and better salaries. The table grape and wine boycott that the UFW maintained from 1965 to 1970 achieved health and safety regulations that had previously seemed impossible for agricultural workers. Chávez continued to serve as a visible, influential advocate for farm laborers throughout the 1970s, 1980s, and early 1990s, always calling for more humane and healthier working and living conditions.

César Estrada Chávez was born in Yuma, Arizona, on March 31, 1927. After his father was swindled out of his small business and the government seized his grandfather's farm, Chávez's family moved to California and joined the migrant farm labor force. Chávez attended 37 schools before graduating from the eighth grade, at which time his father suffered an accident that left him incapacitated. To support his family, Chávez began to work full time as a farm laborer until he enlisted in the Navy at the age of 17.

First subjected to racial and linguistic prejudice in the English-only, skin-color-segregated California schools, Chávez grew even more aware of racism in the United States during his two-year stint in the Navy. While on leave, Chávez went to a movie theater in Delano, California, and was arrested for refusing to respect its segregationist seating policy. Chávez married Helen Fabela in 1948 and settled with their growing family—they eventually had eight children—in Delano, California.

Chávez was introduced to community organizing in 1952 in the Sal Si Puedes neighborhood of San Jose, California, where he was living temporarily as a migrant farm worker. Fred Ross and Father Donald McDonnell of the Community Service Organization (CSO) quickly identified Chávez as a charismatic leader and recruited him to work for the CSO on a voter registration drive. McDonnell served as a mentor to Chávez, introducing him to the nonviolent organizing techniques of Mahatma Gandhi and the respect for all life forms of St. Francis of Assisi. In 1958 Chávez became the national director of the CSO. His major victory while at CSO was forcing the government to investigate the corrupt hiring practices of the government's Farm Placement Service, which favored low-paid Mexican *braceros* over migrant farm workers who were U.S. citizens.

By 1961, Chávez wanted to focus exclusively on problems faced by farm workers, so he left the CSO and in 1962 founded the National Farm Workers Association (NFWA). Chávez was soon joined by former CSO organizer DOLORES HUERTA, and together they chose grape pickers as their first group of workers to organize. The first major action of the NWFA was in 1965, when it joined the Agricultural Workers Organizing Committee (AWOC) in a strike. Inspired by the AWOC success, the NWFA initiated its first strike in September 1965 after the grape pickers at Lucas and Sons' farm walked off the job. When the strike was declared illegal, the NFWA resorted to another tactic, a five-year nationally coordinated boycott of table grapes and wine.

Chávez and Huerta knew that concern for farm worker welfare would not be enough to convince American consumers to boycott grapes and wine. Farm laborers, among the lowest paid workers in the United States, were a population mostly ignored by mainstream Americans. Pesticides, however, did concern the American public, especially in the years following RACHEL CARSON's *Silent*

Spring. By focusing on pesticides, the NWFA was able to appeal to consumer self-interest and at the same time push growers on an important safety issue for workers. The NWFA ran farm worker clinics throughout California that were tracking pesticide poisonings among farm workers. Two nurses, Peggy McGivern and MARION MOSES, collected data, worked with medical experts to devise a proposal for a better pesticide policy, and toured the country to educate boycott organizers on the dangers of pesticides in the food stream. The NFWA's legal team, working with California Rural Legal Assistance, began to sue individual growers for exposing workers to dangerous levels of pesticides and withholding information about which pesticides were applied. Even as late as 1969, one California judge declared that he saw no good reason to release documents that described the types of pesticides used and the dates and locations where they were applied, nor did he understand why it would be beneficial to require growers to post notices in fields where pesticides had recently been applied.

With a boycott in full swing and an evergrowing union membership (at its peak about 50,000 members), Chávez decided to undertake a water-only, 25-day fast in 1968. A powerful symbol, the fast allowed Chávez a poignant way to declare his solidarity with the suffering of farm workers and to declare a stance of noncooperation with supermarkets, which continued to stock boycotted grapes.

By 1970—when 75 percent of grape pickers were NWFA members, such major political figures as Robert F. Kennedy and Walter Mondale had sided with the NWFA, and the boycott was cutting deeply into grape and wine sales—the majority of growers finally signed a contract that protected agricultural workers in ways they had never enjoyed before. Among the health and safety gains: certain pesticides, including dichlordiphenyltrichlor (DDT) and parathion, would no longer be used; the union could have free access to records of pesticide application; any application of organophosphates had to be approved by a union committee; and whenever the highly toxic organophosphates were used, workers were given cholinesterase tests to measure their organophosphate blood levels. Thanks in part to the impetus of the NWFA, DDT was banned by the Environmental Protection Agency (EPA) in 1972.

Grape workers organized and protected, the NWFA moved on to organize a lettuce boycott. When courts ordered that the lettuce boycott be lifted, the NWFA refused, and Chávez was jailed for 14 days. NWFA supporters maintained a 24-hour vigil outside the jail for the duration of his incarceration.

The NWFA was chartered by the American Federation of Labor–Congress of Industrial Organizations (AFL-CIO) and became the United Farm Workers in 1972. The UFW by no means won all of its battles. When the 1970 contracts with the UFW expired in 1972, many growers signed with the Teamsters Union, which did not include a health and safety clause in its contracts, and threatened those growers who maintained contracts with the UFW. The UFW declared a new boycott against producers who signed with the Teamsters.

Throughout the 1980s, Chávez continued to fight against pesticide abuse in agroindustry. In 1987, he and RALPH NADER jointly called for a boycott of all grapes sprayed with pesticides that the EPA had declared hazardous. Chávez fasted for 36 days in 1988 to bring attention to the children of farm workers dying of cancers most likely caused by pesticide exposure.

Chávez led the UFW until his death, April 23, 1993. He died in San Luis, Arizona, during his sleep. Before his death, in 1990, Chávez had been awarded Mexico's *Águila Azteca*, that country's highest civilian award. Posthumously, he was given the Presidential Medal of Freedom in 1994, and also in 1994, his birthday, March 31, was designated a California state holiday.

BIBLIOGRAPHY

Conord, Bruce, *César Chávez*, 1992; Faistein, Mark, *César Chávez*, 1994; Levy, Jacques E., *César Chávez: An Autobiography of La Causa*, 1975; Griswold del Castillo, Richard and Richard A Garcia,., *César Chávez: a Triumph of Spirit*, 1995; Mattheissen, Peter, *Sal Si Puedes: César Chávez and the New American Revolution*, 1969; Orosco, Jose Antonio, *César Chávez and the Common Sense of Nonviolence*, 2008; Pulido, Laura, *Latino Environmental Struggles in the Southwest*, 1991; Ross, Fred, *Conquering Goliath: César Chávez at the Beginning*, 1989; United Farm Workers, www.ufw.org/.

Chavis, Benjamin
(January 22, 1948–)
Civil Rights and Environmental Justice Activist, Executive Director of the National Association for the Advancement of Colored People

Former executive director of the National Association for the Advancement of Colored People (NAACP) Benjamin Chavis coined the term *environmental racism* in 1982, when, while working for the United Church of Christ's Racial Justice Commission, he decried the frequent practice of siting toxic dumps and industries in areas settled predominantly by racial minorities. After he cosigned a letter to the ten largest national environmental organizations in 1990 asking why there were no people of color on their boards of directors and why they were ignoring the problem of environmental racism, most of the "Group of 10" began to work more actively with minority populations and the environmental problems they face.

Benjamin Franklin Chavis Jr. was born on January 22, 1948, in Oxford, North Carolina. He was one of four children of Benjamin F. Chavis Sr., a bricklayer and orphanage administrator, and Elizabeth Chavis, a schoolteacher. His parents told him early in his life of his great-great-grandfather, John Chavis, a freed slave who was the first Black graduate of Princeton University and worked for White slaveholders in North Carolina as a private teacher for their children. When he was discovered teaching slave children to read, a violation of a state law, he was beaten to death by Whites. Chavis grew up with an awareness of racial injustice and led a reform movement at the age of 13 when he entered Oxford's Whites-only library and attempted to borrow a book. The librarians told him to leave, Chavis asked why, the librarians called his parents, other people got involved, and soon the library was open to all townspeople, regardless of race. As a teenager, Chavis joined the NAACP and the Southern Christian Leadership Conference (SCLC). He went to Washington, D.C., with the local NAACP youth council for the March on Washington in 1963 and heard Martin Luther King Jr. give his renowned "I Have a Dream" speech.

Chavis entered the all-Black St. Augustine's College in Raleigh, then transferred to the University of North Carolina in Charlotte, where he was one of 14 Black students in the university, and the only one majoring in sciences. He organized his fellow Black students and campaigned for a Black student union and a Black studies department. Chavis worked as the western North Carolina coordinator for the SCLC, and during the summers he worked for the Raleigh office of the United Church of Christ's Commission for Racial Justice (CRJ). He graduated with his B.A. in chemistry in 1969 and taught high school chemistry for a year in Oxford, before moving on to full-time civil rights work at the CRJ.

In 1971 Chavis was asked by the CRJ to go to work in the newly desegregated schools in Wilmington, North Carolina, to work with Black students who were being discriminated against by White students and school administrators. The tension in Wilmington quickly accelerated, and a White-owned grocery store was burned. Chavis and nine others were indicted with arson and conspiracy charges. The jury, composed of ten White people, some of them known members of the Ku Klux Klan, and two Black people, found Chavis guilty and he was sentenced to 34 years in prison. Chavis served four years, beginning in 1976. During his time in prison, Chavis studied at Duke University and received a degree in divinity, taught a seminar in Black church studies at Duke, worked in leadership roles for the National Alliance Against Racism and Political Repression and the Southern Organizing Committee for Economic and Social Justice, and wrote a book of prayers, *Psalms from Prison*. Amnesty International and the United Church of Christ, in the meantime, were working on his behalf, since the trial had been flawed and he was considered a political prisoner. In 1980 he was freed after three important witnesses recanted their testimony, claiming that they had been pressured into testifying against the "Wilmington Ten" by local police.

Upon his release, Chavis was ordained as a minister in the United Church of Christ, and resumed working for the CRJ. In 1982, he became involved in the struggle against the siting of a toxic polychlorinated biphenyl (PCB) landfill in Warren County, North Carolina, just east of his native Oxford. Warren County was one of the poorest counties in the state, with a population that was 64 percent Black. The county was a poor choice for the landfill because the water table was high and most residents used wells for their drinking water. Local citizens organized themselves and were supported by several nationally known civil rights and labor leaders, including Chavis, yet the state began hauling the PCB-contaminated soil to the dump site. In September 1982, Chavis was arrested along with more than 400 other protesters for blocking the dump trucks' access to the site. Environmental justice scholar ROBERT BULLARD says that this protest "marked the first time anyone in the United States had been jailed trying to halt a toxic waste landfill."

Chavis commissioned CRJ director of research Charles Lee to perform a national study, "Toxic Wastes and Race in the United States," which showed that polluting industry and waste processing sites were predominantly sited in areas inhabited by racial minorities. Chavis is credited with coining the term *environmental racism* to describe the problem. He was such an effective spokesman for the movement for environmental justice—which works for an end to environmental racism—that the Bill Clinton–AL GORE team appointed him to their transition team.

In 1990, Chavis, along with several other representatives of the growing environmental justice movement, cosigned a letter addressed to the ten largest mainstream environmental organizations in the United States: the Sierra Club, the National Wildlife Federation, the Audubon Society, the Natural Resource Defense Council, the National Parks and Conservation Association, the Wilderness Society, the Izaak Walton League, the Environmental Defense Fund, the Environmental Policy Center, and Friends of the Earth. The letter chastised the "Group of 10" for their overwhelming whiteness and for their lack of action on issues of environmental racism. More money and effort were being spent on struggles in other developing countries than on combating environmental threats to poor racial minorities in this country, the signers complained, and they demanded action. Most of the "Group of 10" acknowledged that their boards and staffs were too White, and they responded with recruitment drives for minority employees and board members. During the 1990s there was a notable increase in attention from many of these groups to problems of environmental racism.

Chavis left the CRJ in 1993 when he was named executive director of the NAACP. He held that post for 16 months, reaching out to young Black people and to other Black organizations, including the Nation of Islam, in an attempt to increase membership. That he did; 160,000 new members signed up during his first year. But Chavis was fired in August 1994 after the board discovered that he had made unauthorized use of NAACP funds to settle with an employee who had filed a sexual discrimination suit.

Chavis joined the Nation of Islam shortly after leaving the NAACP, and changed his name to Benjamin Mohammed. In 2001 he founded the Hip-Hop Summit Action Network, which harnesses the popularity of the Hip Hop movement to encourage and empower youth to work for a better future. His latest project is a chain of hip-hop restaurants, HipHopSodaShops, selling healthy food and drinks, which he sees as an opportunity to offer a practical lesson in financial literacy for youth. Chavis Mohammed has six children, four from his first marriage and two from his second, to Martha Chavis.

BIBLIOGRAPHY

Anaya, Toney, and Benjamin Chavis Jr., "Race and the Environment: Protecting the Have-Nots," *Atlanta Constitution*, 1991; Bullard, Robert, *Dumping in Dixie*, 1990; "Hip-Hop Summit Action Network," hsan.org; Kotlowitz, "A Bridge Too Far? Benjamin Chavis," *New York Times*, 1994; Lewis, Neil A., "Seasoned by Civil Rights Struggle," *New York Times*, 1993, Waldron, Clarence, "Ben Chavis announces plans for hip-hop restaurants," *Jet*, 2007.

Christy, Elizabeth
(1945 – 1985)
Founder of Green Guerillas, Urban Gardener

Elizabeth "Liz" Christy founded the Green Guerillas, an urban gardening activist group known for planting the first community garden in New York City. As an artist living in Manhattan's East Village in the 1960s and 1970s, Christy worked with communities to instill hope and bring beauty and vitality to the places around them. Known for her innovative work in planting beautiful, creative gardens in unlikely places, Christy is credited for starting the modern community gardening movement in New York City.

Christy was born in 1945 in New York City. In 1973 she created the Green Guerillas to help increase the amount of green space in Manhattan. The group's first project was a garden on the corner of Bowery and Houston Streets. Christy described her inspiration for starting this urban gardening project in an account of coming home from work and seeing a young boy playing in an old, discarded refrigerator that had been dumped in the vacant lot next to her painting studio. Upon returning the boy to his family, the boy's mother told Christy that she should do something about the condition of the abandoned lot, which was littered with garbage and debris such as old mattresses and oil drums.

Christy proposed the idea of a garden and enlisted the help of friends from all walks of life to volunteer their time, energy, and creative planting skills to grow a garden out of a pile of rubble with a base of eight inches of gravel. The determined Green Guerillas hung up a sheet on a fencepost that read "Watch this plot of land be turned into a garden in 24 hours." They then embarked on the massive undertaking of cleaning up the abandoned lot in preparation to plant, and within twenty-four hours created a garden that included an abundance of seedlings, crabapple trees, and wisteria vines. Slowly, people in the neighborhood began to take interest in the gardening project, and within months the small group of gardeners had grown to include many dedicated locals. When city officials began to take notice of the gardeners' efforts they initially gave them a hard time about trespassing on the unused lot. After Christy got the *New York Daily News* to run an article on the efforts of the group to clean up and create gardens in this unlikely location, the Green Guerillas were granted permission to rent the site for $1 per month starting in 1974. The garden was named "Bowery Houston Community Farm and Garden" and included sixty beds of vegetables such as cucumbers and tomatoes, as well as herbs, wildflowers, vines, and trees. In 1976 the garden won the Mollie Parnis Dress Up Your Neighborhood Award, which was funded by the dress designer to encourage communities to take pride in the appearance of their neighborhoods.

Christy and the Green Guerillas used creative techniques to adapt their planting efforts to the hostile ground conditions in New York. The group became known for their use of "seed bombs," in which balloons or old Christmas ornaments were packed with local wildflower seeds, fertilizer, and water and thrown into inaccessible places to green them.

For her pioneering work in gardening in New York City, Christy was awarded the first "Urban Forestry Award" by the American Forestry Association. She also served on the Council on the Environment New York City as the first director of the Open Space Greening Program in 1975 and continued in that position until her death in 1985. The program loaned gardening tools and books, gave lectures, as well as supported gardeners with on-site gardening assistance in all five boroughs of New York City. She launched the Plant-A-Lot program to provide funding to dedicated gardening projects. In 1978 the parks department started a program called Green Thumb to support gardeners. In the late 1980s, there were estimated to be over 800 community gardens, and according to Green Thumb, these gardens produced over $1 million of produce annually.

Gardens give communities a means to take action to reduce crime and grow healthy foods, in addition to cleaning up and taking pride in their neighborhood. Currently the original garden planted by Liz Christy and the Green Guerillas is still maintained by an all-volunteer group of dedicated gardeners and is open year round. The garden has a pond with fish and turtles, a beehive that produces over 100 pounds of honey annually, wildflowers, fruit trees, grape vines, and berries. Despite recent threats to the garden by nearby building construction and development, it continues to thrive.

Liz Christy passed away at age 39 from cancer, and the "Bowery Houston Community Farm and Garden" was renamed the "Liz Christy Bowery-Houston Garden" in her memory in 1986. Today, it remains the oldest all-volunteer garden in Manhattan. In the Green Guerillas and other community gardening groups, Christy's passion for creating gardens and art in unlikely places lives on. In her spirit, the groups strive for the sustainability and continued growth of urban gardening in New York City. The Green Guerillas maintain offices in Manhattan and Brooklyn and continue to offer support to garden enthusiasts interested in starting/maintaining urban gardens, educating young gardeners, and helping people to take an active role in their community.

BIBLIOGRAPHY

www.ecotippingpoints.org/ETP-Stories/indepth/newyorkgarden.html; www.greenthumbnyc.org/; www.newvillage.net/Journal/Issue1/1briefgreening.html; www.lizchristygarden.org; www.pps.org/great_public_spaces/one?public_place_id=45.

Cizik, Richard
(September 1, 1951-)
Christian Minister, Environmentalist

Since 1992 the Reverend Richard Cizik has spearheaded efforts to mobilize the Christian community to counteract the dangers of global warming as well as to support "Creation Care" and "Stewardship" of our Earth.

Richard Cizik was born on September 1, 1951 to Nora and Ervin in Quincy, Washington. As a young farm boy in the Pacific Northwest, Cizik observed his family's farm lose income more than once from nature's wrath upon their cherry crop. He graduated with a B.A. in political science from Whitworth College, received a M.A. in public affairs from George Washington University, and earned a Master of Divinity from Denver Seminary.

His conversion to biblical environmentalism was not unlike his decision to follow and preach the teachings of Jesus Christ. While attending a conference at Oxford University, Rev. Cizik heard Sir John Houghton, an evangelical scientist, speak on millennial ice-core data and ensuing shrinking of the polar ice caps.

"I realized all at once, with sudden awe, that climate change is a phenomenon of truly biblical proportions," Cizik told *Grist Magazine*.

His "green evangelism" with Creation Care and the National Association of Evangelicals has influenced many to show concern for the environment. He distinguishes "creation care" from other environmentalism for its roots, "not in politics or ideology, but in the scriptures." Cizik cites *Genesis 2:15* and *Revelation 11:18* to support his position.

On speaking tours throughout the country, his adamant stance has rattled the ears of polluters and wanton consumers alike: "Destroyers beware. Take heed. It was by and for Christ that this Earth was made, which means it is sinfully wrong — it is a tragedy of enormous proportions — to destroy, degrade, or despoil it. He who has ears, let him hear."

In 2004, under Cizik's guidance, the National Association of Evangelicals (NAE) formally endorsed seven principals for Christian political engagement in "For the Health of the Nation." The document called upon evangelicals to work to safeguard the sanctity of life and traditional family values; to fight for justice for the poor; to work to promote peace and restrain violence; to end torture, rape, and slavery; to promote human rights and religious freedom for all; and last, but certainly not least, to preserve God's creation.

Richard Cizik (Photograph courtesy of Richard Cizik)

On this last point, the NAE board wrote unambiguously: "We affirm that God-given dominion is a sacred responsibility to steward the Earth….We urge government to encourage fuel efficiency, reduce pollution, encourage sustainable use of natural resources, and provide for the proper care of wildlife and their natural habitats."

Cizik has preached: "Unlike our evangelical fathers who sat on their hands and tolerated racism…we will not have to apologize to our children for doing nothing about what is a threat to our entire biosphere."

Not everyone has been pleased with NAE's broader mandate. Focus on the Family's James Dobson, along with several other influential right-wing Christian leaders, publicly demanded the firing of Cizik over his "preoccupation" with global warming. They wanted the 30 million-member organization to stay focused on what they described as "the great moral issues of our time": opposing abortion and gay rights. Dobson and his allies wrote that global warming is an unproven theory. But the NAE has steadfastly stood by their vice-president of government affairs.

Cizik regularly testifies before Congress on the need to promote renewable energy, strengthen laws to protect our air and water, as well as a host of other social justice issues, including debt relief for poor countries and for the U.S. military to stop utilizing torture techniques when interrogating prisoners.

In 2008, *Time Magazine* named Cizik one of the world's top 100 leaders. In addition to his position with the NAE, Cizik sits on the advisory boards of the Pew Forum on Religion and Public Life and the Institute on Religion and Public Policy.

He is married to Virginia Jackson Lutz. Cizik is the father of two boys, Rich, Jr. and John. They live in Fredericksburg, Virginia.

BIBLIOGRAPHY

Hightower, Jim, and Susan DeMarco, Swim Against the Current: Even a Dead Fish Can Go With the Flow, 2008; www.creationcare.org/; www.nae.net/images/civic_responsibility.pdf; www.coloradoindependent.com/view/greening-the; www.time.com/time/specials/2007/article/0,28804,1733748_1733754_1736213,00.html; www.grist.org/news/maindish/2005/10/05/cizik/; www.thegreatwarming.com/revrichardcizik.html; www.coloradoindependent.com/view/as-cizik-crusades.

Clawson, Marion

(August 10, 1905–April 12, 1998)
Agricultural Economist, Public Lands Policy Analyst, Director of Resources for the Future

Agricultural economist Marion Clawson had a significant impact on public lands policy over the course of his 70-year career. He is well known for his insightful critical analyses of agriculture and recreation on federal lands. He served as director of the Bureau of Land Management from 1948 to 1953, directed and held various offices at the nonprofit organization Resources for the Future (RFF), and wrote many books on the topic of federal land use policy. He was one of the first analysts to apply the principles of social science to forestry, outdoor recreation, and agriculture and was a pioneer of the "multiple use" concept used in public lands management.

Son of William Ennes and Agnes Thompson Clawson, Marion Clawson was born on August 10, 1905, in Elko, Nevada, where he grew up. Clawson graduated from the University of

Nevada in 1926 with a B.S. in agriculture. Three years later, in 1929, he earned an M.S. in agriculture and economics, also from the University of Nevada. During the time he was working on his master's degree he was employed as an agricultural economist at the University of Nevada's experimental agriculture station. Upon receiving his master's degree, Clawson moved to Washington, D.C., to become an agricultural economist at the Bureau of Agricultural Economics. He remained in Washington until 1938, when he relocated to Berkeley, California, and continued to work for the bureau as an agricultural economist. He also became involved in land use on the Columbia Basin and in California's Central Valley during this time, acting as head of research and planning for both of these areas from 1940 to 1942 and 1942 to 1945, respectively. Clawson earned a Ph.D. in economics from Harvard University in 1943.

In 1947, Clawson joined the U.S. Department of the Interior. He worked as regional administrator in San Francisco, California, for a year before moving back to Washington, D.C., in 1948. Clawson served as the second director of the Bureau of Land Management (BLM) from 1948 to 1953. When he arrived at the BLM, the agency was primarily concerned with the management of ranch land and with extractive industries. "The bulk of our land was grazing land and our administration of that land was of great importance to the ranchers who used it," he stated in a 1989 interview with the *Journal of Forestry*. The BLM was also heavily involved with oil and gas developers and, in the West, the timber industry. There was literally no official recognition of the value of recreation and conservation on the federally owned lands that the BLM was responsible for managing. The BLM had been attempting to establish itself as an important natural resource "production" agency, along much the same lines as the U.S. Forest Service during this same time period, and the policies created to manage the federal lands were, according to Clawson, "totally unrelated to reality and much criticized by the field people." He changed this by introducing the concept of economic policy analysis to the BLM. This was the first instance in which a federal land management bureau utilized this tool, which measures the effectiveness of a given policy based on economic factors. At the time, Clawson did not think of it as policy analysis, so much as he considered it to be a matter of practical efficiency. Through this efficiency, he was able to "find" up to 25 percent more funding for his district managers.

Clawson was discharged as BLM administrator in 1953 when the newly elected president, Dwight Eisenhower, appointed Douglas McKay to the post of secretary of the interior. Clawson spent the next two years in Israel as a member of the BLM economic advisory staff. He returned to the United States in 1955, accepting a position with a nonprofit research and educational organization, Resources for the Future, where he stayed until his death in 1998. Clawson acted as director of the land use and management program for 18 years and then served as the organization's acting president, vice president, and consultant, consecutively. He became a senior fellow emeritus in 1979. Clawson believed that RFF's greatest influence was exerted through the graduate students who were exposed to the institution's work and who then brought that experience to government and private businesses. And while the specific policy results brought about by the activities of RFF are difficult to pin down, they manifest, Clawson believed, in the actions of policy makers influenced and inspired by the organization's work.

Clawson wrote extensively on the subject of public lands policy, particularly focusing on national forests, national parks, and recreation. He published more than 30 books on these issues, including *Uncle Sam's Acres* (1951) and *Federal Lands: Their Use and Management* (1957), which are considered classic primers on public lands history and administration. He also wrote such important works as *Economics of Outdoor Recreation* (1966), *Forests for Whom and for What?*

(1975), *Federal Lands Revisited* (1983), and in 1987, his autobiography, *From Sagebrush to Sage: The Making of a Natural Resource Economist*. He also contributed to many professional journals, *Journal of Forestry*, *Journal of Business Administration*, and *Journal of Forest History* included.

Clawson will be remembered for his contributions to the fields of agricultural economics and public lands administration. He was one of the first analysts to apply the principles of social science to forestry, outdoor recreation, and agriculture, analyzing natural resource policy with a consideration for ecological, economical, and sociocultural factors.

Clawson was a member of the American Agricultural Economics Association, the American Society for Range Management, and the American Academy of Arts and Sciences. He married three times, first to Clara Partridge in 1931, second to Mary Montgomery in 1947, and third to Nora Roots in 1972. He had four children, two each from his first two marriages. Clawson died on April 12, 1998, in Washington, D.C., during surgery for a hernia.

BIBLIOGRAPHY

Clawson, Marion, *From Sagebrush to Sage: The Making of a Natural Resource Economist*, 1987; Dowie, Mark, *Losing Ground: American Environmentalism at the Close of the Twentieth Century*, 1995; Healy, Robert G., and William E. Shands, "A Conversation with Marion Clawson: How Times (and Foresters) Have Changed," *Journal Of Forestry*, 1989; Norgaard, Richard B., "From Sagebrush to Sage: The Making of a Natural Resource Economist," *Quarterly Review of Biology*, 1990; Sedjo, Roger A., *Marion Clawson's Contribution to Forestry*, 1999.

Cobb, John B., Jr.

(February 9, 1925–)
Theologian

A theologian who has worked primarily in academic contexts, John Cobb Jr. has, since the early 1970s, called for an integration of Christian and environmental thought. Cobb is a "process" theologian, who emphasizes the importance of interdisciplinary and interfaith work. He has articulated a revision of Christian theology that responds to the pressing social issues of our time and reimagines humankind's relation to the natural order. In particular, Cobb has stressed the importance of shifting Christian thought away from human dominion over the earth toward an ethic of stewardship.

John B. Cobb Jr. was born in Japan on February 9, 1925. The youngest of three children, he lived in Japan with his parents, who were Methodist missionaries, until 1940, when Americans were urged to leave the country because of the outbreak of World War II. Cobb moved to Georgia, the home state of both his parents, where he lived with his grandmother and went to Emory Junior College at Oxford, Georgia. In 1943, before he finished his studies, Cobb joined the United States Army, where he was assigned to the Japanese language program. His army experiences had a profound shaping effect on Cobb's thought because he was exposed for the first time to non-Protestant intellectuals, primarily Jews and Irish Catholics. He came to understand the limits of his Protestant beliefs and sought a wider understanding of twentieth-century ideas. Upon leaving the service, Cobb enrolled at the University of Chicago, eventually settling in the Divinity School.

Dr. John B. Cobb (Photograph courtesy of Center for Process Studies)

While there, Cobb's thought was shaped primarily by two people: Richard McKeon and Charles Hartshorne. McKeon led Cobb to a stance of philosophical relativism, that is, to the belief that all major systems of philosophical thought are capable of arriving at considerable truth. Hartshorne introduced Cobb to the ideas of Alfred North Whitehead. Whitehead reversed the Platonic celebration of the ideal, by emphasizing the importance of process. In Whitehead's thought, actuality is in process, and anything outside process is abstract and therefore lacking in causal efficacy. Whitehead's thought thus values the life of the world over the realm of ideal forms. Cobb's career has been in large part an effort to adapt Whitehead's thought for Christian theology. Cobb graduated from the University of Chicago with a Ph.D. in 1952 and took a position at Emory University's School of Theology. In 1957, Cobb was invited to take a position in California's Claremont School of Theology and Claremont Graduate School, where he taught until his retirement.

Cobb's engagement with environmental issues began in 1969, when he read PAUL EHRLICH's *The Population Bomb*. In the introduction to *Sustainability: Economics, Ecology & Justice (1992)*, Cobb says that Ehrlich opened his eyes to current and impending ecological disasters and made him reorder his priorities accordingly. During this time Cobb also read LYNN WHITE JR.'s essay "The Historical Roots of the Environmental Crisis," which taught him that Christian theology fostered attitudes that supported exploitation of the natural world. Cobb's ecological awakening led him to organize in 1970 a conference on "Theology of Survival," to establish a chapter of Zero Population Growth, and to serve as chair of the ecojustice task force of the Southern California Ecumenical Conference. Cobb also began studying the ideas of architect PAOLO SOLERI and economist HERMAN DALY. In 1972, he organized a conference, "Alternatives to Catastrophe," at which both Soleri and Daly spoke, and published his own book, *Is It Too Late? A Theology of Ecology*. In this book Cobb returns to the tradition of process philosophy and finds strands of thought useful for "ecological thinking." In particular, Cobb discovers within process philosophy ideas to counter anthropocentric and dualistic thinking, both of which lead to ecologically destructive relationships between humankind and the natural world.

In 1973, Cobb, together with David Griffin, founded the Center for Process Studies at the Claremont School of Theology. Cobb became convinced of the value of process theology for solving social and political crises and founded the center to encourage increased interdisciplinary work. Cobb sees the separation between disciplines as contributing to destructive social and environmental practices and has worked to build dialogues between disparate fields. His own work has exemplified this principle. In 1982, he collaborated with biologist Charles Birch to write *The Liberation of Life: From the Cell to the Community*, which proposed an ecological approach to the biological understanding of life instead of a mechanistic one. It thereby also challenged the traditional separation of science and theology. Cobb also returned to his early involvement with Japanese ideas in his 1982 *Beyond Dialogue: Toward a Mutual Transformation of Buddhism and Christianity*, again challenging a separation between Eastern and Western thought. *For the Common Good: Redirecting the Economy toward Community, the Environment, and a Sustainable Future*, co-written in 1989 with Herman Daly and Clifford Cobb, offered a profound critique of traditional economics and proposed a new, more humanistic and environmentally sustainable approach. *For the Common Good* won a 1992 Grawemeyer Award for Ideas Improving World Order. In addition to *Sustainability*, he subsequently published *Sustainining the Common Good* (1994), and *The Earthist Challenge to Economism* (1999).

Cobb's career has been devoted to creating a Christian theology responsive to present-day political concerns. In recent years he has joined efforts to address Christianity's antigay and misogynist strands. He helped found the Mobilization for the Human Family, now named Progressive Christians Uniting, a group of liberal church leaders organized to counter the Christian right. As chair of its Reflection Committee, he edited in 2002 *Christianity and Religious Diversity*, explaining how Christians can respond to other religions without betraying to their own beliefs, and how the other religious traditions present in the U.S. today can actually be of benefit to the spiritual growth of Christians. Two other volumes produced by this group are *Progressive Christians Speak* and *Resistance: The New Role of Progressive Christians*.

Cobb retired from Claremont's School of Theology in 1990. He continues to co-direct the Center for Process Studies and lives in Claremont.

BIBLIOGRAPHY

"Boston Collaborative Encyclopedia of Western Theology," people.bu.edu/wwildman/bce; "Center for Process Studies," www.ctr4process.org; Griffin, David Ray, and Joseph C. Hough, *Theology and the University: Essays in Honor of John B. Cobb, Jr.*, 1991.

Colborn, Theo
(March 28, 1927–)
Zoologist

Our Stolen Future, written in 1996 by Theo Colborn with coauthors John Peterson Myers and Dianne Dumanoski, alerted the world to a serious yet largely unrecognized chemical contamination problem. Present on earth since their introduction by industry as early as the 1920s, many chlorine- and petroleum-derived chemicals, chemical by-products, and chemical breakdown products proliferating the food web are toxic in the most minute quantities. They have already affected the sexual development and the endocrine and immune systems of many animal species at the top of aquatic food chains and have caused neurodevelopmental and neuromuscular problems in a sizable segment of human children. Colborn coordinates research efforts by scientists all over the world and works with environmental groups, government agencies, and the chemical industry toward the phaseout of these so-called endocrine-disrupting chemicals.

Theodora Decker Colborn was born on March 28, 1927, in Plainfield, New Jersey. From a very early age, she was attracted to water, and she spent as much time as she could playing in a creek that flowed past the farm where she lived. Her mother loved gardening, flowers, and birds and instilled a love for all of these in her daughter. Colborn attended Rutgers University, earning a degree in pharmacy in 1947. She and her husband, Harry Colborn, whom she met at Rutgers, took over the Colborn family pharmacy in New Jersey and soon opened two more. They had four children before deciding in 1962 to escape the hassle and fast pace of their life in New Jersey and move to Colorado. After a brief stint in Boulder, where Colborn did a semester of graduate work in pharmacy, the family settled in the valley of the North Fork of the Gunnison River in western Colorado, and began to raise sheep.

The pastoral beauty of the valley was disturbed in the early 1970s, the federal government decided to expand coal mining activity near her home. Colborn and several friends founded the Western Slope Energy Research Center (WSERC) to promote sustainable mining. Once recognized by the Sierra Club as one of the most efficient grassroots organizations in the country, WSERC nonetheless lost many of its battles. It was through this experience that Colborn learned the importance of impeccable—not anecdotal—scientific information. In 1978 she began a master's degree program in freshwater ecology at Western State College of Colorado in Gunnison. She spent summers at the Rocky Mountain Biological Laboratory, studying aquatic insects in the area's streams to find out if they were accurate indicators of ecosystem health and meeting world-renowned scientists who would later provide crucial support for her work. While at Western State she organized a series of conferences on water issues, the first national and international meetings of their type at the college, which attracted scientists, policy makers, environmental activists, and officials from government agencies.

In addition to the heightened effectiveness that association with an academic institution granted her, Colborn found herself fascinated by ecological science. Free at this point in her life of the constraints of motherhood, since her children were all grown, she entered the University of Wisconsin at Madison's Ph.D. program in zoology in 1982. Her professor there was Stanley Dodson, whom she had studied under at the Rocky Mountain Biology Laboratory; he helped her design a distributed program that included epidemiology, toxicology, and water chemistry. After she got her Ph.D. in 1985, Colborn was awarded a fellowship with the congressional Office of Technology Assessment (OTA) in Washington, D.C.

After two years at the OTA, Colborn was invited to join a team at the Conservation Foundation (later merged with the World Wildlife Fund), also in Washington, D.C., to provide the science for a book on the state of the Great Lakes ecosystem, which is contaminated by massive quantities of industrial pollutants. Colborn found that animals in the lakes were disappearing but not because they had cancer. Instead, animals that ate fish were having difficulty reproducing, and those that were able to reproduce were bearing offspring that suffered a suite of health effects that suggested that their endocrine, immune, and reproductive systems were being undermined before they were born, preventing them from surviving to adulthood. As she searched for the chemical contaminants responsible for this problem, Colborn discovered that many of the possible culprits shared a damning characteristic: they altered animals' endocrine systems by interfering with hormones' ability to transmit intricate hormonal messages that control how an individual is constructed and functions later in life. Other scientists who had become aware of this problem before Colborn, including psychologists Sandra and Joseph Jacobson of Detroit, had already discovered this problem of prenatal exposure in human babies whose mothers ate Great Lakes fish.

Her work quite promising yet still far from conclusive, Colborn received support from the W. Alton Jones Foundation in 1990, which allowed her to focus entirely on the effects of transgeneral exposure to contaminants. The W. Alton Jones Foundation's director, zoologist John Peterson Myers, was intrigued by Colborn's work. He gave her the opportunity to convoke the first Wingspread Work Session in July 1991, which brought together 21 scientists to share findings and contemplate the implications of this research. The scientists collectively came up with the term *endocrine disruption* at this session, and at its conclusion signed a consensus statement recommending the phaseout of endocrine disruptors. They also contributed peer-reviewed papers to a technical volume entitled *Chemically Induced Alteration in Sexual and Functional Development: The Wildlife/Human Connection*, which was edited by Colborn and her assistant at World Wildlife Fund, Coralie Clement, and published in 1992. This book caught the attention of industry and the public health community but was too technical to be accessible to most lay readers. Colborn organized five more Wingspread Work Sessions between 1993 and 1996, each of which resulted in better-coordinated research and further consensus statements.

Knowing that the threats of endocrine disruptors would be ignored unless more people learned about them, Colborn collaborated with Myers and Dianne Dumanoski on *Our Stolen Future*, published in 1996. This book traces Colborn's steps as she pieced together the endocrine disruptor thesis, explaining the complexities of it for lay readers. The book describes the effect of endocrine-disrupting chemicals on wildlife and explores what humans suffer as well. There is already evidence that sperm count is declining, there is a higher rate of abnormalities in the development of sexual organs, and testicular cancer is increasing, to name a few of the problems that studies on the human population have revealed. As dangerous as the organochlorines that bioaccumulate (or become more concentrated each step up the food chain), so too are other types of chemicals that do not build up in human tissue and are found in food or products that people encounter every day at home, work, school, and in their cars. Bisphenol A, for example, is an estrogen-mimicking plastic monomer that was first used in the 1920s and currently occurs in many man-made products, including baby bottles and hikers' water bottles. Estrogen disruptors can penetrate the wombs of female lab animals, and a great deal has been discovered over the past decade about what they do in humans. What may be most troubling to readers of *Our Stolen Future* and policy makers is that there is no safe dose for some of these chemicals, and there is no safe haven from them. Unfortunately, the U.S. government has failed to support research to design screens and assays to test chemicals for endocrine-disrupting effects.

As those familiar with the history of RACHEL CARSON's 1962 *Silent Spring* might have predicted, *Our Stolen Future* was met with a virulent counterattack by the chlorine industry, and there have been more and more, very sophisticated, attacks over time from petroleum, plastics, chemical, food packaging, and pesticides corporations and trade associations. This should be of no surprise because the most egregious and widespread endocrine disruptors are derived as by-products from the processing of fossil fuels.

According to *Sierra* writer David Helvarg, the original multimillion-dollar smear campaign targeting the book was coordinated and funded by the Chlorine Chemistry Council (CCC), an industry group representing this country's major chlorine manufacturers. Today, well-coordinated international public relations corporations are handling the spin on every aspect of the endocrine disruptor issue. Despite this discrediting attempt, *Our Stolen Future* has been translated into eighteen languages and has been through many printings.

Endocrine disruption has now become a new biomedical discipline that involves highly-respected scientists from the fields of neurodevelopmental biology, epidemiology, biochemistry, physiology, embryology, cancer research, and others. The discipline has many prestigious and influential researchers. The Environmental Protection Agency, the National Academy of Sciences, and the President's National Science and Technology Council have all prioritized the issue.

Colborn has received many recognitions and awards, among which are the 1999 Norwegian International Rachel Carson Award, the 2000 International Blue Planet Prize, the 2003 Society of Toxicology and Environmental Chemistry Rachel Carson Award, the 2003 Center for Science in the Public Interest Rachel Carson Award, and she was chosen as one of *Time*'s Environmental Heroes in 2007.

Colborn is Professor Emeritus at the University of Florida, Gainesville, and is President of The Endocrine Disruption Exchange (TEDX), a non-profit organization based in Paonia, Colorado, which has built and maintains a rich database about the effects on humans and animals of low or ambient exposure to chemicals. Colborn resides in Paonia, Colorado.

BIBLIOGRAPHY

Burger, Alyssa, "Sex Offenders," *E Magazine*, 1996; Helvarg, David, "Poison Pens," *Sierra*, 1997; Lerner, Michael, "Crossed Signals," *Whole Earth Review*, 1997; "Our Stolen Future," www.ourstolenfuture.org; "The Endocrine Disruption Exchange," www.endocrinedisruption.com; Wapner, Kenneth, "Theo Colborn Studies Waterways and Wildlife," *Amicus Journal*, 1995.

Colby, William

(May 28, 1875–November 9, 1964)
Secretary and Director of the Sierra Club

Few Sierra Club members have been more enthusiastic or more boundless in their energy when it came to conservation than William Colby. A key member of the Sierra Club after JOHN MUIR's death in 1914, Colby served as a director for 49 years. During his lifetime, he contributed substantially to the saving of redwoods, the enlargement of Sequoia National Park, and the establishment of Kings Canyon and Olympic National Parks. However, Colby is probably best remembered for his participation in the battle for the Hetch Hetchy Valley, where his ability as a determined and eloquent protector of nature came to the fore.

William E. Colby, born May 28, 1875, in Benecia, California, was one of five children of Gilbert and Caroline (Smith) Colby. Their untimely deaths left Colby an orphan at age six, and he was brought up by a legal-minded aunt. Influenced by his aunt, Colby, who had once expressed interest in becoming a naturalist like his hero and future comrade-in-arms, John Muir, took an early interest in the law.

Colby started at the University of California but was forced to drop out owing to financial problems. He began teaching in an Oakland preparatory school, but the ambitious Colby would not be denied his goal. He made two round-trips daily across the bay, one to attend an early morning class at Hastings Law School and another to attend more classes in the afternoon after his teaching duties were done for the day. He graduated in 1898 from Hastings Law School. Tired from the rigor of work and study, Colby gladly accepted a post with the Sierra Club as its representative in the Yosemite Valley. Colby's enthusiasm for the mountains and the many Sierra Club friends he had made on his first trip into the Sierra a few years earlier won him his appointment, and in 1900, he became the club's recording secretary. In 1901, Colby initiated the annual high trips that began the club's popular outings program; he also led these trips until 1929. As Colby gained prominence within the Sierra Club, he started his career as an attorney with a Bay area law firm. During the course of that career, he achieved considerable respect as an attorney who specialized in mining and water law, which served him well in his conservation work.

By 1905, Colby's principal activity in the Sierra Club had become the protection of the Hetch Hetchy Valley. Plans to dam the Tuolumne River at the bottom of the valley to provide water for the growing city of San Francisco were made more urgent after the city's devastating earthquake in April 1906. The plan was met by stern conservationist opposition; the Hetch Hetchy Valley lay within the confines of Yosemite National Park. Damming protected land would set a dangerous precedent.

During the struggle to preserve Hetch Hetchy, Colby worked in close relation with John Muir, the leading figure and spokesperson in the efforts to prevent the dam from being built. Together, they wrote countless letters and pamphlets advocating the protection of Hetch Hetchy. Colby's careful technical arguments complemented Muir's stirring rhetoric to create emotional but rational pleas in favor of the valley. Often Muir and his arguments were dismissed as misanthropic and impractical. Colby, with his experience as a mining lawyer, worked to control Muir's zeal and to deal with the technical problems a dam would create in Yosemite National Park. Interestingly, the law firm where Colby worked was one of the leading proponents of the proposed dam, so Colby often had to pull strings from a distance so as not to jeopardize his job.

Division within the Sierra Club regarding the Hetch Hetchy Valley led Colby to establish a separate organization called the Society for the Preservation of National Parks in 1907 in order to ease the growing rift within the outdoors club. With Muir as president, this organization was composed of a network of Sierra Club council members from all over the country, making the Hetch Hetchy campaign national and relieving much of the pressure from the San Francisco members of the Sierra Club.

Ultimately, Hetch Hetchy, which became a national *cause célèbre*, was approved for damming in 1913 after almost a decade of struggle. While this case did set the dangerous precedent of violating a national park, Colby was at least able to appreciate one positive outcome of the experience: the conscience of the nation had been awakened. As Colby wrote 30 years later in the first *Sierra Club Handbook*, "While this particular battle was lost… it has deterred others from attempting similar inroads."

Nevertheless, the loss of the Hetch Hetchy was enough to kill John Muir, who died the following year. After his death, Colby's prominence in the Sierra Club grew. He served as a director for the next 49 years. During this time, he was active in leading directives to protect forests and establish national parks. In 1927, he became the first chairman of the California State Park Commission. Colby also suggested the creation of the John Muir Trail in honor of his friend and the Sierra Club's inspirational first president.

After a lifetime of service to the Sierra Club and the cause of conservation, Colby became the first recipient of the John Muir Award, the Sierra Club's highest recognition for achievement in conservation. Colby died November 9, 1964, at his home in Big Sur, California.

BIBLIOGRAPHY

Cohen, Michael P. *The History of the Sierra Club, 1892–1970*, 1988; Jones, Holway R., *John Muir and the Sierra Club: The Battle for Yosemite*, 1965; Righter, Robert W., *The Battle over Hetch Hetchy: America's Most Controversial Dam and the Birth of Modern Environmentalism*, 2006; Wolar, Glynn Gary, "The Conceptualization and Development of Pedestrian Recreational Wilderness Trails in the American West, 1890–1940: A Landscape History," Ph.D. Dissertation, University of Idaho, 1998.

Cole, Thomas
(February 1, 1801–February 11, 1848)
Landscape Painter, Founder of the Hudson River School of Painting

Thomas Cole, the founder of the famous Hudson River School, the first American painting movement, portrayed the grandeur of wilderness in the United States through his landscape paintings. In doing so, he began an artistic tradition that helped to define the ways that Americans interact with and appreciate nature.

Thomas Cole was born on February 1, 1801, in Bolton-le-Moor, Lancashire, England, to James and Mary Cole. His father was an unsuccessful muslin manufacturer, who was unable to keep up with the trend toward mechanization that was occurring in that region, the center of England's textile manufacturing trade and the very cradle of the industrial revolution. Cole's parents encouraged his artistic interests but could not pay for an artistic education. He did attend a boarding school for a short time in Chester and at the age of 14 was apprenticed to a designer of calico prints at a calico print-works in Chorley. Later, he apprenticed with a wood engraver in Liverpool. In 1818, after James Cole's business failed in the depression following the Napoleonic Wars, the Cole family emigrated to the United States, arriving in Philadelphia in 1819. Here, Cole worked as a wood engraver. After a year in Philadelphia, Cole and his family moved to Steubenville, Ohio, where Cole worked as a wood-block carver in his father's wallpaper factory for two years.

It was in Ohio that Cole had something of an awakening after making the acquaintance of a traveling portraitist by the name of Stein. Cole was inspired, and although he had had no formal instruction in painting, he set out in February 1822 to become an artist himself. He traveled around the countryside painting portraits to survive. He had always had a great appreciation for nature, taking long hikes as a child and later exploring the Ohio River. The turning point in his artistic career occurred in May 1823, when he decided to take his notebook into the woods and work from nature. He drew a picture of a gnarled tree trunk, his first nonhuman subject. Once winter fell, Cole returned to Philadelphia to live in a bare, unheated room. He used the tablecloth his mother had given him when he left home as a blanket; it had been the only item she had had that could provide some warmth. Cole haunted the Pennsylvania Academy of Fine Arts with the single-minded purpose of learning how to translate his passion for the natural world into paintings. Cole studied the paintings on view, including landscapes painted by Thomas Birch and Thomas Doughty, two prominent landscape artists of the time.

In 1825, Cole moved to New York and began to exhibit his work. He displayed three of his Hudson River Valley landscapes in a store window. They were well reviewed, and more importantly for Cole, were noticed and purchased by three influential painters, John Trumbull, Asher Durand, and William Cullen Bryant. The prominent Trumbull, who was at that time president of the American Academy of the Arts, is said to have praised Cole for accomplishing in his landscapes what he himself had been trying in vain to do for years. Trumbull arranged for the exhibition of Cole's work in the American Academy and introduced him to a network of wealthy patrons and collectors.

Cole's landscape paintings were revolutionary. Until this point, nature had been primarily depicted as a backdrop for historical paintings featuring famous people acting out well-known situations. Cole changed all of this by making nature itself the powerful, dynamic subject of his paintings. According to author James Thomas Flexner, "Cole was developing a landscape style that did not so much break with the vernacular tradition as transform it." He was painting with an exuberance and sense of importance that had never before been brought to the American landscape. Cole believed in the primacy of the subject. To him, techniques such as use of color and shading were to remain subservient to the subject and were never to be ends in and of themselves. In his portrayals of vast landscapes he deliberately created visual and symbolic oppositions—storm and sunshine, wilderness and human society—to produce a type of exhilaration similar to that experienced when looking at actual landscape panoramas. In the process, he literally helped to invent the way that Americans view wilderness.

The three paintings that he sold in 1825, including the well-known *Lake with Dead Trees (Catskill)*, with their moodiness and power, established the style that would become Cole's signature. Their sale marks the birth of the Hudson River School of Painting and Cole's initiation as its founder. The Hudson River School was the first American movement in painting. It would eventually include such painters as Frederic Church, Asher B. Durand, and ALBERT BIERSTADT. These artists dominated painting in the United States from the 1850s to the 1870s, creating large-scale works that captured the beauty and splendor of the wilderness.

In 1829, on a grant from a Baltimore art collector, Cole traveled to Europe. He visited his native England and Italy. While in Italy he had the idea for a series of five paintings that would track the course of a civilization from its beginning to its end. After he returned to the United States in 1832, a New York art collector named Luman Reed commissioned Cole to paint the series, which he called *The Course of Empire*. These paintings, completed in 1836, were not as well received publicly as his pure landscapes had been, owing to their moral undertones.

Cole settled in Catskill, New York, in 1833, where he boarded with the family of John Alexander Thompson at Cedar Grove, a house surrounded by 88 acres of woods on three sides. Cole married Maria Bartow, one of Thompson's nieces, in 1836. They continued living at Cedar Grove and had four children together, Theodore, Mary, Emily, and Thomas. Cole continued to paint during this time, producing several hundred paintings while at Cedar Grove. When the Catskill-Canajoharie Railroad cut through the woods north toward Albany, Cole became one of the first conservationists in the United States before the word *conservation* even existed with its present meaning. In an article for *National Parks* magazine, Lynne Bertrand quotes him as having said, "Beauty should be of some value among us that where it is not necessary to destroy a tree or a grove, the hand of the woodsman should be checked."

Cole lived at Cedar Grove for 12 years. He died, apparently of pleurisy, February 11, 1848, at the age of 47. Some of his most significant works include: *Lake With Dead Trees (Catskill)*, 1825; *The Oxbow*, 1836; and *The Voyage of Life*, 1839–1840.

BIBLIOGRAPHY

Baigell, Matthew, *Thomas Cole*, 1981; Bertrand, Lynne, "The American Canvas," *National Parks*, 1989; Flexner, James Thomas, *That Wilder Image*, 1962; Powell, Earl A., *Thomas Cole*, 1990.

Collom, Jack

(November 8, 1931–)
Poet, Teacher

Jack Collom is a poet from Colorado who teaches poetry and ecology up and down the Rocky Mountains, from Taos, New Mexico, to Salmon, Idaho. He has written tirelessly about his environs, both outer and inner, since his first book of verse, *Blue Heron & IBC*, was published in 1972. At Naropa University, where he has taught in the Jack Kerouac School of Disembodied Poetics since 1986, Collom has developed eco-lit curricula as well as pedagogies for elementary and secondary schools to activate poetry and ecology simultaneously in the classroom.

Jack Collom was born John Aldridge Collom on November 8, 1931, in Chicago, Illinois. His parents were secondary school teachers who encouraged young Jack's interest in nature. A bird-watcher from the age of 11, Jack Collom has always been a nonviolent outdoorsman, preferring birding and trekking over hunting and trapping. In 1947, when he was 16 years old, his family moved to the small cold town of Fraser, Colorado. He graduated from high school in a class of four, going on to forestry school at what is now Colorado State University at Fort Collins.

After a stint in the Air Force in Germany and North Africa, Collom spent the late 1950s and early 1960s learning his chops at verse writing in and around New York City and other places. He began working in factories in Connecticut to support his poetry habit and his family. He edited the literary magazine *The* from 1966 to 1977.

By 1974 he was working in "Poetry in the Schools" programs in Colorado, Wyoming, and Nebraska, and in 1980 he became a full-time poet in the public schools of New York City. The early teaching approaches that he developed are presented in his book, *Moving Windows* (1985). A variety of writing experiments that are especially appropriate in conjunction with ecological study are included in *Poetry Everywhere* (1994). In that book, and as a first assignment for any group, Collom asks students to write a list of "Things to Save," including both personal possessions and the wonders of our planet earth. Other forms Collom is wont to assign include "Compost-based Poems," "Place Poems," "Recipes" (how to make a horse, a planet, for example), and "Talking to Animals."

Collom always has researched the animals treated in his poems, and he has a penchant for small vertebrates. Animals of particular interest to Collom are mice, fox, passenger pigeons, the blue heron, as well as migratory birds. His latest book, *Exchanges of Earth & Sky* (2005) is a collage of poems and bird materials.

In addition to his 23 books of poetry, Collom has written essays on eco-poetics in which he explains his unique and creative approach to impending ecological collapse. He wrote in his 1994 essay, "On, at, around Active Eco-Lit," "Perhaps some poetry, in its eco-response, can reach forward in time, and humanize or enchant scientific prophecy." Like many poets, he is annoyed by pure sci-

Jack Collom (Photograph by a teacher at Whittier School, Boulder, CO)

ence's tendency to quantify all things. In the same essay, he advised, "'Out there' is the sense of an endless supply, & endlessness equals unpredictability. Once things can be counted, they're almost gone." The 2005 volume of the journal *ecopoetics*, published by Jonathon Skinner, includes more than 70 pages of Collom's writings on nature.

Collom continues to teach at Naropa University, where he received the 2001 President's Award for Faculty. He has received two Poetry Fellowships from the National Endowment for the Arts. In 2008 he travelled to Brussels, Belgium to read poetry and give the plenary address at a conference at the Université Libre de Bruxelles on "Poetic Ecologies."

Currently, Collom is assembling a collection of his best poetry and experimental writing, called *Second Nature*.

Collom resides in Boulder, Colorado, with his wife, Jennifer Heath. He has four grown children, Nat, Chris, Franz, and Sierra.

BIBLIOGRAPHY

Collom, Jack, "An Ecosystem of Writing Ideas," *jack magazine*, www.jackmagazine.com/issue2; Collom, Jack, *Arguing with Something Plato Said*, 1990; Collom, Jack, *Blue Heron & IBC*, 1972; Jack Collom, "On, at, around Active Eco-Lit," *Annals of the Jack Kerouac School of Disembodied Poetics*, Anne Waldman and Andrew Schelling, eds. 1994.

Commoner, Barry

(May 28, 1917–)
Biologist, Activist, Founder of the Center for the Biology of Natural Systems

One of the founding fathers of the modern U.S. environmental movement, Barry Commoner has since the 1950s advocated the correction of environmental problems at their source. Commoner's Center for the Biology of Natural Systems at Queens College, New York, has researched and proposed solutions to a variety of environmental threats, including air pollution, nuclear power, soil and water contamination, and waste disposal. Commoner's focus on problems that affect the public, together with his desire to publicize his common-sense solutions, has motivated him to write five books and even to run for president on the Citizen's Party ticket in 1980.

Barry Commoner was born on May 28, 1917, in New York City. An uncle gave him a microscope as a child, and Commoner spent his free time gathering and examining specimens from Brooklyn's Prospect Park. Commoner studied zoology at Columbia College, graduating in 1937 with honors. He then moved on to Harvard University, where he earned an M.A. in 1938 and a Ph.D. in 1941, both in biology. After a year of teaching at Queens College, Commoner was drafted by the Navy Reserve. An early assignment was to design a method to spray Pacific island beaches with dichlordiphenyltrichlor (DDT) before Navy troops invaded them, and when he tested the procedure on the New Jersey shore, a huge fish kill resulted. This was Commoner's first personal experience with a phenomenon he has seen repeated many times: that society learns about the pitfalls of a product or technology only after it has adopted it and become dependent upon it.

Following his discharge from the Navy and a two-year stint as associate editor of *Science Illustrated* magazine, Commoner accepted a position in the botany department at Washington University in Saint Louis, Missouri. By 1953, Commoner had risen to full professor of botany and became the department's chair in 1965. His research at that point in his career was on the tobacco mosaic virus. Commoner felt that some of the discoveries he was making about the virus might be applied to viruses occurring in humans, and his work was funded in part by a pharmaceutical company and the American Cancer Society. Commoner was responsible for some of the earliest findings about the association between free radicals and cancer.

At the same time that his academic career was blossoming, Commoner's conscience drew him toward research that would address some of the environmental problems that had emerged since the end of World War II. Nuclear fallout was an urgent concern, since the United States and the Soviet Union in the early 1950s were making frequent atmospheric tests of nuclear bombs. Commoner, together with Linus Pauling and Margaret Mead, convinced their scientific colleagues to form study groups and lobby the government about this and other problems. Commoner helped form and for 17 years served on the board of directors of the Scientists' Institute for Public Information, which made scientific information available to the public.

By 1966, Commoner had decided to wrap up his studies of tobacco viruses and devote all of his energies to solving environmental problems. With a $4.25 million grant from the U.S. Public Health Service, Commoner established the Center for the Biology of Natural Systems (CBNC) at Washington University, which would coordinate a multidisciplinary group of researchers, including economists, biophysicists, sanitary engineers, anthropologists, and the like, to study the "real-world problems" resulting from society's dependence on electricity, automobiles, detergents, insecticides, plastics, and so on.

The lessons that Commoner has drawn from CBNC's studies and history are that environmental problems are best solved at their source. For example, in a 1990 interview in *Mother Earth News*, Commoner decries the regulatory approach used by most legislation. The Clean Air Act of 1970, for example, required a 90 percent reduction of carbon monoxide, hydrocarbons, and ozone and set a seven-year deadline for that goal. It was not achieved by 1977, nor by 1982, nor even by 1987; in fact levels started to rise after 1982. The only dramatic improvement in air quality was an 86 percent drop in lead content, a result of the banning of leaded gasoline. Commoner recommends the same tactic with pesticide contamination of soil and water: a ban on pesticides. When CBNC studied the productivity of organic farms in the midwestern United States, it found that they were 8.5 percent less productive but that farmers made the same amount of money per acre because they did not have to purchase expensive pesticides. To halt air pollution caused by fossil fuel–fired electric plants, Commoner says that at the very least, natural gas should be burned to generate electricity, and it would be even better to use methane gas produced by manure or coastal algae, or solar energy gathered by photovoltaic cells. In a 2007 *New York Times* interview, when asked about global warming, Commoner said that "the only rational answer is to change the way in which we do transportation, energy production, agriculture and a good deal of manufacturing."

Commoner's ideas, by his own admission, would be difficult to implement in an economic system such as ours that encourages short-term gain even at the expense of the environment. He is a proponent of more government control over certain industries. In his view, for example, the government should mandate what types of fuels can be used in electric plants or automobiles. Because his ideas could be implemented more effectively if the government assumed more control over environmental issues, Commoner agreed to run for president on the Citizens Party ticket in 1980. The Citizens Party advocated public control of the energy industry and a sharp reduction in defense spending. Ronald Reagan won that election, but Commoner did garner 250,000 votes.

In 1981, CBNC moved to Queens College at the City University of New York. Commoner stepped down from teaching at the age of 70 in 1987 and from the direction of the CBNS in 2000. He has two children from his 1946 marriage to Gloria Gordon and has been married to Lisa Feiner since 1980.

BIBLIOGRAPHY

"Center for the Biology of Natural Systems," www.cbns.qc.edu; Commoner, Barry, "Environmental Democracy Is the Planet's Best Hope, *Utne Reader*, 1990; Commoner, Barry, *Making Peace with the Planet*, 1990; Egan, Michael, *Barry Commoner and the Science of Survival*, 2007; Nixon, Will, "Barry Commoner: Earth's Advocate," *In These Times*, 1991; "The Ploughboy Interview," *Mother Earth News*, 1990; Strong, Douglas, *Dreamers and Defenders, American Conservationists*, 1988; Vinciguerra, Thomas, "At 90, an Environmentalist From the 70s Still Has Hope," *New York Times*, 2007.

Connett, Ellen, and Paul Connett

(June 21, 1943– ; October 20, 1940–)
Secretary of American Environmental Health Studies Project; Executive Director of American Environmental Health Studies Project

Paul and Ellen Connett provide solid scientific information and networking support to communities throughout the world that are fighting municipal solid waste incinerators and fluoridation of their water systems. Since 1985 they have published newsletters, provided on-line data bases of articles and reports, produced videos, and Paul Connett has given more than 2,000 talks worldwide, about these issues. The Connetts worked independently until 2001, when they assumed the direction of the American Environmental Health Studies Project, with Paul Connett serving as executive director and Ellen Connett as secretary.

Ellen Langle was born on June 21, 1943, in Brooklyn, New York, and was raised in Dumont, New Jersey. She moved to New York City during the 1960s, worked for an advertising agency, and in her free time became involved in the American Committee to Keep Biafra Alive. Through this work she met Paul Connett.

Paul Connett was born on October 20, 1940, in Sussex, England. He graduated with honors from Cambridge University, earning a B.A. in natural sciences in 1962. After teaching high school for four years, he moved to the United States and commenced a doctoral degree program in biochemistry. Quickly Connett was swept up by the anti–Vietnam War movement, and he left the program. In New York City, at a meeting about the situation in Biafra, Connett met Ellen Langle. They began working together on political issues and married in 1970.

The couple moved to England in 1970. They worked for one year opposing the war in East Pakistan, now Bangladesh. Ellen Connett and Roger Moody, an editor at *Peace News* in London, were cofounders of Operation Omega, a group that defied the blockade by delivering much-needed supplies to the besieged country. She and Operation Omega member Gordon Slaven were captured by the West Pakistan army, charged with illegal entry, and sentenced to two years in prison. They served two months and were released in December 1971 when the Indian army liberated Jessore, East Pakistan, where the prison was located. After the war the Connetts lived in London, where Paul Connett taught general studies at a technical college and Ellen Connett raised their three sons. They were particularly concerned about nuclear power plants and worked against the proposed expansion of the Windscale nuclear plant (now known as Sellafield). The Connetts relocated to the United States in 1979, when Paul Connett entered a Ph.D. program in chemistry at Dartmouth College. He graduated in 1983 and that same year accepted the position he held until retiring in 2006, as professor of chemistry at Saint Lawrence University in Canton, New York.

The Connetts believed that their days of activism had ended and that they could expect the quiet life of an academic family. Paul Connett was looking forward to devoting himself to teaching, and he began hosting a weekly program at the local public radio station.

In 1985, however, they learned of a plan to site a municipal waste incinerator in their rural county. Ellen Connett, who was then working at St. Lawrence University as a periodicals clerk, searched the library's journal archives, and the couple discovered that the incinerator would present a serious health risk. In 1977 it had been discovered that dioxin, a highly toxic substance, for which there is no safe dose, is created as a by-product when chlorinated substances are burned. Chlorine is prevalent in municipal waste, occurring in low levels in any bleached cotton or paper product and at significantly higher levels in polyvinyl chloride (PVC) plastic. A health risk assessment was performed for the proposed incinerator in 1985, which assessed only inhalation as the route of exposure to dioxin. Paul Connett believed that ingestion might present a greater risk. He and Tom Webster, who worked with BARRY COMMONER at the Center for the Biology of Natural Systems, published what became the first study on the uptake of dioxin in cows' milk from the dioxin emitted by municipal solid waste incinerators. That study showed that dioxin emitted by trash incinerator smokestacks near grazing cows presented a far greater route of exposure than inhalation, owing to the direct deposition of dioxin onto the pasture and its uptake by the grazing cows. Thus, anyone consuming beef or milk from the area (the county was then the second-largest milk producer in the state) was potentially exposed to very high levels of dioxin. Connett and Webster went on to publish six more scientific papers on dioxins, all of which were published in *Chemosphere* and presented at the International Symposia on Dioxin and Related Compounds. It is now accepted that the major route of exposure to dioxin is through the ingestion of milk, meat, and fish. Of concern is that the fetus and breast-fed baby are exposed to the highest levels of dioxin in the human species.

During the mid-1980s hundreds of incinerators were proposed throughout the country. The Connetts shared information with other communities through their newsletter *Waste Not*, which by 1988 came out weekly and was sent to hundreds of citizen activists. Each two-page issue of *Waste Not* documented incinerator proposals countrywide, tracked industry proponents as they traveled from community to community, described their arguments, offered scientifically sound responses to these arguments, hailed victories against incinerators, and mourned defeats. The Connetts published *Waste Not* until 2000. Almost 300 back issues are available online at the American Environmental Health Studies Project website (americanhealthstudies.org).

Paul Connett gained a reputation for his articulate, scientifically sound testimony, and he was invited to attend public hearings on incinerators all over the country. Since 1985 he has made more than 2,000 presentations to a wide variety of audiences, usually pro bono, in 49 states, 5 Canadian provinces, and 43 foreign countries. He has devoted three sabbaticals and most of his vacation time to being on call for activists in need. The Connetts, together with Tom Webster and Billie Elmore, launched the Citizens Conferences on Dioxin. The first two conferences were held in 1991 and 1994. In 1996, they worked with several other groups, including the Citizens Clearinghouse on Hazardous Waste, to coorganize the Third Citizens Conference on Dioxin.

The St. Lawrence County municipal solid waste incinerator debate lasted five and a half years; the proposal was finally defeated by a narrow margin of county legislators in July 1990. During the period between 1985 and 1993, incinerator proposals were defeated in more than 300 communities across the nation. The last municipal solid waste incinerator was built in the United States in 1995. The incinerator industry has moved abroad, however, and incinerators are being proposed in Asia, Latin America, and some European countries. Most of Paul Connett's current presentations are done abroad at the request of local grassroots activists.

Between 1985 and 1994, Paul Connett, together with Robert Baily, a professor of fine arts at St. Lawrence University, produced 41 videos that document the dangers of incineration and safer alternatives for Video-Active Productions. The videos' topics range from the poisoning of a South African community from the operations of a medical waste incinerator and a hazardous waste landfill to video interviews with fluoride researchers. Starting in 1997, he produced 25 videos on topics of environmental justice, waste, and fluoride toxicity for Grassroots and Global Video Videotapes. His son, Michael Connett, is coproducer of the fluoride series.

In 2001, Paul Connett took over as executive director of the American Environmental Health Studies Project (AEHSP), which had been founded five years earlier by by Oak Ridge, Tennessee activists Cliff Honicker and Jacqueline Kittrell, whose area of concern was workers' and community exposure to nuclear radiation near nuclear weapons plants, but who had also support campaigns against a hazardous and radioactive wate incinerator. Honicker and Kittrell were no longer unable to run AEHSP, and so the Connetts took it over, Paul as Executive Director and Ellen as Secretary. AEHSP currently serves as umbrella for several projects, including the Fluoride Action Network, BurnBarrel—an organization working to raise awareness about and end the common but toxic practice of backyard waste burning—and the current manifestation of the Connetts' work on hazardous waste: "Zero Waste & Sustainability." The AEHSP website hosts the archives of *Waste Not* and catalogs for Paul Connett's videos.

Since 1996 the Connetts have worked on issues related to the toxicity of fluoride. Paul Connett co-founded the Fluoride Action Network (FAN), a large Internet-based coalition of scientists, dentists, and doctors devoted to providing up-to-date information on fluoride to citizens, scientists and policy-makers. Ellen Connett became director of FAN's Pesticides Project, which hosts the only online database of more than 300 mainly fluorinated, and some fluoride, pesticides. Since 2004 FAN has submitted formal objections to the U.S. Environmental Protection Agency's (EPA) first-time approval of the fumigant sulfuryl fluoride. This is a highly toxic neurotoxin which, according to the EPA, is the second largest source of fluoride exposure for people living in the U.S. because of the very high fluoride tolerances approved for post-harvest and processed foods. As of mid-2008, FAN, together with the Environmental Working Group and Beyond Pesticides, were in the middle of an administrative procedure with the EPA on their request for a hearing on their objections to sulfuryl fluoride. If granted, it would be the first time a hearing was held where the EPA was challenged on the first-time approval of a pesticide. If denied, the groups plan to sue the EPA.

The Connetts have received many awards for their work. They shared the Conservationist of the Year award in 1990 from the Environmental Planning Lobby in Albany, New York. Paul Connett received a Leadership Award from the National Campaign Against the Misuse of Pesticides in 2000. Ellen Connett was appointed in 2000 to the board of the Citizens Environmental Coalition, based in Albany, New York.

The Connetts reside in Canton, New York.

BIBLIOGRAPHY

"American Environmental Health Studies Project," www.americanhealthstudies.org; Connett, Paul, "The Disposable Society," *Ecology, Economics, and Ethics: The Broken Circle*, F. H. Borman and S. R. Kellert, eds., 1991; Connett, Paul, and Ellen Connett, "Municipal Waste Incineration: Wrong Answer to the Wrong Question," *The Ecologist*, 1994; Schwab, Jim, *Deeper Shades of Green*, 1994; "Fluoride Action Network," www.FluorideAlert.org.

Conway, Stuart

(July 17, 1953 -)
Co-founder and International Director of Trees, Water & People, Watershed Manager

Stuart Conway is the co-founder and international director of Trees, Water & People (TWP), a nonprofit organization that works for an environmentally sustainable future through reforestation, watershed management, promoting renewable energy, appropriate technology, and environmental education programs. With its headquarters in Ft. Collins, Colorado, TWP strives to promote the involvement and collaboration of local people in the conservation and management of natural resources to work towards sustainability in the communities in which they live.

Conway was born in Cleveland, Ohio, in 1953. He joined the Peace Corps with his wife, Jennie Bramhall in 1984, and they worked in Guatemala for three years. Conway graduated in 1983 with a bachelor's degree in Forest Management from Colorado State University and earned a masters degree in International Development and Agroforestry from Cornell University in 1989. He directed the New Forest Project in Washington, D.C., for eight years and developed reforestation and watershed protection programs in the Philippines, Central America, and Africa.

Trees, Water, & People was founded in 1998 by Conway and fellow conservationist Richard Fox. Fox serves as the organization's National Director, overseeing programs, largely in the Rocky Mountains, that focus on renewable and alternative energy and watershed protection in communities in Colorado and Wyoming. TWP's national sector also works with Native American communities and recently installed over 200 solar heating systems in South Dakota reservations to heat homes more efficiently. In his role as International Director, Conway coordinates programs in El Salvador, Honduras, Guatemala, Haiti, Nicaragua, and Brazil. Primary projects include forest replacement and reforestation, protecting watersheds, promoting renewable energy, and appropriate technology such as efficient cooking stoves. Both national and international efforts focus on environmental education and revolve around the belief that people need to be involved in caring for the natural resources in the area in which they live. TWP also promotes awareness by hosting Eco-Tours and Work Tours to Central America to observe and participate in conservation efforts such as building fuel-efficient stoves and planting trees in addition to cultural activities and sightseeing.

Over 65 percent of the forests in Central America have been destroyed in the past 30 years. Since its start 10 years ago, Trees, Water & People has planted more than two million trees in Central America in an effort to re-establish this precious natural resource. These trees make up forests that control erosion, protect water supplies, and maintain climate patterns by removing greenhouse gasses from the air. Reforestation efforts focus not only on planting trees but also on the establishment of local tree nurseries with microcredit loans.

In addition to saving forests by re-planting trees, TWP also works to significantly reduce the rate at which this natural resource is destroyed by human consumption. One of TWP's largest and most successful projects is its fuel-efficient stove project in Honduras, established in 1998. In collaboration with local communities and the Honduran Association for Development (AHDESA), TWP developed the *Justa* stove, a fuel-efficient cooking stove designed to reduce wood usage for fuel to conserve trees and reduce emissions. The stoves burn 70 percent less wood, create less toxic smoke, and burn hotter than the traditional open cooking fires used by most communities in Central America. According to a TWP press release on the organization's 10th anniversary, the 25,000 fuel-efficient cooking stoves built in Central America and Haiti have prevented over 175,000 tons of carbon emissions. In addition to reducing emissions, *Justa* stoves improve health by producing very little indoor smoke. As the majority of families in Central America prepare food on open wood fires, usually indoors without much ventilation, daily cooking often leads to health problems such as heart and lung disease, with the highest rates occurring in women and children from the toxic smoke in the kitchens. With a metal chimney, these stoves remove 80 percent of the toxic gases, including carbon monoxide, emitted by burning wood. *Justa* stoves also save families time and money by requiring them to obtain and burn less wood for fuel and support the local communities by creating jobs to build them. Due to the success of the Honduras stove program, TWP introduced similar stove programs in Guatemala, Nicaragua, El Salvador, and Haiti between 1998 and 2007.

Stuart Conway was awarded the E-chievement Award in 2001 from *e-town*, a nationally broadcast radio show that appears weekly on National Public Radio, for his work on community reforestation and improved stoves in Central America. In 2005 TWP and AHDESA won the Ashden Award for Sustainable Energy, known as the "Green Oscar" for their stove project in Honduras. The Project was also awarded a $132,000 grant from the United States Environmental Protection Agency, which was used for a micro-credit program to help families with the $65–$70 cost of a stove over a year. TWP's work in Central America was also featured on *Earth Pulse, Heroes for the Planet*, a television program that appeared on the National Geographic Channel and was sponsored by the Ford Motor Company. TWP's tribal solar and tree planting program appeared on *CNN International News*.

In addition to his role as TWP's International Director, Conway currently serves on the Board of Directors for TWP, as well as being a founding Board Member and Vice President of the Rocky Mountain Sustainable Living Association (RMSLA), and a founding Board Member of Engineers in Technical Humanitarian Overseas Support (ETHOS). He also served on the Board of Directors of Friends of Guatemala, a Returned Peace Corps Volunteer group dedicated to helping students in Guatemala with scholarships.

BIBLIOGRAPHY

Bhagat, Brook and Bhagat, Gaurav, "Trees Water & People: Planting Trees, Protecting Watersheds, and more…" *EcoWorld Nature & Technology in Harmony*, 2005; www.ashdenawards.org/winners/trees; www.etown.org; www.handsontv.info/series6/04_Energy_Matters_reports/report5.html; www.repp.org/discussiongroups/resources/stoves/TWP/justa/Justa_stoveone-pager.pdf; www.treeswaterpeople.org.

Cook, Richard A.

(February 25, 1960 -)
Sustainable Urban Designer, Principle Owner/Chief Architect of Cook+Fox Architects

Richard Cook is an architect specializing in design that restores and regenerates the urban environment. A Partner at Cook+Fox Architects in New York City, he is among the vanguard of the high-performance building movement, often termed sustainable or green design. Cook helped design the first skyscraper to seek a

Richard A. Cook (Photograph courtesy of Gunther Intelmann for Cook+Fox Architects)

LEED Platinum (Leadership in Energy and Environment Design) certification from the United States Green Building Council for the 55-story Bank of America Tower at One Bryant Park in Midtown Manhattan, as well as the first project of any type in New York, the Cook+Fox Office at 641 Avenue of the Americas, to earn the LEED Platinum certification.

Richard Allan Cook was born on February 25, 1960, in Massachusetts. He grew up in central New York and lives in the region to this day. He attended Syracuse University, where he studied architecture and was awarded the Norman J. Wiedersom Travel Fellowship for study in Florence, Italy. He graduated *cum laude* in 1983 with a Bachelor of Architecture and was the winner of the Soling Student Design Competition. He went on to work in New York City, first with his future business partner at Fox & Fowle Architects, and later as the principal at Richard Cook & Associates, a firm known for its expertise working in historic landmark districts.

Since teaming up in 2003 with Robert F. Fox, Jr., the designer of the Condé Nast headquarters at 4 Times Square, which in the late 1990s set the standard for energy efficient high rises, Cook has integrated work in historic areas with sustainable architectural design. The firm's award-winning 2005 Front Street project in the Historic South Street Seaport at the southern tip of Manhattan, has 14 mixed-use buildings that are cooled with ten 1,500-foot-deep geothermal wells.

Designing One Bryant Park in Midtown Manhattan was an enormous undertaking. The 2.2 million-square-foot, 55-floor monolith was, at its time, the second tallest building in New York City and the largest development site in Midtown. In addition to employing leading-edge strategies for a healthy and productive, daylit work environment, the project included an Urban Garden Room, expanded and improved public circulation space, and the restoration of the Henry Miller's Theater, which first opened its doors in 1918.

In December 2006, Cook+Fox's office at 641 Avenue of the Americas in New York City was the first project in New York State to earn LEED Platinum certification, under LEED for Commercial Interiors. Cook, Fox and two other partners have also formed a consulting company, Terrapin Bright Green, to provide environmental strategic thinking and planning services to developers, business leaders, and policymakers. Cook addresses the topic of green architecture frequently in the media, having appeared on PBS, NPR, and in *Wired Magazine*, and he delivers speeches in many venues.

At the United Nations in 2005 he posed a vision of buildings as mostly self-sufficient citizens in an urban community, and explained how One Bryant Park "will use fifty percent less energy than a conventional building, discharge zero storm water to the city's sewer system, generate seventy percent of its annual energy needs on site, and ninety percent of the construction debris will be recycled." Its design incorporates natural resources, such as the sun, available to that particular location, and rainwater, another free resource, which averages four feet per year in Manhattan, using it to flush toilets and in the cooling system, reducing the building's fresh water usage by approximately fifty percent. Waterless urinals at One Bryant Park alone will save 3.4 million more gallons of water per year. The 4.6 megawatt natural gas cogeneration plant, which generates about two-thirds of the energy the building needs annually, is connected to a state-of-the-art thermal storage system and has a payback period in reduced energy costs of less than four years.

The quality of the indoor environment at One Bryant Park was a top priority, with heating/cooling supplied through an under-floor displacement air ventilation system. Workers and visitors breathe air that is ninety-five percent free of particulates, ozone, and volatile organic compounds, whereas a typical building will only filter out thirty-five percent.

Eco-efficient strategies are but a transition into what architect WILLIAM MCDONOUGH and German chemist Michael Braungart have termed eco-effectiveness, nothing short of a new Industrial Revolution. *Cradle to Cradle* (2002). In his current work, Richard Cook is pursuing architecture that explores a new aesthetic while restoring human and natural environments, informed by concepts such as biophilia and biomimicry. (See E.O. Wilson and Janine Benyus).

Richard Cook sits on the Board of Directors in the Tri-State area for HOPE Worldwide, an international non-governmental organization providing sustainable, community-based services for those in need. He lives in Rockland County with his wife, Ellen, and their twin sons.

BIBLIOGRAPHY

Cook, Richard A., AIA, Partner, Cook+Fox Architects, with Alice Hartley, *What Is Free?: How Sustainable Architecture Acts and Interacts Differently*, speech to the United Nations Economic and Social Council, Conference on Planning Sustainable Urban Growth and Sustainable Architecture, New York City, 6 June 2005, www.un.org/docs/ecosoc/meetings/2005/docs/Cook.pdf; Mueller, Tom, "Biomimetics: Design by Nature," *National Geographic*, April 2008; McGuigan, Cathleen, "Designing Light and Air," *Newsweek*, March 8, 2008; "Meet Richard Cook, Architect" *Time for Kids*, Specials, EARTH DAY 2007, www.timeforkids.com/TFK/kids/specials/articles/0,28285,1608119,00.html; "Meet Rick Cook, Beau Ideal of Green Architects," March 24, 2006 www.treehugger.com/files/2006/03/lime_meet_rick.php; Feder, Barnaby J., "Environmentally Conscious Developers Try to Turn Green Into Platinum," *New York Times*, August 25, 2004; Lyne, Jack, "Bank of America Begins Work on $1-Billion NYC Tower," www.siteselection.com/ssinsider/snapshot/sf040816.htm.; terrapinbrightgreen.com; www.cookplusfox.com; www.usgbc.org.

Cooper, James Fenimore

(September 15, 1789–September 14, 1851)
Novelist

James Fenimore Cooper earned his place as one of the founders of American fiction when he wrote the Leatherstocking Tales—stories about Natty Bumppo, a rugged frontiersman who lived in the late eighteenth and early nineteenth centuries. Generations of readers have since enjoyed these tales of adventure set in the backwoods and forests of the early United States. Cooper wrote many other novels as well and became known for his detailed descriptions of a beautiful natural world and for his resounding criticism of wasteful and destructive pioneering practices in the United States. His novels helped to define the American identity of the times and to document the excesses of civilization on the new frontier.

James Fenimore Cooper was born in Burlington, New Jersey, on September 15, 1789. His father, Judge William Cooper, was a wealthy landowner who founded Cooperstown in central New York State, where the family moved when James was one year old. At the age of 14, Cooper entered Yale, but he was thrown out for misconduct after a year. Following that, he became a sailor for a year in preparation for entering the Navy, which he did in 1808. After three and a half years of service, the last year of which was spent on furlough, he resigned from the Navy and began a career as a gentleman farmer. He married Susan Augusta DeLancey in 1811 and eventually settled at Angevine Farm near Scarsdale, New York, and had five daughters and two sons. Cooper's ambitions as a gentleman farmer were proving difficult, because although his father left an immense estate when he died, he also left sizable debts, and Cooper and his family had to struggle with financial crisis.

It was only after these various trials and travails that Cooper began his literary career. He was 31 years old when he wrote his first novel, *Precaution* (1820), and it was a flop. The next book he wrote was a patriotic tale of the American Revolution called *The Spy* (1821). It appealed to the American sense of adventure and national loyalty and met immediate success. Cooper's career took off. With his next book, *The Pioneers* (1823), which takes place in 1793–1794 near Lake Otsego, New York, he introduced to the world the character of Natty Bumppo, also known as Leatherstocking. By the end of his career, Cooper had written four more tales about Natty Bumppo, including *The Last of the Mohicans* (1826), *The Prairie* (1827), *The Pathfinder* (1840), and *The Deerslayer* (1841), known collectively as the Leatherstocking Tales.

Leatherstocking claims a unique place in literary history as the first American fictional hero. The United States in the late eighteenth and early nineteenth centuries was stepping toward autonomy and working hard to become established as a nation of power. This involved a national mentality of conquering and civilizing the wildness of the physical environment and the native people who lived in it. Settlements were expanding farther and farther into the frontier, uprooting everything in their path. The encroachment of civilization cramped Leatherstocking, who lived in a rough hut by Lake Otsego, close to the town of Templeton (modeled after Cooperstown). Leatherstocking's way of life was to live off the land, never taking more than he needed to sustain himself. Like the Native Americans he interacted with, he was extremely adept at reading the woodlands for subtle cues. He exemplified a way of life that was in tune with his natural surroundings, in sharp contrast to what he called the "wasty ways" of the settlers living nearby. There are endless descriptions in this book and other Leatherstocking Tales of the senseless destruction that was common on the frontier: frenzied killing of passenger pigeons, heedless cutting of trees, netting fish in such huge quantities that most of them went to waste. Most of the settlers at this time fell into the all-too-common American habit of mistaking abundance for inexhaustibility, and Leatherstocking made a lonely stand for a more disciplined approach. In the end, though, unable to bear the sound of axes felling trees and unable to trust that the people around him would learn to be less selfish, he moved halfway across the continent to escape. Cooper clearly wished that more Americans would follow Leatherstocking's moral path, and his stories have left us with questions just as pertinent today: can a society bent on progress survive its wasteful and destructive ways?

In the midst of writing these and other novels, Cooper and his family moved to Europe, where they lived from 1826 until 1833, mainly in Paris and Italy. His novels gave Europeans a portrait of American life, and during his time there he was a literary spokesperson for the United States and defended it in his writing. However, on his return to the United States he became disgusted with the abuses of democracy and what he considered to be the tyranny of the majority. He began writing satire and nonfiction, much of which contained candid political criticism—something that made him very unpopular and earned him many enemies. This phase of his career brought on increasing controversy and struggles with a libelous press, though he did manage to resolve much of it and return to writing fiction. By the end of his life he had written over 50 books.

James Fenimore Cooper died on September 14, 1851, in Cooperstown, New York.

BIBLIOGRAPHY

Axelrad, Allan M., *History and Utopia: A Study of the World View of James Fenimore Cooper;* 1978, www.oneonta.edu/external/cooper/writings/utopia.html; Ringe, Donald A., *James Fenimore Cooper,* 1962; Schwarz, Frederic D., "Cooper's Coup," *American Heritage,* 1998; Spiller, Robert E., *Fenimore Cooper, Critic of His Times,* 1931; Taylor, Alan, "Fenimore Cooper's America," *History Today,* 1996.

Costle, Douglas

(July 27, 1939–)
Administrator of the Environmental Protection Agency

Douglas Michael Costle is a lawyer, civil servant, and activist. His environmental career has spanned nearly 40 years and includes such accomplishments as helping to create the Environmental Protection Agency (EPA) in 1970 and serving as its head from 1977 to 1981.

Douglas Michael Costle was born on July 27, 1939, in Long Beach, California. Soon thereafter, his parents, Michael and Shirley Joan, moved the family to Seattle, Washington, where Costle spent his adolescent years, attending Jane Addams Junior High School and Lincoln High School. After graduating from high school, Costle entered Harvard University, where he earned a B.A. degree in 1961. Three years later, in 1964, he received a J.D. degree from the University of Chicago.

Costle began his career as a trial attorney with the civil rights division of the U.S. Department of Justice in Washington, D.C. After a year in this capacity, he transferred to the Department of Commerce, where he remained until 1967, serving as an attorney for the Economic Development Administration. Costle entered into private law practice in

1967 as an associate with Kelso, Cotton, Seligman and Ray, a San Francisco law firm. In 1968, he became a senior associate with another San Francisco law firm, Marshall, Kaplan, Gans and Kahn.

Costle returned to Washington in 1969, accepting a position as senior staff associate for environment and natural resources of the President's Advisory Council on Executive Organization. It was in this position that Costle contributed significantly to the creation of the Environmental Protection Agency, an independent agency of the U.S. government responsible for the protection and maintenance of the environment for future generations. The EPA effectively replaced the former Environmental Health Service, focusing on the control of air and water pollution through the integration of research, monitoring, and enforcement. Costle lobbied to be appointed as assistant administrator of the new agency but was not awarded the position by President Nixon. Costle maintained an association with the EPA for another year, however, acting as a consultant and also serving on the President's Council on Environmental Quality.

In 1971, Costle was a fellow at the Smithsonian's Woodrow Wilson International Center for Scholars. In 1972, he became deputy commissioner for the Department of Environmental Protection in Connecticut. He was appointed commissioner in 1973 by Connecticut governor Thomas Meskill. As commissioner, Costle gained a reputation as an effective and fair administrator. He instituted a penalty program, referred to as the "Connecticut Plan," that required polluters not only to equip their plants with the proper means to prevent pollution, but also to pay fines equal to what they would have paid had they complied with environmental regulations in the first place. Both environmental and industrial interests praised the plan as fair. Costle resigned from the Connecticut Department of Environmental Protection in 1975 and accepted a position as assistant director of the Congressional Budget Office in charge of natural resources and commerce. He kept this position for a year and a half before being appointed by Pres. Jimmy Carter to the post of administrator of the EPA. Costle acted as EPA administrator from 1977 to 1981.

Costle's relatively late appointment as head of the EPA in the Carter administration was questioned by some who saw him as something of a "compromise candidate." A top EPA official wondered, in a 1977 *Newsweek* article, whether or not Costle had "the horsepower and the guts" to stand up to industry and enforce the country's growing number of environmental regulations effectively. However, under Costle's direction, the EPA grew to hire 600 new employees, and it increased its budget from $2.7 billion to $5.5 billion. Costle emphasized the use of scientific data in creating and enforcing environmental policy, leading the agency in a cautious, deliberate manner. He made a controversial decision to delay the imposition of new automobile emission standards and allowed work to continue on a nuclear power plant project in Seabrook, New Hampshire. He also negotiated what he referred to as "the largest environmental agreement in the history of the steel industry" with United States Steel, which reduced air and water pollution from several large Pittsburgh steel facilities. While with the EPA, Costle endorsed the "bubble concept," which treats polluting plants as if they are under a single bubble that covers the entire facility and allows pollution reductions to be made in the manner most cost effective for the polluter. Costle declared that the EPA was a public health agency and was instrumental in the adoption of the famous Superfund toxic waste cleanup legislation created by the Comprehensive Environmental Response Compensation and Liability Act (CERCLA).

After leaving the EPA in 1981, Costle practiced law with the private firms Wald, Harkrader & Ross and Updike, Kelley & Spellacy, and was dean of the Vermont Law School from 1987 to 1991. In recent years he has worked with public relations firms in the areas of digital media's influence on consumer purchasing, opposition research, and performance measurement.

Costle has also remained active in environmental affairs. He cofounded and acted as executive committee chair for the Environmental Certification Corporation and was chair of the United States/People's Republic of China Environmental Protection Protocol. He served as dean of the University of Vermont Law School from 1987 to 1991. In 1993, he joined the Institute for Sustainable Communities (ISC) as chair of the board of directors. ISC is a nonprofit organization that provides technical training and financial support to communities in an effort to foster environmental protection and economic and social well being. It was founded by former Vermont governor Madeleine M. Kunin in 1991, and it focuses on encouraging civic participation in strong democratic institutions that encompass a diverse array of interests in decision-making processes. Costle believes strongly that economic development and environmental protection are not mutually exclusive concepts but in fact actually reinforce each other. The ISC works on both fronts through its four foci: community development and environmental action; democracy building; environmental training; and environmental and civic education. Costle served on the board of this organization until his retirement in 1999.

Costle married Elizabeth Holmes Rowe in 1965; they have two grown children, Douglas Michael and Caroline Elizabeth.

BIBLIOGRAPHY
Costle, Douglas, *Our Environmental Future: challenges and opportunities*, 1996; "Institute for Sustainable Communities," www.iscvt.org; Langway, Lynn, "The EPA's New Man," *Newsweek*, 1977.

Cowles, Henry
(February 27, 1869–September 12, 1939)
Botanist, Ecologist

In 1899 Henry Cowles published "The Ecological Relations of the Vegetation of the Sand Dunes of Lake Michigan," a work now regarded as one of the founding moments of modern ecology. Cowles's work in this and in later publications helped transform botany from a system of classification and catalog to the scientific study of plants in their environment. Cowles studied ecological succession and pioneered the view that ecology is dynamic, shaped by relationships among species, individuals, and their environment.

Born in Kensington, Connecticut, on February 27, 1869, Henry Chandler Cowles attended local public schools and graduated from New Britain High School. He went to Oberlin College in Ohio and graduated in 1893. In 1894 he began teaching natural science at Gates College in Nebraska but left after one year to study geology at the University of Chicago. There he worked with Thomas Chamberlin and Rollin Salisbury, both of whom practiced a dynamic approach to geology. Cowles eventually switched his field to botany, attracted by John Merle Coulter, who had recently been recruited by the university to start a department of botany.

Coulter introduced Cowles to the work of European botanist Eugenius Warming, who was evolving an ecological approach to the study of plants. Cowles combined his work in botany with his background in geology and began his doctoral research on the succession of plants on the Indiana Dunes at the southern end of Lake Michigan. The dunes provided an ideal site for Cowles's study because their advance caused the rapid succession of plant species. Cowles came to see succession not simply as the product of competition between species but as a more complex process involving the struggle of individuals with their environment. Cowles's work challenged the view that succession was always progressive—the result of strong species squeezing out the weak—and argued that sometimes succession had destructive, negative results. Cowles finished the dissertation, "An Ecological Study of the Sand Dune Flora of Northern Indiana," in 1898 and received his Ph.D. in botany from the University of Chicago. In 1899 he published his results in the *Botanical Gazette*, under the title "The Ecological Relations of the Vegetation of the Sand Dunes of Lake Michigan."

This work initiated a school of ecology known as "dynamics," that is, focused on describing and understanding processes of change in ecosystems. Cowles argued that dynamics were a key component of arriving at accurate botanical classification. His ideas were part of a growing scientific interest in dynamics, derived in part from Darwin. A central idea of the dynamic school is the "climax" community, a stage of equilibrium reached in a particular ecosystem in which plant communities are stable and self-sustaining. Cowles argued for a subtle, complex view of the climax stage. His work showed that what looks self-sustaining can in fact prove self-destructive if, for example, one species crowds out neighboring species necessary to the health of the whole ecosystem.

Cowles followed his first studies on the Indiana Dunes with work on the surrounding ecosystem, publishing his results in 1901 in a paper entitled, "The Physiographic Ecology of Chicago and Vicinity." This paper is given credit as the first formal study to systematically employ the concepts of succession and climax. He also made comparative studies of dunes on Cape Cod. In 1911, Cowles became full professor at the University of Chicago and in 1925 was appointed chair of the botany department. He held the position until his retirement. As a teacher, Cowles was remembered for his use of photography and other methods that took students out of the classroom and into the field. His photographs—slides and prints—were recently rediscovered and are on display at the University of Chicago. He is credited with generating enthusiasm for the emerging field of ecology and created a large and loyal following of students who went on to careers in a variety of scientific fields.

Cowles worked with a number of influential scientists, including Sir Arthur George Tansley, who first coined the term and concept of the ecosystem, and ecologist Frederick Clements. His work on the dunes of Lake Michigan also attracted the attention of landscape designer Jens Jensen. In 1914, Cowles, along with several of his students, founded the Ecological Society of America. In 1926 he was appointed editor of the *Botanical Gazette*. Cowles used his influence to help establish the Illinois state parks system and the forest preserves of Cook County. He was a charter member of the Illinois State Academy of Science. He served as president of the Chicago Academy of Science, the Association of American Geographers, the Botanical Society of America, and the phytogeography and ecology section of the International Botanical Congress.

Cowles retired from the University of Chicago in 1934. He died at his home in Chicago on September 12, 1939, after a long illness.

BIBLIOGRAPHY

Cassidy, Victor M., *Henry Chandler Cowles: Pioneer Ecologist*, 2007; Cooper, William, "Henry Chandler Cowles," *Ecology*, 1935; Golley, Frank, *A History of the Ecosystem Concept in Ecology*, 1993; Yoe, Mary Ruth, "The Once & Future Scenes," *University of Chicago Magazine*, 1997.

Cox, Paul
(October 10, 1953–)
Ethnobotanist

Ethnobotanist Paul Cox shared a Goldman Environmental Prize in 1997 with Fuiono Senio, high chief of the village of Falealupo, Western Samoa, for their cooperative role in saving a 30,000-acre rain forest outside Falealupo from imminent destruction. The Falealupo reserve is a model of sustainable use: villagers harvest plants for medicinal or traditional uses, an arboreal walkway used by ecotourists and researchers provides the village with an extra source of income, and the forest continues to flourish. A specialist on the ethnobotany of the Samoa islands, Cox also directed the National Tropical Botanical Garden in Hawai'i from 1998 till 2004, and in 2004 founded the Institute for EthnoMedicine.

Paul Alan Cox was born in Salt Lake City, Utah, on October 10, 1953, to a family long devoted to conservation. His great grandfather helped establish Arbor Day in Utah; his grandfather founded wildfowl preserves and fish hatcheries in the West and played a lead role in establishing the elk preserve in Jackson Hole, Wyoming. Cox's mother, a fisheries biologist, and his father, a conservation officer, both worked for the U.S. Fish and Wildlife Service; and his father also worked for the National Park Service and in the state park system of Utah as superintendent. Cox spent much of his childhood outdoors, accompanying his parents on their duties, and they both encouraged their son's early interest in plants. When he became fascinated with a rare plant, *Darlingtonia californica*, at the age of ten, for instance, they drove him to the California coast near Crescent City, where one of two natural populations grow.

When Cox was 19 years old, he was called to serve as a missionary by the Church of Jesus Christ of Latter-day Saints. He began his two years of service in the small, remote village of Safune, on the island of Savaii, Western Samoa. The village's high chief, Aumalosi, taught Cox the chiefly version of Samoan, a dialect reserved for chiefs and almost never taught to *palagi*, or foreigners. Cox still does not understand why he was chosen for such instruction, but he proved a facile learner and now speaks the dialect well. This fluency has been of great use in his ethnobotanical studies and conservationist efforts in Samoa, since both entail complex interactions with Samoan people.

Cox returned to Utah in 1975 and resumed studies at Brigham Young University (BYU), graduating with a B.S. in botany in 1976. He then earned two master's degrees in 1978, one from the University of Wales in ecology and the other in biology from Harvard University. Harvard awarded him a Ph.D. in 1981. At Harvard, Cox was deeply influenced by Prof. RICHARD EVANS SCHULTES, who upon learning that he was fluent in Samoan, encouraged him to begin ethnobotanical studies there. After a two-year stint at Miller Institute for Basic Research in Science at the University of California, Berkeley, from 1981 to 1983, Cox was offered a professorship in the botany department at BYU.

Cox was devastated by the death of his mother, in 1984, of breast cancer. In his grief, he vowed that he would dedicate his life to searching for a cure to that disease. His training led him to believe that of the many medicinal plants growing in tropical rain forests, at least one might hold a cure for cancer. Two months after his mother's death, Cox learned that he had won a National Science Foundation Presidential Young Investigator Award to fund any research project of his choosing. So, in 1984, Cox was able to return to the island of Savaii in Western Samoa to begin what would become a long and fruitful career studying the medicinal plants of its lush rain forests. This time, he was accompanied by his wife, Barbara, and their four children. Living in a *fale* (an open-air Samoan-style home) on the beach in the village of Falealupo, the family readily integrated into the village's social life. Cox studied with local healers, and he gathered specimens of medicinal plants that he felt might offer cures for cancer to be screened by the National Cancer Institute (NCI) in Washington, D.C. During his stay in Falealupo that year, Cox made two discoveries that would fuel his later conservationist efforts: that the Western Samoan flying fox, a large flying fox bat of the rain forest, was facing extinction and that the village of Falealupo was being forced by the Western Samoa government to build a new school for its children, which was such an expensive endeavor that the village had to sell logging rights to its rain forest to pay for it.

Cox used funds from his National Science Foundation award to fund a study of the Western Samoan flying fox. He returned in 1988 to help his research team set up their study in Falealupo, and while he was there, he learned that the company that had been granted the logging rights to the forest in return for a down payment on the village school had just begun cutting trees. Cox and the researchers visited the logging site and were horrified. Cox writes in his 1997 memoir *Nafanua* that watching the rain forest fall reminded him painfully of watching his mother succumb to cancer. Just as he would have done anything for her comfort and survival, he felt compelled to save the Falealupo rain forest. A few days later he made a daring proposal to the village Council of Chiefs: that he himself would pay for the village school and pay off the logging company's down payment on the school, so that the forest could remain standing. After several days of debating the offer—controversial because Samoans have many times in their history been taken advantage of by power-hungry *palagi*—High Chief Fuiono Senio convinced the Council to accept it. Fuiono then ran three miles to the logging site, machete in hand, and forced the loggers to leave.

Cox returned to the United States and raised money to buy back the lease from the logging company and to pay for the new school. He and Barbara had decided to sell their own home to raise the necessary funds, but that became unnecessary when other donors contributed to the fund. Soon Cox was able to return and sign the official contract in which the villagers promised to protect the rain forest for 50 years, extracting forest products in a sustainable manner only for medicines and other traditional uses. They also vowed to protect the endangered Western Samoan flying fox. He later returned to help construct an aerial walkway and observation platform 100 feet above ground. Designed for researchers and tourists who pay entrance fees, this provides additional income to the village, where the average per capita yearly income is under $100. For his leadership in saving the village's rain forest, the Council of Chiefs bestowed a unique honor on Cox, the title of Nafanua, or Goddess of War, which he still holds today and which entails a lifelong responsibility for the well-being of the village. Cox and Fuiono Senio were jointly awarded a 1997 Goldman Environmental Prize for saving the Falealupo rain forest.

In addition to this achievement, Cox also lobbied successfully for an act setting up a national park in American Samoa, which protected habitat of the flying fox. It was signed into law in 1988. Although he had been unable to persuade the U.S. Fish and Wildlife Service that the flying fox merited listing as an endangered or threatened species, Cox and several members of his research team attended the 1989 conference of the Convention on International Trade in Endangered Species (CITES), whose delegates voted to prohibit commercial traffic of the Western Samoan flying fox and six other species of Pacific Island flying foxes. One of the plants from the Falealupo forest that Cox sent to NCI yielded prostratin, a new anti–acquired immunodeficiency syndrome (AIDS) drug, and in accordance with his contract with NCI, the Samoan people will share half of NCI's royalty income. Cox has signed a similar agreement with Nu Skin International, which has a line of botanical products that Cox helped formulate. Nu Skin funded the aerial walkway in Falealupo, a water catchment scheme, and other projects in Samoa and other islands. These projects of Nu Skin's "Force for Good" campaign are funded via contributions to Seacology, a nonprofit organization that seeks to preserve the ecosystems and cultures of islands throughout the world and on whose scientific advisory board Cox sits.

Cox continues to visit Samoa at least once a year for his on-going ethnobotanical research. He has served as the King Carl XVI Gustaf Professor of Environmental Science at the Swedish Biodiversity Centre, where he works closely with the king and studies medicinal plants used by the Lappish reindeer herders above the Arctic Circle. Cox directed the congressionally chartered National Tropical Botanical Garden in Hawai'i from 1998 to 2004.

During these years, Cox began researching the causes of a neurological disease called by islanders "lyticobodig", that has affected people on the island of Guam throughout history. He and his team of researchers hypothesize that it affects people who have eaten flying foxes, which in turn have consumed and concentrated toxins from native cycads, primitive plants that look like tiny palms or tree ferns. In 2004 Cox founded the Institute for Ethno-Medicine to search for cures to motor neuron diseases like "lyticobodig" and ALS (Amytrophic Lateral Schlerosis) by studying the health of indigenous peoples. Cox is Executive Director of the Institute, specializing in Ethnobotany and Drug Discovery, and also serves on the Institute's Board of Directors.

BIBLIOGRAPHY

Balick, Michael, and Paul Cox, *Plants, People, and Culture: The Science of Ethnobotany*, 1996; Cox, Paul, *Nafanua: Saving the Samoan Rain Forest*, 1997; Hallowell, Christopher, "The Plant Hunter," *Time*, 1997; Hallowell, Christopher, "Rainforest Pharmacist," *Audubon*, 1999; Maiello, Michael, "Best Natural Preservative: Money," *Forbes*, 2002; "National Tropical Botanical Garden," www.ntbg.org/; "The Seacology Foundation," www.seacology.org; Weiner, Jonathon, "The Tangle," *New Yorker*, 2005; Willis, Monica Michael, "The Plant Detective," *Country Living*, 1998.

Craighead, Frank, and John Craighead
(August 14, 1916–October 21, 2001), (August 14, 1916–)
Wildlife Biologists

Wildlife biologists Frank and John Craighead became famous for their research on the grizzly bears of Yellowstone National Park and their commitment to sharing their research with the general public via articles for *National Geographic* magazine and several educational and documentary films. Through their research, they pioneered the use of radio tracking collars and satellite telemetry in the 1960s and early 1970s. In addition to their work with wildlife, they were particularly concerned about preserving the pristine rivers of the Northern Rockies and provided the impetus and much of the wording for the 1968 Wild and Scenic Rivers Act.

Frank Cooper Jr. and John Johnson Craighead, identical twins, were born on August 14, 1916, in Washington, D.C. Their father, Frank Craighead Sr., was chief of the Bureau of Forest Entomology in the U.S. Department of Agriculture in Washington, D.C. Upon his retirement to Florida, Frank Sr. authored books on the orchids, air plants, and trees of southern Florida and published many papers about the region's changing ecology. As teenagers,

Frank and John became interested in falconry, and at the age of 21, they cowrote "Adventures with Birds of Prey" for *National Geographic*, the first of their 20 articles for that magazine. Their first book, *Hawks in the Hand*, was published in 1939. The Craigheads attended Pennsylvania State University, each receiving a B.A. in science in 1939. They each earned M.S. degrees in ecology and wildlife management in 1940 from the University of Michigan. In 1940, with a National Geographic Society grant, they traveled to India, and as guests of Prince Dharmakumarsinhji, they trained and flew falcons, coursed cheetah at antelope, and participated in the pomp and ceremony of the royal family. They served as lieutenants in the Naval Reserve during World War II, organizing the Navy's Land Survival Training Program and writing the manual *How to Survive on Land and Sea*. This garnered them a special citation in 1946 from the secretary of the navy. The brothers returned to the University of Michigan after the war to earn their Ph.D.s in vertebrate ecology in 1950. Their doctoral research, done with fellowships from the Wildlife Management Institute, compared the annual predation of complete raptor communities in Michigan and Wyoming. It resulted in the 1956 publication of *Hawks, Owls and Wildlife*, which set a new standard for the scientific study of raptors and their role in ecosystems.

John Craighead worked for the U.S. Fish and Wildlife Service as a wildlife biologist, led the Montana Cooperative Wildlife Research Unit, and was professor of zoology and forestry at the University of Montana from 1952 to 1977, earning the Outstanding Educator of America award in 1973. During this same period, Frank Craighead managed the Desert Game Range for bighorn sheep in Nevada, worked as a wildlife biologist for the U.S. Forest Service, founded the Outdoor Recreation Institute in 1955, and took a post as senior research associate and adjunct professor at the State University of New York (SUNY) at Albany. The brothers carried out research together, individually, and with other biologists in a variety of areas, including water quality in western rivers, aquatic insects, air quality in Yellowstone, and such wildlife species as elk, Canada geese, the golden eagle and other raptors, mountain lions, magpies, and pheasants. Together the Craigheads wrote the Peterson field guide *Rocky Mountain Wildflowers* in 1964.

The Craigheads were invited in 1959 to study grizzly bears in Yellowstone National Park, home to the largest remnant population of that species. They spent 12 years in this endeavor, pioneering the use of radio tracking (and later satellite tracking) to study the physiology and ecology of wild grizzlies. Their study compiled the most extensive population data on the grizzlies, which led to a much more complete understanding of the grizzlies' interaction with their ecosystem. When Yellowstone officials announced plans to rapidly close down the park's refuse dumps, the Craigheads warned that this would put the grizzlies in danger. They had discovered that the bears did not distinguish between natural food sources and nonnatural ones and they correctly predicted that the sudden disappearance of a major food source resulted in bears' becoming nuisances in nearby areas inhabited by humans. The Park Service not only did not heed the Craigheads' warning, it forced the Craigheads to leave their research base in the park in 1971, and the study of the Yellowstone grizzly came under strict government control.

The Craigheads' 12 years of research yielded important biological data and evidence of misguided management that led to the 1975 listing of the grizzly as a threatened species. During the 1980s, their controversy with the National Park Service began to heal, and they were able to collaborate with Park Service biologists and other scientific groups trying to facilitate the recovery of the species. Their work with the grizzlies resulted in dozens of technical papers, several articles for *National Geographic* and other popular magazines, and the National Geographic Society documentary film *Grizzly* (1967), which featured the brothers. Frank Craighead's *Track of the Grizzly* (1979) was published by the Sierra Club. John

Craighead wrote two technical books. *A Definitive System for Analysis of Grizzly Bear Habitat and Other Wilderness Resources* (1983) explains how Landsat multispectral imagery using on-the-ground botanical data and computer technology can be used to map and evaluate the vegetation complexes and landform characteristics of large expanses of remote wilderness. His second book, *The Grizzly Bears of Yellowstone: Their Ecology in the Yellowstone Ecosystem, 1959–1992*, was coauthored with Jay Sumner and John Mitchell in 1994. Both books won The Wildlife Society's publication of the year award. In his acceptance speech for the award to the latter book, John Craighead summed up how grizzly bear protection fits into wilderness conservation as a whole: "To preserve the grizzly bear in its natural state, we must keep, intact, the entire spectrum of biodiversity present within its public-land habitat in the Northern Rockies. Concomitantly by preserving the grizzly we automatically preserve the great biodiversity that is its environment."

When the Craigheads first traveled west early in their careers, they were impressed by the region's wild rivers. They boated many of them and advocated classifying them according to their natural assets and recreational potential and preserving the most pristine in their wild state. They published a classification system, listing specific data necessary for classification purposes. They drafted legislation that eventually became the Wild and Scenic Rivers Act. With a strong lobbying effort from STEWART BRANDBORG's Wilderness Society, the bill was signed into law in 1968. This dedication was recognized by the National Geographic Society, which featured the Craigheads in its 1970 documentary film *Wild River*.

Once the Craigheads retired from their respective academic positions, they each devoted themselves to their own nonprofit wildlife research institutes.

Frank Craighead's Outdoor Recreation Institute changed its name in 1980 to the Craighead Environmental Research Institute (CERI). It is currently codirected by his sons Frank Lance Craighead and Charles Craighead and his daughter-in-law, April Hudoff Craighead. Frank Lance is an assistant professor of biology at Montana State University, Charles is a wildlife biologist who authors books and produces conservation documentaries, and April is a biologist. The mission of CERI is "to increase humankind's understanding, appreciation, and protection of our natural environment; particularly wildlife populations and wild landscapes," and it works in four program areas: nature reserve design that accommodates movement through corridors; conservation biology and genetics; Geographic Information Systems for conservation; and conservation education. In 1994, Frank Craighead published *For Everything There Is a Season: The Sequence of Natural Events in the Grand Teton–Yellowstone Areas*, which describes the seasonal changes for plants and ecosystems that he observed during his 50 years in the field.

Upon John Craighead's retirement in 1977, he founded and directed the Wildlife-Wildlands Institute in Missoula, Montana, which plans, coordinates, and conducts research projects on wildlife and wildlands. Through the institute, John Craighead and his colleagues developed a system for botanically describing and mapping wilderness ecosystems and conducted a variety of research programs. The institute was renamed the Craighead Wildlife-Wildlands Institute, Inc., in 1987. John Craighead served as its president from 1987 to 1990 and currently serves as the chairman of its board of directors, responsible for setting the institute's goals and direction, developing policy, and soliciting financial support. His sons, John Willis and Derek, are director designate and president, respectively.

The Craigheads have been honored for their contributions to conservation through innovation and leadership in scientific inquiry, public education, and promotion of science-based environmental policy. They have shared many accolades for their work, including the 1970 Distinguished Alumnus Award and the 1973 Alumni Fellow Award from

Pennsylvania State University; the National Geographic Society's John Oliver La Gorce gold medal in 1979; and the 1988 National Geographic Centennial Award, which recognized the "fifteen individuals who symbolize the best in their fields." John Craighead received the Aldo Leopold Award from The Wildlife Society in 1998.

Frank Craighead died on October 21, 2001; John Craighead resides in Missoula, Montana.

BIBLIOGRAPHY
"Craighead Environmental Research Institute," www.grizzlybear.org/; Croke, Vicki Constantine, "The Brothers Wild," *Washington Post Magazine*, 2007; Devlin, Sherry, "John and Frank Craighead," *Missoulian's 100 Montanans, Our Pick of the Most Influential Figures of the 20th Century*, 2000; Puckett, Karl, "John and Frank Craighead," *Great Falls Tribune 100 Montanans of the 20th Century*," 1999; Martin, Douglas, "Frank Craighead, 85, an Outdoorsman and a Protector of the Grizzly, Dies," *New York Times*, 2001; Stroud, Richard, *National Leaders of American Conservation*, 1986; Weaver, John L., "John and Frank Craighead," *Wildlife Society Bulletin*, 1996.

Cronon, William
(September 11, 1954–)
Environmental Historian

One of the leading American environmental historians of his generation, William Cronon has written extensively on a variety of topics ranging from indigenous land use in New England to problems with the modern environmental movement. As Frederick Jackson Turner Professor and Vilas Resarch Professor of History, Geography, and Environmental Studies at the University of Wisconsin at Madison, one of the elite universities for environmental studies, Cronon's academic work in environmental history demands the respect of his peers and influences both social and natural scientists whose focus is environmental studies.

William John Cronon was born September 11, 1954, in New Haven, Connecticut, to E. David, a historian, and Mary Jean Hotmar Cronon, a nurse. He grew up in Madison, Wisconsin, and studied at the University of Wisconsin at Madison, where he majored in English and history. He graduated with honors in 1976 and won a Rhodes Scholarship to study at Oxford University for two years, between 1976 and 1978. Returning to the United States, he completed his M.A. and M.Phil. at Yale University in 1979 and 1980 respectively. Between 1976 and 1982, Cronon was a Danforth Fellow. Cronon then went back to Oxford University, where he earned his D.Phil. in 1981. Returning to the United States, Cronon taught western American and urban history at Yale University and earned his Ph.D. in 1990. He taught at Yale for over a decade before becoming the Frederick Jackson Turner Professor of History, Geography, and Environmental Studies at the University of Wisconsin at Madison in 1992, a position he still holds. In 2003 he was named Vilas Research Professor at UW-Madison—this is the university's most distinguished chaired professorship.

Cronon has written extensively. His first book, *Changes in the Land: Indians, Colonists, and the Ecology of New England* (1983), was a study of how the New England landscape changed with the arrival of Europeans to the region and their colonization. In 1984, the work was awarded the Francis Parkman Prize of the Society of American Historians.

In 1991, Cronon's *Nature's Metropolis: Chicago and the Great West*, was published. A study of Chicago's relationship with the natural-resource-rich American West, the book won several prizes, including the *Chicago Tribune*'s Heartland Prize for the best literary work of nonfiction published during the previous year (1992), the esteemed Bancroft Prize for the best work in American history (1992), the George Perkins Marsh Prize from the American Society for Environmental History (1993), and the Charles A. Weyerhauser Award from the Forest History Society (1993). *Nature's Metropolis* was also one of three nominees for the Pulitzer Prize in history in 1992.

His essay, "The Trouble with Wilderness or Getting Back to the Wrong Nature," published in his book *Uncommon Ground: Toward Reinventing Nature* (1995), sparked considerable controversy among academics and environmentalists alike. Cronon argued that wilderness was nothing but a cultural construction and examined the implications of different cultural ideas of nature for modern environmental problems. Poet and naturalist GARY SNYDER, among others, took issue with Cronon's contention that nature and wilderness were cultural constructions. Cronon is currently at work on several projects, including a local history of Portage, Wisconsin, which will explore ways of integrating environmental and social historical methods with nontraditional narrative literary forms. He is also completing a book entitled *Saving Nature In Time: The Past and Future of Environmentalism*, based on a series of lectures he gave at Queens University in Belfast in 2001, on the relationship between environmental history and environmentalism.

Cronon was president of the American Society for Environmental History and has served on the editorial boards of several environmental history journals. He is the general editor of the Weyerhauser Environmental Books Series for the University of Washington. During the spring semester of 1994, Cronon organized and chaired a faculty research seminar on the theme of "Reinventing Nature" at the University of California's Humanities Research Institute in Irvine, California. In January 1996, he became director of the Honors Program for the College of Letters and Science at the University of Wisconsin at Madison, and from 1997 to 2000 he served as the founding faculty director of the new Chadbourne Residential College at the University of Wisconsin at Madison. Cronon is a member of the Governing Council of The Wilderness Society and of the National Board of the Trust for Public Land. In 2008, Cronon received the highest scholarly awards bestowed by the American Society for Environmental History, and the Forest History Society.

Cronon has been involved with the University of Wisconsin, Madison's Lakeshore Nature Reserve; he chaired the committee that produced a master plan for it in 2006 and worked to produce a website about it, which includes an award-winning interactive map of it that he helped design. (www.lakeshorepreserve.wisc.edu)

Avocationally, Cronon enjoys hiking, backpacking, swimming, and cross-country skiing. He is also active in the Wilderness Society. Cronon continues to live and teach in Madison, Wisconsin.

BIBLIOGRAPHY

Cronon, William, "A Place for Stories: Nature, History, and Narrative," *The Journal of American History*, 1992; Cronon, William, "The Uses of Environmental History," *Environmental History Review*, 1993; Cronon, William, ed., *Uncommon Ground: Rethinking the Human Place in Nature*, 1995, "William Cronon," www.williamcronon.net.

American Environmental Leaders

From Colonial Times to the Present

D

Daly, Herman

(July 21, 1938–)
Economist

Economist Herman Daly has challenged many assumptions of traditional economics regarding the idea that supply is infinite and that growth can continue indefinitely. He is author or coauthor of several influential books, including *Steady State Economics* (1977), *For the Common Good: Redirecting the Economy towards Community, the Environment, and a Sustainable Future* (1989), and *An Introduction to Ecological Economics* (1997). He believes that economic restrictions should be imposed that would limit resource consumption, discourage waste, and ultimately lead to economically and ecologically sustainable societies.

Herman E. Daly was born on July 21, 1938, in Houston, Texas, where, as a child, he was exposed to the rich cultural diversity of that city. He developed a special interest in Latin American culture and decided he wanted to help poorer, developing countries achieve a standard of living equal to that of the United States. He felt that the field of economics would be the ideal vehicle for him to help to bring about this change. He attended Rice University, receiving a B.A. degree in 1960, and continued his education at Vanderbilt University, where he earned a Ph.D. in 1967. Meanwhile he had accepted a position as assistant professor of economics at Louisiana State University in Baton Rouge. Daly taught at Louisiana State University, first as an assistant professor and later as full professor, from 1964 until 1988.

In 1967, Daly traveled to the northeastern Brazilian state of Ceará as a Fulbright scholar and Ford Foundation Visiting Scholar to teach economics at the University of Fortaleza. It was while in Brazil that Daly experienced an economic and ecological awakening. His eyes were opened to the real and dramatic danger posed by population growth in Brazil, and he came to the realization that, just as surely as there is a limited number of bodies the earth can support, there must be a similar limit to the amount of sustainable commodities available as well. He realized, in short, that there must be a limit to economic growth. This was a revolutionary realization, coming as it did from a person who up until this point in his life had been a "traditional economist," which is to say, an economist who believes that the solution to every problem is growth. In a 1980 interview with *The Mother Earth News*, Daly stated that "most economists do agree on the basic theory that the economy is a machine that continually needs to be fueled and made

Herman Daly (Photograph courtesy of University of Maryland)

bigger." Daly's idea that economic growth cannot be sustained indefinitely is in direct opposition to the traditional economic perspective.

Daly returned to the United States in 1968, and in 1973 he edited his first book, a collection of essays entitled *Toward a Steady State Economy*. This book attempted to expose the fundamental fallacy inherent in traditional, as Daly put it in his 1980 interview, "growthmania" economics. Daly expanded further on this theme in 1977 with the publication of *Steady State Economics*. Daly's version of economics takes into account such factors as sunshine, population growth, and the first and second laws of thermodynamics (energy cannot be created or destroyed, and everything in the universe trends toward disorder). Daly uses these limiting factors to suggest practical policy changes that would create an economy based on sustainability rather than growth. To achieve sustainability, he believes, we should establish economic and social limits that reflect the natural world's limits. For example, we should recognize solar power as the ultimate source of all energy, calculate what it costs to produce a given unit of usable solar energy, and use that figure to determine the cost of energy derived from depletable sources such as coal and oil. He finds it completely illogical that the current economy makes solar power uneconomical in comparison with the rapidly extracted "sunshine of Paleozoic summers" (fossil fuels), when in reality, solar power is the most economically and environmentally sound power source we have at our disposal.

Daly left Louisiana State University in 1988 for a position with the World Bank as senior economist. Given his visionary and heretical views on economics, many thought that Daly would not last long at the World Bank. However, he stayed for six years, until 1994. While at the World Bank, Daly introduced the idea that natural resources such as forests, soils, clean water, and clean air should be considered "natural capital" and should not be "spent" by developing countries in order to make a quick profit. He criticized the Gross National Product as an inaccurate indication of a country's prosperity, introducing the concept of the Index of Sustainable Economic Welfare as a more accurate indication of a country's economic well being.

In a speech he made just before leaving the World Bank in 1994, Daly prescribed a series of remedies for what he saw as the 50-year-old institution's "middle-aged infirmities." He recommended that labor and income be taxed less, because they ought to be encouraged, but that the consumption of energy and the depletion of natural resources be taxed more, in order to discourage them. It should, in other words, be less expensive to earn and more expensive to waste. Another of his recommendations was that we should move away from the ideology of international free trade and, instead, begin to think in terms of national production for internal markets. Daly also suggested that natural capital be treated as monetary capital, that it be invested in and increased.

Since 1994, Daly has served as a senior research scholar at the University of Maryland's School of Public Affairs. He is the author of several important books in addition to *Steady State Economics*. In 1980 *Economics, Ecology and Ethics* came out, and in 1989 he published *For the Common Good: Redirecting the Economy towards Community, the Environment and a Sustainable Future* (coauthored with JOHN B. COBB JR. and Clifford W. Cobb; this book won the Grawemeyer Award for ideas for improving World Order). This book, directed toward a general audience, offers a profound critique of traditional economics and advocates a more environmentally sustainable and humanistic approach. In 1997, he wrote *An Introduction to Ecological Economics*, which was coauthored with several others. This book describes the emergence of the field of ecological economics as a "transdisciplinary" science whose practitioners dedicate themselves to understanding the interrelationships between natural and human systems in an attempt to encourage sustainable human activities. Daly thinks of economics as a branch of biology, since both fields focus on the exchange of resources between organisms. Ecology and economics, he explains, are both derived from the same Greek root word of *oikos*, which means "household." Where ecology is the study of the "household," economics is its management. *Ecological Economics: Principles and Applications*, co-written with Joshua Farley in 2004, is a seminal textbook for a new generation studying economics in this context.

Daly has received the Honorary Right Livelihood Award (considered Sweden's version of the Nobel Prize), the Heineken Prize for Environmental Science from the Royal Netherlands Academy of Arts and Sciences, Norway's Sophie Prize, and the Medal of the Presidency of the Italian Republic. Daly is married and has two children.

BIBLIOGRAPHY

Daly, Herman E., "A steady state economy,," *The Ecologist*, 2008; Logan, William Bryant, "What Is Prosperity?" *Whole Earth Review*, 1995; McDaniel, Carl, *Wisdom for a livable planet: the visionary work of Terri Swearingen, Dave Foreman, Wes Jackson, Helena Norberg-Hodge, Werner Fornos, Herman Daly, Stephen Schneider, and David Orr*, 2005; Meadows, Donella, "Daly Medicine: The End of the World Bank as We Know It?" *Amicus Journal*, 1994; Stone, Pat, "Herman E. Daly Steady State Economics," *Mother Earth News*, 1980; "University of Maryland School of Public Policy Faculty and Staff Profiles: Herman Daly," www.publicpolicy.umd.edu/facstaff/faculty/Daly.html.

Darley, Julian and Celine Fanny Rich
(August 5, 1958– ; October 26, 1967–)
Founders of Post Carbon Institute and Meta Foundation

Julian Darley and Celine Rich have passionately devoted their lives to public service and the pursuit of environmental sustainability and relocalization. As founders and directors of Post Carbon Institute in Eugene, Oregon, Darley and Rich assist communities to increase their independence and adapt to living sustainably in an energy constrained world.

Darley, born in London in 1958, to Peter and Betty Murden, was the eldest of two children. He received a BA with Honors in Music and Russian from Nottingham University in 1981. After writing and directing documentary films and music videos for six years in London with his own production company, Darley moved to Hollywood, where he doctored a variety of scripts for feature films. In 1990, Darley returned to Europe, working as a language instructor in Spain, Germany, Italy and France. Much of the urgency found in Darley's future environmental work was undoubtedly informed by this vast travel and global work experience. From 1995-1997, Darley taught story structure, editing and Web production at the University of Texas at Austin. Here, with his Broadcast Radio News class, Darley produced a weekly one-hour current affairs show on NPR that reached throughout central Texas, a stepping stone to the groundbreaking work Darley would undertake with Global Public Media. After receiving his MA in Mass Communication and Journalism from the University of Texas at Austin, Darley returned to London to work as a research assistant. He acquired his MSc in Social Research

Julian Darley (Photograph courtesy of Post Carbon Institute) and the Environment at the Center for Environmental Strategy, through the University of Surrey. In 2000, Darley relocated yet again, to Vancouver, Canada, where he and Celine Rich began their work.

Rich, born in Victoria, Canada, in 1967, to Cliff and Heather Rich, was the eldest of two children. After receiving a Marketing Certificate from Kwantlen College in Richmond, British Columbia, in 1987, Rich became publicly active in the Vancouver area. Working as Executive Director of The Discovery Project for South East Vancouver, Rich spearheaded various public awareness and fundraising projects to bring together the private and public sectors, increase community development, and promote positivity. Simultaneously, Rich coordinated various projects emphasizing the importance and nature of public art. Such projects included designing and placing benches in community parks, mural painting, implementing art projects within inner city parks, and lecturing throughout Canada on community art and civic participation. In 1997, Rich received her BA in Fine Arts from the Emily Carr Institute of Art and Design. In 1999, she acquired her MA in Design for the Environment from the Chelsea College of Art and Design in London. And in 2000, she began working as Program Manager for the City of Vancouver while joining forces with Julian Darley.

Meta Foundation, created by Darley and Rich in the year 2000, grew from a need they saw for new public methods of discussing and tackling overwhelmingly complex environmental issues, a more open forum, so to speak, than those provided in mainstream public media. Meta Foundation was born as an umbrella organization to support and assist other organizations working on these environmental issues. Global Public Media, established in 2001 as the first initiative of Meta Foundation, became that open forum: an Internet broadcasting station providing in-depth environmental news and analysis by world renowned experts in a variety of different fields. Every unedited interview and issue discussed at Global Public Media is archived and remains available to the public at large.

As Global Public Media began its work, Darley and Rich were introduced to the concept of Peak Oil—the idea that, in the near future, the global production of oil will reach its peak and begin to decline. Their extensive research on this issue and its subsequent effects shifted the focus of Meta Foundation, and led to the establishment of Post Carbon Institute. With most of their support coming from the United States, Meta Foundation was moved to Eugene, Oregon, and incorporated as a nonprofit entity in 2003. As public interest in the work of Meta Foundation grew, Post Carbon Institute rallied the most prominent Peak Oil experts to serve on their board of directors. The necessity and urgency of the issues around Peak Oil, alongside the rapid success and public support of Post Carbon Institute, led to the removal of Meta Foundation as the umbrella organization. Today, Darley and Rich's Post Carbon Institute remains a thriving parent organization to numerous public initiatives and ideas.

The mission of Post Carbon Institute is to "assist communities in the effort to Relocalize and adapt to an energy constrained world." Relocalization involves rebuilding communities and societies to produce food and energy locally, as well as returning to a shared and local currency, governance and culture. Through Relocalization, energy security is increased, local economies gain strength, and social and environmental conditions improve drastically.

Post Carbon Institute acts as a think tank, a reservoir of information and proactive strategies, that community groups, governments, businesses and organizations can employ in their efforts to Relocalize. Through its five major programs—Global Public Media, The Oil Depletion Protocol, Post Carbon Cities, The Relocalization Network and Local Energy Farms—Post Carbon Institute has been an invaluable asset for numerous cities and communities. In the fall of 2007, Post Carbon Institute released *Post Carbon Cities: Planning for Energy and Climate Uncertainty*, a guidebook for local governments. Through their website, Post Carbon Institute offers up-to-date energy bulletins and featured blogs, with Darley and Rich frequently contributing entries. Every month a newsletter is published, as well as an annual report on all Post Carbon Institute's activities.

In 2004, Darley authored *High Noon for Natural Gas: The New Energy Crisis*, outlining the world's ill-advised dependence on natural gas as another non-renewable energy source. In 2006, Darley, Rich and David Room co-authored *Relocalize Now!: Getting Ready for Climate Change and the End of Cheap Oil*, analyzing many of the ideas continually put into practice by Post Carbon Institute.

Both Darley and Rich serve as President and Executive Director, respectively, of Post Carbon Institute. They can be reached through Post Carbon Institute's website. They were married on Earth Day 2000 and live in Sebastopol, California, with their son Raphael Rex Darley.

BIBLIOGRAPHY

Darley, Julian, *High Noon for Natural Gas: The New Energy Crisis*, 2004; Darley, Julian, Rich, Celine and Room, David, *Relocalize Now!: Getting Ready for Climate Change and the End of Cheap Oil*, 2006; www.peakmoment.tv, Peak Moment 14: Building a Relocalization Network, Interview with Celine Rich and Julian Darley; www.howtoboilafrog.com, Interview: Julian Darley; www.postcarbon.org; www.globalpublicmedia.com.

Darling, Jay Norwood "Ding"
(October 21, 1876–February 12, 1962)
Cartoonist, Cofounder of the National Wildlife Federation

Pulitzer Prize–winning cartoonist Jay Norwood "Ding" Darling is known in conservation history for his efforts to restore wildfowl habitat during the 1930s and as one of the founders of what is now the National Wildlife Federation.

Jay Norwood Darling was born on October 21, 1876, in Horwood, Michigan. The son of a minister who moved his family to various towns in Michigan, Indiana, and Iowa, Darling grew up exploring the countryside and hunting ducks in lush midwestern wetlands. He was seduced by the power of cartoons as an eight-year-old, when his father received a postcard with a friend's hand-penned cartoon lampooning the ministry. Darling watched his father laugh harder than he had ever seen him laugh before. The boy copied the cartoon and filled many notebooks with cartoon exercises from a correspondence course. As a student at Beloit College in Beloit, Wisconsin, Darling was suspended for a year after the school yearbook published his cartoon of the faculty as young ballerinas lined up at the barre. Darling did graduate with a B.A. from Beloit in 1900; later the school also bestowed on him an honorary Doctorate of Letters.

After graduating from Beloit, Darling immediately went to work for the *Sioux City Journal* as a reporter, photographer, and cartoonist. Quickly he distinguished himself as a talented cartoonist. He moved to the *Des Moines Register and Leader* in 1906, introducing himself with a cartoon about that city's serious air pollution from the soft coal burned in furnaces: a monk (*moine* in French means "monk") smoking a "soft coal" pipe and blowing big black smoke rings. Apart

DARLING, JAY NORWOOD "DING"

Jay Norwood "Ding" Darling, "Father of the Federal 'Duck Stamp.'" Since 1934, the more than $700 million in sales raised from the stamps has been used to acquire more than 5.2 million acres of habitat for the National Wildlife Refuge System. (Photograph courtesy of Smithsonian institute/U.S. Fish and Wildlife Service)

from a short episode in New York City with the *Globe* syndicate, Darling remained with the *Register and Leader* (which later became the *Register)* for the rest of his cartooning career, selling cartoons to syndicates and appearing, at his peak, in 300 newspapers. Darling's pen could be acid, his opinions strong. His ability to distill national problems into

A judge closely inspects Federal Duck Stamp Contest entries. (Photograph courtesy of Gary Tucker/U.S. Fish and Wildlife Service)

simple attention-grabbing images made him a force that all major politicians had to recognize and reckon with. Though his subjects were mostly political, Darling frequently delved into the environmental issues of the day: erosion, industrial contamination of waterways, and greedy hunters and anglers. A survey of newspaper editors named him the country's best cartoonist in 1934, and he won two Pulitzer prizes, in 1923 and 1942.

Darling, a Republican, was critical of Pres. FRANKLIN D. ROOSEVELT's New Deal social policies as well as his lack of response to the crisis that threatened Darling's beloved ducks. The dustbowl conditions of the early 1930s had dried up the wetlands that waterfowl used as breeding and feeding grounds, and their numbers diminished drastically. Although Darling supported outspoken prowildlife advocates such as WILLIAM TEMPLE HORNADAY and ROSALIE EDGE, who called for shortening the hunting season and cutting bag limits, he restrained himself from blatant criticism, because responsibility for this problem fell to Roosevelt's secretary of agriculture, Henry Wallace, a fellow Republican and a close friend. In 1933, Wallace invited Darling to serve on a special Presidential Commission on Wildlife Restoration, charged with devising a strategy for saving the ducks. The committee, which included wildlife management expert ALDO LEOPOLD, issued recommendations to budget $17 million to purchase several million acres of submarginal farmland for conversion into wetland waterfowl refuges. A few months later, in the spring of 1934, Darling was invited to become chief of the U.S. Biological Survey and try to implement this recommendation. Despite the huge pay cut entailed (Darling was then earning $100,000 for his cartoons, and the Biological Survey chief earned $8,000), Darling accepted the challenge.

Conservation historians still speculate that Roosevelt offered Darling this post to quell Republican conservationist critics. While that might have been the case, during his 20 months in the post Darling was allotted $14.5 million to establish 19 major wildfowl refuges and 13 secondary ones, on a total of 840,000 acres of reclaimed farmland. Roosevelt, who at the same time was trying unsuccessfully to wrestle Congress for money to rebuild inner-city tenements and fortify New Deal welfare programs, was envious of Darling's congressional support. But for Darling's ambitious save-the-duck plan to succeed, this was not enough. He raised more money through his one-dollar duck stamps that hunters had to buy and affix to their hunting licenses. The gun and ammunition industries offered more support, with a pledge of 10 percent of their annual sales to raise a ten-million-dollar endowment fund for wildlife protection. Darling applauded, but Roosevelt declined the offer because it was conditional on canceling the 10 percent federal excise tax on all guns and ammunitions sold in the United States. Disappointed, Darling resigned and returned to cartooning in the fall of 1935.

Darling remained active in wildlife conservation. He helped form the American Wildlife Institute (AWI) as a lobby for all industries that benefited from hunting, including the gun and ammunition industries, automobile manufacturers, and oil and railway companies. Chaired by the top executives of these companies, the AWI favored restoration of wildlife habitat and game management and gave research money to 10 land-grant colleges to promote scholarship in these fields. The AWI, with support from Roosevelt's staff and endorsements from 36,000 wildlife groups, organized the largest-ever wildlife conference in February 1936 in Washington, D.C. The conference resulted in the founding of the General Wild Life Fund (GWLF), whose new membership immediately elected Darling as president. He led the GWLF as it successfully pushed Congress to pass the 1937 Pittman-Robertson bill, essentially the same plan as the one the guns and ammunition industries had proposed two years earlier. GWLF changed its name to the National Wildlife Federation (NWF) in 1938. Disenchanted with the NWF because it acted too often as a lobbying arm for the gun industry, Darling moved on to become more active in the National Audubon Society. During the remainder of his life, Darling focused on two conservation projects in particular: the preservation of the Lewis and Clark Trail and the protection of Captiva and Sanibel Islands off the Gulf Coast of Florida, where he spent his winters with his wife, Genevieve Pendleton, and their two children. A wildlife refuge on Sanibel Island was named for him after his death.

Darling continued his cartooning until illness debilitated him in 1949. He died in Des Moines on February 12, 1962, after a series of strokes.

BIBLIOGRAPHY

Fox, Stephen, *The American Conservation Movement: John Muir and His Legacy*, 1981; Lendt, David, *The Life of Jay Norwood Darling*, 1989; Mahoney, Tom, "How to Be a Cartoonist," in John E. Drewry, ed., *More Post Biographies*, 1947.

David, Laurie Ellen
(March 22, 1958–)
Climate Change Activist, Producer, Author

Best known for co-producing AL GORE'S Academy Award winning documentary *An Inconvenient Truth*, Laurie David is a Hollywood-based climate change activist. David is the founder of the Stop Global Warming Virtual March, an environmental awareness effort bringing together Hollywood royalty, political leaders, business leaders, and everyday Americans to change policy. David has written several books on global warming and has produced many award-winning cable and broadcast programs on the subject of global warming. She brings her long-standing connections to A-list comedians and writers (from her previous career in talent management) to her current environmental projects, guaranteeing a wider audience for global warming content and pulling the subject firmly into mainstream popular culture.

Born Laurie Ellen Lennard on March 22, 1958, David began her career in Cincinnati, Ohio as a copywriter for a car dealership. After writing her first television commercial, she became an associate editor for *Tee-Shirt Weekly*, where she had the opportunity to interview veteran rock and rollers about concert tees, which led to a job as reporter for *Record World*. When *Late Night with David Letterman* had an opening for a music researcher, she took it, eventually becoming a booker of comedic acts for the show during the 1980s. That's where she met Larry David–co-creator of *Seinfeld* and creator and lead character of *Curb Your Enthusiasm*. They were married in 1993, but after 14 years they were divorced (in 2007). After Letterman, David went on to form her own talent management company. Upon moving to Los Angeles, David became vice-president of comedy development for Fox Television, developing sitcoms. She has produced comedy specials for HBO and MTV.

David credits her mid-career move into environmental advocacy to a meeting she had with ROBERT F. KENNEDY, JR., founder of the Riverkeeper Project. She met him while serving as a member of the board of the Natural Resources Defense Council, which she'd been on since 1999. Davis came out of that meeting agreeing with Kennedy that environmental protection is a civil-rights issue, and began working on environmental issues full time. She started holding get-togethers in her Hollywood home for 50 to 150 Hollywood celebrities at a time. These became influential eco-salons where she solicited money and commitments of personal involvement from California's well-known and well-off. Through these salons Davis has raised millions of dollars, and attracted stars like Tom Hanks, Sheryl Crow, and Jack Black to work for her cause. She lobbies television producers to feature the Toyota Prius in shows like *24* and *Alias*.

After the 2004 presidential election, which she saw as a great catastrophe for environmentalism, David contacted her mentor Kennedy and two of the NRDC's leaders to create a virtual march to stop global warming. She wanted to craft an internet march that could

Laurie David (Photograph courtesy of lauriedavid.com)

continue until "we were millions strong, combining all our voices into one loud, clear cry for action." David partnered with environmental and web organizing groups that include the Sierra Club, Union of Concerned Scientists, Care2, Netroots, Tides, National Wildlife Federation, myspace.com, and the National Council of Churches. She then recruited prominent Republican Senator (and 2006 Republican presidential candidate) John McCain, to demonstrate that the environment is a post-party issue. The Stop Global Warming Virtual March only requires an email address for participation, and has more than a million participants.

On May 27, 2004, David was asked to moderate a town hall meeting on global warming in New York City as part of the opening of the climate change disaster picture *The Day After Tomorrow*. One of the panelists was Al Gore, who presented a 10-minute section of his slideshow on global warming. David was so impressed by the presentation that she met with Gore and began to extensively promote it. A national and international tour ensued. The presentation was in so much demand that David and Gore saw that a feature-length film could strategically meet that demand and extend the reach of the presentation's message. It went on to win the Academy Award for best documentary of 2006 as well as best song, "I Need to Wake Up." Grossing $49 million at the box office, the film is to date the fourth-highest grossing documentary. Gore's companion 2006 book reached number one on *The New York Times* best-seller list. The film received a rare special recognition from The Humanitas Prize.

David is criticized as a "GulfStream Liberal" for maintaining that it is unnecessary to lower one's standard of living in order to advance green politics. David says her work is with the "grass-tops" as well as the grass-roots.

In 2007 she launched the Stop Global Warming College Tour. She currently writes a blog on *The Huffington Post*, and is a fundraiser for Democratic candidates. David has authored the bestselling book *Stop Global Warming: The Solution is You!* and *The Down to Earth Guide to Global Warming*. She has appeared on *The Oprah Winfrey Show*, guest edits *Elle Magazine*, and writes and is profiled in many national magazines. In 2007, David received the Feminist Majority's Eleanor Roosevelt Award, Audubon Society's RACHEL CARSON Award, and National Wildlife Federation's Conservation Achievement Award for Special Achievement. In 2006 David was honored by *Glamour* magazine as a "Woman of the Year."

She lives in Los Angeles with two daughters, Cazzie and Romy.

BIBLIOGRAPHY

David, Laurie, *Stop Global Warming: The Solution is You – An Activists Guide*, Fulcrum Publishing, 2006; David, Laurie and Cambria Gordon, *The Down-to-Earth Guide to Global Warming*, 2007; www.stopglobalwarming.org; www.lauriedavid.com/bio.html; newsbusters.org/node/11995; www.npr.org/templates/story/story.php?storyId=9969008.

Dawson, Richard
(August 2, 1935–)
Educator

Richard Dawson is considered a founding father of environmental education, especially in Kansas City, where he taught biology and environmental science for 42 years, from 1958 until 2000. Recipient of numerous awards for excellent teaching, Dawson is an innovator. He set up outdoor ecological laboratories for high school students in the 1960s, designed high school curricula in the areas of world futuristics and bioethics, and was known for a unique approach to science teaching whereby he asked his students to hone their observational skills by writing poetry.

Richard Glen Dawson was born on August 2, 1935, in Columbia, Missouri. An artist uncle gave him a book of JOHN JAMES AUDUBON's bird paintings while Dawson was in grade school, which helped inspire his lifelong fascination with nature. As a high school student he led field trips for the Burroughs Nature Club, Kansas City's Audubon Society, and developed a nature center at the local Camp Lake of the Woods, where he fell in love with teaching children about "critters."

Dawson attended Carleton College in Northfield, Minnesota, which is endowed with a 700-acre arboretum. He transformed the footpaths through the "Arb" into self-guiding nature trails, with numbered stakes and a monthly descriptive booklet to point out seasonal plants and other wildlife, and he painted interpretive habitat displays that were erected along the trails. Dawson met his wife, Ellie, also a nature educator, when she came to a meeting of the Carleton Natural History Club. Dawson, who was president of the club, invited her to accompany him on setting up the next month's guide. They married in 1959 and later had two daughters, Andrea and Carolyn.

Following his graduation from Carleton with a B.A. in biology (1957), Dawson earned an M.S. in biology from the University of Michigan (1958) and returned to Kansas City to teach at Shawnee Mission North High School. By the mid-1960s, Dawson was already distinguishing himself as a tireless and inventive biology teacher. He established an Environmental Science Camp at a 300-acre outdoor recreation site in Kansas City's Swope Park in 1964, the first of its kind in the region, and directed summer programs there for 18 years until the tax money that funded it dried up. Dawson's unique summer camp programs combined regular camp activities such as horseback riding, archery, cookout/campouts with ecology activities, with staffed habitat studies and campers' individual research projects culminating in presenta-

Richard Dawson (Photograph courtesy of Richard Dawson)

tions for parents. In 1965, Dawson led an effort to convert a former restaurant into the Lakeside Nature Center, Kansas City's first public environmental education center. During the school year, Dawson held class on the ecologically valuable vacant lands near Shawnee Mission North and invited students on camping trips in Swope Park on weekends. Dawson proposed a formal outdoor laboratory composed of 24 acres of forest, fields, pond, and stream adjacent to Shawnee Mission South High School in 1968. When the school board agreed, Dawson transferred to Shawnee Mission South and set up the Shawnee Mission Environmental Science Laboratory.

In addition to his work setting up areas for outdoor environmental education, Dawson is recognized for the classroom curricula he developed. In his "Science and Survival" course, students studied contemporary science and environmental issues, formed opinions about pertinent public policy, and then wrote letters to elected officials and newspapers. The "World Futuristics" course that Dawson designed in 1974 was the first of its kind in the United States. Asking students to imagine the type of world they wanted to bequeath to their children, Dawson encouraged long-range planning skills and worked with issues such as resource availability, pollution, and population dynamics, using computer-generated forecasting graphs, simulation games, trend extension, cross-impact matrices, and more techniques. In 1992, Dawson was invited by the Woodrow Wilson Fellowship Foundation to work with a team at Princeton University to design curricula for incorporating bioethics issues into biology courses to teach critical thinking and decision making in areas such as genetics, reproduction, and environmental problems.

Dawson's innovations and teaching methods earned him numerous professional awards, ranging from Outstanding Biology Teacher Award of the Midwest region from the National Association of Biology Teachers in 1968, to Kansas Master Teacher Award from Emporia State University in 1986, to a spot in the Mid-America Education Hall of Fame at Kansas City Kansas Community College (1998).

Nominators for the Hall of Fame recognition described another of Dawson's approaches to teaching. He asked his students to write poetry. "The young people are encouraged to examine leaves, insects, everything amazing in the world of nature, and then to express the emotions evoked," wrote literature teacher Rowena Unger Turk on Dawson's nomination form. Dawson published booklets of student poetry, and he shared his own poetry with his students as well. From his booklet *Buffalo Chip:*

> *Black Oak*
> Summer's warm rushing winds
> Twist and crack the brittle trunk
> Until the oak's crown crashes.
> Vulnerable now, the fractured bole
> Softens to the fungus touch
> For woodpecker carpentry.
> Pewee, Nuthatch, Chickadee
> Inheriting these holes
> Protect unbroken trees.

Dawson retired from teaching in 2000. He now works with Kansas City Wildlands, primarily in restoration. He helps clear invastives, burns, and plants wildflower seedlings in prairies and limestone prairie glades in local parks and wildlife areas.

BIBLIOGRAPHY

Dawson, Richard, *Buffalo Chip and Other Biological Droppings*, 1993; Dawson, Richard, "A Natural History Camp for Pre-Teens," *The American Biology Teacher*, 1967; Hoskins, Alan, "Environmental Pioneer Dawson Selected to Education Hall of Fame," *Kansas City Kansan*, 1998.

DeBonis, Jeff
(March 18, 1951–)
Forester, Founder of Association of Forest Service Employees for Environmental Ethics and Public Employees for Environmental Ethics

As a U.S. Forest Service employee who spoke out in 1989 against the ecologically destructive forest management practices of the agency, Jeff DeBonis was a pioneer whistle-blower. Since then, he has organized two nonprofit organizations, the Association of Forest Service Employees for Environmental Ethics (AFSEE) and Public Employees for Environmental Responsibility (PEER), both of which organize and support environmental activism and whistle-blowing among public employees.

Jeffery Nicholas DeBonis was born on March 18, 1951. He grew up in Bedford, Massachusetts, where the Shawsheen River ran behind his house. He spent a significant amount of time on and along the river as a child. When his family arrived in Bedford, the river was healthy and full of native fish such as eastern pickerel, shiners, sunfish, and brook trout. DeBonis remembers that pollution had killed the river by the time he was in 11th grade.

DeBonis attended Colorado State University in Fort Collins, Colorado, graduating in 1974 with a B.S. degree in forestry. He spent his next three years in El Salvador with the U.S. Peace Corps, where he worked with El Salvadoran government agencies, nongovernmental organizations (NGOs), and private citizens on reforestation and soil conservation projects. He lived in remote villages, instructing small groups of farmers on how to utilize appropriate soil conservation and forest management techniques on their land. He also helped to develop a large-scale experimental reforestation project in conjunction with the United Nations and NGOs. The purpose of this project was to reintroduce native hardwood species into degraded, clear-cut forest lands. His experiences with the massive clear-cuts of El Salvador made a lasting impression on him.

After returning to the United States, DeBonis began his career with the U.S. Forest Service in 1978. He would remain with the forest service until 1991. His career as a forester has been well documented in Todd Wilkinson's *Science under Siege*, in a chapter revealingly entitled "Confessions of a Timber Beast." Wilkinson writes, "During a career that spanned thirteen years, DeBonis had a role in delivering billions of board feet of lumber into the laps of local timber mills in the Pacific Northwest…. His decisions brought down tree trunks a millennium old, killed fish, displaced grizzly bears, and spotted owls, carved up mountainsides into rectangles of visual blight and cost taxpayers at least tens of millions of dollars in losses through publicly subsidized road construction." During his time with the U.S. Forest Service, DeBonis was a timber-sale planner. It was his job to decide how big the clear-cuts would be and where the trees would fall.

DeBonis, however, will not be remembered for his role in harvesting national forests in the United States. He will be remembered for speaking out against the ecologically unsound practices of the U.S. Forest Service and for attempting to reform this bureaucracy from within. According to DeBonis, the beginnings of his apprehension about the U.S. Forest Service management policies date back to 1978 when he was a forester trainee on the Kootenai National Forest out of Troy, Montana. The clear-cutting of forests, the resulting erosion, and the decimation of trout fisheries reminded him of El Salvador. He was also concerned with the Forest Service management imperative to produce timber outputs, creating a system that rewarded those who cut down more trees.

Jeff DeBonis (Photograph by Susan Denzer DeBonis)

The turning point in DeBonis's career came in 1989. After attending a seminar in Eugene, Oregon, on ancient forests, he wrote a two-page memorandum and distributed it throughout the Forest Service using the agency's computerized communications system, its equivalent of e-mail. In the memo, DeBonis attacked the Forests Service's position as "an advocate of the timber industry's agenda," calling for greater attention to conservation and stewardship. He also stated that the Forest Service should look to the "conservation community" for assistance "in developing a strategy which will contribute to an ecologically sustainable lifestyle in the 21st century."

This memo caused quite a stir throughout the agency and in the timber industry. DeBonis had broken an unspoken law of the Forest Service in speaking out against its policies. He was not alone, however, in feeling that the Forest Service should reevaluate its practices. In the months following the distribution of his memo, DeBonis was contacted by hundreds of fellow Forest Service employees who wanted to speak out but were afraid. The Association of Forest Service Employees for Environmental Ethics grew out of his organizational efforts during this time. DeBonis had become a self-described "whistle-blower," intent on exposing (in his own words) "the Forest Service's willful violation of the spirit and intent of environmental laws that resulted in extensive over-cutting of national forests." He organized his fellow employees around these issues, encouraging diverse opinions and freedom of speech in an agency not known to foster such behavior.

DeBonis acted as executive director of AFSEEE (which has dropped the *A* and is now simply known as FSEEE) until 1991, when he left the Forest Service to concentrate on environmental advocacy through nonprofit organizations. In 1992, he left AFSEEE and founded another nonprofit group, Public Employees for Environmental Responsibility. PEER is an advocacy-oriented organization that works to protect the environment through organizing and supporting public employees. PEER has supported dozens of environmental whistle-blowers throughout the United States and has helped to organize hundreds of public employees as environmental activists in federal and state enforcement and land management agencies. Under the direction of DeBonis, PEER also worked on many environmental issues, challenging enforcement of national and state environmental protection laws, as well as combating overgrazing and overcutting on federal lands, threats to endangered species, toxic pollution, and corporate timber theft. PEER has also sued and won numerous court decisions on behalf of employee activists and the environment, conducted advocacy surveys of entire agencies, and disclosed environmental damage and illegal activities in numerous federal and state agencies. PEER is unique among environmental organizations in that it provides inside information, often from anonymous sources, the sources themselves being the ones required by inappropriate agency policies to cause environmental degradation. PEER has provided a forum where these policies can be brought to light by those most familiar with their ill effects and has given a voice and an opportunity to act to countless environmentally concerned public employees.

DeBonis resigned his position as executive director of PEER in 1997. He serves on the Advisory Board of the Native Forest Council, whose mission is "to fully protect and preserve every acre of publicly owned land" in the USA, and works as a Senior Associate for TREC, Training Resources. for the Environmental Community, which provides targeted strategic training for organizations that work towards protection of wildlands in the Western United States.

DeBonis has received many awards for his advocacy and environmental accomplishments. Included among these are the Alliance for the Wild Rockies Conservation Award, 1989; Giraffe Award for Environmental Whistleblowing from the Giraffe Foundation, 1989; the Environmental Leadership Award from the California League of Conservation Voters,

1995; and the National Conservation Achievement Award from the National Wildlife Federation, 1996. DeBonis lives in Hood River, Oregon.

BIBLIOGRAPHY

DeBonis, Jeff, "Natural Resource Agencies: Questioning the Paradigm," in *A New Century for Natural Resources Management*, edited by Richard L. Knight and Sarah F. Bates, 1995; Ervin, Keith, "Voice of Doubt Sickened by Timber Practices Condoned by the Government, Forester Spoke Out," *Seattle Times*, 1990; "Forest Service Employees for Environmental Ethics," www.fseee.org; McLean, Herbert, "A Very Hot Potato," *American Forests*, 1990; "Native Forest Council," www.forestcouncil.org; Nilsen, Richard, "Reforming the Forest Service from Within," *Whole Earth Review*, 1989; "Public Employees for Environmental Responsibility," www.peer.org; Wilkinson, Todd, *Science under Siege*, 1998.

Desser, Christina Louise
(September 24, 1954–)
Artist, Writer, Organizer, Attorney

Chris Desser has been active in the environmental movement for her entire professional career. She cofounded the Muir Investment Trust and has practiced land use and environmental law, acted as project director for the Migratory Species Project during the 1990s, and served on numerous boards of directors and advisory boards for foundations and nonprofit organizations with environmental foci. As executive director of Earth Day 1990, she redefined grassroots environmental organizational strategies and opened the eyes of environmentalists to the possibilities afforded by effective use of the media. As coordinator of the Funders Working Group on New Technologies, she has been deeply engaged in the health, safety, environmental, and policy issues implicated in biotechnology. Desser's current project is an art installation entitled "The Catalog of Extinct Experience."

Christina Louise Desser was born on September 24, 1954, in Los Angeles, California. She was the first of two children born to Alan and Shirley Desser. She has a younger brother, Jim. As a child and young adult her experiences in the natural world shaped her perspective and commitment to environmental activism. She skied, rock climbed, and backpacked extensively in the Sierra Nevada and in the Rocky Mountains, swam in mountain lakes, and body surfed in the Pacific Ocean. Desser traveled frequently during her formative years, with her family and on her own. She still does. She has had some penetrating and heartbreaking experiences in her travels. During the 1960s in coastal Mexico, she saw the remains of slaughtered sea turtles floating in the Sea of Cortez. In Yalta, in the 1970s, she took a midnight swim in the Black Sea; when she returned to the same spot the next day, she found an oil sheen polluting the water she had been swimming in.

Desser was in high school during the first Earth Day celebration in 1970. This event underscored for her the threats facing the environment and demonstrated to her the importance of the political process to environmental change. In 1972, motivated to help the effort to end the Vietnam War, Desser joined George McGovern's presidential campaign. She was the youngest member of the national staff. In this campaign she began to develop her political organizing and media skills. She remained politically active throughout her time at the University of California at Berkeley, where she studied philosophy and rhetoric. In 1978 she took two years off from school to work at *Rolling Stone* magazine and to serve as assistant to the director of ACTION, a government agency, now defunct, that oversaw the Peace Corps and Volunteers in Service to America (VISTA). She graduated from Berkeley in 1978 with honors. Desser studied law at the McGeorge School of Law at the University of the Pacific. During this time she interned at the Environmental Defense Fund and wrote a manual about California's pesticide regulations. She received her J.D. degree in 1983 and went to work with Manatt, Phelps, Rothenberg and Tunney in Los Angeles, practicing land use and environmental law until 1987. She then served as deputy city attorney for land use in San Francisco until 1989. According to Desser, practicing environmental law deepened her understanding of how the political process can be brought to bear on environmental issues.

In 1989, Desser left law to organize Earth Day 1990. Earth Day afforded her an opportunity to use the power of the media and political-campaign-style organizing to mobilize a large environmental constituency. This approach, novel at the time, was dramatically successful. Earth Day 1990 culminated in the largest grassroots demonstration in history, with 200 million participants in 140 countries. It confirmed the potential of political organization to those in the environmental movement, which, owing to Earth Day 1990's example, has since become more savvy about the power and uses of media and organizing by constituency.

In 1991, Desser cofounded the Muir Investment Trust, the first socially responsible and environmentally sound municipal bond mutual fund. She remained with the Muir Investment Trust until 1992. In 1993 she designed the Migratory Species Project in San Francisco to promote the understanding of interconnection and interdependence by linking communities along important migratory routes. In 1999, California governor Gray Davis appointed Desser to the California Coastal Commission, a twelve-member commission responsible for managing the conservation of California's coastal resources through a comprehensive planning and regulatory program. Desser became the coordinator of the Funders Working Group on New Technology in 1999. This group raises awareness and promotes activism on the myriad environmental and health issues raised by emerging technologies, as well as its threat to democracy and dissent She co-edited and contributed to a collection of essays examining such issues: *Living with the Genie: Technology and the Quest for Human Mastery*, published in 2003.

Desser co-founded Women's Voices Women Vote in 2003, a project to increase the participation of single women in the electoral process. Currently she is at work on The Catalog of Extinct Experience, "an art installation exploring extinct and vanishing experiences in the natural world—like sipping water from a stream or seeing stars in the sky…" Desser has said that she experiences violence to the environment in an almost physical way, a way that literally requires action of her. When she walks through a clear-cut forest or stands before an oil-fouled ocean, it pains her so deeply, and with such awareness, that it calls for action.

Desser has served on the Boards of many companies, foundations, and non-profit organizations including Patagonia, Rainforest Action Network, Rockwood Leadership Program and Women Donors Network. She is a Fellow at On the Commons. She has practiced meditation in various Buddhist traditions for more than 20 years and practices yoga daily. She lives in San Francisco, California, with her husband, Kirk Marckwald.

BIBLIOGRAPHY

Desser, Christina, *California's New Pesticide Regulations and You. A Guide to What They*

Say. What Your Rights Are. What You Can Do, 1982; Desser, Christina, "Making the Connections," *Inquiring Mind*, 1996; Desser, Christina, "Manufactured Reality and the Extinction of Experience," *Wild Duck Review*, 2002; Desser, Christina, "Transgenics: Unnatural Selection or Bad Choice," *Wild Duck Review*, 1999; "Onthecommons.org," www.onthecommons.org.

Devall, Bill

(December 2, 1938–)
Deep Ecologist, Activist

Bill Devall has dedicated his life and work to the protection of the environment, both actively and intellectually. After his move to California in the late 1960s, Devall was a regular participant in countless nonviolent demonstrations to preserve redwood forests, establish wilderness areas, and protect coastlines. Intellectually, Devall has been one of the leading proponents in the United States of deep ecology, a biocentric movement that challenges practical and philosophical contemporary anthropocentric conceptualizations of resource management.

William Bert Devall was born December 2, 1938, in Kansas City, Kansas, to William and Marie (Culp) Devall at the tail end of the Great Depression. His father worked in the steel industry, and his mother, the first person in her family to receive a college education, was a schoolteacher who became a housewife. Devall was raised in the suburbs of Kansas City and was educated primarily during the quiet decade of the 1950s. Growing up outside of such cities as Kansas City and Denver and never spending much time away from the manicured suburbs, Devall's early impressions of nature bordered on the romantic and the mystical. His parents taught him to admire nature but from a distance. Their first family vacation, in 1947, was an auto trip through the Colorado Rockies. They looked at the scenery from the windows of the car but did not hike into the mountains or sleep outside under the stars.

Upon completion of his B.A. in sociology from the University of Kansas in 1960, Devall earned an M.A. in sociology at the University of Hawaii in 1962. He wrote his doctoral dissertation—on the Sierra Club—at the University of Oregon, where he received his Ph.D. in 1970.

Devall's first involvement in the conservation movement came when he went to Humboldt County, California, in 1968 to teach at Humboldt State University. There, he was inspired by DAVID BROWER, who was then executive director of the Sierra Club. He was also inspired by local Sierra Club activists who faced great adversity as they fought for the establishment of Redwood National Park. Devall's first real activism came two years later, in 1970, when he helped to organize local participation for the first Earth Day. From that point on, Devall was committed to conservation activism and has worked on almost every campaign for the protection of California wilderness, including its coastal land and forests. His activism has always been based on principles of nonviolent, direct action.

While developing his own thoughts on social science, philosophy, and ecology, Devall was heavily influenced by the writings of Paul Shepard, ALDO LEOPOLD, and JOHN MUIR. With his discovery of Norwegian philosopher Arne Naess's short, but highly influential, paper on a new theory called deep ecology, "The Shallow and the Deep, Long-Range Ecology Movement" (published in *Inquiry* in 1973), Devall found direction and a philosophical framework for his own ideas and thoughts. Along with GEORGE SESSIONS, with whom he has worked closely, Devall became an advocate for the deep, long-range ecology movement in the United States. Together they edited the seminal text, *Deep Ecology: Living as if Nature Mattered*, in 1985.

During the 1980s, Devall was active with the Earth First! movement through all of its various metamorphoses. He served as president of the Earth First! Foundation (later renamed the Fund for Wild Nature) from 1984 to 1989. As an academic, however, he was never really accepted by the self-proclaimed "rednecks for wilderness," the urban anarchists, or the feminists who influenced the movement during the latter half of the decade. A close friend and associate of DAVE FOREMAN, Devall resigned from the Earth First! Foundation in 1990 at the same time that Foreman left the movement. Around the same time, he and Foreman were invited by DOUG TOMPKINS, an environmentalist and outdoors clothing manufacturer, to discuss the need for a foundation to promote the deep, long-range ecology movement. Tompkins then established the Foundation for Deep Ecology, and Devall's association with the foundation led to his work on many projects sponsored by the foundation, including the 1993 publication of *Clearcut: The Tragedy of Industrial Forestry*.

Devall retired from the Department of Sociology at Humboldt State University in 1995.

BIBLIOGRAPHY

Devall, Bill, *Bioregion on the Edge*, 1999; Devall, Bill, "The Deep, Long-Range Ecology Movement: 1960-2000—A Review," *Ethics & the Environment*, 2001; Devall, Bill, *Living Richly in an Age of Limits*, 1992; Devall, Bill, *Simple in Means, Rich in Ends*, 1988; Devall, Bill, and George Sessions, eds., *Deep Ecology*, 1985.

Devoto, Bernard

(January 11, 1897–November 13, 1955)
Writer, Historian

Bernard Devoto was a Pulitzer Prize–winning author, historian, and social critic. From his position as editor of "The Easy Chair" in *Harper's Magazine* from 1935 to 1955, he contributed greatly to the early conservation movement, fueling public sentiment that would eventually result in the preservation of Dinosaur National Monument and in such legislation as the 1964 Wilderness Act. He was named an honorary lifetime member of the Sierra Club.

Bernard Augustine Devoto was born January 11, 1897, in Ogden, Utah, to Florian and Rhoda Dye Devoto. His family was a microcosmic representation of the small community in which it lived. His mother was Mormon, his father Catholic, and Devoto, as it would later turn out, a serious practitioner of neither religion. Devoto's education began at a convent school and continued in public schools. He graduated from Ogden High School in 1914. Growing up, he experienced all of the freedoms that go along with a frontier childhood. He spent his time hiking, climbing, and camping in the wilderness of northern Utah.

Devoto attended the University of Utah for one year (1914–1915), where he helped to organize a chapter of the intercollegiate Socialist Society, quickly disbanded by the university administration. This event, along with the dismissal of four unorthodox faculty members, disgusted Devoto, and he left for Harvard in 1915. His focus at this time was primarily on philosophy, though he studied writing and continued to act as an intellectual revolutionary. Upon the declaration of war, Devoto enlisted and was commissioned a lieutenant of infantry in 1918. He was not sent overseas. Instead, he spent the next two years, until the armistice, at Camp Perry in Ohio teaching marksmanship. In 1920, he returned to Harvard and received his degree "as of the class of 1918."

After graduating, Devoto returned to Utah. In 1921, he took a job as a teacher at the North Junior High School in Ogden. He was definitely not what people had come to expect from a junior high school teacher in Ogden, Utah. His sharp tongue and his willingness to use profanity fascinated his students but shocked and offended their parents and his fellow teachers.

He accepted a position teaching English at Northwestern University in 1922. He taught at Northwestern for five years, gaining a reputation as one of the best teachers on campus and attracting large numbers of students to his classes, with his sarcastic showmanship and tough but fair grading practices. While there, he met and married Helen Avis MacAir, with whom he would have two sons, Gordon King and Mark Bernard. Devoto refused to study for a Ph.D., but his success with the students and his growing prominence as a writer brought him an assistant professorship in 1927. His first book, *The Crooked Mile*, had been published in 1924 and his second, *The Chariot of Fire*, in 1926. During these years, he also wrote many articles for such magazines as *Harper's* and *The Saturday Evening Post*.

Finding it difficult to continue balancing his teaching with his writing, Devoto resigned his professorship in 1927 and moved with his family to Cambridge, Massachusetts, planning to do nothing more than write. He alternated between whipping up potboilers under the pseudonym John August to pay the bills and producing serious works of social history and biography such as *Mark Twain's America*, 1932, and *We Accept with Pleasure*, 1934. He was an instructor and lecturer at Harvard from 1929 to 1936. And, in 1935, he became the editor of the "Easy Chair" of *Harper's*, a position he held for 20 years.

It was in this capacity that Devoto had his greatest impact as a conservationist. He used this platform to express his views on public lands and the federal responsibilities for their management. He compiled these views into a series of conservation essays and published them in 1952 in his four-page column, "The Easy Chair." In 1953, Devoto wrote four "Easy Chair" columns in relation to public-lands issues, going so far in one of them as to suggest that Congress close the national parks until it saw fit to allocate enough money to allow them to run properly. He lit many fires with his articles in *Harper's*, fires that would help lead to the passage of the Wilderness Act in 1964 and to other major conservation legislation during the Kennedy and Johnson administrations.

Devoto also contributed to the movement that would eventually erupt into the struggle to save Dinosaur National Monument in 1956. The essays and articles he produced in the name of conservation were works that he was proud of, because they validated his position as a professional journalist and as a controversialist. They also gave his reforming impulses, which can be traced all the way back to his early college days, a cause and a purpose. Wallace Stegner writes, "His conservation writings record a continuous controversy unmarred by any scramble for personal advantage or any impulse towards self justification, a controversy in every way dignified by concern for public good and for the future of the West."

Devoto did not live to see many of the successes of the conservation movement he helped to fuel. He died of a heart attack on November 13, 1955.

Bibliography

Bowen, Catherine Drinker, Edith R. Mirrielees, Arthur M. Schlesinger, and Wallace Stegner, *Four Portraits of One Subject: Bernard Devoto*, 1963; Burrows, Russell, *Bernard Devoto*, Western Writers Series, 1997; Fish, Peter, "The Prescient Historian," *Sunset*, 1996; Lapham, Lewis H., "Alms for Oblivion," *Harper's*, 1997; Stegner, Wallace, *The Uneasy Chair*, 1973.

DiCaprio, Leonardo
(November 11, 1974—)
Actor, Director, Producer of *The 11th Hour*

Film superstar Leonardo DiCaprio of *Titanic* (1997) fame won a Golden Globe Award in 2005 for his leading role as filmmaker and entrepreneur Howard Hughes. He has starred in many other high grossing films such as *Romeo and Juliet* and *Blood Diamond*, and has been nominated five additional times for Golden Globe Awards and three times for Academy Awards. In 2007 he produced, co-wrote and narrated *The 11th Hour*, a feature-length documentary about saving humanity from ecological collapse. It received the Jules Verne Adventure Film Festival Audience Choice Award, the Best Documentary Feature Diversity Award from the Multicultural Motion Picture Association, and the Clarion Award from the International Visual Communications Association.

Leonardo Wilhelm DiCaprio was born on November 11, 1974, in Los Angeles, California, to George and Irmalin DiCaprio, a comic distributor and a legal secretary who would go on to manage her son's career. He grew up in Los Angeles, where he attended the Los Angeles Center for Enriched Studies, a school for gifted students, and the John Marshall High School. He currently has homes in Los Angeles, in New York, and owns a small island in Belize, where he is planning to build an eco-friendly resort run with renewable energy. DiCaprio began acting as a child on television, and would have his first significant film part in *This Boy's Life* (1993), co-starring Robert DeNiro.

Although DiCaprio's concern for the environment preceded his stardom, the money and fame garnered from *Titanic* (1997) and *The Man in the Iron Mask* (1998) enabled him to embark in earnest on his environmental activism and philanthropy. He established the Leonardo DiCaprio Foundation in 1998. He began networking with leaders such as Nobel Laureate AL GORE in the fight to combat global warming. He served as national chairman of Earth Day in 2000. In 2003 the Natural Resources Defense Council (NRDC) opened a new green building in Santa Monica, California, featuring DiCaprio's e-Activism Computer Zone, which aims to galvanize young people into lifelong environmentalism. The following year he joined NRDC's Board of Trustees as well as the Board of Directors of Global Green USA, an affiliate of Green Cross International. Global Green is especially active in affordable green housing design.

DiCaprio's foundation website calls for personal action pledges, such as stopping the use of plastic shopping bags, and contains a plethora of resources to get informed and bring about change. Among the website's prominent links are two short environmental education films that DiCaprio co-wrote and narrated. *Global Warming* (2003) was inspired by Thom Hartmann's *Last Hours of Ancient Sunlight* (1998), and is about the causes and solutions to climate change. It calls for "the separation of oil and state." *Water Planet* (2005) is about the causes and solutions to freshwater pollution and shortages. DiCaprio made both films with Global Green USA and the Tree Media Group, an independent media organization that aims to support and sustain civil society.

In 2004 DiCaprio traveled to fourteen cities to stump for presidential candidate John Kerry, co-author of *This Moment on Earth* (2007) and longtime environmentalist whose command of and commitment to progressive green policy has often been obscured by the mainstream media. In 2005 DiCaprio amplified the tone and tenor of his activism. "We must not allow Congress and big oil companies to do what they want with our national wilderness areas. They are part of our heritage. We can't let these corporate powerhouses fool us into thinking that our only energy resource is oil. We need our government to encourage innovation."

DiCaprio was to team up once again with the Tree Media Group to make *The 11th Hour*, released in 2007. Sisters Leila Conners Petersen and Nadia Conners, founders of Tree Media, directed the film, and DiCaprio produced, narrated, and helped edit it. Fifty luminaries in areas like energy and sustainability were interviewed so as to explain the magnitude of the problem and the immense promise of green design and action. Those featured range from former CIA Director James Woolsey, to climate change author and activist BILL MCKIBBEN, and Nobel Peace Prize laureate Wangari Maathai. The interviews were shot in DiCaprio's mother's garage, and stock footage was used to depict environmental calamities like droughts, floods and glacier collapses, as well as the hope of green buildings and intelligent design systems which often involve mimicking natural systems that have been around for millions of years.

The central point of *The 11th Hour*, DiCaprio said upon its release, is that "we could reduce our footprint on this planet by 90 percent with technologies that are already there and available. We don't have to invent anything new, even at this point."

Leonardo DiCaprio's foundation was honored in 2001 by Environment Now with the Martin Litton Environmental Warrior Award, and Global Green USA presented DiCaprio with the Environmental Leadership Award in 2003. His mother Irmalin DiCaprio, the president of his foundation, was honored at Global Green Millennium Awards for her Environmental Community Leadership.

DiCaprio continues to produce films. His company, Appian Way, has adapted Kurt Eichenwald's *Conspiracy of Fools* (2005), about the collapse of the Houston-based energy company Enron. He is also helping to create a reality TV show called E-topia to showcase green building methods and materials. *The 11th Hour* will tour campuses in 2008-2009, and includes curriculum aids on its website, www.11thhouraction.com.

BIBLIOGRAPHY

Roberts, Sheila, "Leonardo DiCaprio Interview, The 11th Hour," www.MoviesOnline.ca (2007); Tim Sohn, "Green Giants," *Outside Magazine, The Green Issue*, April, 2007; DiCaprio, Leonardo, *Waterkeeper Magazine*, Winter 2005; Clough,Cari-Lynn, "Off-Screen Hero," www.ukula.com; www.leonardodicaprio.org; www.leonardodicaprio.com; www.11thhouraction.com; www.treemedia.com.

Dilg, Will

(1867–March 8, 1927)
Founder of Izaak Walton League of America

Publicist and advertising man Will Dilg led 53 fishermen and hunters to found the Izaak Walton League of America (IWLA) in 1922. Although his time at the helm of the new organization was short, Dilg's charismatic leadership gave the IWLA the push it needed to become the first nationwide conservation organization and the largest one of its time.

Little is known of the early life of Williamson H. Dilg, who was born during the fall of 1867 in Milwaukee, Wisconsin. He was an advertising man and a publicist by profession, a fisherman by vocation. He contributed articles to hunting and fishing publications. According to a story cited by writer Stephen Fox, Dilg was moved to dedicate his life to preserving opportunities for young boys to enjoy outdoor experiences after his own son died. Dilg and 53 other sportsmen founded the Izaak Walton League of America with the goal of saving "outdoor America for future generations," according to the IWLA's official history. The problem they were most concerned about was the degradation of the country's best fishing streams due to contamination by industry and raw sewage and to sedimentation caused by soil erosion. They named their organization after the seventeenth-century British fisherman who wrote the conservationist classic *The Compleat Angler*. The IWLA was modeled on fraternal orders such as the Kiwanis Club. Within a few years of its founding it boasted 100,000 members, most of whom lived in the Midwest.

In August 1922, Dilg founded IWLA's publication, the monthly *Outdoor America* (renamed *Izaak Walton League Monthly* during its first year). Dilg wanted *Outdoor America* to appeal to a large, mainstream audience and was able to woo many famous American writers to contribute free articles. Dilg's editorials decried industrial civilization and yearned for the calm of nature. *Outdoor America* became the conservation movement's largest publication and served as a powerful recruitment tool.

In 1923, Dilg learned of a private developer's plan to drain the river bottoms of the Upper Mississippi basin. This was Chicagoan Dilg's favorite place to fish—he spent two months every year fishing there. The river bottoms were also the best spawning grounds for black bass, Dilg's favorite game fish. Dilg mounted an energetic and successful assault on this plan. He moved to Washington, D.C., with an army of IWLA staff members and set up an office in a suite at the New Willard Hotel. His goal was to have a 300-mile stretch of the Upper Mississippi declared a federal wildlife refuge. Dilg and his staff wrote the Upper Mississippi River Wild Life and Fish Refuge bill, recruited two fellow sportsmen legislators to introduce it, and lobbied hard to assure its passage. With help from secretary of commerce and veteran angler Herbert Hoover, Dilg convinced Pres. Calvin Coolidge to sign the bill. No expense had been spared on this project; the conservation movement had never before seen a conservationist effort of this magnitude.

The IWLA annual meetings were huge occasions in which Dilg and other members of the IWLA's brotherhood expounded on the glory of their struggle. Conservationists from the Audubon Society, the Boone and Crockett Club, and other organizations who attended the IWLA meetings were astounded. Their members were primarily of the privileged elite classes of the eastern seaboard, staid and dignified. But at the IWLA, the crowd was uninhibited. Dilg was not a member of the privileged elite; he had made his money in the brash business of advertising. At the annual meetings, compared by some observers to revivalist meetings, religious metaphors flowed freely, reports Stephen Fox: members compared Dilg to St. Paul, to Stephen rousing a crusade, to David fighting Goliath. Dilg, for his part, frequently referred to "the God of Nature" as his savior and the object of his passion.

But within a few years, Dilg's weaknesses became apparent to other leaders of the IWLA. Despite the strength of the organization and the wealth and generosity of a number of the board members, Dilg's activities hemorrhaged the organization's treasury. Dilg had outspent the organization's budget by 100 percent. His lobbying efforts for the Upper Mississippi protection bill had cost more than any similar conservationist effort before it. *Outdoor America* ran a deficit too. To replenish its accounts, *Outdoor America* began to accept large advertisements from the gun and ammunition industry, which Dilg strongly opposed. But he was not in a position to impose his commitment to independence. Further weakening him was throat cancer, which had been diagnosed in 1924.

Other leaders of the IWLA decided that Dilg had to be deposed for the organization to continue. Dilg was forced out of *Outdoor America* in 1925, and at the annual meeting of April 1926 he was removed from his post as president, by a vote of over two-thirds of the members. He tried to fight but at this point was too weak. Dilg dedicated the remainder of his life in Washington, D.C., to efforts to convince the president to establish a Conservation Department in his cabinet.

The IWLA has continued its advocacy for clean water and healthy forests and was an important actor in much of the landmark conservation legislation of the twentieth century.

Dilg died of throat cancer on March 8, 1927, in Washington, D.C.

BIBLIOGRAPHY

Fox, Stephen, *The American Conservation Movement: John Muir and His Legacy*, 1981; "Izaac Walton League of America," www.iwla.org; Stroud, Richard, ed., *National Leaders of American Conservation*, 1985.

Dingell, John, Jr.

(July 8, 1926–)
U.S. Representative from Michigan

John Dingell Jr. has been a member of the U.S. House of Representatives since 1955. During his more than 50 years in Congress, he has been involved with the creation of many important pieces of environmental legislation, including the National Environmental Policy Act of 1970, the Marine Mammal Protection Act of 1972, the Endangered Species Act of 1973, and the 1990 Amendments to the Clean Air Act.

John David Dingell Jr. was born on July 8, 1926, in Colorado Springs, Colorado, to John David Dingell and Grace Bigler Dingell. The family moved to Detroit, Michigan, in the late 1920s. Dingell's father, a New Deal Democrat and an advocate of a national health insurance program, was elected to the U.S. House of Representatives in 1932. Dingell attended private elementary and secondary schools in Washington, D.C., and served as a page in the House of Representatives from 1938 to 1943.

From 1944 to 1946, Dingell served as an infantryman in the United States Army. He was discharged with the rank of 2nd lieutenant following the completion of World War II. Later that year, he entered Georgetown University. He graduated in 1949 with a B.S. degree in chemistry, and in 1952 he earned a law degree from Georgetown. In 1952, Dingell accepted a position as research assistant to U.S. circuit judge Theodore Levine. Dingell became assistant prosecuting attorney in Wayne County, Michigan, which includes Detroit and its suburbs, a position he occupied from 1954 to 1955. In September of 1955, Dingell's father died in the middle of his term in the House of Representatives. Dingell ran in a special election to fill the vacated position and was elected, at the age of 29, to succeed his father as representative of the Sixteenth Congressional District in Detroit.

Dingell began his career as representative by supporting strong civil rights legislation: introducing a bill in 1956 that led to the creation of the Civil Rights Division in the Justice Department and proposing legislation that prohibited segregated hospitals from receiving federal aid. He was especially active in environmental issues as well. In 1963, Dingell organized a group of House representatives in criticizing the United States Public Health Service's apparent unconcern with the ability of streams and lakes to support wildlife. Two years later, in 1965, Dingell helped to create a bill that required rural water and sewage treatment plants that were built with federal funds to comply with all federal water pollution standards.

In 1966, Dingell was appointed to the position of chairman of the Fisheries and Wildlife Conservation subcommittee of the Energy and Commerce committee of the House of Representatives. From this position, Dingell was able to secure important pieces of environmental legislation. He introduced the House version of what was to become the National Environmental Policy Act of 1970. He was floor manager of the Marine Mammal Protection Act of 1972, and he helped to draft the Endangered Species Act of 1973, a bill that requires the U.S. Fish and Wildlife Service to list threatened or endangered species and work toward the recovery of viable populations and also prohibits any federal projects from destroying the habitat of an endangered species. Dingell became chairman of the Commerce Committee's energy and power subcommittee in 1975, a move that marked his increasing prominence in the House of Representatives. Energy was an important national issue in the mid-1970s, owing to the Arab oil embargo of 1973 and 1974, and Dingell was in a key position to help formulate energy policy. He backed government regulations and price controls to conserve U.S. energy resources, and he was an important participant in creating the Energy Policy and Conservation Act, a bill that provided the president the authority to set domestic oil prices, ration gasoline, and establish energy conservation plans. Dingell also supported Pres. JIMMY CARTER's efforts to reduce energy consumption through a combination of taxes and other federal regulatory actions.

Dingell assumed the chair of the Energy and Commerce Committee (now called the Commerce Committee) in 1980, also acting as chair of its Oversights and Investigations subcommittee. From these positions Dingell began to wield significant power in the House of Representatives. The Commerce Committee was one of the House's most powerful, because of its far-reaching jurisdiction. It was concerned with everything from health and the environment to communications, consumer protection, and trade. One important investigation conducted by this committee under Dingell's direction was into the criminal misconduct of Environmental Protection Agency (EPA) personnel in managing the toxic cleanup money made available in the "Superfund" clause of the Comprehensive Environmental Response Compensation and Liability Act (CERCLA). This 1983 investigation led to the resignation of Pres. Ronald Reagan's EPA administrator, Anne Gorsuch, and to a perjury conviction for one of her deputies, Rita Lavelle.

Dingell's district is one of the most heavily industrialized in the country. It includes a large number of autoworkers and union members and is home to the main Ford automobile plant. So, while Dingell has been an important player in creating environmental legislation, he has also been an ardent supporter of the auto industry. He long opposed stricter air quality standards, understanding that such legislation would have a negative impact on his constituents. It was not until 1990 that shifting congressional interests and power led him to support a clean air bill for the sake of his own political survival. Dingell did help to author, and was a supporter of that year's Amendments to the Clean Air Act. His leadership on the Amended Clean Air Act is credited for its almost unanimous passage through Congress.

Most recently, Dingell has resolved to lead Congress on the issue of Global Warming. He co-sponsored the Energy Independence and Security Act, passed by the House in 2007, which increases fuel economy standards for vehicles and buildings and appliances. He has proposed policy ideas on reducing greenhouse gas emissions by 60 to 80 percent by the year 2050, through a "cap and trade" program, through which companies would be allowed to emit a certain amount of greenhouse gasses, and if they came in under that limit, could sell this "credit" to other companies unable to comply with their limit. Leadership from Dingell on this issue—because traditionally he has been so protective of industry—is said to be key to its general acceptance in Congress.

Dingell has been elected to more consecutive terms than any other living member of Congress in the House of Representatives and is the second-longest serving Congressperson in history. He lives with his second wife, Debbie Dingell, in Virginia.

BIBLIOGRAPHY
Cifelli, Anna, "Capitol Hill's One-Man Gauntlet," *Fortune*, 1985; Hook, Janet, "By Shifting Tactics on Clean Air, Dingell Guarded His Power," *Congressional Quarterly Weekly Report*, 1990; Mason, Milo, "Interview: U.S. Representative John D. Dingell (D-MI)," *Natural Resources & Environment*, 2008; Noah, Timothy, "Corporate Watchdog." *Newsweek*, 1987; Raine, Harrison, and Gary Cohen, "Congress's Most Feared Democrat," *U.S. News and World Report*, 1991; Von Drehle, David, "A Mastodon Takes On Global Warming," *Time*, 2007.

Dittmar, Hank

(January 12, 1956–)
Advocate for Sustainable Cities and Transport, Urban Planner

Hank Dittmar has dedicated his career to promoting sustainable transportation and urban planning. He has founded and/or directed a number of organizations dedicated to these fields, including the Surface Transportation Policy Project, the Metropolitan Working Group of President Clinton's Council on Sustainable Development, the Great American Station Foundation, and Reconnecting America. Currently, he serves as the Chief Executive of The Prince's Foundation for the Built Environment in London, and chairs the Board of the Congress for New Urbanism.

Henry Eric ("Hank") Dittmar was born on January 12, 1956, in Oklahoma City, Oklahoma, and was inspired to become active in environmental issues on the first Earth Day, in 1970. He attended Northwestern University, receiving a B.S. in communication studies in 1976, and went on to earn a master's degree in community and regional planning from the

University of Texas at Austin in 1980, where he contributed to the development of Texas's Coastal Zone Management legislation.

Dittmar was responsible for coordination of public transit systems in the nine-county San Francisco Bay area from 1980 to 1983 and worked as a transit planner for the municipal bus service of Santa Monica, California, from 1983 to 1984. He directed the Santa Monica airport from 1984 to 1989, where he developed the nation's most advanced airport noise ordinance. While managing the departments of legislation and finance for the metropolitan Transportation Commission in Oakland, from 1989 to 1993, he helped San Francisco replace the earthquake-damaged Embarcadero Freeway with a surface boulevard and a streetcar line.

In 1993, Dittmar became executive director of the Surface Transportation Policy Project, a national, nonprofit coalition of more than 200 organizations dedicated to ensuring that environmental policy and government investments help to support a strong economy, promote energy conservation, protect environmental quality, and build more equitable and livable communities. Specifically, STPP focused on documenting and publicizing the tremendous quality of life impacts of auto dependency and personal and societal solutions to the problem. STPP publishes *Transfer*, a biweekly e-mail newsletter, and *Progress*, a bimonthly forum for transportation and community issues. It also published numerous reports in tune with its mission statement that "we emphasize the needs of people, rather than vehicles, in assuring access to jobs, services, and recreational opportunities." Among its reports (available for purchase on its web site) are "Road Work Ahead: Is Construction Worth the Wait?" (which reveals that road construction delays are not usually offset by the later gains in travel time), and "High Mileage Moms" (which describes the heavy driving routine of the typical homemaker). The coalition's policy publications have been widely credited with providing Congress with the intellectual underpinnings for both the 1991 Intermodal Surface Transportation Efficiency Act (ISTEA) and the 1998 TEA-21 legislation.

Dittmar was appointed by President Bill Clinton to the White House Advisory Committee on Transportation and Greenhouse Gas Emissions in 1994 and to the President's Council on Sustainable Development's Metropolitan Working Group in 1996, for which he was chair. His major emphasis during his five years at STPP was to manage its campaign to pass TEA-21. President George Bush had signed ISTEA in 1991, which acknowledged aspects of transportation policy that had not been included in previous legislation. ISTEA represented "a shift from a highway building era to an era of managing our transportation system in a way that balances mobility and accessibility concerns with environmental priorities," according to a 1997 STPP report. Despite its high-reaching goals, however, a study by the General Accounting Office found that the Department of Transportation's research agenda did not meet ISTEA goals, especially in the areas of sustainable development and intermodalism (the use of more than one mode of transportation during a trip, driving an automobile to a train station, then taking a train to complete the trip, for example).

Under Dittmar's leadership, STPP responded to this weakness by organizing a workshop for experts to develop a proposed research agenda that could be incorporated into the ISTEA reauthorization bill, TEA-21, and by working to establish a national network of regional activists who sought to force state departments of transportation to implement the progressive aspects of the new legislation. Dittmar also recommended discontinuing the funding of research on the Automated Highway System, which would have removed urban freeway lanes from ordinary use and restricted them to use by specially equipped cars that would have been electronically controlled by a central computer to operate in high-speed platoons as close as 18 inches apart. Recommendations were also made to research the relationship between travel behavior, land use, and transportation and to study how the boom in information technology has affected transportation and the sustainability of communities. The TEA-21 legislation responded to these recommendations by discontinuing the Automated Highway System and by calling for the creation of a National Transportation and the Environment Cooperative Research Program, now being designed by the National Research Council.

After the passage of TEA-21 in June, 1998, Dittmar left STPP and moved to New Mexico to work on transportation issues at the grassroots level. He became president and chief executive officer of the Great American Station Foundation, which promotes the revitalization of historic train stations (and in turn the community centers surrounding them) by offering funding for their renovation. The Great American Station Foundation facilitated a grant for the renovation of some 35 stations around the U.S., including the historic station in Las Vegas, New Mexico, which was converted into the terminal for Greyhound and Amtrak and the seat of the Las Vegas chamber of commerce. The Great American Station Foundation grew into Reconnecting America in 2002, with the mission to help communities create more effective and efficient transportation and in turn revitalize city centers and suburban neighborhoods. Dittmar was President and CEO of Reconnecting America until 2005, when he became Chief Executive for the Prince's Foundation for the Built Environment.

This organization, one of 17 charities established by HRH Prince Charles of Wales, seeks to improve the quality of people's lives by teaching and practicing timeless and ecological ways of planning designing and building. The Foundation engages in live projects as urban designer and master planner thorough a unique method of community engagement and design called Enquiry by Design. It is involved in dozens of projects across the UK and abroad, including the remediation of BP's oldest refinery and its conversion to an urban village, the development of Sherford an urban extension to Plymouth, England as a an exemplar of sustainable development, and a project in Rose Town in Kingston, Jamaica to revitalize an inner city neighbourhood and reclaim it from gang violence. The Prince's Foundation promotes location efficiency and has demonstrated that a combination of residential density, mixed use, walkability and access to public transport can reduce car travel and carbon emission, improve health and increase quality of life.

Dittmar has served on numerous boards of directors of transit and planning-oriented groups, including the Institute for Location Efficiency, the Center for Neighborhood Technology, the Environmental Leadership Project, the Biodiversity Project, and the League of Conservation Voters. He is Chair of the Board of the Congress for New Urbanism. In 2008, he was awarded the Seaside Prize, in recognition to his contribution to more sustainable cities. Dittmar lives with his wife, Kelle, and their twins, Cole and Clara, in London. In addition to his work on transit issues, he is a published poet and short story writer.

BIBLIOGRAPHY

Dittmar, Hank, *Transport and Neighbourhoods*, 2008; Dittmar, Hank, *The New Transit Town: Best Practices in Transit-Oriented Development*, 2003; Dittmar, Hank, "Sprawl, the automobile and affording the American dream," in *Sustainable Planet*, edited by Juliet Schor and B.S. Taylor, 2002; Horan, Thomas A., Hank Dittmar, and Daniel R. Jordan, "ISTEA and the New Era in Transportation Policy: Sustainable Communities from a Federal Initiative," *Toward Sustainable Communities: Transition and Transformations in Environmental Policy*, 1999; Lockwood, Charles, "Q & A with Hank Dittmar," *Urban Land*, 2007; "Reconnecting America," reconnectingamerica.org; "Surface Transportation Policy Project" www.transact.org/; "The Prince's Foundation for the Built Environment," www.princes-foundation.org; "Transportation Equity Act for the 21st Century," www.fhwa.dot.gov/tea21

Dombeck, Michael

(September 21, 1948–)
Chief of U.S. Forest Service, Fisheries Biologist

Michael Dombeck, who served as fourteenth chief of the U.S. Forest Service (USFS) from 1997 until 2001, steered the Forest Service on a new course: away from its former promotion of timber extraction above all other uses and toward the broader goal of promoting the long-term ecological health of the land it manages.

Michael P. Dombeck was born on September 21, 1948, in Stevens Point, Wisconsin, and grew up in the Chequamegon National Forest in northern Wisconsin where his parents ran a general store. Dombeck's first summer jobs included working in the family store, taking care of seasonal homes, and after two summers cutting pulpwood he turned to guiding fishermen, which he continued for 11 years until 1977. He earned his B.S. degree in biology and general science from the University of Wisconsin-Stevens Point in 1971 and an M.S.T. degree in biology education there in 1974. While at Stevens Point, Dombeck read ALDO LEOPOLD's *A Sand County Almanac*, which still governs his thinking on natural resource management. Dombeck taught high school sciences and college zoology; he continued his studies at the University of Minnesota, obtaining an M.S. in zoology in 1977, and at Iowa State University, where he was awarded a Ph.D. in fisheries biology in 1984.

In 1978, Dombeck started working as a fisheries biologist for the USFS at Upper Michigan's Hiawatha National Forest. He worked in the USFS's fisheries program as its Pacific Southwest Region manager from 1985 to 1987 and then as its national manager in Washington, D.C., until 1989, when he joined the Department of the Interior's Bureau of Land Management (BLM), working first as science advisor and special assistant to the director, then in 1993 as acting assistant secretary in land and minerals management, and in late 1993 to 1994 as chief of staff to the assistant secretary of land and minerals management. President Clinton nominated Dombeck for director of the BLM in early 1994, but western Republican congresspeople, who generally favor extraction interests and the rights of ranchers to graze their livestock on government land for minimal leasing fees, successfully opposed the nomination because of Dombeck's commitment to conservation. President Clinton maintained Dombeck as acting director of the BLM, a position not requiring congressional confirmation, for three years until the retirement of thirteenth USFS chief Jack Ward Thomas in 1996. Since congressional approval is not required for USFS chiefs, Clinton was able to appoint Dombeck

Michael Dombeck (Photograph courtesy of University of Wisconsin-Stevens Point)

to that position in December 1996. He is the only person to have served as head of the nation's two largest land management agencies, the USFS and the BLM.

Dombeck inherited an agency with internal strife and public concerns, that some had said lost its way as it continued to transition away from large-scale harvest of old-growth forests that began during World War II. From the beginnings of the USFS under founding chief GIFFORD PINCHOT, its goal has been to facilitate extraction of timber from the national forests in the United States. Pinchot's vision was to manage extraction so that it would allow a sustainable yield over the long term. But largely as a result of WWII, the goal of sustainability was cast aside and the USFS moved into large-scale timber harvest. By the 1980s, timber companies were taking 10 to 12 billion board feet annually from national forests; clear-cuts were scarring even the steepest mountain forests, and the resulting erosion was contaminating streams and rivers and causing landslides. USFS managers were caught between lawsuits from environmentalists about the agency's violation of environmental protection laws, continuous pressure from industries and the Reagan Administration to allow more extraction, and the agency's own muddled bureaucracy. President Clinton's naming of Dombeck as USFS chief in 1996 was a response to public protest about the crisis in national forests.

Dombeck, still influenced by the land ethic as articulated by Aldo Leopold, immediately called for a shift in USFS priorities. On July 1, 1998 he wrote to employees "If we are to redeem our role as conservation leaders, it is not enough to be loyal to the Forest Service organization. *First and foremost*, we must be loyal to our land ethic. In fifty years, we will not be remembered for the resources we developed; we will be thanked for those we maintained and restored for future generations." He declared that the USFS would no longer prioritize timber extraction over all other activity in national forests and that the long-term health of the land should be the basis on which decisions are made about what is allowed in national forests. He called for a new approach of "collaborative stewardship," which would seek public participation in an effort to balance the varied activities in national forests, including timber and mineral extraction, grazing, hunting and fishing, and other forms of recreation.

Some western Republicans, such as Rep. Helen Chenoweth and Sen. Larry Craig, both of Idaho, were not happy with Dombeck's work at the USFS and called him to testify before congressional committees almost monthly after he became USFS chief. Despite their attempts to stop him, Dombeck was able to repair some key structural flaws at the USFS and make major policy changes. He replaced all six deputy chiefs, some of whom were viewed as obstacles to changes needed to move the agency into the 21st century, and assembled a team who supported change in agency direction. He authorized and published a report that showed how the USFS actually lost money on its timber sales. In 1998 Dombeck declared an 18-month moratorium on building new roads in the most remote areas of national forests until the USFS could determine a long-term road policy that would allow for the maintenance of existing, heavily used roads, the construction of those roads deemed necessary, and the designation of areas that would be kept roadless in perpetuity.

Throughout his four-year tenure as USFS Chief, Dombeck was known for his patience and diplomacy in dealing with lawmakers who opposed his reforms and with the residents of towns neighboring national forests who were despondent at the decline of the logging industry. Dombeck urged long-term thinking at the policymaking level and for towns whose economies were dependent upon unsustainable resource extraction.

Dombeck has been the recipient of serveral awards in recognition of his role in redefining the USFS: the National Wildlife Federation's Conservationist of the Year in 2002, the LADY BIRD JOHNSON Conservation Award in 2002, the Audubon Medal in 2002, and the Distinguished Service Award from the Society for Conservation Biology in 2003. As the capstone to his life-long career in public service, he was granted the highest award in federal service, the Presidential Rank—Distinguished Executive Award. The *New York Times* wrote that he was the "most conservation minded Forest Service Chief since Gifford Pinchot."

Dombeck currently is UW System Fellow and Professor of Global Conservation at the University of Wisconsin-Stevens Point. He has authored, co-authored, and edited over 200 popular and scholarly publications, including the books *Watershed Restoration: Principles and Practices* (1997), and *From Conquest to Conservation: Our Public Lands Legacy* (2003). To the general public, Dombeck advises a return to his intellectual mentor Aldo Leopold's land ethic. Specifically, Dombeck urges Americans to take the long view—first and foremost to ask what we want the land to look like in 50 and 100 years, and then make conscientious decisions about resource consumption so that we do not lead other countries with more lenient environmental protection policies to overharvest their natural resources to meet our immense demand.

Dombeck lives near Stevens Point with his wife Patricia. They have one daughter, Mary, who served in the Peace Corps in Africa and is studying veterinary medicine.

BIBLIOGRAPHY

Anderson, H. Michael, "Reshaping National Forest Policy," *Issues in Science and Technology*, 1999; Annin, Peter, "Saving the Tall Timber: The U.S. Forest Service Turns a Bit More Green," *Newsweek*, 1999; "Homepage of Michael P. Dombeck," www.uwsp.edu/cnr/gem/Dombeck/; Kriz, Margaret, "Fighting over Forests," *National Journal*, 1998; Lewis, Daniel, "The Trailblazer," *New York Times Magazine*, 1999; Sudetic, C., "The forest for the trees," *Rolling Stone*, 2001; "United States Forest Service," http://www.fs.fed.us/.

Donovan, Richard

(August 6, 1952–)
Chief of Forestry and Deputy Director, Rainforest Alliance

Richard Donovan oversees the Rainforest Alliance's SmartWood program, which certifies wood and wood products grown and harvested in an environmentally responsible manner in more than 60 countries around the world. A founding member of the Forest Stewardship Council (FSC), the international body that accredits wood certification programs such as SmartWood, Donovan helped write the "Principles and Criteria for Natural Forest Management," the document upon which the FSC bases its decisions to accredit certification programs.

Richard Zell Donovan was born on August 6, 1952, in Englewood, New Jersey. His parents were both from northern Minnesota, where three generations of his mother's family ran a sawmill from the late 1800s until 1954. As a young man, Donovan learned how to work as a woodcutter and logger in the north woods, skills and practical experience that have served him well during his career. Donovan attended Wabash College in Crawfordsville, Indiana, from 1970 to 1972, before transferring to the University of South Florida. He spent four months at the National University of Mexico in Mexico, ultimately graduating from USF with a double major in Latin American history and romance languages in 1974.

Richard Donovan (Photograph courtesy of Richard Donovan)

Upon graduation, Donovan moved to Maine and worked as an activist on forest issues in the region and with the Alaska Coalition on the Alaska Lands bill. Donovan enlisted in the Peace Corps in 1975 and was sent to Paraguay, where he spent three and a half years working with Paraguay's National Environmental Sanitation Service. Upon his return to the United States, Donovan worked in northern Minnesota as a woodcutter and in 1979 entered the Antioch New England Graduate School to study natural resources management and administration. His major research project there was to assess the quality of forest management in Vermont's municipal forests and analyze their history; it culminated in recommendations to the public and the private sector about more effective ways that municipal forests could be managed for multiple purposes, including watershed protection, recreation, education, and timber and nontimber forest products extraction.

Donovan graduated from Antioch with an M.S. in 1981 and throughout most of the rest of the 1980s worked as a consultant on natural resource management projects in developing countries and North America, most of that time with ARD, Inc., a Vermont-based international consulting firm. He spent three and a half years in Costa Rica from 1987 to 1990 as a World Wildlife Fund (WWF) senior fellow, during which time he designed and implemented an integrated conservation/community development project in a recently settled buffer zone of Costa Rica's spectacular Corcovado National Park. The BOSCOSA Forest Conservation and Management project offered environmentally sustainable alternatives to *campesinos*, who generally practiced traditional, environmentally destructive slash-and-burn agricultural techniques. Through BOSCOSA, *campesinos* established and managed tree and agroforestry plantations and managed natural forest for timber and nontimber products, watershed protection, and ecotourism.

Donovan returned to Vermont in 1990, where he continued his work on conservation and development as a senior fellow with WWF and also taught in the University of Vermont's Environmental Program and School of Natural Resources. In mid-1992, he became director of the Rainforest Alliance's SmartWood Program. SmartWood, established in 1989, was the first timber certification program in the world and was the first of the Rainforest Alliance's ecological certification programs (the Rainforest Alliance also certifies tropical agricultural crops such as bananas, coffee, cocoa, oranges, and more through its Sustainable Agriculture Division, cofounded by CHRIS WILLE).

SmartWood works for forest conservation by certifying wood and wood products that are grown and harvested responsibly from natural forests and tree plantations in tropical, temperate, and boreal forest regions. Its global network of regional nonprofit certifying organizations assesses companies and awards a seal of approval to those that comply with SmartWood's stringent environmental, economic, and social criteria. Once a company's forest products have been certified by SmartWood, they can be marketed to customers who are often willing to pay more for them, and this provides an economic incentive that SmartWood hopes will motivate more forest managers to manage their forests in a more sustainable manner and earn certification. The SmartWood seal has become a mark of excellence in forestry, to the point where many public and private forestry operations seek to become certified for public recognition and peer credibility. Since its founding, the program has certified almost 400 different forest management operations on more than 100,000,000 million acres. Certified wood from these areas is manufactured into certified products ranging from plywood to flooring to furniture to musical instruments. The companies that do this processing receive "chain of custody" certification; SmartWood has certified more than 2,000 such companies. Overall, SmartWood has certified operations in 66 countries.

In addtion to SmartWood, the Rainforest Alliance Forestry Division now also includes the TREES Program (Training, Research, Education, Extension and Sourcing), which implements projects with small and medium-sized forest enterprises throughout the Americas and China, and a Markets Program, that provides "SmartSource" support for companies seeking to "green" their supply chain around the globe.

Rainforest Alliance (and SmartWood) is proud of its many success stories on both the environmental and the socioeconomic fronts. Among them is one on which it collaborates with its Brazilian partner Imaflora, which established a guitar-making school in the Amazon outpost of Manaus, where poor children can go after their regular classes to learn to make guitars and other stringed instruments with nonendangered wood species of the Amazon rain forest. Not only has this helped protect the endangered woods with which guitars are traditionally made, it has taught at-risk children a marketable skill and has engendered in them an appreciation for conservation.

Another success story is taking place in the Maya Biosphere Reserve in Guatemala's Peten region. This area of more than 5 million acres, established and given protective status in 1990, has a section where sustainable low-impact agriculture and timber extraction is allowed. Allowing multiple use was a controversial decision, as most traditional environmental groups believe that full preservation is a better strategy for protection of biodiversity. SmartWood has certified operations on about 60 percent of the land where multiple use is allowed and the Rainforest Alliance has promoted environmentally-sustainable economic activities via micro-grants to people who use the rainforest resources to make furniture and establish butterfly farms, among other low-impact, sustainable activities. A recent study has revealed that this approach has been very successful: the deforestation rate in certified areas is twenty times less that that in non-certified areas, and there is no virtually no burning in certified areas whereas in non-certified areas between seven and 20 percent of the forest is burnt every year. Rainforest Alliance's work clearly demonstrates that there are no panaceas for stopping deforestation or forest degradation—the answers lie in a combination of effective sustainable forest management and protected areas.

With the ecocertification boom that began after the renewed public interest in the environment after Earth Day 1990, Donovan and others serious about certification realized that their efforts would be for naught if other certifying entities began offering less stringent certifications. During 1991 and 1992, Donovan worked with a number of international and regional organizations in Europe, the Americas, Melanesia, and Asia to develop the concept of an international body for reviewing and approving forest management certifiers. This idea led to the formation in 1993 of the Forest Stewardship Council, an internationally recognized organization based in Oaxaca, Mexico, that evaluates, monitors, and accredits certification bodies like SmartWood. Donovan cochaired the committee that wrote FSC's "Principles and Criteria for Forest Management," the seminal document upon which all FSC-approved certifications are based. Since its formation, the accredited certification organizations in the FSC system have certified approximately 10,000 forest management and forest products operations covering more than 250 million acres in some 79 countries.

Donovan directs Rainforest Alliance's forestry activities from its Forestry Division headquarters in Richmond, Vermont. He resides in the nearby town of Jericho with his wife, Karen, a special education teacher. Their two children, Andrew and Emily, live nearby. The Donovan family all continue their ancestral tradition of heating their homes with firewood harvested from local forests.

BIBLIOGRAPHY
Ervin, J., R. Donovan, et al., eds., *Forest Products Certification: Opportunities and Constraints*, 1996; "Forest Stewardship Council," www.fscus.org/; "Rainforest Alliance," www.rainforest-alliance.org/; Smart Wood," www.smartwood.org/.

Douglas, Marjory Stoneman
(April 7, 1890–May 14, 1998)
Writer, Founder of Friends of the Everglades

Variously referred to as the Everglades' "patron saint," "empress," "champion," and "one of the true guiding lights," writer Marjory Stoneman Douglas started the movement to save the Florida Everglades from development with her best-selling *The Everglades: River of Grass*, published in 1947. Through this book and other writings and her fierce grassroots activism, Douglas fought for the preservation of this unique ecosystem and was one of the few environmentalists who lived long enough to enjoy the fruits of her labor. The year before she died, Everglades National Park was expanded significantly, and the federal government announced rehabilitation plans to undo the decades of damage that development and agriculture had inflicted upon it.

Marjory Stoneman Douglas was born in Minneapolis on April 7, 1890, to Lillian Trefethen Stoneman and Frank Bryant Stoneman. While she was still very young, her mother, a concert violinist, left Marjory's father and took her to her grandparents' home in Taunton, Massachusetts. Douglas was raised on stories told by her French grandmother and was encouraged by high school teachers to write. She attended Wellesley College, graduating with a B.A. in English composition in 1912. At Wellesley, Douglas was elected class orator and published her work in the college's literary magazine. In 1914, she married Kenneth Douglas, who was 30 years older than she and turned out to be an alcoholic check forger. She divorced him three years later and never remarried. In 1915, after her mother had died, Douglas moved to Miami, Florida, to be closer to her father, who had founded the *Miami Herald*. She worked as a reporter for the *Herald* until the United States entered World War I. She joined the Red Cross and worked in its publicity department, traveling throughout Europe to write articles about child refugee relief. When she returned to Miami in 1920, she worked as an assistant editor at the *Herald* for three more years before leaving to write short stories. Her stories, many of which were set in a region unfamiliar to most readers—southern Florida—met rapid success. Over a period of 15 years, 40 of her stories were published in the *Saturday Evening Post*, and other magazines such as *Collier's, Woman's Home Companion*, and *Reader's Digest* published many more. She won second place in the 1928 O. Henry Memorial Prize, and in 1937 her "Story of a Homely Woman" was included in an anthology of the best stories published in the *Post*.

An avid student of Florida's geography and history, Douglas was especially interested in the area west of Miami that most Floridians considered a useless, pest-infested swamp. The Everglades is a huge marshy area that originally extended south from Lake Okeechobee to the Gulf of Mexico, covering approximately one-third of the Florida peninsula. A shallow, slightly inclined pan of water covered with saw grass, it serves as a giant water purifier. Water originally drained out of Lake Okeechobee slowly through the Everglades, the entire trip to the ocean lasting a full year. The Everglades' ability to soak up excess rainfall gave it an important role in flood control, and it stored water that evaporated into north-blowing clouds that hydrate central and northern Florida. Farmers, developers, and industrialists did not recognize the ecological importance of the Everglades and as early as the mid-1800s sought to "reclaim" the land for other uses. The 1850 federal Swamp and Overflowed Lands Act turned over the Everglades to the state of Florida on the condition that it drain the area. More than 400 miles of drainage canals were built by the 1930s to divert water from the region; in later years the U.S. Army Corps of Engineers increased the canal network to 1,400 miles and built levees that locked up water in reservoirs for irrigation. Seven massive pumping systems were set up to protect crops on the reclaimed land from inundation. Douglas's father denounced this work in a *Herald* editorial in 1905, and his daughter also believed that the area deserved more respect for its natural features and its ecological significance. In 1927 she joined a citizen's committee that lobbied for the Everglades' protection as a national park.

In the 1930s, Douglas successfully pitched a nonfiction piece about the threats of wildlife poaching in the Everglades to the editor of the *Saturday Evening Post*, and by 1941 she had started work on her famous *The Everglades: River of Grass*, published first in 1947 and still in print. Douglas spent five years exploring the Everglades by canoe, row boat, and swamp buggy and on foot to research the book and in the process realized that her love for the area would convert her into a lifelong activist to protect it. The book reveals to lay readers not only the complexity of the water cycle and wetland ecology, but also the history of human interaction with the area—how indigenous people learned to live off the Everglades and the clumsy attempts of white colonists to convert them into the dry land that they knew how to use. This human history was the first documentation of its kind about the Everglades.

The book was an immediate success, with the first printing of 7,500 copies selling out in just a month. In that same year, 1947, Everglades National Park was established, protecting over a million areas of the Everglades. But the area remained under siege, because it was surrounded by agriculture and contaminated by pesticide- and fertilizer-laden runoff. Developers ate further into the Everglades to build housing and industry, and the east-west Everglades Highway impeded water flow.

The Everglades remained in print throughout the 1950s and 1960s, earning the Everglades a widening group of admirers. Local conservation groups continued to push for more protection, but it was not until 1969, when Douglas was 79 years old, that she became a full-time activist for the Everglades. In that year, the twin threats of an oil refinery on Biscayne Bay south of Miami and a jetport in the middle of the Everglades emerged. Douglas founded Friends of the Everglades, a local, grassroots group that anyone could join for a dollar, and became its first president. The group defeated the refinery and the jetport and lobbied to improve the north-south flow of water. In a 1999 article for *International Wildlife*, Douglas recalled that the proponent of the refinery really did the environmental movement a great deed: "His idea was so ridiculous and it stimulated such widespread opposition that many people who'd otherwise been sitting back were enlisted in the environmental movement right then."

Douglas devoted the last 30 years of her long life to the continuing struggle to protect the Everglades. She continued to address any group that invited her, despite her age and worsening blindness. Friends of the Everglades grew to 5,000 members and in concert with major national conservation organizations successfully lobbied for a major restoration project for the Everglades. Florida voters voted in 1996 for a constitutional amendment to clean up the Everglades but against a penny-a-pound tax on sugar that would have paid for it. The Clinton administration stepped in and agreed to buy 50,000 acres of sugarcane fields surrounding Everglades National Park. The U.S. Army Corps of Engineers and the South Florida Water Management District were assigned the task of restoring water flow in this area with $1.5 billion from the federal government. After Douglas's death two years later, Vice President AL GORE said that "Marjory was one of the true guiding lights. I am thankful she lived long enough to see the fruits of her good efforts." Douglas was honored for her work with a Presidential Medal of Freedom in 1993. A nature center in Key Biscayne, the Department of Environmental Protection building in Tallahassee, and several schools and parks in south Florida have been named after her.

Douglas lived alone for more than 70 years in a thatched cottage that she designed herself in the Coconut Grove neighborhood of Miami. She died on May 14, 1998, at home.

BIBLIOGRAPHY

Breton, Mary Joy, *Women Pioneers for the Environment*, 1998; Douglas, Marjory Stoneman, "A Dollar for the Everglades," *International Wildlife*, 1999; Douglas, Marjory Stoneman with John Rothchild, *Marjory Stoneman Douglas: Voice of the River*, 1987; "Friends of the Everglades," www.everglades.org/; Grunwald, Michael, *The Swamp: the Everglades, Florida and the politics of paradise*, 2006; Lim, Grace, and Patrick Rogers, "Lady Everglades," *People Weekly*, 1998; Severo, Richard, "Marjory Douglas, Champion of Everglades, Dies at 108," *New York Times*, 1998.

Douglas, William Orville
(October 16, 1898–January 19, 1980)
Supreme Court Justice

In 1939, at the age of 40, William Orville Douglas became the second youngest appointee to the U.S. Supreme Court. While his years on the Supreme Court were hardly free from controversy (twice his foes tried to impeach him), many observers now regard Douglas as one of the finest justices in the Court's history. Douglas was an ardent defender of the nation's wild areas when environmental cases were heard by the Supreme Court, writing eloquent minority opinions. He is also remembered for leading two major grassroots preservation battles in the 1950s and for his books on nature, which were widely read and highly acclaimed.

William Orville Douglas was born October 16, 1898, in Maine, Minnesota, to Julia Fisk Bickford Douglas and William Douglas, a Presbyterian minister. Douglas's family did not stay long in Minnesota, as the elder Douglas transferred to a new pastorate in Estrella, California, followed shortly by another move to Cleveland, Washington. In Washington, Orville, as he was known in his youth, first came across the awesome natural features of the Pacific Northwest that would influence much of his later career. The Cascade Mountains were 40 miles to the west of Cleveland, and the Columbia River was 30 miles to the south. Spending formative years in such spectacular country endowed him with a lifelong emotional and spiritual tie to that landscape.

In 1904, not long after the family's arrival in Washington, the elder Douglas died of complications following surgery for stomach ulcers. Julia Douglas moved her family of three young children to Yakima, Washington, where they bought a house with part of the life insurance money her husband had left behind. She invested the rest in a highly speculative irrigation project that soon failed. Housed but penniless, Orville Douglas took odd jobs washing store windows, sweeping floors, and picking fruit in the fertile Yakima Valley. This early experience instilled in him a deep sympathy for the poor, which later influenced a significant number of his decisions on the U.S. Supreme Court.

Although poverty undoubtedly influenced Douglas's views, another factor even more profoundly shaped the course of his life. While still in Minnesota, Douglas had contracted a minor case of polio. As a young boy, his legs remained weak, and he was bullied at school. Determined to rise above his peers, Douglas quickly climbed to the top of his class. He also strengthened his legs by regular walking in the foothills north of Yakima, which tightened his bond to the magnificent northwestern landscape.

Finishing school, Douglas earned a scholarship to Whitman College. To supplement the scholarship, Douglas worked summers as a farmhand, meeting radical members of the Wobblies, the Industrial Workers of the World, who recruited members from among farm laborers. His success at Whitman led to a short stint teaching in Yakima and then to Columbia Law School in 1922. He was admitted to the New York bar in 1926 but continued teaching at Columbia until 1928, when he accepted an offer at Yale University Law School. In 1932, he was named Sterling Professor of Law, a title he held until being appointed to the Supreme Court. In the midst of the Depression, in 1934, Douglas was asked to direct a protective committee study by the U.S. Securities and Exchange Commission (SEC). The study lasted two years, at the end of which Douglas was named commissioner of the SEC, and chairman in 1937. In 1939, he was appointed to the Supreme Court.

Pres. FRANKLIN D. ROOSEVELT wanted to appoint a westerner to the nation's highest tribunal to balance regional representation on the Court. Douglas's 1939 appointment was mildly controversial; despite growing up in Washington, Douglas had spent his entire adult career as a member of the Eastern intelligentsia and boasted a meteoric career. Nevertheless, Douglas quickly showed himself to be a genuine westerner, cultivating an image as a rugged individualist, expert outdoorsman, and determined conservationist.

The majority of Douglas's successful conservation battles were personal, however, not issues he ruled upon as Supreme Court Justice. His first publicized conservation battle involved the Chesapeake & Ohio Canal near Washington, D.C., which some had hoped to turn into a scenic highway. Douglas frequently hiked along the historic canal and enjoyed both its wildlife and its solitude. In 1954, he challenged the editors of the *Washington Post*, who had endorsed the idea of a parkway, to hike the 189-mile canal from Washington to Cumberland, Maryland. Douglas's weighty influence as a Supreme Court justice attracted the attention of the Wilderness Society and other environmentally concerned individuals. The editors of the *Post* accepted Douglas's challenge and ultimately changed their opinion. The well-publicized hike generated all kinds of interest and annual reunion hikes to maintain the issue's prominence. In 1961, Pres. Dwight D. Eisenhower declared the C & O Canal a national monument, and in 1971 it was declared a national historic park.

Douglas's next fight was in 1958, to prevent the building of a road along an ocean beach in Olympic National Park in Washington State. Local business interests were lobbying for a new road that would wind along the beach to make the area more accessible to automobiles. Having hiked the beach before, Douglas felt it possessed a special quality worthy of protection. Along the lines of his successful C & O Canal protest, Douglas and local activist POLLY DYER organized a three-day, 22-mile hike along the primitive beach to gain publicity for the beach's protection. This tactic succeeded again, and the road was never built.

Douglas's interests in preserving hiking or outdoors areas were not simply for aesthetic values or interests. In his first book of nature writing, *My Wilderness: The Pacific West*, published in 1960, Douglas explained the deeper issues involved in the 1958 fight. Providing both a natural and cultural history of the region, Douglas offered a number of ecological lessons relevant to the proposed road and its impact on both terrestrial and marine wildlife.

For most of Douglas's tenure on the Supreme Court, few environmentally charged cases came to the tribunal. When they did, Douglas likely dissented from the majority opinion in favor of environmental protection but was largely unable to change existing environmental law. Nevertheless, his activity in the public forum and his eloquence on environmental matters remain a significant aspect of his lasting environmental legacy.

Douglas died January 19, 1980, at Walter Reed Army Hospital in Washington, D.C., with his children and wife at his side. In 1984, Douglas received the posthumous honor of having 166,000 rugged, roadless acres adjacent to Mt. Ranier National Park designated the "William O. Douglas Wilderness."

BIBLIOGRAPHY

Bosmajian, Haig, "The Imprint of the Cascade Country on William O. Douglas," *Journal of the West*, 1993; Douglas, William O., *My Wilderness: East to Katahdin*, 1961; Douglas, William O., *My Wilderness: The Pacific West*, 1960; Douglas, William O., *A Wilderness Bill of Rights*, 1965; Sowards, Adam M., "William O. Douglas: The Environmental Justice and the American West," in Regan Lutz and Benson Tong, eds., *The Human Tradition in the American West*, 2001.

Dowie, Mark

(May 20, 1939–)
Investigative Reporter, Editor, Publisher

Mark Dowie's journalism career, which includes working as publisher and editor of *Mother Jones* magazine, has earned him 17 major journalism awards for his coverage of important social and environmental issues. While working at *Mother Jones*, Dowie broke the stories on the Dalkon Shield and the Ford Pinto and helped launch provocative investigations of unethical corporate practices. Through the course of his investigative reporting, Dowie became critical of the current mainstream environmental movement, believing that it should abandon diplomatic tactics and attempts at "win-win" capitulation with corporate polluters. In his book *Losing Ground: American Environmentalism at the Close of the Twentieth Century* (1995), nominated for a Pulitzer Prize, he promotes a new form of environmentalism, one that is diverse in class, race, and gender and strongly linked to grassroots human rights movements.

Mark Dowie was born in Toronto, Ontario, on May 20, 1939, the son of Ian and Shan (Campbell) Dowie. When he was eight years old his family moved to Cleveland, Ohio. He attended Denison University, receiving his B.A. in English in 1962. From the time he graduated from college to the time he went into journalism, Dowie pursued several careers, many of which prepared him well for investigative reporting. He worked in metal prospecting and investment banking and then helped operate a cattle ranch in Wyoming in the early 1960s. He then moved to San Francisco, where he went to graduate school in economics at the University of California; he later coordinated long-range economic planning at Industrial Indemnity from 1966 to 1969. He eventually became involved in prisoners' rights and acted as executive director of Transitions, Incorporated, an employment project for ex-prisoners, from 1969 to 1974. In 1974, he published *Transitions to Freedom: Comparative Community Response to the Return of Imprisoned Convicts*, the first step in his career in journalism.

In 1976, Dowie began working for *Mother Jones*, a newly launched progressive magazine offering investigative articles and promoting activism and social change. By getting involved at such an early stage at the magazine, he was able to influence its scope and help the magazine break new ground. He wrote a landmark investigative article for *Mother Jones* in 1977 about Ford Motor Company's safety problems. Titled "Pinto Madness," the article stated publicly for the first time that Ford Motor Company had made unethical decisions regarding the production of the Ford Pinto by opting for maximum profit instead of safety. Dowie made the claim that in order to make the Pinto lightweight and inexpensive, certain safety measures were neglected, leaving the fuel tank unnecessarily vulnerable to rupture in the event of rear-end collisions. Furthermore, Ford engineers were aware of this defect through pre-production crash tests, but they proceeded with the manufacturing process anyway, since the assembly-line machinery was already set up for production. Dowie went on to expose the fact that Ford Motor Company spent eight years fighting against and effectively delaying the implementation of a governmental safety standard that would have forced the company to redesign the Pinto's unsafe gas tank. The article won a National Magazine Award from the Columbia University School of Journalism in 1978.

Dowie had also written an earlier article for the magazine revealing the corporate history of the Dalkon Shield, a poorly designed intrauterine device that killed at least 17 women and injured hundreds more before a federal investigation forced its manufacturers to take it off the market. In researching corporate documents on the case, Dowie had noticed that the total number of the devices far exceeded the sum of those sold and recalled in the United States. He discovered that one million of the dangerous Dalkon Shields had been exported to 42 countries, many of them poor, developing countries. Over the next three years, Dowie gathered information on many similar cases involving unsafe products banned in the United States, such as toxic pesticides, tainted foods, known carcinogens, and defective medical devices that were being "dumped" on other countries. *Mother Jones* assembled an investigative team to write up a special report on U.S. policies that allowed corporations to sell shiploads of these products, mostly to Third World nations. In an attempt to pressure the Carter administration and Congress into banning the practice, *Mother Jones* staff delivered copies of the issue with the investigative report on dumping to every embassy in Washington, D.C., to all delegations at the U.N., and to major newspapers throughout the world.

Dowie was publisher of *Mother Jones* from 1977 to 1980 and then editor from 1980 to 1985, and during his years at the magazine he was responsible for many revealing and environmentally relevant investigative reports. He left the magazine in the mid-1980s, but continued writing. In 1995, Dowie published *Losing Ground: American Environmentalism at the Close of the Twentieth Century*, a critique of the mainstream environmental movement. In the book, he made clear his frustration that the movement had not lived up to its potential and was in fact "courting irrelevance." He followed the history of environmentalism, starting with conservation notions at the turn of the century, up to the debut of the conception of the "environment" as including both the human and the natural habitat, which occurred with the publication of RACHEL CARSON's *Silent Spring* (1962). But increasing motivation over the next two decades to preserve wilderness and enact environmental legislation was roadblocked during the 1980s by the Reagan administration. During the 1990s, Dowie wrote, environmentalism was shackled by a bureaucratic attempt to find a happy medium between politicians and corporate polluters. The mainstream environmental groups were becoming too close to and too much like the industries they claimed to fight, and phrases such as "nonadversarial dialogue" became their buzzwords. The hope Dowie held for the future of environmentalism lay in true grassroots movements linked to civil rights, involved men and women of all cultures and races, and included urban as well as rural issues. The diversity and activism of these groups would make them able to more powerfully assert society's rights to a satisfactory environment, Dowie believed.

After the publication of *Losing Ground*, Dowie turned his attention on foundations in the United States and in 2001 published *American Foundations: An Investigative History*. This book examines the role in our society of the 50,000 American foundations—and the $400 billion in assets that they control.

In addition to his research and writing, Dowie teaches at the University of California, Berkeley's Graduate School of Journalism.

BIBLIOGRAPHY

Dowie, Mark, "A Case of Corporate Malpractice: The Corporate History of the Dalkon Shield Intrauterine Device," *Mother Jones*, 1976; Dowie, Mark, *Losing Ground: American Environmentalism at the Close of the Twentieth Century*, 1995; Dowie, Mark, "Pinto Madness," *Mother Jones*, 1977; Dowie, Mark, "The Hidden Cost of Paradise," *Stanford Social Innovation Review*, 2006; Hochschild, Adam, "Dumping Our Mistakes on the World," *Mother Jones*, 1979.

Downing, Andrew Jackson
(October 30, 1815—1852)
Landscape Designer, Writer, Horticulturist

A.J. Downing, horticulturist, landscape designer, architect, and writer, is considered the "father of landscape gardening and of public parks" in America. He designed and landscaped the grounds for the Capitol, the White House and the Smithsonian Institute. Downing was a lifelong advocate for public parks so that the urban rich and poor alike could have beautiful, natural places to visit.

Born Andrew Jackson Downing on October 30, 1815, in Newburgh, New York, A.J. Downing grew up in an environment dedicated to plants, where his father owned a nursery specializing in apples and pears. Downing was born at a time when America was seeing unprecedented wealth and the development of a new, bourgeois society that had the time and money to spend on beautifying their lifestyles. Downing, with his brother, began working in his father's nursery at a young age and in 1838 became sole owner. This was also the year he married a grandniece of JOHN QUINCY ADAMS.

Downing, a voracious reader, began writing articles for various magazines when he was only 17, mainly about landscape gardening. His greatest influence was the English horticultural writer, J.C. Loudon, who proselytized for simple but beautiful styles as a means of enriching one's life and for public spaces to be enjoyed by all classes.

Downing became a landscape designer and founded and edited the magazine *The Horticulturist*. In 1841, at the age of 26, Downing published his first book that would make him famous: *A Treatise on the Theory and Practice of Landscape Gardening, Adapted to North America: With a View to the Improvement of Country Residences*. His other books include *Cottage Residences* (1842), *Fruit and Fruit Trees of America* (1845), and *The Architecture of Country Houses, Including Designs for Cottages, Farm Houses, and Villas* (1850). In all of his books, Downing called for urban planning and home designs that complement nature.

In *Rural Essays*, he writes:

> "The taste of an individual, as well as that of a nation, will be in direct proportion to the profound sensibility with which he perceives the beautiful in natural scenery. Open wide, therefore, the doors of your libraries and picture galleries all ye true republicans! Build halls where knowledge shall be freely diffused among men, and not shut up within the narrow walls of narrower institutions. Plant spacious parks in your cities, and unclose their gates as wide as the gates of morning to the whole people."

In 1850, Downing was commissioned to design and landscape the grounds for the Capitol, the White House and the Smithsonian Institute. His design for Lafayette Park remains unchanged to this day. This was the same year that he traveled to England to study English landscape design and met the young architect Calvert Vaux. Vaux returned to America with Downing and they partnered in designing and landscaping country estates along the Hudson River. Downing introduced Vaux to his friend, FREDERICK LAW OLMSTEAD, and the three men began designing plans for a large park in New York City that would include gardens, zoos, concert halls, art galleries, a science museum, horticultural societies and a free dairy. The park was intended to be a place for all classes of society to enjoy nature.

In 1852 at the age of 36, while designing the plans for the park, the paddle steamer that Downing and his family took to travel from Newburgh to New York City caught on fire and Downing drowned. Vaux and Olmsted continued their work on what was to become Central Park. After his death, his wife, Caroline, made an urn for Downing which now resides at the Smithsonian Institute.

BIBLIOGRAPHY

Downing, Andrew Jackson, preface to *A Treatise on the Theory and Practice of Landscape Gardening*, 1841; Elliott, Charles, "A.J. Downing, Garden Evangelist," *Horticulture*; www.fredericklawolmsted.com/ajdowning.htm; www.uvm.edu/pss/ppp/ajd.htm; hcs.osu.edu/hort/history/159.html; www.gardenvisit.com/biography/andrew_jackson_downing; www.buffaloah.com/a/archsty/ital/index.html#era.

Drayton, William
(June 15, 1943–)
Social Entrepreneur, Founder and President of Ashoka

William Drayton founded the international fellowship Ashoka in 1980 to enable "social entrepreneurs" (highly ethical, motivated people with revolutionary ideas for improving society, who possess the problem-solving ability to implement them) to devote themselves full time to putting into practice their vision of change. Ashoka's fellowships—which take the form of a living expense stipend for three years—generally come at the crucial point in which its fellows are just launching their projects. Ashoka support allows them to develop and disseminate their ideas and to build stable institutions through which they can continue to work after the financial support ceases. More than 2,000 Ashoka fellows work in 60 countries worldwide, on projects concerning virtually every aspect of human need.

Born on June 15, 1943, in New York City, William Drayton was a natural entrepreneur from an early age. One of the first entrepreneurial experiences he remembers was selling small items to his parents' dinner guests; another was publishing an elementary school newspaper with 60 pages of advertising. At Phillips Academy, Drayton founded the Asia Society, which became one of the school's most popular student organizations. While studying at Harvard, Drayton created the Ashoka Table, dinners at which prominent government, union, and religious leaders explained, off the record, the inner workings of their organizations. Drayton founded Yale Legislative Services at Yale Law School, which at its peak attracted one-third of the law school's student body. Drayton graduated with an A.B. from Harvard College in 1965; earned his M.A. from Balliol College, Oxford University, in 1967; and received his J.D. from Yale Law School in 1970.

Drayton began working for New York–based McKinsey & Company in 1970, helping a wide range of clients (government, corporations, foundations) solve management and policy problems. He taught at Stanford Law School from 1975 to 1976 and taught regulatory and management reform at Harvard's John F. Kennedy School of Government in 1977. He worked with President JIMMY CARTER's transition planning team, designing regulatory and management reform programs for such areas as airline and trucking deregulation and civil service reform. During Carter's term in office, Drayton served as assistant administrator of the Environmental Protection Agency (EPA). Among his chief accomplishments was the design and implementation of a flexible, market-like approach to regulation that encouraged industry to meet environmental goals in efficient, yet enforceable ways. He proposed tradeable pollution rights, similar to what the presidential administration of Bill Clinton implemented 20 years later in its attempt to decrease emissions of ozone-depleting gasses. When President Reagan's administration took over in 1981 and tried to weaken the EPA, Drayton became president of Save EPA, an association of prominent environmental managers that worked to limit the damage. Save EPA was renamed Environmental Safety in 1983. It serves as a monitor of the EPA and offers pro bono counsel and analysis to senior executive branch and legislative leaders. Drayton still serves as its chair.

During the late 1970s Drayton and a group of friends began laying the foundation for what officially in 1980 became Ashoka. The organization was named for an Indian leader of the third century B.C. who, after successfully uniting India by force, was stricken by great remorse. Ashoka renounced violence and dedicated the rest of his life to promoting social welfare, economic justice, and religious tolerance. Drayton and his covisionaries spent their vacations during the late 1970s looking for people who embodied Ashoka's approach. They traveled in India, Indonesia, and Venezuela, countries selected for their variation in size and culture, seeking effective innovators who dedicated themselves to the public good. They amassed a database that included hundreds of "social entrepreneurs."

By 1981 Ashoka had raised enough funds to begin its second phase: offering fellowships to selected social entrepreneurs whose work in the fields of environment, poverty alleviation, women's issues, and disability was very promising and who were at the particularly vulnerable early stages of their innovative projects. With a goal similar to that of venture capital investors, Ashoka sought fellows whose innovations for the public good would yield great social "profit" if moderate funding came at the right time.

Ashoka fellows are selected through a rigorous process consisting of several screenings, reference checks, and interviews with in-country and out-of-country Ashoka representatives. The fellowships take the form of a stipend for living expenses for three years and are tailored to the fellow's needs. Ashoka does not fund projects; it expects its fellows to mobilize financing from local sources or to make the project self-financing.

In 1984, Drayton was awarded a $200,000 MacArthur Foundation grant. This enabled him to quit his job at McKinsey & Company and dedicate himself full-time to Ashoka. He has raised millions of dollars, mostly from U.S. and international foundations, and has allied with several major global companies that donate expertise to support Ashoka's social entrepreneurs.

One of the more than 2,000 fellows working in 60 countries is Albina Ruíz Ríos, of Lima, Peru, who developed a successful program to pick up garbage in poor neighborhoods where the government had discontinued its garbage collection service. She set up several microbusinesses that hired employees from the neighborhoods as garbage collectors. Residents are encouraged to pay the monthly fee for the collection through incentives. Prompt payers in a neighborhood built on a barren hillside get a tree planted in their front yard and a sticker for their window that says "This house is clean." The household with the most prompt payment record gets gifts such as food baskets. These poor neighborhoods have better payment records than Lima's wealthier neighborhoods with government garbage collection. Currently, more than three million low-income Limeños are clients of Ruíz Ríos's companies. Her case illustrates the approach of Ashoka: contributing to substantial social change that affects a large number of people, by investing in a single individual with the outstanding qualities of a social entrepreneur.

One of Ashoka's criteria is that the work of fellows be replicable, so that it can be implemented elsewhere. Ashoka looks for people that Drayton says will leave their "scratch on history," people who will set or change national or regional patterns. After the initial fellowship ceases, support continues in the form of a lifelong association with Ashoka and its worldwide network of social entrepreneurs.

In addition to serving as President of Ashoka, Drayton works with several other organizations. He is chair of three groups: Youth Venture (www.genv.net), which helps community groups provide youth with the support they need to undertake their own projects, ranging from producing their own radio programs to setting up a teen counseling phone service; Get America Working (www.getamericaworking.org), which works to create job opportunities for this country's unemployed; and Community Greens (www.communitygreens.org), an organization that promotes the development of open spaces that will be collectively owned and cared for by those whose homes are adjacent to them. Drayton has received many awards for his work: The Yale School of Management gave him the 1987 Award for Entrepreneurial Excellence; he received the 1995 National Public Service Award from the National Academy of Public Administration and the American Society for Public Administration; in 1996 he was elected Member of the American Academy of Arts and Sciences in 2005 he was selected by both *U.S. News and World Report* and Harvard's Center for Public Leadership as one of America's Best Leaders, and in 2006 Harvard University recognized him as one of its 100 most influential alumni.

BIBLIOGRAPHY

"Ashoka," www.ashoka.org; Bornstein, David, "Changing the World on a Shoestring," *Atlantic Monthly*, 1999; Hammonds, Keith H., "A Lever Long Enough to Move the World," *Fast Company*, 2005; Holmstrom, David, "Change Happens, One Entrepreneur at a Time," *Christian Science Monitor*, 1999; Hsu, Caroline, "Entrepreneur for Social Change," *U. S. News and World Report*, 2005.

Drury, Newton
(April 9, 1889–December 14, 1978)
National Park Service Director

Generally castigated for allowing Bureau of Reclamation surveyors to study dam sites in Dinosaur National Monument in 1941 and for his involvement (or lack thereof) in the Echo Park controversy of 1949–1956, Newton Drury's positive work as director of the National Park Service (NPS) from 1940 to 1951 has gone largely unnoticed. The conventional criticism of Drury's tenure tends to ignore his first nine years as director, when he successfully arrested proposals to exploit park resources for the World War II effort and fought against the Bridge Canyon and Glacier View Dams. In an age of high development, Drury believed that the federal government had a duty to protect places where the aesthetic should have primacy over the economic. This commitment, which bucked the tradition of the period's often blind pursuit of economic interests, ensured that national parks in the United States would remain intact for future generations.

Newton Bishop Drury, the son of Wells, a newspaper editor in Virginia City, Nevada, and San Francisco, California, and Ella Bishop Drury, was born April 9, 1889, in San Francisco. Drury attended the University of California, Berkeley, and graduated in 1912. He worked at the university for several years following his graduation, teaching English and forensics and assisting the university's president, then served in World War I with the Army Balloon Corps. After the armistice, he returned to San Francisco and together with his brother Aubrey, who eventually wrote a highly acclaimed guidebook to California, ran an advertising and public relations agency. In 1919, Drury became the first executive secretary (the functional equivalent of executive director today) of the Save-the-Redwoods League. This organization, which was founded with the help of National Park Service director STEPHEN MATHER, managed during Drury's 21-year tenure to directly purchase some 50,000 acres of redwood groves and convince the state of California to buy nearly half a million acres more for state parks. Some historians consider this Drury's greatest contribution to conservation.

Drury declined appointment as director of the National Park Service when HORACE ALBRIGHT retired in 1933, because he opposed Albright's expansion into areas that Drury felt were more the concern of state and local governments. Like many preservationists, Drury had grown alarmed by the direction the NPS took during the New Deal. In an effort to create jobs for organizations such as the Civilian Conservation Corps (CCC), the size and nature of the agency's jurisdiction expanded to include not only new national parkland (some of which many preservationists saw as less than worthy of the name), but also a host of monuments, historic sites, and buildings. Drury, who was a purist, believed that the NPS should revert to its original mission of managing and preserving natural areas of truly spectacular natural beauty.

By 1940, when NPS director Arno Cammerer suffered a heart attack and resigned, the Park Service's reputation as a preservation agency had suffered greatly. The National Parks Association, a nonprofit organization that monitored the NPS and defended national parks from private incursions and commercial interests, had opposed some park proposals on the grounds that the land was not suitable for parks. Groups such as the Wilderness Society and the Sierra Club objected to CCC developments within the parks. In order to avoid further controversy, Secretary of the Interior HAROLD ICKES decided to look outside the Park Service for a new director whose preservationist credentials were impeccable. Drury's work with Save-the-Redwoods had gained him a national reputation, and his character was exactly what Ickes was looking for. Even though he had declined the position seven years earlier, Drury accepted this offer and on August 20, 1940, became the National Park Service's fourth director, the first without any prior Park Service responsibilities.

Less eager than his predecessors to expand the Park System, Drury opposed NPS involvement in areas he judged not to meet national park standards. Fewer than 20 new areas were added during Drury's 11 years as director, and most were small. The largest—Coulee Dam National Recreation Area (99,000 acres) and Theodore Roosevelt National Memorial Park (70,000 acres)—were both areas that Stephen Mather, the first director of the National Park Service, had opposed. That Drury's tenure coincided with World War II might also have contributed to Drury's less-than-eager approach to enlarge the National Park System.

Drury might have had a greater effect on the Park Service had his directorship not coincided with World War II. When the war began, the Park Service and other "nonessential" agencies were moved to Chicago. This move resulted in the agency's lack of contact with Congress and Congress's subsequent 50 percent reduction in park budgets and staffing to help fund the war effort. Nevertheless, Drury fought hard to prevent the exploitation of the natural resources in the national parks to aid the war effort. The problems only intensified after the war, as the agency did not return to Washington, D.C., until 1947. While its budget increased somewhat during the following two years, the Korean War in 1949 threatened further cuts. Albright, who continued to be an influential adviser to NPS directors, and conservation groups such as the Sierra Club and the Wilderness Society lobbied hard to prevent the threatened cuts. Weakened by his distance from Congress, Drury witnessed such groups becoming prominent in battling his causes for him. As such, Drury's work as director is often considered weak.

Nevertheless, Drury was successful in the fight against the Glacier View Dam, which the Army Corps of Engineers sought to build in Glacier National Park in the late 1940s. He also led the struggle against the construction of Bridge Canyon Dam, which would have affected Grand Canyon National Park and Monument. Such activity suggests that Drury was not the timid appeaser many historians have described.

Drury was also active, though arguably equally ineffective, in the controversy that led to his resignation. The Bureau of Reclamation wanted to build dams in Dinosaur National Monument, and in 1944 Drury approved a Park Service study of Dinosaur that suggested that dams could be constructed within the monument. To protect the purity of the national monument concept, the area would be downgraded to a national recreation area. The report was given to the Bureau of Reclamation, which began planning for the dams. In 1947, Drury visited Dinosaur National Monument for the first time. Impressed by the scenery, Drury immediately regretted having originally supported the dam proposal. In 1948, the Park Service submitted a report to the Bureau of Reclamation stating that a dam would be incompatible with Dinosaur National Monument. Feeling betrayed, the Bureau of Reclamation leaked the report to dam supporters, who demanded that Congress approve the dam. Under siege, Drury agreed to a compromise that would allow dams in the monument but at different, less damaging sites than had originally been proposed. But the situation was already too polarized, with other park officials opposed to any dams. Accused of hypocrisy by the Bureau of Reclamation, Drury was forced to resign by Interior Secretary Oscar L. Chapman in 1951, leaving other dam opponents, such as the Sierra Club, to win glory in preventing the dams after years of debate.

In 1951, Drury became director of the California Division of Beaches and Parks. During his tenure there, much of the State Park System's share of shore oil royalties, which had been suspended in 1947, began to flow once again. The extra income allowed Drury to expand the system so that, by 1959, when he retired at the age of 70, the California State Park System was composed of 150 beaches, parks, and historic monuments, which covered 615,000 acres.

Drury was the recipient of two Pugsley awards, one in 1940 and the other in 1950, given by the American Academy for Park and Recreation Administration to recognize contributions to and development of public parks in the U.S.

Drury died in Berkeley, California, December 14, 1978. He was 89 years old.

Bibliography

Harvey, Mark, *A Symbol of Wilderness: Echo Park and the American Conservation Movement*, 1994; Ise, John, *Our National Park Policy: A Critical History*, 1961; Neel, Susan Rhoades, "Irreconcilable Differences: Reclamation, Preservation and the Origins of the Echo Park Controversy," Ph.D. dissertation, UCLA, 1990; "Newton Drury," www.rpts.tamu.edu/Pugsley/Drury.htm; Pearson, Byron, "Newton Drury of the National Park Service: A Reappraisal," in *Pacific Historical Review*, 1999; Shankland, Robert, *Steve Mather of the National Parks*, 1970.

Dubos, René

(February 20, 1901–February 20, 1982)
Microbiologist

René Dubos was a soil microbiologist who discovered the enzymes in soil microbes that were used as the world's first antibiotic drugs. In his work, he learned that the environmental conditions to which soil microbes are subjected will affect their many characteristics and capabilities. Transferring this observation to the larger world, Dubos discovered that all organisms are affected in this way by their environment: their environment helps determine which of their varied capabilities emerge. Dubos was disturbed by wanton environmental destruction and in the early 1960s became an outspoken advocate for the nascent environmental movement of that time.

René Jules Dubos was born in Saint-Brice, France, a small village outside of Paris, on February 20, 1901. A severe case of rheumatic fever at the age of eight robbed him of his aspirations to race bicycles or play professional tennis. His convalescence included long walks in the countryside, and Dubos developed an appreciation during this period of that area's beautiful pastoral landscape. As a teenager he read an essay by philosopher Hippolyte Taine about the effect that that particular landscape had on French fable-writer La Fontaine, whose stories most French children grow up hearing. The idea that an environment had a great effect upon its inhabitants was one that Dubos would return to throughout his professional life.

Dubos and his parents moved to Paris and opened a butcher shop just before World War I broke out. His father was soon called to military service and died of a war injury when Dubos was 18 years old. Dubos finished secondary school on scholarship and was set to attend a college that specialized in physics and chemistry, when his rheumatic fever recurred. Once he recovered, there was only one college in Paris that was still accepting new students so late into the school year, the National Institute of Agronomy. He enrolled there and graduated with a B.S. degree in 1921, but so disliked his courses that he determined to never again enter a laboratory. Dubos moved in 1922 to Rome, where he worked as associate editor for an agricultural journal. While in Rome, he read a paper by Russian soil bacteriologist Sergei Winogradsky that immediately made sense to him and inspired him to return to microbiology. The paper postulated that soil microbes should not be isolated and studied in laboratories but instead must be studied in their own environment so that their interactions with other soil bacteria can be observed.

Dubos traveled to the United States in hopes that he could study there. On board the ship, Dubos met Selman Waksman, a soil scientist from Rutgers University whom he had previously led on a tour of Rome. Waksman and another colleague whom Dubos had met in Rome, Jacob Lipman, set up Dubos at Rutgers, and within three years he had earned his Ph.D. in soil microbiology. Dubos's thesis was about how environmental conditions determine the ability of soil bacteria to digest cellulose. In 1927, after receiving his Ph.D., Dubos met Oswald Avery at the Rockefeller Institute for Medical Research. Avery was a physician who was researching pneumococcus, the bacteria that causes lobar pneumonia. Avery believed that the cure for pneumonia lay in discovering how to dissolve the polysaccharide capsule encasing pneumococcus. Dubos offered to test soil bacteria for such an agent—cellulose is a polysaccharide commonly found in soil, so he felt it was likely that another soil microbe might digest the pneumococcus polysaccharide. Avery helped Dubos obtain a fellowship to the Rockefeller Institute, and Dubos set out into the bogs of New Jersey in search of the right bacterium. Within three years, Dubos had discovered a bacterium that could eat the polysaccharide capsule and isolated the particular enzyme that digested it. Work on the enzyme as a cure for pneumonia would have continued had it not been for the emergence of sulfa drugs as an effective cure for the disease.

What was most interesting to Dubos about this project was that the bacterium in question produced the enzyme it needed to digest the polysaccharide only when there was no other food source available. This was an observation that Dubos realized had many implications: organisms have diverse capabilities, and many of these capabilities will emerge only in response to certain environmental conditions.

Dubos continued his work to develop new antibacterial substances during the 1930s. In 1939 he discovered tyrothricin, which contained the antibacterials gramicidin and tyrocidine. He insisted that the drugs he discovered be referred to as antibacterial or antimicrobial as opposed to "antibiotic" (or "antilife"), because he felt these were medicines that restored life.

In 1942, Dubos's wife Marie Louise Bonnet died of tuberculosis. His grief at her loss led him to look for a cure for the disease and also to question why the disease, which she had had as a child, reemerged at that time. Dubos had moved to Harvard in 1942 but returned to the Rockefeller Institute two years later to open a department dedicated to tuberculosis research. By 1947 he had discovered a way to breed large numbers of the tuberculosis bacilli without their mutating to become vastly different from the form that causes tuberculosis in humans. This enabled other researchers to develop the Bacille Capmette-guérin (BCG) vaccine, still used today. His research on the causes of tuberculosis also led him to believe that people's early environment and nutrition have a long-term effect on their health. He believed that a healthy child would have a much better chance for a long, healthy life and that social reforms that would improve environment and nutrition for all children were of moral necessity. Dubos's second wife, Jean Porter, whom he married in 1946, also contracted tuberculosis but managed to recover. Together, they wrote the 1952 exploration of the disease, *The White Plague: Tuberculosis, Man, and Society*.

The realization that illness is caused by more than just microbes, together with his deep humanism, led him to write prolifically for a general audience about medicine, human adaptability, and the environment. His three books *Man Adapting*, *Man, Medicine and Environment*, and *So Human an Animal* celebrate the ability of all organisms to adapt to varied environments but also reveal humanity's particularly awesome adaptation skills as a double-edged sword. Humans are so adaptable that they could very easily adapt to the worst manifestations of modern life: pollution, a landscape devoid of beauty, a joyless life. Despite this worry, however, Dubos parted from the emerging environmental movement of the 1970s with his insistence that people were not enemies of nature but rather had the potential to restore health to their environment. Dubos believed that people need to understand the value of a healthy natural environment and that they must protect it in order to live to their full potential. He believed that a healthy environment was a natural right. He was inspired by a grassroots movement in Queens, New York, to clean up Jamaica Bay and resist the expansion of Kennedy Airport onto a landfill in the bay. A peninsula into the bay is now named Dubos Point Wetland Park.

Dubos received many awards and honorary degrees for his work in health and the environment. After his retirement from Rockefeller University in 1971, he became professor of environmental studies at the State University of New York, College at Purchase, and was an adviser at Richmond College on Staten Island. Dubos and his wife divided their time between their apartment in Manhattan and their estate in Garrison, New York, where they planted many trees and gardens. René Dubos died from heart failure in New York City on February 20, 1982, his 81st birthday.

BIBLIOGRAPHY
Moberg, Carol L., and Zanvil A. Cohn, "René Jules Dubos," *Scientific American*, 1991; Moberg, Carol L., and Zanvil A. Cohn, eds., *Launching the Antibiotic Era: Personal Accounts of the Discovery and Use of the First Antibiotics*, 1990; Piel, Gerard, and Osborn Segerberg Jr., eds., *The World of René Dubos: A Collection from his Writings*, 1990.

Dunlap, Louise
(February 7, 1946—)
Lobbyist, Co-founder of the Environmental Policy Institute and Environmental Policy Center

In 1976, Louise Dunlap became the first woman to hold the position of chief executive at a major U.S. environmental organization. In 1972, she co-founded the Environmental Policy Institute and Environmental Policy Center, and served as the president of these organizations from 1976 until 1986. Under her leadership these two groups grew to lead the largest environmental lobbying staff in Washington.

Louise Dunlap was born February 7, 1946 in Lancaster, Pennsylvania. She graduated from Duke University in 1968, and went on to be legislative assistant to the President of the National Parks and Conservation Association. From there she moved on to Friends of the Earth, where she served as Assistant Legislative Director from 1971 until 1972. During her tenure with the Environmental Policy Institute and Environmental Policy Center, she organized and led the seven-year national citizens' effort to enact the Surface Mine Control & Reclamation Act of 1977. This federal legislation requires the coal industry to restore farmlands, protect streams and wetlands, and to return mountain lands to their original contours and in a condition suitable for use equal to or better than their prior condition. Because of persistent violations of the law, she has joined citizen efforts to ban mountaintop mining.

In 1981, Dunlap joined forces with her husband and partner, Joe Browder, to form Dunlap & Browder, Inc., consultants to national and global energy, natural resource and industrial companies, to governments, Native American tribes, and to public interest organizations. Louise Dunlap and Joe Browder provide pro bono services to defend communities and environmental values.

From 1987 through 2002, Dunlap served as Washington, D.C. advisor on energy efficiency and transportation technologies and fuels for the California Energy Commission. She also served as advisor to the Chair of the California Air Resources Board and to the California

Louise Dunlap (Photograph courtesy of Louisa Santarelli Koplan)

Energy Commission Chairman regarding the Clean Air Act of 1990. She continues to advise CEC and the Natural Resources Defense Council on energy efficiency issues. She was a key strategist working to pass the Alternative Motor Fuels Act of 1988, which provided incentives for automobile companies to produce cars powered by alternative fuels. Additionally, she worked toward the development of the Energy Policy Acts of 1992, 2005 and subsequent federal energy and environmental policies. For more than ten years she and Joe Browder have advised Honda on environmental issues such as climate change and fuel efficiency.

In addition to having served as a member of the Board of Visitors of the Duke University Nicholas School of the Environment, Dunlap was a founding member of Duke University's Women's Studies Council, Senator Jay Rockefeller's National Alternative Fuels Task Force, and of the Democratic Women's Leadership Forum. Her leadership positions also include serving as Chair of the WLF Environment and Energy Task Force and serving on the boards of the League of Conservation Voters, Clean Water Fund, Scenic America, Environmental Policy Institute, and National Clean Air Coalition.

Dunlap has received numerous honors for her work, including recognition at a ceremony on the National Mall in commemoration of the 10th anniversary of the federal surface mine reclamation law in 1987. She also received recognition for global environmental leadership that year from the Friends of the United Nations Environment Programme. In 2008, the Pennsylvania AML campaign presented her with the Watershed Hero Award for her three-year effort helping achieve 2006 Congressional Renewal of the Abandoned Mine Lands Program of the federal strip mine reclamation law.

Dunlap lives in Fairhaven, Maryland, with her husband Joe Browder. She is currently working on advancement of the federal tax incentive programs for energy-efficient commercial buildings, schools, homes, and equipment included in the Energy Act of 2005. These programs are designed to significantly reduce greenhouse gas emission, the risks of electrical power blackouts, and reduce increases in the price of natural gas. She also focuses on programs to more accurately account for the environmental costs of coal production.

BIBLIOGRAPHY

Dunlap and Browder, Inc., www.dunlapbrowder.org/; "Controlling the Strippers," *TIME* Magazine Online. Oct. 22, 1973, www.time.com/time/magazine/article/0,9171,908078,00.html?promoid=googlep; Kenny, Robyn, "Surface Mining Control and Reclamation Act of 1977, United States," *Encyclopedia of Earth*, www.eoearth.org/article/Surface_Mining_Control_and_Reclamation_Act_of_1977,_United_States.

Durning, Alan

(November 7, 1964–)
Founder and Director of Sightline Institute, Writer

Alan Durning is founder and director of Sightline Institute, a private, nonprofit research organization that seeks to foster a sustainable economy and way of life in the Pacific Northwest. Durning has authored and contributed to numerous publications on a wide range of socioenvironmental topics.

Alan Durning (Photograph by Amy Chan).

Alan Thein Durning, the son of Marvin and Jean Durning, was born November 7, 1964, in Seattle, Washington. Durning grew up in Seattle but came from a family that had always roamed widely. Consequently, he aspired to the life of a world traveler, so much so that after his name in his grandmother's guest book, Durning, at the age of 11, wrote the title "world traveler."

Durning attended Oberlin College in Oberlin, Ohio, where he graduated with high honors in 1986, studying environmental policy but majoring in philosophy. While there, he also earned a Bachelor of Music degree from Oberlin Conservatory in trombone performance (he no longer plays). Shortly after college, Durning moved to Washington, D.C., where he joined the staff of the Worldwatch Institute, a research center that monitors the world's social and ecological health. After a few years of 70-hour weeks, Durning was promoted and began traveling the world, studying everything from poverty to atmospheric chemistry. "It was urgent stuff," he wrote in his award-winning book, *This Place on Earth*, "documenting injustice, testifying before Congress, jet-setting on behalf of future generations."

During this "jet-setting" period, Durning experienced something of an epiphany in the Philippines, while interviewing members of remote hill tribes about their land and livelihood. He met with an old, traditional priestess who asked him about his homeland. Durning did not know what to say. Home—when he was there—was Washington, D.C., a city he did not hold dear to his heart; crime and poverty were rampant. Durning abashedly replied that in the United States, people had careers, not places. Durning recalls that the old woman looked at him with pity. It was this encounter that persuaded Durning to focus on local issues rather than global ones.

Looking for a place to call home, Durning left Washington, D.C., and returned to Seattle. There, in 1993, he founded Northwest Environment Watch—which changed its name to Sightline Institute in 2006—a wholly independent research center designed to foster an environmentally sound economy and way of life in the Pacific Northwest—the biological region stretching from southeast Alaska to northern California and from the Pacific to the crest of the Rocky Mountains. Sightline Institute is predicated on the belief that if an environmentally sustainable economy cannot be created in the greenest part of history's richest civilization, it probably cannot be done. If it can be done, the Pacific Northwest will set an example for the world.

Sightline Institute serves as a monitor of the region's environmental conditions and a pathfinder for routes toward a lasting economy. Through action-oriented interdisciplinary research, Sightline Institute provides northwesterners with reliable information about what sustainable development is and how to achieve it. Five thousand residents of the Pacific Northwest a day consult Sightline Institute's daily blog or the many publications available on its website. Its newest publication is *Cascadia Scorecard*, which monitors regional socioenvironmental trends, for example per-person use of electricity, diesel and gasoline; suburban sprawl; and middle-class income.

According to its mission statement, Sightline Institute identifies and promotes long-term solutions for reconciling people and place, economy and ecology. One of its major tools is its series of publications, for which Durning is a prolific writer. The books in the series inform both generalists and experts of cutting-edge findings on a wide range of topics, such as the current health of ecosystems, the relationship between cars and cities, and the creation of green jobs. Durning's own publications include *This Place on Earth*, published in 1996, which was the winner of the 1997 Governor's Writers Award. *This Place on Earth* is part autobiographical as it recounts Durning's return to Seattle with his wife and family, the evolution of his own bioregional thinking, and the development of Sightline Institute. Sightline publications that Durning has written or contribute to include *Cascade Scorecard (2007)*, *Green-Collar Jobs* (1999), *Tax Shift* (1998), *Misplaced Blame* (1997), *The Car and the City* (1996), and *How Much Is Enough?* (1992), which has been translated into seven languages. As a general theme, Durning's work focuses on socially and ecologically sustainable living.

Durning has also coauthored seven of the Worldwatch Institute's State of the World reports and two of its Vital Signs reports. His articles have been published in *World Watch*, *Washington Post*, *Los Angeles Times*, *New York Times*, *Christian Science Monitor*, *International Herald Tribune*, *Foreign Policy*, *Sierra*, *Utne Reader*, *Technology Review*, and more than 100 other periodicals. A sought-after keynote speaker, he has lectured at the White House, major universities, and numerous conferences. In 1996, Durning was awarded a Building Economic Alternatives award by Co-op America for his work.

Durning continues to live and work in Seattle. He has three children, Gary, Kathryn, and Peter.

BIBLIOGRAPHY

Dietrich, William, "Seeing Green," *Seattle Times*, 2006; Durning, Alan, *Green-Collar Jobs: Working in the New Northwest*, 1999; Durning, Alan, and Yoram Bauman, *Tax Shift: How to Help the Economy, Improve the Environment, and Get the Tax Man off Our Backs*, 1998; Durning, Alan, and Christopher Crowther, *Misplaced Blame: The Real Roots of Population Growth*, 1997; Durning, Alan, and John C. Ryan, *Stuff: The Secret Lives of Everyday Things*, 1997; Roberts, Paul, "The Durning Point," *Utne Reader*, 1996; Ryan, John C., *State of the Northwest*, 1994; "Sightline Institute," www.sightline.org.

Dutcher, William
(January 20, 1846–July 1, 1920)
Amateur Ornithologist, First President of National Audubon Society

William Dutcher, a successful insurance agent for Prudential Life and expert amateur ornithologist, was a leader for the bird-protection legislation movement of the late nineteenth century and early twentieth century and a pioneer of the National Audubon Society's sanctuary program.

William Dutcher was born on January 20, 1846, in Shelton, New Jersey, and went to work at age 13. With little formal education,

William Dutcher (Library of Congress, Prints & Photographs Division, LC-USZ62-83949).

Dutcher became a very successful businessman and expert birder. His acquaintances spoke of "extraordinary personal qualities" that offset his lack of formal education. His interest in birds was showcased through his interest in hunting birds and his impressive collection of bird specimens from the Long Island and New Jersey shores. He wrote numerous respected scientific papers about birdlife in the region.

The American Ornithologists Union (AOU), at the American Museum of Natural History in New York, was founded in 1883 for "the protection and study of birds." That same year, Dutcher was elected as an associate member. He served as its treasurer for 14 years and rapidly became one of the most active members of its Committee on Bird Protection. He was especially interested in legislation that would protect North American birds, and with the Committee, he drafted model state legislation for nongame bird protection in 1886. During the late 1800s, birds were in high demand for their plumage, which was used to decorate women's hats and considered high fashion at the time.

In 1898, Senator George F. Hoar of Massachusetts introduced a bill in Congress that would have outlawed the importation, sale, or shipment of millinery plumes in the United States. The bill did not gain the support of the AOU, and many claimed that this was a primary reason for its failure. Congressman John F. Lacey of Iowa introduced a similar bill, called the Lacey Act, that prohibited intrastate shipment of birds and other animals if it violated state law, using the commerce clause from the U.S. Constitution that allows the federal government to regulate state trade. The AOU joined the effort to lobby for the Lacey bill, and it was passed in 1900. However, only five states had bird-protection legislation at the time.

The bird-protection movement by 1900 was fragmented. There were Audubon bird-watching and protection groups in many states, and some were passing bird-protection legislation, but Audubon groups were not unified in a singular effort. Dutcher suggested forming a union of state Audubon societies to create an impressive national front. In 1901, at a meeting of state Audubon groups, members decided that a national committee should be formed, and Dutcher was elected chairman. By 1903, there were 37 state societies, most of which were part of the national committee.

With the passage of the Lacey Act as well as the passage of bird-protection legislation by a growing number of states, Dutcher recognized the need for enforcement of the law on the ground in the individual states. In 1900, he initiated an enforcement system that evolved into the successful Audubon sanctuary and warden system. With the fundraising help of New Hampshire AOU member Abbott H. Thayer, the program began with the hiring of wardens to protect seabird colonies. The first wardens recruited were lighthouse keepers who were hired to post No Trespassing signs and watch the coast for bird poachers. By 1901, 27 wardens were working for the program. Dutcher organized questionnaires for the wardens to complete that provided a wealth of information about bird habitat, mating, and hatching. For example, the questionnaires included information about where the largest breeding colonies of each species were along the eastern seaboard.

By January 1903, the national committee of Audubon societies, under Dutcher's leadership, had fallen $700 in debt. An anonymous benefactor promised a legacy of $100,000 to be given to the Audubon Society if it incorporated immediately and promised to broaden its focus to include wild animals as well as birds. In 1905, the National Association of Audubon Societies for the Protection of Wild Birds and Animals was officially incorporated.

To help run the organization, Dutcher hired T. Gilbert Pearson as the first salaried, full-time Audubon executive. Together they supervised the warden system, lobbied for more bird-protection legislation, and initiated a bird education program for children. While Dutcher grew more fanatical in his belief for bird protection toward the end of his career (he eventually came to disagree with the taking of scientific specimens), Pearson served as a middle-of-the-road figure. Pearson was also effective as a fundraiser and public speaker for the association.

Dutcher's budgeting woes continued until 1907, when the association accumulated $8,000 worth of debt. Dutcher, responsible for the mismanaging, was reprimanded by the board of directors, and his control of the budget was limited. He resigned as president but was reinstated shortly after.

Dutcher remained dedicated to his work on bird-protection issues despite his managerial problems. Through education and legislation, Dutcher made significant progress in the work toward bird protection. As early as 1902, Dutcher insisted that educational programs would be essential to the success of the Audubon movement. He wrote educational leaflets for the National Committee of Audubon Societies until 1910. Each leaflet, focusing on one bird, consisted of four pages of text that described the bird's habitat and actions, accompanied by illustrations. At the end of the leaflet were tips for teachers and students on studying the bird. The education program did not do as well as Dutcher had hoped, largely for lack of funds, until 1906. At that time Margaret Olivia Slocum Sage, widow of Russell Sage, established the Russell Sage Foundation, which gave money for the education program. By 1915, there were 152,164 children enrolled in 7,728 Junior Audubon classes.

Toward the end of his career, in 1910, Dutcher was instrumental in the passage of the Audubon Plumage Bill in New York by Gov. Charles Evans Hughes. The bill prohibited the sale or possession of plumage of birds in the same family of any species protected in New York, including herons, egrets, gulls, terns, and songbirds. It gave milliners a year to use the prohibited feathers they had in stock. Although the law pertained only to New York, that state was the main center of the millinery activity. While Pearson lobbied for the bill, Dutcher was the mastermind behind it.

On October 19, 1910, Dutcher suffered a paralyzing stroke that prohibited him from speaking or writing again, although he lived for ten more years. Dutcher retained the title of president while Pearson succeeded him as executive officer of the Audubon Association. Dutcher died July 1, 1920.

BIBLIOGRAPHY

Fox, Stephen, *The American Conservation Movement, John Muir and His Legacy*, 1981; Graham, Frank, Jr., *The Audubon Ark*, 1990; Stroud, Richard, ed., *National Leaders of American Conservation*, 1985.

Dyer, Polly

(February 4, 1920–)
Wilderness Preservation Activist

Polly Dyer has been a major force behind wilderness protection efforts in the Pacific Northwest. She was one of the few women involved in the conservation debates of the 1950s and 1960s, and once her talent for organizing environmental activists was revealed, she quickly rose to coordinate protection campaigns for Olympic, Mt. Rainier, and North Cascades National Parks. She has cofounded four regional conservation organizations and two state chapters for national groups, and for 40 years, from 1964 to 2004, she organized Northwest Wilderness Conferences, initially for the Federation of Western Outdoor Clubs, and after 1984 under the auspices of the Northwest Wilderness and Park Conference.

Polly Dyer was born Pauline Tomkiel on February 4, 1920, in Honolulu, Hawaii. Her father was a career officer in the United States Coast Guard, and the family moved frequently. It was not until they moved to Ketchikan, Alaska, in 1940 that Dyer discovered wilderness and an appreciation and love for the natural world. She explored the natural areas near Ketchikan, and one day climbed to the top of Deer Mountain, where she was awed by the beautiful, wild expanse in view. During another hike up Deer Mountain, she met John Dyer, a young chemical engineer and world-class rock climber who had moved to Ketchikan from the San Francisco Bay area in 1943. The two married in 1945. John Dyer had been an officer for the Bay Area chapter of the Sierra Club, and Polly Dyer quickly became interested in the club's conservation work. Together they were active in a local Ketchikan conservation group that John had helped found.

The Dyers remained involved in conservation causes when they moved to Berkeley, California, in 1947 and then to Auburn, Washington, in 1950. In Washington, they and another couple cofounded the Pacific Northwest chapter of the Sierra Club, the club's first definitive step toward becoming a national organization. They also joined the Mountaineers, a Washington-based hiking and conservation organization. The couple backpacked in the Cascade and Olympic mountain ranges, and Polly Dyer led a Girl Scout troop, emphasizing hiking over arts and crafts.

Dyer became secretary for the Mountaineers' Conservation Committee in 1952, and in 1953 she represented the Mountaineers on the Washington governor's Olympic National Park Review Committee, to study and make recommendations for the possible removal of the west-side forests from the park. Two other conservationist women served on the 14-member committee, which was dominated by men (and one other woman) sympathetic to the timber industry. The committee's majority preferred reducing the size of the park, but its report recommended instead that a study be made by a "higher authority." The conservationist forces, joined by two other members representing trade unions, wrote a minority report to oppose reduction. It was known that the governor agreed with the majority, but Dyer and the other conservationists had mobilized their organizations to send so many letters to the committee that he subsequently responded that there was no need for further study.

This was the first of what would be Dyer's many major organizing efforts on behalf of wilderness preservation. She continued to defend Olympic National Park from constant attempts during the 1950s by the timber industry to log the parks, even testifying before the U.S. Senate in 1955. Rayonier, a timber company owning substantial forest land on the Olympic Peninsula, tried to ridicule Dyer and other women preservationists in a full-page national magazine advertisement that showed women scolding loggers. The advertisement explained that the women proposed wasting potential timber because they believed that trees should "reach maturity, die, topple over, and rot."

In 1956, a scenic highway was proposed for the new coastal strip of Olympic National Park, the longest roadless portion of coastline in the continental United States. Brainstorming with colleagues from the Wilderness Society (TWS) about how to defeat this proposal, Dyer responded enthusiastically to TWS executive secretary HOWARD ZAHNISER's suggestion to invite Supreme Court justice WILLIAM O. DOUGLAS to lead a hike along the stretch. This hike would be similar to the well-publicized three-day hike he had led along the Chesapeake and Ohio Canal in 1954. Participants on that trek had been well-known conservationists and writers and editors from the *Washington Post*. The hike had convinced them to oppose plans to build an expressway there and instead to support Douglas's proposal to establish a national historic park. Douglas agreed to the Olympic Coast hike, and Dyer coordinated the 22-mile trip in August 1958. Seventy-two people participated, including the nation's best-known conservationists and several journalists. A 1964 reunion hike along the southern part of the park's coastal area drew more than 150 participants and once again drew public attention to the pristine, roadless beauty of the area. At the 2008 50th anniverary commemoration of the hike, Polly Dyer—at 88 years of age—was given a standing ovation before she able to say a word at the panel discussion she took part in.

In 1957, Dyer cofounded the North Cascades Conservation Council, the idea originating at a meeting in her living room. The council fought for national park designation for an area of mountainous national forest in northwest Washington that was slated for logging. Finally in 1968 the North Cascades National Park Complex, which includes Ross Lake and Lake Chelan National Recreation Areas, was designated. Dyer opposed the construction of the North Cascades Scenic Highway during the 1960s for its intrusion on unspoiled wilderness and was one of two women who accompanied Gov. Dan Evans on a 20-person horseback survey of the route.

Although Governor Evans supported the road project and presided at the opening of the road in 1972, he was a committed environmentalist, and he and Dyer remained allies. They had first worked together in the early 1960s, when he was a state legislator, on a bill that regulated billboards. Dyer participated in the lobbying effort for the Wilderness Act of 1964 and contributed some of its language. As governor, Evans appointed Dyer to the Forest Practices Board in 1974. She convinced him to add seven more miles of roadless coastline to Olympic National Park, including Shi Shi Beach and Point of the Arches. Once Evans was elected U.S. senator, Dyer worked with him to have areas within Olympic, Mount Rainier, and North Cascades National Parks designated as wilderness under the Wilderness Act, protecting them from logging, road building, new mining claims, dams, and off-the-road vehicles.

In addition to these major preservation accomplishments, Dyer has cofounded several state preservation groups. She cofounded Mount Rainier National Park Associates in 1958. She and three others from the governor's 1950s Olympic National Park Review Committee were invited to join the board of trustees of Olympic Park Associates. Both organizations act as watchdogs over their respective national parks. She has served on the boards of both of these groups and is currently president of Olympic Park Associates. In 1984 she cofounded and for two years served as president of the Puget Soundkeeper Alliance, which works with automotive shops, shipyards, and marinas along the sound to reduce water pollution. Dyer cofounded in 2003 the Olympic Coast Alliance (OCA), a nonprofit organization focused on the northwestern section of the Olympic Peninsula and works "...to assure a healthy coastal ecosystem through public education and outreach, conservation issue advocacy, Olympic Coast

National Marine Sanctuary support, stewardship programs, and a strong working relationship with coastal tribes," Dyer served as the OCA's first president.

Dyer organized biennial wilderness conferences for the Federation of Western Outdoor Clubs from 1964 to 1974 and then in 1984 to celebrate the 20th anniversary of the Wilderness Act, under the auspices of the Northwest Wilderness and Park Conference. These conferences have enthused and rallied activists, helped them network more effectively, and brought in new recruits to learn more about wilderness and how they could contribute to the effort.

Although all of the work mentioned thus far has been done as a volunteer, Dyer worked from 1974 to 1994 as continuing environmental education director at the University of Washington's Institute for Environmental Studies. Dyer earned a B.A. in geography in 1970 from the University of Washington.

Dyer's husband, John, to whom she had been married almost 63 years, passed away at the age of 97 in 2008. Dyer continues to reside in northeast Seattle.

BIBLIOGRAPHY

Breton, Mary Joy, *Women Pioneers for the Environment*, 1998; Kaufman, Polly Welts, *National Parks and the Woman's Voice*, 1996; "Olympic Coast Alliance," www.olympiccoast.org; Pryne, Eric, "A Fighter by Nature, Longtime Conservation Leader in the State Doesn't Plan to Slow Down in Retirement," *Seattle Times*, 1994; Urbani de la Paz, Diane, "Justice served: Memories shared of historic hike on Peninsula's Pacific coast led by William O. Douglas," *Peninsula Daily News*, 2008.

American Environmental Leaders

From Colonial Times to the Present

E

Earle, Sylvia

(August 30, 1935–)
Marine Botanist, Oceanographer

Sylvia Earle has spent almost 6,000 hours underwater exploring and studying the life of the oceans, earning the nickname "Her Royal Deepness." Her explorations have given her a vast appreciation of the ocean as a living system, one upon which the health of the planet is utterly dependent. As the most famous woman marine scientist of our time, she is highly visible, and she has used this attention to speak out against the harmful effects of pollution, development, and overfishing on the earth's seas. She is leading a project called Sustainable Seas Expeditions, in which her goal is to dive in submersibles in all 12 of the U.S. marine sanctuaries to document the wildlife there and to try to understand some of the long-term effects of environmental abuse.

Born on August 30, 1935, in Gibbstown, New Jersey, Sylvia Alice Earle was raised with her two brothers on a small farm near Camden. Her interest in the oceans started early, on vacations to the New Jersey shore. Curious, she read all she could find about oceans and began recording her observations in a notebook. Although neither of her parents had been to college, they valued education and encouraged her love of exploring. When she was 12 years old her family moved to Clearwater, Florida, and suddenly the Gulf of Mexico was at her back door. Someone gave her a pair of goggles, which opened a new underwater world and increased her desire to learn more about the oceans. She finished high school at the age of 16, and though her parents were unable to help her financially, she began studying at Florida State University, paying her way by working in a laboratory. She earned her B.S. in marine biology and had graduated by the time she was 19 years old. It was during this time that she decided to study marine plants. Understanding the vegetation, she discovered, is the first step to understanding how the whole ecosystem works.

After earning her master's degree in 1955 from Duke University, she began work on her Ph.D., continuing her study of plant life in the Gulf of Mexico. During this time she married and her attention turned to having a family. In the next few years two children arrived, but she was able to continue working on her dissertation—"Phaeophyta of the Eastern Gulf of Mexico." When it was completed in 1966, it caused a sensation in the oceanographic community by giving the world its first glimpse at the marine plant species in the Gulf of Mexico. She has continued her effort to catalog the plant and animal species of the oceans to help people understand and protect this largely unexplored ecosystem.

Until this time, most of what was known about life in the oceans was learned from dead specimens. Inspired by Jane Goodall, who studied chimpanzees in their own habitat, Earle wanted to do the same for marine plants and animals. In 1970 she was selected to participate in Tektite, a project sponsored by the United States Navy, the Department of the Interior, and the National Aeronautics and Space Administration (NASA). It allowed scientists to live in an enclosed laboratory 50 feet under water to conduct extended research projects. She and four other women lived and worked there for two weeks, and she treasured the chance to get to know some of the ocean creatures on their own terms.

The Tektite mission brought Earle new recognition and national attention. She used this opportunity to raise public awareness of the oceans and began speaking out against the damage being done to the oceans by development along coastal areas, pollution and dumping of chemicals, overharvesting of fish, and other environmental hazards. In addition to her ongoing research projects, she began writing books and producing films, always advocating greater care for the oceans of the world. She has also been ever-mindful of how little we actually know. Less than one-tenth of 1 percent of the ocean has been explored, and she emphasizes that it is difficult yet essential to protect marine species.

In continuing to push the boundaries of underwater exploration, Earle has been confronted with shortcomings in existing technology. In 1979 she made a record-breaking dive to 1,250 feet below surface in a special pressurized "Jim" suit near the Hawaiian island of Oahu. She was able to explore the depths for two and a half hours, untethered, yet this only fueled her desire to dive deeper. In the 1980s she and engineer Graham Hawkes started Deep Ocean Technologies, a company dedicated to developing tools for oceanic work and exploration. In 1984, using one of their innovative Deep Rover submersibles, Earle made another record-breaking dive, this time to 3,280 feet.

Earle continued through the 1990s to pursue her goal of helping people understand the role of oceans in maintaining the health of the planet. In 1990 she was appointed chief scientist of the National Oceanic and Atmospheric Administration (NOAA), where, among other duties, she was responsible for monitoring ocean health. As part of her work with NOAA she traveled to Kuwait and reported on the environmental damage caused when 11 million barrels of oil spilled into the Persian Gulf during the Gulf War. Frustrated with the bureaucracy facing a political appointee, she left the post in 1992 and continues to struggle with disappointment in a government that has no underwater equivalent of NASA, despite the fact that oceans cover 75 percent of the earth and that 90 percent of all known organisms live there. Earle has been a highly visible environmentalist—from 1998 until 2003 she led a project called Sustainable Seas Expeditions, which documented the wildlife in U.S. marine sanctuaries. These marine reserves, administered by NOAA, make up about 18,000 square miles of the coastal waters of the United States and are largely unexplored. Declines in numerous fish species, widespread coral loss, and other signs of increasing ecological damage made the Sustainable Seas project even more important. It created baseline data for monitoring the future health of these reserves and for educating the public about protecting the diversity there. The project was a collaboration between NOAA and the National Geographic Society, funded by the Richard and Rhonda Goldman fund. Findings from this project are archived and can be accessed at www.oceanservice.noaa.gov/websites/retiredsites/supp_SSEretired.html.

Sylvia Earle has been married three times and raised four children. She is active in environmental organizations, including serving as a board member of Ocean Conservancy. She is in high demand as a lecturer, encouraging her audiences to think of the ocean as a cornerstone of the life-support system for the whole planet. She lives in Oakland, California.

BIBLIOGRAPHY

Conley, Andrea, *Window on the Deep*, 1991; Earle, Sylvia A., *Dive! My Adventures in the Deep Frontier*, 1999; Earle, Sylvia A., *Sea Change: A Message of the Oceans*, 1995; Glausiuz, Josie, "Earle of the Sea," *Discover*, 2000; "Ocean Conservancy," www.oceanconservancy.org; Pangea Digflital Pictures, *Oceanography/with Dr. Sylvia Earle* (video recording), 1995; Plummer, William, "Depth Charger," *People Weekly*, 2000; Wexler, Mark, "Sylvia Earle's Excellent Adventure," *National Wildlife*, 1999; White, Wallace, "Her Deepness," *New Yorker*, 1989.

Edge, Rosalie

(November 3, 1877–November 30, 1962)
Conservation Activist

Bird-watcher and environmental reformer Rosalie Edge was the first woman to become prominent in the American conservation movement. She established the Emergency Conservation Committee (ECC) in 1929 to investigate misdeeds of the National Audubon Society, of which she was a life member. She published numerous pamphlets describing environmental problems and recommending solutions and provided occasional testimony to the U.S. Congress about conservation issues. In addition to personally purchasing the land for Hawk Mountain Sanctuary in Pennsylvania, she fought successfully for the establishment of Olympic and Kings Canyon National Parks and for the expansion of Yosemite National Park. She lost a campaign in the 1930s to reform the U.S. Biological Survey, but her complaints were later addressed by the U.S. Fish and Wildlife Service during the 1960s and 1970s.

Mabel Rosalie Edge was born Mabel Rosalie Barrow in New York City on November 3, 1877. Cousin to author Charles Dickens and painter James McNeill Whistler, Edge was raised as a member of the privileged elite. She attended private schools but got into trouble for asking too many questions and annoying her teachers. She met her husband, British engineer Charles Noel Edge, on a trip to England and shortly after their marriage moved to the Orient, where he sold locomotives. They had two children and spent some time in England before returning to the United States. Edge became involved with the women's suffrage movement and served as treasurer for the New York Women's Suffrage Party. In 1915, when the family bought a vacation house in Rye, New York, Edge began noticing the area's birdlife.

Soon she joined the Audubon Society as a life member and came to know the zoologists at the American Museum of Natural History. One of them, Dr. Willard Van Name, was especially concerned about the dangers facing birds. They were hunted for sport and for their plumes, and although the Audubon Society had fought hard for federal laws to protect birds during the first two decades of the century, Van Name believed that the society was not doing enough to advocate the laws' strict enforcement. He wrote a pamphlet about the situation and mailed a copy to Edge, who was then vacationing in Paris. She read it and returned home in time for the Audubon Society's 1929 annual meeting. The board of directors and Audubon's president T. Gilbert Pearson were taken aback by Edge's forceful questions about how the Audubon Society was addressing the problems Van Name brought up. Instead of responding to her concerns, Pearson complained that she had spoiled the meeting. There was no time to see the movie that had been scheduled, lunch was getting cold, and the official photographer for the annual society photograph had been kept waiting too long.

Far from discouraging Edge, this rebuff fueled her drive to reform the Audubon Society. Edge formed the Emergency Conservation Committee with Van Name and journalist Irving Brant shortly after the annual meeting. From that year on, she and her small group of allies attended every Audubon Society annual meeting. The formerly subdued gatherings became lively happenings. Crowds attended, eager to witness the scandal Edge inevitably stirred. President Pearson felt the heat. The ECC publicized his collusion with sportsmen and the hunting industry and decried the commissions he earned from the generous contributions by these interests.

In 1932 Edge discovered that the Audubon Society was earning "rent" from its Paul Rainey Wildlife Sanctuary in Louisiana. The Audubon Society had been leasing trapping rights to local muskrat trappers and had earned some $100,000 in royalties from the almost 300,000 muskrat pelts obtained. Infuriated, Edge brought this up at the 1932 annual meeting. Pearson and the board justified it, saying that muskrats were eating the vegetation that the endangered blue goose depended upon, and that furthermore, the money raised was necessary for the depression-depleted coffers of the Society. Edge published a pamphlet on the situation, and after fighting in court to obtain Audubon's mailing list, she sent a pamphlet to every member of the National Audubon Society. Audubon Society membership plummeted from 8,400 to 3,400, but Pearson remained in place. Finally in 1934, Pearson was forced by his board to resign, and the new president, John Baker, put an end to the trapping.

This fight won, and confident that the Audubon Society was in better hands, Edge turned her focus to the federal government's conservation policies. She fought with the U.S. Biological Survey, which at that time appeased farmers and ranchers with an aggressive antipredator policy. She argued that predators were given unjustifiably bad press and that they actually helped farmers by preying on destructive rodents. One of her pamphlets deconstructed the popular myth that eagles routinely carried off human babies. Although the Biological Survey ignored her concerns at the time, when reformers took up the cause during the 1960s and 1970s, the later-reorganized U.S. Fish and Wildlife Service did cease its predator program.

Edge's concern for birds of prey led her to found a sanctuary for them along the Pennsylvania mountain ridge they follow on their southward migration. Edge visited the Kittatinny ridge one fall and found scores of hunters lying in wait for the hawks and shooting them for sport by the thousands. Edge believed that three-peaked Hawk Mountain, in the middle of the migration corridor, would serve as a valuable refuge, and she used $2,500 of her inheritance to purchase it in 1934. The ECC raised more funds to hire a caretaker and build hawk shelters at Hawk Mountain Sanctuary.

During the 1930s Edge joined with other conservationists to fight for the creation of two new national parks in the West: Olympic National Park and Kings Canyon National Park, established in 1938 and 1940, respectively. She was the principal proponent of the enlargement of Yosemite National Park, which resulted in the addition of 6,000 acres of old-growth sugar pine forest in 1937. Edge also joined the fight against the dam in Dinosaur National Monument's Echo Park in the 1950s.

Edge kept the ECC going as long as she lived. Since it was essentially a one-person organization during her last years, it folded after her death, but Hawk Mountain Sanctuary still exists and is administered by an association that she founded for that purpose. The National Audubon Society eventually expressed public appreciation for her persistent activism, treating her to a standing ovation at the 1962 annual meeting just a few weeks before her death. Edge died on November 30, 1962, in New York City.

BIBLIOGRAPHY

Broun, Maurice, *Hawks Aloft: The Story of Hawk Mountain*, 1949; Fox, Stephen, *The American Conservation Movement: John Muir and His Legacy*, 1981; Graham, Frank, Jr., *Man's Dominion: The Story of Conservation in America*, 1971; "Hawk Mountain Sanctuary," www.hawkmountain.org/; Kaufman, Polly Welts, *National Parks and the Woman's Voice*, 1996; Taylor, Robert Lewis, "Oh, Hawk of Mercy," *New Yorker*, 1948.

Ehrenfeld, David

(January 15, 1938–)
Founder and Editor of *Conservation Biology*, Ecologist

David Ehrenfeld is a professor at Rutgers University who specializes in conservation ecology and its role in an increasingly technological world. He has gained attention for his leadership in the journal *Conservation Biology*, of which he was the founding editor, and through the books he has written. In his influential writings, he often focuses on society's obsession with power and technology and on how that obsession affects our relationship with the natural world.

David William Ehrenfeld was born January 15, 1938, in New York City to Irving and Anne (Shapiro) Ehrenfeld. He attended Harvard University, where he earned his bachelor's degree in history in 1959, and then attended Harvard Medical School, receiving his M.D. in 1963. At the University of Florida he did doctoral research on the orientation and navigation of sea turtles and received his Ph.D. in zoology in 1966. The next year, Ehrenfeld accepted an assistant professor position at Columbia University in New York and three years later became an associate professor of biology. In 1970, he and June Gardner, a plant ecologist, were married. They would later have four children: Kate, Jane, Jonathan, and Samuel. Ehrenfeld stayed at Columbia University until 1974, when he took a position as professor of biology at Rutgers University in New Brunswick, New Jersey.

In 1978, Ehrenfeld's book *The Arrogance of Humanism* came out. In it, he sets out to remind the world of its failures—and does so by commenting on soil depletion, technological mistakes such as dichlordiphenyltrichlor (DDT), plant and animal extinctions, and the concurrent rise in social violence. Rather than point a finger at capitalism or overpopulation or any of the other usual targets of environmentalists, Ehrenfeld blames the philosophy of humanism and its defining principle of supreme faith in human reason. He believes that humans are having a fatal love affair with technology and control and that problems arise when the only socially acceptable solution is to apply reason over emotion. It is an example of hubris to believe that all problems are soluble by people, he writes, and such intellectual arrogance simply reduces nature, thereby reducing conservation as well. *The Arrogance of Humanism* became a much-discussed and influential book that has gone into nine printings. The influence of his ideas is still felt more than 20 years later, with contemporary ecologists discussing the underlying assumptions of ecosystem management as to whether or not they imply a demonstration of human arrogance.

In 1987 Ehrenfeld founded and became editor of *Conservation Biology*, a scientific journal that deals with ecologically important studies and issues that contribute to the preservation of species and habitats. It is supported by the Society of Conservation Biology, which is committed to examining the scientific basis of conservation in order to counter environmental deterioration. Articles in the journal cover topics such as analyses of species declines, population modeling, discussions of vertebrates as indicator species, recommendations for management decisions and practices, the impacts of game ranching and poaching, and many others. *Conservation Biology*, now accepted as required reading for ecologists throughout the world, remains instrumental in the effort to move conservation biology to the forefront of the sciences. In the past decade it has become the most frequently cited journal in its field. Ehrenfeld also has compiled selected articles from the journal into a series of six volumes titled *Readings from Conservation Biology*, which cover a broad range of topics—illustrating the diversity of approaches to conservation decisions.

Ehrenfeld's book *Beginning Again: People and Nature in the New Millennium*, published in 1993, further builds on a foundation of ecology. He maintains that many of the problems in the relationship between humans and nature that have accompanied the end of the twentieth century lie in an obsession with control. The ability to manipulate the world is new and addictive, he says, and it overlooks complexity and diversity—the backbones of the natural world. This fixation with control has also led to a growing tendency toward overmanagement, which serves to disconnect those in power from those doing the groundwork—in other words, those who really understand what's going on. In searching for solutions for these disturbing trends, Ehrenfeld relies on the understanding gained by ecologists, who study the particularities of life in diverse systems. He discusses restoration ecology, saying that although species cannot be reconstructed, ecosystems can—as long as it is recognized that restoration is never as good as preserving the land in the first place. In the last chapter of the book, titled "Life in the New Millennium," Ehrenfeld emphasizes that the ultimate success in conservation will depend on a revision of everyday living—not just in increased efforts to save the world. When people who are not even making efforts at conservation are able to live in a way that is compatible with the existence of other native species in the region, then the destructive changing of nature will end. In other words, he concludes, conservation has to start at home.

Swimming Lessons: Keeping Afloat in the Age of Technology was published in 2002. It describes the enormous changes that our world is undergoing due to great advances in technology, most of them negative and disruptive, and provides suggestions for "keeping afloat".

Since 1989, Ehrenfeld has been a regular columnist for *Orion*, a magazine dedicated to characterizing humans' responsibilities to the environment, exploring the ethic of stewardship, and cultivating nature literacy. In his column, Ehrenfeld sometimes deals with biological issues, such as woodland restoration or biotechnology. But often his topics go beyond biology to explore things like the modern lifestyle and its disconnection from the outdoors or the problems that arise from the reliance on expert knowledge, which usually ignores cultural wisdom. A common theme for Ehrenfeld is that society's concept of progress leaves little room for traditional knowledge or for anyone with concerns for the future, and yet traditional wisdom can often hold brilliant solutions to problems that people face today.

In 1993 he stepped down as editor of *Conservation Biology* and now serves as a consulting editor. He continues his work at Rutgers University, where he teaches general ecology, field ecology, and conservation ecology. He makes his home in Highland Park, New Jersey.

BIBLIOGRAPHY

Ehrenfeld, David, *The Arrogance of Humanism*, 1978; Ehrenfeld, David, *Beginning Again: People and Nature in the New Millennium*, 1993; Ehrenfeld, David, *Swimming Lessons: Keeping Afloat in the Age of Technology*, 2002; Norton, Bryan G., "Beginning Again: People and Nature in the New Millennium," *BioScience*, 1994; Stanley, T. R., "Ecosystem Management and the Arrogance of Humanism," *Conservation Biology*, 1995.

Ehrlich, Anne, and Paul Ehrlich

(November 17, 1933– ; May 29, 1932–)
Biological Researcher; Population Biologist

Anne and Paul Ehrlich are well-known spokespeople for the conservation and population control movements in the United States. They have cowritten eleven books, all of which send a straightforward, hard-hitting message about the environmental dangers that face the planet and its living inhabitants. Paul Ehrlich—whose academic specialty is entomology and who cofounded the field of coevolution—emerged in popular media during the 1960s and 1970s when he issued dire predictions about population growth and the ensuing scarcity of the earth's resources. His best-selling *The Population Bomb*, published in 1968, warned of the devastation that would be suffered by a population grown too big. The Ehrlichs work out of Stanford University's Center for Conservation Biology, which they helped found in 1984.

Anne Fitzhugh Howland was born on November 17, 1933, in Des Moines, Iowa. As a child, she developed an interest in nature through outdoor activities, nature studies in school, and summer camps.

Paul Ralph Ehrlich was born on May 29, 1932, in Philadelphia and raised in Maplewood, New Jersey. As a child, he chased butterflies and caught and dissected frogs; as a teen, he was encouraged in a serious study of butterflies by a mentor at the American Museum of Natural History in Manhattan. Ehrlich studied at the University of Pennsylvania, graduating in 1953 with a B.S. in zoology.

The Ehrlichs met at the University of Kansas; Anne studied there from 1952 to 1955, and Paul earned his M.A. there in 1955 and his Ph.D. in 1957. They married and established a close collaborative relationship. Paul Ehrlich accepted a position in Stanford University's Department of Biological Sciences in 1959. Specializing in evolution, population dynamics, and ecology, he has studied butterflies, snake mites, birds, and coral reef fishes. With botanist PETER RAVEN, Paul Ehrlich discovered and described a phenomenon they called "coevolution," complex interactions between species that influence the way they evolve. Anne Ehrlich focused on raising their daughter, Lisa Marie, during the 1950s and early 1960s. She illustrated Paul Ehrlich's identification key *How to Know the Butterflies*, published in 1961, and joined Stanford's Department of Biological Sciences in 1962.

The Ehrlichs first became interested as teenagers in environmental problems caused by overpopulation. They both read *Our Plundered Planet*, by HENRY FAIRFIELD OSBORN JR., and Paul Ehrlich also read *Road to Survival*, by WILLIAM VOGT. The writers of both books warned that overpopulation and abuse of natural resources could lead to widespread famine and impoverishment. During a sabbatical in 1966, the Ehrlich family traveled to India and was horrified by the conditions in the poorest part of Delhi, where people were living on the street, barely surviving. This seemed to be a worst-case scenario for overpopulation, and Paul Ehrlich described it in *The Population Bomb*, which was published in 1968 and quickly rose to best-seller status.

An appearance on the *Tonight Show* shortly after *The Population Bomb* came out thrust Paul Ehrlich into the public spotlight. He announced publicly that he had had a vasectomy and founded the organization Zero Population Growth to promote smaller families in the United States. He argued for a "luxury tax" on such items as diapers and baby food and supported a proposal that the U.S. government not send food aid to countries such as India that had not taken any measures to curb population growth.

The Population Explosion, which the Ehrlichs cowrote in 1990, provides an update to *The Population Bomb*, detailing environmental problems created by overpopulation. It

Anne and Paul Ehrlich (Photograph courtesy of Anne and Paul Ehrlich)

emphasizes that wealthy countries, even though their populations are not increasing at the same rate as poorer countries, cause more environmental problems because they consume natural resources and pollute on a much greater scale.

In addition to *The Population Explosion*, the Ehrlichs have cowritten ten other books. They write in a clear and compelling manner to make their books accessible to lay readers. This dedication to the education of nonscientists about science and conservation issues, as well as their vanguard research and compelling arguments for conservation, has made the couple prominent spokespeople for the environment. *Extinction: The Causes and Consequences of the Disappearance of Species* (1981), in addition to being an entertaining primer on evolution and extinction, describes the dangers that will result from the widespread loss of biodiversity currently taking place on planet earth. Their memorable metaphor for disappearing species on earth, rivets being popped out of an airplane one by one, has been adopted and widely cited by the biodiversity conservation movement. The central problem leading to loss of biodiversity and other environmental problems, in their analysis, is that the human enterprise—which includes the global population's size and growth, its consumption, and technologies—is highly unsustainable and is becoming more so as both the population and each person's consumption increase. The inequitable rich/poor gap makes the unsustainable situation even more unstable. The Ehrlichs describe the causes and effects of inequity in *The Stork and the Plow* (1995), cowritten with Gretchen Daily.

The Ehrlichs have been especially concerned about what they call the "brownlash," an attempt by anticonservationists to convince the public that environmentalists are overly pessimistic and exaggerate the dangers to the planet. In their books and articles, the brownlashers claim that human activity has negatively affected only a very small portion of the planet, that nature is incredibly resilient and capable of recovering from any destruction that does occur, and that technology and human innovation will prevail and solve serious environmental problems. The Ehrlichs' *Betrayal of Science and Reason: How Anti-Environmental Rhetoric Threatens Our Future* (1996) debunks outrageous statements one by one, tracing misunderstandings, miscalculations, and misleading statements.

The Ehrlichs' latest book is *One with Nineveh: Politics, Consumption and the Human Future* (2004). In it, they describe the three major and interlocking problems facing today's world: overpopulation, overconsumption, and political and economic inequity and recommend steps we can take to avert global disaster and achieve a sustainable society.

Anne Ehrlich became senior research associate for the Department of Biology in 1975 and began teaching an environmental policy course for Stanford's Human Biology program in 1981. Together, the Ehrlichs helped found the Center for Conservation Biology (CCB) at Stanford in 1984; it has become an influential research and teaching center for the field of conservation biology and also studies such questions as population growth, environmental deterioration, and use of natural resources. Anne Ehrlich serves as its policy coordinator, and Paul Ehrlich is its president.

In addition to her writings and work at the Center for Conservation Biology, Anne Ehrlich has worked as an outside consultant to the Global 2000 Report of the White House Council on Environmental Quality (1977–1980), as an adviser for the Fate of the Earth Conferences in 1981 and 1984, and as a commissioner for the Greater London Area War Risk Study (GLAWARS; 1985–1986) of the Greater London City Council. She was elected a member of the American Academy of Arts in 1998 and holds two honorary degrees. She has served on the boards of directors of numerous nonprofit organizations, including the Sierra Club; the Pacific Institute for Studies in Environment, Development, and Security; the Rocky Mountain Biological Laboratory; Friends of the Earth; and the Ploughshares Fund. She received the 1985 Raymond B. Bragg Award for Distinguished Service and also in 1985 was honored by the American Humanists Association.

Paul Ehrlich, the Bing Professor of Population Studies at Stanford University, has received several honorary degrees, a MacArthur Prize Fellowship, the 1990 Crafoord Prize of the Royal Swedish Academy of Science (which he shared with entomologist E. O. WILSON), the JOHN MUIR Award of the Sierra Club, the 1987 Gold Medal Award of World Wildlife Fund International, the 1993 Volvo Environmental Prize, the Blue Planet Prize in 1999, and in 2001 both the Distinguished Scientist Award from the American Institute of Biological Sciences and the Eminent Ecologist Award from the Ecological Society of America.

Paul and Anne Ehrlich shared the 1994 United Nations Environmental Programme Sasakawa Environment Prize, the 1995 Heinz Award, the 1996 Distinguished Peace Leader Award from the Nuclear Age Peace Foundation, and, most recently, in 1998, the prestigious Tyler Award.

BIBLIOGRAPHY

"A Winning Partnership," *Environmental Health Perspectives*, 1998; "Center for Conservation Biology," www.stanford.edu/group/CCB/; Ehrlich, Paul, *A World of Wounds: Ecologists and the Human Dilemma*, 1997; Ehrlich, Paul, and Anne Ehrlich, *Healing the Planet: Strategies for Resolving the Environmental Crisis*, 1991; "Heinz Awards," www.heinzawards.net.

Eisner, Thomas
(June 25, 1929–)
Entomologist

Thomas Eisner's life work has been focused on insects, and he is especially known for his discoveries about how insects communicate with one another by secreting certain chemicals. His work has led him to cofound (along with his colleague Jerrold Meinwald) the new field of chemical ecology, and to contribute widely to such disciplines as comparative behavior and biocommunications. Eisner has been a leader in the movement to conserve endangered environments and promotes bioprospecting, the search for useful substances occurring naturally, to make nature more economically valuable.

Thomas Eisner was born on June 25, 1929, in Berlin, Germany. His family moved to Barcelona when Hitler ascended to power in 1933. Then the Spanish Civil War erupted, and after a brief stay in France and Argentina, his family emigrated to Uruguay, where he spent the remainder of his childhood. Eisner's parents believe their son learned to walk in order to chase insects in the backyard, and Eisner tells a story about how as a young boy in Barcelona, he was in a sandbox one day, intently observing some pill bugs. A tremendous explosion shook his neighborhood—one of the first acts of terrorism of the Spanish Civil War. But instead of frightening the boy, it annoyed him because the ensuing chaos interrupted his session with the bugs! As well as indulging his intense interest in insects, his parents instilled him with a love of music and an unusual olfactory ability. His father, a chemist, concocted perfumes and creams at home, and they opened his nose to a world of subtle scents.

When Eisner's family moved to New York in 1947, Eisner applied to Cornell University but was not admitted, mostly owing to his poor English. He went to Champlain College in Plattsburgh, New York, and after two years there, transferred to Harvard, where he earned a B.A. in 1951 and a Ph.D. in 1955. Eisner married Maria Lobell and became a naturalized U.S. citizen in 1952. He was offered a teaching position at Cornell University in 1957 and has taught there ever. He is the Jacob Gould Schurman Professor Emeritus of Chemical Ecology. Eisner codirected the Cornell Institute for Research in Chemical Ecology from 1993 till 2006, and was a senior fellow at the Cornell Center for the Environment. He is one of the most popular lecturers on campus.

In the 1991 documentary film *The Bug Man of Ithaca*, Eisner is a convincing advocate for insects. He reveals one caterpillar's defensive strategy: it hides itself from predators by sewing itself a costume of pieces of the flower it eats. He shows how the green lacewing's larvae, which eat woolly alder aphids, pick the wool off each aphid before eating it and stick the wool onto their own bodies. Still other insects fit into a complex ecological web. As a stink bug stuck in a spider web dies and is devoured by the spider, its stench attracts other flies that in turn get stuck in the web. Another spider finds a moth in its web, tastes it, and if it does not like the moth, frees it. Certain caterpillars feed on poisonous plants, whose distasteful flavor remains in their bodies once they transform into moths. Spliced into this film are cuts from some of Hollywood's insect horror movies, which by the end of *Bug Man* seem crass compared to the brilliance of bugs as revealed by Eisner.

Eisner is best known for his research into the ways that insects defend themselves and communicate with one another using chemicals. One of Eisner's most famous discoveries was of the defense system of the bombardier beetle, which shoots hot poison from the tip of its abdomen at a rate of 500 shots per second. Eisner and Meinwald have discovered a

Thomas Eisner (Photograph by Susan Middleton & David Liittschwager)

chemical in millipedes that could be used as a nerve drug, a substance in fireflies that serves as a cardiac stimulant, and a cockroach repellent that occurs in an endangered mint.

Learning about the potentially useful chemicals manufactured by plants and animals led Eisner to develop a field he calls "chemical prospecting," which involves scouring natural habitats for potential medicines, pesticides, and chemicals of use to industry. Eisner sees four benefits from chemical prospecting: new jobs for local people, new opportunities for investment, more funds for conservation, and a stronger scientific infrastructure in biodiverse countries. This will help developing countries, especially in their quest for funds for conservation. Eisner helped convince the Merck & Company pharmaceutical giant to sign an agreement with the Costa Rican National Biodiversity Institute (INBio), whereby Merck paid INBio half a million dollars per year in return for being provided with samples of what INBio researchers believed might be useful pharmaceutical substances.

Eisner has written six books. His latest works include a book of photos of leaves changing color, *Chromatic Fantasy* (2000); *For Love of Insects* (2003), a collection of photos and narratives about some of Eisner's favorite bugs; and co-authored in 2005 with his wife Maria Eisner and Melody Siegler, another book of photos and descriptions of chemical defenses, *Secret Weapons*.

Eisner has received many awards for his work in chemical ecology and conservation, including Harvard University's Centennial Medal, the 1990 Tyler Prize, the 1994 National Medal of Science, and the National Conservation Achievement Award from the National Wildlife Foundation in 1996. He sits on the boards of directors of the Union of Concerned Scientists and the Center for Plant Conservation of the Missouri Botanical Garden. Eisner resides in Ithaca, New York.

BIBLIOGRAPHY
Ackerman, Diane, *The Rarest of the Rare: Vanishing Animals, Timeless Worlds*, 1995; Eisner, Thomas, and Jerrold Meinwald, eds., *Chemical Ecology: The Chemistry of Biotic Interaction*, 1995; Eisner, Thomas, and Edward O. Wilson, eds., *The Insects: Readings from Scientific American*, 1997; Canadian Broadcasting Corporation, *The Bug Man of Ithaca*, (video recording) 1991; Wilson, E. O., *Naturalist*, 1994.

Ellis, Juliet
Environmental Health Advocate, Executive Director of Urban Habitat

The executive director of the Oakland, California non-profit Urban Habitat, Juliet Ellis took the helm in 2001 from renowned environmentalist CARL ANTHONY, who had been with the organization since its inception in 1989. Ellis has led the organization, often through effective coalition work, to significant victories for residents of Oakland and the entire San Francisco Bay region in the areas of improved public transportation, affordable housing, and environmental health. Under her tutelage, Urban Habitat engages in popular education through the ongoing publication of materials such as the *Race, Poverty and the Environment* journal, and with its Leadership Institute, which prepares residents from underserved communities to participate more fully in the local public policy organizations that impact their lives.

Juliet Ellis obtained a B.S. in marketing from Ball State University in Muncie, Indiana in 1995 and a Masters in business administration from San Francisco State University in 2001. Before directing Urban Habitat, Ellis was the associate program officer for Neighborhood and Community Development at the San Francisco Foundation.

Transportation justice is one of Urban Habitat's signature program areas. In 2006 the organization helped secure $120 billion over 25 years for public transportation projects in the nine-county Bay Area from the Metropolitan Transportation Commission. This amount includes $359 million for the Lifeline Program, which is dedicated to serving low-income communities. Moreover, Urban Habitat has developed a Transportation Justice Equity Platform that has been endorsed by 15 organizations. This initiative aims to affect the area's Regional Transportation Plan on behalf of low-income communities so they can receive an equitable amount of transportation funding and investment.

The organization has also been involved in the areas of land use planning through the Community Capital Investment Initiative, specifically in the city of Richmond. A low-income waterfront community and the site of a Chevron oil refinery, it is one of the Bay Area neighborhoods being targeted for investment and urban renewal without the displacement of its current moderate- and low-income residents.

One of the means supported by Urban Habitat to create a permanent barrier against gentrification is turning apartment buildings into cooperatives through community land trusts. A successful local example is San Francisco's 53 Columbus building, located in prime real estate between Chinatown and the Financial District. It now boasts affordable apartments in perpetuity for tenants to own based on their ability to pay, and resale is restricted to other low-income earners.

Another program area for Urban Habitat is environmental health and justice. In 2002, Urban Habitat and 14 other area organizations created the Bay Area Working Group on the Precautionary Principle, which seeks to keep substances that haven't been proven safe from being used in consumer products or released into the environment, instead of waiting for proof of direct links between chemical exposure and illness to discontinue use. The precautionary principle requires that producers, not the public, show that they have selected the safest alternative.

As a result of the efforts of the Working Group, in June 2003 and June 2005 precautionary principle policies were approved in San Francisco, and in March 2006 one was approved in Berkeley. These new policies require that any purchases made by these localities apply the precautionary principle to items bought with public funds. Despite the fact that the precautionary principle forms part of European environmental laws, and is central to the 1992 Rio Declaration which the United States signed, it is generally not part of U.S. law, so these Bay Area policies are nothing short of groundbreaking for the country, showcasing the possibilities at the local level in the face of inaction at the national level.

Urban Habitat is also supporting the Oakland Apollo Alliance's Green-Collar Jobs campaign, and Mayor Ron Dellums's efforts to preserve industrial land to bring in thousands of these well-paying jobs in the fields of renewable energy. Dellums has signed the Green Corridor Initiative with other cities so as to start the production of biosynthetic fuels and solar cells.

In addition to the work she does for and on behalf of her organization, Ellis serves on the board of directors of the David Brower Center, the Transportation and Land Use Coalition, the Oakland Homeless and Low-Income Task Force, and the Ella Baker Center for Human Rights. In 2001 *Ebony* magazine listed Ellis as one of the up-and-coming leaders under 30. She lives in the San Francisco Bay Area.

BIBLIOGRAPHY

www.urbanhabitat.org; www.takingprecaution.org.

Elton, Charles S.
(March 29, 1900–May 1, 1991)
Ecologist, Founder and Editor of *Journal of Animal Ecology*

One of the founders of the science of ecology, Charles Elton influenced the creation of the field by coupling natural history with quantitative and experimental research. His first book, *Animal Ecology* (1927), was lauded not just for its treatment of animal communities, but for the principles of ecology he established in the areas of food chains, ecological niches, and the structures of feeding relationships in ecosystems. To this day, Elton's work is cited more than any other single ecologist in the field.

Charles Sutherland Elton was born in Manchester, England, on March 29, 1900. His parents were literary scholar Oliver Elton and children's writer Leticia Maynard Elton. His mother hailed from Scotland's Isle of Coll, whose natural landscape Elton explored thoroughly with his older brother Geoffrey Yorke, who died suddenly in 1927. Elton credited his brother with being the first to suggest to him that the ecological web of life is governed by certain principles. Elton attended Oxford University's Liverpool College, graduating with first class honors in zoology in 1922. In 1923 he was appointed to a teaching position at Oxford, where he spent his entire career until retirement in 1967.

During his undergraduate years Elton was a research assistant to Julian S. Huxley, with whom he made a series of trips to the Arctic in 1921, 1923 and 1924. The ecological survey of Arctic vertebrates expanded with each subsequent trip, culminating in the publication of his research in the *British Journal of Experimental Biology* in 1924. He went back to Spitsbergen in 1930 after becoming a biological consultant in 1925 to the Hudson Bay Company. He undertook studies in the fluctuations of furbearing animals as revealed in the records of trappers dating back to 1736.

In 1930 Elton published *Animal Ecology and Evolution*, in which he posited that animals migrate and select their environments in periods of stress, such as extreme climate conditions, as opposed to the environment making a natural selection of animals. After the book went out of print in 1968, Mathew Liebold and Timothy Wootton, two professors at the department of Ecology and Evolution at the University of Chicago, succeeded in having their university press print a new edition of the book in 2001, to which they wrote an extensive foreword geared for their students and the general interested public.

Elton helped to spawn the sub-discipline of invasion biology when he published *The Ecology of Invasions by Animals and Plants* (1958). With the reprinting of that book in 2000, also by the University of Chicago Press, Elton's work continues to reach both students of ecology and the wider public with what is now considered one of the central scientific books of the 20th century. On the occasion of the 50th anniversary of the book's publication in 2008, South Africa's Centre of Excellence for Invasion Biology at Stellenbosch University is celebrating Elton's book for being cited more than any other single publication in the field.

In 1932 he established the Bureau of Animal Population at Oxford. It became a global center for the collection of animal data, and an international research institute, attracting scholars from many countries. Among them were many Rhodes, Fulbright, and Rockefeller scholars from the U.S., such as EUGENE ODUM, who wrote with his brother one of the first textbooks on ecology in 1953, and Thomas Park, zoologist at the University of Chicago from 1949 to 1974 and past president of the Ecological Society of America.

Also in 1932 Elton founded and edited the *Journal of Animal Ecology*. In 1936 Oxford's

Corpus Christi College elected him senior research fellow. At the outset of World War II, Britain's Agricultural Research Council sought the aid of Elton's Bureau of Animal Population for finding ways to control rodent pests. His work helped to save food supplies in a critical period. In 1942 Elton published *Voles, Mice and Lemmings*, and in 1954 "The Control of Rats and Mice" in the *Journal of Ecology*.

The Ecology of Invasions by Animals and Plants started out as a series of three BBC radio broadcasts in 1957 titled *Balance and Barrier*. In them, and the subsequent book, Elton covered faunal and floral history, the structure and dynamics of populations, and conservation. He quotes fiction writers, poets, and prophets, and recounts humorous tales of globalization such as a friend's astonishment upon returning from Egypt to find small beetles hatching out of his shirt buttons, which were made from a type of palm nut. "The larvae had gone on living in the stuff, having apparently passed through the manufacturing process like... Chaplin in *Modern Times*."

Although Elton details the successful introduction of species such as various Pacific salmon to other parts of the world, he concentrates on destructive ecological explosions such as the worldwide pandemic influenza following World War I, and the American chestnut blight caused by a parasitic fungus originating in Asia, brought to the U.S. on nursery plants. The world is even more interconnected today than it was in the late 1950s, and the ecological meltdowns brought about by species invasions are probably more numerous. Since Elton made observations about the role of climate in population fluctuations from the beginning of his career, he would not be surprised by how global warming has accelerated this trend, by allowing for the proliferation of species that heretofore had not been able to thrive in certain regions, and extinguishing others that haven't been able to adapt or migrate. Since Elton's time, great progress has been made in quantifying the economic costs of species invasions and the loss biodiversity.

Notably, like biologist RACHEL CARSON, whose 1962 groundbreaking book *Silent Spring* called for more restrained use of chemical pesticides, Elton in *The Ecology of Invasions* also urges for biotic alternatives to synthetic chlorinated hydrocarbons and organophosphate pesticides, particularly for agriculture, where DDT had already been shown to decrease soil productivity, depress the growth of seedling crop plants, and increase the resistance of some crop pests. Both would be pleased with the 2004 Stockholm Convention's ban of DDT for agricultural use. Also like Carson, Elton was above all a committed conservationist. He was instrumental in establishing the Nature Conservancy Council in 1949. He urged careful stewardship and environmental management of humanity's territorial commons, whether they are wild lands or those exploited by humans, so as to attain an equilibrium of "refuge, beauty and interest, and security."

Elton's habitat studies of many years formed the basis of his last book *The Pattern of Animal Communities* (1966). After retiring from Oxford University in 1967, he studied tropical America. Elton was a foreign member of the American Academy of Arts and Science. In 1961 he became a life member and eminent ecologist of the Ecological Society of America. He received the gold medal of the Linnean Society in 1967, and the Royal Society's Darwin Medal in 1970. He died on May 1, 1991 in Oxford.

BIBLIOGRAPHY

Elton, Charles S., *Animal Ecology*, 1927, 2001; Elton, Charles S., *The Ecology of Invasions by Animals and Plants*, 1958, 2000; Crowcroft, Peter, *Elton's Ecologists: A History of the Bureau of Animal Population*, 2001; "Elton, Charles Sutherland (England 1900-1991)," *Some Biogeographers, Evolutionists and Ecologists: Chrono-Biographical Sketches*, www.wku.edu/~smithch/chronob/ELTO1900.htm; "Elton, Charles," www.britannica.com/eb/article-2093;

"Charles Sutherland Elton," en.wikipedia.org/wiki/Charles_Sutherland_Elton; "Announcement of a symposium: Fifty years of invasion ecology—the legacy of Charles Elton," academic.sun.ac.za/cib/events/Elton_CIB-symposium.htm; Lambert, Bruce, "Thomas Park, 83, Dies of Cancer; helped Ecology Become Science," *The New York Times*, April 4, 1992.

Emerson, Ralph Waldo
(May 25, 1803–April 27, 1882)
Writer

From the mid-nineteenth century on, Ralph Waldo Emerson has been cited by writers and naturalists as inspiration for their interest in the natural world. A leader of the American transcendentalist movement beginning in the mid-1830s, Ralph Waldo Emerson spoke and wrote about nature as a revealer of spiritual truths, declaring in his essay "Nature" that "every natural fact is a symbol of some spiritual fact." His work as philosopher, orator, theologian, and poet remains a prerequisite in the study of American literature, history, theology, and the natural sciences.

Ralph Waldo Emerson was born in Boston on May 25, 1803, when some areas of Boston were still half-rural. Like many naturalists, as a child he was drawn to open fields, ponds, and sylvan places. His father, Rev. William Emerson, died when Ralph Waldo was seven years old, and it was only through great resourcefulness that his mother succeeded in sending all six sons to Harvard College. Young Ralph Waldo was greatly encouraged by his aunt, Mary Moody Emerson, who enjoyed his poetry and provided him with literature from around the world. Emerson graduated at 18 years of age and took the pulpit of Boston's Second Unitarian Church at the age of 27. He continued to build on his studies and became increasingly convinced that deeper knowledge of the natural world would not only attest to the glory of God, but would also build one's moral foundation. He stated in a sermon called "Astronomy" that "religion will become purer and truer by the progress of science. This consideration ought to secure our interest in the book of nature."

By 1832, Emerson's curious mind led him away from the ministry and toward natural history. He went to Europe and visited the Jardin des Plantes at the Musée d'Histoire Naturelle in Paris, after which he wrote in his journal, "I am moved by strange sympathies, I say continually, I will be a naturalist." He referred back to this experience in his work continuously over the next decades. Emerson returned to the United States and began lecturing at the Natural History Society in Boston and so embarked on a career as a prophetic orator whose addresses were often published as essays and were disseminated by New England church ministers and literati. Rather than return to the pulpit, Emerson preferred to work as a free agent, organizing his own speaking engagements by renting a hall and paying himself with the proceeds.

Emerson's 1836 essay "Nature" presents his theory that the natural world is emblematic of larger truths: "1) Words are signs of natural facts. 2) Particular natural facts are symbols of particular spiritual facts. 3) Nature is the symbol of spirit." Criticism immediately followed its publication, as church officials recognized Emerson's ideas as an attack on the authority of organized Christianity. Emerson's

Ralph Waldo Emerson (Library of Congress, Prints & Photographs Division, LC-USZ62-73430).

"Nature" and the ensuing discussion in ecclesiastic circles led to a loosely organized movement in New England called transcendentalism. Transcendentalists referred to the book-length essay as "the Bible," and they would gather at Emerson's Concord home for transcendentalist meetings. Transcendentalists held the Neoplatonic and Kantian notion of a parallel between the material world and the higher realms, and they regarded nature as a source of divine truth about the spirit and the human mind.

In 1841, while living in Concord, Massachusetts, Emerson took in a handy young writer, HENRY DAVID THOREAU, who in exchange for chores had a place to live and a visionary mentor in Emerson. Thoreau put Emerson's philosophy to the test by practicing it in the woods of Concord and northern New England and chronicling his experience in the American literary classic *Walden*. While Emerson and Thoreau did not agree about everything, they spoke and wrote on nature's behalf like none other before them. The magazine *The Dial*, which Emerson published with Margaret Fuller from 1840 to 1844, became an outlet for their transcendentalist writing. Emerson's productive relationship with Thoreau lasted until Thoreau's untimely death in 1862 of tuberculosis. The late twentieth century's ecology movement in the United States, nature writing, and the spread of Buddhist philosophy in the United States all claim some influence from the combined literary efforts of Emerson and Thoreau.

Some of Emerson's most quoted essays are "The American Scholar," which Oliver Wendell Holmes called the United States's "intellectual Declaration of Independence," and "The Poet," an essay pored over by WALT WHITMAN, Emily Dickinson, and a generation of American poets. Perhaps Emerson's most famous essay was "Self-Reliance," which reified the American characteristic trait of rugged individualism.

Critics were later to say that Emerson spent too much time doing desk work to be a true naturalist and that he preferred his creature comforts to the rugged lifestyles of Henry David Thoreau and JOHN MUIR. Late in Emerson's life he invited Muir to come to New England as his guest, advising that the solitude of the wilderness "is a sublime mistress, but an intolerable wife." But what Emerson may have lacked in woodsmanship and natural scientific knowledge, he made up for with his flair for the romantic, and his enthusiastic romanticism led many people into the woods and into the study of natural history. He also remained au courant in the natural science study of his day, reading extensively on developments in the field. As laudatory of natural scientific inquiry as he could be in his speeches and essays, he also admonished the direction of science when it became strictly empirical and denied the spiritual aspect.

Among the lasting works of Ralph Waldo Emerson, his essays and sermons are most widely known, but his journals (from a journal-writing practice that began when he was eight years old and continued until his death) especially chart his studies of the natural environment. Ultimately, Emerson was not a naturalist but a writer, public speaker, poet, and perhaps the first American philosopher. His work has had a lasting impact on American theology, environmental study, poetry, and nature writing.

At 79 years of age, on April 27, 1882, Emerson died from pneumonia that he had contracted walking in a spring rain without a coat or hat. He is buried in Sleepy Hollow Cemetery in Concord, Massachusetts, the town he called home for most of his life.

BIBLIOGRAPHY

Bosco, Ronald and Joel Myerson, *Emerson in His Own Time: a biographical chronicle of his life, drawn from recollections, interviews, and memoirs by family, friends, and associates*, 2003; Brooks, Van Wyck, *The Life of Emerson*, 1932; Elder, John, ed., *American Nature Writers*, Vol. 1, 1996; Paul, Sherman, *Emerson: Angle of Vision: Man and Nature in the American Experience*, 1952; Richardson, Robert D., *Emerson: The Mind on Fire, A Biography*, 1995; Smith, Harmon, *My Friend, My Friend: the story of Thoreau's relationship with Emerson*, 1999.

American Environmental Leaders

From Colonial Times to the Present

F

Figueroa, Rogelio

(September 13, 1963–)
Gubernatorial Candidate for the Commonwealth of Puerto Rico, Entrepreneur, Columnist

The 2008 candidate for governor of the Commonwealth of Puerto Rico for the newly registered party *Puertorriqueños por Puerto Rico* (Puerto Ricans for Puerto Rico), Rogelio Figueroa is an entrepreneur in green buildings, and a specialist in industrial processes used by cosmetics, food, pharmaceutical, and biotechnology firms. He started and managed a technical services company serving the pharmaceutical and biotechnology industry in Puerto Rico for over a decade, and has been a community activist long impassioned by environmental conservation and managed growth. He writes a regular column for Puerto Rico's leading daily *El Nuevo Día* on many topics of the day, including energy independence and the use of renewable technologies, better quality of life through conservation, and the development of infrastructure fostering less reliance on personal automobiles.

Rogelio Figueroa García, the youngest of nine children, was born on September 13, 1963, to Sotero Figueroa Pomales, an agricultural worker and small farmer, and Juanita García Noble, a homemaker. He grew up in a rural area within the eastern town of Ceiba, surrounded largely by unspoiled coastal vegetation. His advocacy for vulnerable communities and environmentally sustainable development stems from growing up around hardworking people, amid stunning natural beauty. Figueroa received a B.S. *magna cum laude* in Chemical Engineering from the Colegio Universitario de Mayagüez in 1986, and an M.A. in Chemical Engineering from Ohio State University in 1988.

In the mid-1990s Figueroa first became influenced by the thinking of PAUL HAWKEN, particularly his renowned book *The Ecology of Commerce* (1993). The author posits his "comprehensive outcome" principle, which takes into account the results of commercial activity on all parties, not just direct participants. This principle seeks to include, not externalize and ignore, the costs of environmental and/or community degradation in business calculations. As has happened in so many places around the world, Figueroa observed how urban sprawl was swallowing swath upon swath of previously lush greenery in the archipelago of mainland Puerto Rico, Vieques, and Culebra, and the fossil fuel industry was polluting air and land for all through refineries, power generation, and highways perpetually clogged with gasoline-burning cars. So he decided in the mid-1990s that he wanted to start a new political party modeled on the Green parties of Europe to address environmentally and socially critical issues. It was to be a process that would take several years.

He founded the company Anovis Corporation in 1996, which assists pharmaceutical and biotechnology companies operating in Puerto Rico in the areas of compliance with federal regulations, advanced documentation, and other "trouble shooting" technical services. The company's name stands for "A New Vision of Knowledge" and Figueroa's goal was to teach his staff that "anything is possible." In the meantime, Figueroa brought this can-do attitude to many grassroots environmental efforts, such as fighting to preserve forests and sustainable coastal development in Toa Baja, and working as an advocate with the Ceiba Development Alliance (APRODEC) for his home community in the long struggle regarding the development of the closed Roosevelt Roads Naval Station in Ceiba.

In 2003 Figueroa helped found *Puertorriqueños por Puerto Rico*, an organization seeking participation in the electoral arena. Its platform fosters unity among all Puerto Ricans based on four goals: citizen participation, sustainable economic growth, effective governmental administration, and improved quality of life. Figueroa ran for governor as a write-in candidate in 2004. After managing Anovis for many years, he sold his shares in 2006 to finance the registration of *Puertorriqueños por Puerto Rico* as an official party. By 2007 PPR had collected enough valid signatures to become certified as an official commonwealth-wide party, with access to government funds for its operations. Figueroa has been compared with Barack Obama, and his party is running a full slate of candidates throughout all of Puerto Rico for the November 2008 elections, including the environmental consultant and former U.S. Marine Carlos Alberto Velázquez for Puerto Rico's Resident Commissioner in the U.S. Congress.

Figueroa remains active in the private sector with EcoUrbana, a green buildings firm helping residential and commercial property owners retrofit their buildings with climate-moderating roofing and other cooling elements, solar systems for hot water and energy generation, and rainwater collection and treatment tanks. He serves as a watchdog on Puerto Rico's environmental policy issues, most recently lobbying for stalled bills in both chambers of the Puerto Rican legislature on tax incentives for solar and wind energy, "net metering," whereby energy companies would have to pay citizens for excess energy they give back to the grid, and prioritizing loans to small renewable energy firms.

He lives in San Juan, Puerto Rico.

BIBLIOGRAPHY

Staff Writers, "Local Firm Helps Multinational Companies Comply," *Caribbean Business*, 21 August 2003; "Forty Under Forty 2003," *Caribbean Business*, 2003; Martínez Rodríguez, Eugenio, "Rogelio Figueroa y su promesa verde," wikeo.com, June 2005; falcon.blogsome.co/entrevista-a-rogelio-figueroa/; www.porpuertorico.com; www.ecourbana.com; www.anovis.com.

Fontenot, Willie

(November 26, 1942–)
Community Liaison Officer in the Louisiana Attorney General's Office

Willie Fontenot worked for 27 years as an environmental specialist in the Citizens Access Unit of the Louisiana attorney general's office, until his retirement in 2005. He has helped organize nearly 500 citizens' groups throughout Louisiana and 30 other states to solve environmental problems faced by their communities. Fontenot also works with other state and national environmental organizations, including Clean Water Action, the Mississippi River Basin Alliance, and the Louisiana Environmental Action Network.

William Alexander Fontenot was born on November 26, 1942, in Opelousas, Louisiana, one of eight children. His early environmental education came from his father, who subscribed to several natural history magazines and was concerned about the effects of the campaign to eradicate fire ants in the Deep South in the 1950s by poisoning them with chlordane in ground-up corn cobs. Fontenot enrolled at the University of Southwest Louisiana (USL) in 1960 but left in 1961 to serve for four years in the United States Navy. Returning from military service, he reenrolled at USL and graduated with a B.A. in political science in 1969.

Fontenot moved to New Orleans in 1970. From 1970 to 1975, he worked in retail and

Willie Fontenot (Photograph by Mary Fontenot).

business, owning an antique and traditional craft store with his wife from 1973 to 1975. When he learned about the area's severe environmental problems in 1970, he joined the local environmental movement. Lake Pontchartrain was fouled by pollutants from industry, dredging for clam shells, and sewage. Local developers were using the state highway department and the Corps of Engineers to push several projects that would have led to the draining and development of 300,000 acres of coastal wetlands around New Orleans. (Today most of these wetlands are preserved in Bayou Savage National Wildlife Refuge in New Orleans East and Jean Lafitte National Park south of the city.) Fontenot joined the Sierra Club in 1972, becoming chair of its New Orleans Group in 1973 and then chair of the Delta (Louisiana and Mississippi) chapter in 1974. He ran as the environmental candidate for the First Congressional District seat of Louisiana in 1974, losing the election but succeeding in drawing attention to the environment. He volunteered as vice president and director of community services at the Ecology Center of Louisiana, Inc., a clearinghouse where many local environmental groups held meetings and had offices. In 1975 Fontenot moved into full-time remunerated work for the environment, when he was hired as the executive director of the Louisiana Wildlife Federation, the state affiliate of the National Wildlife Federation. This position, as well as his prior volunteer work, provided him with knowledge about the workings of government regulatory agencies and effective strategies for working against pollution.

In 1978 Louisiana attorney general William J. Guste Jr. was encouraged by a staff attorney, Richard M. Troy, to hire Fontenot to help citizens understand how to deal with environmental problems and get better access to governmental agencies. Fontenot recalls that Attorney General Guste was aware of an inherent conflict of interest for government officials and agencies. The government has a constitutional obligation to protect resources and the environment, yet it is also charged with promoting economic development. When a regulatory agency approves any project or plan, the government employees involved generally become advocates for it. Explains Fontenot: "They become friends [with the project promoters] technocrat to technocrat, they have empathy. Then [when the project is environmentally destructive], citizens come in, upset and frustrated, and to the technocrats they seem unreasonable." Fontenot worked with Troy and the attorney general to create a job description for helping citizen organizations become involved in the regulatory process.

Fontenot was hired as an "investigator" in 1978, and although his job title later changed to "community liaison officer," his duties did not change. Attorney General Richard P. Ieyoub, who served from 1991 to 2003, described Fontenot's responsibilities as becoming "involved with communities, groups, people, and public officials who are facing environmental threats; and to help them organize, approach government, gain access to information, and interact with regulatory agencies effectively." In many states, when citizens try to contact the government and get information or complain about an environmental problem, they are shuffled around between offices and frequently do not find the person who can respond to their problem. In Louisiana they were sent straight to the one person charged with helping them, Willie Fontenot. (Only one other state, West Virginia, has a similar office.)

During his tenure, Fontenot helped organize almost 500 citizens groups and guided them in their struggle to solve environmental problems in their communities. He traveled throughout the poor, rural parts of the state, meeting with members in living rooms and on front porches. Most groups were quite small when he was first contacted, just three to five people. Fontenot reminded such groups of Margaret Mead's observation: "Never doubt that a small group of thoughtful and committed individuals can change the world; indeed it is the only thing that ever has." Fontenot encouraged the groups, taught them research techniques and helped them find the resources they need, and accompanied them when they met with officials and agencies.

Among the hundreds of successes of the groups he helped, he recalls the work of the residents of rural, Gulf coast Vermilion Parish. In mid-1978, Vermilion Parish resident Gay Hanks called him and complained of trucks dumping toxic waste in 13 commercial dump sites in the parish and randomly in drainage ditches that farmers used to irrigate their rice and crawfish fields. She was worried about the health effects for local people; her 15-year-old daughter had just died of leukemia. With advice and encouragement from Fontenot, she and four others founded the Vermilion Association to Protect the Environment. They organized the neighbors of each of the 13 commercial dump sites to photograph the sites and keep logs of when trucks were coming in. They organized residents to turn out en masse to hearings and meetings with officials, and by the late 1980s, they had succeeded in having 12 of the 13 commercial dump sites shut down and had convinced the EPA to designate three of them as Superfund sites. They also fought off more than 20 more proposed dumps in the parish.

Another landmark citizens response that Fontenot cites is the Ascension Parish "Save Ourselves" organization, headed by local citizen Teresa Robert, which fought a hazardous waste incinerator proposed by IT Corporation in the courts. Save Ourselves based its suit on Article 9, Section 1 of the Louisiana Constitution, which states that "the important natural resources of the state including air and water and the healthful, scenic, esthetic and historic qualities of the environment shall be protected, replenished and restored, as much as possible, consistent with the health, safety and welfare of the people." The battle began in 1980, and five years later, the Louisiana supreme court declared that this constitutional mandate superceded other state agency regulations. The ruling (452 So.2d 1152, SOS v ECC) has been an important precedent for dozens of other suits in the state.

Fontenot also worked with Mary McCastle and the group she helped form in Alsen, Louisiana, The Coalition for Community Action, to oppose another hazardous waste disposal facility, similar to the one fought by Save Ourselves. Ultimately, McCastle and Coalition for Community Action were successful in their opposition to a Rollins Environmental Services commercial hazardous waste disposal facility, and Fontenot credits them for forcing industry and government regulatory officials to pay attention to the needs and demands of communities of color. He believes that this effort represents the earliest success in the area of environmental justice in the nation.

Fontenot's 27 years with the Attorney General's office came to an end in April of 2005. He was escorting a group of University students who were studying environmental justice in the area. They met with Baton Rouge mayor Kip Holden, and their next stop was across the street from the Baton Rouge Exxon/Mobil plant, where some students got out of the van to take photos. Two off-duty law enforcement officials working as plant security approached them and demanded identity cards from the whole group; one member of the group asked what they would do with the cards, and the security officers called for backup. The officers complained about Fontenot to the Attorney General's office, and the Attorney General gave him an ultimatum—retire or be fired. Fontenot opted to retire. A national campaign to pressure the Attorney General to reinstate Fontenot was unsuccessful.

Since his forced retirement, Fontenot has been doing the same sort of community networking and organizing, but on an independent, voluntary basis. He continues to be involved in a number of environmental and community organizations. He has served on the boards of several regional groups: the Louisiana Environmental Action Network; the Mississippi River Basin Alliance; and the Labor Neighbor Project. He is a member of the Environmental Protection Agency's Citizens Advisory Committee of the Gulf of Mexico, and serves on the board of the national organization Clean Water Fund and on committees of Clean Water Action. In 2000, Fontenot collaborated with Laura Dunn of Two Birds Film company on the production of *Green*, a documentary about environmental "injustice" in "Cancer Alley," the section of the Mississippi River between Baton Rouge and New Orleans. *Green* won an Academy Award in 2001, in the Student category.

Fontenot resides in Baton Rouge with his wife, Mary Umland Fontenot. Mary Fontenot currently serves as a community organizer and networker in the office of the Mayor of Baton Rouge—similar to what Willie did for the Attorney General's office. The Fontenots have two grown children, Jacques Alexandre and Dona Frere.

BIBLIOGRAPHY

Anderson, Bob, "Fontenot's a People Helper," *Baton Rouge Morning Advocate*, 1982; Chase, Steve, "Petrochemical Industry in Louisiana: Students Fight Corporate Intimidation," *Clean Water Action News*, 2005; Ellis, William S., "The Mississippi River under Siege," *The National Geographic Special Edition on Water*, 1993; Mackey, Debra, "Prayer, Preparation, and Persistence: A Conversation with Willie Fontenot," *Whole Terrain*, 2003-4, www.wholeterrain.org/issue_12/WillieFontenotInterview.cfm; Schwab, Jim, *Deeper Shades of Green*, 1994; St. Claire, Jeffrey, "The Scourging of Willie Fontenot," *Counterpunch*, www.counterpunch.org/stclair04132005.html.

Foreman, Dave
(October 18, 1946–)
Conservation Activist, Cofounder of Earth First!

Wilderness lover and conservationist Dave Foreman is best known—infamous to some—for the 10 years he spent as an ecowarrior. Working with a loosely knit but large group of individuals under the Earth First! banner, Foreman advocated radical measures to defend wilderness, ranging from sabotage to civil disobedience. He was arrested in 1989 and tried with the so-called Arizona Five on grounds of sabotaging nuclear plants in the Southwest. But this represents only part of Foreman's conservationist career, which also has included an eight-year stint on the staff of the Wilderness Society (TWS), serving on the board of the Sierra Club, coordinating the Wildlands Project, which has designed a wilderness recovery plan for North America, and most recently, founding the Rewilding Institute, which works to educate laypeople and conservationists about its continental-scale conservation strategy.

Dave Foreman was born on October 18, 1946, in Albuquerque, New Mexico, to Skip and Lorane Foreman. His father was an air force sergeant who moved his family frequently. As a child, Foreman sought solace in whatever natural areas were close to his family's current residence. He attended the University of New Mexico, earning a B.A. in history in 1968. As a college student, Foreman campaigned for Republican Barry Goldwater in his 1964 bid for the presidency. He also joined the conservative Young Americans for Freedom and chaired a group called Students for Victory in VietNam. After graduation, Foreman joined the Marines but was dishonorably discharged two months later. He had spent one of his two months in the brig for insubordination and for going absent without leave. Returning to New Mexico, Foreman taught on a Zuni Indian reservation and became a horseshoer in the northern part of the state before beginning his conservationist career.

Foreman joined the staff of the Wilderness Society in 1972 as its Southwest representative and went to Washington, D.C., in 1977 as a TWS lobbyist. There, he recalled in a 1985 *Mother Earth News* interview, he felt that TWS was being lobbied by the government instead of the other way around. Foreman worked with TWS on negotiations with the U.S. Forest Service about RARE II (Roadless Area Review Evaluation II), which proposed that 65 million of the last remaining 80 million acres of untouched wilderness be opened to mining and logging. TWS, he claimed, had presented convincing evidence and arguments for a greater degree of wilderness preservation in a polite and rational manner but nonetheless lost its case. And worse, TWS discouraged its members from trying to appeal RARE II because it was concerned that the meager conservation gains from RARE II would be lost in any litigation.

That experience sent an embittered Foreman back west in 1979. With four friends, Bart Koehler and Susan Morgan (both ex-TWS staff), HOWIE WOLKE (a one-time Friends of the Earth representative), and ex-yippie Mike Roselle, Foreman drove a Volkswagen van down to the Pinacate desert in Mexico. They mused on the ineffectiveness of mainstream conservation organizations, whose administrators seemed more eager to compromise with the government than to change government policies. During that trip, Earth First! was born. Inspired by EDWARD ABBEY's 1975 novel *The Monkeywrench Gang*, Earth First! was a loose confederation of ecoactivists who swore that they would make "No Compromise in Defense of Mother Earth." Although the group had no formal members, no constitution, no officers, no bylaws, and no nonprofit status, Foreman became its best-known spokesperson because he edited its newsletter.

Earth First!'s first public action took place at the 1981 spring equinox, when Foreman and some others draped a 300-foot black plastic streamer off the Glen Canyon dam to simulate a huge crack. (The Glen Canyon dam, on the Arizona-Utah border, was built as a result of a compromise that the Sierra Club under then-president DAVID BROWER had made in 1959. It agreed to allow the dam to be built if Dinosaur National Monument would be spared flooding.)

Earth First!ers meet at seasonal gatherings to define priorities and plan actions and through the 1980s succeeded in halting many environmentally destructive projects that the more mainstream conservationists could not stop with their traditional strategies. Earth First!'s successes usually involved large protests that drew media attention to the targeted environmental destruction. While Earth First!'s sabotage or civil disobedience delayed the loggers, miners, or road-builders, other groups with legal staffs were able to have court orders drawn up to halt the destruction. This was the case in a 1982 action at a Getty Oil road-building and gas-drilling operation, at a 1983 California old-growth redwood grove, and later in 1983 at a road-building project near the Siskiyou National Forest in Oregon. At the latter action, Foreman himself blocked a logging road and was seriously injured when he was dragged for 100 yards under a Plumley Construction Company pickup truck.

Foreman wrote *Ecodefense: A Field Guide to Monkeywrenching* in 1985, a manual for Earth First!ers. It was his authorship of this guide that put the Federal Bureau of Investigation on his trail. Foreman and four others (Mark Davis, Mark Baker, Peg Millet, and Ilse Asplund) were arrested in May 1989 and accused of sabotaging various nuclear installations in the Southwest. The main piece of evidence against Foreman was that his book was found on the dash of the car of the other defendants when they were caught torching an electric pole that carried power generated by the Palo Verde Nuclear Generating Station. The 1991 trial of the "Arizona Five" resulted in jail terms for all but Foreman, who pled guilty to a felony conspiracy charge in return for a five-year delay on his sentence and a reduction, at that time, of his felony to a misdemeanor. Following the trial, Foreman distanced himself from Earth First!, claiming that many Earth First!ers were straying from the main point of the group and allying themselves with socially progressive causes.

Foreman and his wife, nurse Nancy Morton, whom he married during the 1986 Earth First! Round River Rendezvous, continue their conservationist work, albeit with more mainstream environmental groups. Foreman has worked with the Sierra Club, of which he has been a member since 1973 and the Wildlands Project, which is designing a plan for a recuperation of North America's rich wilderness and is working with environmental groups such as the Sierra Club to put this plan gradually into place. Foreman founded the Rewilding Institute to further develop and promote continental-scale conservation, which would provide the habitat necessary for recovering viable populations of large carnivores. They live in Tucson, Arizona.

BIBLIOGRAPHY

Berger, John J., "Tree Shakers," *Omni*, 1986; Bergman, B. J., "Wild at Heart," *Sierra*, 1998; Bookchin, Murray, and Dave Foreman, *Defending the Earth: A Dialogue between Murray Bookchin and Dave Foreman*, 1990; Foreman, Dave, *Confessions of an Eco-Warrior*, 1991; Foreman, Dave, *Rewilding North America: a vision for conservation in the 21st century*, 2004; Looney, Douglass, "Protector or Provocateur?" *Sports Illustrated*, 1991; McDaniel, Carl, *Wisdom for a livable planet: the visionary work of Terri Swearingen, Dave Foreman, Wes Jackson, Helena Norberg-Hodge, Werner Fornos, Herman Daly, Stephen Schneider, and David Orr*, 2005; "The Ploughboy Interview: Dave Foreman: No Compromise in Defense of Mother Earth," *Mother Earth News*, 1985; "The Rewilding Institute," www.rewilding.org; Zakin, Susan, *Coyotes and Town Dogs: Earth First and the Environmental Movement*, 1993.

Fossey, Dian

(January 16, 1932–December 24, 1985)
Zoologist, Founder of Karisoke Research Center

Author of *Gorillas in the Mist* (1983), Dian Fossey was the world's foremost expert on the mountain gorillas of central Africa. Fossey established the Karisoke Research Center in Rwanda, where she spent more than 13 years studying the endangered species. Fossey gathered extensive scientific evidence about the gorillas' behavior, fought off poachers and other threats to their continued existence, and brought their plight to the attention of the world. Without Fossey's efforts, the mountain gorilla would almost certainly be extinct.

Dian Fossey was born on January 16, 1932, in San Francisco. After graduating from high school, she enrolled in the preveterinary medicine program at the University of California, Davis, and later transferred to San Jose State College. She received a bachelor's degree in occupational therapy from San Jose State College in 1954. She moved to Kentucky and worked as the director of the occupational therapy department at the Kosair Crippled Children's Hospital in Louisville. In 1963 she took out a loan to finance a safari trip to Africa, where she first saw a mountain gorilla and met the anthropologists Louis and Mary Leakey. In 1966 Louis Leakey went to Louisville to recruit Fossey for a long-term gorilla study project. Fossey was at first uncertain that she had the appropriate training, but Leakey assured her he was looking for someone who could bring a fresh approach, as well as great determination, to the project. In preparation for the trip, Fossey had her appendix removed prophylactically to demonstrate her determination, before realizing that Leakey had made the suggestion in jest.

Fossey began her study with Jane Goodall in Tanzania, where she learned something of Goodall's methods of studying chimpanzees. Fossey then went to the Republic of Congo (later Zaire) and began her research on the gorillas. On July 10, 1967, Fossey was taken into custody and kept for two weeks, during which time she saw many of her fellow captives tortured and killed and she herself was repeatedly raped. She managed to escape and was able to cross the border into Uganda. On September 24, 1967, she established the Karisoke Research Center in the Parc National des Vulcans in Rwanda. In 1970 she started doctoral studies at Cambridge University. She received her Ph.D. in zoology in 1976.

Fossey's work dramatically changed both the scientific and popular understanding of gorillas. Prior to Fossey's research, gorillas suffered from the "King Kong myth" and were seen as dangerous, hyperaggressive monsters. Fossey demonstrated that mountain gorillas are largely peaceful, family-oriented vegetarians. She described their personalities and family structure, identifying the individual gorillas she studied by name. She described the relations between gorillas and documented the devastation created by poachers. Adult gorillas will fight fiercely to protect their young, and poachers have to kill many adults to capture a single baby. One of the most famous cases involved an adult male gorilla she called "Digit," who was killed while protecting his family. CBS *Evening News* announced the death, and a fund was established in his name. Fossey's work was both scientifically rigorous and engaging for general readers and thus was effective in serving the interests of preservation.

Fossey fought passionately in defense of the gorillas, against poachers, farmers, and sometimes even game preserve officials. Rwanda is a poor nation with a rapidly growing population, and the small park surrounding the research station was seen as potential agricultural land. Poachers are a major threat to gorilla survival, because collecting gorillas for zoos and for trophies is a profitable busi-

Dian Fossey plays with a group of young mountain gorillas in Rwanda's Virunga Mountains in central Africa. (October 5, 1982) (AP Images).

ness. Fossey had violent confrontations with armed poachers, and at one point kidnapped the child of a poacher whom she offered to exchange for a captured baby gorilla. Park rangers sometimes cooperated with poachers, so Fossey's relationship with wildlife officials was uncertain and often overtly hostile. She organized volunteer patrols to fight against poachers, because she believed that park officials were not active enough or completely trustworthy.

In 1980, suffering from physical exhaustion, Fossey took a leave of absence from the research center and accepted a three-year post at Cornell University. While there she finished work on *Gorillas in the Mist*. Fossey returned to Rwanda in 1983, heartened by the enthusiastic reception of the book. On December 27, 1985, her body was found in her camp in the Viruga Mountains in Rwanda. She had been hacked to death by a machete. A number of theories have been advanced about motive for the murder and the identity of the murderer, though no definitive answers have ever been found. In 1988, a movie starring Sigourney Weaver was made of *Gorillas in the Mist*. Today, the mountain gorillas are in a much less precarious position. Increased tourism in the park has been a boon to the local economy, so there is far greater local incentive to preserve Fossey's beloved gorillas. Once thought to have dwindled to as few as 250, the gorilla population is now believed to have risen to more than 500.

BIBLIOGRAPHY

Biermann, Carol, Louise Grinstein, and Rose Rose, *Women in the Biological Sciences*, 1997; Crouse, Debby, "Up Close with Gorillas," *International Wildlife*, 1988; De la Bédoyère and Dian Fossey, *No one loved gorillas more: Dian Fossey, letters from the mist*, 2005; Montgomery, Sy, *Walking with the Great Apes: Jane Goodall, Dian Fossey, Birutae Galdikas*, 1991, Weber, William and Amy Vedder, *In the Kingdom of Gorillas: fragile species in a dangerous land*, 2001.

Franklin, Jerry
(October 27, 1936–)
Forester, Plant Ecologist

After an intensive, 20-year study of old-growth forest, U.S. Forest Service plant ecologist and professor of forestry Jerry Franklin during the late 1980s developed an ecosystem management approach called New Forestry, which melded two goals that had traditionally been considered contradictory: maintaining the ecological health of old-growth forests and logging them. New Forestry emerged as a promising alternative when the northern spotted owl was listed as an endangered species in 1990, obligating the U.S. Forest Service to protect its old-growth forest habitat. In 1993, Franklin was invited by Pres. Bill Clinton to serve on the Ecological and Economic Assessments Roundtable at the White House Forest Conference and on the Executive Committee of the White House Ecosystem Management Assessment Team. He is credited with convincing President Clinton to significantly reduce logging of old-growth forests and set up a 9.5-million-acre system of old-growth forest and riparian reserves. At this point, with much respected research to support it, Franklin's "New Forestry" has been accepted by environmentalists and the timber industry alike.

Jerry Forest Franklin was born on October 27, 1936, in Waldport, Oregon. He was raised in Camas, Washington, a small town on the Columbia River dominated by a large pulp mill. His father, a worker in the pulp plant, instilled a love of forests in his son. As a youth, Franklin camped with the Boy Scouts in nearby Gifford Pinchot National Forest and enjoyed long solitary hikes in the woods. He decided at an early age that he would become a forester. He earned his B.A. in forest management in 1959 from Oregon State University (OSU), the leading forestry school in the Northwest at that time. He earned an M.A. in forest management from OSU in 1961 and a Ph.D. in botany from Washington State University in 1966.

From 1959 until 1975, Franklin was employed as a research forester at the Pacific Northwest Research Station in Corvallis, Oregon. In 1969, he became deputy director of the Coniferous Forest Biome study for the United Nations' International Biological Program, a large-scale study of the earth's major ecosystems. Research by Franklin's team at the H. J. Andrews Experimental Forest, which is attached to and managed by the Pacific Northwest Research Station, was the first ever done on the old-growth coniferous forest ecosystem. Traditional forestry maintained that old-growth forests—those made up primarily of mature trees, many of them 200 or 300 feet high and several hundred years old—had reached their peak; they were no longer growing in height or girth. The approach of traditional forestry was to harvest these old giants and replace them with easy-to-harvest tree plantations. During the National Science Foundation–funded biome study and those that followed it during the 1970s and 1980s, Franklin and his associates were able to synthesize their discoveries and for the first time weave together a portrait of the complex ecological system of the old-growth forests of the Pacific Northwest.

William Dietrich's *The Final Forest* describes some of the many intricate ecological cycles that Franklin's team discovered: the clean, relatively silt-free streams and rivers of old-growth forests provide habitat for hatching insects and attract spawning salmon, who die upon laying their eggs. Rotting salmon carcasses fertilize trees. As insects die and fall into the streams, they feed recently hatched baby salmon. Biologist Chris Maser's observations revealed the relationship between tree voles and mycorrhizal fungi, which live on the root hairs of trees and help them extract nutrients from soil. Voles inhabit the upper reaches of old-growth trees but descend to dig the truffle-like fruit of mychorrhizal fungi. As voles move along the forest floor in search of truffles, they defecate, dispersing the fungi's spores.

Such elegant ecological relationships disappear when a forest is clear-cut. Humus, the nutrient-rich top layer of soil, erodes, making it harder for plants to grow; robbed of their habitat, animals leave; mudslides and flooding are more likely since vegetation does not capture and slow the movement of water over the land; and siltation fouls streams and rivers. During a 1986 sabbatical at Harvard Forest from Oregon State University—where he taught in the Departments of Forest Science and Botany from 1975 to 1992—Franklin learned that clear-cutting in dispersed patches can compromise conditions in the remaining forested areas, due to what came to be called "edge effects." In subsequent research with his student Jiquan Chen, he documented edge effects in old-growth forests as far as 800 feet away from cutover edges.

Franklin devised a system of techniques that he called New Forestry to meld the goals of ecological health and timber extraction. The New Forestry approach to ecosystem management was inspired by Franklin's knowledge of old-growth forest ecology and from his observations of the important role in ecological restoration played by small mammals inhabiting brush remaining at Mount St. Helens shortly after its 1980 volcanic eruption. New Forestry advocates "messy" logging, which allows some live trees and dead snags to remain standing and leaves fallen logs and other debris on the ground to anchor and nurture the soil and to provide habitat for wildlife. Seedlings of various useful tree species are planted, in an attempt to replicate the diversity of the forest. Cut areas are clustered together to minimize the need for logging roads.

New Forestry burst into public view when the northern spotted owl was listed as an endangered species in 1990. Eric Forsman, a biologist who had worked at H. J. Andrews at the same time that Franklin was forest officer there, studied the previously unknown but now famous northern spotted owl and determined that it was an indicator species for the health of old-growth forests in the Pacific Northwest. Indicator species are important because the health of their populations is indicative of the health of the ecosystem in general. Once the northern spotted owl was listed, the U.S. Forest Service was legally obligated to protect its habitat—large expanses of old-growth forests.

Pres. Bill Clinton convoked a Forest Conference in Portland, Oregon, in 1993 and assigned a team of scientists, including Franklin, to devise a plan to protect the spotted owl without completely crippling the timber industry. Franklin's New Forestry emerged as a promising approach, and Franklin quickly rose as its main spokesperson. He was appointed to the Executive Committee of the White House Ecosystem Management Assessment Team in 1993, which is credited for convincing Pres. Clinton to establish a system of old-growth forest reserves, expand stream buffers, and cut logging in national forests by 80 percent.

Although New Forestry was criticized early on by traditional foresters who felt that its guidelines were not specific enough and that it was too young to be proven to work and by environmentalists who feared that it might justify extensive cutting of old growth, Franklin and others have continued to refine the concept, and it has gained respect and has become accepted by the forestry industry over time. Foresters experiment with New Forestry techniques at the H. J. Andrews Experimental Forest and in U.S. national forests. The faculty at the Department of Forestry Science at Oregon State University, considered to be the Vatican of forestry programs, has recruited specialists and become a national leader in the fields that Franklin pioneered: forest restoration and ecosystem management. With Kathryn Kohm, Franklin coedited *Creating a Forestry for the Twenty-first Century: The Science of Ecosystem Management* in 1996, to which more than 50 authors contributed chapters on aspects of New Forestry ranging from ecological processes and management systems to forest economics. In recent years Franklin has published extensively in his current research fields: ecological forestry, disturbances, ecosystem structure and function, and stand development.

Franklin is the recipient of many honors and awards, including the Heinz Award for the Environment in 2005, the LaRoe Award from the Society for Conservation Biology in 2004 for lifetime scientific contributions to conservation biology, the Leadership in Action Award from the U.S. Chapter of the International Association for Landscape Ecology in 2001, the Murie Award from the Wilderness Society in 1998, the 1996 William B. Greeley Award from the American Forests Association, and the Barrington Moore Award for Outstanding Achievement in Forest Research from the Society of American Foresters in 1986. Since 1986, Franklin has been a professor of Ecosystem Enalysis at the University of Washington's College of Forest Resources.

Franklin lives with his wife, Phyllis, in Issquah, Washington, on the outskirts of Seattle.

BIBLIOGRAPHY

Associated Press, "Experimental Forest Provides Scientists with Information," *Oregon News*, 1998; Dietrich, William, *The Final Forest: The Battle for the Last Great Trees of the Pacific Northwest*, 1992; "Dr. Jerry Franklin," faculty.washington.edu/jff; Durbin, Kathie, "Reformation in the Vatican of Sawlog Forestry: History Takes Oregon State for a Ride," *High Country News*, 1995; "The Heinz Awards," www.heinzawards.net; Kohm, Kathryn A., and Jerry F. Franklin, *Creating a Forestry for the Twenty-first Century: The Science of Ecosystem Management*, 1996; Luoma, Jon, *The Hidden Forest*, 1999.

Frome, Michael

(May 25, 1920–)
Environmental Journalist

Michael Frome chose to dedicate himself to environmental journalism at a time when there was very little information in the media about environmental issues. During the 1960s and 1970s he rose to become one of the nation's foremost conservation writers, known for his investigations of environmental crimes and his willingness to name perpetrators. He was fired in 1971 by *American Forests* and in 1974 by *Field &*

Stream for resisting their censorship of his work; both of these firings received widespread attention in other national media. Frome has written 18 books about the environment and efforts to protect it, plus several outdoor travel guides.

Michael Frome was born on May 25, 1920, in New York City to William and Henrietta (Marks) Frome. His journalistic career began at Dewitt Clinton High School, where he wrote for the *Clinton News*. He attended City College of New York (now City College of the City University of New York) immediately after graduating from high school but left in 1941 to work as a copyboy for the *Washington Post* and International News Service, taking dictated stories by phone from reporters. He volunteered during World War II as a navigator for the U.S. Army Air Corps, flying transport missions all over the world, and then after the war returned to the *Washington Post* as a reporter. In spring 1946 he joined a United Nations relief mission to Czechoslovakia and Poland and wrote a series of front-page *Post* articles about those countries' postwar recovery efforts. From 1947 to 1957 he worked as editor of travel publications for the American Automobile Association (AAA) and began to freelance travel articles for such publications as *Holiday*, *Woman's Day*, *Parade*, *Changing Times*, the *New York Times*, the *Christian Science Monitor*, and the *Chicago Tribune*. One of his assignments at the AAA was to develop and promote a campaign for antibillboard legislation, which allowed him to coordinate with national conservation organizations. Through these contacts, as well as his research trips to national parks throughout the United States, Frome became committed to wilderness preservation. Knowing that the public would not support conservation without good information on the issue, he became concerned about the dearth of conservation news in the mainstream media.

In 1959, after writing several travel guides, he began to focus his writing on environmental issues. His first book in this vein was *Whose Woods These Are—The Story of the National Forests* (1962), a history of the U.S. Forest Service (USFS) and guide to national forests. That was followed up with a book he initially had conceived as a history and travel guide for Great Smoky Mountain National Park. Upon learning that the National Park Service was planning an ill-conceived highway and development scheme for that park that would have developed large areas of pristine forest, Frome was moved to assume the role of advocate. The resulting book, *Strangers in High Places*, published in 1966, argued convincingly against the plan. Park officials reacted by banning his book from park bookshops, but the proposed road was never built.

His reputation for good writing and strong advocacy established, Frome became a columnist for *American Forests* in 1966 and for *Field & Stream* in 1967. A freelance article for *Holiday* in 1966, "The Politics of Conservation," probed a question that bothered Frome: why politicians were not responding adequately to a growing public concern for wilderness preservation. This is a problem that Frome has returned to many times over during his career.

Although his columns were popular among readers of *American Forests* and *Forest & Stream*, Frome was fired from both publications in the early 1970s for resisting censorship. For *American Forests*, published by the American Forestry Association, whose board of directors was made up primarily of foresters associated with the timber industry and the USFS, Frome wrote critically about clearcutting of national forests, decrying what he saw as an overemphasis on timber production by a government agency that was also charged with responsible stewardship of public lands. When William Towell, executive director of the American Forestry Association, wrote a memorandum in 1971 to the editor of *American Forests* demanding that Frome cease his criticism of the USFS and the timber industry and focus on other less controversial issues, Frome protested, and was fired. His dismissal, however, caused more trouble for the American Forestry Association than for Frome himself. Former interior secretary STEWART UDALL and Jeff Stansbury wrote about his firing for the Los Angeles Times Syndicate: "How to Kill a Conservation Organization... Obituary for the American Forestry Association"; a colleague wrote a tribute in *Field & Stream* entitled "How the Clearcutters Tried to Gag Mike Frome"; and many of Frome's fans wrote letters of protest to the editor of *American Forests*.

Frome continued writing for the larger and more influential *Field & Stream*, but soon he faced opposition from publishers there as well. Although he did not write from the perspective of an outdoorsman, his focus on conservation was welcomed by hunters and anglers concerned about disappearing natural habitat. He wrote about the effects on wildlife of logging, dam building, wetland drainage, and other intrusive activities; named names of individuals and companies responsible for the damage; and gave suggestions for getting involved. As part of this effort to encourage activism, Frome coordinated a "Rate Your Candidate" feature in election years 1968, 1970, and 1972, in which congresspeople were rated according to their commitment and effectiveness on conservation issues. "Rate Your Candidate" upset those members of Congress who were given poor ratings, one of whom chaired the subcommittee that ruled on broadcasting relations. This was of especial concern to the Columbia Broadcasting System (CBS), the media conglomerate that owned *Field & Stream*, and the magazine discontinued the feature. By 1974, a new editor at *Field & Stream* was actively censoring Frome's work. Frome was told to write about conservation problems in general rather than describing specific crises and referring to specific culprits. Because he would not comply with this order, Frome was fired in late 1974. Conservationists reacted immediately. Individuals picketed CBS's Washington headquarters, and organization heads (as well as some members of Congress) wrote letters of protest to the chair of the board of CBS. *Time* featured the story in its November 4, 1974, issue.

Following this, Frome went on to write columns for *Defenders of Wildlife* for 18 years and for the *Los Angeles Times* and *Western Outdoors* as well. He has written 12 books since 1974, including *Battle for the Wilderness* (1974, revised in 1997), which recounts the long fight to pass the Wilderness Act of 1964 and describes the process for designation of wilderness. *Conscience of a Conservationist* (1989) is a collection of some of his best-known essays and articles, including exposés and conservation histories. *Regreening the National Parks* (1992) elaborates on a theme he has revisited frequently since 1962, the overdevelopment of national parks and other natural sites. Frome believes that rather than defining its primary mission as providing recreational opportunities, the National Park Service should acknowledge the importance of providing sanctuaries for wildlife. He advocates such changes to park visitation policy as determining the human carrying capacity of each park and limiting visitorship to that number, limiting automobile access to some parks, and deemphasizing the role of concessions. *Green Ink: An Introduction to Environmental Journalism* (1998) is both a memoir and a primer for good environmental writing.

Frome's latest titles include *Greenspeak: Fifty Years of Environmental Muckraking & Advocacy* (2002), which are transcripts of speeches he has given since about 1960, on virtually every issue related to conservation, and the autobiographical *Rebel on the Road* (2007).

In addition to practicing environmental journalism, Frome has taught courses on the topic. He has taught at the University of Vermont (1978), the Pinchot Institute for Conservation Studies in Milford, Pennsylvania (1981), the College of Forestry at the University of Idaho (1982–1986), the SIGURD OLSON Environmental Institute at Northland College in Ashland, Wisconsin (1986–1987), and the Huxley College of Environmental Studies at

Western Washington University in Bellingham, where he developed an environmental journalism program (1987–1995).

Frome has received many awards and recognitions, including the Thomas Wolfe Memorial Literary Award (1967); Trout Unlimited's Trout Conservationist of the Year (1972); a Mort Weisinger Award, presented by the American Society of Journalists and Authors for the best Magazine Article of the Year for his 1981 five-part series "The Ungreening of the National Parks" (published in *Travel Agent* and subsequently in *National Parks* Magazine and in the book *National Parks in Crisis*); and the National Parks and Conservation Association's MARJORY STONEMAN DOUGLAS Award (1986). The University of Idaho offers the Michael Frome Scholarship for Excellence in Conservation Writing in his honor. He completed his doctorate in environmental studies through the Union Institute in 1993 and was named Outstanding Alumnus of the Year in 1999.

Frome lives with his wife, June Eastvold, a Lutheran pastor, in Wisconsin. He has two adult children.

BIBLIOGRAPHY

Frome, Michael, *Green Ink*, 1998; McNulty, Tim, "Respect for the Earth, Respect for Michael Frome," *Seattle Times*, 1996; "Michael Frome. Papers, 1959–1989," www.lib.uidaho.edu/special-collections/Manuscripts/mg174.htm.

Fuller, Buckminster

(July 12, 1895–July 1, 1983)
Architect, Inventor

Buckminster Fuller is most often remembered as an architect who designed buildings with an eye for the future. His lifelong goal was to develop a science of design that would solve the world's major problems, such as poverty and housing shortages, while conserving finite resources. Frustrated by the obvious discrepancy between the advanced state of available technology and its haphazard and mediocre applications to ordinary life, he continually and loudly advocated for holding technology to a higher standard. He was ahead of his time in supporting the use of renewable energy resources, which he always incorporated into his designs—claiming that our perceived energy crisis is actually a crisis of ignorance.

Richard Buckminster Fuller Jr. was born on July 12, 1895, in the Boston suburb of Milton, Massachusetts, the second of four children of Richard Buckminster and Caroline Wolcott (Andrews) Fuller. His father was a successful Boston tea and leather merchant who died when his son was 15. Buckminster was born cross-eyed and abnormally farsighted and for several years only saw large patterns and blurred colors. He got glasses when he was four and could suddenly see real details, yet his perception of patterns stayed with him and influenced the way he thought. He went to school at Milton Academy, where he excelled in math and science, and in 1913 he enrolled in Harvard University, where four previous generations of Fullers had received their education. However, he had long been frustrated with formal academics, often feeling that his teachers lacked adequate answers to his questions. By the middle of his first year at Harvard he had become impatient with school and ran off to New York City, where he squandered his tuition entertaining a girl he knew in the chorus line of a current

Buckminster Fuller, the originator of the geodesic principle, stands outside one of his dome houses February 2, 1971. (AP Images/Jim Palmer).

theatrical show—and all her friends and coworkers. His spree resulted in his expulsion from Harvard. A week later his family arranged for him to work in a cotton mill in Quebec, which was not altogether unfortunate for him, as he learned about machines and mechanics and ended up an enthusiastic technician. Having supposedly demonstrated his reliability, he was readmitted to Harvard, only to have his disinclination for conventional education get the best of him; once again he was expelled for irresponsibility. At this point he went to work as a meat lugger at Armour and Company in New York.

In early 1917 he enlisted in the navy and was assigned to active duty, and a few months later he married Anne Hewlett. By the time the war ended, Fuller had gained important experience involving the mechanics of ships and their equipment; perhaps more relevant was his glimpse at the technology necessary to protect people from the hostile weather conditions found at sea. In 1919 he returned to work at Armour and Company as an assistant export manager; there he stayed until 1922. At that point, he went into business with his architect father-in-law, forming Stockade Company, which manufactured a new form of fibrous cinder blocks. That same year his first daughter, Alexandra, died at the age of four—after suffering from a series of epidemic infections aggravated by poor housing conditions during the war. Fuller was shattered by her death and took years to emerge from a profound depression. Shortly after the birth of a second daughter, Allegra, in 1927, he lost his job at Stockade Company, which brought him near the point of suicide. But after a period of self-analysis, he emerged from his emotional crisis and resolved to renounce financial and personal gain and to use his talents to help humankind. He believed that worldwide needs, such as housing, could be met by taking advantage of all relevant scientific principles and technical designs, which could be implemented in such a way as to conserve resources and still be practical and cost-effective.

Fuller moved his family to Chicago and began the process of turning his meditations into realities. This led to the invention of several revolutionary structures, all of which adhered to his principle of doing more with less. Some of Fuller's other inventions include the Dymaxion house, whose name was coined by Fuller's publicist from "dynamism," "maximum," and "ions," all favorite words in Fuller's vocabulary. The Dymaxion house, a family dwelling that was to be mass-produced to cut down on energy expenditure, was to serve as a prototype for a worldwide housing industry. It incorporated a number of highly sophisticated labor-saving devices, such as compressed air and vacuum units that took care of dusting; laundry machines that washed, dried, and conveyed clothing to storage units; and revolving shelves that were rigged to move at the interruption of a light beam. Fuller intended to construct the houses using inexpensive, efficient materials, such as casein—a translucent sheeting made from vegetable refuse, which was to be used for the walls, windows, and ceilings. And, perhaps most remarkably considering that this was in the late 1920s, Fuller planned for the use of renewable energy (such as solar and wind-generated) that could be channeled directly into the house to work as electricity or air conditioning or could be stored in batteries for future use. The general public was perhaps not ready for these ideas, and the Dymaxion house never got beyond the stage of models. In 1932 he founded the Dymaxion Corporation to produce his inventions, including the Dymaxion car and a Dymaxion world map that showed all the continents on a flat surface without distortion. He invented a board game called the World Game, which utilized a large-scale Dymaxion Map for displaying world resources and allowed players to strategize resource-conserving solutions to global problems.

Fuller is most famous for his geodesic dome design, which demonstrates enormous strength with minimal quantities of materials. A dome can cover large areas of space without internal supports, since pressure applied to its surface is dissipated along the entire structure; and in fact it grows relatively lighter and stronger the larger it is. Geodesic domes are also extremely easy and quick to construct and use such a comparatively small amount of materials that they are dramatically more cost-effective than any other housing structure available. Fuller gained recognition for his design in 1953 when Ford Motor Company commissioned him to build a 93-foot cover for their Dearborn plant rotunda, and he was then increasingly in demand to build similar structures. He created them for the air force, the Union Tank Car Company, the Missouri Botanical Gardens, and an international trade fair in Afghanistan. Others began appearing in Tokyo, New Delhi, Bangkok, and Moscow.

Fuller was truly ahead of his time. Many of his inventions, considered impractical at the time, have gradually come into circulation over the years. Long before most people became concerned about energy conservation, he decried the inefficiency in most mechanical gadgetry—he once calculated that fully 96 percent of worldwide energy expenditure (most of which comes from nonrenewable sources) is wasted on friction, bad design, and general carelessness. His belief was that architects and engineers should be held to a higher level of responsibility on behalf of all humanity.

During the course of his career, he was awarded 25 U.S. patents, received 47 honorary doctorates, received dozens of awards in architecture and design, and circled the globe 57 times, lecturing to millions. On July 1, 1983, he died at his wife's deathbed in a hospital in Los Angeles.

BIBLIOGRAPHY

Baldwin, J., *BuckyWorks: Buckminster Fuller's ideas for today*, 1996; "Buckminster Fuller Institute," www.bfi.org; Fuller, Buckminster, *Ideas and Integrities*, 1963; Fuller, R. Buckminster, and Robert Marks, *The Dymaxion World of Buckminster Fuller*, 1960; Gabel, Medard and Jim Walker, "The Anticipatory Leader: Buckminster Fuller's Principles for Making the World Work," *The Futurist*, 2006; Kenner, Hugh, *Bucky: A Guided Tour of Buckminster Fuller*, 1973; McHale, John, *R. Buckminster Fuller*, 1962; Scanlon, Matt, "The Mind Behind the Dome," *Mother Earth News*, 1999.

Fuller, Kathryn

(July 8, 1946–)
President and Chief Executive Officer of World Wildlife Fund

Kathryn Fuller served as president and chief executive officer of the World Wildlife Fund (WWF) from 1989 till 2005. She arrived to this post after leading that organization's Trade Record Analysis of Flora and Fauna in Commerce (TRAFFIC) program to monitor international trade in endangered species, directing public policy, and serving as its executive vice president. Previous to her work at WWF, Fuller helped create a Wildlife and Marine Resources Section at the U.S. Department of Justice.

Kathryn Fuller was born in New York City on July 8, 1946, the eldest of three children. Brought up in Westchester County just to the north of New York City, Fuller was from the very beginning interested in nature and the outdoors. Her mother, Carol Fuller, was an amateur naturalist dedicated to conservation and raised her children on books including accounts of naturalists and explorers, such as Jane Goodall, whose articles about chimpanzees in Tanzania were just being published for the first time in *National Geographic* magazine. Fuller attended Brown University, initially studying biology but switching to major in English after her biology classes proved to be premed rather than nature oriented. She graduated in 1968.

Fuller designed computer systems for Yale University's library and the American Chemical Society before taking a job in 1971 at Harvard's Museum of Comparative Zoology. In her free time, Fuller audited Harvard classes. One of her favorites was given by entomologist EDWARD O. WILSON, who rekindled her commitment to pursue a career in conservation. Fuller accepted an invitation from ecologists Richard and Runi Estes in 1972 to accompany them to Tanzania to study wildebeest migration. It was during this two-month trip that Fuller finally got to see firsthand the wilds that she had been daydreaming about since childhood and also that she realized how crucial conservation would be to the survival of such spectacular wildlands.

Upon her return from Tanzania, Fuller enrolled in law school in Texas, hoping to become a wildlife lawyer. After graduating in 1976 from the University of Texas School of Law in Austin and clerking for a Texas U.S. District Court judge for one year, Fuller moved to Washington, D.C., and joined the Department of Justice. She began working for the Land and Natural Resource division of the Department of Justice in 1979 and helped set up the new Wildlife and Marine Resources Section there. She worked on cases pertaining to endangered species, fisheries, and the Lacey Act of 1900, which prohibits the importation or state-to-state transport of poached wildlife. During the early 1980s, while at the Department of Justice, Fuller enrolled in a master's degree program in marine, estuarine, and environmental studies at the University of Maryland. This, she thought, would allow her to further develop her scientific knowledge.

In 1982, when the youngest of her three children was born, Fuller left the Department of Justice to work as a private consultant in conservation. She was hired by the World Wildlife Fund to research all national and international laws that fell within the domain of the Lacey Act. Within a year she became an employee of WWF and directed WWF's TRAFFIC program, which monitors international wildlife trade and works to strengthen protection of threatened or endangered species. Fuller moved up the ranks of WWF, becoming executive vice president in 1987. When WWF president and chief executive officer (CEO) WILLIAM K. REILLY was named Environmental Protection Agency administrator by President Bush in 1989, Fuller was elected president and CEO of the organization, a post she kept until 2005.

WWF, perhaps the world's best-known conservation organization with over one million U.S. members, has sponsored more than 2,000 projects in some 100 countries. Its efforts are directed toward three global goals: "protecting endangered spaces, saving endangered species, and addressing global threats." Under Fuller's leadership, WWF acknowledged that conservation efforts will not succeed unless human needs are addressed. One of her accomplishments during the mid-1980s was to help engineer many "debt-for-nature" swaps, through which countries rich in biodiversity but in debt to international financial institutions had portions of their debts forgiven in exchange for a commitment to conserve natural resources. This was seen as a win-win solution to the paralyzing external debts that many developing countries suffer. Current WWF conservation projects are designed with participation from local people, in order to address their needs and assure their full support. WWF has also worked on global threats to nature, such as climate change and the accumulation of toxic and persistent chemicals.

When Fuller left WWF, the organization set up the Kathryn Fuller Science for Nature Fund, which operates four programs: Fuller Fellowships, to support scientists earlier in their careers to work on conservation issues of importance; an annual Science for Nature Symposium to discuss an emerging scientific issue pertinent to conservation; bimonthly Science for Nature Seminars in which scientists visit WWF's Washington D.C. headquarters to present cutting-edge science-based conservation research; and a Visiting Scientist program, in which a senior scientist spends a sabbatical at WWF.

For her work in conservation, Fuller has received a United Nations Environmental Programme Global 500 Award, was given Brown University's 1990 William Rogers Outstanding Graduate Award, and has received several honorary degrees. Fuller is currently Chair of the Ford Foundation Board of Trustees, and serves on the boards of Resources for the Future and the Smithsonian Institution's National Museum of Natural History.

BIBLIOGRAPHY

Breton, Mary Joy, *Women Pioneers for the Environment*, 1998; "Ford Foundation," www.fordfound.org; Hitt, Greg, "Animal Passions," *Harpers Bazaar*, 1991; "Kathryn S. Fuller," *Current Biography Yearbook*, 1994; "World Wildlife Fund," www.worldwildlife.org.

Futrell, J. William
(July 6, 1935–)
Attorney, President of Sustainable Development Law Associates

J. William Futrell served as president and chief executive officer of the Environmental Law Institute (ELI) for 23 years, from 1980 until 2003, and is credited for making this national, nonprofit research and educational institution a leader in advancing environmental protection by improving law, management, and policy throughout the world. Since 2003, he has served as President of Sustainable Development Law Associates, which seeks to encourage the growth of sustainable development law, which includes statutes, regulations, and decisions that prevent, mitigate, or punish unsustainable conduct.

John William Futrell was born on July 6, 1935, in Alexandria, Louisiana, to J. W. and Sarah Ruth (Hitesman) Futrell. Growing up in rural Louisiana, he was most influenced by the Methodist Church and the Boy Scouts, with whom he explored the Kisatchie National Forest woodlands that surrounded his home. In high school, he first read Albert Schweitzer's *Out of My Life and Thought* and was moved by its call for reverence of life. His church activities at college led to participation in sit-ins to desegregate church facilities in Louisiana, an experience that spurred a lifelong commitment to civil rights and that demonstrated how law and religion interact. He earned his B.A. in philosophy at Tulane University in 1957, was commissioned a second lieutenant in the United States Marine Corps, and received a Fulbright Scholarship to study recent German history and economics at the Free University of Berlin. This opportunity—which inspired his longstanding commitment to international work—led to his assignment to the Office of Naval Intelligence at the U.S. Mission in West Berlin. From 1960 to 1962, he served in East Asia, in turn commanding an artillery battery and a military police company and teaching a course on survival skills. These years taught him that communism posed a fundamental challenge to religious and democratic values.

Futrell earned his LL.B. from Columbia University's School of Law in 1965 and that same year became a law clerk for federal judge Edwin Hunter of the U.S. District Court, Western District of Louisiana, where he participated in desegregation cases for seven of the state's 64 parishes. He worked as a trial attorney for the New Orleans firm Lemle & Kelleher from 1966 to 1971, during which time he became interested in the new field of environmental law. Environmental law was just then emerging as a result of a broad social movement and citizen protests, which led to the passage of a dozen statutes and hundreds of regulations in a few short years. Futrell became one of the first environmental law professors in 1971, teaching at the universities of Alabama and Georgia from 1974 to 1979. Aside from his law practice and teaching, he organized Sierra Club groups in the southern United States and became southern regional vice president of the Sierra Club in 1971. Elected to the Sierra Club Board of Directors in 1971, he led campaigns for better coastal zone management and ocean protection, wilderness expansion, and urban environment. As Sierrra Club president in 1978, he worked to forge alliances with civil rights groups, an effort that led to the City Care Conference in Detroit in 1979 and the City Care movement.

Futrell was awarded a fellowship from the Wilson Center at the Smithsonian Institution for the academic year 1979–1980, during which he wrote and lectured on the relationship of administrative agency law and practice to nonprofit organizations and citizen participation. In 1980 he became president and chief executive officer of the Environmental Law Institute. ELI had been founded in 1969 by the Public Law Education Institute and the Conservation Foundation to train lawyers and other professionals to work in the new field of environmental law, and Futrell has developed and nurtured the organization as it has grown to become a major influence in the shaping of national environmental policy and law.

In addition to providing continuing environmental education to lawyers through its annual environmental law intensive and about 50 seminars and courses per year held throughout the country, ELI offers its educational services to corporate and public interest members as well. The Corporate Program offers training in environmental law issues to the environmental staff members of these companies. ELI bills this program as a way in which "forward-thinking businesses and their environmental professionals" can promote "environmental leadership in the business community." ELI's Public Interest Program offers a special membership category for public interest and citizen advocacy groups. Public interest members enrich ELI's seminars about specific environmental topics and issues, and ELI in turn helps assure that their viewpoints are heard by corporations and government agencies such as the Environmental Protection Agency and the National Oceanic and Atmospheric Administration. These "professional dialogues" convene a diverse group of experts to develop implementable solutions to pressing environmental problems.

ELI publishes three periodicals that have become major sources of environmental law, policy, and management information: the monthly *ELR—The Environmental Law Reporter*; *The Environmental Forum*, a bimonthly journal with articles on environmental management issues by lawyers, corporate executives, politicians, Environmental Protection Agency administrators, and citizen activists; and *National Wetlands Newsletter*, which specializes in wetlands regulation, policy, and science. Much of the material in these journals is published electronically on ELI's web site (www.eli.org). In addition, ELI publishes several research reports per year, concise summaries of the policy studies undertaken by EPI's staff. Research topics include air and water pollution, wetlands, economics, state environmental law, and toxic substances and hazardous waste.

Approximately one-third of ELI's work is done outside of the United States. Projects emphasize capacity building for environmental groups and government agencies in India, Mexico, Ukraine, and Uganda, among other countries. Since 1993, Futrell has served as the North American vice chair of the International Union for the Conservation of Nature (IUCN) Commission on Environmental Law, working with the IUCN staff in Switzerland and with the six other vice chairs from the other regions to make the international network a reality. Futrell continues to work with the IUCN Commission on Environmental Law to make presentations internationally on international and national environmental law and its applications to conservation issues.

Futrell has published many articles on topics ranging from environmental ethics to environmental law and constitutional rights, to hazardous waste management, to the National Environmental Policy Act. Responding to a mandate from the 1992 United Nations Earth Summit, Futrell and the ELI staff developed a blueprint for a new approach to environmental law. In the 1993 ELI book *Sustainable Environmental Law*, Futrell and the other contributors charted a shift from traditional environmental law—"a massive legal response aimed at curbing pollution and conserving resources"—to a new approach that would not eliminate the earlier approach but would "shift the focus to causes of impacts." Through this new approach, environmental concerns have been integrated into the development law of real estate, insurance, and other fields. In 2003, when Futrell retired from ELI, he went on to found Sustainable Development Law Associates.

Futrell lives in Arlington, Virginia, with his wife, Iva Macdonald Futrell. They have two adult children, Sarah and Daniel.

BIBLIOGRAPHY

Campbell-Mohn, Celia, ed., *Sustainable Environmental Law*, 1993; "Environmental Law Institute," www.eli.org; Futrell, J. William, "Environmental Ethics, Legal Ethics, and Codes of Professional Responsibility," *Loyola (Los Angeles) Law Review*, 1994; Futrell, J. William, "Love for the Land and Justice for Its People," Sierra Club History Series, Regional Oral History Office, The Bancroft Library, University of California, 1984; Futrell, J. William, "The Transition to Sustainable Development Law," *Pace Environmental Law Review*, 2003; Futrell, J. William, "Defining Sustainable Development Law," *American Bar Association Natural Resources & Environment*, 2004.

American Environmental Leaders

From Colonial Times to the Present

Gagliano, Sherwood M.

(1935–)
Geomorphologist, President of Coastal Environments, Inc. (CEI)

Sherwood M. Gagliano is coastal Louisiana's Chicken Little, the first person to decry not that the sky was falling, but that the land was sinking. Prior to Gagliano's 1970 groundbreaking report, it was believed that the Delta system was replenishing coastal wetlands and estuaries in a phenomenon called coastal equilibrium. But "Woody" Gagliano, a young scientist fresh out of Louisiana State University, recognized that his home state was actually losing landmass up to 16.5 square miles a year. Ever since, he's been on a mission to understand the significant erosion of coastal Louisiana and, if possible, to rectify it.

Sherwood Gagliano was born in New Orleans, Louisiana on December 10, 1935. As a young man, he explored the marshes of southern Louisiana, and made his first observations of wetland erosion as a high school student who was interested in archaeology. Gagliano noticed that the shell heaps left behind by Native Americans were sinking. His interest was perked. Gagliano sought an academic career at Louisiana State University, first receiving a B.S. in geology before going on to graduate work in the Geography Department where he earned a doctorate in 1967. In the mid-1960s he was asked by LSU's Coastal Studies Institute to head the research funded by the Army Corps of Engineers to study the potential effects of re-directing water from the Mississippi to New Mexico and Texas. His findings were presented to the 1970 National Academy of Sciences meeting in Houston. Gagliano predicted Louisiana would lose 500 square miles of coastal wetlands by 2000 without even considering re-channeling water to the Southwest.

Over the years, Gagliano championed important causes and cures for the rapid erosion of Louisiana. By 1990, the U.S. Congress was utilizing Gagliano's findings to help enact the Coastal Wetlands Planning, Protection and Restoration Act, previously known as the Breaux-Johnston Bill. It provided $50 million a year on wetlands restoration projects. Knowing that $50 million would not be enough given the scope of the work, Gagliano proposed a project called the Third Delta Conveyance Channel, a $2 billion dollar piece of a $14 billion dollar Coast 2050 proposal for wetlands restoration and hurricane protection. The Conveyance Channel, developed by Gagliano and his associate, Johannes van Beek, is a monumental project to divert 200,000 cubic feet per second of Mississippi River water several miles downstream to the Barataria and the Terrebonne Estuary. Gagliano believes this will stabilize the marshland quickly.

After years of study, Gagliano is convinced that active tectonic faults below Louisiana are also a major cause of the erosion of Louisiana's landmass, in addition to the man-made levees, on and off-shore drilling, and wetland draining. He testified before U.S. Congress after the devastating Hurricane Katrina in 2005 that stressed fault lines were just as much culpable for the breaking of the levees as the surge of water from the river, the U.S. Army Corps-built levees, or anything else that caused the devastating flooding of New Orleans. Gagliano urges to incorporate seismic data into the considerations of rebuilding in Louisiana and wetland restoration.

"Hurricane protection and wetland restoration have been regarded as a battle against the erosive forces of the sea, a horizontal engagement. Findings of the tectonic studies indicate that the dominant processes are geological and the changes are vertical, thus requiring a fundamental shift in battle strategy," Gagliano told Congress in 2005.

Gagliano spent 12 years on the faculty of the Coastal Studies Institute and the Department of Geography and Marine Sciences at LSU before founding, in 1972, Coastal Environments, Inc. (CEI), an applied science and planning firm, providing environmental research and consulting to private and government entities, where he remains president today. Dr. Gagliano is a member of the Geological Society of America, the American Association of Petroleum Geologists, the Society for Sedimentary Geology, the Society of American Archaeology, the Society of Sigma Xi, and was the founding president of the Louisiana Archaeological Society.

Gagliano recently served as an advisor to the state of Louisiana as they developed a new state agency–the Coastal Protection and Restoration Authority of Louisiana. The agency is formulating a master plan of coastal restoration and storm protection.

Currently he lives in Baton Rouge, Louisiana, with his wife, Betty Huxen Gagliano.

BIBLIOGRAPHY

Schleifstein, Mark, "Early warning went unheeded," www.pulitzer.org/year/1997/public-service/works/3-3/; Grunwald, Michael and Susan B. Glasser, "The Slow Drowning of New Orleans," *Washington Post*, www.washingtonpost.com/wp-dyn/content/article/2005/10/08/AR2005100801458_pf.html; Masson, Todd, "Plan in place to create two new deltas," www.louisianasportsman.com/stories/2003/paradise-lost/plan-in-place.htm; Gagliano, Sherwood, PhD., "Effects of Earthquakes, Fault Movements, and Subsidence on the South Louisiana Landscape," and "Effects of Geological Faults on Levee Failures in South Louisiana," www.coastalenv.com/html/publications.html.

Geisel, Theodor (Dr. Seuss)
(March 2, 1904–September 24, 1991)
Children's Author and Illustrator

As a writer and illustrator of over 40 much-beloved children's books, Theodor Geisel (Dr. Seuss) has had a unique influence on four generations of Americans. In an era when children's books were dry and didactic, his whimsical and imaginative stories revived children's interest in reading—while also exposing such dangers as war, prejudice, or wasting natural resources. His classic book, *The Lorax* (1971), addresses the theme of conservation with the story of an ecosystem that becomes dismally polluted and deserted as a consequence of an individual's self-interest and greed. For many young children, *The Lorax* may be their introduction to environmental issues and may have a lasting influence on their thinking and sense of responsibility.

Theodor Seuss Geisel was born on March 2, 1904, in Springfield, Massachusetts, and grew up there with his older sister, Margaretha. His father, Theodor Robert Geisel, was the manager of a brewery and later, during Prohibition, served as a park superintendent. His mother, Henrietta Seuss Geisel, discovered young Ted's love of rhymes and fostered his awareness of the pleasure of words. In high school, his teachers found him bright, but not dedicated; and to fellow students he was funny and charming. In 1921 he entered Dartmouth College, planning to major in English. Before long he had made himself a fixture at the offices of the Dartmouth humor magazine, *Jack-O-Lantern*, and by his junior year he was editor in chief. As graduation approached, he faced questions from his father

Theodor Geisel reads from his book "Horton Hears a Who!" to Lucinda Bell at his home in La Jolla, Calif., June 20, 1956. (AP Images)

regarding his plans, and he jokingly wrote back that he would be attending Oxford University on a fellowship. His father, proudly believing it, had an announcement published in the newspaper. Upon graduating in 1925, Ted had to confess that there was no fellowship. His father insisted that the family must simply find a way to send Ted to England anyway, and that fall he was enrolled at Lincoln College in Oxford. He found his graduate studies there to be tedious and abandoned them after a year. The experience was not a total loss, however, as he met the woman he would eventually marry, a fellow American student named Helen Palmer.

In 1927, Geisel settled in New York, got a job as a writer and artist with *Judge* magazine, and married Helen. Geisel signed "Seuss" on his cartoons for the magazine, explaining to those who knew him that he was saving his full name for a "serious" novel he hoped to write someday. After a time he added "Dr." to the name to compensate for the doctorate he never earned at Oxford. Geisel also worked as a freelance cartoonist and essayist, and throughout the 1930s his creative ideas were seen on the pages of *Vanity Fair*, *Redbook*, and the *Saturday Evening Post*. Later, before his enlistment in the Army Signal Corps in 1943, Geisel wrote political cartoons, lashing out at the evils of fascism and racism that accompanied World War II.

His first children's book was written in 1936, about a boy who imagines a fantastic parade of scenes on the street as he walks to school, instead of the drab horse and wagon that passes by. It was called *And to Think That I Saw It on Mulberry Street* and was rejected by 27 publishers as being too different from other children's books. It was finally published in 1937 when an old Dartmouth friend who was junior editor at Vanguard Press convinced his superiors to give Geisel's book a chance. This was the breakthrough that would shape his career.

Geisel went on to write over 40 children's books, all of them in his exuberant style—giddy illustrations and silly, rollicking verse. In the era of mundane Dick and Jane primers, his books were a breath of fresh air to children and parents alike. Geisel avoids preaching in his books, yet underlying the humor is often a moral emphasizing strong values important for readers of any age. In *The Lorax*, which Geisel listed as his favorite of all the books he wrote, he unabashedly voices his fears about the detrimental effects of greed and pollution on the environment. It tells the story of a creature called the Once-ler, who happens upon a beautiful place where Truffula Trees grow, Swomee-Swans sing, and Brown Bar-Ba-Loots frisk about in the shade. Filled with entrepreneurial ambition, the Once-ler proceeds to cut down the Truffula Trees and manufacture Thneeds, which resemble misshapen hairy pink underwear—and everyone starts buying them in great quantities. As the trees continue to fall, the Lorax appears, crying out against this destruction and calling the Once-ler "crazy with greed." The Once-ler replies that business is business, saying:

> Well, I have my rights, sir, and I'm telling you
> I intend to go on doing just what I do!
> And, for your information, you Lorax,
>   I'm figgering
> on biggering, and biggering, and biggering, and
>   BIGGERING,
> turning MORE Truffula Trees into Thneeds
> which everyone, EVERYONE, EVERYONE
>   needs!

Soon the trees are gone, the sky is smothered with smog, and the water is brown with pollution. The Swomee-Swans and all the other creatures have long since left. The Lorax appears a final time, gives the Once-ler a mournful look, and departs—leaving behind a rock etched with the word "UNLESS." Years pass in this wasteland where only Gricklegrass grows in place of the Truffula Trees, and at the end of the book the Once-ler, now filled with remorse and worry over what he caused, explains the meaning of the Lorax's message: Unless someone starts to care, things are not going to get any better. But the story ends with hope: one Truffula Tree seed has been saved, and the Once-ler urges the reader to plant it and care for it.

Published in 1971, *The Lorax* was ahead of its time, and it took a decade before its popularity soared. But its influence was clear, to the point where it was seen as a threat to some in the timber industry. In 1989, in the logging town of Laytonville, California, a campaign was initiated to remove the book from the second-grade reading list after the child of a logging-equipment salesman read the book at school and then came home and questioned his father's motives. A media frenzy ensued, and eventually the school-board president closed the debate and left *The Lorax* on the shelves. *The Lorax* has proven to be an effective educational tool. Children who read the story can identify with it, giving them a taste of how costly an individual's selfish actions can be and cultivating a sense of commitment to protecting the environment. Like many books, this one can have a powerful and lasting influence on a child's thinking.

Though he and his wife never had children of their own, Geisel's love of children is apparent in his books. He won many awards, including Oscars, Emmys, and a Pulitzer. And 30 years after his graduation, Dartmouth bestowed an honorary doctorate on him, making "Dr." Seuss legitimate. In 1967, after 40 years of marriage, his wife, Helen, took her own life. Geisel married Audrey Stone the next year, and they lived in La Jolla, California, for over 20 years, until his death. Theodor Geisel died on September 24, 1991, in La Jolla.

BIBLIOGRAPHY

Cohen, Charles D., *The Seuss, the Whole Suess, and Nothing but the Seuss: a Visual Biography of Theodore Suess Giesel*, 2004; Fensch, Thomas, *The Man Who was Dr. Seuss: the Life and Work of Theodore Geisel*, 2000; Fensch, Thomas, ed., *Of Sneetches and Whos and the Good Dr. Seuss: Essays on the Writings and Life of Theodor Geisel*, 1997; Kanfer, Stefan, "The Doctor Beloved by All: Theodor Seuss Geisel," *Time*, 1991; Morgan, Judith, and Neil Morgan, *Dr. Seuss and Mr. Geisel: A Biography*, 1995; Nell, Philip, *Dr. Seuss: An American Icon*, 2005 Zicht, Jennifer, "In Pursuit of the Lorax: Who's in Charge of the Last Truffula Seed?" *EPA Journal*, 1991.

Gelbspan, Ross
(June 1, 1939–)
Journalist, Writer

Ross Gelbspan, a journalist and writer, was at the forefront of the movement to expose to public attention the disastrous consequences of global warming, which has propelled the climate into instability and exacerbates virtually every other environmental problem. Through his intensive investigations, he helped launch a campaign to disclose the truth about issues surrounding the global addiction to oil and coal and the environmental damage this causes by trapping heat in the atmosphere. His book *The Heat Is On: The High Stakes Battle over Earth's Threatened Climate* (1997), the first book for a general readership on the topic of global warming, definitively brings home the imminence of climate change brought about by combustion of fossil fuels and examines the campaign of deliberate confusion of the public by well-funded public relations professionals in the big coal and oil companies. His 2004 follow-up, *The Boiling Point*, analyzes the reasons that the U.S. has been the last country in the world to acknowledge global warming, and proposes solutions to the crisis.

Ross Gelbspan was born on June 1, 1939, in Chicago, Illinois, and grew up there. He received his B.A. in political science and English from Kenyon College in Gambier, Ohio, in 1960. After a year of graduate study at the Johns Hopkins School of Advanced International Studies in Washington, D.C., he took a reporting job at the *Philadelphia Bulletin* and then switched to the *Washington Post* in the early 1960s. He later moved to New York City and worked for the *Village Voice* during the late 1960s and early 1970s. In 1971, he wrote a series on the Soviet underground for which he spent a month in the Soviet Union interviewing dissidents and human rights advocates. He began reporting on environmental affairs in 1972 when he covered the first United Nations environmental conference in Stockholm, Sweden. This was also where he met Anne Charlotte Brostrom, whom he married in 1973. At around this time Gelbspan accepted the position of national news editor for Scripps Howard News Service, based in New York. He also taught journalism as an adjunct professor at Columbia University.

In 1979 the *Boston Globe* hired Gelbspan as a senior editor. In his capacity as special projects editor, he conceived, directed, and edited a series of articles on job discrimination against African Americans in Boston-area corporations, universities, unions, newspapers, and state and city government. The series won a Pulitzer Prize in 1984. In 1992 he coauthored a front-page series for the *Globe* on the 1992 United Nations Conference on Environment and Development in Rio. In 1993 Gelbspan retired from the *Boston Globe* and started writing a novel, but he found himself getting more and more involved in the global warming issue instead. In 1995 he coauthored an article for the *Washington Post* on the link between the spread of infectious diseases and changes in climate. He found that although the article was well received, a number of readers wrote and assured him there was no proven link between fossil fuel combustion and global climate change. Their response made him wonder why there was such a controversy over the validity of global warming. He began to investigate the politics surrounding the issue more deeply and quickly discovered the main reason for the public confusion. Since the 1992 Earth Summit, a band of several high profile "greenhouse skeptic" scientists had helped to create a widespread public belief that the issue of climate change is filled with uncertainties and hardly cause for alarm. In 1995 Gelbspan wrote an article disclosing the fact that many of these skeptic scientists receive fuel industry funding. The article appeared on the cover of the December issue of

Harper's Magazine. Gelbspan took the main ideas from this article, which was nominated for a National Magazine Award, and expanded them into a book called *The Heat Is On: The High Stakes Battle over Earth's Threatened Climate* (1997). The book was published in paperback in 1998 as: *The Heat Is On: The Climate Crisis, the Cover-up, the Prescription*.

The Heat Is On began with a scientific explanation of global warming and how it was related to human activities. Each year humans cause six billion tons of carbon to be released into the lower atmosphere through the burning of fossil fuels and deforestation. This carbon builds up and traps heat, causing some of the erratic and increasingly unstable weather patterns around the world. As Gelbspan pointed out, global temperature records already bore witness to climate change: 1997 had just replaced 1995 as the hottest year ever recorded, the five hottest consecutive years on record began in 1991, and the 11 hottest years in recorded history had occurred since 1980. The planet was heating at a faster rate than at any time in the previous 10,000 years. Other consequences of alterations in the atmosphere included altered drought and rainfall patterns, temperature extremes, and more severe storms. To leading climate scientists, the congregation of so many strange weather events worldwide was an early symptom of a rise in the average global temperature. Gelbspan affirmed that scientific opinion was virtually unanimous in agreement that industrial activity was having an effect on the earth's atmosphere and that climate change was happening, yet the United States stood alone in questioning the reality of the situation.

Gelbspan devoted much of the book to examining the campaign of deception by coal and oil companies that kept many people in this country confused and misinformed. He expanded on the links between the greenhouse critics and the coal and oil industries that, together, constituted the biggest single industry in history. For example, in 1993 alone the American Petroleum Institute spent nearly the same amount on public relations as the entire expenditure budget combined of the nation's five major environmental groups that focused on climate change. Gelbspan also discussed the influence of the fossil fuel industries on congressional leaders who fought to defund climate research and who were even able to tie up international negotiations to reduce carbon emissions. Though there is no quick or easy solution to the problem, Gelbspan did make recommendations—for example, transferring government subsidies and tax incentives away from fossil fuels and into renewable energy. His book carried a powerful and influential message, and not surprisingly, it was also the subject of numerous loud attacks by the fossil fuel lobby.

After the book's publication, Gelbspan traveled and spoke extensively on global climate change. He appeared on *ABC News Nightline* and the National Public Radio shows *All Things Considered* and *Talk of the Nation*. He was invited to the World Economic Forum in Davos, Switzerland, in 1998, where he addressed heads of state, government ministers, and leaders of multinational corporations. With Dr. Paul Epstein of Harvard Medical School and the Intergovernmental Panel on Climate Change (which the United Nations formed in 1988 to address the climate crisis), Gelbspan brought together a group of people in 1998 to work out a set of solution strategies. This group, which includes scientists, energy company presidents, economists, and other specialists, came up with a World Energy Modernization Plan that contains a set of prescriptions, including the elimination of national subsidies for fossil fuels and the use of revenues from a tax on international currency transactions to finance the development of alternative energy technologies for developing nations. Gelbspan continues to be involved in this group as it works to accelerate international climate negotiations.

Gelbspan published *The Boiling Point* in 2004. This book resoundingly criticizes politicians, the coal and petroleum industries, journalists, and even environmental organizations. Big oil and coal have committed the most egregious offenses with its misinformation campaigns and manipulation of politicians and journalists—but elected officials and the press should have resisted them, Gelbspan holds. His criticism of environmental organization centers on their prioritization of their own institutional agendas rather than this major and urgent problem. Gelbspan proposes solutions to the problem based on those of the World Energy Modernization Plan—these have, in the years since they were first presented, been enthusiastically received by many policy makers and leaders.

Gelbspan maintains a climate change information website, "The heat is online," which contains a plethora of up-to-date information and links about global warming. He and his wife, who is a nonprofit developer with the Women's Institute for Housing and Economic Development, make their home in Brookline, Massachusetts. They have two grown daughters, Thea and Joby.

BIBLIOGRAPHY

Dunn, Seth, "The Heat Is On: The High Stakes Battle over Earth's Threatened Environment," *World Watch*, 1998; Gelbspan, Ross, *The Boiling Point*, 2004; Gelbspan, Ross, "Global Warming: The Heat Is On," *Alternative Radio*, 1998; Gelbspan, Ross, "The Heat Is On," *Harper's Magazine*, 1995; Gelbspan, Ross, *The Heat Is On: The High Stakes Battle over Earth's Threatened Environment*, 1997; Gore, Al, "'Boiling Point': Who's to Blame for Global Warming," *New York Times Book Review*, 2004; "The Heat Is Online," www.heatisonline.org; Simonsen, Kevin, "The Heat Is On: The High Stakes Battle over Earth's Threatened Environment," *Ecology Law Quarterly*, 1998.

Gibbs, Lois

(June 25, 1951–)
Activist, Founder of the Center for Health, Environment and Justice

As a mother of small children and a housewife in the subdivision of Love Canal in Niagara Falls, New York, Lois Gibbs's life was transformed when she and her neighbors discovered in 1978 that their neighborhood was built on a toxic waste dump and that levels of toxic chemicals in their homes and the local elementary school were high enough to cause birth defects, cancers, and a host of other health problems. Taking the helm of the Love Canal Homeowners Association, Gibbs worked to assure relocation and compensation for all of the neighbors who were affected. After relocating her family to Washington, D.C., Gibbs founded the Citizens Clearinghouse on Hazardous Waste in 1981 (now the Center for Health, Environment and Justice—CHEJ), an organization dedicated to helping community organizations facing similar toxic waste issues. Now commonly referred to as the "mother of Superfund" (the federal program to clean up toxic waste sites), Gibbs's work through CHEJ has inspired and aided more than 8,000 grassroots organizations to demand accountability from industrial polluters and the U.S. government.

Lois Marie Gibbs was born on June 25, 1951, in Buffalo, New York. Until 1978, she was a shy homemaker, married to chemical plant worker Harry Gibbs, and the mother of two children. In 1972, the Gibbses bought a home in the modest Love Canal subdivision of Niagara Falls, named after entrepreneur William Love, who dug the canal in the late 1800s to link the Upper and Lower Niagara Rivers.

Halted by an economic depression, all that was left of the project was a 60-foot-wide by 3,000-foot-long pit that later became a dump site used by the Niagara Falls municipality, the United States Army, and the Hooker Chemical Corporation. When the pit was filled to capacity and covered with soil, Hooker sold the land to the local board of education for one dollar, on the condition that Hooker would be free of any future liability. A school and houses were built on the site in the 1950s, and except for strong fumes and strange substances surfacing in peoples' yards and in the school's playground, Love Canal's past was forgotten.

In 1978, after a series of articles on local hazardous waste problems by reporter MICHAEL BROWN was published in the *Niagara Gazette*, Gibbs began to wonder if her five-year-old son Michael's epilepsy and urinary and respiratory problems could be caused by the chemicals. Since the focus was initially on the elementary school built right in the middle of the former canal, she asked Michael's pediatrician to write a letter to the school board requesting that he be transferred to a school in a safer area of town. The school board refused. Gibbs realized that her son would continue to suffer unless she conquered her shyness and began to fight. Her first step was to write and circulate among her neighbors a petition calling for the closure of the elementary school. In addition to gathering signatures, Gibbs heard of horrifying health problems and of residents' fears that their homes would soon be worthless and they would have no way to escape the polluted neighborhood. In August 1978, Gibbs and two neighbors took the petition with 161 signatures to the state capital of Albany to present it to the State Health Commission. They were surprised by the commissioner's response: to close the school and to recommend that all pregnant women and children living closest to the school leave the area. Within a week after that meeting, President JIMMY CARTER declared Love Canal a federal emergency area and allocated funds to relocate the 239 families living in the first two rings of homes around the school.

But that is where rapid government response ended, recounts Gibbs in her memoir, *Love Canal: My Story*. The next two years were a nightmare for the remaining neighbors living on the canal but farther away from the school. A "clean-up" effort involving channels that would drain toxic leachate out of the area was undertaken by the state health department, but residents were doubtful that it would solve the problem. In addition, as machinery dug into the toxic ground, more chemicals were released, and the area became even more dangerous to inhabit.

Gibbs became president of the Love Canal Homeowners Association (LCHA), a group residents formed so that they would have a say in the future of the area. She spent virtually all of her time spearheading a fight to get the government to purchase Love Canal homes at a fair price so that Love Canal residents could move away and regain their health. Gibbs worked without a salary full time at the LCHA office at the closed school, and her home became an after-hours meeting place for residents, officials, and reporters. Gibbs helped with the neighborhood health surveys, designed by scientist and ally of the homeowners Dr. Beverly Pagen. Gibbs became a practiced public speaker, testifying about Love Canal in Albany and for the U.S. Congress. She served as an advocate for residents, continually pressing government agencies for relocation funds. But it was not until the Environmental Protection Agency (EPA) released its study in May 1980 showing that residents exhibited chromosomal damage, and angry Love Canal residents took two EPA representatives hostage, that President Carter finally agreed to evacuate all Love Canal families who wished to leave. Carter first provided for temporary relocation and then in October 1980 allocated federal money to fund permanent relocations for all Love Canal residents wanting to leave. As a response to the pressure that Gibbs and her neighbors had put on the federal government, the Federal Superfund Program was established in 1980 to clean up toxic waste sites similar to Love Canal.

Gibbs relocated to Washington, D.C., with her two children. Thousands of Americans were contacting her to request her advice and assistance in dealing with toxic hazards in their own neighborhoods, and in 1981 she founded the Citizens Clearinghouse for Hazardous Wastes (now CHEJ) to respond. Staffed by scientists and organizers, CHEJ helps grassroots groups facing local environmental problems involving toxic waste, solid waste, air pollution, incinerators, medical and radioactive waste, pesticides, sewage, and industrial pollution. CHEJ produces books and information packets, responds to questions on environmental hazards, and produces both a monthly and quarterly magazine. It has served as an important informational and networking link for more than 8,000 communities throughout the country, with a commitment to helping grassroots groups be independent and self-sufficient. Additional accomplishments by CHEJ include successfully lobbying the government to provide communities near Superfund Sites with up to $50,000 in technical assistance grants; coordinating efforts to pass Right-to-Know laws that give people access to information about the chemicals stored, disposed of, and released near their homes; helping convince McDonalds to stop using styrofoam hamburger packages; and many more campaigns.

For her courage and effectiveness at Love Canal and her work at CHEJ, Gibbs received the Goldman Environmental Prize in 1991 the Heinz Award in the Environment in 1998, the 1999 John Gardner Leadership Award, was recognized by *Outside* magazine as one of the "Top Ten Who Made A Difference," and was nominated for the Nobel Peace Prize in 2003. Gibbs lives in Virginia with her husband and one of her four children.

BIBLIOGRAPHY

Berger, Rose Marie, "What Sustains over the Long Haul?" *Sojourners*, 1997; Breton, Mary Joy, *Women Pioneers for the Environment*, 1998; "The Center for Health, Environment and Justice," www.chej.org; Gibbs, Lois Marie, *Love Canal: My Story*, 1982; Gibbs, Lois Marie, *Love Canal: the story contiues...*, 1998; Gibbs, Lois Marie, and the Citizens Clearinghouse for Hazardous Waste, *Dying from Dioxin: A Citizens Guide to Reclaiming Our Health and Rebuilding Democracy*, 1995; Shribman, David, "Lois Gibbs: A Woman Transformed by a Cause," *New York Times*, 1981.

Gleason, Henry Allan
(January 2, 1882–1975)
Botanist, Ecologist, Taxonomist

Henry Allan Gleason was a noted botanist, taxonomist, and ecologist. Breaking away from the popular theory of association succession of plant development proposed by ecologist Frederic Clements, Gleason developed the individualistic concept of ecology. His species-individualistic model has since become predominantly used in studying community ecology.

Born in Dalton City, Illinois, on January 2, 1882, Henry Allan Gleason began studying botany at 13 and began contributing to *The American Naturalist* while still in high school. He went on to graduate with a B.S. and M.A. from the University of Illinois. He spent a year as a fellow at the University of Ohio and a summer studying invertebrates on the Isle Royale, sponsored by the University of Michigan. He then went on to get a Ph.D. in taxonomy from Columbia University in 1906.

Gleason held teaching positions at the University of Illinois and the University of Michigan before spending a year studying tropical vegetation in Ceylon, Java, and the Philippines. After giving a lecture in 1918 on his findings during his travels, he was offered a position at The New York Botanical Gardens. At the Botanical Gardens he served as curator, head curator, assistant director, and acting director, and was responsible for the South American collection there.

Gleason served as editor for *Garden Journal*, *Addisonia*, and the *Bulletin*. He edited the revised editions of *North American Flora* and *Plants of the Vicinity of New York*. Gleason wrote *The New Britton and Brown Illustrated Flora of the Northeastern United States and Adjacent Canada* (1952). Co-authoring with Arthur Cronquist, Gleason also wrote *The Natural Geography of Plants* (1964) and the *Manual of Vascular Plants of the Northeastern United States and Adjacent Canada* (1963, repr. 1991).

As Vice President of the Pacaraima-Venezuela Expedition co-sponsored by the Garden, the American Museum of Natural History, and the National Geographic Society, Gleason is credited with 235 contributions to the field of vascular botany.

In his early studies, Gleason utilized the concepts of plant association and development theorized by Frederic Clements. But eventually he began to express doubts about Clements's theories, claiming the association concept underestimated the real diversity of plants, and eventually developed the species-individualistic model. Where Clements theorized that plant communities consist of predictable groups of species that are linked by obligatory interactions with one another, Gleason proclaimed that plant communities are chance assemblages of species that live in the same place only because they share similar abiotic tolerances and need similar resources.

In 1939, in his first published article about his new concept, "The Individualistic Concept of the Plant Association" he wrote " … it may be said that environment varies constantly in time and continuously in space; environment selects from all available immigrants those species which constitute the present vegetation, and as a result vegetation varies constantly in time and continuously in space."

Gleason's individualistic-species model eventually widely influenced ecological and geographical studies of vegetation and is currently used to document individual plant responses to global warming.

He died in 1975.

BIBLIOGRAPHY

The New York Botanical Library International Plant Science Center Mertz Library Archives and Manuscript Collections; *Henry Allan Gleason*, Columbia Encyclopedia; http://bio.research.ucsc.edu/~barrylab/classes/ecology/20C-L24-Communities.htm; geography.berkeley.edu/ProgramCourses/CoursePagesFA2002/geog148/Lectures/Lecture06/VegetationConcepts.html; sciweb.nybg.org/Science2/libr/finding_guide/glearec.asp.

Gold, Lou

(March 5, 1938–)
Storyteller, Wilderness Advocate

Political scientist Lou Gold quit academia in 1973 and moved to Oregon where he fell in love with the old-growth forest of the Klamath-Siskiyou bioregion and decided to devote the rest of his life to celebrating and protecting wilderness. For more than a decade, starting in 1983, Gold spent every summer camped on top of Bald Mountain in the Siskiyou wilderness area of southwestern Oregon. He spent the fall and winter months touring the United States, lecturing about ancient forests and the dangers they faced. Gold's effectiveness in gaining fans for forests is obvious to U.S. Forest Service officials, who say they can trace Gold's lecture route by the postmarks on letters they receive decrying their permissive policies.

Lou Gold was born in Chicago, Illinois, in 1938. He led an urban childhood but enjoyed exploring the lagoon at Chicago's Garfield Park, his main contact with "wilderness." Gold studied at the Illinois Institute of Technology, receiving a B.S. degree in political science in 1959 and continuing on there to do graduate work until 1961. He left Illinois for Columbia University, where he studied for three more years, until becoming a popular professor of political science at Oberlin College (1964–1966) and at the University of Illinois (1967–1973).

By the early 1970s, Gold began feeling that his life was not whole and that his work was not as meaningful as he had hoped it would be. So in 1973, he quit academia and moved west to Takilma, Oregon, where some close friends lived. He became a carpenter and cabinetmaker, in the hopes that working with his hands would make him happier. In his free time, Gold explored the rugged, 700,000-acre Klamath-Siskiyou bioregion straddling southwestern Oregon and northwestern California. Gold and his neighbors knew how special the area was, and in recent years the incredible biodiversity of that region has been recognized by such organizations as the World Wildlife Fund, the International Union for the Conservation of Nature, and the Wildlands Project. The area boasts the nation's highest concentration of Wild and Scenic Rivers and the largest remaining unprotected roadless forests.

During the late 1970s and early 1980s, the U.S. Forest Service was initiating construction of a road through the Siskiyou National Forest (one of five national forests in the Klamath-Siskiyou bioregion), to facilitate the logging that was to commence there. Local environmentalists protested the road building, and Gold decided to join them. He was arrested for the first time during a May 1983 road blockade, when he and seven others sat down in front of a bulldozer and refused to let it pass. Gold and the others were granted their freedom on the condition that they not enter national forest land for one year. But within a few days Gold returned. He declared that he was there in peace, in order to bear witness to the destruction of the forest and pray for its safety. Gold took off on a pack trip, climbing Bald Mountain, a 3,800-foot peak whose summit afforded a magnificent 360-degree view. He decided to camp under the luxuriant branches of a large tree near its summit. He constructed a Native American–inspired medicine wheel on the mountain's flat top and prayed there every day. He was delighted to find that within a few days of his arrival the animals were no longer afraid of him. His friends packed in food for him, and surprised hikers were delighted by his mission and often donated supplies for his stay. In his copious free time on top of Bald Mountain, Gold carved walking sticks to give to each of the hikers he met during the summer.

Despite his hopes that life in the wilderness would bring him the peace he sought, Gold was haunted by questions. As he wrote in his "Bald Mountain Vigil," "What sense does it make to ask a society that discards its old people to save its old trees? What sense does it make to ask a society that regularly abuses its children to preserve the forest for our great, great grandchildren? What sense does it make to ask a government, which is continually preparing for war, to maintain the peacefulness of the natural world?" He also caught his mind "concocting great dramas, holding arguments with the logging industry or delivering self-righteous lectures to the Josephine County Court." Eventually, through meditation and soul-searching, Gold realized that he did not know how to stop the road building and logging that was happening in the forests below Bald Mountain and that the best he could do was to pray from his mountaintop spot and to talk to anyone he could about the problem.

His original intention was to stay on Bald Mountain forever. However, the darkness, cold, and precipitation of fall convinced him that it would be better not to spend winters there. When he descended the mountain in September, he was immediately arrested for violating his promise not to enter national forest land during that year.

The next summer Gold again climbed Bald Mountain and within a few days met a group of 4-H campers there. Several of them helped Gold clean up the mountaintop (the Forest Service had demolished a lookout there, and each winter's snows and winds unearthed more rubble) and construct his medicine wheel. One of the most enthusiastic volunteers was the son of the local national forest supervisor. He brought his father up a few weeks later, and instead of evicting Gold for violating a rule that visitors can camp for no longer than two weeks in any spot, the supervisor arranged to haul down the hundreds of pounds of rubble that Gold and his 4-H volunteers had cleaned up and asked Gold to sign a volunteer agreement to maintain nearby trails. From that moment until he stopped summering on Bald Mountain in the mid-1990s, Gold served as a volunteer caretaker of the area.

Gold found that he was happy alone on Bald Mountain but that he was even happier when he was able to serve as storyteller and host to visitors. He then decided that he could use his formidable lecturing skills from his university days and put together a slide show and talk. He spent 15 falls and winters on a lecture circuit, talking to students, clubs, conservation organizations, any group interested in his message. His presentation received rave reviews, and the U.S. Forest Service claimed it knew where Gold had spoken last from the barrage of mail it received from that place.

Gold decided in 1999 to change careers and has embarked on a new path as a painter. He works closely with the Siskiyou Regional Education Project, a wilderness protection and advocacy organization, but currently resides in Brazil, where he is an active blogger on environmental and spiritual topics.

BIBLIOGRAPHY

Gold, Lou, "Bald Mountain Vigil," in Cass Adams, ed., *The Soul Unearthed*, 1996; Norman, Michael, "Lessons: A Former Professor Comes Down from a Mountain to Offer Insights about Nature," *New York Times*, 1988; "Siskiyou Regional Education Project," www.siskiyou.org; "Visionshare," lougold.blogspot.com; Watkins, T. H., "The Laughing Prophet of Bald Mountain," *Orion*, 1990.

Golten, Robert
(February 2, 1933–)
Attorney, Professor of Law

Attorney Robert Golten has dedicated his career to helping the disenfranchised, be they marginalized people or endangered species, and to training law students to do the same. He is known for litigating the first successful case based on the Endangered Species Act (ESA), for his effective mediation skills in controversies with several competing interests, and for founding the country's first environmental legal clinic, at the University of Colorado law school.

Robert Joseph Golten was born in Chicago on February 2, 1933. He muses that his beloved Chicago Cubs inspired him to work on behalf of the underdog and also believes that being Jewish might have influenced him to pursue a career dedicated to "redressing the imbalance of power." Golten attended the University of Michigan, graduating in 1954 with an A.B. cum laude and honors in economics. He went to Harvard University's law school, graduating in 1959.

Robert Golten (Photograph courtesy of University of Denver)

Following two years in a conventional law practice, and after planting job seeds in Washington D.C., Golten went overseas to sell mutual funds to expatriate Americans in Europe. He was then offered a job as corporate counsel for the parent mutual fund company. After thinking seriously about it—it would have been a glamorous and lucrative job—Golten, Calvinist that he was, decided against taking it and instead went to Washington, D.C., to work for the Justice Department. He moved to the Office of Economic Opportunity in 1965, serving as general counsel of the Job Corps program. From 1970 to 1974, Golten was a trial attorney for the District of Columbia's Public Defender office. He began teaching at American University's law school in 1970 as well, specializing in psychiatry and law and professional responsibility. There he initiated what was to become the first of his legal clinics: students worked with him to defend mental patients who had been involuntarily committed to a large public mental institution. Golten immediately recognized the multiplier effect of working with students: many more indigent or low income clients could be served, at no cost to them, when the students got involved.

In 1974, Golten was recruited by the National Wildlife Federation (NWF) into the field of environmental law. He won the nation's first suit based on the Environmental Species Act, a 1975 case (*National Wildlife Federation* v. *Coleman*) in Mississippi that prevented a highway interchange from being built through the last remaining habitat of 40 endangered Mississippi sandhill cranes. Golten had overwhelming evidence that the ESA would be violated if the highway were built, but the real estate developers who owned the land at the proposed highway interchanges apparently enjoyed considerable political influence, and the judge (later impeached) ruled that a compromise could be forged for both "cranes and lanes." Golten achieved a reversal of this decision from the Fifth Circuit Court, and later recalled, "That put me on the environmental map."

Golten was capable of more than feisty advocacy. In 1976 he was called to the I'on swamp in Francis Marion National Forest, one of the last sites where the very endangered and soon to be extinct Bachman's warbler had been seen. The U.S. Forest Service (USFS) was planning to allow timber cutting in the swamp, and local environmentalists wanted Golten to help them prevent it. Since he could foresee problems with a traditional lawsuit (e.g., proving that the warbler still existed), Golten asked for permission to mediate and obtained a compromise with the USFS, whereby upland pines would be cut but not the lower hardwoods crucial to the swamp habitat. Golten's effectiveness as a mediator pleased him, because he felt that reason and dialogue were often better tactics for long-term success than hard-core litigation.

In 1978, Golten moved his family, wife Mary Margaret Addison and daughters Ryan and Lauren, to Boulder, Colorado, to set up what was to become the nation's first natural resource litigation clinic established in a law school. The NWF paid Golten's salary, and the University of Colorado (CU) Law School provided an office, institutional support, and student interns. The litigation clinic allowed students—early on graduate students at Colorado State University's Natural Resources school as well as CU's law students, but later just law students—to research issues such as land use, timber management, mineral development, water resources, and fish and wildlife management. The most famous struggle in which the litigation clinic participated involved the proposed Two Forks dam. The Two Forks project, scheduled for construction near Deckers, Colorado, would have dammed the South Platte River, eliminating an ecologically important stretch of the riverine habitat and with it a highly prized trout fishery near the major urban area of Denver.

WILLIAM K. REILLY, then the administrator of the Environmental Protection Agency, finally rejected the dam in 1991 and instead adopted the environmentalists' alternative model for conserving and delivering water to Denver.

After leaving the Natural Resource Litigation Clinic in 1984, Golten worked for a private law firm in Boulder on various American Indian, natural resources, and land use issues. He also served as county attorney in Summit County, Colorado, during 1985 to 1988, acting director for the Native American Rights Fund legal services support center in 1988, and special land use counsel for Jefferson County, Colorado, in 1989. In 1992 he started an American Indian law clinic at the University of Colorado, directing it until 1996.

In addition to a small private law practice, he teaches at the University of Denver (DU). In 1998 he founded, and has since directed, the Center for International Human Rights Law and Advocacy at DU's Josef Korbel School of International Studies. This Center focuses attention particularly, but not only, on indigenous people worldwide in cases involving land and natural resource issues. In concert with the American Bar Association, he has helped start legal-aid clinics in developing countries—in Slovakia (1996), Uganda (1998) and Azerbaijan (2000); and consulted with legal-aid clinics in Moldova (1998) and Kyrgystan and Kazakhstan (2001). He has served on the board of directors and is currently an advisor to Global Response, which responds to imminent environmental threats worldwide with letter-writing campaigns and political and citizen action.

Golten resides in Boulder with his second wife, Joan Brett.

BIBLIOGRAPHY

Bingham, Gail, *Resolving Environmental Disputes : A Decade of Experience*, 1986; Malmsbury, Todd, "Environmentalist Believes Political Power Remains," *Boulder Daily Camera*, 1981; Neuschaefer, Nan, "Environmental Law: New Field," *Boulder Daily Camera*, 1979.

Goodman, Paul

(September 9, 1911–August 3, 1972)
Writer, Social Critic

Paul Goodman was a social critic with multiple and varied targets; as an anarchist pacifist, he decried militarism, he criticized traditional schooling, and he attacked the government's bureaucracy and centralism. He approached the reconstruction of society with imagination and creativity, ever providing what he called "practical proposals" for change. It is mainly for his pioneering proposals in the area of urban planning—especially those put forth in the 1947 book *Communitas* that he cowrote with his brother Percival—that he is considered an important influence on the environmental movement.

Paul Goodman was born on September 9, 1911, in Greenwich Village, New York City, the youngest of Barnett and Augusta Goodman's three children. Before he was born, his father suffered a business failure and deserted the family. Goodman received an excellent education at a public magnet school and attended religious school as well. He studied at the College of the City of New York with philosopher Morris Raphael Cohen, from whom Goodman learned to question the status quo and think critically. He graduated with a B.A. in 1931 and then worked reading movie scripts at home while continuing to attend classes as an auditor at different colleges and universities in Manhattan, participating in discussions and writing papers. One of the papers he wrote for Columbia professor Richard McKeon was published in the *Journal of Philosophy* in 1934. During the mid-1930s, Goodman began publishing his prose, poetry, and criticism regularly in avant garde literary magazines.

When professor McKeon moved to the University of Chicago in the late 1930s, he invited Goodman to join him and begin work on a doctorate. Goodman did so but was expelled one year later for his sexual behavior—propositioning young men. Goodman, a bisexual who fathered three children during his two common-law marriages, encountered similar problems with the administrations of the Manumit School of Progressive Education in Pawling, New York, and Black Mountain College in North Carolina. Goodman eventually was awarded his Ph.D. from the University of Chicago (in 1954), and his doctoral thesis, *The Structure of Literature*, was published by the University of Chicago Press.

Goodman wrote prolifically during the 1940s; he published poetry, fiction, plays, literary criticism, and in 1947, *Communitas: Means of Livelihood and Ways of Life*, cowritten with his brother Percival. This book, published during the post–World War II construction boom, was revolutionary in that it was among the first American works to insist that cities did not have to be crowded and unhealthy, designed to facilitate industry and commerce, but instead could be planned with aesthetics, recreation, and quality of life in mind. The book analyzes how different city plans deal with transportation and quality of life for their residents. While earlier planners, BENTON MACKAYE and FREDERICK LAW OLMSTED, JR., for example, had hoped that the automobile would improve the lives of urban workers by allowing them to commute between their work in cities and their homes in garden-filled suburbs, the Goodmans recognized that dependence upon the automobile was a terrible trade-off, because ensuing congestion and demolition of neighborhoods for highways diminished everyone's quality of life. The Goodmans provided suggestions for the renewal of New York City, such as banning cars from Manhattan, reducing pollution in the rivers, converting the island's riverfront into a swimmable beach, and building a "garden city" where people could work, recreate, and live comfortably within the city. Few read the book upon its first publication, but it was more widely read when it was reissued in 1960 with a cover quote from LEWIS MUMFORD. The book's recommendations for New York City were taken up in the 1960s by a group of activist planners called Urban Underground. Although never implemented as Goodman had envisioned, Goodman's utopian ideas nevertheless served as inspiration that change was possible, according to Urban Underground member and environmental historian ROBERT GOTTLIEB.

Goodman's restless intellect shifted foci often throughout his life; his receptivity and flexibility served him as he explored a number of fields during the 1950s and 1960s. He underwent psychotherapy during the late 1940s and early 1950s, and he quickly became an expert on it, cowriting *Gestalt Therapy* with Dr. Fritz Perls and Ralph Hefferline in 1951 and working half-time as a lay psychotherapist at the New York Institute for Gestalt Therapy. His interest in psychology is reflected in the work he wrote for the Living Theatre of New York City, which was deeply psychological in nature. Facing rejection by mainstream publishers and critics during most of the 1950s and living in virtual poverty, Goodman's view became increasingly cynical. In 1960 when his book *Growing Up Absurd* was published by Random House, he shot into public view. *Growing Up Absurd* criticized society in the United States of the 1950s for its conformism, for its discouragement of creativity, honesty, and true community. The book resonated with youth of the day, and he became a popular speaker at college campuses—he spoke at over 100 during this period—as students erupted into rebellion with the Berkeley Free Speech movement and massive nationwide protests against the Vietnam War. Goodman sympathized with young people's disgust with "the system," drawing connections between society's excessive consumerism, developers' eagerness to turn rich land into parking lots, and the U.S. government's use of napalm in Vietnam to defoliate jungles in its attempts to uncover guerrillas.

He had written pacifist reflections on the military draft during the 1940s, when he was draft age, and republished them during the 1960s. He urged young people not to aid and abet a violent state and to break the government's laws if they were in conflict with moral law. Goodman's son Matthew, a student at Cornell University, participated in the first public burning of draft cards at New York's Central Park in the spring of 1967.

In addition to editing the radical newspaper *Liberation* with activist and organizer David Dellinger from 1962 to 1970, Goodman wrote at least one book per year during the 1960s. *The Community of Scholars* (1962) and *Compulsory Mis-Education* (1964) criticized traditional universities, advocating instead student-centered institutions with a stronger sense of community. These are considered primers for the alternative education movement, inspiring the creation of many experimental free schools. His other books provided critiques of society in the United States for its various flaws, including militarism, centrism, rigid hierarchy, bureaucracy, and rigidity in terms of the sexual behaviors it permitted.

In addition to writing, Goodman taught during the 1960s as guest professor at the University of Wisconsin–Madison, the Experimental College of San Francisco State College, and the University of Hawaii–Honolulu and worked as a fellow at the Institute for Policy Studies in Washington, D.C.

Although initially excited by the potential of the 1960s youth movement to bring about major structural changes in the tradition of Martin Luther's reforming the church and Thomas Jefferson's constructing a new democratic nation, Goodman was eventually disappointed by the movement's stubborn, unrealistic goals. He faded out of the public eye when students rejected his critiques of their movement. Goodman never completely recovered from the tragic death in 1967 of his son Matthew, who fell to his death while picking huckleberries in the mountains near his father's New Hampshire farm, one week before having to report to an FBI office for his draft resistance.

Paul Goodman died of a heart attack on August 3, 1972, at his farm in Groveton, New Hampshire. He left two surviving daughters, Susan and Daisy.

BIBLIOGRAPHY

DeLeon, David, *Leaders from the 1960s: A Biographical Sourcebook of American Activism*, 1994; Goodman, Paul, *Crazy Hope and Finite Experience: the Final Essays of Paul Goodman*, edited by Taylor Stoehr, 1997; Gottlieb, Robert, *Forcing the Spring: The Transformation of the American Environmental Movement*, 1993; Ostriker, Alicia, *Paul Goodman*, 1976; Parisi, Peter, ed., *Artist of the Actual: Essays on Paul Goodman*, 1986; Widmer, Kingsley, *Paul Goodman*, 1980.

Gore, Albert, Jr.
(March 31, 1948–)
Author, Politician, Venture Capitalist

Politician Al Gore—who served as representative and senator from Tennessee, vice president under Pres. Clinton, and presidential candidate in 2000—is perhaps this country's most famous contemporary environmental activist. As such a high-profile figure, has brought climate change and other environmental problems into public focus, first through his book *Earth in the Balance* (1992) and more recently with his award-winning documentary *An Inconvenient Truth* (2006). Gore shared the 2007 Nobel Peace Prize with the IPCC—the Intergovernmental Panel on Climate Change—the IPCC was honored for creating "an ever-broader informed consensus about the connection between human activities and global warming," and Gore for being "probably the single individual who has done most to create greater worldwide understanding of the measures that need to be adopted."

Albert Arnold Gore Jr. was born March 31, 1948, in Washington, D.C., to Senator Albert Gore Sr. and Pauline (LaFon) Gore. Gore grew up in a political atmosphere in the nation's capital. He graduated cum laude from Harvard in 1969 and served a tour of duty in Vietnam as an army reporter. Gore married Mary Elizabeth ("Tipper") Aitcheson in 1970. When he returned from Vietnam, Gore began reporting for the Nashville *Tennessean* while attending divinity school at Vanderbilt University Graduate School of Religion. He later studied law at Vanderbilt, before giving it up to run for a seat in the U.S. House of Representatives in 1976. At the age of 30, Gore won this election and began what would be a long and successful political career.

During the eight years he served as a Democrat in the House of Representatives, Gore became increasingly interested and active in environmental issues and was known for his depth of knowledge about nuclear weapons, in particular. He led the first congressional hearing on toxic waste and was the catalyst behind the passage of the 1980 Superfund bill, which set up a fund to clean up toxic waste sites. His environmental record was marred by his support for two Tennessee Valley Authority environmental fiascoes: the Tellico Dam, which was opposed by environmentalists because it was thought to threaten the endangered snail darter, and the Clinch River experimental nuclear "breeder" reactor. The former was built; the latter was not; Gore supported both projects because of the jobs they would offer Tennesseeans. Gore left the House of Representatives in 1984, when he won a seat in the Senate, and he served as a senator until winning the vice presidency in 1992.

Gore began writing *Earth in the Balance* in 1989, after his son, Albert III, was hit by a car and severely injured. Gore later explained that this trauma had prompted him to reevaluate serious life issues, and he started to consider the effect an environmentally unstable world would have on the future of his four children. The book was a resounding success both on the market and among the critics, because Gore effectively synthesized a variety of complex environmental issues and explained them in lay terms. In the second section of this book, Gore presented a series of solutions to these problems. He drew from his experience in legislating environmental laws and policies to outline the more complex facets of global warming, acid rain, deforestation, and overpopulation. His understanding of these issues was indisputable, and his proposed market-based solutions were pragmatic, though controversial. Many conservative critics disparaged Gore's proposed solutions as being economically implausible.

The solutions section of *Earth in the Balance* received the most media attention during the 1992 presidential campaign; environmental issues were a major aspect of the Democratic platform. Gore proposed a unified global effort, with rich and poor nations working together to stem the tide of population growth and environmental degradation inflicted by existing economic and political strategies. Such a plan would work under the umbrella of a United Nations Stewardship Council, which would monitor events and policies that were detrimental to the planet.

Gore's nomination as vice president earned the Democratic ticket the endorsement of many major environmental organizations, whose leaders were optimistic that Gore would be able to push Clinton to adopt a pro-environment agenda. Gore was able to convince Clinton to resist the antienvironmental offenses of the right-wing 104th Congress, elected in a conservative backlash in 1994; to negotiate the successful Kyoto Protocol for reducing greenhouse gas emissions; and to designate several new national parks and monuments in the West, including the spectacular 1.7-million-acre Grand Staircase–Escalante National Monument in Utah. However, Gore failed to obtain many significant gains that he had reportedly lobbied hard for. For example, during the administration's first year in office, Gore tried to persuade the president to impose a new tax on energy consumption, but Clinton refused, afraid the middle class would revolt. Clinton also refused Gore's plea to raise fuel efficiency standards for automobiles, before the 104th Congress revoked the president's unilateral power to do so. Nor could Gore prevent the president from backtracking on issues of livestock grazing on public lands, mining reform, and the 1995 salvage-logging rider, which suspended all environmental regulations of logging in damaged forests, a piece of legislation that environmentalists universally considered disastrous.

Despite these setbacks, Gore continued to promote himself as an environmentalist during his 2000 campaign as Democratic nominee for president. *Earth in the Balance* was reissued in time for the campaign with a new, updated introduction; in interviews Gore reiterated his commitment to its ambitious goals. Although Gore won the popular vote, and actually earned more votes in the election than any previous Democratic candidate for president, a controversy over mishandled votes in Florida put the decision into the hands of the U.S. Supreme Court, which gave the presidency to George W. Bush.

After this defeat, Gore withdrew from politics and spent some time in contemplation about his next move. He decided to re-focus his energies on the environment, specifically the issue of climate change, and developed a slide show that he would go on to present more than 1000 times. At one presentation in 2004, following the premier of the climate change thriller *The Day After Tomorrow*, LAURIE DAVID and Lawrence Bender—film producers by profession—were in the audience. They and their friend, film director Davis Guggenheim, were struck by Gore's show, and the idea for the film was born. In *An Inconvenient Truth* Gore gives clear and effectively illustrated explanations of incontrovertible scientific evidence of global warming, how politics and economics have accelerated it, and suggestions for reversing or slowing it. It become one of the highest-grossing documentary films ever, and won several awards, including an Academy Award, the Humanitas Prize, and best documentary from a number of film critics' societies. Gore issued a companion volume with the film, *An Inconvenient Truth: The Planetary Emergency of Global Warming and What We Can Do About It*.

Together with the Intergovernmental Panel on Climate Change of the World Meterological Organization and the United Nations Environment Program, Gore was awarded the 2007 Nobel Peace Prize for efforts "to build up and disseminate greater knowledge about man-made climate change, and to lay the foundations for the measures that are needed to counteract such change." Gore told *Time* that "It's the greatest honor I could ever have, but it's hard to celebrate recognition of an effort that has thus far failed. I'm not finished, but thus far, I have failed. We have all failed." He went on to say that the changes necessary for reversing global warming are unprecedented, and would best be compared to the efforts citizens make "when nations mobilize for war."

Gore's 2007 book, *The Assault on Reason*, analyzes our main political, environmental and economic problems and argues that the public must resist the "infotainment"-cum-news-and-analysis offered on mainstream television and seek real, solid information about the issues. This will allow, he believes, for a true, participatory democracy, in which we can arrive at solutions to the grave problems confronting our world.

In addition to his work as a writer and Gore in recent years has become a businessman, founding a London-based venture capital firm, Generation Investment Management, to fund companies devoted to sustainability, and joining Kleiner Perkins, a Silicon Valley-based venture firm that funds "clean" technologies.

Gore and his wife Tipper make their home in Tennessee, where Gore has been a livestock and tobacco farmer since the early 1970s.

BIBLIOGRAPHY

Baden, John A., ed., *Environmental Gore: A Constructive Response to Earth in the Balance*, 1994; Burns, James MacGregor, and Georgia J. Sorenson, *Dead Center: Clinton-Gore Leadership and the Perils of Moderation*, 1999; Clinton, Bill, and Al Gore Jr., *Putting People First: How We Can All Change America*, 1992; Gore, Al, Jr., *Earth in the Balance*, 1992, 2000; "An Inconvenient Truth," www.climatecrisis.net; "Peace 2007," www.nobelprize.org/nobel_prizes/peace/laureates/2007/; Rauber, Paul, "The Great Green Hope," *Sierra*, 1997; Walsh, Bryan, "The Gore Interview," *Time*, 2007.

Gottlieb, Robert

(February 21, 1944–)
Professor, Urban Planner, Activist

Urban planner, activist, and professor of urban and environmental policy, Robert Gottlieb attempts to widen what is traditionally thought of as the environmental agenda in his writings, research projects, and college courses. Gottlieb believes strongly that there must be a link between research and action, and he has worked with community, environmental, and labor groups to try to bring about environmental change in such areas as water policy, food policy, transportation and land use policy, and industry production issues.

Robert Gottlieb was born on February 21, 1944, in Brooklyn, New York, in a household where radical politics was a mainstay. As a teenager Gottlieb was involved in this country's earliest protests against atomic testing and its radioactive fallout. Gottlieb attended Reed College in Portland, Oregon, and spent a year in Strasbourg, France, where he became involved with the International Situationists, a European-based group that prefigured many of the themes of the New Left, including its critique of a mass consumer and "spectacle" society. At Reed, Gottlieb majored in French literature, and upon graduating in 1965, he joined Students for a Democratic Society, a national political organization that was prominent in the New Left political movement responsible for many of the major youth and anti–Vietnam War actions of the 1960s.

Gottlieb returned to New York City after graduation and, while studying sociology at the New School for Social Research, founded and directed the Movement for a Democratic Society and cofounded several affiliated organizations, including the Urban Underground (or Planners for a Democratic Society). These groups, all founded between 1967 and 1969, represented an early marriage of radical politics and environmentalism. They translated the environmentally oriented utopian ideas of such radical thinkers as MURRAY BOOKCHIN and PAUL GOODMAN into action strategies, including, for example, limiting the access of cars into Manhattan.

In 1969, as several of the New Left groups began to implode, Gottlieb journeyed west. Many young New Yorkers were at this time moving to San Francisco, famous for its accommodation of those looking for an alternative lifestyle. When Gottlieb would mention to acquaintances en route that he was interested in Los Angeles, the response would be quizzical. Los Angeles was viewed as a conservative heartland, not a place of interest to a radical activist interested in environmental and urban planning issues. But Gottlieb saw Los Angeles as a challenge and opportunity in relation to his radical environmentalist perspective, given its role as the original city of sprawl and, at the same time, its emerging dynamic of new ethnically and culturally diverse communities connecting with the region's long history of experimentation that Carey McWilliams (who became an important influence on Gottlieb's own research and writing) had previously described.

One of Gottlieb's first activities in California was to cofound and manage the Midnight Special, a cooperatively owned bookstore in Venice. After he left the Midnight Special in 1973, he began lecturing on politics and social movements, urban planning, and the history of the Los Angeles region at various local universities, including the California Institute of the Arts, University of California, Los Angeles (UCLA), Peoples College of Law, and California State University at Los Angeles. During this period he undertook his investigation of the history of the power structure, the political dynamics, and the land use issues of the Los Angeles area. This resulted in his first book—*Thinking Big: The Story of the* Los Angeles Times, *Its Publishers, and Their In-*

Robert Gottlieb (Photograph courtesy of Urban & Environmental Policy Institute)

fluence on Southern California—which was cowritten with Irene Wolt and published in 1977.

Since this first project, Gottlieb has continued to write prolifically on topics that reflect his wide range of interests, all of which are based on the common theme of the link of social movements and progressive politics with environmentalism. Since 1977, he has published ten more books, chapters in more than a dozen books, and more than several hundred articles in scholarly journals and magazines of general interest.

Far from remaining at his desk or inside the confines of an ivory tower, Gottlieb has been an active participant in the issues he studies. For example, in 1986 he served as faculty coordinator for a conference, "International Green Movements and the Prospects for a New Environmentalism," at UCLA that brought together academics and activists to explore opportunities for a more expansive environmental movement and its place among movements for change. Twelve years later, he hosted a conference at Occidental College, "Progressive L.A.: A Conference on Social Movements in Los Angeles—Uncovering Our Past and Envisioning Our Future," that helped launch the development of the Progressive Los Angeles Network (PLAN), an innovative marriage of progressive policy analysts and activists, including environmental activists. While serving from 1980 to 1987 as director of the Metropolitan Water District of Southern California, the largest water district in the country, Gottlieb challenged the dominant water industry perspective of ever-expanding water supplies imported from distant places to fuel the continuing expansion of the region. Gottlieb identified the need for a new water "ethic of place" and a "community value" rather than "commodity value" to water. He further elaborated these ideas in his two books on water policy, *A Life of Its Own: The Politics and Power of Water* (1988) and *Thirst for Growth: Water Agencies as Hidden Government in California* (1991), and in his many articles on this subject. Interested in issues of materials use and production and waste generation and disposal, and inspired by a student project he helped supervise, Gottlieb studied the struggles of such Los Angeles area grassroots groups as Mothers of East Los Angeles and Concerned Citizens of South Central against proposed waste incineration facilities in their communities. He documented these and other struggles, within the context of a history of waste generation and disposal policies, in his book *War on Waste* (1989), coauthored with his former student Louis Blumberg.

The rise of the antitoxics groups of the 1980s, which Gottlieb helped document, has been associated with the development of an environmental justice movement that challenged the range of environmental burdens, such as waste incinerators and other hazardous facilities, imposed on low-income neighborhoods and communities of color. Gottlieb's major study of environmentalism and the roots of the environmental justice movement, *Forcing the Spring* (1993, revised edition 2005), helped place in historical perspective and make more coherent this more recent development of a dynamic and broader-based environmental movement. His subsequent book, *Environmentalism Unbound* (2001), linked this perspective on an "environmentalism of daily life" to the groundbreaking work associated with the Urban & Environmental Policy Institute (UEPI) in Los Angeles (www.uepi.oxy.edu) which he directs. Along these lines, Gottlieb also began to explore issues of production and the workplace and industrial environmental policy through the Pollution Prevention Center that he cofounded in 1991 and still directs today (as part of UEPI).

Gottlieb has stretched his conception of what should be included in the environmental agenda even further, engaging in such diverse issues as cleaning clothes, janitorial work, and cultivation, production, and access to food. In 1992, while he was teaching at UCLA's Graduate School of Architecture and Urban Planning, his students became interested in food issues and persuaded him to supervise a research project on the topic. They were interested in the price and availability of food, its quality, and how a community's food system is experienced. The students' work became a new point of departure for Gottlieb, who saw an emerging community food security movement as directly addressing social, environmental, community health, and production issues. Through subsequent research projects and programs, Gottlieb helped develop new innovative policy and programmatic initiatives (such as the development of farm to school programs for low-income elementary schools (www.farmtoschool.org) and the passage in 1996 and subsequent reauthorization through the Farm Bill of the Community Food Projects federal legislation), as well as new movement groups (such as the Community Food Security Coalition). Gottlieb argues that these food issues resonate for people as a daily life concern and can embody an aspect of the new environmentalism.

Most recently, Gottlieb has published two books about Los Angeles. The first, *The Next Los Angeles: The Struggle for a Livable City* (co-authored with Mark Vallianatos, Regina Freer and Peter Dreier, 2006) draws on the development of "Progressive L.A.", which linked community activists with researchers and policy analysts in order to develop a progressive agenda and vision for Los Angeles. His most recent work, *Reinventing Los Angeles* (2007), further draws on his experience of UEPI, including the re-envisioning of the L.A. River and ArroyoFest, an extraordinary event where the Pasadena Freeway was closed for a bike ride and a walk ON the freeway to highlight the important of alternatives to the car and the freeway.

Gottlieb is currently Professor of Urban and Environmental Policy at Occidental College and director of the Urban and Environmental Policy Institute. He edits two book series for MIT Press: Urban and Industrial Environments, and Food, Health and Environment. He resides in Santa Monica.

BIBLIOGRAPHY

Gottlieb, Robert, "Beyond NEPA and Earth Day: Reconstructing the Past and Envisioning a Future for Environmentalism," *Environmental History Review*, 1995; Gottlieb, Robert, "The Meaning of Place: Reimagining Community in a Changing West," in Hal K. Rothman, ed., *Reopening the American West*, 1998; Gottlieb, Robert, and Louis Blumberg, "Rethinking Place, Reinventing Nature: An Environmental Justice Perspective on the Public Lands," *George Wright Forum*, 1996; Gottlieb, Robert, and Andrea Brown, "Janitorial Cleaning Products: It's Not Just What Gets Used, But How It Gets Used That Counts," *Pollution Prevention Review*, 1998; Gottlieb, Robert, and Andrew Fisher, "'First Feed the Face': Environmental Justice and Community Food Security," *Antipode*, 1996; "Robert Gottlieb: Henry R. Luce Professor of Urban Environmental Studies," employees.oxy.edu/gottlieb/; "UEPI bios - Bob Gottlieb," departments.oxy.edu/uepi/bios/gottlieb.htm.

Gould, Stephen Jay
(September 10, 1941–May 20, 2002)
Paleontologist, Writer

In addition to his highly productive scholarly career, Stephen Jay Gould dedicated his life to presenting the modes, implications, benefits, and shortcomings of science to a literate public. In his scientific research and thought, Gould defined and participated in crucial debates of the biological and geological sciences, particularly with regard to the theory of evolution, the interpretation of fossil evidence, and the meaning of diversity and change in biology. His forwarding of these debates influenced our understanding of nature, our recognition of the human impact on the natural environment, and, ultimately, a significant portion of the environmentalist rhetoric. A leading evolutionary theoretician, Gould, with his more than 20 books and over 1000 essays, reviews, and articles, was a popular and well-known writer and lecturer on scientific topics.

Stephen Jay Gould was born September 10, 1941, in New York City. When he was five years old, he was taken to the American Museum of Natural History by his father, a court stenographer with an avocational interest in natural history. Gould's fascination with paleontology developed throughout his childhood and teenage years, rivaling his passion for the New York Yankees. He completed his undergraduate degree in geology at Antioch College in 1963 and returned to New York for doctoral studies in paleontology at Columbia University, completing his studies in 1967.

In the course of his graduate studies, Gould became very aware of problems surrounding ecosystem disruption by humans. Working in Bermuda on his dissertation, which examined a remarkable Bermudian land snail named *Peocilozonites*, Gould watched the population of this snail become completely eliminated, by accident, as a result of biological control.

In order to control *Otola*, an imported edible snail that had escaped from a garden and spread throughout the island as an agricultural pest, authorities introduced a "cannibal" snail from Florida, called *Euglandina*. Rather than controlling the *Otola* populations, *Euglandina* devastated the *Peocilozonites*. Returning in 1973, Gould was unable to find a single *Peocilozonite* on the island. This experience led Gould to argue for environmental protection, not from an ecological perspective but rather from an emotional humanistic point of view. Preaching for a humanist ecology to complement our scientific understanding for the need for biodiversity, Gould argues, in his 1993 collection of essays, *Eight Little Piggies*, that "we cannot win this battle to save species and environments without forging an emotional bond between ourselves and nature... for we will not fight to save what we do not love." Many of Gould's other writings also reflect his strong sense of environmental ethics.

In 1967, Gould became assistant professor of geology and assistant curator of invertebrate paleontology at the Museum of Comparative Zoology at Harvard University. In 1971, he became associate professor and associate curator; in 1973, he became professor of geology and zoology and curator of invertebrate paleontology at the Museum of Comparative Zoology and an adjunct member of the Department of the History of Science. During this time, Gould gained a reputation as one of Harvard's most visible and engaging instructors, offering courses in paleontology, biology, geology, and the history of science. In 1982, he was named Alexander Agassiz Professor of Zoology.

In 1974, Gould initiated a monthly series of essays for *Natural History*, under the title, "This View of Life." Writing on such topics as "Size and Shape," "Sizing Up Human Intelligence," and the "Race Problem," Gould established himself as a widely respected writer and was often praised for reviving the popular scientific essay. His critical genre of science writing represented a marked change from the traditional and traditionally dull, didactic style that had preceded his work. Gould's *Natural History* submissions also helped forward his notions of an environmental ethics to a widespread audience.

Among Gould's more famous pursuits was certainly his critique of the central concepts of Darwinism and his notion of the "punctuated equilibrium." This theory, which he formulated with his colleague, Niles Eldredge, in 1972, postulates that species tend to mutate aimlessly, within the expected bounds of statistical variation, and that radical evolution is concentrated in relatively rapid events of speciation—within geologically short periods of 100,000 years or so. Gould's and Eldredge's punctuated equilibrium theory modifies the theory of evolution that had been accepted previously, which held that evolution took place gradually, as slow, continuous transformations of established lineages. While his theory of punctuated equilibrium has stimulated endless debates since the mid-1970s, Gould maintained that it filled a void in Darwin's theory. Darwin himself struggled to explain gaps in fossil records that could not be explained if evolution moved forward as the accretion of many small changes. Gould's final and monumental *The Structure of Evolutionary Theory* (2002) describes and discusses in detail the historical on-going debate about Darwinian evolution, and the evolution of the theory itself, with contributions to it over time from other theorists.

Gould's high visibility as a leading Harvard academic, his critical voice, and his enthusiasm for debate prompted him to enter into scientific, cultural, and political controversies. His participation in the debate surrounding "creationist science" made him a prominent detractor of this cause. He openly opposed legislation to require its teaching alongside Darwinian evolution and testified in several court cases concerned with this issue. As the chief evolutionist in the United States, he stood out as a lightning rod for advocates of creationism, as made obvious by the endless

Internet bulletin boards offering discussion threads on this or related topics.

The recipient of more than 40 honorary degrees, more than a dozen literary awards, and countless academic medals and awards, Gould's work was among the most highly respected in the United States of scholars in any field. Gould died of cancer on May 20, 2002.

BIBLIOGRAPHY
Allmon, Warren, Kelley, Patricia, and Robert Ross, *Stephen Jay Gould: Reflections on his View of Life*, 2009; Gould, Stephen Jay, *Full House: The Spread of Excellence from Plato to Darwin*, 1996; Gould, Stephen Jay, *The Mismeasure of Man*, 1981; Gould, Stephen Jay, *The Panda's Thumb*, 1981; Gould, Stephen Jay, *Wonderful Life: The Burgess Shale and the Nature of History*, 1989; Gould, Stephen Jay, McGarr, Paul, and Steven P. R. Rose, *The Richness of Life: the Essential Stephen Jay Gould*, 2007; "Stephen Jay Gould Online Archive," www.sjgonline.org.

Gray, Asa
(November 18, 1810–January 30, 1888)
Botanist

Few Americans, past or present, have moved their disciplines and the general understanding and perception of nature forward more substantially than nineteenth-century botanist Asa Gray. Gray was a pioneer and master in the field of plant geography and became the most persistent and effective advocate in the United States of Charles Darwin's theory of evolution. Gray's contributions in botany and to the creation of the Botanical Museum at Harvard University, to which he donated his immense collection of American flora, were instrumental in the development of the appreciation of nature in the United States.

Asa Gray was born November 18, 1810, in Sauquot, New York, the eldest of the eight children of Moses Gray, a farmer and tanner, and his wife, Roxana Howard. Gray attended the Clinton Grammar School, nine miles from his home, and transferred to Fairfield Academy, where he received his first lessons in natural science. Gray was drawn to botany at the age of 17, after reading an entry about the field in Brewster's *Edinburgh Encyclopedia*. He bought Amos Eaton's *Manual of Botany* that winter and immersed himself in it until spring, when he could put his newfound knowledge to practice.

Gray received his degree in medicine from the Fairfield Medical School in 1831, but already his heart was devoted to botany and he never did take up the practice of medicine. One of his earliest professional acquaintances was with Dr. John Torrey, a scientist whose early attempts to categorize plant species into broader plant families represented the first steps toward our modern classification system. Torrey quickly became Gray's friend and mentor. Gray spent 11 years teaching, traveling, collecting, and working as Torrey's assistant in his home in New York. Living in the Torreys' home, Gray benefited from the daily association with Torrey, while Mrs. Torrey worked to improve his taste, manners, and general culture. More important was Gray's immersion in the scientific community of New York. In December 1834, for the first time, Gray read two scientific papers before the New York Lyceum of Natural History. The following year, he moved permanently to New York to be close to Torrey. Gray's first major publication, *Elements of Botany*, was published in April 1836, and that summer he was appointed botanist of a projected government expedition to the South Seas. Delays and complications led to his resignation before the ship sailed. Instead, he became librarian and curator of the New York Lyceum of Natural History until 1838, when he accepted a professorship of botany at the University of Michigan. He spent the next year in Europe, purchasing books for the university and studying various specimens and hybridizations of American plants in European herbaria. The trip was successful and initiated lifelong friendships with several European botanists.

In 1842, after further expeditions to Virginia and the mountains of North Carolina, the first edition of Gray's *Botanical Text-Book* was published. He was offered the Fisher professorship of natural history at Harvard, and without ever having the time to assume his teaching duties at the University of Michigan, he accepted it. Already, Gray was the universally acknowledged leader in American botany. Gray's connections with European and North American botanists allowed Gray's herbarium at Harvard to thrive and serve as a general nucleus for the identification of newly discovered North American plants.

After a year-long engagement, in 1848 Gray married Jane Lathrop Loring, who survived him to edit his autobiography and letters. He traveled extensively in the ensuing years and created the Harvard Department of Botany, training many of the eminent botanists of the next generation. Gray held several distinguished positions in academic societies and was one of the founders of the National Academy of Sciences.

Gray was also a prolific writer. His frequent contributions to the *American Journal of Science* constitute an impressive and authoritative history of botany extending over half a century. He wrote less frequently for a variety of other periodicals and also published five important textbooks. In all, Gray produced more than 350 books, monographs, and shorter papers furthering the understanding and acceptance of descriptive botany in North America. Timing certainly played a role in Gray's success as a botanist. He lived at a time when exploration of the rich and diverse flora of North America was accelerating. The clarity and accuracy of Gray's prose made his writing accessible to the lay public as well as to scientists.

In September 1857, Charles Darwin wrote Gray a now-famous letter in which he outlined his theory of the evolution of species by means of natural selection and sent Gray an advance copy of *The Origin of Species*. The eminent American botanist championed Darwin's theory, and Darwin prized Gray as one of his most influential supporters and most searching critics. Much to the disappointment of many of Darwin's agnostic disciples, however, Gray continued to consider himself a theist. Gray believed that religion and Darwin's theory of natural selection were not in conflict. While it seemed that he had one foot in each camp, Gray anticipated later discoveries by Gregor Mendel and Hugo De Vries by suggesting that variations were not physical, but physiological, thereby allowing himself to maintain his faith in God as Creator and his belief in Darwin's theory of evolution.

In 1872, Gray retired from teaching, and in 1873, CHARLES SPRAGUE SARGENT succeeded him as director of the Botanical Garden. Gray donated his herbarium, containing some 200,000 specimens, and his library of 2,200 volumes to Harvard University upon the completion of a fireproof building designed for them. Gray continued his work and held onto his Fisher professorship until his death on January 30, 1888. He died at home, in Cambridge, Massachusetts, one month after a paralytic stroke. Appropriately, his last act was a letter to a fellow botanist, gently scolding him for coining a superfluous plant name.

BIBLIOGRAPHY

Dupree, A. Hunter, *Asa Gray: American Botanist, Friend of Darwin*, 1988; Gray, Jane Loring, ed., *Letters of Asa Gray*, 1893; Miles, Sara Joan, "Charles Darwin and Asa Gray Discuss Teleology and Design", in *Perspectives on Science and Christian Faith*, 2001; Sargent, Charles Sprague, ed., *Scientific Papers of Asa Gray*, 1889.

Grinnell, George Bird

(September 20, 1849–April 11, 1938)
Cofounder of the Audubon Society, Cofounder of the Boone and Crockett Club, Editor and Publisher of *Forest and Stream*

George Bird Grinnell was an avid explorer of the American West and a prolific writer. The articles and editorials he wrote for his magazine, *Forest and Stream*, issued rallying calls for the conservation of big game animals and birds and more stringent protection of the national parks. His readers were urged to join the two major conservation-oriented organizations he helped found, the Audubon Society and the Boone and Crockett Club. Ethnologists laud his contribution to the field of American Indian studies. He wrote ten books about Plains Indians and their folklore.

George Bird Grinnell was born in Brooklyn, New York, on September 20, 1849, to a well-off family. At the age of eight, he moved with his family to a house on the estate of the Audubon family in northern Manhattan. Madame Audubon, the widow of the artist and naturalist JOHN JAMES AUDUBON, ran a day school in her family's mansion in Audubon Park. While not at school, Grinnell and a band of friends who also lived on the estate had the run of the place, which extended all the way to the Hudson River. His interest in natural history and love for exploring developed at Audubon Park, along with a mischieviousness that marked his early years. At the age of 12, he and some other boys from Audubon Park were arrested for skinny-dipping in the river and were actually put in jail until their parents could pick them up. Grinnell was expelled from Yale University for climbing a lightning rod and painting his class's graduation year on the face of the college clock. He was readmitted after he passed his class exams and he earned a B.A. in 1870.

The summer after graduation, Grinnell left on the first of what would be 40 trips west during his lifetime. On this first trip, he accompanied a Yale fossil-collecting expedition to Kansas, Wyoming, Utah, and Nebraska. Upon his return, Grinnell moved to New York to help his father run the family dry goods business during the year, escaping for trips west to hunt, explore, and learn more about the Indians in the summer. In 1874, Grinnell reached a turning point in his life and career. He sold the family business and devoted himself wholly to science. Yale's Peabody Museum offered him employment as an osteology assistant, and he began working toward a Ph.D. in paleontology. During the summers, Grinnell continued to travel west. He served as naturalist for Col. George Custer on his Black Hills expedition in 1873, and made another trip west in 1875 to Yellowstone, writing an acclaimed account of the wildlife he observed there. While at Yale, Grinnell also began writing for *Forest and Stream*, a high-profile conservationist magazine with a readership of influential sportsmen. In 1880, after receiving his Ph.D., he bought majority rights to

George B. Grinnell and his wife on Grinnell Glacier. (Library of Congress, Prints & Photographs Division, LC-USZ62-93186)

the magazine and became editor and publisher. Grinnell's frequent articles and editorials called attention to the environmental problems of the day, including diminishing game, depletion of forests, water pollution, and endangered watersheds. Sportsmen formed 342 known conservation clubs throughout the country in response to *Forest and Stream*'s call for activism. When Grinnell became concerned in 1887 about the disappearance of birds that were valued for their plumes, he began publishing *Audubon Magazine*, devoted solely to bird protection. During the mere two years that he published *Audubon Magazine*, some 19 regional Audubon societies were founded with a total of about 50,000 members. The year 1900 marked the passage of the Lacey Act, for which Audubon members had lobbied heavily. It outlawed interstate commerce of protected birds killed by hunters, greatly decreasing the financial incentive for hunters interested in plume birds. That year, Grinnell resumed publishing a bird-oriented magazine, *Bird Lore*, which in 1904 became *Audubon*, and the scattered Audubon societies joined together under the banner of the National Audubon Society.

One of Grinnell's most influential readers was THEODORE ROOSEVELT. Roosevelt first went to meet Grinnell after *Forest and Stream* criticized his book *Hunting Trips of a Ranchman* (1886). They soon became friends, vowing to further the conservationist cause together. In 1887 they cofounded the Boone and Crockett Club, whose membership requirements included having killed at least one adult male of three separate species of big game. The first stated goal of the club was "to promote manly sport with the rifle," but the club's objectives were quickly distilled into the conservationist goals of protecting big game animals and their habitats. The club was particularly effective in its fight to maintain the wildness of Yellowstone, which had been declared a national park in 1872. The influential members of the Boone and Crockett Club lobbied Congress to prevent railway and concessions companies from cutting forests, killing animals, and even marring natural geysers in their attempts to transform the park into a huge, profitable resort. The club was also instrumental in the founding of Glacier National Park (1910), which Grinnell had first surveyed in 1885.

Roosevelt and Grinnell coedited the Boone and Crockett Club's publications during the 1890s. They put out three books together, *American Big Game Hunting* (1893), *Hunting in Many Lands* (1895), and *Trail and Campfire* (1897).

Grinnell's service to the conservation movement was vast: he helped establish the American Game Association in 1911, he served as president of ROBERT STERLING YARD's National Parks Association in 1925, he helped found the New York Zoological Society in 1895 and served as a trustee, and he was a member of the federal advisory board for the Migratory Bird Act.

In addition to his conservationist activities, Grinnell was an active advocate for the Plains Indians, with whom he had become familiar during his trips west. Presidents Cleveland and Roosevelt depended upon Grinnell to advise them on Indian affairs, and they both dispatched him to mediate land disagreements between Indians and White settlers. Grinnell developed many strong, long-lasting friendships with Indian chiefs, especially White Calf of the Blackfeet. Grinnell wrote ethnographic descriptions of the Pawnee, Blackfeet, and Cheyenne peoples and transcribed many folktales.

Grinnell married Elizabeth Kirby Curtis Williams in 1902, when he was 52 years old. Grinnell died in New York City on April 11, 1938, at the age of 88, after a long illness.

BIBLIOGRAPHY

Cutright, Paul Russell, *Theodore Roosevelt: The Making of a Conservationist*, 1985; Diettert, Gerald A., *Grinnell's Glacier: George Bird Grinnell and Glacier National Park*, 1992; Evans, Robley, *George Bird Grinnell*, 1996; Parsons, Cynthia, and Schulyer M. Meyer, *George Bird Grinnell, A Biographical Sketch*, 1993; Punke, Michael, *Last Stand: George Bird Grinnell, the Battle to Save the Buffalo, and the Birth of the New West*, 2007

Grogan, Pete
(February 19, 1949–)
Recycling Expert

Pete Grogan cofounded the grassroots recycling organization Eco-Cycle in Boulder, Colorado, in 1976, along with Roy Young. He directed Eco-Cycle until 1987, fostering its growth as it became the largest nonprofit recycling organization in the nation. He then became an international recycling consultant with R.W. Beck, assisting numerous local and state governments in the development of their recycling programs. At his current position of manager of market development for International Paper, Grogan works to increase paper recovery in North America in order to supply a demand for recovered paper worldwide, and particularly in China.

Peter Laurence Grogan was born on February 19, 1949, in Newark, New Jersey. As a young child vacationing at the beach, he spent summer evenings with his family on the boardwalk, watching boats at sea that appeared to be on fire. One evening when he asked about this, his parents told him that they were actually barges that hauled garbage out to sea, burned it, and then dumped it into the ocean. The next day, swimming in the ocean, he noticed that it was full of tiny bits of incinerated garbage! This experience, at the age of five, was the root of Grogan's environmentalism, he now believes. Grogan's parents had learned to recycle during World War II and continued to do so after the war. The family diligently separated newspapers and magazines to give to a local ragman or the Salvation Army when they came through their neighborhood. Once Grogan left home, he was amazed at the waste generated by most households.

Grogan studied psychology at the University of Colorado–Boulder, graduating with a B.A. in 1974. One of his first jobs was with a local program for juvenile offenders. Grogan

Pete Grogan (Photograph by Dave Putnam)

wanted to experiment with sports therapy, but there were no funds available for sporting equipment. To raise the money, he and the teenagers collected recyclables from residents until they had raised a few thousand dollars. After he stopped the collections, people continued to call him to request pickups.

That was the inspiration for Eco-Cycle, a residential recyclable material collection program that he and friend Roy Young founded in 1976. For the first year, Grogan and Young volunteered their time; they coordinated truck rental, recruited community organizations to provide 40 volunteers to collect the recyclables in return for a donation of $500 to their organization, and sold the material to recycling processors. Because of their success and their potential as a model for other communities, the EPA agreed to fund the program if it could also get financial support from the governments of the city of Boulder and Boulder County. With that seed money in place, Eco-Cycle grew and reached financial self-sufficiency.

Grogan's contacts with the university psychology department helped him encourage wide participation in Eco-Cycle. A block-leader program enlisted volunteers who distributed Eco-Cycle's newsletters and posted signs to remind their neighbors of the monthly pickups. Prof. Stuart Cook of the Department of Psychology at the University of Colorado hypothesized that uniform recycling bins would increase participation levels, so he obtained research funds to buy bins and to pay graduate students for a study. Bins were distributed to 1,000 homes on specific blocks in different neighborhoods and indeed participation with the bins increased significantly. Today, thousands of cities provide residents with containers.

In 1987, when recycling was coming into vogue throughout the country, Grogan decided to leave Eco-Cycle and begin helping others to plan and implement recycling programs. He spent the next seven years as a consultant with R.W. Beck and Associates, which offers consulting services to government and industry throughout North America and Asia in recycling, composting, and solid waste planning; design of material recovery facilities; and other related areas. He also helped the paper and plastic industries increase their recovery of recyclable waste products.

From 1994 until 2008, Grogan managed market development activities for Weyerhaeuser Recycling, one of the world's three largest paper recyclers, based in Tacoma, Washington. Weyerhaeuser Recycling buys recovered paper and repulps it into newsprint and corrugated containers. He works with legislative bodies and paper trade associations to promote the growth of paper recycling and recovery. The United States is currently approaching 50 percent paper recovery. Grogan is working to increase that percentage and to ensure that swings in the international market do not threaten the economic viability of recycling paper.

Grogan is a popular speaker, appearing frequently at recycling conferences in the United States, Canada, Mexico, and Europe. He gave the keynote address at the White House Summit on Recycling in 1998. In his speeches, Grogan maintains that in an energy-tense world, everyone should engage in recycling all materials. The U.S will be at a strategic disadvantage long term because of all the resources that have been sent to landfills instead of recycling facilities. Americans have been taught to think that resources are unlimited, but in fact they do have limits. We are beginning to understand that there is a limit to oil, however, thanks to the emergence of the concept of 'peak oil.'

Grogan was a member of the board of directors of the National Recycling Coalition from 1982 to 1987 and again from 1989 to 1994, serving as president from 1992 to 1993. He is curently a member of the board of the Institute for Scrap Recycling Industries. Grogan received the Outstanding Alumni Award from the University of Colorado in 2004, and was recognized in 2006 with the National Recycling Coalition's Lifetime Achievement Award and Recycler of the Year Award.

BIBLIOGRAPHY

Booth, Michael, "Recycling Guru Laments Colorado's Waste," *Denver Post*, 1999; Grogan, Peter, "Emerald City Looks to Tomorrow," *Bio-Cycle*, 1998; Grogan, Peter, "Recyclables like Bananas Need Buyers," *Bio-Cycle*, 1997.

Grossman, Richard L.

(1943–)
Activist, Director of Environmentalists for Full Employment, Cofounder of Program on Corporations, Law and Democracy

Richard L. Grossman helped bring about the passage of the first antinuclear ballot initiative, in California in 1976. As director of Environmentalists for Full Employment (EFFE) from 1976 to 1985, he initiated cooperation among environmental and labor groups. Today he focuses on stimulating debate among environmental and social activists that challenges the authority of corporations.

Born in Brooklyn, New York, in 1943, Richard L. Grossman was a member of a family that, early in his life, instilled in him an appreciation for justice and democracy. His family, he says, was always very clear about what was right and what wrong. He graduated with a B.A. from Columbia University in 1965 and joined the Peace Corps, where he was a teacher in a small town on the Filipino island of Leyte. He was in the Philippines from 1965 to 1967, a series of years he found very instructive. Living there—in a former American colony—during the Vietnam War, he gained a new perspective on the United States and the rest of the world. He remembers the people of the Philippines as being very patient with the "young arrogant Americans."

Upon returning to the United States in 1967, Grossman participated as an adult education teacher in various War on Poverty Program efforts throughout the country. Then, from 1971 to 1972, he farmed in the Hudson Valley of New York, wrote a novel that was not published, and wrote and published several short stories. In 1973, Grossman took a position in California as a writer and production worker for the San Francisco *Phoenix*, a biweekly newspaper. He also cofounded and published a literary magazine entitled *Gallimaufry* and was a fellow with the CORO Foundation for Public Affairs during these years.

In 1974, he became involved with the antinuclear protest movement in California. He was an organizer for California Proposition 15, the first antinuclear initiative on a state ballot, challenging government officials and utility providers to actually engage in a meaningful debate on the subject of nuclear power and attempting to force them outside of their "no nukes, no jobs" mantra. The ballot initiative was successfully passed into law in 1976. Owing to his efforts in organizing, Grossman was offered the position of director of Environmentalists For Full Employment in Washington, D.C., in 1976. He accepted the offer and left California. He acted as director of EFFE from 1976 to 1985, helping to build a foundation of unity and cooperation between labor and environmental organizations. A large part of his responsibility was to provide support for local unions interested in protesting potential nuclear power generator projects in their neighborhoods. The American Federation of Labor–Congress of Industrial Organizations (AFL-CIO) was, at that time, a staunch supporter of nuclear power projects, and local unions that wanted to protest their construction could not do so without facing recriminations from the national labor organization. Grossman created a coalition of antinuclear unions that broke the public unity of unions, allowing many local unions to protest nuclear projects. During his time as director of EFFE, Grossman also organized a giant labor/environmental conference in Pittsburgh that attracted thousands of workers and environmentalists.

After leaving EFFE in 1985, Grossman became a guest fellow at the Institute for Policy Studies in Washington, D.C., and was executive director of Greenpeace USA for a short time during 1985 and 1986. In 1987, he cofounded the Stop the Poisoning (STP) schools project at the Highlander Center in Tennessee. These schools, which concentrated on ending corporate poisoning, were modeled after the citizenship schools that the Highlander Center ran for the civil rights movement. Grossman helped to organize an STP committee composed of people from all over the South who lived in at-risk communities. The committee met once or twice a month. Participants came to strategize and compare notes, and they eventually became quite skilled at stopping particular corporate assaults on the health and well-being of their communities. However, Grossman saw that while these dump-by-dump and chemical plant-by-chemical plant victories were very important, there simply was not enough time in the world to combat each of these problems one at a time. He saw people organizing, educating, and passing new laws, yet somehow the destruction continued. He began wondering about the causes behind the fact that corporations have such a large degree of decision-making power in our society, while the best that ordinary people can normally do is react to the decisions and try to make things, as he says, "less bad."

In 1992, Grossman left the STP schools project to concentrate his efforts on exploring and challenging the existing power structure that so effectively recognizes the authority of corporations while completely disregarding the power of people in the United States. To this end, he cofounded the Program on Corporations, Law and Democracy (POCLAD) in 1993. POCLAD's official mission is "to instigate democratic conversations and actions that contest the authority of corporations to define our cultures, govern our nations, and plunder the earth." POCLAD works to replace the illegitimate power of corporate institutions with democracy. Corporate power, according to Grossman, is illegitimate simply because it is not constitutional and has usurped the authority of a sovereign people. Corporations make decisions that have a fundamental impact on our lives. They decide things like how our health, food, and energy services operate. These are decisions that should, he says, be made instead by elected officials.

According to Grossman, in order to reclaim these decision-making powers, Americans need to stop treating organizations as if they were entities subject to the Bill of Rights (which they are; legally a corporation has the right to free speech, while an employee on company property does not) and instead redefine corporations as public instruments subordinate to the people. Corporations should no longer be treated as private contracts but should be treated as limited, subordinate institutions. Grossman provides a simple example of what this means practically, in an interview published in *Corporate Crime Reporter*. He says we should tell Exxon,

> Your job is to find oil. Dig it up. Refine it. Get it where it needs to go. Your job is not to write environmental laws. Your job is not to write the worker laws. Your job is not to educate people on how to use energy. Your job is not to tell us the future. Your job is not to influence how we think. Your job is not to lobby. Your job is not to get involved in any elections. Your job is not to give any charitable contributions. Your job is not to endow chairs in universities. Your job is to get the oil and bring it back. Your job is not to be a cultural, political institution.

Grossman has written hundreds of newspaper and magazine articles, and he has written and coauthored several books, including *Fear at Work*, *Job Blackmail, Labor and the Environment*, and a frequently reprinted pamphlet entitled *Taking Care of Business: Citizenship and the Charter of Incorporation*.

In 2005, Grossman left POCLAD and joined the staff of the Community Environmental Legal Defense Fund as historian and educational director. He had been informally advising this non-profit law firm—located in Chambersburg, Pennsylvania—since its founding in 1995. With the Fund he co-founded Democracy Schools in 2003. These Schools—which have been taught in more than 20 states—explore law, histories, andsrategies with communities seeking to stop unwanted corporate and governmnet assaults. Grossman's work with the Legal Defense Fund has also involved drafting municipal ordinances that ban specific corporate action, and that strip corporations of illegitimate constitutional privileges and powers.

Grossman lives in the Catskill Mountains of New York. He is writing a book on the "crisis of strategy" characterizing political action today: so much hope, energy and resources poured into resisting one corporate attack at a time…over and over again. He believes that breaking free from this crisis of failed strategy requires understanding and challenging the nation's basic constitutional theory and doctrine. His book, among other things will examine celebrated aspects of history, from the Revolution and the U.S.'s slave and property Constitution, to the anti-democratic foundations of Anglo-American jurisprudence and the "rule of law," to the "limited victories" of people's struggles, that have prevented true democratic self-governance.

BIBLIOGRAPHY

"The Community Environmental Legal Defense Fund," www.celdf.org; "Corporate Crime Reporter—Interview With Richard Grossman," www.ratical.org/corporations/CCRivRG1197.txt; Grossman, Richard L., "After Seattle… The WTO, The US Constitution and Self Government," *By What Authority*, www.poclad.org/bwa/fall99.htm, 1999; Kazis, Richard, and Richard L. Grossman, *Fear at Work: Job Blackmail. Labor and the Environment*, 1982; "Richard Grossman Biography from Americans Who Tell the Truth," www.americanswhotellthetruth.org/pgs/portraits/Richard_Grossman.html.

Gussow, Joan Dye

(October 4, 1928–)
Nutrition Educator, Author

Troubled by trends in agriculture and food processing, Joan Dye Gussow has sought to educate people on the complexities of the food system in the United States and its impact on human nutrition and the environment. She is an emerita professor of nutrition and education at Columbia University Teachers College and has written about consumer food choices, food systems, and prospects for the future. With the growing popularity of convenience foods—which are often highly processed and heavily packaged—the diets of most people are becoming radically disconnected from the raw materials produced by farmers, and Gussow has made a career of trying to reverse this trend. She is a dedicated gardener and champions a greater reliance on fresh, locally grown foods instead of products of the multinational food industry.

Joan Dye was born on October 4, 1928, in Alhambra, California, the daughter of Chester and Joyce (Fisher) Dye. She attended Pomona College in Pomona, California, receiving her B.A. in zoology-chemistry in 1950. She then moved to New York City, where she took a job as a researcher for Time, Incorporated. In 1956 she left that job and became a freelance writer for Street and Smith Publications, and on October 21 of that year she married Alan M. Gussow, an artist. She and Alan had two sons, Adam and Seth. During the mid-1960s, she worked as an editorial and research assistant at Yeshiva University and then held a similar position at Albert Einstein College of Medicine, from 1966 until 1969. In 1970 she began working as an instructor in nutrition education for Columbia University Teachers College. She received her master's in community nutrition education from Columbia University in 1974, where she also received her doctorate in nutrition education in 1975. At that point she became assistant professor of nutrition and education and chairperson of the nutrition program.

Gussow's original area of specialization was nutrition education, and she has always worked at generating resistance to nutrition miseducation in the United States. But she also knows that the realities of agriculture and food production are invisible to a great majority of food consumers and that in order to make the right nutrition decisions, people need to have a better understanding of where the food comes from. Hoping to reach a wider audience, she began writing magazine articles and books. In 1978 her book, *The Feeding Web: Issues in Nutritional Ecology*, was published, which dealt with some of the problems with the existing industrial food systems and how they shape consumer food choices.

Current agricultural patterns are shaped by the effort to make nature conform to industry's need for uniformity, durability, and low raw materials costs. Gussow's writings explain how these demands have unleashed destructive forces on farming's resource base, threatening long-term sustainability. Of primary importance in countering these trends is the need to encourage more localized food production in order to keep consumers closer to their food sources and lower the energy costs of transport, processing, and distribution. In an article she wrote for *Food Monitor* in 1985, Gussow points out other problems with a globalized food supply—such as contamination disasters in which tainted food gets dispersed over great distances. She illustrates this with an example of a polychlorinated biphenyl (PCB) spill at a packing plant in Billings, Montana, in 1979 in which PCBs got into meat meal used for animal food. By the time the problem was discovered, contamination had spread to 18 states and British Columbia, and 1.2 million chickens, 5,300 hogs, 30,000 turkeys, 800,000 pounds of animal

Joan Gussow (Photograph courtesy of *The Valley Table*).

feed, and 74,000 bakery items had to be destroyed. Despite an apparently elaborate system of safeguards, this was by no means an isolated incident; and Gussow reminds readers of the vulnerability inherent in such large distribution systems.

Gussow continued to examine problems with the food industry in *Chicken Little, Tomato Sauce and Agriculture: Who Will Produce Tomorrow's Food* (1991), where she tackles the issues of biotechnology, consumer preference, and alternatives to current unsustainable agriculture patterns. Part of the book's title comes from Frederik Pohl's 1952 science fiction classic *The Space Merchants*, which features a product of misguided technology called "chicken little"—a headless, featherless, wingless lump of flesh fed by tubes, created to feed a growing global population. Gussow comments on so-called technological "progress" in the food industries and questions what drives it. She reveals that the number of food items available in a typical supermarket has increased from 800 around 1930 to over 30,000 today, with an average of 15,000 new products introduced a year. Consumers are bombarded with choices, and are directed by advertising toward food selections that are instant, artificial, disposable, individually portioned, and overpackaged. Gussow condemns this current trend as intolerably wasteful. When it comes to making food choices, she recommends keeping it simple and advises consumers not to eat anything their ancestors would not recognize. She also points out that although the food industry has become a daunting force that may seem impervious to change, consumer concern really is capable of creating pressure on the food system. In her fight to help reform some of the problems in large-scale industrial food systems, Gussow has come to believe that food is an indication of other problems and that the way to engage people in helping to sustain the processes that supply their food is to get them to care about the environment as a whole.

As a nutritionist, Gussow advises people to eat whole foods and to eat lower on the food chain; as an environmentalist her advice would be the same, and she would also advocate buying food locally and eating seasonally. Proving that it is possible to live year-round off a home garden, Gussow buys very little from grocery stores and for produce relies entirely on what she grows. She retired from Columbia Teachers College in 1994 but continues to teach her signature course "Nutritional Ecology" as an emerita professor. She has served as a member of the U.S. Department of Agriculture's National Organic Standards Board and the Food Advisory Committee of the U.S, Food and Drug Administration, and has chaired the boards of the Society for Nutrition Education, the National Gardening Association, the Jessie Smith Noyes Foundation and Just Food. She currently serves on the boards of Just Food and the Frontera Farmer Foundation, and is on the Governing Board of Trustees of her village.

Gussow tends the garden that she and her late husband designed for their home on the west bank of the Hudson River in Piermont, New York. Her latest book, *This Organic Life* (2001), details the trials and tribulations, and most importantly—the joys and rewards—of being a mini-farmer.

BIBLIOGRAPHY

"Faculty Profile: Gussow," www.tc.columbia.edu/faculty/index.htm?facid=jeg30; Fraser, Laura, "Homegrown Harvest," *Health*, 1997; Gussow, Joan Dye, *Chicken Little, Tomato Sauce and Agriculture*, 1991; Gussow, Joan Dye, *The Feeding Web: Issues in Nutritional Ecology*, 1978; Gussow, Joan Dye, "PCBs for Breakfast and Other Problems with a Food System Gone Awry," *Food Monitor*, 1982; Liebman, Bonnie, "A Chicken Little in Our Future?" *Nutrition Action Healthletter*, 1991.

Guthrie, Woody

(July 14, 1912–October 3, 1967)
Singer, Songwriter

A refugee of the dust bowl of the 1930s, hobo, and champion of the working man, Woody Guthrie wrote more than 1,000 folksongs, including such classics as "This Land Is Your Land" and "Pastures of Plenty" that Americans still sing today. His songs instilled generations of Americans with a deep pride in the natural beauty of the land and the humble people on it. As an advocate for marginalized populations, be they migrant workers or lonesome hobos of the Depression, his work was a source of inspiration for many underdog causes, including the antinuclear movement, farmworker solidarity, and regional save-the-river campaigns all over the North American continent.

Woodrow Wilson Guthrie was born on July 14, 1912, in Okemah, Oklahoma, to Nora Belle (Tanner) and Charlie Guthrie, a real estate agent and district clerk. Guthrie's childhood was wracked with natural and unnatural disasters. When he was six, his 14-year-old sis-

Woody Guthrie (Library of Congress, Prints & Photographs Division, NYWT&S Collection, LC-USZ62-130859).

ter Clara's dress caught on fire while she was doing household chores, and she died. Another sister, Mary Josephine, was born in 1922, just as Charlie Guthrie's real estate business died out and he lost reelection as district clerk. His mother began to show signs at this time of the disease that would eventually claim her life and Woody's as well, Huntington's chorea.

After Charlie Guthrie committed his ailing wife to an asylum and moved to Pampa, Texas, with his youngest children, 15-year-old Woody began living outdoors and found that he enjoyed it. One family took him in and taught him some music. Guthrie learned to play jaw harp and the harmonica, beat rhythm with carved animal bones, and began singing his way out of the hard times that had befallen his family. The year 1929 brought the stock market crash, the beginning of the Great Depression, a worsening drought in Texas and Oklahoma, and the death of Guthrie's mother.

Guthrie married Mary Jennings in 1933. While awaiting the birth of their first child in Pampa, Texas, in 1935, they witnessed a devastating dust storm. The winds blew across the Great Plains carrying hundreds of thousands of tons of Oklahoma and Texas Panhandle topsoil into the sky. Farms in South Dakota, Colorado, Iowa, Arkansas, Missouri, Nebraska, Kansas, Oklahoma, and Texas—and the life savings of the farmers as well—were blown away. Guthrie recorded the storm's horror in his song "Dust Storm Disaster."

> We saw outside our window
> Where wheat fields they had grown,
> Was now a rippling ocean
> Of dust the wind had blown.
>
> We loaded our jalopies
> And piled our families in,
> We rattled down the highway
> To never come back again.©

This dust storm and the many others Guthrie observed yielded him more than a song. The dust bowl—the result of a protracted drought that parched fields left fallow owing to the reduced demand for wheat during the Great Depression—was a formative political experience for Guthrie. What made the situation worse for small farmers was the mechanization of agriculture, which pushed small undercapitalized farmers off the land, because only large, highly capitalized agribusiness could afford modern combines and harvesters. The drought exacerbated bad circumstances for the small farmer in the Wheat Belt, and many undertook a great migration westward.

Guthrie began hopping freight trains, to Oklahoma, Arkansas, and eventually California. The songs he wrote during his wanderings, to his surprise, had a profound effect upon his listeners. In 1937 Guthrie went to California and, with his cousin Jack Guthrie, created "The Oklahoma (Jack) and Woody Show" on KFVD in Los Angeles. Woody's popularity among the migrants in California grew as he sang their tales. For KFVD, he covered migrant camp conditions in northern California. Guthrie became more politicized after seeing the camps, and by 1939 his work on behalf of the Communist Party led to a rift with the radio station.

On New Year's Day 1940, Woody Guthrie set out for New York City, hitchhiking from Pampa, Texas. On the trip he heard the entire country singing along with Kate Smith's "God Bless America," and he wrote a retort he called "God Blessed America for Me," which he later renamed "This Land Is Your Land." The song has come to stand as an anthem for the environment, celebrating America's spectacular landscape and emphasizing that the beauty and bounty of the United States belong to the people of the land. Two stanzas were deleted from Guthrie's first recording of it:

> As I went walking, I saw a sign there,
> And on the sign it said "Trespassing."
> But on the other side it didn't say nothing,
> That side was made for you and me.
> In the shadow of the steeple I saw my people,
> By the relief office I saw my people—
> As they stood hungry, I stood there asking
> Is this land made for you and me.©

In March 1940, Woody sang "This Land Is Your Land" at a benefit for West Coast migrant workers. At this performance he met folklorist Alan Lomax and PETE SEEGER, who befriended him and collaborated with him on many later recordings. Lomax recorded Guthrie for the Library of Congress, which was followed by recordings for Victor Records and radio appearances. Lomax recommended Guthrie for a part in the documentary film to promote the Bonneville Power Administration and the Coulee Dam project. Guthrie spent a month at the project's site, writing 26 songs that are compiled in the Columbia River Collection, including "Roll On Columbia":

> Green Douglas firs where the waters cut through
> Down her wild mountains and canyons she flew,
> Canadian Northwest to the ocean so blue,
> Roll on, Columbia, Roll on.©

1941 was an important year for Guthrie. He joined the Almanac Singers with Pete Seeger, Lee Hays, Millard Lampell, and others and published his memoir *Bound for Glory*, which received rave reviews. That same year, after eight years of marriage, most of which Guthrie spent on the road, Mary Guthrie gave her husband an ultimatum: that he choose to live at home with his family or leave them permanently. He chose the latter and soon fell in love with Marjorie Greenblatt Mazia, a dancer he met in New York. They married in 1945 and had four children. World War II interrupted his career, but Guthrie joined the merchant marine with song mate Cisco Houston, and together they chronicled in song this phase of U.S. history.

After the war ended, Guthrie reunited with Pete Seeger and returned to recording songs for the labor movement. However, once communist witch hunts began in the spring of 1947, with Pres. Harry Truman's Executive Order 9835 to track down disloyal Americans, Guthrie's career faltered. The unions that he and Seeger had hoped to collaborate with had blacklisted them as probable communists and members of subversive organizations, and his concerts began to be canceled unexpectedly. By 1949, Guthrie had begun losing his concentration, drinking alcohol more heavily, and disappearing more frequently. In 1952 he was diagnosed with Huntington's chorea, an incurable disease of the nervous system. He divorced Marjorie in 1952 and married Anneke Van Kirk Marshall, with whom he lived briefly in a community of black-listed entertainers in Topanga Canyon, California. He spent the last 15 years of his life in and out of hospitals, until his death in Creedmore State Hospital in Queens, New York, on October 3, 1967.

BIBLIOGRAPHY

Cray, Ed, and Studs Terkel, *Ramblin' Man: the Life and Times of Woody Guthrie*, 2006; Guthrie, Woody, *Bound for Glory*, 1941, 1995; Guthrie, Woody, *Pastures of Plenty*, ed. Dave Marsh and Harold Leventhal, 1990; Guthrie, Woody, *Seeds of Man: An Experience Lived and Dreamed*, 1995; Jackson, Mark Allan, *Prophet Singer: the Voice and Vision of Woody Guthrie*, 2007; Klein, Joe, *Woody Guthrie: A Life*, 1980, revised, 1999; Partridge, Elizabeth,

This Land was Made for You and Me: The Life and Songs of Woody Guthrie, 2002; Santelli, Robert, and Emily Davidson, eds. *Hard Travelin': The Life and Legacy of Woody Guthrie*, 1999; Yates, Janelle, *Guthrie: American Balladeer*, 1995.

Gutiérrez, Juana Beatriz

(1932–)
Cofounder and President of Mothers of East Los Angeles

Juana Beatriz Gutiérrez was instrumental in founding Las Madres del Este Los Angeles–Santa Isabel (the Mothers of East Los Angeles), or MELA, a nonprofit group of women activists who have agitated and organized to improve conditions in their neighborhood since 1985. She is now president of this organization, which came into existence to protest the construction of a state prison in East Los Angeles. Since that time, MELA has been active in protesting many other environmentally and socially unsound projects in East Los Angeles and elsewhere. Currently, it operates the Mothers of East Los Angeles Water Conservation Program.

Born in the north-central region of Mexico in the town of Sombrete, Zacatecas, in 1932, Juana Beatriz Gutiérrez grew up in Ciudad Juárez near El Paso, Texas. She moved to the United States in 1956 and married Ricardo Gutiérrez, who was then a marine. He later became a warehouse shift manager in Los Angeles, California. Gutiérrez and her husband have lived in the Boyle Heights section of East Los Angeles for the past 40 years, where they have raised 9 children.

Gutiérrez became concerned about the safety of her children in 1979 when drug dealers and gang members began assembling on a regular basis in the park across the street from her house. In response to their presence, she organized a neighborhood watch program and became president of the local Parent Teachers Association. Also, she and her husband began organizing after-school activities in the park for the children of the neighborhood. Thus began her role as a leader in organizing effective community responses to threats to the health, safety, and happiness of her neighborhood.

In 1985, California state officials announced plans to construct a $100 million state prison on Santa Fe Avenue in East Los Angeles, prompting Gutiérrez, with the help of California assemblywoman Gloria Molina, to organize a group to oppose the construction of the prison. Upon the advice of a local priest, Father Moretta from Resurrection Church, they named the group Mothers of East Los Angeles. Gutiérrez and several other women from her neighborhood, including AURORA CASTILLO, collected 1,500 signatures on a petition against the building of the prison. They gave this petition to Molina to take to the State Assembly in Sacramento. Gutiérrez also organized community demonstrations protesting the prison and participated in the Earth Day 1990 festival in Exposition Park, distributing educational materials and T-shirts and raising funds through the sale of tamales. MELA became adept at attracting media attention, especially utilizing protest marches to draw regional, and even national, focus to their cause. Their campaign ended successfully in 1992, with the passing of a law that prohibited the building of any state prison in East Los Angeles.

The Mothers of East Los Angeles next acted in response to the proposed construction of a hazardous waste incinerator in the industrial town of Vernon, just one mile from Gutiérrez's home. This incinerator would have further degraded the already overburdened air of East Los Angeles by burning up to 22,500 tons of commercial hazardous waste per day. In 1982, MELA led 500 protesters to a Department of Health Services meeting and demanded that an environmental impact review be conducted. MELA also threatened to sue the city of Vernon as well as California Thermal Treatment Systems, the company that planned to build and operate the incinerator. In response to the rising tide of opposition to the incinerator, Tom Bradley, who was then mayor of Los Angeles, eventually joined Las Madres in denouncing the project, and it was defeated.

In the years since these successes, Las Madres has continued combating the construction of toxic facilities and other health-threatening projects in East Los Angeles and elsewhere. MELA was a part of the coalition organized to protest the diverting of an oil pipeline away from the wealthy, politically connected cities of Santa Monica and Pacific Palisades and through the low-income communities of East Los Angeles. The group also joined the protest against the construction of a cyanide hexavalent chromium treatment plant next to Huntington Park High School, fought against the spraying of insecticide, and marched against a toxic waste incinerator planned for the Latino farming community of Kettleman City.

Gutiérrez's most recent project with MELA has been the Mothers of East Los Angeles Water Conservation Program. This program, launched in 1992, has focused on replacing old water-guzzling toilets and shower heads to conserve water and has also served to invigorate the neighborhood's economy. The primary objective of this program is to get Angelenos (residents of a naturally water-poor city) to trade in their old 7-gallon toilets for new 3.5-gallon toilets provided by the Los Angeles Department of Water and Power (DWP). DWP has calculated that 48 million gallons of water would be conserved daily if all Los Angeles residents were equipped with these Ultra Low Flush Toilets. Residents can obtain these low-flush toilets simply by showing up at MELA's headquarters at the Gutiérrez house with identification and their DWP bill. They are given an Ultra Low Flush Toilet, as well as instructions on how to install it. When they bring back their old toilet to be recycled, they get a low-flow showerhead. This program has led to the installation of 50,000 low-flush toilets since 1992. The water conservation program employs 25 full-time and three part-time staff members. Its profits are channeled into community projects: for instance, paying high school students to go door to door encouraging mothers to have their children fully immunized and tested for lead poisoning and hiring teams of students to go out in the morning before school to sweep streets and paint over graffiti.

Gutiérrez, along with MELA, has become a political force to be reckoned with in East Los Angeles, not to mention in the rest of California. She sees her neighborhood group's emergence as such a force on toxic-waste and other issues as natural. She sees the environment not as something "out there," but rather as the entire physical and social setting where people live and work every day. The poverty and violence in inner city Los Angeles, then, are just as much a part of her environment as the toxic lead levels and air pollution; all problems she faces in attempting to help her neighborhood stay healthy and safe. She is quoted in Steve Lerner's *Eco-pioneers* as saying that her organization is "not economically rich—but culturally wealthy; not politically powerful—but community conscious; not mainstream educated—but armed with knowledge, commitment, and determination that only a mother can possess; The Mothers of East Los Angeles–Santa Isabel is an organization striving to protect the health and safety of East Los Angeles Neighborhoods."

Gutiérrez's work has been recognized through numerous honors and awards. She was named 1988 Woman of the Year by the California State Legislature. She received the

Pope John Paul II Benemereti Award in 1992 and the Mexican Mother of the Year Award in 1993.

BIBLIOGRAPHY
Bullard, Robert, ed., *Unequal Protection: Environmental Justice and Communities of Color*, 1994; Lerner, Steve, *Eco-pioneers: Practical Visionaries Solving Today's Environmental Problems*, 1997; "National Women's History Project," www.nwhp.org/whm/gutierrez_bio.php; Rosenblum, Sarah H and Juana Beatriz Gutierrez, *A Journey to South Mott Street: Where Motherhood, Grassroots Activism and Civil Action Meet*, 2007; Schwab, Jim, *Deeper Shades of Green*, 1994.

American Environmental Leaders

From Colonial Times to the Present

Hair, Jay

(November 30, 1945–November 15, 2002)
President of the National Wildlife Federation

Jay Hair was head of the National Wildlife Federation (NWF), one of the most prominent and important conservation organizations in the United States, for the 15 years from 1981 to 1996. It was largely during Hair's term as president that this organization evolved from its role as an advocacy group for hunters and fishermen to the influential position in the environmental world that it occupies today.

Jay Dee Hair was born on November 30, 1945, in Miami, Florida. When he was three months old his parents divorced, and Hair moved with his mother, Ruth, and his two siblings, to Leota, Indiana, where Ruth's family maintained a farm. Hair lived on the farm for the first 11 years of his life, catching fish in the farm ponds and learning to hunt with the help of his uncles. In 1957, Hair's mother remarried, and the family moved to Landenberg, Pennsylvania. Hair's stepfather, William Johnson, was a DuPont chemical engineer, and he encouraged Hair to excel academically. Hair attended Avon Grove High School in West Grove, Pennsylvania, where he was president of his senior class. After graduating from high school in 1963, Hair entered Clemson University in South Carolina. He earned a B.S. degree in biology four years later, in 1967. He remained at Clemson for two more years to complete an M.S. degree in biology, as well.

Upon receiving his M.S. degree in 1969, Hair moved to Edmonton, Canada, to work as a graduate research fellow in the Department of Zoology at the University of Alberta. He remained in this post for one year. In 1970, he was commissioned as a second lieutenant in the United States Army, and he left the United States for Vietnam, where he served as a public health specialist. After one year of service, Hair returned to the University of Alberta and completed his Ph.D. in zoology in 1975. In the meantime, Hair had accepted a position as assistant professor of wildlife biology in the Department of Entomology, Fisheries and Wildlife at Clemson University in 1973, a position he occupied until 1977. During his time as assistant professor at Clemson, Hair also worked as a research and management consultant to the South Carolina Wildlife and Marine Resources Department from 1976 to 1977. Hair left Clemson in 1977 for North Carolina State University in Raleigh, where he served as administrator of the fisheries and wildlife sciences division, as well as associate professor of zoology and forestry. He worked in Raleigh until 1981, holding a second position as well, this one with the U.S. Department of the Interior as special assistant from 1978 to 1980, in which he helped to develop national fish and wildlife policy.

The National Wildlife Federation is one of the largest, most influential private, nonprofit conservation-education organizations in the United States. Founded in 1936, its mission is "to educate and inspire" individuals to conserve wildlife and other natural resources, in an effort to promote an environmentally sustainable future. Hair had been heavily involved with the NWF after attending his first meeting of the organization in South Carolina in 1974. He became president of the South Carolina Wildlife Federation in 1976, the year in which that group was named the NWF's outstanding affiliate of the year. And, in 1981, after learning that the NWF was conducting a search for a new president to replace Thomas Kimball, who had held the post since 1960, Hair applied for the position. He was elected president of the NWF at the age of 35. Hair served as the NWF president for the next 15 years, moving the organization away from its conservative stance on many environmental issues and into the environmental mainstream. Hair revitalized the sportsman image of NWF, creating a larger, more active, more diverse, and more influential organization. During his tenure, membership grew from 4.2 million in 1981 to nearly 6 million in 1994, and the NWF annual operating budget more than doubled, reaching $90 million in 1990.

As president of NWF, Hair played a significant role in many national environmental issues. In one of his first publicly visible actions as president of the NWF, he criticized the actions of James Watt, President Reagan's secretary of the interior. Watt was a strong supporter of development, and during his time as secretary he caused an uproar in the environmental community by advocating development on public lands and by supporting oil drilling in wildlife preserves. Hair, along with other well-known environmentalists, called for Watts's resignation, an outcry that made front-page news across the Unites States. Hair was also the first head of a major environmental organization to arrive on the scene in Prince William Sound when the *Exxon Valdez* spilled its 11 million gallons of oil in 1989. He used the opportunity to speak with the national press about the dangers of drilling and transporting oil in ecologically sensitive locations. The NWF and the Natural Resources Defense Council successfully sued Exxon, requiring the company to establish a fund for the continuation of cleanup and to provide assistance to those Alaskans who suffered financially from the spill.

Despite his criticism of Exxon, Hair believed that business and industry could play an important role in the environmental movement. He created the Corporate Conservation Council, whose members include such companies as DuPont, Monsanto, ARCO, Ciba Geigy, and others, each of which pays a $10,000 membership fee and is invited to seminars and on special excursions. Many corporate representatives have also been invited to sit on NWF's board of directors. In one well-known case, described in MARK DOWIE's *Losing Ground*, this has been controversial for the organization. The chief executive officer of Waste Management, Inc., known for its violations of toxic release regulations, not only sat on the board but was the recipient of Hair's personal intervention on its behalf. Hair helped Waste Management persuade the Environmental Protection Administration (EPA) director under President Bush, WILLIAM K. REILLY, to override EPA policies and issue permits to two stalled Waste Management projects. Congress investigated, and Hair eventually admitted that his involvement had been a mistake.

Hair left the NWF in 1995. He served for two years, 1994 to 1996, as President of the World Conservation Union (IUCN), a global network of governmental and non-governmental environmental organizations, private companies, and community groups.

Beginning in 1996, Hair worked in a variety of roles for governmental and non-governmental organizations and private companies. That year, he was commissioned by the International Finance Corporation (IFC), the private sector arm of the World Bank, to review the IFC's handling of the environmental and social mitigation aspects of the Pangue hydroelectric project on the Bio Bio River in Chile, which the IFC helped to finance. The "Hair report," as it has come to be known, contains strong criticisms of the practices followed by the IFC in the development of this controversial $367 million hydroelectric dam. In 1998, Hair became executive vice president of business development for a company called GreaterGood.com. This company operates "shopping villages" on the Internet, which link to the home pages of nonprofit groups. The nonprofits use these "villages" to sell merchandise, operating under the assumption that having their merchandise grouped in one location on the Internet will lead to an increase in membership and support for the nonprofit organizations. Hair also served as Secretary General for the International Council on Mining and Metals, dedicated to improving the public image of the mining and metals industry and by increasing its contributions to sustainable development.

Hair received many awards for his environmental efforts, including the Edward J. Cleary

Award from the National Academy of Environmental Engineers in 1989 and the National Park Foundation Theodore and Conrad Wirth Environmental Award in 1990.

Hair battled bone marrow disease for the last five years of his life, and died on November 15, 2002. He is survived by his two children and his wife, Leah.

BIBLIOGRAPHY
Allen, Thomas B., *Guardian of the Wild*, 1987; Dowie, Mark, *Losing Ground*, 1995; "Greater Good," www.greatergood.com; Kinch, John A., *Newsmakers*, 1994; Mosher, Lawrence, "Washington's Green Giants," *The Amicus Journal*, 1989.

Hamilton, Alice
(February 27, 1869–September 22, 1970)
Physician, Social Reformer

In a time when occupational health and safety were hardly considered, Alice Hamilton became an active advocate against the use of industrial toxins and hazardous working conditions. A lifelong proponent of social justice and pacifism, Hamilton is most widely recognized for her endeavors to detect and combat the medical problems caused by industrialization. Through her tireless efforts, toxic substances in the lead, mining, painting, pottery, and rayon industries were exposed, and legislation was passed to protect workers.

The second of the five children of Montgomery Hamilton, a wholesale grocer, and Gertrude Pond, Alice Hamilton was born in New York City on February 27, 1869. She grew up in a secure material and financial environment on her grandmother's estate in Fort Wayne, Indiana, after her father's business failure. Taught only by her parents and tutors, Hamilton received little formal training except in languages until 1886, when she entered Miss Porter's School in Farmington, Connecticut. Hamilton's mother always encouraged her children to follow their minds and inclinations.

Hamilton's decision to pursue a career in medicine was influenced by two main factors: first, it was one of the few professional fields open to women in the latter half of the nineteenth century, and second, as she stated in her autobiography, "as a doctor I could go anywhere I pleased… and be quite sure that I could be of use anywhere." Hamilton started in medicine at the University of Michigan in March 1892, after studying science at the Fort Wayne College of Medicine. She received her M.D. the following year and interned in Minneapolis and Boston. She returned to the University of Michigan in 1895 to work in the bacteriology laboratory of F. G. Novy but left that fall to travel to Germany with her sister Edith, a noted Greek scholar. In Germany, Hamilton studied bacteriology and pathology at the universities of Leipzig and Munich. Returning to the United States, she trained for a year at Johns Hopkins Medical School before taking a job in 1897 as a professor of pathology at the Woman's Medical School at Northwestern University, a position that she held until the Woman's Medical School closed in 1902. Hamilton accepted a position as a bacteriologist at the Memorial Institute for Infectious Diseases, but before starting there, she studied briefly at the Pasteur Institute in Paris.

When Hamilton returned to Chicago in the autumn, she found that the city had been struck by a typhoid epidemic. Hamilton gained acclaim for a paper presented to the

Chicago Medical Society that suggested that flies were the agents in spreading the disease. While her theory proved to be wrong—it was later discovered that the epidemic had stemmed from a break in the local pumping station that had allowed sewage to escape into the water pipes—Hamilton and her work were gaining respect.

Prior to the closing of the Woman's Medical School, Hamilton became a resident at Hull House, a settlement designed by its founder JANE ADDAMS to give care and counsel to Chicago's poor and sick. At Hull House, Hamilton witnessed firsthand the disease, disability, and premature death common to workers in certain industries. Upon reading Sir Thomas Oliver's 1902 book *Dangerous Trades*, Hamilton began her lifelong mission to oppose and treat the excesses of industrialization. She quickly learned that occupational safety laws, workers' compensation laws, and effective factory-inspection systems in the United States lagged far behind those in European countries such as Germany and England and began to use her growing reputation to publicize these problems.

In 1908, Hamilton was named to the Illinois Commission of Occupational Diseases by Gov. Charles S. Deneen. The commission's preliminary investigation revealed the need for a larger study that, in 1910, Hamilton directed. A year later, Hamilton accepted an appointment as special investigator for the U.S. Bureau of Labor. Her work required that she make field investigations of mines, mills, and smelters. Her first statistical study—on lead, the most widely used industrial poison—documented the alarmingly high mortality and morbidity rates of workers exposed to the poison. She later produced similar studies on aniline dyes, picric acid, arsenic, carbon monoxide, and other industrial poisons. During World War I, Hamilton investigated the high explosives industry and revealed that nitrous fumes were the cause of a great number of supposedly natural deaths. In spite of trying not to sensationalize her findings, Hamilton became widely known as a crusader for public health and an advocate of other social causes such as woman suffrage, birth control, a federal child labor law, state health insurance, and workers' compensation.

Hamilton was also a pacifist and accompanied Jane Addams to the International Congress of Women at The Hague as well as on a mission to the war capitals to present the women's peace proposals. In 1919, she investigated the famine in Germany and became involved in the Quaker famine relief effort. That same year she was named the first female faculty member of Harvard University as an assistant professor of industrial medicine. Hamilton suffered much discrimination as the university's first female professor. She was denied access to the Harvard Club and to participation in graduation ceremonies. Nevertheless her classic textbook, *Industrial Poisons in the United States* (1925), established her as one of the world's leading authorities on the subject. During this time she was also successful in persuading the surgeon general to investigate the dangerous effects of tetraethyl lead and radium.

While at Harvard, Hamilton maintained her international contacts. She served two terms on the Health Committee of the League of Nations (1924–1930) and became an ardent proponent of the league. In 1924, she was the only woman delegate on the League of Nations Health Commission to the USSR. Concluding that "there was more industrial hygiene in Russia than industry," Hamilton admired certain aspects of the Bolshevik system but deplored its suppression of free speech. Of Nazi Germany, which she visited in 1933, Hamilton was far more critical; from a very early stage, she felt that the United States should oppose Hitler.

Hamilton retired from Harvard in 1935 and moved to Hadlyme, Connecticut. She remained publicly active, however, and in 1935 accepted a position as consultant to the Division of Labor Standards in the U.S. Department of Labor. In 1937 and 1938, Hamilton conducted her last field investigation, a survey of the viscose rayon industry. She successfully demonstrated that rayon processes involved a high level of toxicity, a finding that resulted in Pennsylvania's first compensation law for occupational diseases.

Hamilton, who never married, published her autobiography in 1943. Between 1944 and 1949, she served as president of the National Consumers' League. In her later years, Hamilton continued to be politically active and vocal, advancing causes of social justice and pacifism; she withdrew her opposition to the equal rights amendment in 1952 and in 1963 called for an end to U.S. military involvement in Vietnam. Hamilton died of a stroke in her home in Hadlyme, Connecticut, on September 22, 1970; she was 101.

BIBLIOGRAPHY

Fee, Elizabeth and Theodore M. Brown, "Alice Hamilton: Settlement Physician, Occupational Health Pioneer," *American Journal of Public Health*, 2001; Grant, Madeline P., *Alice Hamilton: Pioneer Doctor in Industrial Medicine*, 1967; Hamilton, Alice, *Exploring the Dangerous Trades: The Autobiography of Alice Hamilton, M.D.*, 1943; Sicherman, Barbara, *Alice Hamilton: A Life in Letters*, 1984; Slaight, Wilma Ruth, "Alice Hamilton: First Lady of Industrial Medicine," Ph.D. dissertation, Case Western Reserve University, 1974; Young, Angela Nugent, "Interpreting the Dangerous Trades: Workers' Health in America and the Career of Alice Hamilton, 1910–1935," Ph.D. dissertation, Brown University, 1982.

Hansen, James E.
(March 29, 1941–)
Professor, Climatologist, Writer, Director of the National Aeronautics and Space Administration's Goddard Institute for Space Studies

The director of the National Aeronautics and Space Administration's Goddard Institute for Space Studies in New York since 1981, and an adjunct professor at Columbia University's Earth Institute since 1985, James Hansen is a climatologist known as the Paul Revere of global warming. He has studied the earth's atmosphere and global surface temperatures since the mid-1970s, and has published and lectured widely in scientific and public policy arenas, calling attention to the dangers posed by the rate and amount of human-generated greenhouse gas emissions, as well as to the potential for renewal posed by this crisis. He also communicates directly with the general public through appearances on television programs such as *60 Minutes*, and by written commentaries in publications such as *The London Times*, *The Nation*, and his own website.

James Edward Hansen was born on March 29, 1941, on a farm in Charter Oak Township, Iowa, and grew up in Denison, Iowa, the fifth of seven children. He attended the University of Iowa, receiving his B.A. in Physics and Mathematics in 1963. From 1963 to 1966 he went through a NASA Graduate Traineeship, earning an M.A. in Astronomy from the University of Iowa in 1965, and studying astrophysics at the universities of Kyoto and Tokyo between 1965 and 1966. In 1967 he received a Ph.D. in Physics from the University of Iowa. His dissertation was about the atmosphere of the planet Venus. While at the University of Iowa, he met his lifelong mentor James Van Allen, who discovered the radiation belts encircling Earth. Hansen married Anniek Dekkers Hansen of the Netherlands in 1971, and has two children, Erik and Christine. He resides in Kintnersville, Pennsylvania.

James E. Hansen (Photograph courtesy of James E. Hansen; Source: NASA-GISS)

Hansen first used the term "global warming" in 1981 to describe the effect of the energy imbalance to Earth's atmosphere caused by human emissions of gases such as carbon dioxide, methane, nitrous oxide, and halocarbons. During the 1980s he testified before the U.S. Congress on multiple occasions, but it was after his 1988 testimony to committees in the U.S. Senate and House of Representatives that his term "global warming" gained wide currency. He demonstrated that CO_2 emissions were the preeminent cause of global warming due to their long atmospheric lifetime. One-third of CO_2 emissions remain in the atmosphere for 100 years, and about one-fifth lasts over 1,000 years.

Hansen has made several recommendations on behalf of every person, species, and indeed all matter on the home planet Earth. These include a complete moratorium on building new coal-fired plants that do not capture and sequester CO_2 and imposing a price on carbon emissions, which could take the form of fuel taxes, industry cap-and-trade schemes, and individual allowances. He also has called for substantial incentives for energy efficiency and conservation, an improvement in national building and vehicle efficiency standards, and a halt to deforestation.

Despite his mild manners, Hansen has been a figure of some notoriety since 1989 when the executive branch's Office of Management and Budget altered the text of his testimony before Congress to minimize the implications of his scientific research into global warming. In December of 2005 the public affairs office of NASA, his own agency, sought to control his contacts with the press and the nature of the information he could disseminate. However, Hansen continued to speak freely and in March 2006 NASA backed him and others by establishing new rules to allow open communication between NASA scientists and the press. He continues to call for eliminating White House approval and editing of peer-reviewed scientific work presented to Congress by technical civil servants, which he has said is just as bad during Democratic or Republican administrations. Hansen has also called for political campaign finance reform so that fossil-fuel interests aren't able to exert undue influence over the representatives charged with conducting the public's business, and for a global grassroots movement to engender significant changes in climate policies. Yet Hansen is not happiest when whistle-blowing, but when scientifically quantifying global warming and options for dealing with it.

Hansen's lab uses 10,000 temperature gauges around the planet to monitor Earth's temperature on a monthly basis. They use satellite data and climate modeling to show what is happening now, and what is projected to happen to Earth's climate in the next decades and centuries; the accelerated melting of the Greenland ice sheet and of Arctic Ocean ice, which could be ice-free by 2012. Hansen argues that ice sheet disintegration could soon reach a tipping point after which humans won't be able to control the consequences of the planet's accelerated warming. The sea level rise and the warming of the oceans (and the consequent warming of the atmosphere because while ice reflects heat away from Earth, water absorbs it) will cause severe inundation and storms in the world's coastal areas.

In a 2008 interview on the nationally syndicated radio program *Democracy Now!* Hansen explained, "The main problem is fossil fuel use. We cannot put all of the fossil fuel—the carbon dioxide from all the fossil fuels back into the atmosphere without creating a completely different planet. The last time that carbon dioxide was in the atmosphere, there was no ice on the planet. It was a completely different planet. And we have to realize we are either going to have to leave a lot of the fossil fuels in the ground, or else we're going to have to capture the carbon dioxide when the fossil fuels are burned. And that just is not well understood, and the fossil fuel companies would rather that you didn't understand that."

An urgency to the work of Hansen and other scientists is fueled by the findings. His early warnings about global warming have been validated repeatedly in many reports, the most widely disseminated of which was the United Nation's Intergovernmental Panel on Climate Change, which shared the Nobel Peace Prize that year with former Vice President AL GORE.

Hansen also has received numerous honors and awards. In 1996 he was elected a member of the National Academy of Sciences. Since 2000 he has been the recipient of three GISS Best Scientific Publication awards through a peer vote process. In 2001 he was honored with the John Heinz Environmental Award, and in 2002 he received the American Geophysical Union's Roger Revelle Medal. In 2006 he was named to the Time 100, *Time* magazine's list of the world's 100 most influential people, and he was given the World Wildlife Fund Duke of Edinburgh Award from Prince Philip. In 2007 the American Physical Society awarded him the Leo Szilard Lectureship Award.

Hansen's concern for science education in the U.S. led him in 1994 to found the Institute on Climate and Planets with Carolyn Harris. It is a government, university, and business collaboration developed at NASA's Goddard Institute and involves New York City high school and college science teachers and students in cutting-edge climate research during summer vacations.

BIBLIOGRAPHY

Democracy Now! Interview, March 21, 2008, www.democracynow.org/2008/3/21/censoring_science_inside_the_political_attack; Bowen, Mark, *Censoring Science*, 2007; Johansen, Bruce E., "The Paul Revere of Global Warming (James E. Hansen of NASA) (Biography)," *The Progressive*, 2006; Hansen, James E. "Climate Change: On the Edge," *The Independent, UK*, 2007; Hansen, James E., "Why We Can't Wait," *The Nation*, 2007; "Dr. James E. Hansen," www.columbia.edu/~jeh1/.

Hardin, Garrett

(April 21, 1915–September 14, 2003)
Biologist, Human Ecologist

Biologist and human ecologist Garrett Hardin was known for his bold assertions about difficult issues facing humanity. His famous 1968 essay, "The Tragedy of the Commons," warns that unless there are strict regulations in place, people will destroy the land, water, and air that they share. His 1974 article for *BioScience*, "Living on a Lifeboat," proclaimed that it was irresponsible for wealthy nations to share resources with poor countries unless the poor countries had population control policies in place and the wealthy countries donated expertise and technology for improvement along with the material aid. Controversial as they may be, Hardin's opinions inspired new fields of studies and fruitful debates among scholars.

Garrett Hardin was born on April 21, 1915, in Dallas, Texas. His father worked in the offices of the Illinois Central Railroad and was transferred every few years. Hardin grew up in five different midwestern cities but spent every summer on his grandfather's Missouri farm. He contracted polio at the age of four, which weakened and shortened his right leg. In his Chicago high school he excelled in both writing and drama and was awarded scholarships to a drama school as well as to the University of Chicago. Realizing that his handicap would relegate him to a limited number of roles, Hardin opted for the University of Chicago, where he studied under ecologist W. A. Allee, one of the only scholars at the time who taught that unimpeded population growth would be a major challenge to life on earth. Hardin majored in zoology and graduated in 1936. He continued studying at Stanford University, earning a Ph.D. in 1941 in biology. He stayed at Stanford on a fellowship from the Carnegie Institute in Washington to study algae and its potential as a food source, but in 1946 he stepped down, because he had come to believe that increasing the production of food would only aggravate population problems. He was hired at the University of California–Santa Barbara as assistant professor of bacteriology in 1946 and stayed there his entire career. He was named full professor of biology in 1957 and in 1960 began teaching human ecology.

Hardin began to diversify in 1949 with his popular textbook *Biology: Its Human Implication*. He wrote the scripts for and starred in teaching films and during the 1950s became interested in genetics and evolution. He wrote *Nature and Man's Fate* in 1959, which continues to be a useful introduction to evolution, the history of evolutionary theory, and its moral and social implications. In 1960, Hardin designed a course in human ecology. It dealt with controversial issues such as evolution and population growth. At that time abortion was illegal and socially taboo, but Hardin included it in his course. He became an advocate of freeing women from what he termed "compulsory pregnancy" and lectured throughout the United States on the need to legalize abortion. Abortion did not become legal until the *Roe* vs. *Wade* ruling in 1973, but in 1963 Pres. Lyndon B. Johnson signed the nation's first birth control bill, and in 1964 the first federally funded family planning program was established in Corpus Christi, Texas.

Hardin's "The Tragedy of the Commons" was published in *Science* in December 1968 and provided a philosophical and historical context for the population concerns that were popularized by PAUL EHRLICH's *The Population Bomb*, also published in 1968. "The Tragedy of the Commons" challenges the thesis of economist Adam Smith, who believed that decisions about individual behavior made by rational human beings would always lead, in the long run, to the greater good for all. Instead, Hardin expanded upon the argument of William Forster Lloyd, a nineteenth-century Oxford philosopher who described what happened when pastures held in common (or "commons") were open to all herdsmen. Each would try to gain the greatest individual benefit, running as many animals as possible. But eventually the pasture would be depleted, and no one would be able to use it. Hardin's conclusion was that "freedom in a commons brings ruin to all" and that the only way to avoid disaster was to establish a policy of "mutual coercion, mutually agreed upon," which would regulate behavior. "The Tragedy of the Commons" was reprinted in dozens of anthologies and was made part of the curriculum for courses in biological and social sciences.

For Hardin, limiting population growth was basic to avoiding degradation of the commons. More people leads to more resource use, which leads to the speedy depletion of those resources. He advocated worldwide population growth policies, with limits to the number of children one could have. Bearing as many children as they wish brings satisfaction to parents, but the presence of too many children leads a society to economic and environmental disaster. "Freedom to breed will bring ruin to all," he told a biographer for the 1974 edition of *Contemporary Biography*. During the 1970s Hardin wrote about pollution disposal as an additional problem of the commons. With increases in population and its ensuing production, more and more waste is generated, yet there is no growth in areas that can be used for waste disposal.

Hardin wrote another seminal piece for *BioScience* in 1974, "Living on a Lifeboat." Here he wrote that countries were like lifeboats, each having only a limited supply of the essentials for survival. Poor countries' lifeboats were much more crowded and supplies were shorter. Wealthier nations had more food and water and fewer citizens but should refrain from sharing with the poor unless the poor nation had a strict population control policy in place. Wealthy donors, in his opinion, should also share technology and expertise to help the poorer countries become self-sufficient. Hardin favors restrictions on immigration into the United States for similar reasons: emigration serves as a pressure valve for poor nations, and this release of pressure only delays the poor countries' solutions to their problems.

Hardin's analyses have been controversial, earning him stars in some camps and attacks in others. Respondents to the lifeboat article point out that the world did not start out with wealthy and poor nations; rather, many wealthy nations gained their wealth by pilfering resources from poor nations; also, they say, cooperation among nations is potentially necessary for the survival of all nations. The authors of *Environment*'s 30th anniversary revisitation of "The Tragedy of the Commons" cite many examples in which communities have been able to regulate their own use of natural resources more successfully than when an outside regulator such as the government intervenes. Yet despite critiques of the essay, Hardin's point that commons are delicate and must be protected from overuse was seminal for much recent work on issues of population control, conservation of resources, and sustainable development.

During the 1990s, Hardin actively supported the theory that intelligence was race-based, and wrote in his 1999 book *The Ostrich Factor: Our Population Myopia* that affirmative action was a form of racism. In this book he also proposed an official limitation of reproductive rights as a way to reduce population growth.

Hardin and his wife, Jane Coe Swanson, whom he married in 1941, had four children. Garrett and Jane were members of the Hemlock Society (now called Compassion & Choices) which supports members in their choice of when to die. They committed suicide together at home in Santa Barbara, on September 14, 2003.

BIBLIOGRAPHY

Burger, Joanna, and Michael Gochfeld, "The Tragedy of the Commons 30 Years Later,"

Environment, 1998; "The Garrett Hardin Society," www.garretthardinsciety.org; Hardin, Garrett, "Extensions of 'The Tragedy of the Commons,'" *Science*, 1998; Hardin, Garrett, *Living within Limits: Ecology, Economics, and Population Taboos*, 1993; Hardin, Garrett, *The Ostrich Factor: Our Population Myopia*, 1999; Ostrom, Elinor, Joanna Burger, Christopher B. Field, Richard B. Norgaard, and David Policansky, "Revisiting the Commons: Local Lessons, Global Challenges," *Science*, 1999; Spencer, Cathy, "Garrett Hardin Interview," *Omni*, 1992.

Harrelson, Woody

(July 23, 1961–)
Actor, Cofounder of Oasis Preserve International

Woody Harrelson was first known to millions of American television viewers as Woody Boyd, an endearing, dimwitted bartender on the very popular situation comedy series of the 1980s and 1990s, *Cheers*. Nominated five times for an Emmy for this role, Harrelson won the award in 1989. Harrelson has since appeared and starred in many major Hollywood films, including *The People vs. Larry Flint*, *Indecent Proposal*, and *Natural Born Killers*. Harrelson is also a well-known celebrity activist who has participated in many public acts of civil disobedience to protect the environment. His activism has included protesting the logging of ancient redwood forests, advocating for the legalization of hemp, and withholding federal income taxes. He is also the cofounder of Oasis Preserve International, an international nonprofit organization to protect sensitive rain forests in Latin America.

Woodrow Tracy Harrelson, the second of three boys, was born in Midland, Texas, on July 23, 1961. His father, Charles Harrelson, abandoned his family when Harrelson was seven years old. He was a gambler who was soon convicted of murder and sent to prison. Harrelson's mother, Diane, a legal secretary, divorced Harrelson's father and raised her three sons on her own with great financial difficulty. As a young child, Harrelson was prescribed the drug Ritalin for hyperactivity and violence. When his difficulties continued, Harrelson was given a scholarship to Briarwood, a private school in Houston for children with learning disabilities. When Harrelson was 12, his family moved to Lebanon, Ohio, where he performed in his first theatrical production. Harrelson's father was released from prison in 1978 during Harrelson's senior year at Lebanon High School but was arrested a year later, charged once again with murder, and sentenced to two life terms. He died in a high-security federal prison in Florence, Colorado, in 2007.

Despite his difficulties, Harrelson was an intelligent student and maintained good grades in school. In 1979, Harrelson won a scholarship to Hanover College in Indiana. A theology major, Harrelson began college with very conservative religious and political views and voted for Ronald Reagan in 1980. During his junior year of college, however, Harrelson began to pursue his interest in the theater as well as to experiment with drugs and alcohol. He appeared in several college theatrical performances before graduating with a B.A. in theater arts in 1983. Harrelson moved to New York City after graduating from Hanover, and his first break came in 1984 when he was hired as an understudy in the Broadway play *Biloxi Blues* by Neil Simon. Shortly thereafter he was cast with a small part in the Hollywood film, *Wildcats*. While filming in Hollywood, Harrelson decided to audition for a role on a popular television series, even though he felt television was a step down from the theater. Offered the part and given 24 hours to decide, Harrelson said yes and became Woody Boyd on *Cheers*.

Harrelson's success gave him the opportunity to play many small parts in feature films, such as *Casualties of War*, *Cool Blue*, *L.A. Story*, and *Ted and Venus*. His first major movie role was in *Doc Hollywood* in 1991, with Michael J. Fox. Harrelson continued to perform in theatrical productions, as well, including *The Boys Next Door*, *The Zoo Story*, and *Brooklyn Laundry*. Harrelson's first starring role in a Hollywood movie was in 1992 with *White Men Can't Jump*. Shortly thereafter he was cast in a leading role in the movie *Indecent Exposure*.

After *Cheers* went off the air, Harrelson began to focus on his film career. His most controversial film to date was Oliver Stone's *Natural Born Killers* in 1994. Due to its theme of violence, the film received a great deal of media attention. Harrelson went on to star in another controversial film, *The People vs. Larry Flint*, a biographical drama about the publisher of the pornography magazine *Hustler*, for which Harrelson received an Oscar nomination, but which was criticized by feminist organizations in the U.S. Harrelson continued on to leading roles in *Welcome to Sarajevo*, *The Thin Red Line*, and *The Walker*, and a minor role in the Academy Award-winning *No Country for Old Men*.

In his personal life, Harrelson has struggled with a self-admitted addiction to fame, power, violence, and sex. In 1990, he came to the realization that he was unhappy and decided to embark on a spiritual search. Traveling to Peru, India, and Africa, Harrelson became a strict vegetarian and began practicing holistic healing and yoga. In the early 1990s, Harrelson began to speak out publicly on issues of environmental preservation, hemp legalization, racism, and sexism, and he voiced his opposition to the Persian Gulf War. His first well-known act of civil disobedience was in 1995 when Harrelson withheld money from the Internal Revenue Service and wrote them a letter explaining that he could not support the government's disregard for the environment. A very outspoken hemp advocate, Harrelson was arrested in Kentucky in August 1996 for planting four seeds of industrial hemp. Harrelson says that industrial hemp is a very important source of ecologically friendly fiber and that the distinction must be made between industrial hemp and marijuana. A couple of months later, in November 1996, Harrelson was arrested on the Golden Gate Bridge in San Francisco along with eight others protesting the logging of ancient redwoods in northern California; he was fined and sentenced to community service. In August 1997 Harrelson posted bail for a young man who was arrested for growing marijuana; he was a medical marijuana proponent and amateur scientist experimenting with different plants for the treatment of cancer. Harrelson now feels that many people did not understand these actions—though they did attract media attention to the issue.

Woody Harrelson married his long-time partner and second wife, Laura Louie, in 1998. In 2001, he and a group of friends and family partly biked and partly drove a biodiesel-powered bus 1500 miles along the West Coast to promote sustainability. A documentary film *Go Further* as well as a handbook *How to Go Further* (2003) resulted from that trip, and Harrelson and his wife launched their environmentally-oriented website Voiceyourself.com at that time.

In recent years, Harrelson moved to a sustainable, solar community on the island of Maui, Hawai'i, where about 90 percent of what his family eats is grown locally. He acknowledges that air travel is his "worst transgression."

Harrelson has donated his time and energy to many environmental organizations, including American Oceans Campaign, Rainforest Action Network, and Surfrider Foundation.

Both Harrelson and his wife are yoga instructors, and Laura is cofounder of Yoganics food products.

BIBLIOGRAPHY

Carr, David, "Loves the Beach, the Planet and Movies," *New York Times*, 2007; "Crusader Woody Supports the Legalization of Hemp," *People Weekly*, 1996; Dicum, Gregory, "Walking the Talk: Woody Harrelson's Sustainable Life," *SFGate*, 2003, www.sfgate.com; Schick, Elizabeth, ed., "Woody Harrelson," *Current Biography Yearbook*, 1997; Wood, Campbell, "Woody Harrelson: Acting on His Convictions," *E*, 1997; Woody Harrelson and Laura Louie's Voice Yourself, www.voiceyourself.com.

Harry, Debra

(July 9, 1957–)
Executive Director of the Indigenous Peoples Council on Biocolonialism

Debra Harry's career has focused on rebuilding indigenous communities after the destructive impacts of colonization and protecting the human and collective rights of indigenous peoples. Most recently, her work has centered on protecting the genetic resources of indigenous peoples from exploitation by corporate, scientific, and government interests. She is an expert in nonprofit management and encourages communities to initiate their own programs and generate culturally appropriate solutions from within. As a recipient of a three-year Kellogg Foundation leadership fellowship in 1994, she studied the field of human genetic research and its implications for indigenous peoples. Currently she is the executive director of the Indigenous Peoples Council on Biocolonialism (IPCB), which she founded in 1998.

Debra Harry was born in Reno, Nevada, on July 9, 1957, to Floyd Harry and Charlotte Davis. A Northern Paiute, she grew up on the Pyramid Lake Reservation and graduated from Fernley High School. At age 21 she became an activist and community organizer against the MX land-based missile system that was proposed for Nevada and Utah and also opposed plans for uranium mining in Nevada.

Throughout her twenties Harry continued to work with Native American rights and community development efforts, specializing in nonprofit management. In 1981, Harry become a board member of the Tribal Sovereignty Program, which later became the Seventh Generation Fund, a national foundation established to provide philanthropic support to Native American communities. In 1985, she served as program officer at the Seventh Generation Fund. She is a faculty member of the Fund Raising School at Indiana University, in Indianapolis. In the early 1990s she served as the capital campaign manager for the Institute of American Indian Arts (IAIA) in Santa Fe, New Mexico. She was responsible for major gift development, volunteer management, and campaign management. The campaign raised $4.9 million, providing the necessary funds to support the IAIA's museum for student and alumni work. The museum, housed in a renovated historic building, is located in downtown Santa Fe.

Harry received her M.S. degree in community economic development from New Hampshire College in 1994. That same year she also received a Kellogg Foundation Leadership Fellowship and studied the implications of human genetic research for indigenous peoples. In 1998, she founded the IPCB to assist indigenous peoples in the protection of their genetic resources, indigenous knowledge, and cultural and human rights from the negative effects of biotechnology. For the past ten years she has been an activist, researcher, and frequent speaker on the topics of human rights, genetic research, race relations, and community development.

Harry considers herself to be a continuing link in a struggle for indigenous peoples' survival that began centuries ago. In an interview, Harry said, "Since the first contact with western civilization, all of our attention and energies have been devoted to responding to external assaults on our sovereignty and human rights. Native people have never been passive—we can't afford to be because we have responsibilities to insure the wellbeing of our future generations. They have a right to live free from oppression and external control." The problems facing indigenous people today include forced economic dependency, erosion of sovereignty, appropriation of natural resources, diminished territories, racism, and now, biopiracy, or unethical appropriation of their genetic resources. Harry's interest in biodiversity runs parallel to her work on human rights. They are both ethical issues in which the dominant society repeatedly refuses to recognize the indigenous peoples' right to self determination.

Much of the earth's genetic and cultural diversity is found within indigenous territories. Unfortunately, this diversity is viewed as a commodity by many governments and corporations. The immense resources of technology-rich countries are being pooled in worldwide public and private collaborations in order to carry out genetic research. These efforts, combined with increased technological capabilities for genetic sequencing, are fueling a worldwide effort to collect genetic samples from plants that produce foods or medicines, from animals, and from diverse human populations. The genetic resources that indigenous societies have nurtured, and that in turn have nurtured their lives for centuries, are at risk of genetic theft. The patents and profits from products that come from appropriated indigenous biological resources and knowledge do not benefit the tribes, but rather go to shareholders and those who can afford to buy the products. Greed, racism, and oppression are at the heart of the matter because the human and collective rights of indigenous people are often violated in the quest to own and control the world's genetic resources. The biodiversity that exists on indigenous land is not there by chance. A thorough knowledge of the land, species, and natural cycles creates a respect for the ecosystem that allows indigenous people to live on their land without exploiting it for profit. Yet, the rights of indigenous people to use, control, and protect the resources within their territories are under constant pressure from a dominant society built upon extraction and commodification of natural resources.

The field of human genetic engineering has potential to further exploit indigenous people as genetic material is collected, studied, and commercialized by scientific, corporate, and government interests. Unique genetic patterns can be patented under U.S. patent law, turning life and human traits into property. Harry finds this to be unethical for a variety of reasons, the most basic being the idea that the human genetic code can be privatized for profit. Other disturbing aspects are that blood samples have been taken from indigenous people without fully informed consent and that the genetic material is then made available to other researchers for secondary uses unknown to the original donors. Indigenous people cannot control who has access to the samples or how those samples are manipulated or commercialized. "We must set limits on what is acceptable." Harry says. "Patenting life is not acceptable, and many people would fundamentally agree with that. Human genetic materials are passed down from our ancestors, and belong to our future generations. It is not a commodity to bought, sold, owned, or manipulated."

Harry founded the IPCB in order to "assist indigenous peoples in the protection of their genetic resources, indigenous knowledge, and cultural and human rights from the negative effects of biotechnology... [and provide] educational and technical support to indigenous peoples in the protection of their biological resources, cultural integrity, knowledge, and collective rights." IPCB projects include a genetic research database that tracks genetic research affecting indigenous peoples as well as community education, technical assistance, and intervention programs. To prevent exploitation of indigenous peoples, the IPCB provides technical expertise to tribes that are affected by genetic research.

Harry has authored numerous briefing papers and articles on the topic of genetic research and its impact on native peoples. In 2003 she produced a documentary film, *The Leech and the Earthworm*, to inform and illustrate through interviews, historical footage, and creative use of images, how biopiracy is a contemporary form of colonialism and exploitation.

Although Harry's work takes her on frequent travel around the United States and internationally, she maintains her residence in Nixon, Nevada.

BIBLIOGRAPHY

Harry, Debra, "Acts of Self-Determination and Self-Defense: Indigenous Peoples' Response to Bio-Colonialism," in *Rights and Liberties in the Biotech Age: Why We Need a Genetic Bill of Rights*, edited by Krimsky, Sheldon and Peter Shorett, 2005; Harry, Debra, "Globalization and Indigenous Peoples," *National Network of Grantmakers Newsletter*, 2000; Harry, Debra, and Frank Dukepoo, *Indians, Genes and Genetics: What Indians Should Know about the New Biotechnology*, 1998; "Indigenous Peoples Council on Biocolonialism," www.ipcb.org/; "Race to Crack the Code, an Interview with Debra Harry," *Midwest Soarring Wings*, 1999.

Harvey, Dorothy Webster
(October 25, 1915–)
Environmental Activist, Writer

Writer, activist, and environmental researcher Dorothy Harvey spent twelve years working against environmental exploitation in Utah. She was primarily concerned with the development of water resources in that arid state, especially the massive Central Utah Project (CUP), which was designed to take water from high in the Uinta Mountain range southward into the Uinta Basin. By diverting water from the streams to the west along a 100-mile aqueduct, the project would have left the streams parched and the range without an adequate water supply. Through fund-raising efforts she mounted a major public education campaign in Utah about the growing concerns of biologists and recreation users regarding the CUP and its potentially negative impact upon Utah's wilderness areas.

Dorothy Davis Alexandria Webster was born on October 25, 1915, in Galt, Ontario, Canada. She was one of two children born to Charles Webster, an engineer, and Maude Davis, a schoolteacher. She survived the depression and worked at various jobs for a few years after graduating from high school. In 1937, thanks to family members who supported her quest for education, she was accepted at the University of Michigan and focused on American Studies, but she never finished her degree. It was there that she met and eventually married William R. Harvey, an engineering student.

Dorothy Harvey (Photograph by Mark Harvey)

During and after World War II, she followed her husband to jobs in Maryland and Maine until the couple settled in Madison, Wisconsin, in 1949. Later ordained an Episcopal priest, her husband was assigned to St. James Church in Manitowoc, Wisconsin, and kept that position for the next 28 years. In the meantime, Dorothy Harvey bore four children, Kathleen, Patricia, Pamela, and Mark; took a position as a school secretary; and wrote an advertising column for the *Manitowoc Herald Times* under the pseudonym "Sadie Snooper."

During the 1960s, during annual treks to the Rocky Mountain states, visiting various national parks, Harvey and her family became enthralled by the scenery, wildlife, and backcountry wilderness. These experiences later inspired Harvey's activism in wilderness designation efforts by the Sierra Club, the Wilderness Society, and other groups. Throughout, she saw herself as a devout Christian endeavoring to protect God's creation.

Harvey's early environmental activism was centered on wilderness designation in Wisconsin. She volunteered for the Sierra Club to lead a series of studies of the surrounding national forest and roadless areas. But seeing the wilderness in the state of Wisconsin as relatively limited and knowing that there was much more wilderness in the West, very vulnerable to development, Harvey felt "called" to pursue environmental work in the western region of the country.

In 1971, working under Prof. Ross Smith of the University of Nevada, Harvey participated in wilderness studies of the Ruby Mountains within the Humboldt National Forest in Nevada. During the following year, 1972, she led a group of volunteers studying areas in the Payette National Forest of Idaho that had been subjected to excessive logging. Here she was exposed to the politics of resource management within the national forest. Her group became disillusioned as it faced the corporate power of the Boise Cascade Company and a Forest Service administration unwilling to ensure environmental compliance; eventually it disbanded, and she returned to Wisconsin.

During 1973 and 1974, she participated in Sierra Club–sponsored studies of the Uinta Range of northeast Utah. Often working alone, she hiked extensively, encountering a variety of wildlife species and landscapes. While on the north slope of the Wasatch Forest she became acquainted with Jim Kimbal, a wildlife biologist for the U.S. Forest Service, who told her about a project to design logging proposals that would create meadows for elk habitat. Her interest in the project led her to solicit funding for it. Working closely with Kimbal and other biologists, Harvey developed a close relationship with biologists from the Forest Service and from Utah State University. The knowledge she gained from observing their elk habitat research facilitated her efforts to preserve wilderness in the high Uintas.

In 1975 Kimbal suggested she investigate the impact of phosphate mining in the Caribou National Forest in Idaho. She discovered that a third of the forest had been completely denuded of vegetation as a result of the digging of 150-foot canyons to extract the ore, which was not sold but was stored by the company in hopes that it could earn higher profits in the future. She wrote an extensive report on the impact of this activity on the habitat of local wildlife, including the migratory patterns of elk. Unfortunately the Forest Service's hands were tied because of provisions in the 1872 Hard Rock Mining Law, which permitted mining on the public lands without environmental regulations or standards. Despite a state government that sought to exploit rather than to protect the environment, her publications of these abuses increased public awareness and led to curtailment of further developments.

Harvey accepted an investigative assignment from *High Country News* in 1976 and 1977 and began to write about oil shale development within the Uinta Basin of Utah. Fearing the loss of a potential wilderness area, Harvey teamed up with Peter Hovingh, a biochemist from the University of Utah, and led canoe trips on the White River where a dam for the water supply was being proposed. These trips increased awareness of the fragility of the ecosystem and the potentially disastrous impact of a dam upon local flora and fauna. No dam would be built, and eventually oil shale extraction from the basin was determined to be economically unfeasible.

In 1977, a government biologist introduced Harvey to the CUP on a tour of dams currently under construction. The CUP was under development by the U.S. Bureau of Reclamation and the Central Utah Water Conservancy District (CUWCD) in the central and east-central part of Utah. The project provided Utah with the opportunity to use a sizable portion of its allotted share of Colorado River water. This water would be provided to meet the municipal and industrial requirements of the most highly developed part of the state along the Wasatch Front, where population growth and industrial development were continuing at a rapid rate.

Keenly aware of the value of outdoor recreation within the Uinta range and on its southward flowing rivers, Harvey began to organize opposition to the CUP. She felt the Bureau of Reclamation and the state were failing to meet the mandates of the National Environmental Policy Act (NEPA), were basically ignoring the values of outdoor recreation and wilderness, and were willing to sacrifice the rivers for economic benefit. In 1977, she helped to form an anti-CUP grassroots organization, Citizens for a Responsible CUP, whose name changed the following year to Utah Water Resources Council and then again to Intermountain Water Alliance in 1979. The group proved instrumental in informing the public about the state and federal government's plans for water development in Utah and their potential impact upon the environment. It sought to educate the public on the natural value of stream flows and on the fish and wildlife threatened by the CUP. Unfortunately, Harvey and her allies faced a public that maintained a "use it or lose it" mentality and held the conviction that the CUP would "make the desert bloom." She left the state of Utah in 1986 and returned to Wisconsin to be with her husband.

Harvey's efforts laid the groundwork for greater public scrutiny of water development in Utah and fostered a growing awareness of the value of free-flowing rivers. Other groups that spawned in the 1990s, such as the Utah River Council, would continue the efforts she began and ultimately prove successful in saving portions of the Uinta and Bear Rivers from features of the CUP.

Harvey currently resides in Fargo, North Dakota. She continues to support the concept of sustainable water management so that the integrity of the natural systems is maintained and intact ecosystems are preserved. In 2006, she donated 120 boxes of her archived materials on the CUP and National Forest Wilderness to the Special Collections Department at the University of Utah.

BIBLIOGRAPHY

"Central Utah Water Conservancy District," www.cuwcd.com; Harvey, Mark T., *A Symbol of Wilderness: Echo Park and the American Conservation Movement*, 1994; Reisner, Marc P., *Cadillac Desert: The American West and Its Disappearing Water*, 1987; "Utah Rivers Council," www.utahrivers.org.

Hawken, Paul
(February 8, 1946–)
Entrepreneur, Writer

Paul Hawken is an entrepreneur who writes and works in the fields of industrial ecology and sustainability, where he seeks to marry environmentalism with economic and industrial development.

Paul Gerard Hawken was born on February 8, 1946, in San Mateo, California. Involved in the civil rights movement as a young man, he served as press coordinator for the 1965 march on Montgomery, Alabama. He worked in Selma, Alabama, with Martin Luther King's staff, registering the press, giving interviews on national radio, and acting as a marshal for the final march. Later that same year he worked as a staff photographer for the Congress on Racial Equality in New Orleans, where he was kidnapped by the Ku Klux Klan but escaped thanks to intervention by the Federal Bureau of Investigation. The photographs he took during this time were published around the world.

In 1966, he moved to Boston and created the Erewhon Trading Company, the first company in the United States to focus on selling organically produced food. Erewhon introduced many of the health food items that have since become staples: locally produced organic fruits and vegetables, soy sauce, and

Paul Hawken (Photograph courtesy of Paul Hawken)

local spring water, for example. Erewhon was also the first company to produce organically grown rice in the United States. By 1973, Erewhon revenues had risen to $50,000 a day. Erewhon had its own manufacturing facilities and contracted with farmers in 37 states on 56,000 acres of farmland. Erewhon owned two stone mills and two rail cars and leased three warehouses. In 1974, Hawken sold Erewhon, beginning his pattern of founding, successfully leading, and then walking away from businesses.

In 1979, he cofounded the Smith and Hawken mail order gardening supply company with a partner, David Smith. Smith and Hawken originally began as a nonprofit offshoot of Ecology Action, specializing in hand tools used in a type of gardening known as French-intensive/biodynamic gardening. Eventually, the company branched off into other horticultural areas and began importing tools made by a 200-year-old foundry in Lancashire, England. Together, the partners turned Smith and Hawken into a $12 million a year business with four retail store locations and 600,000 yearly catalog customers. More important to Hawken than the bottom line, however, was the philosophy behind the business. Hawken is a noted business theorist whose views on running a business have been widely read and are vastly influential. He expressed in an interview with the magazine *Mother Earth Review* in March 1985, that "a business has to resonate with your sense of who you are, and what you do in the world." All of the other "business things" such as inventory and accounts and budgets and profit should come secondary to the *reason* that business is being done. He urged readers not to "confuse the vehicle with the destination" and said that doing business is nothing more than a way to accomplish something and should never be looked upon as an accomplishment in and of itself.

It was this sense of purpose that led him to leave Smith and Hawken in 1991. In his 1993 book, *The Ecology of Commerce*, he explained his reasons for leaving. "The recycled toner cartridges, the sustainably harvested woods, the replanted trees, the soy based inks were all well and good, but basically we were in the junk mail business. All the recycling in the world would not change the fact that doing business in the latter part of the twentieth century is an energy intensive endeavor that gulps down resources." Even though the business he was running operated in a manner that was 99.9 percent more ecologically sensitive than almost every other business operating in the United States, he was still unable to justify carrying out business in a way that generated so much waste. So, he stopped.

Hawken finds something to be fundamentally wrong with an economic system that makes it cheaper to destroy resources than to sustain them, and he believes that large-scale changes need to be enacted to avoid the continued physical degradation of earth and the consequences that go along with that degradation. He suggests that we create a market where people and businesses are rewarded for internalizing costs, rather than externalizing them. To do this we should, over the course of 20 years, phase out the entire current tax system and replace it with one that would no longer tax those things that we encourage: jobs, profits, income. Instead, we would tax through the utilization of what he calls "green fees." Green fees would adjust the prices of commodities to reflect the actual cost of the commodity being purchased. The price of gasoline, for example, should take into consideration environmental costs such as air pollution, acid rain, and the mitigation of global warming. This type of coversion of the business paradigm and more is described in *Natural Capitalism: Creating the Next Industrial Revolution* (1999), co-written with AMORY LOVINS and HUNTER LOVINS. *Publisher's Weekly* compared this book to FRANCIS MOORE LAPPÉ'S *Diet for a Small Planet* and STEWART BRAND'S *The Whole Earth Catalog* in the revolutionary nature of its ideas and the influence it has had on its readers.

Following the publication of *Natural Capitalism*, Hawken began to focus on the growth of a phenomenon he says has emerged largely beneath the radar: the blooming of hundreds of thousands of non-profit organizations that have emerged in response to social and environmental problems worldwide. In 2007 he published *Blessed Unrest: How the Largest Movement in the World Came into Being and Why No One Saw It Coming*. The book explores the history of the movement, and celebrates the energy and accomplishments of non-profit organizations. Part of what is so important about this movement, according to Hawken, is that it is all about ideas, and a natural effect of ideas is that they "open and liberate." A function of this huge but dispersed movement is that it dissolves "the pathological concentrations of power." Taking his research and writing one step further, Hawken has created a wiki, wiserearth.org, that facilitates involvement and networking between organizations.

Today, Hawken continues to innovate—since 2000 he has founded and/or serves as CEO of three tech companies that exemplify his philosophy: PaxIT, PaxFan, and Groxis.

Hawken is currently involved with several business organizations, including: Global Business Network, a private consulting network of 100 members; Interface, Inc., where he is one of a 12-member group of consultants responsible for turning RAY ANDERSON's Interface into the world's leading industrial ecology company; and Natural Capital Institute, a small research and educational organization that works with companies and individuals to make business a positive force for social justice and the environment. His work with non-profit organizations is varied; he has served on the boards of the Natural Step International, Urban Ecology, the ALDO LEOPOLD Leadership Program, the Materials Efficiency Project, the Center for New American Dream, and Friends of the Earth. He has also received numerous awards for his work on the intersection of environmentalism and industry. He was named "Best of a Generation" by *Esquire* in 1984, was given the Environmental Stewardship Award by the Council on Economic Priorities in 1991, was named "One of 100 Visionaries Who Could Change Our Lives" by the *Utne Reader* in 1995, and was presented with the Green Cross Millennium Award for Individual Environmental Leadership in 2003.

Hawken currently resides with his family in Sausalito, California.

BIBLIOGRAPHY

Frons, Marc, ed., "A Garden-Tool Maker Who's Cultivating Slow Growth," *Business Week*, 1986; Hawken, Paul, *Blessed Unrest*, 2007; Hawken, Paul, *The Ecology of Commerce*, 1993; Hawken, Paul, *Growing a Business*, 1987; Hawken, Paul, *Natural Capitalism*, 1999; Katz, Donald R., "Guru of the New Economy," *Esquire*, 1984; McNally, Terrence, "Paul Hawken: How to Stop Our Political and Economic Systems From Stealing Our Future, Alternet, 2007, www.alternet.org/story/54920/; "Paul Hawken," www.paulhawken.com; "Wiserearth," www.wiserearth.org.

Hayes, Denis

(August 29, 1944–)
Earth Day Organizer

Denis Hayes became famous in 1970 when Sen. GAYLORD NELSON recruited him to organize the first Earth Day. The participation of some 20 million people in Earth Day's varied activities brought the environment to the forefront of the mainstream public. Twenty years later, Hayes became the international chair of the second major Earth Day celebration. The intent of Earth Day II was to remind the public that all of the original environmental problems that Earth Day I addressed were still in existence and that individuals did have the power to respond to these problems by becoming more conscious of the environmental impact of their lifestyle. When he has not been organizing Earth Days, Hayes has worked with government and nonprofit agencies. Since 1992 he's promoted alternative, nonpolluting sources of energy and solutions to the environmental problems that plague the planet today, through his work with Bullit Foundation of Seattle.

Denis Allen Hayes was born in Wisconsin Rapids, Wisconsin, on August 29, 1944, and raised in the small mill town of Camas, Washington. An early impetus to environmental work was the putrid sulfur smell emanating from the town's paper mills. Hayes left Camas for a three-year hitchhiking trip around the world and then entered Stanford University, where he became student body president. Hayes attended Harvard Law School, but once he was invited in 1970 by Wisconsin senator Gaylord Nelson to organize Earth Day, he quit Harvard and moved to Washington, D.C. Thanks to Hayes's energetic publicity and organizing campaign, 20 million schoolchildren, college students, church members, and others participated in the first Earth Day. This show of public concern for the environment helped push Congress into passing the string of environmental legislation that came before it during the 1970s, including the Clean Air Act, the Water Quality Act, the Environmental Protection Act, and the Endangered Species Act.

After Earth Day, Hayes spent a year as a visiting scholar at the Smithsonian Institution (1971–1972) and directed the Illinois State Energy Office in 1974 and 1975. He joined the Worldwatch Institute's staff in 1975, where he researched alternative energy sources, especially solar energy. He wrote *Rays of Hope* in 1977, which described how the United States could kick its fossil fuels habit and convert to solar energy. Next, Pres. JIMMY CARTER named Hayes director of the Solar Energy Research Institute (SERI) in Golden, Colorado. This position lasted only two years, since the Reagan administration took funds away from government agencies such as SERI that were researching alternative energy sources. Hayes moved to San Francisco in 1981 and returned to law school. He practiced corporate law for a short time, then returned to his environmental work.

The year 1990 was a banner year for Hayes. It was the 20th anniversary of Earth Day, and Hayes was the international chair of a celebration by 200 million participants in 3,600 U.S. cities and 141 countries. Hayes saw Earth Day II not as a cure-all for the world's serious environmental problems but rather as an effective means to communicate with the public. Perhaps owing to increased environmental awareness, people made changes in their lifestyle that year. In an *E Magazine* interview in 1995, Hayes cited these statistics: in 1990, 3,000 new curbside recycling programs were initiated, and there was a 100 percent increase in recycling of postconsumer waste that year. Also in 1990, Hayes founded Green Seal (greenseal.org), an organization that independently certifies environmentally friendly products. The program helps consumers support companies doing their part to reduce pollution, and it can help "green" manufacturers reach a conscientious market.

Since 1992 Hayes has been president and CEO of Seattle's Bullit Foundation. The Bullit Foundation provides grants to non-profit organizations in the Pacific Northwest, that work to defend the plants, animals, water, and land. Hayes resides in Seattle, Washington.

BIBLIOGRAPHY
"The Bullit Foundation," www.bullit.org; Cahn, Robert, and Patricia Cahn, "Did Earth Day Change the World?" *Environment*, 1990; DeLeon, David, *Leaders from the 1960s*, 1994; Motavalli, Jim, "Cutting through the Fog: Denis Hayes on Earth Day Strategy," *E Magazine*, 1995.

Hayes, Randy
(July 11, 1950–)
Founder and President of Rain Forest Action Network

Rainforest Action Network (RAN) and its founder and director Randy Hayes were largely responsible for bringing the problem of rain forest deforestation to the attention of the American public during the 1980s and 1990s. RAN's partnerships with grassroots rain forest conservation groups in 60 countries around the world, its effective publicity campaigns in the United States, and its ability to mobilize its 30,000 members have made it an effective, visible force against rain forest destruction. Hayes currently serves as president emeritus of the organization.

Randall Hayes was born on July 11, 1950, in East Liverpool, Ohio, to Ace and Beverly Hayes. Exploring the forests of West Virginia and the swamps of Florida inspired an early interest in nature and in keeping it wild. His father's entrepreneurial spirit and his mother's focus and kindness contributed to Hayes's career choice and success. He earned a B.A. in psychology and sociology from Bowling Green State University in Ohio in 1973 and went on for graduate work in environmental planning at San Francisco State University in 1983. His master's thesis was the film "The Four Corners, A National Sacrifice Area?" that documented the tragic effects of uranium and coal mining on Hopi and Navajo Indian lands in the Four Corners region of the American Southwest. It won the Best Student Documentary award from the Academy of Motion Picture Arts and Sciences in 1983 and served as his introduction to the environmental problems faced by native peoples.

During a 1984 trip to Costa Rica, Hayes was shocked by the rain forest destruction there. He visited a pristine rain forest area where a new road had recently been built. The blood-red clay swath through the forest left an indelible impression on him. After vowing to do something to combat worldwide rain forest destruction, Hayes returned to the United States and in 1985 organized the first international rain forest strategy conference in Sausalito, California. It was attended by about 70 participants from 12 countries, representing several environmental organizations and groups of indigenous peoples. The conference revealed that rain forest destruction was the result of many converging conditions in less-developed countries: official government disrespect for the rights of indigenous people to live in their native rain forests; land ownership inequities that drive landless peasants to slash and burn virgin forests, the only lands left for colonization; and road construction and dam building projects financed by international financial institutions such as the World Bank and the International Monetary Fund. Out of this founding conference, the Rainforest Action Network was born. It existed as a working group of the Earth Island Institute, which nurtured it until 1987, when RAN was large enough to sustain itself.

RAN's first goal was to bring the rain forest issue to public attention. One of its early projects was a well-publicized boycott of Burger King, because that fast-food chain bought beef from Latin America where ranchers graze their cattle on pastures cleared from rain forests. After the boycott cut Burger King's 1987 profits by 12 percent, Burger King officials announced in 1988 that the company would no longer buy its beef in Latin America.

Its effectiveness in mobilizing boycotts established, RAN also came to be known for the creativity and innovation of its direct action protests. Hayes was present at the birth announcement of Earth First!: the draping of a black plastic 300-foot "crack" down the side of the Glen Canyon Dam in March 1981. Inspired by the drama of that event, Hayes has organized RAN volunteers with technical climbing skills to undertake many similar actions. Their first was a 1986 climb of the World Bank building in Washington, D.C., during a meeting of World Bank finance ministers. Activists hung a two-story banner that declared "World Bank Destroys Tropical Rainforests" from the front of the building, and police were not able to cut it down for two days. Hayes later told the *San Francisco Chronicle*, "That image went around the world." The banner revealed what before then had been a little known fact: that World Bank–funded development projects frequently resulted in severe environmental degradation. Public outcry put pressure on the World Bank to develop stricter environmental criteria for its projects, and vocal RAN members helped influence the World Bank's 1994 withdrawal of funding from the environmentally destructive Altamira dam project in Brazil's Amazon Basin.

RAN members work through local chapters or engage in on-line activism, in response to RAN's campaigns. In 2008 these included: "Freedom from Oil" which demands that the auto industry produce zero-emissions vehicles; "Global Finance" which challenges financial institutions to fund renewable energy rather than destructive industries; "Old Growth," which boycotts companies that engage in logging of ancient forests; and "Rainforest Agribusiness," which seeks to stop the conversion of tropical forests to industrial agriculture. RAN coordinates national publicity and letter-writing campaigns, nonviolent direct-action protests, and boycotts of the culprits. In many cases, RAN collaborates not only with local grassroots groups but also with environmental giants such as the Sierra Club, Greenpeace, and the Natural Resource Defense Council.

Hayes has developed, and RAN subscribes to, a 500 Year Plan to "orchestrate an environmental U-turn" for the Earth's forests and the services they provide. The six steps to this plan—available in full on www.ran.org—are paraphrased as follows: 1) acknowledging the global emergency caused by deforestation; 2) clarifying key human and ecological values and goals; 3) determining and implementing a cap on ecologically harmful activities; 4) developing a plan for forest protection that will halt deforestation and promote sustainability; 5) committing to a timetable and a system for verification; and 6) boycotting corporations or governments which don't adhere to the 500 Year plan.

Hayes was a finalist for the 2006 Volvo for Life Environmental Award, and resides in San Francisco.

BIBLIOGRAPHY
Buchanan, Rob, "Looking for Rainforest Heroes," *Outside*, 1992; Freistadt, Margo, "The Man behind the Rainforest Action Network," *San Francisco Chronicle*, 1989; Hayes, Randy, "Activism: You Make the Difference," *Lessons of the Rainforest*, 1990; Hayes, Randy, "Lessons

of the Rain Forest," *Call to Action: Handbook for Ecology, Peace and Justice*, 1990; "Rainforest Action Network," www.ran.org.

Hays, Samuel P.
(April 5, 1921–)
Environmental Historian

Fondly referred to by his colleagues as "the grandfather of environmental history," Samuel Hays has spent a lifetime as a leader and respected writer of the environmental history of the United States. While his writings cover such diverse matters as environment and urbanization, environmental regulation, forest issues, air quality, the role of values, and postwar environmental politics, the consistent thread though all of Hays's work is his deep commitment to environmental issues and to his belief in the importance of history to understanding the environmental impulse, environmental policy, and environmental controversy.

Samuel Pfrimmer Hays was born April 5, 1921, in Corydon, Indiana, the son of Clay Blaine, a small-town lawyer and dairy farmer, and Clara Ridley (Pfrimmer) Hays. His interest in the environment emerged during his boyhood. He acquired some knowledge of conservation from experience with the U.S. Soil Conservation Service on his family's farm and more from a Civilian Conservation Corps camp at a neighboring state forest. In his early twenties, Hays spent two summers at American Friends Service Committee work camps on farms, first at a demonstration farm in eastern Tennessee that was part of the program of the Tennessee Valley Authority, and second at a Farm Security Administration community for farm day laborers in southeastern Missouri. These experiences were augmented between 1943 and 1946, when he worked with the Oregon and California Revested Lands Administration on public forests in western Oregon. His work for the so-called O&C ranged from tree planting and fighting forest fires to cooking and tool maintenance. During this two-and-a-half-year stint, Hays became interested in the agency itself and was made "project education" leader. His new task was to inform members of the camp about the O&C, its history, and its program.

Hays completed his B.A. in psychology at Swarthmore College in 1948 and then moved on to Harvard, where he earned an M.A. in 1949 and a Ph.D. in history in 1953. At Harvard, Hays was able to integrate his interest in conservation with his focus on history. His dissertation dealt with the Progressive movement and conservation. Harvard University Press published the revised dissertation in 1959 as *Conservation and the Gospel of Efficiency*. This work became one of the seminal contributions to the field of environmental history and was reprinted by the University of Pittsburgh Press in 1999. It is as relevant today as it was when it was first published.

Applying to agricultural schools, Hays hoped to teach conservation history but had no success securing employment in his then-obscure field. Instead, he opted for the equally new, but more popular, fields of political, urban, and social history, teaching briefly at the University of Illinois and for seven years at the University of Iowa before accepting the position as chair of the Department of History at the University of Pittsburgh in 1960, where he spent the remainder of his career. During the 12-year hiatus between the publication of *Conservation and the Gospel of Efficiency* and Hays's return to the study of environmental issues, he published widely in the fields of urban political and social history.

Hays's return to historical work on the environment after 1970 coincided with a period of great environmental enthusiasm. The celebration of Earth Day in April 1970, the 1969 passage of the National Environmental Policy Act (NEPA), and the founding of the Environmental Protection Agency in 1971 suggested that the human relationship with the environment was becoming an important—and hitherto relatively unexplored—avenue for historical inquiry. For Hays, it was a return to an area of scholarly and personal interest, but one that was driven by new interests as well. Through the 1970s to the present, Hays has written prolifically in journals and book chapters on conservation history, environmental politics, and the city of Pittsburgh. Not least of these interests was the opportunity to engage in mutual scholarly interests with his wife, Barbara Darrow, a biologist whom he married in 1948. The two collaborated on the highly acclaimed *Beauty, Health and Permanence: Environmental Politics in the United States, 1955–1985* in 1987. At the heart of his work is the relationship between conservationism and politics, as evidenced in all of his books, including his most recent three: *A History of Environmental Politics Since 1945* (2000), *Wars in the Woods* (2006), and *The American People and the National* Forests (with a 2009 publication date), a history of the U.S. Forest Service, focusing on its relationship with U.S. society.

In addition to his books and essays, Hays is an archivist of primary urban and industrial resource materials. His work in collecting archival material for the University of Pittsburgh has earned the History Department its prominence in the field. Hays was responsible for amassing a tangible chronicle of the industrial growth and development of Pittsburgh and the surrounding region. Under his leadership, this collection, known as the Archives of Industrial Society, grew to incorporate original source documents and served as a basis for several dozen doctoral dissertations. The scholarly result was brought together in a volume called *City at the Point: Essays in the Social History of Pittsburgh*, which he edited and which was published by the University of Pittsburgh Press in 1990.

In 1982, a subdivision of the collection was created, the Environmental Archives. It included both Pennsylvania and national environmental records. The Environmental Archives now houses, on a continuing basis, records of the Pennsylvania chapter of the Sierra Club, the Western Pennsylvania Conservancy, and the Pennsylvania Environmental Council. National records include those of Environmentalists for Full Employment, Environmental Action, and the Environmental Action Foundation, one of the sponsor organizations for the first Earth Day in 1970 and no longer in existence. Over the years Hays and his wife have gathered a massive number of documents pertaining to environmental affairs since 1970, featuring citizen organizations from all 50 states as well as national organizations. These are now housed in the Environmental Archives and constitute its largest collection, totaling over 800 linear feet of documents. It includes a major collection of British environmental documents that Hays gathered beginning with his stint as Harmsworth Professor of History at Oxford in 1982–1983, to which a collection from an English environmental historian was added. Hays believes that historians should collect and preserve contemporary material for future study, as it can prove to shed valuable insights on the growth and development of popular movements.

Aside from his academic work, Hays has also been active in environmental affairs, writing countless letters and articles to clarify environmental issues. He has been involved with the Sierra Club on a variety of issues, especially those pertaining to eastern state and national forests. He donated his father's 320-acre dairy farm to the Harrison County, Indiana, Park Board and the Indiana Nature Conservancy, to create the Hayswood Nature Reserve in 1976 and the Indian Creek Woods in 1986. And in 1994 he created an endowment through the Community Endowment for Southern Indiana to support upkeep of Indian Creek Woods. It is perhaps not irrelevant to his personal philosophy of life that in 40 years of teaching at three major universities he has never held a parking permit, always walking daily from his home to his office.

In 1982, Hays received the Theodore C. Blegen Award from the Forest History Society. In 1991, he received the Pennsylvania Governor's Award for Excellence in the Humanities, and in 1993 he was awarded the Historical Society of Western Pennsylvania History Makers Award. More recently, in 1997, the American Society for Environmental History awarded him its first Career Achievement Award for Lifetime Contributions to Environmental History. In 1999 he received a distinguished service award from the Organization of American Historians.

Hays and his wife have four adult children. They retired to Boulder, Colorado in 2000.

BIBLIOGRAPHY

Hays, Samuel P., *American Political History as Social Analysis: Essays by Samuel P. Hays*, 1980; Hays, Samuel P., *Explorations in Environmental History: Essays by Samuel P. Hays*, 1998; Hays, Samuel P., *Response to Industrialization, 1885–1914*, 1957 (revised, 1995); Hays, Samuel P., "Interview," *Environmental History*, www.historycooperative.org/cgi-bin/cite.cgi?=eh/12.3/hays.html, 2007.

Henderson, Hazel

(March 27, 1933–)
Economist, Futurist

Hazel Henderson began her environmental career in New York City by forcing her local television stations to broadcast daily air quality reports, a practice soon adopted by television networks and newspapers nationwide. In the early 1970s, she shifted her focus to economics, and since then she has written numerous articles and books criticizing such traditional economic concepts as the Gross National Product (GNP). She believes that economics must become a multidisciplinary field if it is to successfully create economically and environmentally sustainable policies. She advocates the creation of a sustainable future through the cooperation of local and international grassroots organizations and business enterprises to manage the planet's resources, establishing a "win-win" economy.

Hazel Henderson was born on March 27, 1933, to Kenneth and Dorothy Mustard in Bristol, England. She dropped out of school at the age of 16, and in 1956 she emigrated to the United States, settling in New York City. She became a naturalized citizen in 1962. Henderson became an activist in 1964 when she began a letter-writing campaign in response to the terrible air quality in New York. She wrote letters to the presidents of the major broadcasting networks requesting that an air pollution index be included in the daily weather report. She also sent letters to New York's elected officials and to Newton Minow, chairman of the Federal Communications Commission. Several weeks later, Henderson received a telephone call from an American Broadcasting Companies (ABC) vice president who supported the idea, and not long after, WABC-TV in New York City began broadcasting a daily air pollution index. Other local television stations and newspapers followed suit. Soon, air pollution information was being made available by television stations and newspapers nationwide.

As a follow-up to her success, Henderson and two friends created an organization called Citizens for Clean Air (CCA), in order to inform New York City residents about the health hazards that go along with air pollution. With the help of an advertising agency that was willing to donate time and resources, CCA launched an educational campaign that quickly gained 25,000 members. In recognition of these efforts, Henderson was named Citizen of the Year by the New York Medical Society in 1967.

In the early 1970s, Henderson began to move away from activism and started developing theories about how to bring about major changes in society. In a 1995 interview with David Kupfer in *Whole Earth Review*, Henderson said, "I always knew I was unemployable, so I invented my own job and have been self-employed for 25 years." She calls the job she invented "social innovator." Others have called it "futurist," "alternative political economist," and "visionary." In the early 1970s, Henderson began educating herself on the principles of economics. She also began publishing articles in such periodicals as the *Harvard Business Review*, the *Columbia Journal of World Business*, and *Science*. In 1972, she helped to create the Princeton Center for Alternative Futures, Inc., an organization for which she continues to act as a director.

In 1974, when Congress created the Office of Technology Assessment (OTA), Henderson was appointed to its advisory council as a citizens' advocate. OTA's purpose was to determine the social, environmental, economic, and political consequences of emerging technologies. In *Women Pioneers for the Environment*, Henderson is quoted as saying that her time on the OTA advisory council, as well as her service on panels of the National Science Foundation and the National Academy of Engineering between the years of 1974 and 1980, served as her "Ph.D. course." In 1975, she served on Pres. JIMMY CARTER's election task force on economics, recommending that the President's Council of Economic Advisors be expanded into a multidisciplinary Council of Social Science Advisors.

Henderson published her first book, *Creative Alternative Futures: The End of Economics*, in 1978. In this book, as well as in her second, *The Politics of the Solar Age: Alternatives to Economics* (1981), Henderson makes the case that the focus of economics is much too narrow. She criticizes the use of the GNP as a true indicator of the economic and social health of a country, since the GNP overlooks nearly half of the production occurring in the world—production by unpaid workers, mostly women. The GNP also fails to classify natural resources as assets, actually treating the clean-up of pollution as additional production rather than as an expense. "Trying to run an economy using only economic indicators like the GNP is rather like trying to fly a Boeing 747 with a single oil pressure gauge," she says. "What we need to do is fill out the instrument panel." To this end she has helped to create the Country Future Indicators (CFI) index, which measures how well a country is investing in its own people. To further develop the CFI, Henderson began to collaborate in 1994 with the asset management fund Calvert, and in 2000 Henderson, Calvert, and a group of 12 scholars introduced the Calvert-Henderson Quality of Life Indicators: education, employment, energy, environment, health, human rights, income, infrastructure, national security, public safety, re-creation, and shelter. The project maintains a website (www.calvert-henderson.com) devoted to describing each indicator and showing how the U.S. and the world at large measures up in each area.

Henderson has published several books since the 1990s. In *Paradigms in Progress* (1991), she describes the fundamental differences in the philosophies underlying economics and environmentalism, stressing the fact that economics can only view parts of the environmental problems that must be solved and can, therefore, only provide partial solutions. She prescribes the abandonment of our historical anthropocentric world-view and the embrace of biocentrism with its wider, more encompassing perspective. In order to develop sustainable, ecologically viable forms of productivity, she points out, we need to gain an appreciation for, and an understanding of, the system of interdependent species that makes up the planet upon which we live.

Building a Win-Win World: Life beyond Global Economic Warfare (1996), provides an alternative to what Henderson refers to as today's global economic warfare based on capitalism, nationalism, and overconsumption. Henderson depicts a possible future that would include sustainable development achieved through decentralized enterprise, energy efficiency, recycling, and cooperation. She argues that the United Nations, currently too patriarchal, should be restructured to fill a role as global networker and broker of partnerships between local grassroots groups.

Planetary Citizenship (2004) is the transcription of a discussion between Henderson and Japanese Buddhist teacher Daisaku Ikeda about the current state of global development, how it should evolve, and how each of them came to hold the beliefs and commitments they are so well known for. *Ethical Markets: Growing the Green Economy* (with Simran Sethi, 2006) is the companion volume to Henderson's PBS television series of the same name, and profiles businesses that exemplify environmental sensitivity and social responsibility.

Henderson writes a syndicated editorial column that appears in 27 different languages in over 400 newspapers worldwide. Her articles have appeared in more than 250 periodicals. She travels the world as a lecturer and consultant, and she has taught courses at various academic institutions, including Schumacher College in the UK, Harvard University, Cornell University, and Brown and Dartmouth Colleges. She has been a member of the board of directors for the Worldwatch Institute, the Calvert Social Investment Fund, and many other organizations, but currently dedicates herself full-time to producing her Ethical Markets TV series. In 1995, Henderson was named one of *Utne Reader*'s 120 visionaries who could change our lives, in 1996 she won the Global Citizen Award, and in 2007 she was elected as a Fellow to Great Britain's Royal Society. Henderson lives on a small island off the coast of Florida and has a grown daughter, Alexandra.

BIBLIOGRAPHY

Black, Sherry Salway, "Paradigm in Progress: Life beyond Economics," *Christianity and Crisis*, 1993; Breton, Mary Joy, *Women Pioneers for the Environment*, 1998; "Calvert-Henderson Quality of Life Indicators," www.calvert-henderson.com; "Hazel Henderson presents an informative web site on various topics from around the world!," www.hazelhenderson.com; Kelly, Kevin, ed., "Interview, Hazel Henderson," *Whole Earth Review*, 1988; Kupfer, David, "To Stitch the World Back Together Again," *Whole Earth Review*, 1995.

Hermach, Tim

(1945–)
Founder and Executive Director of Native Forest Council

Tim Hermach believes that like "big tobacco," the big timber corporations that strip-mine the nation's forests have lied to the people, used bribery and extortion to control politicians, and mounted billion-dollar public relations campaigns to mislead the public, and he acts accordingly. He founded Native Forest Council which has taken unprecedented risks to assure the preservation of the nation's remaining native forests as living life-support systems for future generations. The group was the first since Teddy Roosevelt to advocate a total logging ban on public lands, calling their position Zero Cut and, though they were dismissed at the outset as politically unrealistic, powerful environmental groups such as the Sierra Club have now adopted their versions of Zero Cut for public lands. Passionate, outspoken, and uncompromising, Hermach has widened the focus of political debate over logging and forest management practices and has inspired many other progressive and conservative conservation advocates with his simple, clear and compelling can-do arguments.

Tim Hermach was born in 1945 and grew up in Eugene, Oregon, the oldest of four brothers. He spent a lot of time in the woods, often on publicly-owned national forests and Bureau of Land Management (BLM) land, camping, drinking from clear streams, and chasing enormous salmon. As a young boy he worked in the local fields and orchards and in his father's small businesses. After attending the University of Oregon for one year, the urge to travel hit. He toured Europe for 10 months deeply appreciating the different social and political cultures and the acceptance he felt there as an American. Upon his return, his ventures in the corporate world began. Hermach credits the early success of Native Forest Council to his professional experience that taught him clear goals/objectives produce tangible results. By the age of 25 he had already sold encyclopedias, vacuum cleaners, cars, worked for the phone company and for the Department of Defense. He eventually became director of operations for large apparel manufacturing companies such as White Stag (Portland) and Cole of California (Los Angeles). He enjoyed this "corporate time" and was successful for many years. He returned to UO in 1983, graduating with a business degree in 1986.

In 1985, Hermach learned that the U.S. had already logged over 90 percent of its 1.087 billion acres of native forests—public and private. In stark contrast, only 14 percent of the Amazon rain forest had been logged, although that area was receiving much anxious and diversionary attention at the time. By then the forests Hermach had played in as a boy had been stripped bare from ridgetop to ridgetop, and the streambeds had filled with mud. There was little left besides mono-cropped tree plantations. Most of the remaining small percentage of the country's native forests existed on public lands, but they too were subject to logging at taxpayer expense and with little or no accounting for the full costs and losses to the public in public health, wealth and inventory. To do something about this, Hermach became heavily involved with the Sierra Club. But over the next few years, he grew disillusioned with the large national group, realizing that its main strategy for environmental conflict resolution was compromise. As with much of what Hermach calls the "gang-green" environmental establishment, the Sierra Club's highest priority seemed to be political access and the interests of its wealthy donors, and Hermach wanted nothing to do with it.

In 1988, at the suggestion of the former Sierra Club Director, DAVID BROWER, Hermach founded his own organization, Native Forest

Council, with the purpose of disclosing the truth about national forests and the politics (a corporate cesspool of political corruption) that drive their mismanagement. From the start, the group took compelling but controversial stands and maintained that the United States could no longer afford to chip away at the 5-10 percent of native forests that remained unlogged. Arguing that with so little left uncut in the United States, clearly too much compromise had already occurred, Hermach offered a simple solution he calls Zero Cut: to save what's left and to pass national legislation outlawing any and all further logging of native and old-growth forests on publicly owned federal land. At the outset, many dismissed his stance as quixotic and too radical, and his persistent condemnation of repeated and unwarranted compromise gained him no allies among Washington, D.C.–based environmental organizations. Undaunted, he gathered input from more than 200 grassroots organizations, and in 1989 he drafted the Native Forest Protection Act, which called for an immediate halt to old-growth forest logging and a ban on the third-world-colony exporting of unfinished wood products (logs, chips, and pulp) along with American jobs. The act mandated ecological recovery and restoration and included a provision to ensure government accountability.

When Hermach took his proposed legislation to Washington, D.C., he recruited the support of 14 Democrats in Congress, though they all withdrew their backing after being persuaded to by four national environmental groups expressing opposition at being embarrassed, having long maintained it couldn't be done (Sierra Club, National Audubon Society, The Wilderness Society, & the National Wildlife Federation). For the next few years, Hermach persistently stuck with the campaign, hired the PR firm, Fenton Communications, attracting media attention, distributing information, and raising public awareness of the issue. Eventually editorials appeared in several major newspapers, such as the *Washington Post* and the *New York Times*, questioning and criticizing national forest management policy. Growing public concern moved the U.S. Forest Service to adopt new management philosophies that promised to be ecologically sound, but changes were only cosmetic. In 1994, Hermach realized that his original plan, to protect native and old-growth forest while allowing some logging to continue on planted tree plantations and fiber farms, placed too much trust in the Forest Service, which he believed had essentially become a servant of the dishonest and destructive timber industry. Hence, he altered his proposal. His new policy would end public land logging altogether. It met with predictable opposition for all the usual reasons: that it was politically unrealistic, that there would be a loss of jobs, that it would disrupt the liquidation economy of logging communities, and that aging, "crowded" stands of trees needed to be thinned. But the simplicity and explicitness of the Zero Cut proposal, backed up by Hermach's irrefutable moral and economic arguments that the abuse of the nation's forests had gone on too long, appealed to many and reinvigorated much of the grassroots community that had been fighting losing battles against the timber industry.

The issue gained more and more attention, and although there was still no major environmental organization willing to truly back Zero Cut, the public became increasingly critical of governmental forest mis-management practices. Hermach never broke his stride; he continued campaigning for Zero Cut for the next few years—attending conferences, educating the media, and constantly networking by phone and fax. By 1995 he had scored endorsements from the Oregon Natural Resources Council, Greenpeace, the New York City and Long Island chapters of the Audubon Society, and Washington's Inland Empire Public Lands Council. And in 1996, after an exhausting battle in which the Sierra Club's management threw up many obstacles and tried to prevent its membership from voting in favor of it, the club's members officially voted to support Zero Cut.

Finally, in October 1997, nearly ten years after Hermach had introduced the notion of Zero Cut, Cynthia McKinney (D-GA) and Jim Leach (R-IA) introduced a bipartisan proposal called National Forest Protection and Restoration Act (NFPRA) that would phase out all commercial logging within two years. Doing so would protect the country's forest heritage, cut corporate welfare, and save citizen and taxpayer assets and money; the bill also included a provision to assist logging communities with economic recovery and diversification. Though the bill had not yet passed when this edition went to press, its introduction was a victory in itself, dramatically improving the parameters of the political debate and proving that there was broad support of the Zero Cut idea, originally introduced in essence one hundred years earlier by Teddy Roosevelt.

Native Forest Council continues to argue that nature has great but uncounted value, to demand an honest and fully-costed inventory accounting for publicly owned lands, rivers and streams, and to build strong coalitions for uncompromised and honest economic, social, and environmental solutions. It serves as a powerful information clearinghouse for the media and those within the forest movement, and its *Forest Voice* newsletter is read by citizens all over the country. Hermach continues his work as executive director of the group and remains committed to fighting for Zero Cut and the national forests and the soil, air and water, the fish and wildlife, and the climate and weather they produce, and for the total protection of 650 million acres of federally owned public land, rivers, and streams. He is married, has three children and lives in Eugene, Oregon.

BIBLIOGRAPHY

Borowski, John, "Clarion Call of a Modern Day Lorax," Common Dreams, www.commondreams.org/views03/0806-04.htm, 2003; Broydo, Leora, "Mutiny at the Sierra Club," *Mother Jones*, 1998; Hermach, Tim, "True Colors," *Forest Voice*, 1997; Hermach, Tim, "What Is the Value of Our Wilderness?" *Seattle Times*, 1998; Mazza, Patrick, "Sierra Club Supports Zero Cut," *E Magazine*, 1996; "Native Forest Council," www.forestcouncil.org; Sonner, Scott, "Activist Finally Sees Logging Ban Proposed," *Columbian*, 1997.

Hill, Julia Butterfly
(February 18, 1974–)
Forest Activist

Going beyond what most environmental activists would do to save a tree, Julia Butterfly Hill spent two years from 1997 to 1999 in a 200-foot-tall old-growth redwood in northern California, in protest of the notoriously destructive logging practices of Pacific Lumber, a division of the Houston, Texas–based Maxxam Corporation. With support from a dedicated ground crew, she lived on a six-by-eight-foot tarp-covered platform, where she endured high winds and damp cold in the winter and searing heat in the summer. Before coming to an agreement with Pacific Lumber (which owns the property where her tree stands) and leaving her post, she withstood a barrage of scare tactics from the timber company, such as flying a helicopter right above her head, burning slash piles all around her tree, and cutting off her supply crew for over a week. Hill and some of her supporters have created the Circle of Life Foundation in affiliation with the nonprofit

Julia Butterfly Hill descends from a tree on June 10, 2006 after a 19-day stay. (AP Images/Damian Dovarganes)

Trees Foundation, so that they can continue restoration and conservation efforts in forest ecosystems.

Julia Hill was born on February 18, 1974, in Mount Vernon, Missouri, to Dale and Kathy Hill. Her father was an itinerant preacher, and many of Hill's early memories revolve around religion. She and her two brothers were raised nomadically, traveling from town to town, living in a small camping trailer. Her parents lived by putting their faith before their own concerns, and Julia grew up learning to follow her own convictions above everything else. By the time she had reached high school age, her family had settled in Jonesboro, Arkansas, and she began to attend school for the first time.

In the summer of 1996, while working as a bartender in Fayetteville, Arkansas, she was in a nearly fatal car accident. It took ten months of intensive therapy for her to recover her short-term memory and motor skills. The experience changed her, and she promised herself never to take anything for granted again. Determined to travel and discover her purpose in life, she went on a trip with some friends in the summer of 1997 to the West Coast. Hill was awed by the giant redwoods in northern California and resolved to come back and fight to save the remaining stands of these trees from being clear-cut. She returned to Arkansas, sold all but a few of her belongings, bought camping gear, and headed back west in mid-November 1997. When she reached Arcata, California, she got in touch with Earth First! activists who were rallied at their nearby base camp—the center of activity during their campaigns to protest the logging of old-growth trees. Hill was eager to join in their civil-disobedience activities, so when an opportunity arose to participate in a tree sit, she enthusiastically volunteered.

The tree, named Luna by the activists who built the tree-sitting platform on the night of a full moon, was a 1,000-year-old redwood, reaching 200 feet tall at the top of a windy ridgeline. Located on Pacific Lumber property, it was slated to be one of the millions of trees to be cut and sold by the timber company. Pacific Lumber, once a family-owned operation that upheld a policy of long-term sustainable logging, was acquired in the mid-1980s by Maxxam Corporation, headed by chief executive officer Charles Hurwitz. In an effort to pay off the taxpayer-funded $1.6 billion bailout of his bankrupt savings and loan, Hurwitz used high-interest junk bonds to finance his acquisition of Pacific Lumber, which owned rights to a large tract of ancient redwoods in northern California. To restructure his debt, Hurwitz doubled and in some areas tripled the rate of logging, destroying huge tracts of forest, sparking lawsuits, and provoking outraged environmental protests. In December 1996, seven homes in Stafford, California, were completely destroyed by a mudslide caused by Pacific Lumber's clearcut on the steep slope above them, which had left no vegetation to absorb the winter rains.

Hill, who adopted the "forest name" Butterfly, used safety ropes and a harness to climb Luna for her first tree sit, which lasted six days. On December 10, 1997, she and another activist returned for another tree sit, assuming they would stay up for a few weeks. By this time, Pacific Lumber was ready to begin logging the area and had started intimidation tactics—sending a professional climber up after them and cutting down trees all around them. In early January, the activist who had accompanied Hill on the tree sit went back down. She was now on her own, and for the next few months, she endured almost constant harassment from the logging company. They flew their twin-propeller helicopter right over her head, nearly knocking her out of the tree. She managed to catch the act on videotape and sent it to the Federal Aviation Administration, which threatened to revoke the helicopter operator's license if that ever happened again. Pacific Lumber then began posting security guards around the clock under the tree, cutting off Hill's supply crew. The siege lasted ten days, until the guards were pulled out owing to the severe winter storms on the ridge. The El Niño storms of that year were unusually fierce, and Hill on one occasion was battered by a 16-hour storm with winds up to 70 miles per hour and driving sleet. Later, when Pacific Lumber had cut most of the trees around her, they began burning the slash—filling the air with suffocating smoke for six straight days.

Hill accomplished more than she had originally planned when she climbed into the tree—she became an international celebrity. By the end of her two-year stay, she had a cellular phone, a pager, a radio, a walkie-talkie, a video camera, a tape recorder, and a solar-powered battery charger, all of which she used to network with the press and keep in touch with her ground crew. She did countless radio, newspaper, and magazine interviews, and even had television crews climb up the tree to film her. Using the media attention as an opportunity for outreach, Hill spoke out and wrote editorials about her protest. She became a spokesperson—getting the message out to the public about issues such as the Headwaters Forest Agreement, in which the California and U.S. governments agreed to purchase an old-growth grove in Pacific Lumber's Headwaters Forest for $480 million and turn it into a preserve. Hill and her supporters decry the plan since it leaves to the logging company tens of thousands of acres of prime old-growth habitat. She even had the clout to address the floor of the U.S. Senate by speakerphone about the issue.

Along with some of her supporters, Hill created the Circle of Life Foundation, fiscally sponsored by the nonprofit Trees Foundation, to promote the sustainability and preservation of forests. In December 1999, Hill and Pacific Lumber came to an agreement in which she and the Circle of Life Foundation would pay the company $50,000 in return for a promise not to cut Luna and to reserve a 200-foot buffer zone around the tree. Pacific Lumber pledged to donate the money to Humboldt University to be used for forestry research. For her part, Hill agreed not to repeat her tree sit and to give the company 48-hours notice before visiting Luna. On December 18, 1999, she climbed down and touched the ground for the first time in two years. Hill's decision to end her tree sit was publicly criticized by other direct-action forest activists in the area, who said they wished that when Hill decided to leave her post, she had offered them the opportunity to continue the tree sit in Luna.

Hill wrote *The Legacy of Luna* (2000) while she was sitting in Luna, and *One Makes a Difference* (2003), a handbook of tips on how to live a more eco-friendly life. Hill tours the country to publicize the plight of the redwoods and promote sustainable living. She makes her home in Humboldt County, California, where she continues to work with the Circle of Life Foundation to save old-growth forests.

BIBLIOGRAPHY

"Circle of Life," www.circleoflifefoundation.org; Fortgang, Erika, "The Girl in the Tree," *Rolling Stone*, 1999; Hill, Julia Butterfly, *The Legacy of Luna*, 2000; Hill, Julia Butterfly, *One Makes the Difference: Inspiring Actions that Change our World*, 2002; Hornblower, Margot, "An Ecowarrior Who Calls Herself Butterfly Has Set a Tree-squatting Record," *Time*, 1998; Martin, Sam, "Talking to the Trees: an interview with Julia 'Butterfly' Hill," *Mother Earth News*, 2001.

Hoagland, Edward
(December 21, 1932–)
Writer

Edward Hoagland is an essayist, nature writer, novelist, and short story writer, best known for his free-flowing, digressive essays that focus on the interactions between humans and nature. He has written more than 100 of these essays and has published them in book form in seven collections.

Edward Morley Hoagland was born on December 21, 1932, in New York City to Warren Eugene and Helen Morley Hoagland. His father was a financial attorney who, over the course of his career, was employed by Standard Oil and the Defense and State Departments of the U.S. government. As a child, Hoagland had a severe stutter, which led him to seek entertainment and companionship in the woods near his home (his family had moved out of New York City to New Canaan, Connecticut, when he was eight years old) rather than with other children. This speech impediment continued as he grew older and had a profound influence on his writing. In the introduction to the 1993 editions of *The Courage of Turtles* and *Walking the Dead Diamond River*, two essay collections that share the same introduction, Hoagland writes, "I wasn't writing primarily for money or even fame, but simply to speak. A bad stutter had rendered me functionally mute for years, and this [writing] at last was my breakthrough."

As a youth, Hoagland was intrigued by the wild. He rode horseback for a summer in Wyoming, fought forest fires in the Santa Ana Mountains in southern California, and joined the Ringling Bros. and Barnum and Bailey Circus, where he cared for the big cats. Hoagland's first novel, *Cat Man* (1955), was based on his experiences working for the circus. Hoagland entered Harvard University in 1950, graduating in 1954 with an A.B. degree. During his time at Harvard, Hoagland studied with many prominent writers, including John Berryman and Thornton Wilder. Hoagland served in the United States Army for two years from 1955 to 1957, working as a laboratory technician in an army morgue in Phoenixville, Pennsylvania. After his discharge in 1957, Hoagland returned to New York City, where he lived on the Lower East Side and "strode the streets hungering for experience, convinced that every mile I walked the better writer I'd be," as he wrote in the introduction to the 1993 editions of *The Courage of Turtles* and *Walking the Dead Diamond River*.

Hoagland's father was in no way supportive of Hoagland's career choice. His father, in fact, wrote Houghton Mifflin in an attempt to stop the publication of *Cat Man* on the grounds that it was obscene. After his failure to convince Hoagland to pursue another career, or at least to use a pen name, Hoagland's father effectively wrote his son out of his will.

This opposition from his family provided Hoagland with a strong desire to succeed as a writer, and he began publishing numerous pieces in periodicals such as *Paris Review*, the *Transatlantic Review*, and the *New American Review*. As a young writer, Hoagland published three novels—*Cat Man* (1955), *The Circle Home* (1960), and *The Peacock's Tail* (1965)—each of which received varying degrees of critical acclaim and attracted little popular success.

In the summer of 1966, after the breakup of Hoagland's first marriage, he traveled to the wilderness of northwestern British Columbia, where he hiked hundreds of miles on backcountry trails and interviewed about 80 people. They were homesteaders, Native Americans, trappers, and prospectors, and he was struck by their gaiety and consistency, which had grown out of their "long labor of opening a new country to settlement," as he states in the resultant book's introduction. The book, *Notes from the Century Before: A Journal from British Columbia* (1969), asks the simple question, "How shall we live?"; it is considered by many to be the turning point in Hoagland's career. In *Notes from the Century Before*, Hoagland searches for experiences in a wild country before that country disappears. It was his first foray into nonfiction writing, and it was extremely well received by both reviewers and the general public.

Around the time *Notes from the Century Before* was published, Hoagland began to focus on writing essays, a genre to which he found that he was perfectly suited. In the foreword to *City Tales* (1986), he wrote, "I found at the end of the 1960s that what I wanted to do most was tell my own story.... I discovered that the easiest way to do this was by writing directly to the reader without filtering myself through the artifices of fiction." He began publishing essays regularly in journals such as the *Village Voice*, *Harper's*, and the *New American Review*. The subjects of his essays have varied widely, ranging from the Golden Rule to EDWARD ABBEY and horseback riding with his daughter in Wyoming. Hoagland has published seven collections of his essays. His most recent collection, *Tigers and Ice*, published in 1999, contains accounts of trips to India and Antarctica. The essays, like the majority of Hoagland's, mix astute observations of the natural world with thoughtful contemplation of his own life.

Hoagland's nature essays nearly always focus on the interactions between humans and nature. To him, there is no wilderness if there is no one there to observe it. In *American Nature Writers*, David W. Teague refers to a digression on "the American brand of walking" in one of Hoagland's best-known essays, "Walking the Dead Diamond River," which is collected in the 1973 book of the same name. In this digression Hoagland examines the manner in which modern Americans traverse a landscape. Hoagland explores people's relationships with the natural world, providing suggestions on how they might be improved. In this case, he believes that people should learn to travel more gracefully in nature. Teague writes, "In Hoagland's nature essays, then, wild things provide one of his subjects, but people invariably provide the other."

Although many of his essays focus on the natural world, Hoagland is not solely a wilderness writer. He admits to loving the city and is unique among nature writers in that his attention is not held by wilderness alone, but also is focused on humans and the cities they create. He has published essays with such titles as "New York Blues," "City Walking," and "City Rat." And, on the opening page of *Notes from the Century Before*, he writes that the only relief equal to leaving the city is the relief of coming home to it. Hoagland also continues to write fiction. In 1992, he published *The Final Fate of Alligators*, a collection of previously published short stories, and in 2001, his memoir *Compass Points: How I Lived*. He has received many awards for his literary accomplishments, including an O. Henry Award in 1971, a New York State Council on the Arts Award in 1972, a National Endowment for the Arts award in 1982, and a Lanna Foundation Award in 1993. Today, he lives in a country house in Vermont. He is twice divorced and has a daughter, Molly, from his second marriage.

BIBLIOGRAPHY

Hoagland, Edward, *Notes from the Century Before: A Journal from British Columbia*, 1969; Hoagland, Edward, *The Courage of Turtles*, 1993; Moritz, Charles, ed., *Current Biography Yearbook*, 1982; Teague, David W., "Edward Hoagland," *American Nature Writers*, John Elder, ed., 1996.

Hornaday, William Temple
(December 1, 1854–May 7, 1937)
Director of the New York Zoological Park, Wildlife Preservation Activist

William Temple Hornaday was an influential wildlife preservationist active early in the twentieth century. Through his post as director of the New York Zoological Park and member of the influential Boone and Crockett Club, Hornaday worked to save birds, bison, and seals from extinction. Hornaday also founded the Permanent Wild Life Fund (PWLF), which he controlled exclusively. Because of his uncompromising positions and his tendency toward racism, modern environmentalists have allowed Hornaday to fall into obscurity.

William Temple Hornaday was born on December 1, 1854, on his parents' Indiana farm near the town of Plainfield. As a child, his family moved to Iowa, where he roamed woods and marshes, hunting small game with his rifle. While studying zoology at Iowa State Agricultural College, he decided to become a naturalist and taught himself taxidermy. At the end of his sophomore year, he left Iowa for Ward's National Science Establishment in Rochester, New York, a supplier of mounted specimens for museums, where he perfected his taxidermy skills. Ward's sent him on a series of collecting expeditions throughout the 1870s. In 1882, Hornaday became chief taxidermist at the U.S. National Museum in Washington, D.C. He proposed that the National Museum include exhibits with live animals, and soon this idea evolved into a plan for a National Zoological Park.

Hornaday was appointed superintendent of the emerging National Zoo in 1888, but in 1890, after fighting with its board of directors about the zoo's layout, Hornaday quit his job and moved to Buffalo, New York, to work in real estate. He continued writing about taxidermy and wildlife and was offered a job directing the New York Zoological Park (also known as the Bronx Zoo) in 1896. From this influential position, Hornaday led many early-twentieth-century wildlife preservation battles. He became known for his all-or-nothing positions, for the urgency of his battles, and for his acid pen. In his numerous articles and books, Hornaday used xenophobia and racism to argue his views. During different struggles Hornaday vilified Africans, Jews, and recent immigrants from Italy and Germany. Perhaps for this reason, modern environmentalists do not honor him as they do other, less controversial turn-of-the-century conservationists, such as THEODORE ROOSEVELT, GIFFORD PINCHOT, and GEORGE BIRD GRINNELL.

One of Hornaday's early battles was against the decline of bird populations in the United States. Both for sport and market, hunters at the turn of the century were decimating birds valued for their plumes and their flesh. Innovations in technology and transportation were giving hunters advantages they had not enjoyed previously: for example, train routes and roads that penetrated formerly inaccessible wilderness, decoys and highly trained bird dogs, automatic rifles, and new telephone lines that made it easy for hunters to tell their friends where large flocks of birds were roosting. Hornaday by this time had totally renounced hunting and did not tolerate the activity, especially when practiced as an economic activity rather than for sport. He targeted "alien hunters"—mostly Italian immigrants—and successfully lobbied for the Armstrong Fire-Arms Law of 1905, which made it illegal for aliens to carry guns in public places. Hornaday also went after gun manufacturers for their increasingly deadly weapons, but this industry responded with its own proposals for smaller bag limits, shorter hunting seasons, and a new organization called the American Game Protective Association (AGPA). Although Hornaday and the AGPA both fought for the passage of the 1913 Migratory Bird Act, which assigned the Biological Survey the task of regulating the hunting of all migratory waterfowl, Hornaday abhorred the thought of working with the arms industry. When AGPA director John Burnham was nominated for membership in the Boone and Crockett Club, an exclusive organization of big game hunters and conservationists, Hornaday lobbied hard to exclude him.

Hornaday convinced the Boone and Crockett Club to organize the American Bison Society in 1905. This society facilitated the transfer of 15 bison from the New York Zoological Society to the federal government, which used them to produce a new, protected herd at the Wichita Mountains Wildlife Refuge in Oklahoma. This successful program, which Hornaday had first proposed when he was superintendent of the National Zoo, prevented the American bison from going extinct.

Another of Hornaday's causes was the protection of the northern fur seal, whose waterproof fur coat was highly valued. After the 1868 Alaska Purchase, the U.S. government leased hunting privileges on the Pribilof Islands, where the seals bred. The companies that signed contracts with the government were prohibited from killing female seals, but other parties were allowed to hunt the seals from boats at least three miles away from the islands, and these hunters shot the seals indiscriminately. By 1909, the seals' numbers had fallen to about 150,000, and their extinction seemed imminent. Hornaday called his contacts in Congress and gave a fiery, fact-filled speech to the Senate Committee on the Conservation of Natural Resources. The Committee asked Secretary of Commerce and Labor Charles Nagel to cease the hunting contracts. Instead of halting the killing, however, Nagel had the Bureau of Fisheries carry out the 1910 hunt, killing 12,000 seals, of which 8,000 were cubs. Nagel then tried to suppress Hornaday's outraged response. Hornaday published a booklet of their correspondence, including Nagel's threats of suppression, and shocked congressmen passed a law that put a five-year stop on the seal hunt. Hornaday also successfully urged the government to sign a treaty with Great Britain, Russia, and Japan in 1911 to end their seal hunts.

Hornaday remained at the New York Zoological Gardens until his retirement in 1926. He founded the Permanent Wild Life Fund in 1913, convincing Henry Ford, Andrew Carnegie, and George Eastman to contribute to a $100,000 endowment. He made all the decisions at the PWLF, using it as a vehicle for the preservationist lobbying that he could not do with funds from the Zoo. Hornaday continued as chief administrator of the PWLF until his death on May 7, 1937, in Stamford, Connecticut.

BIBLIOGRAPHY

Fox, Stephen, *The American Conservation Movement: John Muir and His Legacy*, 1986; Graham, Frank, Jr., *Man's Dominion: The Story of Conservation in America*, 1971; Hornaday, William Temple, *Wild Life Conservation in Theory and Practice*, 1914; Stroud, Richard,

National Leaders of American Conservation, 1985.

House, Donna
Botanist

"All seeds have stories. The evolution of stories, knowledge, and memories of our ancestors are embedded in them."
—Donna House

Donna House, Dineh (Navajo) and Oneida, integrates traditional knowledge and practices with western science in an attempt to mitigate the impact of human activity on the earth. In all of her multifaceted work—which has included surveying and protecting rare and endangered species on Native land, designing landscapes for museums that celebrate Indigenous People's relationships with the land, helping develop capacity in local Indigenous organizations and assisting communities in protecting traditional plant gathering sites, and working with students at Northern New Mexico Community College (NNMCC) to design a solar car from theory to 1999 Sunrayce—she strives to maintain the philosophy, values, and ethics of her Indigenous heritage.

Donna House, who sees herself as a reflection of her ancestors, all the elements that make up the earth, the millennia of her culture, and the ideas of Native American philosopher and historian Vine Deloria Jr., prefers to present herself in the Dineh way, by first introducing her ancestors. One pair of her maternal great grandparents was forced on the 1864 Long Walk to Fort Sumner, during which thousands of Dineh people perished as they were forced to march to a prison at Fort Sumner in southern New Mexico. The other pair hid in the mountains to escape the forced march.

Her Dineh maternal grandparents were Carrie Nacly (Towering House clan) and Henry Taliman Sr. (Honeycomb House People clan). Her paternal grandparents met at an Indian boarding school in Phoenix; her Dineh grandfather had been abducted by the Bureau school's recruiters, then kept at the school for a decade. His Dineh name was unpronounceable in English, so a girl from the Oneida Turtle Clan, Elizabeth House, gave him her last name and called him Albert. Later, they married and settled on the edge of the Dineh reservation. Donna is the daughter of Carolyn Taliman House (Dineh Towering House Clan) and John House (Oneida Turtle Clan). She was raised in her Dineh maternal Towering House clan, accompanying her grandparents and other members of the community as they gathered plants for food and medicine; she was included in songs, stories, and dances about the plants and animals populating their homeland.

House came to respect the traditional Dineh way of being and seeing the world. She accepts and puts into practice the Dineh view of all beings on earth—plants, animals, and elements such as water and stone—as people, meriting respect just as one would pay another person.

When House entered the University of Utah, she tried to fulfill the requirements of her biology courses without violating her cultural values and ethics. When she was assigned the task of preparing an insect collection for entomology class, House carefully sought out insects that had died of other causes along the Wasatch Mountains. This innovative attitude—meeting the requirements of science while respecting traditional Indigenous knowledge and practice—has allowed House to straddle two worlds and to serve them both. While studying at the University of Utah, House organized and secured funds for a four-day conference there in 1983, during which Utah state and Native government agencies explored how they could collaborate on environmental issues that concerned them both. The meeting spawned a Utah Indian Task Force to address environmental issues.

Upon graduating with a B.A. in environmental science, House accepted a position as coordinator and botanist for the Nature Conservancy's Navajo Natural Heritage Program, the first U.S. program to inventory rare and endangered species on Indian land. She directed, inventoried and worked with communities to develop environmental protection strategies. House then went on to work as a botanical consultant from 1987 until early 1989, surveying and monitoring federally listed threatened and endangered plant species on Native lands and collecting data on economic and cultural use of threatened flora in the U.S. Southwest.

House worked deep in the conflicts of protecting endangered species and culturally rare species on Indian and federal lands. In 1989, the Nature Conservancy asked House to work on protecting one of the rarest plants in Arizona endemic to the Tohono O'odham Nation. House served first as western regional tribal lands protection planner and then in 1991 as western regional tribal lands program director. This one-person program worked to conserve and protect habitat of endangered and threatened species by combining traditional Native knowledge, ethics, values, and practices with scientific information about conservation. In addition to creating a network of Indigenous organizations, scientists, and federal and state land management decision makers, House conducted plant surveys, taught Native communities about environmental protection laws, and helped them develop programs to protect and conserve biological diversity on their lands—in return protecting Native lifeways.

She collaborated with a team of Utah-based botanists to produce *Utah: Threatened, Endangered, and Sensitive Plant Field Guide* in 1991, a book that has been useful to Native caretakers of these plants throughout the region. House's method for working with local Native communities is described in a 1992 Nature Conservancy article: "She makes her pitch at tribal meetings, weaving biological facts and cultural concerns, then waits for someone to come forward and take up the message."

House has recruited such Native conservationists as Tohono O'odham (Papago) Jefford Francisco, a volunteer caretaker of Kearney's blue-star, once considered by federal officials the rarest plant in Arizona. Dineh Jane Nez looks after Navajo sedge, an endangered broomlike grass that grows mostly on the sides of cliffs. In the Nature Conservancy article, Nez articulates a conservation ethic that House believes is an important aspect of Native culture, that to her, the sedge represents "home ... It's part of you. And if [the plant] should disappear a part of you goes, too." House feels that the relationships that Native people have developed over thousands of years with their land are why Indian reservations boast the most pristine landscapes and cleanest water in the country. She believes that protecting the culture, songs, languages, prayers, traditions, and traditional lifeways of Native people is absolutely necessary for the protection of biological diversity.

Although her work revolves around Indigenous Knowledge of *Place*, she continues to challenge the status quo attitude toward protecting biodiversity. Throughout the decades of work, she notes western theories and amendments, and gives her greater respect to Indigenous knowledge, practice and songs.

In 1994, House began to consult and independently research the environmental issues, and policies of Indigenous peoples in regards to Indigenous Traditional Knowledge. House worked as a botanical consultant for the

Smithsonian Institution's National Museum of the American Indian project. This museum, the most recent one to be built on the Washington, D.C., mall, between the Capitol and the National Air and Space Museum, opened in 2004. She and other museum designers met with representatives of Indigenous peoples throughout the hemisphere and incorporated their ideas in determining which cultural information and artifacts to share.

House, one of the team designers, introduced and implemented native plants of the region into habitats/landscape to respect living objects, Indigenous contributions; and educate the public that the earth is alive and land has memory.

The landscaping surrounding the museum, for which House is key designer, is an essential aspect of the design of the museum as a whole. The museum brochure explains that "The grounds honor local Native people by featuring four environments Indigenous to the Chesapeake Bay region ...[and] Cardinal Direction Marker stones from Maryland, Canada, Hawai'i, and Chile share the landscape with more than 40 Grandfather Rocks, reminders of the longevity of Native Americans' relationship to the natural world."

In addition to her hemispheric-level work, House is very active locally. She volunteers at NNMCC in Española, New Mexico, assisting a group of students—mostly Hispanos and Native Americans, immersed in the region's lowrider culture—on the design of a flawless solar-powered car. Neither House nor the students had training in engineering, yet they recruited investors in the project, researched mechanics and solar energy, networked with engineering students and others with specific fields of expertise, and built El Águila, an entrant in the 1999 Sunrayce, a 1,425-mile race from Washington, D.C., to Disney World's Epcot Center, sponsored by General Motors. Although El Águila suffered a solar array battery problem and was disqualified in the second round, House's students were proud to be one of only three community college teams among a field of competitors that included prestigious private and technical universities. House was the only adviser who was a woman of color. A by-product of this project is that the participants have begun to promote the use of solar and other alternative energy sources in their community and at local schools. House sees this project as one that embodies her view of the world as a giant ecosystem, with each member contributing with his or her special gift.

House is a member of the U.S. Fish and Wildlife Service Recovery Team for Endangered Plant Species in Region 2. She is a past member of the American Association for the Advancement of Science's advisory board on the Collaboration for Equity: Women in Science Initiative. She chaired the Utah Endangered and Sensitive Plant Interagency Committee, has been a board member of Tohono O'odham Soil and Water District in Sell, Arizona, and has served on the board of trustees for the Wheelwright Museum of the American Indian. She was activist-in-residence at the A. E. Havens Center for Study of Social Structure and Social Change at the University of Wisconsin, Madison, in 1991 and was the Richard Thompson Memorial Lecturer (an honor dedicated to the perpetuation of moral concerns and humanistic values) at Iowa State University in 1996. She and artist Truman Lowe contributed an installation to the 2006 exhibit "Between the Lakes: Artists Respond to Madison" at the Madison Museum of Contemporary Art, which addressed the loss of biodiversity, life, culture and experience that marks the landscape of the Upper Midwest.

House was honored in 2006 with the American Society of Landscape Architects Travel Award for the National Museum of American Indian landscape; in 2004, the Center of Southwest Studies and Navajo Studies awarded her Recognition for Protecting and Keeping Our Mother Earth Beautiful and Bountiful For All; and in 2001 she received The American Society of Landscape Architects Merit Award with Jones and Jones Architecture for a highway design acknowledging biological and cultural significant sites.

House migrates between a farm along the Río Grande in Northern New Mexico and Teelch'int'í (Cattails Standing in a Row), her ancestral homeland on the Navajo Nation.

BIBLIOGRAPHY
Haithman, Diane, "A Legacy Reclaimed," Los Angeles Times, 2000; "MMOCA: Donna House," www.mmoca.org/exhibitions/exhibitdetails/betweenthelakes/house_00.php; Oldfield, Margery L., and Janis Alcorn, eds., Biodiversity: Culture, Conservation, and Ecodevelopment, 1991; Stolzenburg, William, "Sacred Peaks, Common Grounds," Nature Conservancy, 1992; Young, Wendy, "Navajo Woman Is 'Key Designer' for New Washington Museum," Navajo Times, 1999.

Huerta, Dolores
(April 10, 1930–)
Cofounder of United Farm Workers

A cofounder of the United Farm Workers (UFW) in the 1960s, Dolores Huerta has played numerous pivotal roles in organizing and representing California's farmworkers, many of them migrants, who are generally underpaid and exposed to toxic agrochemicals and who endure unhealthy living conditions. From 1965 to 1970, a UFW table grape and wine boycott brought California's powerful agribusiness interests to the negotiating table, where Huerta helped mediate the first collective bargaining agreement for farmworkers. The contract objective was to improve not only the workers' wages and job security but also community and workplace environments, including sanitation and reduction of exposure to agricultural insecticides. In the years since, Huerta has directed the UFW's political and lobbying efforts, with the use of pesticides still at the forefront of battles waged between the union and growers.

Dolores Huerta was born Dolores Fernández in the small mining town of Dawson, New Mexico, on April 10, 1930. Her father was a coal miner, field-worker, union activist, and state assemblyman. Her parents divorced when she was five, and her mother moved to the agricultural community of Stockton, California. Huerta's mother supported three children as a waitress, cannery worker, and cook before buying and operating a small hotel and restaurant, where she frequently took in migrant farmworker families. That charity inspired Huerta, as did her mother's activities with women's groups providing assistance to the needy. Although she had infrequent contact with her father—who supplemented his miner's wages with migrant labor during beet harvests—Huerta was nevertheless profoundly proud of and influenced by his indignation over poor working conditions and his contributions as secretary-treasurer of a branch of the Congress of Industrial Organizations (CIO).

Huerta married a Stockton High School classmate in 1950 and gave birth to two daughters. The marriage did not last. As a single mother, Huerta worked and attended Stockton College, where she earned a teaching degree. Yet teaching frustrated her: "I couldn't stand seeing kids come to class hungry and needing shoes. I thought I could do more by organizing farm workers than by try-

United Farm Workers co-founder, Dolores Huerta (center) and UFW supporters, applaud after a farm labor bill was passed by the state Assembly at the California state Capitol Aug. 30, 2002. (AP Images/Rich Pedroncelli)

ing to teach their hungry children," she told the San Diego *Union-Tribune* in 1995.

In 1955, she met Fred Ross, an organizer with the Community Service Organization (CSO). Although initially reluctant, Huerta was persuaded to join the CSO because of its Los Angeles successes in building health clinics and registering voters. She became a founding member of the Stockton branch, and as a CSO lobbyist, she helped push through legislation that included requiring businesses to provide pensions to legal immigrants. She worked closely with CÉSAR CHÁVEZ, who became the organization's general director in 1958. By 1962, Chávez had left the CSO and founded the National Farm Workers Association (NFWA). Huerta joined him two years later, and together they chose grape pickers as their first group to organize. There had never before been a systematic effort to improve the labor and wage conditions of field-workers, who were considered too powerless to extract meaningful concessions from growers. Huerta and Chávez confronted a labor force suffering from severe underemployment, low wages, and chronic ill health, owing to pesticide poisoning and such unsanitary living conditions as open sewers and polluted drinking water.

Despite California Department of Food and Agriculture (CDFA) regulations, which extended beyond crop residue and sought to protect birds, mammals, and state waters, any concerns about worker exposure were discredited by all relevant California regulatory bodies. The CDFA did require growers to warn workers of dangers when fields had been sprayed, but it did not restrict growers from sending laborers into contaminated fields. Chemical burns, eye injuries, lung disease, systemic poisoning, cancer, and birth defects were among the deadly hazards affecting farmworkers exposed to pesticides. Most state safety efforts required that workers, rather than growers, carry the entire responsibility for their own welfare. The NFWA, which by 1966 had merged with another farmworkers union to become the United Farm Workers Organizing Committee (UFWOC), initiated lawsuits against individual growers and took an unflinching stance against pesticides.

While consumers might have little interest in the welfare of farmworkers, Huerta and Chávez understood that the purity of their food would be of great concern. In addition to mobilizing a strike against grape growers in the San Joaquin Valley, which eventually extended to the Coachella Valley of southern California, they called for a national boycott of table grapes and wine. Revealing information about pesticide dangers to the public and encouraging safety codes and regulations proved important leverage. Right-to-know laws, essential to the environmental battle, were rare in the 1960s. With health professionals, including volunteer nurse MARION MOSES, Huerta and Chávez began to amass a huge database on health and safety issues for both workers and consumers. Injuries to workers from sulphur, dichlordiphenyltrichlor (DDT), parathion, and other pesticides were drastically underreported, but so were the dangers to the public of pesticides leaking into the food chain. The UFWOC took an active stance in favor of regulations and against a policy of secrecy about the poisons employed by agroindustry.

In 1966, Huerta negotiated the UFWOC's first contract with Schenly Wine Company. She continued to direct the boycott until sales of grapes fell so drastically that on July 29, 1970, Delano-area growers capitulated en masse. The contracts, again negotiated by Huerta, provided a myriad of first-time benefits for grape workers. Union membership swelled to an all-time high of 50,000 members. In 1973, the newly renamed United Farm Workers (UFW) of America was chartered as an independent affiliate of the American Federation of Labor–Congress of Industrial Organizations (AFL-CIO).

Successive UFW strikes against lettuce producers and other agroindustries resulted in the 1975 passage of the Agricultural Labor Relations Act by the California legislature, which guaranteed the rights of California farmworkers to organize and hold elections for union representation. Huerta led the way for further major legislation, such as the removal of citizenship requirements for public assistance, disability, and unemployment benefits for farmworkers and the enactment for Aid to Dependent Children.

In a frequently cited quotation of 1970, Chávez described Huerta as "totally fearless, both mentally and physically." Through the births of nine more children, and more than 22 arrests, Huerta never rested in the fight for La Causa (the farmworker cause). In 1988, she was attacked by a police officer as she was demonstrating in front of the St. Francis Hotel in San Francisco. The incident left her with six broken bones and a ruptured spleen. As a result, the city agreed to change crowd control procedures, eliminating the presence of Special Weapons and Tactics (SWAT) teams at demonstrations. When Gov. Pete Wilson pushed through legislation in 1996 for the extension of the use of methyl bromide, a deadly, odorless gas used as a pesticide on strawberries, Huerta, at age 66, spearheaded the UFW campaign to ban its use.

Currently, Huerta is President of the Dolores Huerta Foundation, which works in California's Central Valley "to inspire and motivate people to organize sustainable communities to attain social justice." The Foundation encourages the formation of Vecinos Unidos chapters, which identify problems in their neighborhood and propose solutions to them, disseminate information, and activate the community. This program has enjoyed many successes in improvement of school and municipal infrastructure for children, holding community clean-ups, and holding regular parent education meetings, among other efforts.

In addition to fighting for farmworkers' and community causes, Huerta has campaigned to get more women elected to public office in California. She has sat on the boards of the Feminist Majority, Latinas for Choice, the California Labor Federation, and National Farm Workers Service Center, among others. With Chávez, she helped create the Farm Workers Credit Union and the Juan De La Cruz Farm Worker Pension Fund. She has served as vice president of the Coalition of Labor Union Women and the California AFL-CIO.

In 1993, the year of Chávez's death, Huerta received the American Civil Liberties Union Roger Baldwin Medal of Liberty Award and the Eugene Debs Outstanding American Award and was inducted into the National Women's Hall of Fame. She was named one of *Ms. Magazine*'s three "Women of the Year" in 1998 and one of *Ladies Home Journal*'s "100 Most Important Women of the 20th Century."

She received the Eleanor D. Roosevelt Human Rights Award the same year, and the Nation/Puffin Award for Creative Citizenship in 2002. Six schools in California, Texas and Colorado have been named for her.

BIBLIOGRAPHY

"Dolores Huerta Foundation," www.doloreshuerta.org; Ferris, Susan, and Richard Sandoval, *The Fight in the Fields: César Chávez and the Farmworkers Movement*, 1997; Genasci, Lisa, "Dolores Huerta: She, Too, Founded UFW, but Still Toils in Chávez' Shadow," *San Diego Union Tribune*, 1995; Griswold del Castillo, Richard, and Richard Garcia, *César Chávez, A Triumph of the Spirit*, 1995; Pulido, Laura, *Environment and Economic Justice, Two Chicano Struggles in the Southwest*, 1996; Telgen, Diana, Jim Kamp, and Eva M. Neito, *Notable Hispanic American Women*, 1993; United Farm Workers, www.ufw.org.

American Environmental Leaders

From Colonial Times to the Present

Ickes, Harold
(March 15, 1874–February 3, 1952)
Secretary of the Interior

Harold Ickes was secretary of the interior between 1933 and 1945 under Presidents FRANKLIN D. ROOSEVELT and Harry Truman. During his term, the longest ever for a secretary of the interior, the Civilian Conservation Corps (CCC) was mobilized to build campgrounds, trails, roads, and phone lines in national parks; the Soil Conservation Service combated the erosion problem that had caused the Midwest dust bowl; and huge public works projects began taking shape. Although the nation was challenged by the Great Depression and World War II, Ickes nevertheless managed to keep conservation as one of the prioritized items on President Roosevelt's list. He was a thinker ahead of his time, warning the nation that if the environment were allowed to deteriorate, huge public expenditures would be necessary to remedy the resulting problems.

Harold LeClair Ickes was born on March 15, 1874, in Frankstown Township, Pennsylvania. His father was an abusive alcoholic, and his mother died when he was 16 years old. Ickes was sent to Chicago to live with his aunt. He studied at the University of Chicago, teaching night school and scrimping on luxuries such as new clothes and using public transportation to make ends meet. He graduated with a B.A. in 1897 but did not participate in the graduation ceremony because he was embarrassed by his shabby clothes. He learned how to write and how Chicago's notorious political machine worked while reporting for the *Chicago Record*. He sided with the poor but was also intrigued by the political bosses. Once he decided to devote himself to political reform, he realized that he would be much better prepared with a law degree. So he studied for one at the University of Chicago, graduating with honors in 1907. Dedicating himself to political reform became more possible after his 1911 marriage to Anna Wilmarth Thompson, whose family's money allowed him to practice law less and politics more.

Ickes was an enthusiastic supporter of Pres. THEODORE ROOSEVELT, but began to court reformist Democrats after Roosevelt's death. He managed the National Progressive League, which supported Franklin D. Roosevelt during the 1932 election. Roosevelt surprised the country by appointing Ickes, who had very little previous experience with the federal government, as secretary of the interior.

Immediately Ickes began to distinguish himself as an effective administrator. As secretary of the interior, he had to oversee the National Park Service, the Bureau of Indian Affairs, the Bureau of Mines, government buildings in Washington, D.C., the General Land Office, the Geological Survey, and more. Ickes made conservationist allies in these offices, depending upon their recommendations for his decisions. He concurred with his first National Park Service director, HORACE ALBRIGHT, who had been with the National Park Service since its 1916 inception, that national parks should be left in as natural a state as possible. His decisive leadership prevented a later National Park Service director from building the infamous Skyline Drive along the crest of Great Smoky National Park. He worked closely with Bureau of Indian Affairs forestry director ROBERT MARSHALL to protect wilderness on Indian reservations from roads and development. Just weeks before the United States entered World War II, Ickes refused to allow the army to use Henry Lake, Utah, as a firing range because the soldiers' activity would threaten the endangered trumpeter swans.

But Ickes was not purely preservationist. Roosevelt's pet project was the Civilian Conservation Corps, which put over two and a

Commissioner John S. Collier stands with the chiefs of the Flathead Indian Tribe as Secretary of Interior, Harold Ickes (seated) signs into law the Wheeler-Hobard bill that provides for Indian self-rule rather than being under the direction of the Bureau of Indian Affairs. (AP Images).

half million young men to work in national forests and national parks and on Army Corps of Engineers construction projects. Under Ickes's supervision, the CCC built campgrounds, trails, roads, and phone lines in national parks. This was done primarily in order to provide jobs for young unemployed men, but also to prepare national parks for more visitors, who would contribute to the economic development of nearby towns. Ickes also oversaw another of Roosevelt's New Deal programs, the Public Works Administration. The projects that Ickes managed included the construction of Hoover Dam, the water system for Denver, Colorado, and the electrification of the Pennsylvania Railroad between Washington, D.C., and New York City.

Ickes combined his concerns for conservation and development when he founded the Soil Conservation Service and appointed soil scientist HUGH HAMMOND BENNETT to head it. Unrestricted livestock grazing on public lands was a main culprit in the Dust Bowl. Ickes was able to address the problem thanks to a bill introduced by Colorado congressman Edward Taylor, which gave the secretary of the interior the power to establish grazing districts and sell grazing permits. This measure decreased erosion and has allowed for some recovery on federal lands.

Ickes's primary administrative goal while secretary of the interior was to consolidate all national resources within the Department of the Interior. He felt that conservation of national forests—which were managed by the Department of Agriculture—would be more successful and efficient if they were managed by the same department that took care of other natural resources, such as the national parks. His struggle, culminating unsuccessfully in 1939, earned him enemies in the U.S. Forest Service and Department of Agriculture.

Ickes never fully recovered from his failure to unite the natural resources within the Department of the Interior. After that setback and further difficulties that arose after Franklin D. Roosevelt died and left a less-conservationist Harry Truman to take over, Ickes resigned from his post.

Ickes's personality is highlighted whenever his name comes up in environmental histories. He was a scrappy, cantankerous man, who trusted no one and was the frequent victim of a paranoid imagination. His caricature-like personality amused his colleagues, however. Franklin D. Roosevelt nicknamed him "Donald Duck," and Robert Marshall recalled being more entertained than disturbed once while Ickes was berating him for some official misbehavior. Despite his crusty personality, however, Ickes was generous and liberal in his thoughts and actions. In the pre–civil rights years of the 1930s, Ickes hired African Americans for important positions in the Department of the Interior and desegregated the Department cafeteria. He believed that Indians had a right to their own culture, was in favor of their being allowed to own land communally, and was against Indian children's being taken from their families in order to attend boarding schools.

In 1945, after his resignation, Ickes moved with his second wife, Jane Dahlman, and their two small children to a farm in Maryland. Ickes continued to write for such national publications as the *New York Post* and the *New Republic*, but according to Dahlman, his lively spirit withered after he left office. He died on February 3, 1952, in Washington, D.C.

BIBLIOGRAPHY
Clarke, Jeanne Nienaber, *Roosevelt's Warrior: Harold L. Ickes and the New Deal*, 1996; Glover, James M., *A Wilderness Original: The Life of Bob Marshall*, 1986; Ickes, Harold, *The Autobiography of a Curmudgeon*, 1943; Strong, Douglas H., *Dreamers & Defenders: American Conservationists*, 1988; Watkins, T. L., *Righteous Pilgrim: The Life and Times of Harold L. Ickes, 1874–1952*, 1990.

Ingram, Helen
(July 12, 1937–)
Public and Environmental Policy Specialist

Known for her public policy research, particularly in relation to resource-use issues, professor and researcher Helen Ingram has made significant contributions to the understanding of federal, state, and local policy design regarding water conservation and American Indian water rights. She has also focused closely on environmental problems along the U.S.-Mexico border region, including issues of water allocation and economic development. Ingram directed the Udall Center for Studies in Public Policy, an organization dedicated to finding new approaches to serious policy issues in the southwest, including American Indian rights, environmental conflict resolution, and U.S.-Mexico border dynamics. She also taught in the political science department at the University of Arizona in Tucson and at the University of California, Irvine.

Helen Hill Ingram was born on July 12, 1937, in Denver, Colorado, to Oliver Weldon Hill, a salesman, and Hazel Margaret (Wickard) Hill, a teacher. She graduated from Oberlin College in 1959, with a B.A. in government. In 1963 she began working as assistant professor of political science at the University of New Mexico in Albuquerque, where she stayed until 1969—meanwhile earning her Ph.D. from Columbia University in 1967. She then served on the political science staff at the National Water Commission in Arlington, Virginia, for two years, before taking a position of associate professor at the University of Arizona in Tucson. During the next few years she also worked at the Institute of Government Research, first as associate director, then by 1974 as director, a post she held until 1977. In that year, Ingram accepted a two-year senior fellowship at the Washington, D.C.–based Resources for the Future. In 1979, she became professor of political science at the University of Arizona and continued to teach there until 1996.

From 1981 to 1983, Ingram served as a consultant for the Office of Technology Assessment in Washington, D.C. She had become interested in water resources in arid environments and in how water often acts as an indicator of how wealth, political power, and economic development are distributed. Early in her research and writing she mainly explored patterns of national politics and the mechanisms by which water resource projects were authorized and funded at the federal level. But her interests began shifting to state and local water policy and its impact on conservation and American Indian water rights, and she especially began to focus on the U.S.-Mexico border region. From 1988 until 1996, Ingram served as director of the Udall Center for Studies in Public Policy, which had been established in 1987 through the University of Arizona. The center sponsors interdisciplinary research that informs policy-making and specializes in issues involving the environment and natural resources, American Indian governance, the U.S.-Mexico border, and economic development. Part of Ingram's work at the Udall Center involved attempting to ameliorate problems in the border region, such as natural resource exploitation and environmental degradation, by rethinking strategies for policy research and implementation so that they respond to the increasing urbanization and economic and political dynamics of the area.

Ingram left the University of Arizona in 1995 to become the Warmington Endowed Chair at the University of California at Irvine, where she held a joint appointment in the Department of Planning, Policy and Design; Criminology, Law and Society; and Political Science. She retired in 2007.

Among the many books on water and natural resource policy that she has authored or edited, some of the more recent include *Routing the Opposition: Social Movements, Public Policy, and Democracy* (2005), *Deserving and Entitled: Social Constructions and Public Policy* (2005), *Reflections on Water: New Approaches to Transboundary Conflicts and Cooperation* (2001), and *Policy Design for Democracy* (1997). She has also contributed numerous articles and reviews to scholarly journals. She is the recipient of many honors and awards, including the Mentor Award, Public Policy Section, American Political Science Association (2007) and the Friends of Universities Council on Water Resources Certificate of Appreciation for her vision and leadership in the advancement of water resources education and research (1998), the Thomas R. Dye Service Award (1997) and the Howard Laswell Award (1995), both from the Policy Studies Organization.

BIBLIOGRAPHY

"Helen Ingram, School of Social Ecology," www.socialecology.uci.edu/faculty/hingram; Ingram, Helen, and F. Lee Brown, *Water and Poverty*, 1987; Ingram, Helen, Nancy K. Laney, and David M. Gillilan, *Divided Waters: Bridging the U.S.-Mexico Border*, 1995; Mumme, Stephen P., "Divided Waters: Bridging the U.S.-Mexico Border," *American Political Science Review*, 1996; Schneider, Anne Larason, and Helen Ingram, *Policy Design for Democracy*, 1997.

American Environmental Leaders

From Colonial Times to the Present

Jackson, Henry
(May 31, 1912–September 1, 1983)
U.S. Senator from Washington

A member of Congress for more than 40 years, Sen. Henry "Scoop" Jackson helped author a number of important pieces of environmental legislation, most notably the landmark National Environmental Policy Act of 1969 (NEPA). He also helped create the Big Cypress National Preserve in Florida, Washington's North Cascades National Park, and California's Redwood National Park. He chaired the Senate Committee on Interior and Insular Affairs and its successor, the Committee on Energy and Natural Resources, from 1963 to 1980 and played a leading role in conservation and energy legislation.

Henry Martin Jackson was born in Everett, Washington, on May 31, 1912, son of Norwegian immigrants. Although he earned a reputation for hard work as a newspaper carrier, his nickname "Scoop" had nothing to do with journalism. One of his sisters gave him the name because she thought he resembled a comic strip character known for getting others to do his work for him. Jackson graduated from Everett High School in 1930 and from the University of Washington's law school in 1935. In 1938 he ran a successful campaign for prosecuting attorney of Snohomish County. As prosecutor he gained attention for tough treatment of gamblers and bootleggers, and in 1940 he parlayed this attention into his election to the U.S. House of Representatives from Washington's Second District. During his time in the House, Jackson concentrated on military affairs and became an expert on nuclear energy. He enlisted in the military and served in World War II until he was recalled to Congress by Pres. FRANKLIN D. ROOSEVELT. Jackson accompanied the army during the liberation of Buchenwald, an experience that shaped his lifelong fight for Israel's security and the rights of Jews in the Soviet Union. While in the House, he became an opponent of the House Un-American Activities Committee and helped craft public land use policy, vital to his Western constituents.

In 1952, a year in which Republicans dominated Congress and Eisenhower was president, Jackson was one of the relatively few new Democrats elected to the Senate. He served on the Armed Services Committee and came to be known as "the Senator from Boeing" and "thc hawk's hawk" because of his unwavering support for the Washington defense contractor and funding requests of the Pentagon. On other issues he was called "the liberal's liberal," backing labor rights, public education, and other social welfare programs. Jackson was an early critic of Sen. Joseph McCarthy and served on the committee that conducted the Army-McCarthy hearings. Jackson also authored the legislation that led to statehood for Alaska and Hawaii.

As a freshman senator, Jackson was appointed to the Interior Committee, where he had jurisdiction over a number of environmental issues important to his constituents, including mining, hydroelectric power development, and national parks. As he rose through the ranks of Senate seniority, Jackson was dubbed, along with Sen. Warren Magnuson, one of the "Gold Dust Twins" of Washington State, able to bring home a wealth of federal dollars. Jackson pushed through a number of hydroelectric projects and was also active in several fights to preserve wilderness areas. His role in the creation of North Cascades National Park exemplifies his approach to conservation. The park in Washington was important to Jackson because he had hiked there as a boy and knew its beauty firsthand. In 1963 President Kennedy appointed a team to study the possibility of creating a park in the northern Cascades, and the team recommended a 700,000-acre site. A group of powerful interests—the Seattle power company, truckers, lumber companies, and those with mining claims—opposed the park. Jackson negotiated a compromise in which a smaller, 500,000-acre park was created. Jackson's version left a corridor in which it was still theoretically possible to mine and log, appeasing economic interests, but which made those activities nearly impossible because of the configuration of the terrain. Jackson was, first and foremost, a politician, master of the science of compromise and deal making.

Jackson's most important environmental legislation was the National Environmental Policy Act, drafted by consultant to the Senate Committee on Interior and Insular Affairs LYNTON CALDWELL, and often called the nation's environmental Magna Carta. In 1959, Sen. James Murray of Montana had introduced a bill called the Resources and Conservation Act. Although it was never passed, the bill contained several provisions later adopted by NEPA, including a declaration of conservation policy and the creation of an advisory council. Various advances in environmental policy were proposed throughout the 1960s, but it was not until 1969 that enough national momentum existed to enact sweeping legislation. In 1969, Jackson introduced S. 1075. The bill was passed out of the Interior Committee on July 9 and passed without further debate or amendment the following day. Meanwhile, similar legislation, introduced by Congressman JOHN DINGELL of Michigan, was pending in the House but was held up in procedural delays. In December 1969, a House-Senate Conference Committee meeting resolved differences between the two bills, and on January 1, 1970, President Nixon signed NEPA into law. The bill stated broad principles of the federal government's role as environmental steward, including the responsibility to "assure for all Americans safe, healthful, productive, and aesthetically and culturally pleasing surroundings" and to "enhance the quality of renewable resources and approach the maximum attainable recycling of depletable resources." One important practical result of NEPA was the creation of the Council on Environmental Quality (CEQ). Modeled after the Council of Economic Advisors, the CEQ was located within the Executive Office of the President and charged with submitting an annual report on the state of the nation's environments. A second provision required all federal agencies to submit an environmental impact statement (EIS) before proceeding with any action "significantly affecting the quality of the human environment." This requirement proved a potent weapon in the hands of environmentalists, who were able to use the courts to stop possibly destructive actions. By 1975, 119 injunctions had been issued on the basis of agencies' failing to complete the appropriate EIS. NEPA and its EIS requirements continue to direct federal policy today, and in fact some credit the act for initiating the concept of environmental assessment policy worldwide.

Jackson's environmental legacy includes a number of other legislative achievements. He was a key supporter of the Wilderness Act of 1964. He was instrumental in the establishment of the Land and Water Conservation Fund, the National Wilderness Preservation System, the Nationwide System of Trails, and the System of Wild and Scenic Rivers. He also helped enact the Surface Mining Control and Reclamation Act, the Alaska National Interest Lands Conservation Act, and the Youth Conservation Corps (now called the Student Conservation Association).

Henry Jackson died on September 1, 1983, at his home in Everett, Washington, while still serving in the Senate. In his remarks at the funeral, Robert M. Humphrey said Jackson "was an environmentalist long before it became fashionable." The Henry M. Jackson Foundation was established in 1983, guided by Jackson's interests and values. The foundation makes grants in four principal areas: international affairs, public service, human rights, and the environment. In 1987 North Cascades National Park was officially dedicated to his memory.

BIBLIOGRAPHY

Canter, Larry, and Ray Clark, *Environmental Policy and NEPA*, 1997; "Henry M. Jackson Foundation," www.hmjackson.org; Kaufman, Robert Gordon, *Henry M. Jackson: a Life in Politics*, 2000; Larsen, Richard, and William Prochnau, *A Certain Democrat*, 1972; Ognibene, Peter, *Scoop: The Life and Politics of Henry M. Jackson*, 1975.

Jackson, Wes

(1936–)
Plant Geneticist, Founder and president of the Land Institute

Wes Jackson, a plant geneticist, is the founder and president of the Land Institute in Salina, Kansas, a research facility that experiments with modern crop-breeding techniques to produce high-yielding perennial grains. Jackson's new approach to agriculture, known as Natural Systems Agriculture (NSA), mimics the workings of natural ecosystems. Jackson is recognized internationally as a leader in the field of sustainable agriculture.

Sharon Wesley Jackson was born in 1936 on a farm in the Kansas River Valley near Topeka, Kansas. He earned a B.A. in biology from Kansas Wesleyan in 1958 and an M.A. in botany from the University of Kansas in 1960. In 1967, he received his Ph.D. in genetics from North Carolina State University. Jackson taught biology at Kansas Wesleyan before moving to Sacramento, California, to accept a job at California State University. There he created the environmental studies program and served as the department chair until 1976, when he left his tenured position. Jackson and his wife, Dana (since divorced), moved back to Kansas to pursue their interest in sustainable agriculture and alternative energy. The Jacksons established the Land Institute on 370 acres located 28 miles south of Salina along the Smoky Hill River. Concerned about soil erosion and depletion, Jackson began to focus on developing a new method of agriculture that would be less detrimental to the soil.

Wes Jackson (Photograph courtesy of The Land Institute)

His Natural Systems Agriculture, outlined in his 1980 book *New Roots for Agriculture*, is patterned after the natural ecosystem of the prairie. Jackson proposed an agricultural system based on perennial grains, reversing 10,000 years of plant breeding focused on high-yielding annuals. Unlike conventional crops, the grains would be planted in polyculture plots containing a mix of plant species. Pests and diseases that run rampant in monoculture fields planted with one plant species would be held in check by the variety of grains growing in close proximity. The fields would not require tilling, thus reducing a major cause of soil erosion. Modern crop-breeding techniques would be used to increase the yield of such native perennial crops as wild rye, Eastern gramagrass, and Illinois bundleflower. In recent years, staff scientists have been crossing domesticated, annual wheat and sunflower plants with their wild, perennial relatives, to create perennial hybrids.

In 1991, the Land Institute set aside 150 acres for a ten-year research and demonstration project; the Sunshine Farm Research Program was established to explore ways to reduce the ecological costs of farming. Sunshine Farm produced livestock and conventional crops without the use of fossil fuels, irrigation, or chemicals and used alternative sources of energy, including wind turbines, draft animals, and tractors powered with soy oil. Innovative management techniques were used to reduce the need for tillage, irrigation, and pest control. The last field season for Sunshine Farm was 2001; data analysis will reveal how much of the farm's productive capacity was devoted to fuel and fertility for the farm.

Jackson is known primarily for his research on perennial grains. However, under his leadership, the Land Institute has initiated programs in other areas, particularly environmental education. The Institute's Prairie Writers Circle contributes op-ed columns and essays about such topics as the problems of industrial agriculture, water quality, and biotechnology to newspapers around the country. Jackson's interest in the role of agriculture in the community led to the establishment of a Rural Community Studies Center in Matfield Green, a village in the Flint Hills about 100 miles southeast of Salina. Educators at the center, founded in 1999, work with local school districts to introduce ecology into the curriculum, with the goal of developing a place-based education. Scientists and historians assist rural communities in balancing economic, social, and environmental factors so that they can become self-sustaining, retaining their young people as well as their topsoil, clean air, and water.

Under Jackson's direction, the Land Institute has grown to include a scientific staff of eight, including plant breeders, an agroecologist, and a plant pathologist and has attracted the attention of researchers around the world. The Land Institute also offers graduate fellowships to young researchers. Funding projects in this nascent stage is literally providing "seed funding" for ideas that could take hold and be funded at a higher level by mainstream universities and research institutes later on in the researchers' careers. Nevertheless, Jackson has struggled to gain credibility for his studies; harvests of the perennial crops have been disappointing, with low yields and other problems. Jackson has also been criticized for failing to address practical issues such as how to harvest multicrop fields and market unfamiliar grains to consumers.

By the mid-1990s, the inability to produce quick, conclusive results led to a drop in funding from the foundations that support the Land Institute. In response, the institute began to develop joint programs with various academic institutes in an effort to build credibility and to bring in funding. One such partnership is the "plant materials centers" project created in conjunction with Kansas State University. Together they set up centers in various locations throughout the United States where ecologists, plant breeders, biotechnologists, and environmental historians apply NSA to various climates and local conditions.

Jackson's vision extends 25 to 50 years into the future. He acknowledges that reversing 10,000 years of domesticated agriculture is a monumental task that will require many years' work and the support of major academic institutions, agribusiness firms, and governmental agencies. Promising work on perennial grains has been done at Texas A & M and Washington State University and by Jackson's daughter, Laura, a biology professor at the University of Northern Iowa.

Wes Jackson has written many scientific papers, which have appeared in such publications as *Cereal Chemistry* and *Ecology* as well as the Institute publication *The Land Report*. Jackson collaborated with his friend WENDELL BERRY on a collection of essays, *Meeting the Expectations of the Land: Essays in Sustainable Agriculture and Stewardship* (it was coedited with Bruce Colman and published in 1984). Jackson was strongly influenced by Berry's idea of stewardship evolving out of an attachment to place. Jackson explored this idea further in *Becoming Native to This Place* (1994) and *Rooted in the Land: Essays on Community and Place*, edited by William Vitek (1996), pointing out the need to integrate agriculture, ecology, and the rural economy to create what he calls a "coherent community."

Jackson lives in Salina, Kansas, and takes pride in the fact that his grandchildren are the sixth generation of his family to live in Kansas. In 1990, he was named a Pew Conservation Scholar by the Pew Charitable Trusts. Jackson received a MacArthur "genius grant" in 1992 in recognition of his innovative ideas, far-reaching vision, and groundbreaking work. And he was recipient of the 2000 "alternative Nobel" prize, Sweden's Right Livelihood Award.

BIBLIOGRAPHY

Canine, Carl, "Wes Jackson," *Smithsonian*, 2005; Jackson, Wes, *Becoming Native to This Place*, 1994; Jackson, Wes, *New Roots for Agriculture*, 1980; "The Land Institute," www.landinstitute.org; Martin, Sam, "Defending Food: A Talk with Dr. Wes Jackson," *Mother Earth News*, 2000; McDaniel, Carl, *Wisdom for a livable planet: the visionary work of Terri Swearingen, Dave Foreman, Wes Jackson, Helena Norberg-Hodge, Werner Fornos, Herman Daly, Stephen Schneider, and David Orr*, 2005; Sanders, Scott Russell, "Lessons from the Land Institute," *Audubon*, 1999; Soule, Judith D., and Jon K. Piper, *Farming in Nature's Image: An Ecological Approach to Agriculture*, 1992.

Jacobson, Michael

(1943–)
Director of Center for Science in the Public Interest, Food Safety Advocate

Michael Jacobson is the Executive Director of the Center for Science in the Public Interest (CSPI). Referred to in the media as the "food police," CSPI is known for raising public awareness of high fat and calorie amounts in popular foods such as movie theater popcorn, and for advocacy of accurate nutrition labeling. Jacobson refers to the group as "food detectives" for their investigations into food additives, labeling and advertising, and social issues such as corporate financing of food research. CSPI strives to educate and support policy makers and the food industry, as well as raise consumer awareness to help people make healthy food choices at home and at restaurants.

Born in 1943, Jacobson was raised in Chicago, Illinois. He earned his Ph.D. in microbiology from the Massachusetts Institute of Technology in 1969. After graduation he decided to use his knowledge and experience to work for health and environmental issues at RALPH NADER'S Center for the Study of Responsive Law, and contributed to a book on food additives.

In February of 1971, Jacobson co-founded CSPI with fellow Nader coworkers, meteorologist James Sullivan and chemist Albert Fritsch. CSPI was founded to encourage scientists to become more socially involved in addressing health and environmental problems through improved government policies and corporate practices. The organization's original focus was threefold with Jacobson working on food issues, Fritsch focusing on toxic chemicals, and Sullivan studying transportation and pollution. After Sullivan and Fritsch left the organization in 1977, CSPI became primarily focused on food issues, in particular the relationship between diet and health. With offices in Washington, DC, and Ottawa and about 60 staff members, CSPI's current program areas include nutrition, food safety, agricultural biotechnology, alcohol abuse prevention, corporate influence on science, diet, and the environment. Funding for CSPI comes from newsletter subscriptions, members, and donors, and the organization does not accept any government or industry funding. In 1974 CSPI first published the *Nutrition Action Healthletter*, a newsletter, published 10 times a year that currently has over 900,000 subscribers in North America.

Since the 1980s, CSPI has advocated for accurate food labeling. Their efforts greatly contributed to the Nutrition Labeling and Education Act in 1990, requiring clear Nutrition Facts labels on nearly all packaged foods. That same year, CSPI's advocacy also contributed to the first federal law defining "organic" foods. In 1993 CSPI started a campaign against trans fats, first fighting for labeling requirements, which were passed in 2003, then working to encourage banning the use of trans fats in food. In December 2006, New York City became the first city to ban trans fats from restaurants.

In 1994 CSPI first looked at Chinese and Italian restaurant food, and was well publicized for referring to fettuccini Alfredo as a "heart attack on a plate." In 1973 CSPI published the *Nutrition Scoreboard* book to educate the public about the dangers of a diet high in saturated fat, sugar, cholesterol and salt, four years before Congress released the Dietary Goals for the United States in 1977, leading to the current Dietary Guidelines for Americans. CSPI's Eating Green program educates consumers about the benefits of a more plant-based diet including more fruits, vegetables, and whole grains. In addition to increasing consumer awareness of unhealthy foods, CSPI also supports additional taxes on fatty, sugary foods, referred to as the "Twinkie tax."

In the early 1980s CSPI began its Alcohol Policies Project to advocate for alcohol prevention policies, and in 1988 the group's efforts led to a federal mandate for health warning labels on all alcoholic beverage containers. As with junk food, CSPI supports increased taxes on alcohol and cuts on advertising that targets young people. *CSPI's Campaign for Alcohol Free Sports TV* encourages sports organizations to consider the message young people receive from beer ads during sports games, and works toward eliminating alcohol-related advertising during broadcasts.

CSPI first started raising awareness of children's health and nutrition issues in the 1970s by advocating for improved food quality in public schools and publishing a *School Lunch Action Guide* in 1976. In 1991 CSPI started a group called Kids Against Junk Food to support children and families in developing and maintaining healthy eating habits. As fast food restaurants such as Pizza Hut and Taco Bell become more and more popular in public high schools, and marketing sponsored directly or indirectly through food companies increases, CSPI continues to work for healthier food in schools. The group has petitioned to ban junk food advertisements from children's television programming to reduce kids' exposure to unhealthy foods.

Consistent with CSPI's priority to promote food safety and consumer awareness is the group's advocacy for scientific integrity relating to nutrition and health. CSPI developed and maintains a database of scientists and doctors with financial connections to corporations (www.integrityinscience.org).

In addition to his work with CSPI, Jacobson also serves as a National Council Member of the Farm Animal Reform Movement, a non-profit organization that promotes eating a plant-based diet. Jacobson has published several books relating to nutrition issues including *What Are we Feeding Our Kids?*, *Six Arguments for a Greener Diet*, and *Restaurant Confidential*. He currently resides in Washington, D.C.

BIBLIOGRAPHY

Jacobson, Michael F. & The Center For Science In The Public Interest, *Six Arguments for a Greener Diet: How a Plant-based Diet Could Save Your Health and the Environment*, 2006; Jacobson, Michael F. & Hurley, Jayne, *Restaurant Confidential: The Shocking Truth about What You're Really Eating When You're Eating Out*, 2002; Jacobson, Michael F. & Maxwell, Bruce, *What Are We Feeding Our Kids?*, 1994; Rocawich, Linda, "Michael Jacobson—Director of the Center for Science in the Public Interest—Interview," *Progressive, The*, Sept 1994. FindArticles.com. 26 May 2008, findarticles.com/p/articles/mi_m1295/is_n9_v58/ai_15754446; www.cspinet.org/.

Janzen, Daniel H.
(January 18, 1939–)
Tropical Ecologist

Biologist Daniel Janzen is as well known for his discoveries about the intricate ecology of tropical ecosystems as he is for his innovations in tropical forest conservation. A pioneer in the field of coevolution (evolutionary change by two species in response to each other), Janzen developed a field course in biology for the Organization of Tropical Studies (OTS) that is still taught today and that has helped train most North American tropical biologists currently active. Janzen's collaboration with Costa Rican scientists and government officials in establishing the Area de Conservación Guanacaste (a 120,000-hectare protected area in northwestern Costa Rica) and in co-founding the Costa Rican National Biodiversity Institute (INBio) have made him an expert in how to facilitate successful conservation and attempt to pay for it in tropical countries that economically are poor, but are rich in ecology and biodiversity.

Daniel Hunt Janzen was born on January 18, 1939, in Milwaukee, Wisconsin, son of an artistic mother and a father who directed the U.S. Fish and Wildlife Service. He was raised in central Minnesota, where he spent as much time as possible hunting and fishing, alone or with his father. Janzen told a *Rolling Stone* reporter that unbeknownst to him at the time, "the hunting and trapping I did as a kid—figuring out where the deer is going to be when and why—was experimental biology." Janzen began collecting specimens as a child. He assembled a vast collection of Minnesota butterflies during preadolescence and went on his first international butterfly-collection expedition (to Mexico) at the age of 15. Janzen married his first wife while at college and supported her, their child, and his studies by trapping fur-bearing animals and hunting meat for their table. He graduated with a degree in entomology and botany in 1961 and rented a U-Haul to tote his butterfly and moth collection to the University of California at Berkeley

(UCB) to study insect ecology and biological control.

In 1963, while in UCB graduate school, Janzen attended a National Science Foundation–supported course in Costa Rica. He was astounded at the richness and diversity of the remaining tropical forests of that country, far more impressive than the few remnants in Mexico, where he was doing his thesis research. While waiting to take his first job at the University of Kansas in 1965, he returned to Costa Rica and designed a course for the Organization of Tropical Studies in tropical biology for graduate students. Most North American tropical biologists currently working throughout the Americas have attended this eight-week course. Students attend a series of mini-seminars in varied ecosystems throughout Costa Rica and then design their own research project. Janzen taught the course until the early 1970s, and since then he has hosted the classes as they visit his base in the Area de Conservación Guanacaste (ACG).

In 1965 Janzen made a discovery about the relationship that has evolved between ants and acacia trees that revolutionized tropical ecology. During a study trip in Mexico, Janzen observed as an ant patrolling the branch of an acacia tree stung and immediately repelled a larger beetle that had alighted on the tree. Janzen discovered that when he removed the ants that lived in the enlarged thorns of the acacia, insects and vertebrates defoliated and eventually killed the tree. The tree's leaves, he told *Omni* interviewer Bill Moseley in 1993, "were like lettuce; there are no chemical defenses." The ant had evolved to provide defensive services for the acacia tree, and in return, the acacia provided room for the ants to live inside the swollen thorns and food in the form of protein-rich bodies on their leaftips and a sweet nectar oozing from glands at the leaf bases. Janzen learned that this relationship had been described a century earlier by English mining engineer Thomas Belt after a visit to Nicaragua, but until Janzen described it in his landmark 1966 paper, "Coevolution of Mutualism between Ants and Acacias in Central America," for *Evolution*, the many good examples of coevolution had been largely ignored to ecologists and evolutionary biologists.

In 1975, Janzen established a research base in Parque Nacional Santa Rosa, one of the largest remaining areas of dry tropical forest in Mesoamerica. He and his wife, biologist Winnie Hallwachs, had become so concerned about the severe threats to wildlands in Costa Rica by 1985, however, that they abandoned many of their field biology studies and focused instead on conservation and restoration of dry tropical forest. Janzen and Hallwachs devised a plan to help the forest regenerate on abandoned pastures and low-grade cropland surrounding the national park. The seeds for the forest trees are distributed mainly by the wind and by fruit-consuming animals. As agoutis, birds, bats, and monkeys travel through the forest munching and carrying fruits, they defecate or bury the seeds, some of which survive as seedlings. Janzen realized that if the degraded pastures surrounding the park were purchased and added to the park, and if the anthropogenic fires were stopped, the forest would regenerate. Santa Rosa was expanded and incorporated into a network of contiguous protected areas in Guanacaste Province that became the ACG (occupying two percent of Costa Rica's total area), an expanse large enough to contain the entire dry forest ecosystem and the neighboring rain forests and cloud forests, to which the dry forest organisms migrate seasonally and to absorb a wide variety of planned light human uses. The expansion effort is still underway, and becomes ever more urgent as global warming is drying the area and making it even more important to protect a diversity of habitats for species protection and migration. Janzen and Hallwachs describe their current efforts and offer an opportunity for online donations on their faculty website, janzen.sas.upenn.edu/saveit.html.

Although Janzen is not by nature a public person or an extrovert, he and Hallwachs became the main international spokespersons and fundraisers for the project. Their reputation grew as they were featured in such magazines as *Smithsonian* and *Rolling Stone*. People became convinced of their vision for the ACG and forest restoration, and Janzen's fame as a wildman—he was reportedly so fascinated by nature that he once allowed a warblefly larva that had burrowed into his leg to mature and emerge just so he could watch the process—encouraged generous contributions. Most of the necessary funds for land purchases were raised, and the ACG now has an endowment fund for many of its administration costs.

Janzen and Hallwachs insist that wildlands need to generate enough money to pay their own administrative costs and provide some economic benefits for residents of surrounding areas, the nation, and the rest of the world. This made Janzen and Hallwachs proponents of biodiversity prospecting—the search for compounds in nature that can be of use to industry: pesticides, foods, medicines, fragrances, and the like—and any other kind of nondamaging uses of wild biodiversity. Janzen and Hallwachs joined with several Costa Rican scientists to found INBio (www.inbio.ac.cr) in 1989 so as to conduct an inventory of the nation's biodiversity. One by-product of the inventory was INBio's ability to facilitate bioprospecting in Costa Rica. Through its path-breaking contracts with Merck & Company, Inc., Givaudan-Roure, and other companies interested in the compounds discovered through bioprospecting, INBio contributes to the costs of conservation and provides jobs to Costa Ricans trained as paraecologists, para-taxonomists, and parabioprospectors. Janzen and Hallwachs have specialized in training rural inhabitants to carry out complex inventory and field research programs, and more than 100 of them manage the complexity of ACG as well as conduct the ongoing biodiversity inventories of ACG. At present, the focus is on a desperate attempt to incorporate the last remaining forest fragments around the margins of ACG, through fundraising for land purchase, helping to raise an endowment for the entire conserved wildlands of Costa Rica, and promoting global bioliteracy through the development of personal DNA barcorders (Holloway, 2006).

The success of Janzen's and Hallwachs's projects can by no means be attributed solely to them, but they deserve credit for their creative thinking, their insistence that conservation will not succeed unless the humans responsible for it recognize its benefits for them, their tenacity for seeing these projects through, and their willingness to serve as spokespersons abroad. Janzen has received numerous awards and recognitions for his work, including the 1984 Crafoord Prize (considered an equivalent of the Nobel Prize for ecology), a 1989 MacArthur grant, and the 1997 Kyoto prize in basic science. Janzen and Hallwachs have donated all of these monetary awards to conservation projects in the ACG.

Janzen and Hallwachs split their time between the University of Pennsylvania and their cinder-block home and laboratory in Sector Santa Rosa of the ACG.

BIBLIOGRAPHY

Adler, Jerry, "Daniel H. Janzen," *Smithsonian*, 2005; Gallagher, Winifred, "Recall of the Wild," *Rolling Stone*, 1988; Holloway, M., "Democratizing Taxonomy," *Conservation in Practice*, 2006; Janzen, Daniel, "Gardenification of Wildland Nature and the Human Footprint," *Science*, 1998; Janzen, D. H., "How to Grow a Wildland: The Gardenification of Nature," *Nature and Human Society: The Quest for a Sustainable World*, Peter Raven and T. Williams, eds., 1999; Janzen, D. H., W. Hallwachs, J. Jiménez, and R. Gámez, "The Role of the Parataxonomists, Inventory Managers, and Taxonomists in Costa Rica's National Biodiversity Inventory," *Biodiversity Prospecting*, W.-V. Reid et al, eds., 1993; Janzen, D. H., ed., *Costa Rican Natural History*, 1983; "Janzen & Hallwachs & caterpillars," janzen.sas.upenn.edu.

Jensen, Derrick
(December 19, 1960-)
Author, Futurist

Derrick Jensen is an American author, proponent of deep ecology, an activist, and one of the loudest voices calling for radical measures to reverse the destruction of the environment. Through his books and frequent speeches, he issues a warning that civilization cannot be redirected at this point; it needs to be overturned to avoid the complete wreckage of nature. He appeals for a hands-on attitude that goes beyond the conventional. Sustainability cannot be achieved within a system that is inherently unsustainable.

Born on December 19, 1960 in Spokane, Washington, Derrick Jensen received a B.S. in Mineral Engineering Physics from the Colorado School of Mines and an M.F.A. in Creative Writing from Eastern Washington University. He has taught creative writing at Pelican Bay State Prison and Eastern Washington University.

Jensen's work underscores the daunting dimension of the environmental reality. With a mix of fact and personal anecdotes he exposes propaganda, and argues that civilization faces total exhaustion. He has been criticized for saying that some kinds of violence are a perfectly valid response to violence, that more extreme measures are necessary to stop the perpetrators of a more serious form of violence.

Having suffered terrible abuse from his father during his childhood, he puts to use his wisdom to portray a similar unhealthy relationship with the natural environment and its indigenous populations. When something unpleasant happens in an abused family, there is often the promise it won't happen again. "When you build a plant that produces toxic chemicals in bulk, how much of a surprise is it when they leak?" wondered Jensen in one of his talks. It is important to recognize that abusers transform things to their own advantage to maintain their dominant position within the relationship. Also, that when individuals put an end to abuse they do so only through volition and ultimately through confrontation. On a planetary scale, it will be very hard to end such a relationship since it has become so pervasive.

Jensen examines our culture's economic system, finding search of the premises that have led to atrocity and destruction. Some of the topics he explores are deforestation, education, surveillance and control.

Derrick Jensen (Photograph courtesy of Derrick Jensen)

Jensen's latest work is *Endgame*, a two-tome book about this inherent unsustainability of civilization. He puts in evidence how unlikely it is that our culture will undergo a voluntary transformation to a sustainable way of living given that the rate of depletion is so much greater than its rate of restoration. The world is blind with useless hope, living in denial of the effects of our actions. Despite his fatalistic views, his thesis can seem more realistic than overly optimistic dreams of green capitalism. Jensen wonders whether it is not worth trying to save a system that is just no good. He maintains that conditions will get much worse before they get any better unless we accept that centuries of human "development" have failed and that we need to dismantle the whole thing and start over. In his view, the sooner we do this, the better.

Jensen has mocked some of the efforts in the mainstream media for being too naïve and for having no impact whatsoever, for serving as seats of conformity for the masses. He wants to invalidate the pacifist fallacy that agreements can be reached with the corporations.

When asked about specifics regarding "bringing down civilization," Jensen explains, "What I really mean is depriving the rich of the ability to steal from the poor and depriving the powerful of the ability to destroy the planet. That's what I really mean."

From 1990 to 2001 Jensen was Associate Editor of *Transitions* magazine. In 1996 he co-founded the Railroads & Clearcuts Campaign, a project that held corporations and governments accountable for their actions. From March 1997 to the present, he has been a member of the Drafting Committee for the articulation of a new food production ethic. He is a member of the Advisory Board of the Native Forest Network, which is a group working for the preservation of forests, and the Advisory Board of Del Norte Association for Cultural Awareness, a regional nonprofit organization. In 2003, *The Culture of Make Believe* was one of two finalists for the J. Anthony Lukas Book Prize and in 2006 Derrick was named "Person of the Year" by Press Action for the publication of *Endgame*.

He has written two unpublished novels: *Songs of the Dead* and *Lives Less Valuable*, both available on his website. He lives in Crescent City, California.

> "The world gives us so very much. It gives us our life. All our neighbors—the ants, spiders, salmon, geese, sharks, seals, cottonwoods, chestnuts—are doing the real work of keeping this planet going. Isn't it time we did our share?"*

BIBLIOGRAPHY

Endgame, Volume I-II: The Problem of Civilization, 2006; Jensen D., *Walking on Water: Reading, Writing, and Revolution*, 2003; www.derrickjensen.org.

Johnson, Glenn S.
(March 24, 1962–)
Environmental Sociologist, Environmental Justice Scholar and Activist

Focusing on issues of environmental justice, and specifically on the impact on communities of color of transportation, urban sprawl, land use policy, regional equity and emergency response and community preparedness. Glenn S. Johnson is an associate professor of sociology at Clark Atlanta University and a research associate at its Environmental Justice Resource Center (EJRC). Johnson has coedited three recent books in the environmental justice field, *Just Transportation* (1997), *Sprawl City* (2000), and *Highway Robbery* (2004), and has co-compiled the *Environmental Justice Curric-*

---

*Jensen, Derrick. *Endgame Volume II Resistance*. New York 2006. (page 885) *ulum Resource Guidebook,* a collection of environmental justice–oriented curricula used by professors at universities throughout the country.

Glenn Steve Johnson was born on March 24, 1962, in Memphis, Tennessee. He attended the University of Tennessee, earning two B.A. degrees (in academic psychology in 1986 and in sociology in 1987), an M.A. in 1991, and a Ph.D. in 1996, both in sociology. For his M.A., he wrote a thesis entitled "What Are Cities Doing with Their Garbage: A Case Study on the Decision-making Process of Solid Waste Disposal of Knoxville, Tennessee." His Ph.D. dissertation further explored the problem of solid waste disposal; it was entitled "Garbage Disposal, A Case Study of the Impact of Environmental Racism on Landfills: The North Hollywood Dump in Memphis, Tennessee." These projects were inspired by the work of Johnson's mentor, sociology professor ROBERT BULLARD, whose research on racial discrimination by solid waste companies led to the first environmentally oriented lawsuit filed under the 1964 Civil Rights Act. Bullard spent the academic year 1987–1988 teaching at the University of Tennessee, during which he and Johnson met, and Johnson became Bullard's research assistant for Bullard's landmark 1990 book, *Dumping in Dixie: Race, Class and Environmental Quality.*

As a graduate student, Johnson was already becoming an active participant in the emerging subfield of environmental sociology that analyzed the environmental justice movement, hosting symposia and presenting papers at numerous sociology conferences starting in 1990. He taught introductory courses in sociology and social problems at the University of Tennessee and classes on race and ethnicity at Knoxville College and worked for a Knoxville-based youth program during 1990 and 1991. Once he had been awarded his Ph.D., Johnson was offered an assistant professorship in sociology at Clark Atlanta University and a position as research associate at the Environmental Justice Resource Center,

Glenn S. Johnson (Photograph courtesy of Glenn S. Johnson)

which Bullard founded in 1994 and still directs.

The EJRC at Clark Atlanta University is a comprehensive, university-based research center whose mission includes education, training, research, and the storage, retrieval, and dissemination of information. EJRC serves as a national clearinghouse, repository, and archive of the largest collection of environmental justice materials in the world (books, reports, monographs, proceedings, photographs, slides, videos, audiotapes, and so on). Its seven major research areas include environmental justice, transportation equity, suburban sprawl/smart growth, sustainable development, regional equity, emergency response and community preparedness and climate justice. EJRC's four major objectives include (1) increasing the quality and quantity of environmental, health, land use, economic development, transportation equity, and smart growth information available to community-based organizations; (2) linking via the Internet the various community-based organizations, networks, and minority leaders working on environmental justice, transportation equity, smart growth, and health/sustainable communities; (3) expanding the focus, stakeholder interaction, and agenda sharing among community-based and national groups; and (4) assisting community stakeholders in implementing environmental, health, energy, transportation equity, sustainability, and smart growth benchmarks they have set for themselves.

One of Johnson's initial projects at the EJRC was to compile the *Environmental Justice Curriculum Resource Guidebook* (with collaborators Robert Bullard and Chad Johnson). This book catalogs a variety of environmental justice–oriented courses offered at colleges and universities throughout the country, among them courses from the disciplines of sociology, urban planning, law, political science, business, health, transportation, public health, natural resources, public administration, waste management, pollution prevention, community health, risk assessment, occupational health and safety, geography, and faith-based. It was first published in 1997, with an update in 2000.

In addition to coediting two special environmental justice issues of the *Race, Gender, and Class* journal of the Race, Gender, and Class Section of the American Sociological Association, Part I in 1997 and Part II in 1998, Johnson has coedited three scholarly books. *Just Transportation: Dismantling Race and Class Barriers to Mobility* (1997), coedited with Robert Bullard, reveals that the wealthy, educated classes receive disproportionately greater transportation benefits than people of color and others at the lower end of the socioeconomic spectrum. In many large cities throughout the United States, new highways connecting new, predominantly White, middle- and upper-class suburbs, take precedence over improving mass transit systems that serve the mostly poor residents of color who live in inner cities and rely on public transportation. Not only is this an issue of equity, it is also one of environmental health. More highways mean more use of automobiles, which results in more pollution, and the poor are generally more seriously afflicted by asthma and other conditions exacerbated by pollution. Contributors to *Just Transportation* detail how transportation problems have affected communities throughout the country, from Harlem to New Orleans, to southern California, to Atlanta and how activists have responded.

Johnson, together with Bullard and EJRC geographical information system specialist Angel Torres, next addressed the issue of urban sprawl with *Sprawl City: Race, Politics, and Planning in Atlanta* (2000). Focusing on sprawl from the dual perspectives of environmental justice and civil rights, this book examines how racial and class divisions are heightened through random, unplanned suburban growth. African Americans, in particular, are prevented from escaping increasingly unbearable inner cities by such obstacles as restrictive zoning practices, inadequate public transportation, and discrimination by real estate brokers, banks, and mortgage companies. The eight suburban counties surrounding Atlanta, which are growing as fast as 6.6 percent per year, provide an illustrative showcase for the environmental and equity problems caused by such rapid growth. The region has become economically and racially polarized; traffic is thick on the highways yet public transportation in the suburbs is sparse; air quality is so bad that the Environmental Protection Agency has classified Atlanta as a "nonattainment area"; each day some 50 acres of forest are leveled and converted into new development. *Sprawl City* contributors are local experts in the fields of law, urban planning, economy, education, and health care.

Johnson's most recent book, also co-authored with Bullard and Torres, is *Highway Robbery: Transportation Racism and New Routes to Equity* (2004). It illustrates the contributions of transportation policy, and transportation tax dollars, to racial and economic inequality. The authors combine academic research and grassroots perspectives to link national inequalities in transportation to larger economic, health, environmental, and quality of life concerns. Defining transportation equity as a critical civil rights issue, this groundbreaking collection details progressive transit activists' efforts to tip the scales of transportation justice. The contributors to *Highway Robbery* are activists, academics, lawyers, clients, planners, and residents who personal transportation experience infuses each perspective.

Johnson is a member of numerous scholarly societies, including the American Sociological Association, Association of Black Sociologists, Southern Sociological Society, Mid-South Sociological Society, Society for International Development, and the Society for the Study of Social Problems. He resides in Stone Mountain, Georgia.

BIBLIOGRAPHY
Bullard, Robert D., and Glenn S. Johnson, eds., *Just Transportation: Dismantling Race and Class Barriers to Mobility*, 1997; Bullard, Robert D., Glenn S. Johnson, and Angel O. Torres, "Atlanta Megasprawl," *Forum for Applied Research and Public Policy*, 1999; Bullard, Robert D., Glenn S. Johnson and Angel O. Torres, "Dismantling Transportation Apartheid in the United States Before and After Disaster Strikes," *Human Rights Magazine-ABA Section of Individual Rights and Responsibilities*, 2007; Bullard, Robert D., Glenn S. Johnson, and Angel O. Torres, eds., *Highway Robbery: Transportation Racism and New Routes to Equity*, 2004; Bullard, Robert D., Glenn S. Johnson, and Angel O. Torres, eds., *Sprawl City: Race, Politics, and Planning in Atlanta*, 2000; "Environmental Justice Resource Center at Clark Atlanta University," www.ejrc.cau.edu; Johnson, Glenn S. and Shirley A. Rainey "Hurricane Katrina: Public Health and Environmental Justice Issues Front and Centered," *Race, Gender & Class*, 2007.

Johnson, Hazel

(January 25, 1935–)
Founder and Executive Director of People for Community Recovery

Hazel Johnson has been called the mother of the environmental justice movement for her three decades of activism to clean up the highly contaminated "toxic doughnut" surrounding her home in the Altgeld Gardens housing development of southeast Chicago. After her husband died suddenly in 1969 of lung cancer and Johnson discovered that many of her neighbors also suffered from cancer, birth deformities, premature deaths, rashes, eye irritation, and respiratory illnesses, Johnson began lobbying for change. She founded People for Community Recovery (PCR) in 1978 and has pushed city, state, and federal authorities to study and correct the area's environmental contamination and resulting health problems. Although by no means have all of the problems of Altgeld Gardens been solved, Johnson and other PCR activists have enjoyed some success: The neighborhood has been hooked up to the municipal water supply because its wells were contaminated; the group successfully demonstrated against the expansion of one landfill and a moratorium on further landfills has been called; and PCR worked with Greenpeace to prevent the construction of an incinerator nearby. For her courage, persistence, and accomplishments, Johnson was presented with the President's Conservation and Challenge Award for Communication and Education in 1992.

Hazel Washington Johnson was born in New Orleans on January 25, 1935; of her parents' four children, she was the only one who survived. Even as a young girl she was opinionated; she shocked her family by declaring that churchgoers were hypocritical. By the time she was 12, her parents had died, and she moved to Los Angeles to live with an aunt for five years. She returned to New Orleans, where she married John Johnson. In the course of their marriage she had seven children, two of whom, Cheryl and Valerie, help in her work now. In 1956 the Johnsons moved to Chicago, and in 1962 they moved into a new complex in the southeast part of the city, Altgeld Gardens, owned by the Chicago Housing Authority. Unbeknownst to her at the time she moved there, the 17-block development, whose residents were all African Americans, had been constructed on top of the old Pullman Railroad dump, in an area of the city that had been used for more than a century as the city's industrial dumping grounds.

In 1969 her husband began to suffer extreme back pain, and within 10 weeks he was dead, a victim of what doctors said was lung cancer. Dumbfounded, Johnson began to listen as her neighbors spoke of cancers, rashes, miscarriages, and hacking coughs in children. After Johnson saw a television report on the high incidence of cancer in South Chicago, she began to suspect that it might be caused by the area's severe contamination. Altgeld Gardens was encircled by what Johnson eventually dubbed "a toxic doughnut": a steel mill, sewage treatment plants, landfills, abandoned factories, chemical companies, and incinerators. Johnson attended a meeting sponsored by the Illinois Environmental Protection Agency (IEPA) on problems in the area, and after she spoke up about the problems she had noticed, she was sent 12 copies of a health evaluation questionnaire to take to some of her neighbors. She made more than 1,000 copies and organized concerned friends and neighbors to canvass the entire neighborhood. The canvassers found that approximately 90 percent of those they surveyed suffered from symptoms that could have been caused by air pollution. However, the IEPA refused to consider the data because it had not been gathered in a sufficiently professional manner. The city of Chicago then conducted a study that showed that African Americans living on Chicago's south side suffered high rates of cancer, but the city did not compare that rate with those of African Americans living elsewhere nor did it look at possible causes of the cancer.

Johnson founded People for Community Recovery in 1978, with an initial goal of lobbying the Chicago Housing Authority for tenant rights. PCR worked to assure that no apartment would be rented unless it was lead free and to have asbestos removed from the buildings as well. In the face of all of the health problems that were surfacing, and the likelihood that they were caused by air and groundwater pollution, PCR soon began to work on larger environmental issues. Because no satisfactory health study had been completed, PCR and the University of Illinois School of Public Health collaborated in 1993 on another survey that had two particularly significant findings: Fifty-one percent of pregnancies involved some abnormalities, and 66 percent of those who experienced symptoms while living at Altgeld Gardens reported relief from them upon leaving the area.

Although the local, state, and federal governments' environmental and health agencies have not come through for the residents of Altgeld Gardens to draw definitive connections between the environmental hazards and residents' health problems, and then to clean up the area, PCR activists were successful in drawing media attention to the problems and in solving some problems by lobbying politicians and through grassroots protest politics. One of residents' main worries was that their water supply—well water—was contaminated. PCR lobbied for and eventually obtained a hookup for Maryland Manor to the municipal water line. Johnson and other PCR activists, along with Greenpeace, organized effective protests to stop the expansion of a local waste management landfill and to prevent the construction of a chemical waste incinerator nearby. She has been arrested twice during these protests. In these struggles, PCR's predominantly African American activists were able to form bonds with predominantly White groups against their common enemies: polluters and the government agencies that do not enforce laws against environmental contamination. Despite the fact that environmental racism has damned 60 percent of African Americans and Latinos to live in areas contaminated by toxic waste (according to the 1987 United Church of Christ Commission on Racial Justice report, *Toxic Wastes and Race in the United States*) and that a study by the *National Law Journal* in 1992 showed that from 1985 to 1991 the [EPA] fined violators of the Clean Water Act from 500 to 1,000 percent more if they polluted White communities than if they polluted communities of color, Johnson understands the necessity of collaboration. She told Josh Getlin of the *Los Angeles Times*, "We all breathe the same air, and everybody has to live on this planet. So if the air is lousy where I live, sooner or later it's gonna get to your home too."

In 1992 Johnson was one of 13 African American delegates to the United Nations Conference on the Environment in Rio de Janeiro. In that same year she received the President's Environmental & Conservation Medal given by then President Bush. In 1995 she was asked to join the EPA's Common Sense Initiative (CSI) which, teamed with polluting industries, was looking for opportunities to write regulation that would emphasize prevention rather than cleanup. In 1997, Johnson helped arrange one of the many "toxic tours" she has conducted since the 1970s; she arranged for 20 members of the Automobile Manufacturing Subcommittee of the CSI to see nine sites around southeast Chicago from an environmental justice perspective. The CSI was disbanded in December 1998, though not without some success in an attempt to balance the burden of reporting required of industry, on the one hand, and the community's right to know, on the other. Johnson sat on the National Environmental Justice Advisory Council that oversaw the siting of landfills and incinerators.

PCR continues to operate out of a storefront in Altgeld Gardens. In addition to its continued work for environmental justice, it offers the 10,000, primarily African American residents of Altgeld Gardens whatever help it can: job training, human immunodeficiency virus (HIV) prevention, advocacy in the courts, and sponsorship of the neighborhood basketball team and a mentoring program for young women. Johnson still resides in Altgeld Gardens.

BIBLIOGRAPHY

Ayres, William, Jean Ann Hunt, and Therese Quinn, *Teaching for Social Justice*, 1998; "Environmental Justice Resource Center: Unsung Heroes and Sheroes on the Front Line for Environmental Justice," www.ejrc.cau.edu/(s)heros.html; Ervin, Mike, "The Toxic Doughnut," *The Progressive*, 1992; Getlin, Josh, "Fighting Her Good Fight," *Los Angeles Times*, 1993; Greenpeace, *Rush to Burn* (video documentary), 1989; Miller, Stuart, "Green at the Grassroots: Women Form the Frontlines of Environmental Activism," *E Magazine*, 1997; "People for Community Recovery," www.geology.wisc.edu/~wang/EJBaldwin/PCR/; Taylor, Dorceta E., "Environmental Justice: The Birth of a Movement," *Dollars & Sense*, 1996.

Johnson, Lady Bird (Claudia Alta)

(December 22, 1912–July 11, 2007)
First Lady, Conservation Activist

Wife of Pres. Lyndon Baines Johnson, Lady Bird Johnson pushed for a variety of reforms as part of her First Lady's campaign for "beautification." Her efforts resulted in the 1965 Highway Beautification Act, which controlled the proliferation of billboards and the spread of roadside junkyards. In 1982 she founded the National Wildflower Research Center, now known as the Lady Bird Johnson Wildflower Center, to "educate people about the environmental necessity, economic value, and natural beauty of native plants."

Claudia Alta Taylor was born on December 22, 1912, in Karnack, Texas, a small town in the eastern part of the state. Taylor had an affluent upbringing; her mother was from a wealthy Alabama family, and her father was a successful businessman. She acquired the nickname "Lady Bird" from a family cook, who said she was as pretty as the ladybird beetle common in the area. Johnson's mother died when Claudia was five, and she was raised thereafter by her father and her mother's sister. As a child Taylor spent a great deal of time alone in the outdoors and later attributed her interest in conservation to a love of the land and natural beauty acquired in childhood. After graduating from high school at age 15, Taylor spent two years boarding at St. Mary's School for Girls in Dallas, before enrolling at the University of Texas. In 1933 she earned a B.A. with honors, which she followed in 1934 with a degree in journalism, also received with honors.

She met Lyndon Johnson in August 1934, and they were married later that year. Her husband's political career advanced swiftly, with his election to the House of Representatives in 1937, and Mrs. Johnson became closely involved in his political life. While he was serving in the Pacific during 1942, she ran his Washington, D.C., office and learned firsthand the nuts and bolts of American politics. In 1943 the Johnsons bought radio station KTBC in Austin, Texas, the beginning of what would be extensive media holdings, managed in large part by Lady Bird. Lyndon Johnson was elected to the Senate in 1948, and after two unsuccessful campaigns for the Democratic nomination to the presidency, he became Pres. John Kennedy's vice president in 1960.

When President Kennedy was assassinated in 1963, and Lyndon Johnson assumed the presidency, Lady Bird Johnson inherited the office of First Lady from the enormously popular Jackie Kennedy. Mrs. Kennedy had used the attention she attracted to push for a well-regarded, historically attuned renovation of the White House, and in the weeks following the assassination, Lady Bird began to feel a responsibility to make a contribution of her own. In the summer of 1964 she made a tour of national parks and Indian reservations in the West. STEWART UDALL, the secretary of the interior, accompanied Mrs. Johnson on this tour, and their discussions and shared appreciation of the beauty of the West contributed to her growing commitment to conservation and beautification. Udall said later that Lady Bird played a pivotal role in galvanizing the president's commitment to preserving natural beauty, a commitment evident in the formation in 1964 of the Task Force on Natural Beauty. When the Task Force made its recommendations in November of that year, after Johnson was elected to another term as president, it focused on preservation of landscape and open space, highway beautification, and creation of and rehabilitation of the nation's urban parks. All of these became important parts of Lady Bird Johnson's agenda: the beautification of America. In Lewis Gould's *Lady Bird Johnson and the Environment*, she is quoted as saying, "'Getting on the subject of beautification is like picking up a tangled skein of wool—all the threads are interwoven, recreation and pollution and mental health, and the crime rate, and rapid transit, and highway beautification, and the war on poverty, and parks—national, state, and local.'" The push for the preservation of national beauty was an integral part of the Johnsons' Great Society vision, an ambitious effort to improve life for all Americans.

One of her first initiatives was the beautification of Washington, D.C., which she hoped could serve as an example for the rest of the nation. A Committee for a More Beautiful Capital was established in early 1965. She spearheaded efforts to clean up and organize neighborhoods, create and renovate parks, plant flowers in public places, and refurbish the Mall, historic sites, and monuments. Mrs. Johnson used her background in journalism to attract favorable publicity for her campaign, which was focused both on the tourist's Washington—monuments, parks, museums—and inner city Washington, which suffered from all the problems of poverty and racism. She was involved in projects that included the designation of Pennsylvania Avenue as a national historic site and Project Pride, which assisted residents of the Shaw neighborhood, one of Washington's poorest, with urban renewal and education programs. Project Pride involved 250 neighborhood children.

Mrs. Johnson faced many obstacles in completing her ambitious slate of projects, including a constant search for private funds and a Congress reluctant to spend money on what was often perceived as frivolous, "feminine" interest in beauty. Congressional opposition was even more intense in the campaign to pass the Highway Beautification Act, the achievement for which Lady Bird Johnson is best known. The billboard lobby fought the act vigorously and found a receptive audience in Congress. Many members of Congress traditionally waged their campaign battles on roadside billboards. Both Johnsons lobbied hard for passage of the act throughout 1965, and with some compromises to the wishes of the Outdoor Advertising Association of America, the bill was signed into law in October of that year. Highway beautification continued to be a focus for Mrs. Johnson throughout the rest of her term as First Lady, along with an increased involvement in creating new national parks. She was particularly active in campaigns to protect the Grand Canyon and establish a national park to preserve California redwoods. Some of the conservationist legislation passed in the final year of Johnson's term in office included setting up the National Wild and Scenic Rivers System and the creation of North Cascades and Redwoods National Parks.

After they left the White House, the Johnsons returned to Texas, where Mrs. Johnson continued her conservation work at the state and local level. Lyndon Johnson died in 1973. Lady Bird Johnson presided over Texas's highway beautification projects into the 1980s. She was active in Austin conservation efforts, including beautifying the riverfront and developing a system of parks and open space. Throughout her career she was particularly drawn to projects involving plant life, and in 1982 she gave $125,000 and 60 acres of land east of Austin to establish the National Wildflower Research Center, which has worked to preserve and promote the conservation of native wildflowers. Lady Bird Johnson died at her home in Texas on July 11, 2007, at the age of 94.

BIBLIOGRAPHY

Gould, Lewis, *Lady Bird Johnson and the Environment*, 1988; Houk, Rose, *A Biography of Lady Bird Johnson*, 2006; Johnson, Claudia, *A White House Diary*, 1970; "Lady Bird Johnson Wildflower Center," www.wildflower.org; "National First Ladies Library," www.firstladies.org; "Lady Bird Johnson: First Lady and Environmentalist", *London Economist*, 2007; Russell, Jan Jarboe, *Lady Bird: a Biography of Mrs. Johnson*, 1999.

Johnson, Robert Underwood
(January 12, 1853–October 14, 1937)
Editor

Editor of the influential national literary magazine *Century*, Robert Underwood Johnson collaborated closely with pioneer conservationist JOHN MUIR. Johnson helped Muir revive his literary career in 1889 and worked closely with him on establishing Yosemite National Park and fighting the Hetch Hetchy dam. Without the boost and friendship of Johnson, Muir might not be known as the wilderness preservation icon he is today.

Robert Underwood Johnson was born in Washington, D.C., on January 12, 1853. He was raised in Centreville, Indiana, and attended Earlham College in Richmond, Indiana. Upon graduation in 1871, Johnson moved to Chicago and worked as a clerk at the textbook publisher Charles Scribner's Sons. Two years later, Scribner's transferred him to its New York City office, where he began working as an editor at *Scribner's Monthly*, which later became the famed *Century*.

Century was the nation's most influential magazine of the late 1800s. It published new work by the nation's top novelists and took reformist editorial positions on such issues of the day as the improvement of tenement housing and corporate control of politics. Its readership consisted of 200,000 well-educated, affluent subscribers, people who wielded influence in their communities. Johnson prepared popular series for the magazine, most notably a collection of memoirs of Civil War combatants from both sides. Somewhat of an elitist, Johnson felt that by working for *Century*, he was contributing to a growing sophistication of tastes and morality of the century-old United States. Johnson rose through the ranks of the magazine, becoming associate editor under editor Richard Gilder in 1881.

During the 1870s, *Century* had published several articles by John Muir. Muir stopped

Robert Underwood Johnson (Library of Congress, Prints & Photographs Division, LC-DIG-npcc-01177)

writing in the 1880s once he became occupied with the day-to-day life on his Martinez, California, farm. Johnson wrote to Muir a few times during the early 1880s, urging him to take up the pen again, but Muir demurred. In 1889, Johnson traveled to California to research a historical series on the California pioneers. He contacted Muir, they met in person, and a mutual affinity bloomed almost instantly.

Stephen Fox, in his *The American Conservation Movement: John Muir and His Legacy*, claims that each man had an ulterior motive for their friendship. Johnson's was to pump Muir for material for *Century*. Muir's was to recruit Johnson to work for the preservation of the Yosemite Valley he so loved. As soon as they met, Muir proposed a hiking trip through Yosemite. Johnson, who was not an outdoorsman yet, was curious to visit Yosemite and agreed. They spent several days in early summer trekking through remote areas that left Johnson breathless with admiration. Muir told Johnson of his worries that Yosemite, owned by the state of California, would be ruined by the unregulated grazing and tree cutting that was already degrading the area. Johnson said he thought the two should work to give Yosemite inviolable status as a national park, just like Yellowstone had gained in 1872. Muir agreed to write two Yosemite *Century* articles if Johnson would propose the idea to his contacts in Washington, D.C.

In March 1890, California congressman William Vandever introduced a bill to convert some 288 square miles of Yosemite into a national park, but Muir felt that 1,500 square miles deserved protection. While Muir was writing his *Century* articles, Johnson testified in favor of the larger park size at the House of Representatives' Commission on Public Lands. Muir's articles appeared in the August and September issues of *Century*; a bill to establish the 1,500-square-mile Yosemite National Park was passed by Congress on September 30, 1890, and signed into law by the president the next day.

Pleased by their success, Muir none-theless worried about the Yosemite's safety. At this time there was no legislation and no national park service to protect national parks from the "utilitarians," as Muir called stockmen, lumbermen, and those who believed in the right to use public lands for economic gain. Again Johnson was to propose a prophetic idea: that they found a "defense association" for Yosemite and Yellowstone. Muir, who was not comfortable in most social situations, was intimidated by the thought of establishing a club. But by 1892, a group of California wilderness proponents formed the Sierra Club to keep the utilitarians out and facilitate the wilderness lovers' exploration of the park. John Muir was persuaded to serve as the Sierra Club's first president; he led annual wilderness trips and enjoyed the opportunity to tell his stories to a receptive crowd.

Johnson persistently urged Muir to continue writing throughout the 1890s. *Century* published Muir's first book, *The Mountains of California*, in 1894, and Muir's famous story about an adventure with his valiant dog, Stickeen. But after Johnson edited down "Stickeen" more than Muir wished, held one article for three years, and rejected another, Muir jumped ship and signed on with Boston publisher Houghton Mifflin. Johnson's and Muir's friendship survived this painful professional split, however, and they collaborated several years later on the fight against the Hetch Hetchy dam.

Hetch Hetchy was a narrow, deep valley carved by the Tuolumne River in northwestern Yosemite. Muir and Johnson agreed that this was one of the most beautiful, wild areas of the park. But to city officials of San Francisco, it seemed an ideal place to build a dam to supply San Francisco with needed water and hydroelectric power. There were several attempts in the first few years of the century to obtain federal permission to dam Hetch Hetchy, but they all failed, due to Interior Secretary Ethan Hitchcock's refusal to permit development in national parks. Once Hitchcock was replaced by an ally of the utilitarian Forest Service director GIFFORD PINCHOT, however, the Hetch Hetchy dam project rolled forward. Muir and Johnson led a national protest against Hetch Hetchy for seven years. They railed against it with their most energetic prose, in articles for *Century*, of which Johnson became editor in 1909; newspaper editorials; and privately published pamphlets. Johnson saw the struggle as one between spirituality and commercialism; he and Muir both referred to the Hetch Hetchy valley as a creation of God that it would be sacrilegious to destroy. Yet the utilitarians prevailed, claiming that if beauty were the criterion, the new reservoir created by the dam would be beautiful too. In December 1913, Pres. Woodrow Wilson signed a bill to grant the Hetch Hetchy valley to San Francisco's water utility for dam construction.

Both Muir and Johnson suffered deep personal setbacks after their defeat. Muir died one year later. Johnson left *Century* during the Hetch Hetchy fight, owing to conflicts with the magazine's business management department. He dedicated the remainder of his career to poetry. During World War I, he organized The American Poets' Ambulances in Italy, a fund for ambulances and field hospitals in Italy. Following the war he was appointed U.S. ambassador to Italy by Pres. Wilson. Although Johnson no longer remained on the forefront of wilderness conservation struggles, he retained his membership in the American Forestry Association, until he resigned in protest when the association came under the control of the lumber industry in the mid-1920s.

Johnson died on October 14, 1937, in New York City. He was married to Katherine McMahon and left two children, Owen and Agness.

BIBLIOGRAPHY
Fox, Stephen, *The American Conservation Movement: John Muir and His Legacy*, 1981; Nash, Roderick, *Wilderness and the American Mind*, rev. ed., 1973; Stroud, Richard, *National Leaders of American Conservation*, 1985.

Jones, Van
(1968–)
Civil Rights and Environmental Justice Activist and Organizer

Van Jones is a leader in the effort to create a nationwide "Green Jobs Corps" to reinvigorate urban employment and to provide a bridge out of poverty through training and development of green collar jobs. Largely due to Jones's efforts spearheading this historic initiative, in 2007 President Bush signed into law the Green Jobs Act of 2007, authorizing $125 million per year to create an Energy Efficiency and Renewable Energy Worker Training Program. Jones works to unite traditionally disparate factions of the progressive movement, believing that it is a contemporary moral imperative to build a green economy strong enough to lift people out of poverty.

Van Jones was born in rural Tennessee in 1968. His grandfather was a bishop in the Methodist church. Jones has a wife, Jana, and a son, Cabral. He graduated with a B.A. degree in 1990 from the University of Tennessee at Martin, which he attended on a minority scholarship (as part of an Affirmative Action program). Interested in journalism, Jones founded an underground college publication, *The 14th Circle*, and helped launch Nashville's community newspaper *The Third Eye* in 1990, as well as interning in several Southern newsrooms before growing disenchanted with mainstream media's inability to report on issues of race and poverty. Admitted to both Yale and Harvard law schools, Jones graduated in 1993 from Yale, where the unequal treatment he saw given to drug users (Yale students were given a year off to clean up, often overseas, while local minority youth were given prison sentences) spurred his interest in social activism. In 1992, the spring the Rodney King uprising happened in Los Angeles, Jones interned in San Francisco as a legal observer for the Lawyers Committee on Civil Rights during demonstrations, where he and hundreds of others were arrested.

Jones was inspired to return to the Bay Area to work with the Lawyers Committee upon graduation. His first assignment as a civil rights attorney was an environmental justice case suing the Chevron refinery in Richmond, California, for environmental racism. With the support of the Lawyers Committee, Jones incubated Bay Area PoliceWatch, a project to provide legal referral services for police abuse victims. In 1996 that project spun off to become the Ella Baker Center for Human Rights, founded by Jones who was and continues to be its executive director.

The Ella Baker Center (EBC), named by Jones for an unsung heroine of the Civil Rights movement, creates projects to reform the prison system and to create opportunities in the green economy for poor communities and communities of color. It is Jones's ability to create collaborations across varied interest groups that accounts for the local and national success of many of the EBC projects.

Books Not Bars is the EBC flagship project addressing youth incarceration, and it is credited with creating a 30 percent drop in the total prison population of California youth. In 2002, Books Not Bars' successful campaign helped stop the construction of an expensive "super-jail" for Oakland's youth. Jones promotes young peoples' ability to become the solution to social problems. For Jones, criminal justice reform means rebuilding the economic infrastructure of urban areas. Jones led the EBC initiative Reclaim the Future in 2005, in collaboration with the Oakland Apollo Alliance and the Oakland electrical union, to model a clean energy jobs coalition, creating the nation's first-ever green enterprise zone. The coalition helped to raise $250,000 from the city government to create a Green Jobs Corps, which is training young people in installation of solar panels, weatherizing buildings, and laying green roofs.

That project went national in 2007 as Green for All, aimed at creating an inclusive green economy strong enough to lift people out of poverty. Jones has said that much of the African American community is economically stranded, and he's created Green for All to replace the vanished blue collar, steppingstone manufacturing jobs with green jobs. The EBC, backed by Speaker Nancy Pelosi (D-CA), achieved a major victory with the passing of the Green Jobs Act of 2007, which will train 35,000 people a year in green trades using the Oakland, California, Green Jobs Corps as a model.

Jones has received the Rockefeller Foundation's Next Generation Leadership Fellowship, the Ashoka Fellowship, the Echoing Green Fellowship, and Reebok's Human Rights Award. He has served on the Boards of the Social Venture Network, National Apollo Alliance, Bioneers, and Rainforest Action Network. Jones is a Senior Fellow with the Center for American Progress. He is a contributing blogger at the Huffington Post, and his essays and writings appear in a number of books. His first book, *The Future's Getting Restless*, will be available October 2008. Van Jones says, "we want green jobs, not jails," and he defines a green collar job as a vocational job in a field that honors the earth.

BIBLIOGRAPHY

The Green Jobs Act of 2007, www.fpif.org/fpiftxt/5233; www.thesunmagazine.org/issues/387/bridging_the_green_divide; www.vanjones.net; article/interview, www.collagefoundation.org/people/people-vanjones.html.

Jontz, Jim

(December 18, 1951–April 14, 2007)
U.S. Representative from Indiana, Organizer

During his three terms in Congress as a representative from Indiana, Jim Jontz was most noted for his opposition to logging in old-growth forests in the Pacific Northwest. First elected to Congress in 1986, Jontz was at the center of the controversy surrounding protection for the spotted owl. He led resistance to resumption of logging after it was halted by concern for the owl and fought for tougher regulation on timber sales in national forests. Defeated in his bid for reelection in 1992, Jontz went on to lead several environmental lobbying and activist groups, including Audubon's Endangered Species Coalition, American Lands Alliance, and the Alliance for Sustainable Jobs and the Environment.

James Jontz was born on December 18, 1951, in Indianapolis, Indiana. He became an Eagle Scout and worked summers leading nature hikes in the Indianapolis city parks, through the Children's Museum. He graduated from Indianapolis's North Central High in 1970 and from Indiana University in Bloomington in 1973. Motivated to fight the construction of a dam in central Indiana, Jontz ran for election the Indiana House of Representatives in 1974. Despite being a Democrat in a traditionally Republican district, and being only 22 years old, Jontz won. He served in the House until 1984 and earned a reputation for hard work and support for working people. Jontz was called a "full-time legislator" in a state where legislators are expected to work only part of the year. While in the House he was particularly active in oversight of the public utilities; he sponsored legislation that encouraged conservation and worked to prevent the state power company from passing costs of a failed nuclear plant back to consumers. Jontz also actively advocated reducing medical costs for the poor and elderly and fought for legislation benefiting women. In 1984 he was elected to the Indiana Senate, again surprising observers by winning in a Republican stronghold.

Jontz left the Indiana Senate in 1986, when he was elected as U.S. representative from the 5th District. He earned a reputation as a critic of monoculture practices, a dangerous stance for someone from a farm state, but he gained the trust of farmers by voicing their issues. Jontz demonstrated that it was possible to simultaneously support the environment and farmers. He argued against the overreliance on pesticides because of the danger to farmers, whose health and land were most directly impacted by exposure to pesticides and their runoff. Jontz was instrumental in passing an amendment to the 1990 Farm Bill that protected farmers' relief benefits from counting against their ability to qualify for other assistance programs such as food stamps. In addition to his work on agricultural issues, Jontz also played a key role in fighting the nuclear power industry by blocking a 1992 provision that would have allowed the industry to pass cleanup costs on to taxpayers. He also worked to protect Indiana's Salt Creek Corridor, a key wetlands habitat.

Jontz's time in Congress was defined by his work to preserve forests. He was especially concerned about private timber sales on public land. The U.S. Forest Service spent millions of dollars every year building roads and marking boundaries so that private logging firms could cut lumber on Forest Service land. Jontz argued that this amounted to a public subsidy of the timber industry, at a habitual loss to taxpayers. He introduced legislation to cut below-cost timber sales and federal outlays for lumber-harvesting support. Jontz received national attention for his efforts to stop logging in old-growth forests in the Northwest, particularly during the 1989–1990 battle over the spotted owl. In

1989, a federal court issued an injunction that blocked cutting on Forest Service land while considering whether cutting would interfere with efforts to protect the endangered owl. Mark Hatfield of Oregon and Brock Adams of Washington sponsored an amendment to an Interior Department appropriations bill that would have lifted the court injunction, and Jontz urged his colleagues to defeat the amendment. The debate was fierce and sharply polarized, and Jontz became a lightning rod for anger from timber interests. In April 1990, a protest was held in Hoquiam, Washington, at which angry loggers burned Jontz in effigy. Undeterred, Jontz introduced the Ancient Forest Protection Act in 1991—this raised public awareness of the problem, but due to opposition by powerful industry interests, was defeated. Jontz was targeted for ouster by the timber industry and in 1992 was defeated in his bid for reelection by Steve Buyer. Jontz then ran for Senate in 1994, challenging incumbent Republican Sen. Richard Lugar, but lost.

Leaving electoral politics and Indiana, Jontz began to work with non-profit environemental organizations. He served as director of the National Audubon Society's Endangered Species Coalition, where he lobbied Congress in support of the Endangered Species Act. In 1995 he became the executive director of the Western Ancient Forest Campaign (WAFC), a coalition of activist groups fighting for wilderness preservation. WAFC was active in the campaign against the North American Free Trade Agreement (NAFTA), which was criticized for promoting free trade at the expense of the environment. WAFC also campaigned in support of environmentalists in developing countries, including a 1997 campaign to block the expansion of NAFTA to South America. Jontz moved to Portland, Oregon in 1999. Through WAFC, he was a participant in the 1995 Sugar Loaf timber protests in Oregon, as well as the 1999 World Trade Organization protests in Seattle. In 1999 WAFC changed its name to American Lands Alliance. Also in 1999, Jontz helped organize the Alliance for Sustainable Jobs and the Environment, an oganization formed to protect the environment and respect workers' rights, and to oppose the practices of 'rogue corporations,' i.e. those companies that abuse the environment and their employees.

Jontz was elected president of Americans for Democratic Action in 1998, and coordinated its Working Families Win project, which worked to bring issues of fair trade and the environment into the focus of presidential and congressional candidates.

Jontz battled colon cancer for two years, and succumbed to it at the age of 55, on April 14, 2007. He was remembered by his colleagues and friends as indefatigable, unrelenting and eternally optimistic.

BIBLIOGRAPHY

"Alliance for Sustainable Jobs and the Environment," www.asje.org; "American Lands," www.americanlands.org; "Americans for Democratic Action," www.adaction.org; Dustin, Thomas, "Jontz's Commitment Paying Off Again," *South Bend Tribune*, 1996; "Jontz, James P.," *Indianapolis Star*, 2007; Lancaster, John, "Debate on Timber Harvesting Is Major Environmental Battle," *Washington Post*, 1989; Nixon, Will, "A Senator for the Ancient Forests, *E Magazine*, 1994.

Jordan, Chris
(1963—)
Photographic artist

Chris Jordan is known for his large photographic images depicting urban settings and the environmental impact of trash. Container yards, landfills, piles of cell phones at electronic recycling centers, his photographs are studies on how numerous and messy humans are. A former corporate lawyer, Jordan uses his art to combat collective ecological disregard of the scale of consumer society.

Chris Jordan was born in San Francisco to Rocky and Susan Jordan, a collector of photographs and a watercolorist respectfully. He grew up surrounded by discussions of images, and wearing a 35-millimeter camera whenever he could. He earned a B.A. in English from University of Texas at Austin in 1988. Wasting no time, he went right to law school (Doctor of Juris Prudence from University of Texas, Austin, Class of 1991). He practiced corporate law for ten years. Throughout the rigors of academic life, his father continued to cultivate his active interest in photographic art, giving his son photo assignments and sharing his notes. "I think my dad secretly knew I should be an artist despite all the outward expectations to take the safe, professional route," Jordan told photo critic Tim Anderson in a 2002 interview.

Living in Seattle, Jordan savored the dark, gray, overcast, urban streetscape. He practiced law by day and photographed the city at night. "Those depressingly gloomy days when the clouds are down around the tops of the buildings and cars drive around all day with their lights on and everyone is ready is commit suicide—that's when I leap out of bed with shouts of joy and spring into action." He would shoot blackened fire escapes, air ducts, subjects that were mundane.

In 2002 at the age of 38 Jordan formally resigned from the bar to make a career leap of faith, from an industry lawyer to an environmental photographer. "I felt I could no longer reconcile representing some of the companies, based on what they were doing."

He began photographing active industrial sites but his goal was "to be able to photograph the way a painter paints—in a loose expressive way." Soon he was producing sensational, complex, relevant, beautiful art. In 2004, he was a finalist for the Honickman First Book Prize in Photography from the Center for Documentary Studies, (juried by Maria Morris Hambourg.) A favorable review in the July 24, 2005 *New York Times Sunday Arts and Leisure* article, "A Great Big Beautiful Pile of Junk" by Philip Gefter expanded Jordan's notoriety as a leader in the eco-arts movement.

"Mr. Jordan is an openly passionate advocate—or maybe a protester. While he is aiming for visually resolved images as an artist, the point is to heighten awareness about our collective environmental disregard. But art and advocacy can be at odds, the goals of one often canceling out the other," wrote Philip Gefter in the *Times*. Jordan explained "My goal is to face the complexity of the issue and honor it."

In 2006 Jordan received an artist's dream come true, a grant from Lannan Foundation to photograph the Gulf Coast damage from the 2005 hurricane season. "In Katrina's Wake, Portraits of Loss From An Unnatural Disaster" (Princeton Architectural Press, 2006), Jordan shows an urban landscape torn asunder, and the sad beauty of the remains of New Orleans.

In his 2007 exhibit "Running the Numbers," Jordan depicts staggering statistics that haunt hypermodern society. Recognizing that numbers alone are never enough to motivate cultural changes, this series seeks to provide statistics in a different way, "to experience the number more directly to the heart," says the

"Plastic Bottles" depicts two million plastic beverage bottles, the number used in the U.S. every five minutes. Archival inkjet prints 60' x 120' 2007 (Chris Jordan: From the series "Running the Numbers: An American Self-Portrait" (2006-2007))

artist, "and see our individual consumer decisions in a new light."

Says Jordan, "One of the huge problems that faces our society right now, is that this problem with our consumerism, and the resulting global warming, worldwide environmental destruction, the toxification of our oceans and the desertification of our agricultural lands, and so on, are not happening because there's an extremely bad person out there who is doing a huge amount of terrible consuming. This is happening because of the tiny incremental harm that every single one of us is doing as an individual. The problem is this cumulative effect from the behaviors of hundreds of millions of individuals. Each person looks around at his or her own behavior, and it doesn't look all that bad. What we each have to expand our consciousness to hold, is that the cumulative effect of hundreds of millions of individual consumer decisions is causing the worldwide destruction of our environment. The hard part of that is the notion of the enormity of the collective."

Solo exhibits of his large photographic images are shown all over the world. In 2007 Chris Jordan's work won international acclaim when it received the Green Leaf Award, Natural World Museum and United Nations

Environment Programme, awarded at the Nobel Peace Center in Oslo, Norway.

Chris Jordan, who lives in Seattle, Washington, also gardens, plays jazz, and is a father.

BIBLIOGRAPHY
Gefter, Philip, *New York Times*, Sunday July 24, 2005, "A Great Big Beautiful Pile of Junk."; *Running the Numbers*, The Morning News, July 23, 2007; Interview by Nicole Pasulka, www.themorningnews.org/archives/galleries/running_the_numbers;Chris Jordan: Photo Essay, *Yes! Magazine*, 2008, www.yesmagazine.org/article.asp?id=2476.

Jukofsky, Diane
(February 11, 1953-)
Director of Communications, Marketing and Education. Rainforest Alliance

As worthy as their causes may be, environmentalist organizations will enjoy meager success unless they are able to effectively publicize the problems they are trying to solve and the solutions they propose. Journalist Diane Jukofsky has devoted her career to helping environmental organizations spread the word and, since 1989, has worked for the Rainforest Alliance. From her office in Costa Rica she directs Communication, Marketing and Education for this organization, overseeing the work of 25 Rainforest Alliance staffers and consultants throughout Latin America and Europe.

Jukofsky was born in Saint Louis, Missouri, on February 11, 1953. She spent her childhood summers at her grandparents' Missouri farm, tending to farm chores alongside her grandmother, Elizabeth Zahorsky Cushing, who had been a founding member of most of the national conservation organizations and was unusually well educated for a girl growing up at the beginning of the twentieth century. At her grandmother's side, Jukofsky learned the names of flowers and constellations and fought her very first environmental battle: a struggle against a dam project on the Meremec River. These experiences are what Jukofsky credits as inspiration for her career.

Diane Jukofsy (Photograph by Chris Wille, Rainforest Alliance)

Jukofsky attended her grandmother's alma mater, Mount Holyoke College, and graduated with a degree in English in 1975. She immediately went to work for the National Wildlife Federation, where she was the assistant director of public information. It was there that she discovered she could combine her academic training with her passion for conservation. Later Jukofsky worked on public relations matters for several nonprofits, including Twin Cities Public Television, the Minnesota

Conservation Federation, Congressman Sam Gejdenson of Connecticut, and Scientists' Institute for Public Information.

During the 1980s, the steep loss of biodiversity in tropical rain forests began to alarm the scientists with whom Jukofsky worked. As the disturbing evidence of the disaster continued to roll in, Jukofsky made a personal commitment to devote herself to rain forest conservation. Along with her husband, CHRIS WILLE, their friend DANIEL KATZ, and several others, she helped found the New York Rainforest Alliance in 1987. Originally it was conceived as a small, local group devoted to rain forest conservation, but it has become an international organization with a multimillion-dollar budget. The Rainforest Alliance distinguishes itself from other rain forest conservation groups through its innovative and economically sound programs to convert rain forest destroyers into allies.

Jukofsky and Wille moved to Costa Rica in 1989 in order to establish the Rainforest Alliance's Conservation Media Center (now called Neotropical Communications) so as to be able to report to conservationists from the site of rain forest destruction. Her Latin America–related projects have varied from helping to launch and manage the Rainforest Alliance's Sustainable Agriculture Program to coordinating public information campaigns for large-scale conservation projects so that vital scientific information may reach the people who can make it succeed, to producing a reference book on world rain forests (*The Encyclopedia of Rainforests*, published in 2002 by Oryx Press), to editing a bilingual on-line reference center for conservation initiatives in Latin America (www.eco-index.org) to publishing the bimonthly, bilingual periodical *Eco-Exchange* (*Ambien-Tema* in Spanish), which covers controversial environmental issues and innovative conservation projects.

Jukofsky's public relations trainings for nonprofit conservation organizations have been especially successful. During the workshops, the staff of a participating organization learns how to communicate more effectively with the press about their work. The final project includes a field trip with journalists to the area the group is trying to conserve. Jukofsky recounts one such expedition in Guatemala:

> It was the first time the Guatemalan journalists had seen a quetzal in the wild (their country's national symbol). When I saw the tears in the eyes of the Guatemalan reporter who watched an emerald green quetzal disappear into the mists of the Sierra de las Minas cloudforest, I knew she would forever understand the passions of those who are fighting to save the reserve. We also showed them a logging operation in the biosphere reserve (which was illegal, but the owner had managed to get permits). The Guatemalan reporters (with a leading daily newspaper and an influential weekly newsmagazine) wrote articles about the operation, which caused quite a stir. As a result, the government rescinded the logging permits. The power of the press! (personal communication, 1998)

The Rainforest Alliance is now active in more than 50 countries worldwide, with an annual budget of $22 million. And Jukofsky now is director of the organization's Communication, Marketing and Education Division, still working to get the word out, but on a large scale.

Jukofsky was elected an honorary member of Sigma Xi, the Scientific Research Society, in 2002. She was the first ever representative of a non-profit conservation organization to be honored in this way. She teaches an on-line class in tropical biodiversity at the New School University and has been a full-time employee of the Rainforest Alliance since 1990. She resides in San José, Costa Rica, with her husband Chris Wille.

BIBLIOGRAPHY

Braus, Judy, ed. *Wow! A Biodiversity Primer*, 1994; "Eco-Index," www.eco-index.org; Jukofsky, Diane, *The Encyclopedia of Rainforests*, 2002; "Rainforest Alliance," www.rainforest-alliance.org.

American Environmental Leaders

From Colonial Times to the Present

K

Kamp, Dick

(August 9, 1948–)
Director of E-Tech International and Border Ecology Project

Richard Kamp is an emergency medical technician, mechanic, environmental researcher, and reporter. He has directed nonprofits coordinating international environmental technical and policy support as well as public health advocacy for two nonprofits internationally and in the United States-Mexico border region. In coordination with his staff, his work has successfully reduced air and water pollution on both sides of the border and since 2004 addressed the environmental impacts of major petrochemical investments. From 1983-2005, Kamp and the Border Ecology Project monitored air, water, hazardous waste, and emergency response issues in the Mexican border zone, and served in the front lines in the battle against natural resource exploitation that degrades the land and the people living on it.

Richard Kamp was born on August 9, 1948 to Ewald and Adele Kamp, who raised their boy near the steel mills, refineries, and coal-burning households of the south side of Chicago, Illinois. He would later say that Chicago in the 1950s made Mexico City seem mildly polluted. His relationship to his environment became public during the 1970s battles against border smelter pollution. At Prescott College in 1983, he earned a B.A. in arid lands studies. His interest in Latin America has focused on impacts of new and old industrialization, as well as litigation, legislation, and development policies in both the United States and Mexico that negatively affect long-term public health conditions in the hemisphere.

The sulfur dioxide (SO_2) and particulates emitting from the "gray triangle" of Arizona-Sonora copper smelters, made the United States-Mexico frontier the largest source of sulphur-dioxide emissions in both countries. In the 1980s, Kamp and the Border Ecology Project (BEP) compiled air quality data, a

Dick Kamp (Photograph by Jane Phillips)

Mexican crop-damage report, and helped conduct clinical studies in Douglas, Arizona to explain the unusually high incidents of the autoimmune disease systemic lupus erythematosus. His 1983-1987 contribution to the drafting and implementation of the United States-Mexico La Paz agreement Annex 4, a binational air quality accord, joint BEP-EDF successful litigation against the Phelps Dodge Douglas smelter, and broad-based public support were key to tremendous improvement of Western air quality. Kamp subsequently forged working groups among civil sector, police, and paramedics for air and hazardous waste and emergency response. The passage and implementation of the Annex 4 agreement cut annual copper smelting SO2 emissions in two countries by 1 million tons annually. The accompanying Annex 3, drafted and implemented simultaneously in January 1987, reduced hazardous waste in the border region by 90 percent within 15 years.

After the passage of the North American Free Trade Agreement (NAFTA), Kamp worked on community capacity building strategies in northern Mexico, and helped incubate nongovernmental projects to promote stronger environmental and social programs. He also participated actively in the NAFTA-created North American Commission on Environment (CEC) from 1993-2000. Kamp's knack for motivating ecologically-minded people and organizations on both sides of the border fence has kept important safeguards in place in an area of the country often relegated to no-man's-land status.

His work on the La Paz agreement has been recognized for more than twenty years. Through a partnership with Wick Newspapers, Kamp's reporting led to a 1988 Pulitzer nomination of the *Sierra Vista Herald* for socially beneficial reporting on border smelter issues.

Through a U.S. presidential appointment, he served as co-chair of the Integrated Border Environmental Program Commission from 1990 to 1992, winning the United Nations Environmental Program Global Youth Award in 1991 for expanding citizen participation in environmental protection. Kamp helped the Environmental Protection Agency (EPA) establish regulations for transportation of hazardous materials across the border during the Clinton administration.

He serves on the board of several cross-border organizations, including Environmental Flying Services, Border Power Plant Working Group, Proyecto Fronterizo de Educación Ambiental SA (Baja California), as well as E-Tech. E-Tech International has been a major force in addressing the impacts of the Peruvian Camisea Natural Gas project as well as Chevron-Texaco dumping in northeastern Ecuador. E-Tech provides international environmental technical consulting and capacity building to communities impacted by industrial development.

But Kamp's environmental day job is environmental liaison to the Wick Newspapers. He lives with his wife, journalist Barbara Ferry, in Santa Fe, New Mexico.

BIBLIOGRAPHY

Kamp, Dick, "Powering up the Border: What's the Rush?" International Relations Center Americas Program, September 5, 2001; Williams, Florence, "Border doesn't block dirty air and water," *High Country News*, March 21, 1994; www.borderecoweb.sdsu.edu/bew/drct_pgs/b/bep.html.

Kane, Hal

(October 9, 1966–)
Writer, Strategic Planner for Nonprofit Organizations

Hal Kane has lent his pen to advance the work of several environmental nonprofit organizations, including the think tanks Worldwatch Institute and Redefining Progress and the advocacy organization Pacific Environment & Resources Center (PERC). His work has focused on the links between development, the environment, population growth, and consumption. His primary area of interest has been how personal choices and lifestyle affect the environment and the economy. He is a prolific writer, with ten books to his name that have been translated into 31 foreign languages.

Hal Moss Kane was born in Ann Arbor, Michigan, on October 9, 1966. His father, Gordon Kane, a professor of particle physics at the University of Michigan, subscribed to journals that covered issues of population and the environment. Kane attributes his interest in these topics to his exposure to them as a budding reader. Through his mother, Lois Kane, who wove and wrote, Kane learned how useful art and words could be for effective communication.

Kane attended the University of Michigan (UM) in Ann Arbor. He intended to study political science but was distressed by the verbose and poorly written texts he was assigned. Knowing that skillful writing would be important in any career choice he made, Kane decided that the best training would be to read good writing and then to learn to write well. So he majored in English language and literature and graduated in 1988. As an undergraduate, Kane organized an annual symposium on venture capital at UM, in which small companies that needed finance could meet potential investors. Kane's experience helping the companies formulate business plans came to be useful as he helped nonprofit groups devise viable financial strategies. During his years at UM Kane also worked for Senators Gary Hart (Colorado) and Don Riegle (Michigan). There, he gained an insider's view of politics and also made the decision not to pursue a career as a staff member for elected officials.

Following his graduation from UM, Kane worked for several environmental organizations, including the Geneva-based Centre for Our Common Future, an organization funded by the United Nations' World Commission on Environment and Development. Kane considers himself lucky to have had the opportunity, at that early point in his career, to draft several speeches for its director, Norwegian prime minister Gro Harlem Brundtland. Kane also wrote and consulted for other nonprofit organizations, including the National Congress of American Indians, Island Press, Partners for Livable Places, and Global Tomorrow Coalition. The U.S. Citizen's Network on the United Nations Conference on the Environment and Development (UNCED) asked Kane to write a book to prepare the American public for the big 1992 conference in Rio. With their support, Kane authored his 1991 *Time for Change: A New Approach to Environment and Development*, which outlines the interconnectedness of economics, the environment, and social issues.

Kane earned an M.A. in international relations and economics from Johns Hopkins University (JHU) in 1992. During the Washington-based time of his studies (he also studied at JHU's Bologna, Italy, campus) he worked as an environmental management fellow for the U.S. Environmental Protection Agency, researching the connections between international trade and the environment.

Following his graduation from JHU, Kane moved on to Worldwatch Institute (WI, www.worldwatch.org), where as a research associate he studied such issues as the sustainability of the world's fisheries, environmental economics, international trade, resource scarcity, hunger, refugees, migration, and population growth and wrote articles for *World Watch*, WI's bimonthly magazine. He cowrote two of WI's *State of the World* books, contributing chapters on industry and the environment for the 1995 edition and on refugees and migrants for the 1996 edition. Kane cofounded a new annual WI series, the *Vital Signs* books, cowriting the editions from 1992 to 1996. This series, which focuses on specific, influential world trends, has proven to be important, selling more than 50,000 copies per year and being translated into 18 languages. Kane also collaborated on a 1994 book with WI director LESTER BROWN, *Full House: Reassessing the World's Population Carrying Capacity*.

In 1997, Kane moved to the San Francisco-based nonprofit think tank Redefining Progress (www.rprogress.org), which states its mission as opening up the debate on the "true meaning of progress, one that goes beyond economic growth to incorporate environmental sustainability and social equity." At Redefining Progress, Kane directed the National Indicators Program, which measures a country's well-being more accurately than the common Gross Domestic Product measure. The Genuine Progress Indicator (GPI), for example, begins with economic output but adds and subtracts other values, including environmental improvement or decline, crime, divorce, unpaid work in the home, commute time, car accidents, and income inequality. In 1998 and 1999, as a senior fellow for Redefining Progress, Kane wrote *Triumph of the Mundane: The Unseen Trends That Shape Our Lives and Environment*, which describes the way of life in the United States today through statistics on the rise of such indicators as the number of people who live alone, the average distance we travel everyday, the frequency with which we move to new homes and new jobs, and many other personal indicators. The book argues that the way lifestyles have changed over the years has dramatically affected the health of our environment and ourselves and has done so more than politics or most of the other factors that we hear about in the news.

From 1998 until 2000 Kane served as executive director of the Pacific Environment & Resources Center (now known as Pacific Environment; www.pacificenvironment.org), a nonprofit environmental organization that has fostered citizen environment movements in Pacific Rim countries such as Russia and China, whose governments have traditionally been closed to public participation. It offers its members the opportunity to visit sites of interest in the United States where potential environmental problems are approached with innovative solutions: well-designed mines, sustainably managed logging sites, and responsible industry, for example, and also monitors the work of bilateral export-credit agencies and international financial institutions and alerts the rest of the world to environmental problems along the Pacific Rim that otherwise would have gone unnoticed.

Kane currently works independently through his own company "The Strategic Pen." He is a popular public speaker, traveling throughout the United States and in foreign countries to give public speeches, to appear on television and radio stations, and to participate in professional conferences. He resides in San Francisco, California.

BIBLIOGRAPHY

Brown, Lester, and Hal Kane, *Full House: Reassessing the World's Population Carrying Capacity*, 1994; Brown, Lester, et al., *Vital Signs*, 1992, 1993, 1994, 1995, 1996; Kane, Hal, *Time for Change: A New Approach to Environment and Development*, 1991; Kane, Hal, *Triumph of the Mundane: The Unseen Trends That Shape Our Lives and Environment*, 2000; "The Strategic Pen and Hal Kane," www.halkane.com.

Katz, Daniel

(November 7, 1961–)
Co-founder and board chair of the Rainforest Alliance

In 1986, at the age of 24, Daniel Katz co-founded the Rainforest Alliance. This organization, which Katz directed until 2000, promotes economically viable and socially desirable alternatives to the destruction of rain forests, through education, social and natural science research, and the establishment of cooperative partnerships with businesses, governments, and local peoples. During Katz's tenure as director, the Rainforest Alliance created independent third-party certification in the fields of forestry, agriculture and tourism.

Daniel Roger Katz was born on November 7, 1961, in Cincinnati, Ohio. Raised in the city, one of his more memorable childhood exposures to nature was seeing Henri Rousseau's primitivist paintings in a children's art book, which even at his young age made an impression. Katz was an energetic organizer and founded a string of clubs in high school and college. He entered Ohio State University in 1979 and studied abroad, in 1981 at the National Chengchi University in Taiwan and from 1983 to 1984 at the Central China University of Science and Technology in Wuhan, People's Republic of China. Katz graduated from Ohio State with a double degree in Chinese and political science in 1984.

In 1985, Katz moved to New York City and did China-related work for a law firm for one year. He attended a small workshop on rain forests in 1986; he found himself fascinated with them and very troubled about the massive deforestation that was not receiving any media attention at the time. With four others who had attended the workshop, Katz created the New York Rainforest Alliance. He quit his job and devoted ten months of full-time work to organize "Tropical Forests, Interdependence and Responsibility," the largest international conference on rain forest conservation that had ever been held. Drawing such well-known figures in rain forest ecology as THOMAS LOVEJOY, PETER RAVEN, and Ghillean Prance, the 1987 conference featured 51 speakers and was attended by some 700 people. The international press covered the event, and Katz and his partners felt that they had successfully challenged scientists and governments to give rain forest conservation the attention it deserved.

Daniel Katz (Photograph by Maggie Lear)

The New York Rainforest Alliance continued to offer lectures and workshops to educate the public about deforestation issues. Katz felt that it was important to begin working in rain forests themselves as well. In 1988 the Rainforest Alliance organized a workshop on the tropical timber industry. This led to the project eventually named SmartWood, the world's first forestry certification program. SmartWood works with forestry operations of all sizes to assess their impact on the environment and awards Forest Stewardship Council (FSC) certification to those companies that manage forests in an environmentally and economically sustainable manner. As of 2008, more than 108 million acres in 64 countries worldwide had been certified by the Rainforest Alliance, making the organization the leading certifier of forestlands to the FSC standards globally. In addition, the Rainforest Alliance's TREES (Training, Extension, Enterprises and Sourcing) program is promoting responsible forest management by working with more than 60 community and indigenous forest enterprises that manage more than 2.4 million acres (more than one million hectares) of forestland. They are working to help these producers manage their land more responsibly and efficiently and link them with buyers and markets for wood products that come from responsibly managed forestlands.

Following the success of SmartWood, the Rainforest Alliance developed the Better Banana Project, a program that certifies banana producers that comply with strict social, economic, and environmental criteria. This project, initiated in 1990, was eventually renamed ECO-O.K. and under the leadership of CHRIS WILLE, headquartered in Costa Rica, was given a big push in 1994 when banana giant Chiquita Brands vowed to certify all of its farms. In 1995, ECO-O.K. was awarded the prestigious Peter F. Drucker award for nonprofit innovation, and in the latter half of the 1990s it gradually expanded to include certifications of other tropical agricultural crops including coffee, citrus, sugarcane, and cacao. Wille has drawn together affiliate conservation organizations in several Latin American countries that make up the Sustainable Agriculture Network (SAN), the group that sets the standard represented by the Rainforest Alliance Certified® seal and for which the Rainforest Alliance serves as secretariat. The SAN standards incorporate the three pillars of sustainable agriculture: economics, ethics and environment. The standards guide farmers in using nature as an ally on the farm and serving as stewards of soils, waters, wildlife, and other natural assets. On certified farms, the people involved in cultivation and harvest enjoy a safe, dignified, and economically just life, and farmers work in concert with local conservationists to promote a healthy habitat for native wildlife on the farm and in neighboring parks and refuges. Farmers are interested both for reasons of conscience and profit; they know that many consumers prefer certified products and will pay more for them. Since the program originated in 1990, certification has been awarded to 31,727 farms that grow tropical crops including coffee, cocoa, bananas, tea, mangos, ferns, flowers and citrus in 19 countries. The amount of coffee purchased from Rainforest Alliance Certified farms has nearly doubled every year for the past five years, from 7 million pounds in 2003 to 91.3 million pounds in 2007.

The Rainforest Alliance also works in sustainable tourism in Latin America, offering training courses to tourism businesses to improve the sustainability of their operations and prepare them for certification from a third-party certifier.

The Rainforest Alliance provides extensive curricula and materials to teachers through its website and links groups of conservation-minded schoolchildren or donors in the United States with specific rain forest-based grassroots organizations abroad.

Because the organization often looked at market-based conservation solutions, Katz decided to study for an executive M.B.A., which he earned in 1996 from New York University.

In 2000, Katz left his position as Executive Director of the Rainforest Alliance, though he continues as Chair of its Board and expert staff member in the areas of nonprofit management and business and the environment. He is currently Director of the Environment Program at The Overbrook Foundation where he directs its environmental giving, in the areas of international biodiversity, conservation, and sustainable consumption and production. At Overbrook, Katz recently launched CatalogChoice.org, a web-based program to help citizens stop receiving unwanted catalogs in the mail. Catalog Choice registered nearly one million users in its first six months of operation. Katz also serves on the boards of other organizations, including People for the American Way Foundation, Gibson Guitar Foundation, and World Parks.

Katz resides in New York City with his wife, Maggie Lear, and their two children.

BIBLIOGRAPHY

Katz, Daniel, and Miles Chapin, *Tales from the Jungle: A Rainforest Reader*, 1995; Katz, Daniel, *Why Freedom Matters: The Spirit of the Declaration of Independence in Prose, Poetry, and Song*, 2003; "Rainforest Alliance," www.rainforest-alliance.org/; Reiss, Bob, *The Road to Extrema*, 1992.

Kaufman, Hugh
(January 14, 1943–)
Hazardous Waste Investigator

Employed by the Environmental Protection Agency (EPA) since its inception in 1971, Hugh Kaufman is best known for his role as a whistleblower, calling attention to EPA's failures and political corruption. Kaufman was a central player in the scandal at EPA in the mid-1980s, which resulted in the ouster of EPA head Anne Gorsuch Burford and the conviction of assistant administrator Rita Lavelle on charges of lying to Congress. Kaufman also worked on drafting two important pieces of legislation, the Superfund Law and the Resource Conservation and Recovery Act. Most recently, Kaufman collaborated on a report that revealed that following the 9/11 attack on the World Trade Centers, the administration of Pres. George W. Bush pressured the EPA to downplay the danger of toxic exposure to first responders and neighbors of the Twin Towers.

Hugh Kaufman was born on January 14, 1943, in Washington, D.C. He was raised in Arlington, Virginia, in one of the few Jewish families in the community. His experience as an outsider growing up contributed to the development of a fighting spirit. He once said his tough-kid approach was to "hit first and ask questions later." Kaufman attended George Washington University, from which he earned a B.S. in 1965 and an M.S. in 1967, both in engineering. After serving in the United States Air Force for four years, Kaufman joined the new Environmental Protection Agency in 1971. Employed first in the noise program, Kaufman was active in creating rules to control noise around highways and airports and helped turn the agency against unlimited landing rights for the Concorde. In 1974 he moved to the hazardous waste division and began on-site investigations for the EPA. The EPA was a new agency, and Kaufman played an important role in developing its toxic waste programs. He compiled reports about hundreds of cases of land, air, and water contamination by hazardous waste, which helped convince Congress to pass the 1976 Resource Conservation and Recovery Act.

The late 1970s saw a dramatic rise in public awareness of the problem of hazardous waste, focused most dramatically on New York's Love Canal case, which made national headlines in 1978. Kaufman helped investigate the case, before Steffen Plehn, deputy assistant administrator for solid waste, recalled Kaufman out of the field and back to headquarters. The agency was afraid of the magnitude of the nation's toxic waste problem and its associated costs, and Plehn ordered Kaufman to stop visiting sites and pressing for clean-up efforts. Kaufman did not comply silently with this order. He and fellow EPA employee WILLIAM SANJOUR gave information to the press and to congressional staff and members, on and off the record, and eventually testified before Congress. Both employees put their jobs at risk and were the targets of internal EPA investigations. Their testimony caused a storm of publicity that helped generate the momentum to pass the landmark 1980 Superfund legislation.

Despite his reputation as a whistleblower, Kaufman managed to keep his job even after President Reagan's election, which brought strong deregulation pressure on the EPA. During this time Kaufman was assistant to the director of the Hazardous Waste Site Control Division; the division was part of the Superfund program, which was led by assistant administrator Rita Lavelle. By March 1982, Kaufman was again in the national news. He appeared before several congressional committees and, on April 24, 1982, on CBS's *60 Minutes*. Kaufman accused the EPA, under the direction of Anne Gorsuch Burford, of failing to meet its legal obligations to enforce environmental regulations. The agency was not spending Superfund allocations to investigate polluters and was cutting illegal sweetheart deals with industry. Kaufman cited a memo from Rita Lavelle to White House counsel Robert J. Perry, in which she accused Perry of "alienating" President Reagan's most important constituency: business. The immediate result of Kaufman's television appearance was an investigation of his activities by the EPA, in which they tapped his phone and photographed Kaufman going into a hotel room with a woman who turned out to be his wife. Congress began an investigation of the EPA, during the course of which Burford invoked executive privilege to keep incriminating documents out of the hands of Congress and EPA critics. In a showdown with Congress, the Reagan administration eventually backed down; President Reagan fired Lavelle and forced Burford's resignation. Lavelle was tried and convicted of perjury and served four months of a six-month sentence. President Reagan appointed a new EPA director, William Ruckelshaus, who had been the agency's first administrator. Ruckelshaus restored order to EPA and returned focus to its enforcement programs.

Kaufman continued to work for the EPA and to serve as an insider advocate for citizens' groups. He was active in the successful fight against a nuclear waste dump proposed for the tiny farming town of Nora, Nebraska, in the late 1980s. In 1993 Kaufman again played the role of whistleblower, this time testifying to Congress about the EPA's issuing a questionable waste-disposal permit to a hazardous waste incinerator next door to an elementary school in East Liverpool, Ohio, operated by Waste Technologies Industry, which had close ties to the Clinton administration. In 1994 Kaufman appeared on Michael Moore's television show *TV Nation*, in a segment called "Sludge Train," about Merco Joint Venture, a reputed mafia project to spread wastewater sludge on a ranch near Sierra Blanca, Texas. Merco successfully sued Kaufman for libel, but an appeals court overturned the verdict and found that Kaufman had not libeled Merco Joint Venture or its venture partners. Kaufman was also a vocal critic of the EPA's plan to clean up the Shattuck Chemical Company waste dump in Denver. Kaufman argued that the plan was not aggressive enough and would eventually lead to groundwater contamination. As a result of his work, the EPA agreed to move the waste to a licensed radioactive waste disposal facility.

As chief investigator for the EPA Ombudsman, Kaufman criticized how the EPA handled the issue of toxics in the air of lower Manhattan after the attack on the World Trade Center, claiming that the EPA succumbed to pressure by the administration of Pres. Bush to downplay the severity of the problem, and used inferior methods to test the toxicity of the air there. Thus, first-responders and neighbors were exposed to toxins much worse than what the EPA reported were present at and near the site. In two other cases—the clean-up of a superfund site in Denver and of another site in Pennsylvania—Kaufman and his boss, Ombudsman Robert Martin, alleged that the administrator of the EPA, Christine Todd Whitman, protected her husband's interests in her handling of a superfund case in Denver and another contaminated site in Pennsylvania. Following this, in 2002, Whitman stripped the office of the Ombudsman of its autonomy; Ombudsman Robert Martin resigned in protest and Kaufman was reassigned.

Kaufman still works for the Environmental Protection Agency in Washington, D.C., and resides in Washington, D.C.

BIBLIOGRAPHY

"Democracy Now: White House Pressured EPA Not to Warn Public about Health Effects of 9/11," www.democracynow.org/2003/8/12/white_house_pressured_epa_not_to; Johnson, Jeffrey, "Hugh Kaufman: EPA Whistle-Blower," *Sierra*, 1988; Johnson, Roberta Ann, "Bureaucratic Whistleblowing and Policy Change," *Western Political Quarterly*, 1990; Mitchell, Greg, *Truth and Consequences*, 1981; Morson, Berny, "The Hero of Shattuck," *Rocky Mountain News*, 1999.

Kellert, Stephen
(October 10, 1944–)
Social Ecologist

A professor of social ecology, Stephen Kellert has spent decades studying the relationship between humans and nature. His research projects have included studies of basic perceptions relating to the conservation of biological diversity, and he has explored and eloquently written about a concept set forth by EDWARD O. WILSON called "biophilia"—the idea that humans possess a deep and biologically based urge to connect with the natural world. Kellert argues that because of this innate affinity for the complexities of nature, natural diversity must be protected for its capacity to enrich and enlarge the human experience. His message takes the rationalization for conservation beyond narrow utilitarian or material needs and makes a new case for preservation of diversity and natural spaces.

Stephen Robert Kellert was born on October 10, 1944, in New Haven, Connecticut. He spent the first five years of his life there, and then his family made a series of moves, mostly within Connecticut. In 1966 he received his bachelor's degree from Cornell University with a major in social psychology and a minor in biology. He earned a Ph.D. from Yale University in 1972 and began teaching and researching there that same year. In 1981, he and Priscilla Whiteman, a teacher, were married. They have two daughters, Emily and Libby. Kellert has continued teaching and conducting research as a professor of social ecology at Yale.

The basic human relationship to nature became the essence of Kellert's work. In the late 1970s and early 1980s he studied human perceptions of animals, including wolves, invertebrates, marine mammals, bears, and diverse endangered species. He also explored the nature-related perspectives of such different groups of people as hunters, birders, farmers, and the general public distinguished by age, gender, socioeconomic status, and place of residence. Through his studies, Kellert began to see recurring patterns of thought in peo-

Stephen Kellert (Photograph by Harold Shapiro)

ple's attitudes toward wildlife and conservation, and it became more and more apparent to him that this reflected a basic tendency in humans to affiliate with nature and diversity.

As these ideas took shape, he became acquainted with the work of Edward O. Wilson, an entomologist at Harvard University. In 1984, Wilson published a book called *Biophilia*, which sought to provide an understanding of how human tendencies to connect with life and natural processes might be the expression of a biological need. Wilson defined *biophilia* as the "innate tendency to focus on life and life-like processes." Kellert and Wilson worked together on this concept when they coedited *The Biophilia Hypothesis*, which was published in 1993. This book brought together 20 scientists from various disciplines, each examining and refining the idea of biophilia in different contexts. The various perspectives—psychological, aesthetic, cultural, ethical, and political—help to frame a broad discussion of biophilia that ultimately goes farther than the standard ecological or economic arguments for the preservation of other species and ecosystems. There are many examples in the book that reinforce the notion that biophilia, and its opposite, biophobia, have evolutionary adaptations. For instance, humans show strong aversions to snakes and spiders with little or no negative reinforcement—while more dangerous modern items such as guns, knives, or electric wires rarely initiate such phobias. Also, people have a common desire to live amid green vegetation and flowers and trees, or near water. Another essay examines the development of myth and the use of natural symbols and how people often ascribe human qualities to animals. As a whole, these essays advance reasons for conservation that are intangible, yet still important: the biophilia concept means that estrangement from the natural world through continued levels of biological destruction could lead to psychological and spiritual impoverishment.

Kellert expanded on this new dimension of conservation in his next book, *The Value of Life: Biological Diversity and Human Society* (1996). Drawing on 20 years of research, he outlines a framework of biologically based values that humans exhibit, such as an aesthetic attraction to nature, a scientific inclination to understand it, a humanistic affection for animals, and others, and then examines differences among varying demographic and cultural groups. In discussing how vital living diversity is, he notes that more Americans visit zoos during an average year than attend all the professional baseball, basketball, and football games together. Visits to national parks and wildlife areas are increasing dramatically, and ecotourism is now the fastest-growing segment of the travel industry. Also, growing numbers of Americans seek wildlife-related diversions such as birding, whale watching, or hunting and fishing. However, in comparing Americans' perceptions of nature with people in other nations, Kellert found that most Americans have a limited understanding of biological processes, and he decries the fact that environmental education receives far too little support. His argument, which illustrates the importance of biological diversity to human psychological health, pleads for greater environmental literacy—both directly, through schools; and indirectly, through mass media.

Building further on these concepts, Kellert wrote another book called *Kinship to Mastery: Biophilia in Human Evolution and Development* (1997). He continues to address concerns over education, since our affinity to nature, though biologically based, is also shaped by mediating influences of learning, culture, and experience. Kellert contends that biophilia is a "weak tendency" and that without positive reinforcement through education and social support it will not develop or thrive. In this book he makes some broad suggestions on how to slow the damage being done to the natural world. These include habitat conservation, integrating nature into people's daily lives, and respecting different cultural attitudes in respecting wildlife. Ultimately the richness of connections with nature will foster a greater quality of life.

Children and Nature, which he co-edited in 2002, explores the influence of nature on children. Contributors to this volume are psychologists, political scientists, primatologists, educators and others—and while there is a great diversity of perspectives, one point of agreement is that exposure to nature is fundamental for a healthy childhood. Also in 2002, Kellert co-edited *The Good in Nature and Humanity: Connecting science, religion, and spirituality with the Natural World*, a collection of 20 essays by major thinkers in the field, that deal with the need to reconcile science and spirituality, faith and reason.

Two of Kellert's most recent books explore how the built environment can help us develop a stronger sense of biophilia: *Building for Life: Designing and Understanding the Human-Nature Connection* (2005) and *Biophilic Design: The Theory, Science, and Practice of Bringing Buildings to Life* (2008), edited by Kellert and two colleagues.

Kellert has received much recognition for his work and many awards. In 1983 he received the Special Achievement Award from the National Wildlife Federation, and in 1985 he received the Best Publication of the Year Award from the International Foundation for Environmental Conservation. He received a Distinguished Individual Achievement Award from the Society for Conservation Biology in 1990, and in 1997 the National Wildlife Federation presented Kellert with its National Conservation Achievement award, recognizing his contributions toward an understanding of how people perceive wildlife and wild places. In 2006, the North American Association for Environmental Education recognized Kellert with its award for Outstanding Contributions to Resarch in Environmental Education. He continues to serve on International Union for the Conservation of Nature Species Survival Commission groups, which he has done since 1992. Kellert has authored more than 100 publications and is the Tweedy/Ordway Professor of Social Ecology at Yale University's School of Forestry and Environmental Studies, and co-directs the Hixon Center for Urban Ecology there.

BIBLIOGRAPHY

Johnson, Andrew, "The Biophilia Hypothesis," *BioScience*, 1994; Kellert, Stephen R., *Kinship to Mastery: Biophilia in Human Evolution and Development*, 1997; Kellert, Stephen R., *The Value of Life: Biological Diversity and Human Society*, 1996; Kellert, Stephen R., and Edward O. Wilson, eds., *The Biophilia Hypothesis*, 1993; "Stephen R. Kellert—Yale School of Forestry & Environmental Studies," www.environment.yale.edu/people/271-Stephen-R.-Kellert/parent:faculty/.

Kendall, Henry
(December 12, 1926–February 15, 1999)
Physicist, Founding Member of the Union of Concerned Scientists

Winner of the 1990 Nobel Prize for Physics for his work in particle physics, Henry Kendall became a vocal critic of nuclear power and the nuclear arms race. Kendall was one of the founding members of the Union of Concerned Scientists (UCS), formed in 1969 to unite scientists to take action against dangerous uses of science and technology. He was particularly influential in the debate over President Reagan's proposed Strategic Defense Initiative (SDI, or "Star Wars") and in calling attention to global warming.

Henry Kendall was born on December 12, 1926, to a wealthy Boston "Brahmin" family. The Kendalls owned the Kendall Company, a health supplies company best known for its Curad line. As a boy, Kendall was more interested in sports than science and was an expert sailor and diver. Upon graduation from high school, he entered the Merchant Marine Academy, where he was studying when the United States dropped the first atomic bomb in 1945. The event awakened Kendall's interest in science, and he entered Amherst College, from which he graduated in 1950 with a B.S. in mathematics.

After graduation, Kendall returned to his interest in the outdoors and operated a diving and salvage operation. He also wrote books about shallow-water diving and underwater photography. Eventually he decided to pursue a career in science, and he earned a Ph.D. in nuclear physics from the Massachusetts Institute of Technology (MIT) in 1955. From 1954 to 1956, Kendall was a National Science Foundation Fellow at Brookhaven National Laboratory and MIT. In 1956 he joined the faculty at Stanford University, where he met Jerome Friedman and Richard Taylor, with whom he would eventually share the Nobel Prize. At the time Stanford had one of the largest particle accelerators in the world and by 1960 had plans to build a new accelerator, two miles in length. Kendall returned to MIT in 1961 and in 1967 began a collaboration with Friedman and Taylor that led to important advances in the understanding of the fundamental nature of matter. Using Stanford's accelerator, they fired electron beams at protons and neutrons and discovered unexpected patterns of deflection. These patterns demonstrated the existence of quarks, up to then only a theoretical proposition. This was the first experimental evidence of subatomic particles. The men's work thus was an important step in the development of the current standard model of the elements of matter.

As a member of the scientific elite, Kendall was in an ideal position to see the ways in which the U.S. military influenced the development and use of science and technology. He served as a consultant to the Department of Defense from 1960 to 1971 and became disturbed by what he saw: the harnessing of the power of science for increasingly destructive ends. At the height of the Vietnam War, Kendall signed the 1968 MIT Faculty Statement that led to the founding of the Union of Concerned Scientists. The statement was a call to scientists and engineers to assume responsibility for the uses of science. The 50 senior faculty who signed proposed, in addition to several other basic ideas, "to initiate a critical and continuing examination of governmental policy in areas where science and technology are of actual or potential significance" and "to devise means for turning research applications away from the present emphasis on military technology toward the solution of pressing environmental and social problems." In early 1969, the group formed the UCS. Kendall was a key figure in the organization from the beginning and served as chairman of the Board of Directors from 1973 until his death.

UCS has been an influential voice in public policy in several areas. One of its initial projects was to call into question the safety of the nation's nuclear arsenal and power plants. In 1977 the UCS issued "Scientists' Declaration on the Nuclear Arms Race," which documented the destructive effects of the Cold War arms buildup. Armed with technical expertise and accepted scientific research, UCS has high credibility with journalists and public officials and used that credibility throughout the 1970s and 1980s to help slow the arms race and close dangerous nuclear plants. Kendall was particularly visible during the fight over the Strategic Defense Initiative, which UCS argued was not only a dangerous escalation of the arms race but also technologically unfeasible. In 1985 UCS issued "Appeal by American Scientists to Ban Space Weapons." SDI eventually died in development. UCS has also been important in publicizing and gaining credibility for theories of global warming. In 1990 it released "Appeal by American Scientists to Prevent Global Warming." In 1992 Kendall authored UCS's "World Scientists' Warning to Humanity," which brought into focus "critical stress" on the environment on a number of fronts, including atmosphere, water, oceans, soil, forests, and living species.

Henry Kendall died on February 15, 1999, while assisting a team from the National Geographic Society in its efforts to map underwater caves in Florida. The cause of death was gastrointestinal hemorrhaging, unrelated to diving. In DAVID BROWER's elegy to Henry Kendall, he reveals that Kendall was an anonymous contributor at essential moments of need, to organizations led by Brower, whose work he believed in, such as the Sierra Club, Friends of the Earth and the Earth Island Institute.

BIBLIOGRAPHY

Brower, David, "Rememberng Henry Kendall, 1927-1999," *Earth Island Journal*, 1999; Chandler, David, "He Still Brown-Bags It," *Boston Globe*, 1990; Oliver, Myrna, "Henry Kendall: Nobel Prize-Winning Nuclear Scientist," *Los Angeles Times*, 1999; "Professor Henry Kendall," *London Times*, 1999; "Union of Concerned Scientists," www.ucsusa.org.

Kennedy, Robert F., Jr.

(January 17, 1954–)
Attorney

Robert F. Kennedy Jr., nephew of Pres. John F. Kennedy and son of Atty. Gen. Robert F. Kennedy, one of the most visible environmental experts and advocates in the country today, is a senior attorney for the Natural Resources Defense Council (NRDC), chief prosecuting attorney for the Hudson Riverkeeper, and director of the environmental law clinic at Pace University Law School in White Plains, New York. He has led Hudson Riverkeeper in more than 200 legal victories over polluters and is best known for negotiating an agreement to protect watersheds surrounding the 19-reservoir water supply of New York City.

Robert Francis Kennedy Jr. was born on January 17, 1954, in Washington, D.C., the third of Robert F. and Ethel Skakel Kennedy's 11 children. He was raised at Hickory Hill, an antebellum estate in McLean, Virginia, across the Potomac from Washington, where his uncle, John F. Kennedy, served as U.S. president from 1961 until his assassination in 1963. Kennedy's devout Catholic parents instilled in their children a profound appreciation for democracy and commitment to social justice. The Kennedy children were frequently reminded that their country had been very good to their family, and they often heard St. Paul's dictum, "To whom much is given, much is expected."

Although Kennedy took seriously the family's debt to society, his early, primary interest was in nature and animals. As a child, he kept a large collection of amphibians, reptiles, and rodents gathered from the streams and forests of Hickory Hill, and when he was 11 years old, his father gave him a red-tailed hawk to train. This awakened what would be a lifelong fascination with raptors. After his father was assassinated in June 1968, Kennedy was sent to board at Millbrook School in upstate New York; the school offered ornithology and natural history curricula and an extracurricular falconry club. Kennedy learned to tame and fly hawks and to trap, band, and release wild raptors. At this point in his life, he hoped to become a veterinarian.

Kennedy attended Harvard College, earning his A.B. in history and literature in 1976. His senior thesis was an analysis of the work of the progressive Alabama federal judge Frank M. Johnson Jr., who desegregated buses and all public facilities, including schools, of Montgomery, Alabama; abolished state poll taxes; ordered that Ku Klux Klan membership lists be published; and reformed the prison system. Kennedy's *Judge Frank M. Johnson, Jr.: A Biography* was published in 1978 by Putnam. Kennedy went on to earn a J.D. degree from the University of Virginia Law School in 1982 and spent one year at the Manhattan district attorney's office prosecuting misdemeanor cases. In 1984 he began work for the Natural Resources Defense Council and the Hudson River Fishermen's Association (HRFA). This organization had been founded in 1966 by Hudson River fishermen angry about the river's contamination and the ensuing decline of the fish population. By the time Kennedy began working with the group, it had a full-time director and "riverkeeper," John Cronin, who patrolled the river to follow up on reports of contamination by the fishermen.

Kennedy's first cases for the HRFA, between 1986 and 1987, were in the town of Newburgh, about 40 miles up the Hudson from Manhattan. Newburgh was run by corrupt politicians who allowed private industry and municipal utilities to poison the Quaissaic tributary and the Hudson River itself. Cronin had been tipped off by local businessman Joe Augustine about the situation, and he, Kennedy, and volunteers from the HRFA collected samples of effluents and stream water that showed undeniably that the Quassaic was being illegally contaminated by 20 separate entities. The New York Department of Environmental Conservation joined with the Fishermen's Association to bring legal action against the polluters. Every polluter—ranging from Mobil Oil to the town water treatment plant to a local textile factory—settled out of court with the plaintiffs, and a well-endowed fund was set up for the cleanup of the Quassaic.

Working on this case proved to be a turning point for Kennedy. Previously, he had not known how to integrate the Kennedy family commitment to social justice with his true love for wildlife and nature. But after learning how environmental contamination affected all of the inhabitants of the Hudson—nonhuman animals and humans alike—he understood that environmental law melded both passions. The success at Newburgh coupled with the challenge of cleaning up the rest of the 315-mile Hudson River convinced Kennedy to accept a position as chief prosecuting attorney for the HRFA (now called the Hudson Riverkeeper). During the Newburgh case, Kennedy had been taking night classes in environmental law at Pace University, and upon his graduation in 1987, Hudson Riverkeeper and Pace agreed to establish a jointly run environmental litigation clinic for Pace University law students. Under supervision by Kennedy and Pace law professor Karl S. Coplan, ten second- and third-year law students spend a year representing Hudson Riverkeeper in federal and state courts and administrative proceedings. Not only have these students gained valuable real-world experience for future careers in environmental law, their work has resulted in ground-breaking decisions in federal courts on decisions under the Clean Water Act and the Resource Conservation and Recovery Act.

Hudson Riverkeeper has been involved in hundreds of legal actions involving the cleanup of the Hudson and Long Island Sound and has forced polluters to pay billions in penalties and remediations. Kennedy is best known for the agreement he forged in 1997 to protect the source of New York City's drinking water. He convinced Republican governor George Pataki—against whom he had campaigned in 1994—to protect the declining watersheds around the 19 upstate reservoirs that provide New York City's drinking water. New York City saved the $8 billion that it would have had to spend on a water filtration plant, and in return, paid watershed protection fees to the municipalities surrounding the reservoirs. Kennedy and Cronin coauthored a 1997 book that described Hudson Riverkeeper and its work, *The Riverkeepers*.

As the accomplishments and the reputation of the Hudson Riverkeeper grew, other water keeper organizations emerged around the country. Currently there are more than 40 similar organizations throughout the United States and Canada. Kennedy serves as national coordinator for the umbrella group, Water Keeper Alliance. In 1999, Kennedy and two partners launched Keeper Springs Mountain Spring Water, a new brand of bottled water, whose after-tax proceeds are channeled to the Water Keeper Alliance.

In addition to his work for Hudson Riverkeeper and Water Keeper Alliance, Kennedy is a senior attorney for the NRDC, where he has played a leading role in a number of international environmental campaigns to preserve endangered ecosystems and the rights of indigenous peoples. These include successful battles to stop such activities as the damming of James Bay in northern Quebec; clear-cut logging in British Columbia's Clayoquot Sound; the Mitsubishi Salt Plant in Laguna San Ignacio, Mexico; the Clifton Cay Development on New Providence Island in the Bahamas; and the Upper Dam on the Bio Bio River in Chile.

In recent years, Kennedy has voiced harsh criticisms of the environmental policies of the administration of Pres. George W. Bush. Kennedy's 2005 book *Crimes Against Nature: Standing Up to Bush and the Kyoto Killers Who are Cashing In on Our World* documents the greed that fuels the energy industry and other polluters, and decries the politics that allow them to do this unimpeded. Kennedy toured the U.S. after the publication of this book, delivering powerful speeches about the need for political change that prioritizes the environment. Interviews with are featured in many popular magazines—he has been very effective at reaching out to the American public.

Kennedy still flies hawks and holds vigil on Schunemunk Ridge overlooking the Hudson River during their annual fall migration to trap, band, and release them as part of an effort to keep tabs on the population. He has a state permit to operate a wildlife rehabilitation center and takes in injured animals, primarily raptors. He has served as president of the New York State Falconers Association.

Kennedy lives with his wife, Mary Richardson, and their three children outside of New York City. He has two older children from a previous marriage.

BIBLIOGRAPHY

Cronin, John, and Robert F. Kennedy Jr., *The Riverkeepers*, 1997; Kennedy, Robert F. Jr., "The Next President's First Task: A Manifesto," *Vanity Fair*, 2008; Leonetti, Carol, "Robert Kennedy, Jr., A Riverkeeper Who Makes the Polluters Pay," *E Magazine*, 1995; "Natural Resources Defense Council—The Earth's Best Defense," www.nrdc.org; Oliver, Joan Duncan, "A Ruffler of Feathers: Eco-Activist Robert F. Kennedy Jr. Stalks Polluters and Avenges

Mother Nature," *Wildlife Conservation*, 1994; "Pace Environmental Litigation Clinic," www.law.pace.edu/envclinic/index.html; "Riverkeeper," www.riverkeeper.org/.

Kingsolver, Barbara

(April 8, 1955–)
Novelist, Gardener

Barbara Kingsolver is a writer and gardener whose first novel, *The Bean Trees*, became an important addition to the canon of American literature. Her fiction has continually been informed by plant and animal life. Millions of readers have had the natural world illuminated by her writing. Her first non-fiction work, *Animal, Vegetable, Miracle: A Year of Food Life* (2007), helped revitalize the locally grown food market.

Barbara Kingsolver was born in Annapolis, Maryland, on April 8 1955 to Wendell R. Kingsolver and Virginia Lee Henry Kingsolver, both of Lexington, Kentucky. Her father was a Navy doctor who later opened a family medical practice in Carlisle, Kentucky. Like her parents, she grew up in eastern Kentucky. In place of a television set, her family had a vegetable garden where her young imagination grew along with an enormous appetite for life. She studied biology, slowly moving westward, first to DePauw University in Indiana, where she earned degrees in biology and English, then further to Tucson, Arizona, where she attained a Masters Degree in animal behavior in 1981 from the University of Arizona. Her older brother also pursued an academic career in biology, her younger sister anthropology. Barbara Kingsolver began her professional life as a science writer for the Arid Lands Institute. After successfully selling articles to national magazines and academic journals (*Mademoiselle, The Progressive, The New York Times, Redbook, The Virginia Quarterly Review,* and *New Mexico Humanities Review*), she ventured into more creative fiction writing.

While pregnant with her first daughter, Camille, Kingsolver's insomnia led to a novel called *The Bean Trees* (1988). It follows a Kentucky woman on her journey west to Tucson. Along the way she was given a baby who she raises with the help of generous Arizona neighbors. Part from becoming a bestseller, *The Bean Trees* became a staple in America's fiction diet.

The voices of Kingsolver the horticulturalist, the botanist, the organic chemist are sewn into her fiction writing. Many of her books incorporate botanical motifs. In *The Poisonwood Bible* (1998) the narrator's ars poetica is Kingsolver's ars poetica:

"In organic chemistry, invertebrate zoology, and the inspired symmetry of Mendelian genetics, I have found a religion that serves. I recite the Periodic Table of Elements like a prayer. I take my examinations as Holy Communion, and the pass of the first semester was a sacrament. My mind is crowded with a forest of facts. Between the trees lie wide-open plains of despair. I skirt around them. I stick to the woods." (page 486)

Other books include: *Holding the Line* (1989), a short story collection called Homeland (1989), *Animal Dreams* (1990), a book of verse titled *Another America* (1992), *Pigs In Heaven* (1993), *Prodigal Summer* (2000), essays in *High Tide In Tucson* (1995), and *Small Wonder* (2002).

Kingsolver's first book of non-fiction, *Animal, Vegetable, Miracle: A Year of Food Life* (2007), was co-written with her husband, an animal psychologist and ecologist, Steven L.

Hopp, and their daughter Camille. After returning to her roots on a farm in Appalachia, her family decided to only eat locally grown food. They chronicle their exploration into the food economy and ecology. The book helped revitalize the locally grown food market and community-supported agricultural groups (CSAs). Kingsolver and leaders in the go-local movement advocate a move away from the industrial food supply for a range of reasons.

"We can start by thinking about farmers every time we eat. How much of my food dollar went to a farmer, to help support sustainable choices? On average, 85 percent of every food dollar goes to the processors, packagers, advertisers and oil companies who profit handsomely from our lack of regard for soil, water, climate and the future," Kingsolver told the Environmental Defense Council newsletter editors.

With more fossil fuels often found in our refrigerators than in our gas tanks, Kingsolver her family, and her readers are shifting to homegrown food in their daily lives.

"We can't wait for radical conservation measures to be imposed on us by our government." She maintains that we can make big changes with small consumer choices.

Kingsolver is an Environmental Defense Council member and lives and writes in southwestern Virginia with free-range chickens, turkeys, Icelandic sheep, and her family.

BIBLIOGRAPHY
Mahoney, Ellen, "How on Earth," October 16, 2007, hoe.kgnu.net/hoeradioshow.php?show_id=314; Environmental Defense Fund newsletter, "Solutions," Vol. 38, No. 4, August 2007; www.kingsolver.com; www.animalvegetablemiracle.org.

Kratt, Chris, and Martin Kratt
(July 19, 1969– ; December 23, 1965–)
Creators and Producers of Children's Wildlife Programs

As creators, executive producers, and stars of *Kratts' Creatures*, a television program designed for school-age children, and the Emmy Award-winning *Zoboomafoo*, designed for preschoolers, Chris and Martin Kratt are redefining children's programming and how future generations will view animals and the world around them. The two programs are designed not only to educate and entertain children but also to empower them to explore the world. The Kratt brothers have also written several wildlife books for children and have produced nature films. Both brothers have a wealth of travel and wildlife experience as "creature adventurers," having filmed all over the world. Together, they formed the Kratt Brothers' Creature Heroes, a not-for-profit organization to stimulate children to become interested and involved in wildlife conservation. With the funds raised, they purchased Grizzly Gulch, a wildlife refuge in Montana, to protect the endangered Great Plains grizzly bear.

Martin Kratt was born December 23, 1965, in Warren, New Jersey. He completed a B.S. in zoology at Duke University in 1990 and was awarded a Richard H. Jenrette Fellowship to the University of North Carolina M.B.A. program. After college, Kratt began his filmmaking career, when he went (with his brother, Chris) to Costa Rica to film wildlife. He later served as an intern at public television station Thirteen/WNET in New York, where he worked on the popular PBS series, *Nature*.

Martin Kratt has been involved in several field training projects involving wildlife, including a training program in breeding endangered species in captivity at the Jersey Wildlife Preservation Trust in England.

Christopher Kratt was born July 19, 1969, also in Warren, New Jersey. He received a B.A. in biology from Carleton College in 1992. He has conducted several field studies in ecology and ecological evolution funded by grants from the Explorers Club and the National Science Foundation. In 1990, he worked as an intern at Conservation International in Washington, D.C., and a year later founded the Carleton Organization for Biodiversity, a group dedicated to increasing public awareness of conservation issues. Upon his graduation from Carleton, he received a Thomas J. Watson Fellowship, which he used to develop wildlife documentaries for children.

Both Kratt brothers are dedicated to teaching young people about wild animals and working for the preservation of endangered species. To that end, in 1990 they founded the Earth Creatures Company, which specializes in wildlife entertainment. In 1996, *Kratts' Creatures*, the first series created by the Kratt Brothers, premiered on PBS. The wildlife program is designed for school-age children; it has attracted enthusiastic viewers of all ages and has received numerous awards—including a 1996 Parents' Choice Award—and widespread critical acclaim; it is seen in 34 countries. Recognizing that there were no wildlife shows specifically designed for preschoolers, the Kratts created and starred in *Zoboomafoo* (zah-BOO-mah-foo), based around a playful leaping lemur. Each episode is based on a separate theme and introduces all kinds of creatures ranging from household pets to camels, tigers, and lesser-known creatures from all over the world. The goal of the program is for young children to befriend animals and to respect and care for the creatures with whom they share the world.

The Kratts' newest television show is *Be the Creature*, a prime-time documentary exploring the biology, physiology, and behavior of such animals as African Wild Dogs, the Japanese Macaque, and the Ethiopian Baboon, that appears on the National Geographic channel.

In addition to their television work, the Kratts have also produced, hosted, and filmed 12 "Earth Creature Reports" for PBS's children's television show, *Real News for Kids*, and produced segments for Nickelodeon's *Video Pen Pals Show*. They have also written several wildlife books for children, which include *Creatures in Crisis*, *Where're the Bears?*, *To Be a Chimpanzee*, and *Going Baboony*.

In 1999, they founded the Kratt Brothers' Creature Heroes, a not-for-profit organization to include and encourage children's involvement in wildlife conservation. They were inspired to do this in 1997, by a letter and check for $3.19 from young Katie O'Connor, who asked them to save animals with her donation. Their first land purchase on behalf of Creature Heroes was at the end of 1999, when with the help of the Nature Conservancy of Montana, they acquired 1,222 acres of Grizzly Gulch, adjacent to the Bob Marshall Wilderness Area and habitat for the endangered Great Plains grizzly bear, the mountain lion, the timber wolf, and elk, among other species. Of the $1.3 million purchase price, $250,000 was raised by children across North America, and the rest was loaned to them. The Kratts toured to fundraise to repay the loan; with the help of Old Navy, half a million dollars was raised during the summer of 2000. .

The Kratt Brothers have won numerous awards for film and children's entertainment, including "Best Children's Film" for *Amazon Adventure* at the 1993 Jackson Hole Wildlife Film Festival and "Best Children's Program" for the premiere episode of *Big Five, Little Five* at the 1996 International Wildlife Film Festival. In September 1998, Secretary of the Interior BRUCE BABBITT presented the Kratt Brothers an award of appreciation for their ongoing commitment and public service on behalf of conservation and environmental education. The honor was bestowed by the U.S. Department of Agriculture for Partners in Conservation Education.

The Kratts continue to be creature adventurers, traveling the world, filming exotic animals for their various wildlife projects, and including children in the many projects. Their Earth Creatures Company currently works out of Toronto.

BIBLIOGRAPHY

"Kratt Brothers: Be the Creature," www.bethecreature.tv; "Kratts' Creatures: PBS Kids GO," www.pbskids.org/krattscreatures; "The Official Kratt Brothers' Website," www.krattbrothers.com/; "PBS: Zoboomafoo," www.pbskids.org/zoboo/.

Krupp, Fred
(March 21, 1954–)
Executive Director of the Environmental Defense Fund, Attorney

As executive director of the Environmental Defense Fund, Fred Krupp is one of the leaders of the "third wave" of environmentalism, whereas environmental organizations work *with* rather than *against* businesses with environmentally destructive practices and policies, to improve those companies' practices and diffuse the traditionally adversarial relationships between environmentalists and corporations. Krupp first came to national attention in 1992 when he negotiated an agreement with McDonald's Corporation to stop using "clamshell" styrofoam containers made with ozone-destroying chlorofluorocarbons (CFCs). Krupp is also recognized for the key role he played in the congressional passage of the Clean Air Act of 1990, and his innovative plan for a national trading system for pollutant emission "credits" was incorporated into the act.

Frederic D. Krupp was born on March 21, 1954, in Mineola, New York, and grew up in Verona, New Jersey. His mother was a high school history teacher, and his father ran a business that processed waste rags that were eventually made into roofing materials. Krupp majored in combined sciences at Yale, where he became interested in finding solutions to environmental problems. He earned his B.S. in 1975. He received his law degree from the University of Michigan in 1978. Krupp formed the law firm Albis & Krupp in 1978 and remained with the partnership until 1984, when he joined Cooper, Whitney, Cochran & Krupp. He married Laurie Devitt, a public health nutritionist, in 1982.

Krupp helped found the Connecticut Fund for the Environment (CFE) in 1978 and served as general counsel for the fund until 1984. In 1979, when he was just 25 years old, Krupp led the CFE in bringing a $1.5 million lawsuit against the Upjohn Corporation for discharging toxic chemicals into the Quinnipiac River in Connecticut. The skillful handling of this bold legal action brought the young lawyer to the attention of the Environmental Defense Fund (EDF), and in 1984, he was offered the position of executive director. A group of concerned citizens in Long Island had founded the Environmental Defense Fund in 1967; inspired by RACHEL CARSON, they sought to block the use of dichlordiphenyltrichlor (DDT) by challenging chemical polluters in court. Krupp's initial goal was to expand the organization's national presence. Under his direction, EDF has grown from 40,000 to 500,000 members. In addition to its innovative, environmentally friendly headquarters in Manhattan, designed by green architect BILL MCDONOUGH, EDF now has offices located in many cities of the U.S, as well as in China. The regional U.S. offices have been successful in raising EDF's profile throughout the nation; they also effect change on the local level by encouraging local governments, businesses, and citizens to seek solutions to regional environmental problems. ED's staff has increased eightfold since 1984, from 50 to 400; the multidisciplinary staff includes scientists, attorneys, and economists. In the last two decades, EDF has moved beyond the national scene, assuming a prominent position on the international environmental scene, particularly in the area of global warming.

Krupp is widely credited with breaking the congressional stalemate over the 1990 Clean Air Act. His innovative plan to reduce acid rain by trading emission "credits" was incorporated into the act. Under Krupp's plan, corporations that reduced sulfur dioxide emissions would be given "credits" that could then be sold to other companies. He achieved further recognition in 1992, negotiating an agreement with McDonalds to substitute cardboard containers for the styrofoam cases the company had been using. A large grassroots consumer campaign led by Penny Newman and LOIS GIBBS had been pushing McDonalds for several years to discontinue using its styrofoam "clam-shell" containers, whose manufacture required ozone-destroying CFCs. McDonalds called upon Krupp to negotiate an agreement in 1992. Krupp catapulted into the national spotlight, and many in the environmental movement claimed this as a symbolic victory. (Newman and Gibbs were disappointed not only because the new bleached paper containers contained little or no recycled content but also because EDF took full credit for the agreement, without acknowledging the gains of the consumer campaign.)

Krupp's willingness to cooperate with major corporations—a tendency that has been called the third wave of environmentalism—has been viewed with suspicion by many environmentalists. But EDF holds that it can often effect change more quickly by working with corporations than against them. During the 1990s, Krupp forged amicable working relations between EDF and global corporations such as Monsanto, Pacific Gas & Electric, and Merck, but was careful, according to MARK DOWIE in *Losing Ground* (1995), to screen out corporate donors to exclude any that "would compromise its negotiating positions or damage its reputation as an independent advocate." EDF accepts no donations or payment from the companies it persuades to make environmental improvements.

In recent years, EDF has worked with FedEx to encourage them to develop a new fleet of hybrid delivery vehicles, with DuPont to reduce the risks of their work in nanotechnology, and has opened an office near the headquarters of Wal-Mart's corporate headquarters to help it improve energy efficiency and and reduce packaging. Krupp helped launch the U.S. Climate Action Partnership and invited dozens of Fortune 500 corporations to participate and call for limits on pollution that contributes to global warming.

EDF has not abandoned its litigious tradition, however; it was preparing to sue Texas utility company TXU to prevent its construction of several new coal-fired power plants, after TXU refused to pursue alternatives. When two private equity groups decided to buy out TXU, however, they chose to negotiate with EDF and the other environmental groups working on the case, and ended up building only three of the 11 new coal plants that had been planned.

Krupp and co-author Miriam Horn published *Earth: The Sequel* in 2008, which was a *New York Times* best-seller and was lauded by New York City mayor Michael Bloomberg as making "it crystal clear that we can build a low-carbon economy while unleashing American entrepreneurs to save the planet, putting optimism back into the environmental story."

Krupp has been a member of the President's Commission on Sustainable Development and the President's Advisory Committee for Trade Policy and Negotiations. Apart from his work with EDF, Krupp is an accomplished rower; he won a gold medal in the 2006 world rowing championship. He was designated in 2007 as one of 16 of "America's best leaders" by *U.S. News & World Report*.

Krupp lives in New Canaan, Connecticut with his wife, Laurie. They have three sons Alex, Jackson, and Zack.

BIBLIOGRAPHY

Dowie, Mark, *Losing Ground*, 1995; "Environmental Defense," www.edf.org; Krupp, Fred, "Business and the Third Wave: Saving the Environment," *Vital Speeches of the Day*, 1992; Krupp, Fred and Miriam Horn, *Earth: the sequel*, 2008; Miller, William H., "Fred Krupp: A Different Kind of Environmentalist," *Industry Week*, 1994; Reed, Susan, "Environmentalist Fred Krupp Helps Crush the Ubiquitous Fast-food Clamshell," *People Weekly*, 1991; Schulte, Bret, "Fred Krupp: environmentalist," *U.S. News & World Report*, 2007.

American Environmental Leaders

From Colonial Times to the Present

LaBudde, Samuel

(July 3, 1956–)
Founder and Director of the Endangered Species Project

Samuel LaBudde is the founder and director of the Endangered Species Project (ESP), an organization that endeavors to curb species extinction through investigations of the illegal wildlife trade, public education campaigns, and wilderness preservation. The recipient of a 1991 Goldman Environmental Award, LaBudde undertook a risky 1988 undercover investigation of dolphin slaughter by the tuna industry. With videotape of this practice in hand, LaBudde helped organize a domestic campaign that resulted in industry reforms and protective legislation, which eventually led to a 95 percent reduction in dolphin kills. LaBudde is also credited for exposing the ecological destruction caused by driftnet fishing. His work on this problem resulted in a 1992 United Nations resolution banning the use of driftnets.

Born in Madison, Wisconsin, on July 3, 1956, to Bessie Freeman and John LaBudde, Samuel Freeman LaBudde (pronounced la-buddy) grew up in southern Indiana. Of mixed French Norwegian and Scotch Cherokee heritage, he was exposed to the regional influences of Hoosier pride and Bible Belt principles throughout his childhood and elementary school years. But in his teens, he transformed into a more rebellious young man: "I think it was an awareness of my own heritage and what happened to the American Indian in this country," LaBudde related in an interview with *The Atlantic Monthly*. "It's essentially the same thing that's been done to the land."

After graduating from high school LaBudde set off on a classic coming-of-age saga of college courses, travel, and outdoor jobs. He spent four years working in the West: He planted trees in the Pacific Northwest, was a technician on a seismic crew, and was a machinist in Alaska. By 1984 he had become increasingly concerned about the deforestation of tropical rain forests, and felt that if he earned a degree in biology he might be able to do something to stop it. He left Alaska and motorcycled to Indiana, where he returned to college and earned a B.S. in biology in 1986. After graduating, LaBudde took a job with the National Marine Fisheries Service (NMFS) as a fisheries biologist on a Japanese trawler in the Bering Sea. Back from his first tour, he was offered a second one, on an American tuna boat based in San Diego. He refused this offer, however, hoping to find a position with an environmental organization.

A few weeks later, while he was waiting in the offices of the Earth Island Institute (EII) for an interview with the Rainforest Action Network (which was than an affiliate of EII), he read in a recent issue of *Earth Island Journal* about how dolphin slaughter by the tuna industry had resulted in a 50- to 75-percent drop in population of the three principal dolphin species. Because tuna frequently school beneath dolphins, commercial tuna fisherman would set the nets around the dolphins in order to catch the tuna. Dolphins would die from exhaustion and muscle fatigue after the chase, or from being caught in the net and suffocated, or when they were pulled through the machinery used to haul in the net. LaBudde learned from EII staff that the biggest impediment to stopping the dolphin killings was the absence of documentation about the problem. He recontacted NMFS to ask for the job on a tuna boat, but learned that NMFS biologists had to sign a nondisclosure statement prohibiting them from speaking about what they saw on board, and that further, no cameras were allowed. So LaBudde sought out Stan Minasian, the director of the Marine Mammal Fund (MMF), to talk about going undercover on a foreign tuna boat. Armed only with his own determination and a promise from the Marine Mammal Fund to supply him with a video camera, LaBudde headed across the Mexican border in September 1987 and got a job aboard a tuna boat. His intent was to obtain graphic footage of the massacre during tuna catches that was needed to raise public consciousness and end the slaughter. Risking exposure and retribution, LaBudde—who says that from his experience waiting tables during college he knew what food was supposed to look like but had never formally prepared a meal for anyone other than himself—worked for 5 months as the cook aboard the Panamanian fishing boat *Maria Luisa*, ultimately securing the film he needed.

After debarking in January, 1988, LaBudde—with support from MMF and EII—set out on a major media campaign on the tuna industry's slaughter of dolphins. LaBudde's footage appeared on most every network's nightly news broadcast and news shows, and a massive boycott of tuna fish was organized and eventually focused on H.J. Heinz corporation, which controlled half of the United States market share of tuna. By April 1990, Heinz announced its decision not to buy or sell tuna that was not dolphin-safe. Congress subsequently passed legislation to heighten dolphin protection and strengthened the dolphin protection clauses of the 1972 Marine Mammal Protection Act in the Act's 1988 and 1994 reauthorizations.

Parallel to his work to protect dolphins, LaBudde also became involved in a fight to ban driftnet fishing. Driftnets (also called gillnets) are ten-meter-deep walls of net made from monofilament fishing line with mesh from two to eight inches wide. They ensnare anything that drifts into them and is large enough to get stuck: squid, billfish, tuna, cetaceans, seabirds, turtles, etc. This practice had been encouraged in East Asia after World War II, but by the late 1980s, when there were more than 1000 vessels each dropping 30 to 40 miles of the net every night in the north Pacific, that marine ecosystem was in extreme danger of collapse. With support from the Hawaiian organization Earthtrust, LaBudde helped organize and lead an expedition on the high seas to document the practice, and wrote a technical paper compiling data about the potential ecological impact of the driftnet fisheries. He provided the report and video to the governments of two dozen southern Pacific nations whose fisheries-dependent economies were most affected by driftnet fishing. Alarmed at the danger to their economies, these governments successfully lobbied the United Nations to pass a 1992 resolution banning driftnet fishing in international waters, and the same year, Pres. Bush signed into law legislation that severely limited the use of coastal driftnets, which essentially made driftnetting economically untenable. LaBudde then spent two years in Europe with Humane Society International on a successful campaign to ban the import of dolphin-deadly tuna and limit the use of driftnets by the European fishing industry.

In recognition of his courageous investigative work and effective public education campaigns, LaBudde was nominated by a network of internationally known environmental organizations and a panel of environmental experts for the 1991 Goldman Prize. He used the $60,000 monetary award to found the Endangered Species Project (ESP), which he directed for 13 years until 2004. ESP worked with other domestic and international non-governmental organizations on investigations and campaigns to protect wildlife and wilderness, providing local activists with video cameras to obtain necessary documentation. ESP financed extensive field investigations throughout Southeast Asia to document illegal trade in tigers and other endangered wildlife. It exposed Vietnam as a center for the Southeast Asian wholesale trade in wildlife and secured international resolutions condemning involvement of China and Taiwan in illegal wildlife trade. Thanks to pressure from ESP and other concerned entities, the U.S. implemented trade sanctions against Taiwan in 1994—the first economic sanctions in history that have been imposed against a country for violations of an international conservation accord. This pressure prompted China, Singapore, South

Korea, and Taiwan to pass laws against trade in tigers. *Crime Against Nature*, a report and video overview that ESP produced in 1994, documents the involvement of organized crime in the illegal wildlife trade and the inability of the Convention on International Trade in Endangered Species (CITES) to regulate it.

In addition to its research and work on policy and legislative matters, ESP contributed to concrete conservation efforts. It helped establish the International Siberian Tiger Sanctuary in Eastern Russia, and worked to set up a bioreserve for gorillas in West Africa.

Despite the positive achievements LaBudde and others can claim, species conservation work is never complete. In 1999, five years after the amendment of the Marine Mammal Protection Act, LaBudde found himself engaged in a lawsuit with other species protection activists—including Humane Society of the United States, Defenders of Wildlife, American Society for the Prevention of Cruelty to Animals, Animal Welfare Institute, and EII—against the United States government for its proposed weakening of dolphin-safe standards. The United States had come under fire by the World Trade Organization for its refusal to import dolphin-deadly tuna from Mexico; this was considered a contravention of international trade rules. A proposal by U.S. Secretary of Commerce William Daley to loosen the definition of "dolphin safe" tuna would have totally undermined much of the earlier work done by LaBudde and his fellow activists. In April 2000, Daley's proposal was struck down.

In 2004, LaBudde closed the doors of ESP and moved his efforts to the International Marine Mammal Project through Earth Island Institute.

LaBudde makes his home in San Francisco. Copies of his video footage showing the devastating effects of tuna nets on dolphins are available through EII; video footage of driftnetting is available through Earthtrust.

BIBLIOGRAPHY

Brower, Kenneth, "The Destruction of Dolphins," *Atlantic Monthly*, 1989; "Earth Island Institute-International Marine Mammal Project" www.earthisland.org/immp; "Earthtrust," www.earthtrust.org; "Goldman Prize: Recipients," www.goldmanprize.org/recipients/recipients.html; Wallace, Aubrey, *Eco-Heroes: Twelve Tales of Environmental Victory*, 1993.

LaDuke, Winona

(August 18, 1959–)
Community Restoration Worker, Cofounder and Cochair of Indigenous Women's Network

Native American economist, writer, and activist Winona LaDuke (Anishinabe) is an advocate for indigenous people throughout the world, promoting indigenous control of traditional homelands. Native peoples have honed sustainable lifestyles that have allowed them to live for thousands of years without damaging the ecology of their homelands, and LaDuke works to nurture that specialized knowledge. She cofounded and cochairs the Indigenous Women's Network, a coalition of Native women who apply traditional knowledge to resolve contemporary problems.

Winona LaDuke, born on August 18, 1959 in California, spent her childhood in Los Angeles

Winona LaDuke (AP Images/Chad Harder)

and in Ashland, Oregon. Her father, Vincent LaDuke, also known as Sun Bear, was an Anishinabe (or Ojibwe, Chippewa) spiritual thinker, writer, actor, and activist who enrolled his daughter as a member of his White Earth reservation and took her with him to powwows and other Native American functions. Both Winona and her father remember that powwow dancing made a deep impression on her. When Winona was five, her parents split up, and she moved with her mother, artist and political activist Betty LaDuke, to Ashland, Oregon. She visited White Earth frequently, and her mother, though not Native American herself, encouraged her to spend summers living with Native peoples in order to learn more about her heritage and Native struggles. Winona LaDuke was recruited by Harvard University, studied economic development there, and graduated in 1982. Upon graduation, she was invited to become high school principal on the White Earth Reservation. Returning to White Earth, she told *People Magazine*, was like coming home for the first time.

LaDuke works to secure Native land tenancy at White Earth, where 90 percent of the 830,000 acres in northwestern Minnesota that were originally declared White Earth Reservation in 1867 are now owned by non-Anishinabe people. With the $20,000 the Reebok Foundation awarded to her in 1988 in recognition of her work championing human rights, LaDuke founded the White Earth Land Recovery Project (WELRP). That seed money was used to purchase 1,000 acres of White Earth land, and the project hopes to acquire hundreds of thousands more.

WELRP has undertaken a number of initiatives to increase their sustainability. At White Earth they are attempting to increase the amount of wind energy they can generate on their land; they collaborate on a national conference about indigenous farming; they are combatting the epidemic of Type 2 diabetes by promoting traditional, local foods. WELRP raises funds through sale of products like jewelry, birch bark baskets and crafts, fry bread mix and more through Native Harvest, a catalog that can be requested by mail, and an online store (www.nativeharvest.com).

In addition to the White Earth Land Recovery Project, LaDuke has worked on many other fronts to fortify Anishinabe culture. She has helped establish an artisan cooperative for traditional handicrafts, set up an Ojibwe language program for children and adults, arranged for all road signs in White Earth to be in the Ojibwe language, and taken legal action to prevent unsuitable development on sacred burial sites.

LaDuke has written three books: *Last Standing Woman* (1997), a novel tracing the history of the Anishinabe people; *All Our Relations: Native Struggles for Land and Life* (1999), which describes how eight Native nations across the United States are struggling to maintain self-determination and community despite threats from outside; and *Recovering the Sacred: The Power of Naming and Claiming* (2005), in which she shows how "naming" and "claiming", sacred elements of Native American spiritual practice and culture, must be regained. What is "sacred" ranges from important mountains and other land features, DNA, foods, and animals."

LaDuke's affiliations and commitments are numerous. She has co-chaired the Indigenous Women's Network, which was founded in 1985 by a coalition of Native women to revitalize indigenous languages and cultures, protect religious and cultural practices, protect the environment, and work toward recovery of indigenous lands. Now she serves on its honorary council. She is a member of the editorial collective that publishes *Indigenous Woman* magazine. Since 1993 LaDuke has organized biannual concert tours with the musical duo Indigo Girls to educate youth about Native issues and raise money for Native environmental causes. She ran for vice president in 1996 and 2000 on the Green Party ticket with RALPH NADER and has served on the board of Greenpeace. She was recognized by *Time* magazine in 1995 as one of the Fifty Leaders for the Future and in *Ms.* magazine in 1998 as one of their Women of the Year.

LaDuke has two children from a marriage to Randy Kapashesit, a Cree from Moose Factory, Ontario, and now lives with her companion, Kevin Gasco, an Odawa coffee roaster from Northern Michigan.

BIBLIOGRAPHY

Barsamian, David, *Winona LaDuke: Activism on and off the Reservation*, audio recording, 1998; Bowermaster, Jon, "Earth of a Nation," *Harpers Bazaar*, 1993; "Indigenous Women's Network," www.indigenouswomen.org; LaDuke, Winona, *Last Standing Woman*, 1997; Paul, Sonya, and Robert Perkinson, "Winona LaDuke," *The Progressive*, 1995; Rosen, Marjorie, and Margaret Nelson, "Friend of the Earth," *People*, 1994; "White Earth Land Recovery Project & Native Harvest," www.nativeharvest.com.

Lammers, Owen

(March 20, 1963–)
Executive Director of Living Rivers, River Advocate

Owen Lammers is the executive director of Living Rivers, the Moab, Utah-based Colorado Riverkeeper that seeks to restore the Colorado River to its former glory, by draining Lake Powell and limiting diversion of its waters for agricultural and municipal use. Prior to founding Living Rivers in 2000, Lammers spent 12 years leading the river advocacy organization International Rivers Network (IRN). IRN is a Berkeley-based group that promotes river management practices that respect both human rights and environmental protection. As head of program development at IRN, Lammers mobilized international campaigns to challenge destructive river development projects around the world and to discourage governments and businesses from financing such projects as the Three Gorges Dam in China.

Owen Thomas Lammers was born on March 20, 1963, in Los Angeles and raised in Walnut Creek and Berkeley, California. His father, Thomas Lammers, is a civil engineer, and his mother, Mary Josephine (Coor) Lammers, is a teacher and moving consultant. Lammers graduated from the University of California at Berkeley in 1986 with a B.S. in natural resources economics. After working for a few years as a real estate appraiser, in 1987 Lammers joined IRN, which at that time was an all-volunteer organization. Lammers plunged into fundraising, and within three months, he was a paid staff member. Over the next 12 years, Lammers worked his way up from administrative director to executive director, eventually becoming vice president for program development. Under his direction, IRN grew from a small volunteer organization to one with 21 staff members, three offices, and a budget of over a million dollars.

In the 1990s, Lammers coordinated international efforts to challenge some of the most destructive river development projects in the world, including the Three Gorges Dam in China and the Maheshwar Dam in India. IRN scored a success by targeting Morgan Stanley Dean Witter because the investment firm had been underwriting securities for the State Development Bank of China, which was helping to finance the Three Gorges project. In response to pressure from environmental groups, including IRN, the shareholders voted to withdraw support for the project and to set guidelines that could prevent the financing of similar projects in the future.

In 1998, IRN was one of three environmental organizations to receive $1 million from the San Francisco–based Richard and Rhoda Goldman Fund, administrator of the prestigious Goldman Environmental Prize. IRN used the money to further support projects in Latin America and Southern Africa. One of the projects supported by IRN is the International Meeting of People Affected by Dams, which held its first meeting in 1997 in Brazil and which works to build an international network of antidam activists.

Lammers, along with Dr. Robert Haas, U.S. poet laureate (1995–1997), helped to create the River of Words Project (www.riverofwords.org), a nonprofit educational program established in 1993. The respected environmental education program distributes curriculum guides that teachers may use to develop activities to teach children about their local watershed; students then create artwork or poetry to submit to an international environmental poetry and art contest. River of Words also offers teacher-training workshops and annually honors a Teacher of the Year.

Lammers's strength as an environmental leader lies in his skill as a campaigner and his ability to mobilize public support. By 1999, IRN had developed from a grassroots activist organization into a well-funded service organization. Lammers felt that it was time to move on. He resigned from IRN in August and within a few months had left Berkeley and moved to Utah. The move was Lammers's response to a growing sense that he could not be a credible environmental leader while spending little time engaged with the natural world. He had been introduced to the red rock country of southern Utah in 1993 when he joined the board of the Four Corners School of Outdoor Education based in Monticello. (He served as a consultant to the school until 1998.) Lammers decided Moab, Utah, was a good place to reestablish his connection to the environment after years of living in the city.

Upon his arrival in Moab, area residents with an interest in restoration of the Colorado River seized the opportunity to organize a group with Lammers at the helm. The idea for GCAN arose out of an informal discussion between Lammers and local river guides and outfitters in a Moab restaurant in late 1999. The group's initial objective was to build public support for the decommissioning of the Glen Canyon dam, with the end goal of draining mammoth Lake Powell. Mobilizing with lightning speed, the group was up and running by January 2000. Lammers enlisted the support of prominent environmentalist DAVID BROWER and set about developing a broad-based membership that included activists, river outfitters, educators, and writers. GCAN began a program of monthly lectures in Moab and established a nonprofit ice cream shop in downtown Moab, with all proceeds going toward restoring the Colorado River watershed.

Three months after GCAN was created, it hosted a Restoration Celebration and Rendezvous in Page and Flagstaff, Arizona. The date of the Rendezvous, March 13, was set to coincide with the 37th anniversary of the start of the filling of Lake Powell and the international Third Annual Day of Action Against Dams and for Rivers, Water, and Life. Eighty-seven-year-old David Brower was the keynote speaker, and Secretary of the Interior BRUCE BABBITT made an appearance wielding a sledgehammer. Two hundred individuals and representatives of 45 organizations signed the Glen Canyon Declaration calling for the decommissioning of Glen Canyon Dam and the draining of Lake Powell.

GCAN changed its name to Living Rivers in 2001, and in 2002, Living Rivers was selected as the Colorado Riverkeeper, by ROBERT F. KENNEDY JR.'s Waterkeeper Alliance. The main goal of Living Rivers is to restore the Colorado River to its original glory by undoing the damage wreaked by dams, pollution, and diversion of its waters. The organization is calling for the revision of the 1922 agreement on how water from the Colorado River is allocated, and for the government to impose water use and efficiency standards for the farmers that use 75 percent of the river's water for irrigation. The Colorado River basin states and Sonora, Mexico have experienced a severe drought since about 1998—with about half of the flow as was normal previously. Yet "federal and state water managers continue to keep their heads in the sand," according to Living Waters' website. Lammars and Living Rivers are working to increase public awareness of this problem and its solutions. One of the most effective responses, says Lammars and Living Rivers, is to destroy the Glen Canyon Dam, which would drain Lake Powell and restore flow through Glen Canyon and Grand Canyon. A response this dramatic would need a swell of public support.

Lammers lives in Moab, Utah.

BIBLIOGRAPHY
"Living Rivers," www.livingrivers.org; "International Rivers Network," www.irn.org; "River of Words," www.riverofwords.org; "The Rivers Movement," *New Internationalist*, 1995.

Lappé, Frances Moore

(February 10, 1944–)
Writer, Cofounder of Institute for Food and Development Policy and Center for Living Democracy

Through her writing and activism, Frances Moore Lappé has fought to dismiss popular myths about the causes of hunger, poverty, and environmental degradation. She has written many books on these subjects, beginning with *Diet for a Small Planet*, the best seller that linked hunger to economic and political issues and urged developed countries to shift from meat production to vegetable production. This groundbreaking book revealed the vast waste of resources incurred by meat production and changed the way millions of people thought about how food choices affect the environment. Lappé was also founder and director of the Institute for Food and Development Policy and more recently with her daughter Anna Lappé launched the Small Planet Institute to promote a new type of democracy worldwide, in which the values of inclusion, fairness and mutual accountability permeate society and governance.

Frances Moore was born on February 10, 1944, in Pendleton, Oregon, to John Gilmer

Moore, a forecaster for the U.S. Weather Service, and Ina (Skrifvars) Moore, a transportation agent for the Corps of Engineers. Her parents' professions made less of an impression on her than their open-minded and progressive home life and volunteer efforts. The family moved to Fort Worth, Texas, when Frances was just a few years old, and with the help of some close friends they founded the First Unitarian Church of Fort Worth. Lappé loved growing up against the backdrop of the church, which provided a forum for discussing and participating in social issues. She attended American University in Washington, D.C., from 1962 to 1963 and then finished up at Earlham College in Richmond, Indiana, earning her B.A. in 1966. In the late 1960s, Lappé headed to Berkeley, California, to study social work in graduate school. But she found herself delving deeper and deeper into the shelves at the campus agricultural library, where she discovered more and more links between food and politics. She began trying to figure out why millions were going hungry despite an apparent bounty of food. In 1967 she married Marc Alan Lappé, a biology research associate, with whom she would have two children, Anna and Anthony. The Lappés' marriage ended in divorce ten years later. She moved to Philadelphia, Pennsylvania after her divorce, in order to work as a community organizer at the Philadelphia Neighborhood Renewal Program, where she stayed two years.

As her interest in agriculture and world hunger grew, Lappé continued to educate herself, taking notes and tacking messages on health food store bulletin boards. She compiled her findings, and in 1971 she published *Diet for a Small Planet*, a book that created a nutrition revolution and changed the way millions of Americans thought about food and world hunger. She pointed out that most of the grain grown on harvested agricultural land is fed to livestock, an extremely inefficient use of energy and farming resources, since a cow must be fed 21 pounds of protein to produce one pound of protein for human consumption. Her book tapped into a powerful well of concern across the country when it showed how this pattern of waste contributes to the overconsumption of resources that the United States had come to be known for. However, Lappé, having grown up eating meatloaf and hamburgers herself, knew that the fixed cultural attitude of the time frowned on vegetarianism and that people were concerned about getting enough protein. So her book explained how to get enough protein without centering one's diet around meat by combining grains with legumes in various combinations, such as beans and rice, beans and tortillas, or soy and rice. This produces a healthy diet rich in protein and makes much better use of the earth's productivity. Lappé accomplished her goal of establishing a sense of the direct impact food choices have on the earth, and her book, which has sold over three million copies, spawned a new wave of environmentally sensitive eating.

In 1975, Lappé cofounded with Joseph Collins the Institute for Food and Development Policy, also known as Food First, in San Francisco, California. The guiding principle of the institute was that the world hunger problem comes not from a scarcity of food, but a scarcity of democracy. The institute studied economics and politics through field research and published reports, articles, pamphlets, school curricula, and study guides. One of the institute's seminal works, *Food First: Beyond the Myth of Scarcity* (1977), written by Lappé and Collins, was internationally recognized as a major achievement in its analysis of global politics surrounding world hunger. They presented the argument that starvation in the world's population is caused not by a scarcity of food supplies or by outmoded farming methods used in developing countries but by political and economic problems such as centralized control of farmland and the colonization of Third World countries by western nations. Lappé and Collins wrote that communities should make it their top priority to become self-reliant in production of food, tools, and fertilizers, though this would require land reform on a grand scale and a return of ownership of local farmland to the people who live on it.

Lappé lectured widely on these issues through the 1980s but eventually began feeling as if public speaking was not enough. She developed the idea that public life must involve dialogue and discourse about the values that inform political views. In 1990 she cofounded with Paul Du Bois the Institute for the Arts of Democracy (now called the Center for Living Democracy) in San Rafael, California, to serve as a catalyst, offering learning tools and training to incorporate a practical vision of democracy into people's lives and get them directly involved in economic and political matters. The center relocated to Brattleboro, Vermont, in 1993 to continue its development, and in 1994 one of its major efforts, the book *The Quickening of America: Rebuilding Our Nation, Remaking Our Lives*, was published. This highly acclaimed, interactive book serves as a guide for the importance of democracy and gives advice on participating in public life.

With her daughter Anna, in 2002, Lappé founded the Small Planet Institute in Cambridge, Massachusetts, to continue promoting the idea that democracy should infuse all institutions, and that democracy itself should be deep and "living," inclusive, fair and responsive. Frances and Anna Lappé have collaborated on a number of book projects, including their 2002 *Hope's Edge: The Next Diet for a Small Planet*, a worldwide discovery of those who have contributed to solving world hunger, and a collection of vegetarian recipes as well. The book won the Nautilus Award for Social Change. Frances Moore Lappé's latest books are her 2006 *Democracy's Edge: Choosing to Save our Country by Bringing Democracy to Life* and *Getting a Grip: Clarity, Creativity, & Courage in a World Gone Mad* (2007).

The Lappés publish, travel, and speak widely, and Anna is becoming a prolific writer in her own right—she published *Grub: Ideas for an Urban Organic Kitchen* in 2006, which exposes and decries industrialized agriculture at the same time that it offers seasonal menues from chef Bryant Terry. Lappé's son Anthony writes and produces television news programming, and is executive editor for Guerrilla News Network. He serves as an advisor to the Small Planet Institute.

In 1987 Frances Moore Lappé won the Right Livelihood Award, sometimes called the "alternative Nobel," And in 2006 she shared with biologist E.O. WILSON recognition from the AltWheels Alternative Transportation Festival for her "Lifetime Service to Increase Planetary Awareness."

BIBLIOGRAPHY

Blanchard, Bob, and Susan Watrous, "Frances Moore Lappé: 'Something New is Possible under the Sun,'" *The Progressive*, 1990; "Food First: Institute for Food and Development Policy," www.foodfirst.org; Lappé, Frances Moore, *Diet for a Small Planet*, 1971; Lappé, Frances Moore, and Joseph Collins, *Food First: Beyond the Myth of Scarcity*, 1977; Lappé, Frances Moore, and Paul Martin Du Bois, *The Quickening of America: Rebuilding Our Nation, Remaking Our Lives*, 1994; "Small Planet Institute," www.smallplanet.org; Turner, Tom, "The World According to Frances Moore Lappé: Food and Democracy Go Hand in Hand," *E Magazine*, 1992.

Leopold, Aldo

(January 11, 1886–April 21, 1948)
Writer, Professor of Wildlife Management, Cofounder of the Wilderness Society

Aldo Leopold is known as the father of environmental ethics and game management. His more than 300 articles record his gradual definition of these two fields, but he is best remembered by the general public as author of *A Sand County Almanac and Sketches Here and There* (1949). This lean, poetic volume, a model for all subsequent nature writers, advocated a change in "the role of *Homo sapiens* from conqueror of the land-community to plain member and citizen of it." Leopold's science and writings have served as inspiration for many environmentalists and conservation organizations, most directly the Wilderness Society, which Leopold helped found.

Born on January 11, 1886, in Burlington, Iowa, Aldo Leopold grew up hunting ducks and partridges in the marshes and woods of Iowa. With the gift of his first rifle at a young age, his father imposed strict hunting rules on the boy, for example, that he could shoot birds only when they were in the air. Leopold went east for preparatory high school and studied forestry at Yale University. After graduating in 1909, he took a job with the U.S. Forest Service and moved to New Mexico, where he worked his way up to supervisor of Carson National Forest.

Leopold quickly began to form his own ideas on conservation. He did not like what he saw happening in national parks in the 1920s. He compared the multitudes of tourists in Yosemite to "wedding guests" consuming "wedding-cake"—the spectacular features like Half Dome, Bridal Veil Falls, and El Capitan. Leopold advocated preservation of wild lands that lacked such impressive scenery but were nonetheless important natural resources and habitat. He worked with New Mexican stockmen to establish the Gila National Forest in 1924, to be used as grazing country by their cattle but to remain undeveloped and inaccessible to tourists.

Once the Gila National Forest was established, Leopold participated eagerly in the extermination of cattle and deer predators such as wolves, but an encounter with a wolf he had just shot awakened him to aspects of ecology that would later help him formulate the science of game management. As Leopold watched the wolf's fading green eyes, he suddenly realized that he had been mistaken to think that predators were exclusively bad and dangerous. As the wolf died, it occurred to him that they belonged to their habitat and that they must play an important role there. This epiphany was promptly confirmed when the deer population surged out of control after Leopold and his Forest Service team had successfully eradicated wolves from the Gila.

Leopold and his wife, Estella Luna Bergere, whom he married in 1912 in New Mexico, moved to Madison, Wisconsin, in 1924. There he continued ruminating on the epiphany he had had with the wolf. He developed a theory of game management and became the University of Wisconsin–Madison's first professor of wildlife management in 1933. His primer, *Game Management*, was also published in 1933 and has guided biologists in managing wildlife ever since. In that book, as well as in his articles written for foresters, sportsmen, conservationists, economists, and the general public, Leopold insisted that a respect for all life forms occurring in a given environment is fundamental for conservation work. This challenged the prevailing basis for conservation of that time, which was that the environment should be conserved primarily to assure future generations a ready supply of natural resources.

Though primarily an academician and scientist, Leopold became active in such conservation organizations as the Izaak Walton

League and the Wilderness Society, of which he was a founding member. Leopold approached his conservation work with the sharp mind of a skeptic, constantly questioning the goals and projects of conservation groups. One of his friends called him a "living question mark."

Leopold enriched his academic career with his work at an old, depleted farm that his family bought in 1935 in Sand County, Wisconsin. Calling it a "living laboratory," the family tried to revive the land by planting trees and nurturing the soil. Leopold recorded the changes on the farm with the passage of seasons and years in *The Sand County Almanac*, now considered an environmental classic. This volume not only lovingly describes what happens in Sand County month by month (the arrival, nesting, and departure south of birds, the growth and blossoming of plants, the rise and fall of rivers and streams), but also proposes new paradigms for how humans can live in greater harmony with their natural environment. Near the end of the book, Leopold articulates his idea for a land ethic—taken for granted by traditional land-based communities, but new to the majority of people who consider themselves civilized:

> The land simply enlarges the boundaries of the community to include soils, water, plants, and animals, or collectively: the land.
>
> This sounds simple: do we not already sing our love for and obligation to the land of the free and the home of the brave? Yes, but just what and whom do we love? Certainly not the soil, which we are sending helter-skelter downriver. Certainly not the waters, which we assume have no function except to turn turbines, float barges, and carry off sewage. Certainly not the plants, of which we exterminate whole communities without batting an eye. Certainly not the animals, of which we have already extirpated many of the largest and most beautiful species. A land ethic of course cannot prevent the alteration, management, and use of these "resources," but it does affirm their right to continued existence, and at least in spots, their continued existence in a natural state.
>
> In short, a land ethic changes the role of *Homo sapiens* from conqueror of the land-community to plain member and citizen of it. It implies respect for his fellow-members, and also respect for the community as such.

Leopold died on April 21, 1948, while fighting a fire on a neighbor's farm. *A Sand County Almanac* was published posthumously, in 1949. His five children all became scientists.

BIBLIOGRAPHY

Callicott, J. Baird, and Eric T. Freyfogle, eds., *For the Health of the Land: Previously Unpublished Essays and Other Writings by Aldo Leopold*, 1999; Flader, Susan, *Thinking like a Mountain: Aldo Leopold and the Evolution of an Ecological Attitude toward Deer, Wolves, and Forests*, 1974; Leopold, Aldo, *Round River; from the journals of Aldo Leopold*, 1953; Loribiecki, Marybeth, *Aldo Leopold: A Fierce Green Fire*, 1996; McCabe, Robert A., *Aldo Leopold, the Professor*, 1987; Meine, Curt, *Aldo Leopold: His Life and Work*; 1988; Nash, Roderick, *Wilderness and the American Mind*, Revised Edition, 1973; Newton, Julianne Lutz, *Aldo Leopold's Odyssey*, 2006; Strong, Douglas H., *Dreamers & Defenders: American Conservationists*, 1988; Tanner, Thomas, ed., *Aldo Leopold: The Man and His Legacy*, 1933.

Lindbergh, Anne Morrow, and Charles Augustus Lindbergh
(June 22, 1906–February 7, 2001; February 4, 1902–August 26, 1974)
Novelist, Poet, Aviator; Aviator, Writer

In a dynamic and world-famous partnership, Charles and Anne Morrow Lindbergh made key contributions to pioneering aviation, exploration, writing, and conservation. In their exploratory flights around the globe, they had many opportunities to view the earth from above and grew concerned that technology and development were causing negative impacts on the environment. Anne was a productive and sensitive writer and used her writing to convey her belief that wilderness should be protected, while Charles used his fame and status to speak out on such conservation issues as saving endangered species. In honor of the Lindberghs' environmental vision, the Charles A. and Anne Morrow Lindbergh Foundation was created to help fund research and educational projects that contribute to a balance between technological advancement and environmental preservation.

Anne Spencer Morrow was born on June 22, 1906, in Englewood, New Jersey, to Dwight Whitney Morrow and Elizabeth Reeve (Cutter) Morrow. Her father, an attorney, later served as ambassador to Mexico from 1927 to 1929 and as Republican senator from New Jersey in 1930 and 1931. Her mother, a poet and educator, was acting president of Smith College from 1939 to 1940 and was an advocate for women's education. Anne grew up with her three siblings in the sheltered comfort of the upper class—traveling with her family on several European tours and attending Miss Chapin's School, a college preparatory school in New York City. Shy and introspective, she filled much of her time with writing. She began studying at Smith College in 1924, majoring in English and continuing her literary efforts. In 1928, the year she graduated with her B.A., she won a prize for the best essay on women of the eighteenth century and had a poem published in *Scribner's Magazine*.

Charles Augustus Lindbergh was born on February 4, 1902, in Detroit, Michigan, to Evangeline (Land) and Charles August Lindbergh and spent most of his childhood years on the family's farm near Little Falls, Minnesota. His parents had little respect for formal education, and when teachers complained that Charles was falling behind, he was pulled out of the school and placed elsewhere. Between the ages of 8 and 16, he attended at least 11 different institutions. After graduating from high school in 1918 in Little Falls, Charles Lindbergh enrolled at the University of Wisconsin in Madison to study engineering. But during his second year, he could no longer resist his growing attraction to flight and enrolled in an aviation school in Lincoln, Nebraska. He went on to become a stunt flier, learning wing walking and parachuting, and then in 1924 joined the army so he could attend the army flight school in San Antonio, Texas. After graduating first in his class, he became the first airmail pilot between Chicago and St. Louis and began plans to attempt the first solo nonstop flight between New York and Paris. On May 20, 1927, Charles Lindbergh left New York in his plane, *The Spirit of St. Louis*, and flew nonstop for 33½ hours to Paris, the first person ever to achieve this.

When news of his accomplishment spread, Charles Lindbergh stepped into the international spotlight. He was awarded the Congressional Medal of Honor by the U.S. government and began flying on tour to promote aviation and express goodwill to other countries. He was invited to the U.S. Embassy in Mexico, where Anne Morrow Lindbergh's father was serving as ambassador. Anne was at the embassy on Christmas break from her junior year of college and met Charles during his

Charles Lindbergh and Anne Morrow Lindbergh (Library of Congress, Prints & Photographs Division, LC-USZ62-116807)

two-week stay there. He took Anne flying, which she found exhilarating, and the two of them began a courtship that they tried to shield from the ever-present press. On May 27, 1929, they succeeded in getting married in Englewood without the press's finding out, though photographers interrupted their honeymoon.

Anne Morrow Lindbergh caught on to her husband's passion for flying, and she herself soon learned to fly. In 1930 she became the first woman in the United States to obtain a glider pilot's license, and she earned her private pilot's license in 1931. Much of their early years of marriage was spent flying all over the globe, exploring and charting routes for commercial air travel. Flying provided the inspiration for Anne Morrow Lindbergh's first book, *North to the Orient* (1935), an account of a survey flight to Asia by way of Canada, Alaska, and Siberia.

In March 1932, the Lindberghs' 21-month-old baby boy, Charles, was kidnapped from their home in Hopewell, New Jersey, and though they paid the ransom, they learned after 72 days that their child had been killed the night of his abduction. The publicity that followed was incessant and unbearable. In 1935, after the birth of their second son and the conclusion of the trial of the man accused of the kidnapping, the Lindberghs moved to England for relative privacy. Anne Morrow Lindbergh continued writing, and in 1938 her next book, *Listen! the Wind*, again based on survey flights she took with her husband, was published. In 1938 the Lindberghs moved to France, and Charles began flying aviation intelligence missions for the U.S. military. In the years following, rumors that many of Charles Lindbergh's beliefs echoed Nazi dogma spread to the United States, and his popularity took an icy plunge. After World War II the Lindbergh family returned to the United States and purchased a home in Darien, Connecticut. In 1955, Anne Morrow Lindbergh's next book appeared. *Gift from the Sea*, her most popular book, contains eight personal essays reflecting on nature, family, the passing of time, and the need to remove oneself occasionally from the routine of everyday life and seek the solitude vital for self-discovery. This book has been hailed as a testimony to the powerful emotional and spiritual value of an intimate relationship with the natural environment. Charles Lindbergh also authored a number of books in his lifetime and is probably best known for the 1954 Pulitzer Prize winner, *The Spirit of St. Louis*, a memoir of his famous flight.

During their travels, the Lindberghs had many opportunities to view the earth's landscapes from the sky. They began noticing changes in the land and became very concerned about the effects of pollution and the disappearance of wild places. Anne Morrow Lindbergh gave voice to these concerns in *Earth Shine* (1969), a book consisting of a pair of essays that illustrate her view that the roots of life are in wilderness. She speaks not only of her fear of the extinction of animal species but also her fear that if wilderness is lost, humans will lose an element vital to their being. In wilderness is renewal she writes, and through that renewal is the possibility of making connections with other life. After many years of privacy, Charles Lindbergh's abiding interest in preserving the environment brought him back into the public eye in the late 1960s, when he began speaking out for conservation. He campaigned to protect endangered species, especially humpback and blue whales. Appointed by the International Union for the Conservation of Nature, he attended the 1966 conference of the International Whaling Commission. He also joined the World Wildlife Fund's Committee of 100, a panel of internationally recognized figures who lobbied heads of state to save endangered wildlife and habitats. His speeches and writings from this time reinforced his belief in the need for both technology and conservation and the necessity of balancing the two. Having pushed the frontiers of aviation technology, Charles Lindbergh was aware of both the achievements of technology and its capacity for destruction. For example, while he supported advancements in aviation, he opposed the development of supersonic transport planes because he feared they would pollute the upper atmosphere. Anne Morrow Lindbergh also believed in balance, and at a conference at Smith College in February 1970, she made a rare public speech, arguing that human values are derived from earth values and therefore the earth must be protected.

The Lindberghs' vision, that the use of technology must be balanced to secure the long-term survival of the earth's life support systems, led to the creation of the Charles A. and Anne Morrow Lindbergh Foundation in 1977. The foundation presents grants each year to research projects that contribute to an equilibrium between technology and environmental preservation and that have included areas of special interest to the Lindberghs, such as exploration, conservation of natural resources, health and population sciences, and wildlife preservation.

Both of the Lindberghs have been presented with numerous honorary degrees and other awards. Charles Lindbergh died of cancer on August 26, 1974, on the island of Maui, Hawaii. Anne Morrow Lindbergh died at her home in Passumpsic, Vermont on February 7, 2001.

BIBLIOGRAPHY
"The Charles A. and Anne Morrow Lindbergh Foundation," http://lindberghfoundation.org; Hertog, Susan, *Anne Morrow Lindbergh: Her Life*, 1999; Lindbergh, Anne Morrow, *Earth Shine*, 1969; Lindbergh, Anne Morrow, *Gift from the Sea*, 1955; Lindbergh, Reeve, *No More Words: a journal of my Mother, Anne Morrow Lindbergh*, 2001; Milton, Joyce, *Loss of Eden: A Biography of Charles and Anne Morrow Lindbergh*, 1993.

Littletree, Alicia
(March 24, 1974–)
Musician, Environmental Organizer

Alicia Littletree was an organizer for Earth First! in northern California during the height of the protests against logging in the 1990s. She was a main protagonist in the struggle to end corporate and government harassment of environmentalists practicing nonviolent direct action protests to protect wilderness.

Alicia Littletree was born on March 24, 1974, in Los Angeles, California, and was raised in Sacramento, the only child of a single mother. She was educated in the public schools, in an accelerated program that featured camping trips and outdoor classes with naturalists. She and the other students in that program were encouraged to rely on their own minds and to develop their imaginations. While in high school, Littletree founded Students for a Green Earth, the school's environmental club. During the first Gulf War in 1991, Littletree joined Sacramento's large protests against the bombing of Iraq, and through those activities, she met a group of Earth First! activists from Humboldt County, on the north California coast.

Littletree moved at the age of 17 to a small cabin on the wooded coast of Humboldt County. She enrolled in an independent high school program there, worked at the Institute for Sustainable Forestry, and attended local Earth First! meetings. Earth First! is a loosely organized group of environmental activists who use nonviolent civil disobedience and direct action to attempt to stop logging, mining, and road building in wild areas. Earth First! works in northern California against clearcutting practiced by large multinational timber corporations in this country's last remaining temperate rain forests, including the last of the ancient redwoods.

It was at Earth First! meetings that Littletree met Earth First! and union organizer and fellow musician JUDI BARI, with whom she was to live and collaborate for the rest of Bari's life. Littletree celebrated her involvement with Earth First! by holding her first tree sit in the spring of 1992 during what is now referred to as the Albion Uprising, a two-month mass protest of Louisiana Pacific's clear-cutting. A tree sit is one of the varied tactics that nonviolent direct action environmentalists use to protect a forest from being cut. It involves climbing a tree and sitting on a branch or a platform, in order to prevent loggers from cutting that tree or any others near it. Littletree's first tree sit lasted nine days, during which she stayed alone aloft in the tree, receiving necessary food, water, and other supplies from a support team on the ground.

Littletree became more involved in Earth First! through the mid-1990s. She helped organize Earth First!'s major protests in the Headwaters forest in 1993 and helped coordinate a 7,000-person rally in the spring of 1996, during which 1,000 people were arrested. In the days following that action, Littletree worked with 13 "affinity groups," tight yet decentralized groups of people collaborating on a nonviolent direct-action protest. The affinity groups shut down the operations of clear-cut giant Pacific Lumber/Maxxam for a full day by blocking every access gate to the forest being cut, holding several tree sits concurrently, and rallying 200 protesters at the company headquarters. Littletree and hundreds more continued on the front lines of the 1996 Pacific Lumber/Maxxam protest for two months.

As well as working with Earth First! to defend the forest, Littletree worked closely with Judi Bari on her court case about the May 24, 1990, car-bombing that had almost killed Bari and injured her passenger Darryl Cherney, another Earth First! activist. Bari and Cherney sued the Oakland police and the Federal Bureau of Investigation (FBI) for false arrest, illegal search and seizure, and conspiracy to violate their first amendment rights by using the bombing to discredit them as terrorists. Littletree worked with the organization set up to coordinate the case, the Redwood Summer Justice Project. She believed that the case was of great importance because it exposed the abuses of rights by the FBI. This has been especially important in recent years since violence against nonviolent environmental activists has become more prevalent and dangerous.

In fall 1999 Littletree helped organize a national meeting of environmental activists suffering corporate and government harassment, which led to the founding of a National Clearinghouse on Intimidation and Disruption to collect reports of harassment from all participating environmental groups and disseminate it to all interested parties, in the hopes that a coordinated response might discourage it. Littletree resides in northern California.

BIBLIOGRAPHY

Hansen, Brian, "Life on the Front Lines," *Colorado Daily*, 1999; Littletree, Alicia, *Uprise Singing: Songs of Redwood Nation Earth First!*, 1995; "Transcript: The Art of Organizing: Creative Activism and Social Change," www.radioproject.org/transcript/1998/9815.html.

Lopez, Barry
(January 6, 1945–)
Writer

As a writer of both fiction and nonfiction, Barry Lopez incorporates elements of imagination, science, and history to create a means of report that many readers find more accurate than work written within the confines of a single discipline. He finds that fiction and nonfiction combined can create an atmosphere in which truth can reveal itself, and he aspires to have his writing serve this shamanic purpose. His growing body of work includes *Desert Notes/River Notes* (1976), *Of Wolves and Men* (1978), *Crow and Weasel* (1990), and *Field Notes* (1994). His 1986 book, *Arctic Dreams*, a contemplative natural history, is widely regarded as his masterpiece.

Born in Port Chester, New York, on January 6, 1945, Barry Holstun Lopez is the son of John Edward Brennan and Mary Frances (Holstun) Brennan, both journalists. When he was three years old, his family moved to southern California; at five, his parents divorced; when he was ten years old, Barry Lopez's mother married Adrian Bernard Lopez. As a boy, Barry Lopez remembers encounters with coyotes, rattlesnakes, deer, and bear. His imagination was captured by the intensity and clarity of these animals, and he idealized their ascetic life and its low impact on the desert landscape. Lopez's prowess with academics earned him a formal education at a Jesuit prep school in New York City and at the University of Notre Dame, where he was awarded an A.B. in 1966 and an M.A. in teaching in 1968. In addition to studying Christian theology, he scoured the full range of Western philosophy and the philosophy of science. Lopez felt that his education benefited him greatly; it endowed him with an appreciation for the rigors of scholarship, the questioning of authority, and a sense of living an ethical life. Yet after completing another year of graduate study in the creative writing program at the University of Oregon in 1969, Lopez felt that his learning was only about to begin. In his essay "The Language of Animals," published in *Wild Earth*, Lopez wrote, "There were other epistemologies out there as valid as the ones I learned in school. Not convinced of the superiority of the latter, I felt ready to consider these other epistemologies, no matter how at odds." This essential curiosity for the unknown or unacknowledged led Lopez in 1970 to commit himself to the life of a nature writer and explorer.

The subject of his first book-length work, *Of Wolves and Men* (1978), was born of this curiosity. In that book he explains his motives: "Let's say there are 8,000 wolves in Alaska. Multiplying by 365, that's about 3 million wolf-days of activity a year. Researchers may see something like 75 different wolves over a period of 25 or 30 hours. That's about 90 wolf-days. Observed behavior amounts to about three one-thousandths of one percent of wolf behavior. The deductions made from such observations represent good guesses, and indicate how incomplete is our sense of worlds outside our own."

Lopez sought to make the wolf less incomplete in his mind by reading all he could about them, then journeying into their territory. While there he became obsessed with the North American polar regions, and repeated excursions into the Arctic tundra resulted in two best-selling books: *Of Wolves and Men* and perhaps his greatest work, *Arctic Dreams: Imagination and Desire in a Northern Landscape* (1986), which won a National Book Award.

His expedition into the North's natural history became a spiritual journey. Studying and hiking the North affected Lopez's imagination profoundly. Icebergs became cathedrals. The bear was the embodiment of intelligence and physical power. Facts about snow geese, seals, and other mammals that traverse the Bering Strait were presented in the book alongside Eskimo myths and folktales. The resourcefulness and physical attributes of the animals of the Arctic amazed Lopez. He traveled the tundra with Eskimos, drawing inspiration from the early documentary filmmaker Robert Flaherty, who made the first full-length documentary film, "Nanook of the North," in 1922. Lopez's study was not anthropological; he didn't learn indigenous languages or hunt with Eskimos, as an anthropologist might have. *Arctic Dreams* is more poetic than anthropological. The reader learns as much about the inner workings of Barry Lopez as about the natural history of the polar regions. However the concluding chapters return to the pure scholarship entailed in writing such a book. Lopez questioned the motives of the ambitious early European expeditions and of Robert Peary, the American who reached the North Pole in 1909. Lopez criticizes these missions after defining, throughout the book, assorted dignified relationships with the land.

Uniting Native American ecological sensibilities and Western science's disciplined inquiry into the natural world is the trademark of Lopez's literary production. He possesses a keen sense for the moment when the geography of land and the geography of mind are synchronized, and he charts those epiphanous "sacred encounters" with the land. *Giving Birth to Thunder, Sleeping with His Daughter* (1977) is a book of allegorical fables that uses American Indian folklore's archetypal trickster character, Coyote. In Lopez's tales, Coyote plays a role that readers can identify as a typically human role: interventionary, impulsive, and ever providing the impetus for situations to which the animal world must adapt or die. In his trilogy *Desert Notes* (1976), *River Notes* (1979), and *Field Notes* (1994), the characters Lopez develops are ones with which he has personal familiarity, aspects of himself perhaps, the transformed scholar. Eccentric academic characters are altered by experiences with nature. In *River Notes*, a visionary naturalist has spiritual insights revealed to him through nature. In the story "Homecoming" in *Field Notes*, the ambition-driven botanist has to stop his career in its tracks to renew his faith and devotion to the land itself. But the land, as much a character as anyone else in his books, is not always a benevolent guru. As in some superstitious tectonic beliefs of our indigenous ancestors, Lopez invokes earthquakes, floods, droughts, and general discord and disharmony to follow the sacrilege of broken promises to the land. In the intermingling of the natural and supernatural, Lopez's fiction can resemble the magical realism of Latin American writers Gabriel García Márquez and Carlos Fuentes.

Barry Lopez can be seen as an Emersonian transcendentalist in that he believes that natural facts reveal spiritual truths and that nature holds power to transform the individual. Like most contemplative nature writers, Lopez treats the mingling of the external landscape and the internal human mind at work. He has likened the awe and wonder that one feels in nature with the passions of falling in love.

Barry Lopez's travel writing appears in literary and environmental journals as well as *Harpers*, *National Geographic*, and the *New York Times Magazine*. His poetic coverage of diverse bioregions—the Great Plains of the Dakotas, Florida's Gulf Coast, the world beneath the ice of Antarctica—make him one of the most popular American nature writers and the recipient of numerous literary awards. Lopez lives near the Mackenzie River on the western slope of the Cascades in Oregon.

BIBLIOGRAPHY

Elder, John, ed., *American Nature Writers*, Vol. 1, 1996; Lopez, Barry, *About This Life: Journeys on the Threshold of Memory*, 1998; Lopez, Barry, *Crossing Open Ground*, 1978; Lopez, Barry, "The Language of Animals," *Wild Earth*, 1998–1999; Lopez, Barry, *Winter Count*, 1976; Murray, John A., "About this Life: A Conversation with Barry Lopez," *The Bloomsbury Review*, 1998; Newell, Mike, *No bottom: in conversation with Barry Lopez*, 2008; Sherman, Paul, "Making the Turn: Rereading Barry Lopez," *For Love of the World: Essays on Nature Writers*, 1992; Tredinnick, Mark, *The Land's Wild Music: encounters with Barry Lopez, Peter Matthiessen, Terry Tempest Williams, and James Galvin*, 2005.

Louv, Richard

(1949–)
Futurist, Biophile, Angler, Author

Richard Louv believes no child should be left inside. He diagnoses the effects of the loss of nature on childhood development, and advises parents to introduce their children to nature, as an antidote to what he calls "nature-deficit disorder," described at length in his 2006 book *Last Child in the Woods*. Louv maintains that our physical, emotional, and spiritual well-being depends upon spending time outside.

Richard Louv grew up wild by 21st century standards. Born on February 15, 1949, in Brooklyn, New York, he was raised in Raytown, Missouri and Shawnee Mission, Kansas. His father was a chemical engineer and his mother was an artist. Richard and his family spent part of each spring protecting box turtles migrating north from Raytown. He most relishes memories of wandering and adventuring in the hills near his neighborhood. He would later wonder if his wasn't the last free-range childhood generation, and if his sons' generation wasn't lacking fundamental, formative time with nature. He attended the University of Kansas, graduating in 1971 with a B.A. in journalism. His powers of observation and skill with language kept him gainfully employed in journalism, working first as a reporter and then as a columnist at the *San Diego Union* and *San Diego Union-Tribune* from 1984 to 2007.

Like many columnists, he began writing books, the first of which was *America II* (Penguin, 1983) about reinvented urban communities, which spring-boarded him into his niche. While raising two sons, Jason and Matthew, with his wife, Kathy, he began contrasting his own childhood in Raytown with his kids' growing up in southern California. As his eldest son hit adolescence, Louv, in a ten-year period, produced five books: *Childhood's Future* (Houghton Mifflin 1990), *101 Things You Can Do for Our Children's Future* (Anchor, 1994), *Fatherlove* (Pocket Books, 1994), *The Web of Life* (1998), and *Fly-Fishing for Sharks* (Simon & Schuster, 2000).

But it was his 2005 book *Last Child in the Woods: Saving Our Children From Nature-Deficit Disorder* (Algonquin), and its updated and expanded edition (2008), that hit a nerve

Richard Louv (Photograph by Robert Burroughs)

with parents and spurred a national movement to "leave no children inside." Louv chronicled the effects of children across the country being deprived of time in nature: diminished use of the senses, attention difficulties, and higher rates of physical and emotional illnesses.

He told Grist.org, "The disorder can be detected in individuals, families, and communities. Nature deficit can even change human behavior in cities, which could ultimately affect their design, since long-standing studies show a relationship between the absence, or inaccessibility, of parks and open space with high crime rates, depression, and other urban maladies."

Louv cites studies that measure the radius kids roam from their house. During a 24-year period from 1970 to 1994, the average kid's radius was reduced 900 percent. He also takes aim at the highly structured, adult-supervised schedules of young people, and decries that kids often spend more than 40 hours a week using electronic devices.

He urges more research into the impact of nature experiences on health, and its impact on nurturing future generations of environmentally-minded people. Louv also encourages parents to cultivate their own enthusiasm for natural places. This enthusiasm, he believes, can help inoculate children from living detached from a vital source of personal well-being.

Louv's lectures and books have motivated groups and individuals get to kids outdoors. In 2007 the US Forest Service started the More Kids in the Woods Program and the National Wildlife Federation launched the first annual "Green Hour" for kids in March. He was a recipient of the Audubon Medal in 2008.

Louv leads Children & Nature Network and is a board member at the environmental nonprofit ecoAmerica. He has advised the Ford Foundation's Leadership for a Changing World's award program and the Scientific Council on the Developing Child. He was also a columnist and member of the editorial advisory board member for *Parents* magazine. In 2008, he was awarded the Audubon Medal by the National Audubon Society. Past recipients have included RACHEL CARSON, E.O. WILSON, and JIMMY CARTER. When he's not fishing and story telling around the country, Richard Louv lives in San Diego with his wife, Kathy Frederick Louv.

BIBLIOGRAPHY

Saving Kids from 'Nature Deficit Disorder,' National Public Radio's Morning Edition May 25, 2005.www.npr.org/templates/story/story.php?storyId=4665933; McKee, Bradford, "Growing Up Denatured," *New York Times*, April 28, 2005; Koch, Wendy, "Nature programs' goal: No child left inside," *USA TODAY*, November 22, 2006; Cooper, Arnie, "Richard Louv Asks Whether We're Raising Our Children Under House Arrest," *The SUN*, February 2007, www.thesunmagazine.org/issues/374/nature_deficit_disorder; www.richardlouv.com; www.childrenandnature.org.

Lovejoy, Thomas

(August 22, 1941–)
Tropical Ecologist, Counselor for Biodiversity and Environmental Affairs at the Smithsonian Institution

Thomas Lovejoy is known for his informed and effective activism about tropical deforestation. During the 1980s, Lovejoy was one of the main voices raising public concern about the destruction of tropical rain forests. He also proposed what has become a successful way to combat tropical deforestation. Through what he called "debt-for-nature swaps," indebted countries would be forgiven a portion of their foreign debt in return for preserving from development an ecologically rich area. Also a respected tropical ecologist, Lovejoy began his Brazil-based Biological Dynamics of Forest Fragments Project in the late 1970s to study the loss of biodiversity when only small patches of forest are left standing. The results of this experiment, which will continue well into the twenty-first century, will help determine how much biodiversity a small and isolated wilderness area can retain.

Thomas Eugene Lovejoy was born in New York City on August 22, 1941, into a wealthy family that owned the Manhattan Life Insurance Company. He was sent to the private boarding school Milbrook, where the founder of the school's zoo, Frank Trevor, encouraged Lovejoy to study field biology. Lovejoy was especially interested in birds. At Yale University, Lovejoy studied under the eminent ecologist Evelyn Hutchinson, who instructed him about the subtleties and complexities of field biology. Lovejoy received a B.S. from Yale in 1964 and a Ph.D. in 1971. His Ph.D. research was carried out in Belem, Brazil, near the mouth of the Amazon River.

Lovejoy joined the Academy of Natural Sciences upon finishing his Ph.D., serving as executive assistant to the science director and assistant to the vice president of resources and planning. In 1973, he moved to the World Wildlife Fund–U.S. (WWF-U.S.), where he remained until 1987, acting as program director (1973–1978), vice president for science (1978–1985), and executive vice president (1985–1987). Lovejoy has also served as chairman of the Wildlife Preservation Trust International and as a member of the Species Survival Commission of the International Union for the Conservation of Nature. For many years Lovejoy has been a research associate at the Smithsonian Tropical Research Institute.

During the late 1970s, Lovejoy initiated what has become one of the largest and longest-term biology field experiments. He was interested in expanding on the island biogeography hypothesis of biologist E. O. WILSON and mathematician Robert MacArthur, which held that the number of species on oceanic islands was predictable and based on the size of the island and its distance from other landforms. Facilitated by a Brazilian law requiring land developers to leave 50 percent of their plots under forest cover, Lovejoy convinced Amazonian cattle ranchers to leave rain forest "islands" of certain sizes sprinkled through their cattle pastures. Working with biologist Rob Birregaard and several Brazilian colleagues, Lovejoy set up the Minimum Critical Size of Ecosystems Project (later renamed the Biological Dynamics of Forest Fragments Project), with 24 forest patches of one, ten, 100, and 200 hectares and a 10,000-hectare control site. Hundreds of researchers have used the plots, and 20 or 30 of them are there at any given time. Although the experiment will continue indefinitely, researchers have already found that the smaller the plot, the more severe the decline of species. Trees die along the edge of the plots, desiccated by the surrounding dry pastures. As they die, so do the animals that depend upon them for food and shelter. What has come to be called the "edge effect" has important implications for those who plan wildlife reserves.

During the mid-1980s, Lovejoy first raised the alarm about tropical deforestation, becoming what Congressman Timothy Wirth called "the Tom Paine of the Rainforest." With his social and political connections, as well as his firsthand knowledge about the political and economic workings of indebted tropical countries, Lovejoy invented and then proposed in the *New York Times* the idea for debt-for-nature swaps. What happened afterwards illustrates an underlying current in Lovejoy's career: he proposes grand ideas, then lets others fine-tune them and implement them. This happened with the Forest Fragments project and with debt-for-nature swaps, dozens of which have been arranged by groups such as Conservation International and the World Wildlife Fund and by several European governments.

Another of Lovejoy's particular abilities is to attract the rich and famous to rain forest conservation. Among those who have visited his Forest Fragments project in Brazil and/or become his influential allies are Sting, Robert Redford, Tom Cruise, Olivia Newton John, and many U.S. politicians. Lovejoy felt that if he could convince at least 15 senators of the importance of tropical conservation, that would be a critical mass for passing important conservation legislation. The late Republican senator H. John Heinz III of Pennsylvania said of Lovejoy that "he makes believers of skeptics," and biologist E. O. Wilson credits Lovejoy with building bridges between science and the public.

Lovejoy and his colleague Robert L. Peters edited the first book, published in 1994, to analyze the effect that global warming would have on biodiversity: *Global Warming and Biological Diversity*. It was widely acclaimed for bringing this issue into the arena of both specialists and the public. In 2002, Lovejoy and colleague Lee Hannah edited *Climate Change and Biodiversity*, a volume with contributions from 66 respected scientists who examine the impact of climate change in the past, present and future and suggest policy and conservation responses. Lovejoy has edited or contributed to a number of other books about biodiversity and threats to it, as well.

Lovejoy continues to contribute to educational and conservation efforts in a variety of ways. He is still a research associate at the Smithsonian Tropical Research Institute, conducting the Biological Dynamics of Forest Fragments project in the Amazon. He participates in the multimedia, multifaceted Paradise Earth project, which is building a physical facility in Arizona and currently hosts the interactive paradiseearth.com. Since 2002 he has directed the Heinz Center for Science, Economics, and the Environment, which convenes business, environmental organizations, academics, and governments to collaborate on designing solutions to environmental problems.

BIBLIOGRAPHY

Gaither, Rowan, "The Natural," *New York*, 1991; "The Heinz Center," www.heinzcenter.org; Laurence, William F., "Fragments of the Forest," *Natural History*, 1998; "Paradise Earth Rainforest Project," www.paradiseearth.org; "Tom Lovejoy and the Last Crusade," *GQ*, 1989; Sun, Marjorie, "How Do You Measure the Lovejoy Effect?" *Science*, 1990.

Lovins, Amory, and Hunter Lovins
(November 13, 1947– ; February 26, 1950–)
Cofounders of Rocky Mountain Institute

Amory Lovins and Hunter Lovins are cofounders of Rocky Mountain Institute (RMI), an independent, nonprofit research and implementation organization that fosters the efficient and sustainable use of resources as a path to global security. Amory Lovins proclaimed that energy waste was a crippling economic and environmental problem in the early 1970s—before the oil embargo of 1972 woke the rest of the world up to that fact—and he innovated the conceptual, technical, and business framework for what has become the $5 billion electricity-saving (or "negawatt") industry in the United States. The Lovinses continue to insist that the solution is not to build more power plants to supply a growing appetite for energy, but rather to reduce society's use of energy through innovation and advanced energy efficiency. Through their work at RMI, and their book *Natural Capitalism* (1999), co-authored with PAUL HAWKEN, their ideas on sustainability have gained a wide audience and have influenced business leaders throughout the world.

Amory Lovins was born on November 13, 1947, in Washington, D.C., to Gerald and Miriam Lovins, a scientist and social services administrator, respectively. He was a frequent participant in national and international science fairs during high school, and one experimental physics project, "Method and Means for Detecting Nuclear Magnetic Resonances," even received a U.S. patent in 1965. Lovins attended Harvard College as a Presidential Scholar for two years but then transferred in 1967 to Magdalen College at Oxford University as an advanced student in theoretical physics. At Oxford's Merton College, where Lovins became a don in 1969, he requested permission to do his doctoral research on energy and resource policy, but he was refused, because at that time energy was not considered worthy of academic study. Rather than pursue another related field, Lovins left Oxford in 1971 to work independently. Serving as the British representative to DAVID BROWER's Friends of the Earth, Lovins pulled off a successful conservation campaign. The mountains surrounding Snowdonia National Park in northern Wales were threatened with copper stripping by the world's largest mining company. Lovins took photographs and wrote text for the coffee-table volume *Eryri: The Mountains of Longing*, which was supplemented by a BBC television program. Public

Hunter Lovins (Photograph courtesy of Natural Capitalism Solutions)

outrage about the threatened destruction, spurred by Lovins's work, halted the project.

Lovins remained headquartered in London throughout the 1970s. During that decade, he worked as an international consultant on energy and resource policy and its link to development, security, and the environment. A 1976 article in *Foreign Affairs* redefined the energy problem, with profound effect: he recommended choosing the cheapest ways (typically efficient use, then appropriate renewable resources) to provide energy in the right amount, quality, and scale to do each desired task. Lovins's 1977 book *Soft Energy Paths: Toward a Durable Peace* inspired a new generation of scientists and decision makers and steered energy companies away from over a trillion dollars in needless investments.

Hunter Sheldon Lovins was born in Middlebury, Vermont, on February 2, 1950, to Farley Hunter Sheldon and Paul Millard Sheldon and was raised in the mountains east of Los Angeles and in the Roaring Fork Valley of Colorado. She learned to ride horses before she could walk and began to ride in rodeos as a teenager, an activity she still enjoys. Her family embarked on camping trips through the western United States and Mexico for weeks at a time, and whenever they witnessed environmental problems, her parents encouraged their children to think about constructive solutions, rather than complaining about the problems. Lovins attended Pitzer College in California, graduating in 1972 with a B.A. in political studies and sociology. She served as assistant director of the California Conservation Project, from 1973 to 1979, attending Loyola law school and receiving her J.D. in 1975. She was admitted to the California bar in 1975 and is still a member. While directing a Los Angeles–based conservation organization called TreePeople in 1976, Lovins came across the energy-efficiency work of Amory Lovins and began to refine its presentation so that it would be more accessible to laypeople. The chief economist of the Atlantic Richfield oil company introduced the two in 1977, and they decided to marry and to integrate careers in 1979. The Lovinses became policy advisers for Friends of the Earth, posts they held until they moved to the rural valley of Old Snowmass, Colorado, to create Rocky Mountain Institute (RMI) in 1982.

The Lovinses designed themselves designed RMI's Snowmass headquarters to showcase energy conservation design. The building was constructed by a group totaling over 100 volunteers; its passive solar features were so effective that bananas could be grown inside despite outdoor temperatures as low as minus-forty-seven degrees Fahrenheit,. Now there is a second location for RMI in Boulder. RMI currently employs more than 80 staff members who form three teams: Built Environment, Energy and Resources, and Transportation Practices; they research and provide consulting services on issues including energy, buildings, communities, climate, transportation and water. In all of these areas, RMI's focus is on profitable routes to sustainability. RMI has formed and spun off four for-profit companies that sell the information it generates. E source, for example, provides technical information on advanced electric efficiency; it was sold in 1999 to the *Financial Times* group. Private donations and research grants provide the rest of RMI's income.

RMI has confidence in the ability of a savvy and efficient private sector to embrace the goal of sustainability; business has been an eager client of RMI's money-saving advice for energy efficiency. RMI's Hypercar Center® and its spinoff, Hypercar, Inc., for example, invented the ultralight hybrid-electric Hypercar® that would use four to eight times less energy than today's cars, emit nothing but hot drinking water, be superior in all respects, and sell for a competitive price. Such cars differ from currently existing electric cars in that they lack heavy batteries and instead are driven by an electric motor powered by a small engine, turbine, or fuel cell on board. The design was placed in the public domain in order to share it with major car companies, and billions of dollars have already been invested in bringing the idea into the marketplace.

The Lovinses together with RMI staff and their collaborators continue to generate unorthodox ideas that make perfect sense for solving world problems. Amory Lovins told *Whole Earth's* PETER WARSHALL in 1998 that the challenge of new solutions usually involves defying status quo, be it in the form of bureaucracy, rigid specifications for technology, or accepted yet inefficient ways of doing things. The Lovinses have authored—individually, together, and with other writers—several hundred articles and 27 books. Their most recent book, *Natural Capitalism* (1999), written with sustainability expert PAUL HAWKEN, explains new business practices, being rapidly adopted, that restore the earth while providing striking profitability and competitive advantage. The book has received widespread praise for its scope and innovative suggestions.

Amory Lovins received the 1999 World Technology Award (Environment), the 1997 Heinz Award, the Onassis Foundation's first Delphi Prize, and a 1993 MacArthur Fellowship. The *Wall Street Journal* predicted that he would be one of 28 people worldwide "most likely to change the course of business in the '90s"; *Newsweek* has called him "one of the Western world's most influential energy thinkers"; and *Car* magazine ranked him the 22nd most powerful person in the global automotive industry. With Hunter Lovins, he has shared the 1999 Lindbergh Award, the 1983 Right Livelihood Award (often called the Alternative Nobel Prize), and a 1982 Mitchell Prize. Hunter Lovins received Loyola's Alumni Award for Outstanding Service in 1975. The Lovinses amicably divorced in 1999, and Hunter Lovins stepped down as co-Executive Director in 2002 to devote more time to promoting natural capitalism. She has founded a thinktank and consulting firm, Natural Capitalism, Inc.

Amory Lovins spends his free time playing and composing for the piano, climbing mountains, tying knots, taking landscape photographs, reading poetry, and studying languages.

Hunter Lovins and her partner, Robbie Noiles, buy, sell, and train horses through their own Nighthawk Horse Company. They play polocrosse, which is like lacrosse but played on horseback, and their team placed second in the 1997 national championship. She helps out on neighboring ranches and rides rodeo, competing in barrel racing. She also works as a fire/rescue/emergency medical technician with her local fire department.

BIBLIOGRAPHY

"HunterLovins.com," www.hunterlovins.com; Kupfer, David, "Amory Lovins," *The Progressive*, 1995; "Natural Capitalism, Inc.," www.natcapinc.com; "Rocky Mountain Institute," www.rmi.org; "The Sage of Old Snowmass," *The Economist*, 1997; Warshall, Peter, "Lockin," *Whole Earth*, 1998.

Luce, Benjamin

(December 15, 1962–)
Author, Energy Expert

Solar energy and anti-corporate activist Ben Luce probably never envisioned himself the activist he became in his mid-40s. Though he dreamed of becoming a composer, Luce ended up pursuing the study of physics. Then, while working at Los

Alamos National Laboratory, he became increasingly interested in the solar energy industry, eventually leaving his work at the lab to become a full-time renewable energy activist. But in 2007, Luce's career took another turn, when he left his position with the New Mexico Coalition for Clean Affordable Energy and blew the whistle on the rampant corporate corruption of politics in New Mexico.

Born on December 15, 1962, in Cambridge, Massachusetts, Luce has a double B.S. in physics and sound recording from the State University of New York at Fredonia. He received his master's degree and a PhD in physics from New York's Clarkson University, then moved to New Mexico for a postdoctoral job at Los Alamos National Laboratory. He worked at the lab, in the field of nonlinear dynamics, from 1993 until 2007. Beginning in the mid-1990s, Luce became increasingly concerned about climate change and in turn, began volunteering as an advocate on renewable energy issues, particularly solar energy, in New Mexico. Then, in 2004, Luce took a leave of absence from his job at Los Alamos and began working as a full-time activist.

As President of the New Mexico Solar Energy Association and co-founder and Director of the New Mexico Coalition for Clean Affordable Energy, Luce advocated passage of a variety of bills in the state, including the solar tax credit, the renewable energy standard (and its subsequent increase), a net metering rule (and its subsequent strengthening) and those related to energy codes for buildings, enhanced solar rights for residents and the inclusion of "solar ready roofs" in the state's building codes.

During that time, he also advocated for energy efficiency, created guidelines for passive solar design, organized energy fairs, visited New Mexico schools and made repeated visits to a wide range of groups, including Kiwanis Clubs, voter groups, churches and environmental organizations, in an effort to educate people concerning the solar energy industry.

As an activist, he worked closely with the New Mexico Public Regulation Commission, the state legislature and Governor Bill Richardson, who appointed Luce to a number of state task forces, including the Climate Change Advisory Group, Task Force on Distributed Solar, Concentrating Solar Task Force and Electricity Transmission Task Force, as well as to the Western Governors Association's Concentrated Solar and Advanced Coal Task Force.

On June 19, 2007, however, Luce announced his break with the governor during a press conference on the steps of the New Mexico State Capitol—locally referred to as the Round House—in Santa Fe. There, Luce announced the creation of a citizens campaign, called Break the Grip!, that would eliminate the hold corporations held over state government in New Mexico. He began his speech by saying:

> This transition has been a bit painful for me, as I'm abandoning positions that I've held for a long time. For the past ten years I really tried to give the existing system here a chance. I thought perhaps if I could just move the ball forward enough incrementally, it would eventually add up to major change.
>
> But my experiences, and the ultimate results, have now caused me to lose faith in the ethical credibility of both the executive branch and the legislature, such as they currently stand, and to believe that we need much more profound change.

Luce attributes his radical change of heart to what he calls "unethical behavior" of the Richardson administration during the 2007 legislative session. The last straw, says Luce, came in May 2007, when Richardson announced his support for nuclear energy the same week that the state's largest electric utility, PNM, appointed James Ferland to head its regulated generation department—a move Luce believes illustrates plans by Richardson and PNM to introduce nuclear generation to New Mexico. (Ferland was the former Vice President of Global Nuclear Field Services for Westinghouse Electric Company. He also served as President and CEO of Louisiana Energy Services, which successfully negotiated with the Richardson administration to locate a controversial uranium enrichment facility in New Mexico.)

Providing a rare insider's look into New Mexico politics, Luce also revealed that the Richardson administration employed a PNM lobbyist, Art Hull, as an on-loan staffer during the legislative session. Luce also broke ranks with other activists working in the state; he claimed that activists working for organizations such as the Natural Resources Defense Council maintained too-close ties with both the Richardson administration and PNM, and he asserted that such groups were more intent on pursuing national goals than protecting the best interest of New Mexicans, particularly those in lower income groups.

During a 2007 interview, Luce had this advice for other energy activists: "Be very careful about incremental progress, which can be used to justify greenwashing a utility or a politician."

Today, Luce lives in Vermont and says he has become "increasingly concerned about the influence of corporations on government." He remains involved in the promotion of solar energy and is working on a school curriculum related to renewable energy and energy efficiency. He also continues promoting better government, in general: "In particular, I'm interested in finding ways to basically remove corporate personhood rights," he says, "which I feel are trampling the rights of the environment and the rights of the public to better our environment."

Bibliography

Luce, Ben, Passive Solar Guidelines for Northern New Mexico, www.nmsea.org/Curriculum/Courses/Passive_Solar_Design/Guidelines/Guidelines.htm; Luce, Ben, New Mexico Solar Energy Association solar curriculum, www.nmsea.org/Curriculum/Listing.htm; Paskus, Laura, "Clean energy insider blows his top in New Mexico," *High Country News*, September 3, 2007, www.hcn.org/servlets/hcn.Article?article_id=17195; Paskus, Laura, "Is Bill Richardson Radioactive?" The Progressive, December 2007.

Lyons, Oren
(1930–)
Onondaga Chief

Faithkeeper of the Onondaga Council of Chiefs, Oren Lyons is also an artist, Hall of Fame lacrosse player, college professor, and internationally recognized leader of environmentalists and indigenous rights activists. Lyons has written and spoken widely about links between ecological crises and suppression of indigenous peoples. He has appeared at numerous international conferences, testified before Congress, and addressed the United Nations General Assembly. He edited an important study of American Indians and democracy, *Exiled in the Land of the Free* (1992), and contributed essays to several other collections, including Bill Willers's *Learning to Listen to the Land* (1991) and Christopher Vecsey's and Robert Venables's *American Indian Environments* (1980). He is professor of American studies at the State University of New York at Buffalo.

Oren Lyons was born in 1930 on Onondaga Indian land in upstate New York, with the name Jo-Ag-Quis-Ho (Bright Sun Makes a Path in the Snow). Lyons was the oldest of eight children. He dropped out of school in the eighth grade and after two years in the army, was earning his living by painting portraits of boxers for local bars. Lyons was also well-known for his abilities at lacrosse, a game invented by Lyons's Iroquois ancestors. The coach of the Syracuse University lacrosse team invited the head of the College of Fine Arts to view Lyons's painting of Jack Dempsey, and despite Lyons's lack of formal education, he was admitted to the university. He was an All-American lacrosse player, and during his senior year, with National Football League Hall of Fame running back Jim Brown on the team, Syracuse went undefeated. (Lyons was elected to the Lacrosse National Hall of Fame in 1993.) He graduated from the College of Fine Arts of Syracuse University in 1958 and was awarded the Orange Key as an outstanding scholar-athlete.

Lyons moved to New York City to pursue a career as a commercial artist. He eventually landed a job with Norcross Greeting Cards, where he rose to become art and planning director, a job that entailed supervising 200 artists. His own painting also gained respect, and Lyons exhibited widely. In 1967, the clan mother of the Turtle Clan chose Lyons to be a faithkeeper, and he returned home to Onondaga. The Onondaga are one tribe in the Iroquois Confederation, and as a tribal chief, Lyons has long fought for recognition of Iroquois sovereignty. He has worked to exempt the nation from federal taxes, helped put forth claims for reparations for stolen lands, and served in the Traditional Circle of Tribal Elders, a council of leaders of Indian nations of North America. He has been particularly active in United Nations work around indigenous people's rights and helped establish the UN Working Group on Indigenous Populations in 1982. In 1990 he was a negotiator between the Mohawk Indians and Canadian government authorities in the standoff at Oka, Quebec, and helped the confrontation end peacefully, with both sides agreeing to look for long-term solutions to Mohawk demands.

The long view is central to Lyons's work and philosophy, shaped fundamentally by Onondaga beliefs. A consistent theme in his work on environmental issues is the need to care for future generations, to make decisions for "the seventh generation to come." He also stresses the belief that humans are connected to and equal with all other things, so that, for instance, how we treat other species will determine human fate as well. When asked by BARRY LOPEZ during an interview for Orion magazine why the seventh generation consideration is so seldom respected, Lyons responded "Human ego is probably the biggest impediment—the amazing ability of any human to perceive themselves as almighty powerful, no matter what…If you can stop thinking about yourself and begin thinking about responsibility, everthing is going to get better. Immediately everything will change."

Lyons has worked as both an activist and a spiritual leader and argues that the separation between the two is artificial and destructive. He has been active in the effort to demonstrate the influence of the Iroquois Confederacy on the Constitution of the United States and emphasizes the spiritual and political connections between the United States and Iroquois nations. Lyons has discussed his ideas in a wide range of publications and events and is a powerful speaker. In 1988 he addressed the first Global Forum of Spiritual and Parliamentary Leaders, held in England. The conference was attended by many influential leaders, including the Dalai Lama and Mother Teresa, and Lyons's speech brought the crowd to its feet. He helped convince the organizers to focus their 1990 meeting in Moscow entirely on environmental issues. In 1992 he led a delegation of the Iroquois Confederacy to the United Nations Conference on Environment and Development in Rio de Janeiro. Lyons's has been an influential voice in discussions of economic development, pointing out that "sustainable development" has often meant destruction of life and land for indigenous peoples. Lyons publishes *Daybreak*, a quarterly journal about issues that impact indigenous people worldwide.

Lyons has received numerous awards and honors for his work in these areas. In 1993, he was awarded the Audubon Medal by the National Audubon Society. In 1995 he was given the Elder and Wiser Award by the Rosa Parks Institute for Human Rights and Self-Development. Oren Lyons is director of the Native American Studies Program and Distinguished Service Professor at the State University of New York at Buffalo.

BIBLIOGRAPHY

Cornell, George, "Blight Knows No Border," *Los Angeles Times*, 1990; Lopez, Barry, "The Leadership Imperative, An Interview with Oren Lyons," *Orion*, 2007; Moyers, Bill, *Oren Lyons the Faithkeeper* (PBS documentary), 1991; "Oren Lyons-Department of American Studies, University at Buffalo," www.americanstudies.buffalo.edu/people/faculty/lyons/; Schneider, Paul, "Respect for the Earth," *Audubon*, 1994; Tucker, Toba, *Haudenosaunee: Portraits of the Onondaga Nation*, 1999.